THE DYNAMICS OF PERSUASION

Persuasion is ubiquitous, pervasive, and inescapable, targeting us on billboards, baseball parks, television programs, and Facebook. Many of us yearn to be more effective persuaders, but how does *persuasion* happen? How can it be harnessed to help people lead healthier, more vibrant lives? Employing social science theories and persuasion scholarship, *The Dynamics of Persuasion* presents answers to these questions.

Organized around major concepts, issues, and persuasion contexts, this text introduces the current body of knowledge on persuasion, using examples found in everyday life. This 5th edition is enhanced by a fully interactive eTextbook component with author-narrated chapter summaries and chapter-by-chapter interactive exercises. The interactive content, an image bank, flashcards, a playlist of video examples, and supportive discussion questions are available online for instructors.

Highlights of this edition include:

- Updates on persuasion theory scholarship, including Fishbein and Azjen's 2010 Reasoned Action Model, cognitive processing models, narrative and persuasion, and interpersonal persuasion;
- New sections addressing ethics in advertising, high-tech media, interpersonal persuasion, and legal issues;
- Increased focus on online persuasion as well as contemporary persuasion in mass media; and
- Case examples demonstrating the global significance of persuasion.

Using theory as the key to unlock the mysteries of contemporary social influence, *The Dynamics of Persuasion* is an engaging text for advanced courses on persuasion in communication, psychology, marketing, and sociology.

Richard M. Perloff, Professor of Communication, has been on the Cleveland State University faculty since 1979. He is a nationally known expert on the third-person effect, the divergent perceptions of mass media impact on others and the self. Dr. Perloff enjoys teaching undergraduate persuasion, graduate persuasion, and political communication courses. He is a fellow of the Midwest Association for Public Opinion Research, writes feature stories for Cleveland weekly newspapers, and has received city and state-wide journalism awards for his work. He lives in Beachwood, Ohio with his family and is an early morning swimmer and newspaper-with-coffee aficionado.

Routledge Communication Series

Jennings Bryant/Dolf Zillmann, Series Editors

Selected titles include:

- Frey: *Group Communication in Context: Studies of Bona Fide Groups, Second Edition*
- Bucy/Holbert: *The Sourcebook for Political Communication Research*
- Heath/Bryant: *Human Communication Theory and Research, Second Edition*
- Stacks/Salwen: *An Integrated Approach to Communication Theory and Research, Second Edition*
- Rubin et al: *Communication Research Measures II*
- Frey/Cissna: *Routledge Handbook of Applied Communication Research*
- Hollingshead/Poole: *Research Methods for Studying Groups and Teams*

THE DYNAMICS OF PERSUASION

Communication and Attitudes in the 21st Century

Fifth Edition

Richard M. Perloff

Routledge
Taylor & Francis Group

NEW YORK AND LONDON

Fifth edition published 2014
by Routledge
711 Third Avenue, New York, NY 10017

Simultaneously published in the UK
by Routledge
2 Park Square, Milton Park, Abingdon, Oxon OX14 4RN

Routledge is an imprint of the Taylor & Francis Group, an informa business

First edition published 1993 by Lawrence Erlbaum Associates

Fourth edition published 2010 by Routledge

Library of Congress Cataloging-in-Publication Data
Perloff, Richard M.
 The dynamics of persuasion : communication and attitudes in the 21st century /
 Richard M. Perloff. — 5th ed.
  p. cm.
 Includes bibliographical references.
 1. Persuasion (Psychology) 2. Mass media—Psychological aspects.
 3. Attitude change. I. Title.
 BF637.P4P39 2013
 153.8'52—dc23   2012036695

ISBN 13: 978-0-415-50742-4 (pbk)

Typeset by Keystroke, Station Road, Codsall, Wolverhampton
Printed and bound by CPI Group (UK) Ltd, Croydon, CR0 4YY

Contents in Brief

Contents

Preface

More than two decades ago, in 1993, Lawrence Erlbaum Associates published the first edition of *The Dynamics of Persuasion*. My attempt at the time was to present an engaging look at persuasive communication theories, research, and applications. Theories were the guidepost, a theme was the interface between the message and the mind, and the emphasis was that you could not understand message effects without appreciating the pathways of the mind. This approach has guided me in the subsequent editions published over the years.

It is interesting that the same theories emphasized back in 1993 continue to dominate the field today. On the one hand, this suggests we could probably benefit from new approaches calling on new concepts or integrating old ones in different ways. In addition, the classic factors—for example, credibility, social attractiveness, and processing persuasive messages—may take on different hues when they are experienced in online contexts that do not resemble the interpersonal arenas in which hypotheses were tested and to which concepts were directed. Does persuasion change when it occurs in contexts mediated by technology and where technology can be sometimes experienced in human terms? Does persuasion change in various ways when the line between persuader and persuaded is no longer simple and static, but occurs online in ways that are frequently blurred, dynamic, and remixed? Research should pursue these questions.

And yet it is important to bear in mind that fundamental verities remain: persuasion *is* persuasion, attitudes are vital and dynamic, and social influence continues to be a complex process fraught with subtle ploys, biased perceptions based on strong habits of the heart, and critically mediated by mental processes, images, and beliefs. With ubiquitous commercials, pervasive political advertising, health campaigns, and omnipresent interpersonal influence attempts, persuasion remains a force to be reckoned with. And, as always, it can be used for morally positive and pernicious purposes, with ethical gray areas galore.

So persuasion remains important. It continues to fascinate. For, as Plato observed, "everything that deceives may be said to enchant."

In writing this fifth edition, I have been attuned to changes in everyday persuasion and the research field, as well as continuities. Thus, I returned to some of the issues—for example, the centrality of theory—that percolated back in 1993. I have also made many changes—in content and form—that I hope will increase the book's utility as a teaching and intellectual tool. In this edition, the following changes have been made:

- Chapters have been streamlined. There are now 14, not 12, chapters. This does not reflect an increase in content areas so much as an attempt to clarify and strengthen readability. The lengthy first chapter has been broken up so that issues are presented more crisply in two chapters. Similarly, the second chapter on attitudes has been divvied up, with one chapter on definitions and structure and a subsequent chapter focusing on strong attitudes. To offer more cohesiveness, the second section of the book is devoted to the nature of attitudes. The material is the same, though updated and organized in a way that should help students better understand theories and applications.
- In a similar fashion, the message chapter has been broken up so that two chapters now cover the message. The message is a centerpiece in persuasion, and I hope this makes it easier to follow the many issues in message processing and effects. Chapter 8, which dealt with personality, has been deleted, given the paucity of research in this area; relevant areas have been moved to other sections of the book. Reflecting the pervasiveness of marketing, the advertising chapter has been re-titled to include mention of marketing; the interface of persuasion and marketing gets additional play in this chapter as well.
- Theory is given a more central role through expanded discussions of relevant concepts and boxes summarizing main points of major theories.
- An entirely new discussion of reasoned action theory is presented. Fishbein and Ajzen revised their theory and integrated it with the Planned Behavior Model in a sweeping book published in 2010, shortly after Martin Fishbein's death. Fishbein contributed immensely to the field and his contributions in specifying and imaginatively conceptualizing attitudes will stand the test of time.
- Ethical discussions get a face-lift in the fifth edition, with an expanded discussion of normative ethical philosophy in Chapter 2, an additional section on the ethics of peripheral processing in the cognitive processing chapter, and a new section in the advertising chapter that explores legal and ethical issues in marketing. Ethics continues to be covered in the discussion of authority, the Milgram study, interpersonal persuasion, and health campaigns.
- The book discusses persuasion and contemporary interactive technologies (Facebook, YouTube, and so forth), with specific discussions of interfaces with

peripheral processing and high-tech marketing. The final chapter explores ways that health communication interventions have migrated to the Web and other interactive contexts.

■ As much as possible, international applications of persuasion that extend beyond America have been added.

■ New scholarship is sprinkled throughout the book, notably a new section on neuro-science and persuasion, new sections on narrative and framing, expanded discussion of the ELM in light of contemporary studies, enhanced description of the Heuristic-Systematic Model, enriched presentation of self-affirmation and cognitive dissonance, additional exploration of interpersonal goals and compliance-gaining, a new section on evaluation research of an anti-drug campaign in Montana, and expanded discussion of interventions to reduce racial disparities in health care in the final chapter.

■ Pictures are sprinkled throughout to break up the text and help offer visual illustrations of concepts.

I hope the new edition provides a good read. And I hope it offers an in-depth introduction to the theories, research, and applications that make persuasion a fascinating area of contemporary life.

Acknowledgments

I want to thank the group of reviewers who read my prospectus for the fifth edition and proffered excellent suggestions, including Linda Brigance of SUNY Fredonia, Bart Collins of Purdue University, Craig Dudczak of Syracuse University, John Pauley of Eastern University, John Powers of Hong Kong Baptist University, Penelope Sheets of the University of Amsterdam, Paul Simpson of the University of Greenwich, Éva Szeli of Arizona State University, Michael Tew of Eastern Michigan University, and Lyn Van Swol of the University of Wisconsin. They viewed the book from a theoretical and pedagogical perspective, and offered many thoughtful ideas that improved the book. I very much appreciated their conscientious approach and perceptive suggestions.

Thank you, as always, to Linda Bathgate, senior editor at Routledge, whose supportive, contagiously positive approach is a wonderful asset. She sees the potential in projects, lending a practical and intellectual vision that is distinctive and much appreciated. Jill D'Urso is a pleasure to work with. She is positive, excellent at integrating ideas, and supportive. Thanks also to Kayley Hoffman for her always-efficient assistance.

Sharon J. Muskin worked expertly and efficiently on innumerable complex computer tasks. Much of the book could not have been completed without her. Her patience and expertise are appreciated.

And thanks on a personal note to my parents: my father, Robert Perloff, for standing as the proud antithesis to provincialism, arguing always for the importance of stretching beyond the narrow confines of the comfortable and familiar; and my mother, Evelyn Perloff, for her endless love of learning and modeling as pure a dedication to work as I know.

My friends, Robert Kraftowitz, Janice Gordon, Joan Arnson, and Ron Arnson were supportive, witty and offered a ballast of good advice on topics that had absolutely nothing to do with attitudes or persuasion. And I thank my family: my 23-year-old son, Michael, whose philosophical insights and wisdom about virtue never cease to inspire; my 16-year-old daughter, Catherine, for her openness to new ideas and resistance to established truths; and my wife, Julie, for timeless advice on psychology, neuroscience, and empirical research, and tolerance for my book-writing ways.

Visual Tour

With Routledge Interactive, you can access your Interactive eTextbook at home, on campus or on the move,* whether online or offline. Your eTextbook offers note sharing and highlighting functionality, as well as exclusive interactive content to enhance your learning experience. The notes you make on your Interactive eTextbook will synchronize with all other versions, creating a personalized version that you can access wherever and whenever you need it.

Throughout the text you will see icons in the margin where further multimedia resources are available via your Interactive eTextbook (see the inside front cover for access details). These include:

Audio summaries

 ■ Author-narrated audio summaries of each chapter introduce students to the key concepts.

Interactive exercises

 ■ Test your knowledge with interactive exercises.

As well as this tailor-made content you can also benefit from the following features:

■ **Search** to find what you need to know.
■ Check the meaning of key terms with the integrated pop-up **glossary**.
■ Follow **hyperlinks** to further online materials.
■ **Notes** can be added to the text, and shared between instructors and students.

*BookShelf will provide access to your eTextbook either online or as a download via your PC, Mac (OS X 10.6>), iPad, iPhone, iPod Touch (iOS 3.2>), Android app or Amazon Kindle Fire.

FOR INSTRUCTORS

- Energize debate in class with videos and further discussion questions from the Instructor eResource:

  www.routledgeinteractive.com/instructors

- Prepare for your course with the Instructor Manual.

- You will also find on the site PowerPoints for your class, explaining the key points in each chapter.

- Enhance your lessons with the textbook's online image bank.

- Instructors using LTi-compliant Learning Management Systems/ Virtual Learning Environments such as BlackBoard can embed the interactive questions within their course module.

  Blackboard

Image Credits

Figures 1.1, 12.1, 12.3 courtesy of iStock

Figure 1.2 courtesy of Benetton

Figures 1.3, 2.1, 2.2, 2.5, 3.1, 4.1, 4.5, 5.3, 6.2a–c, 7.3, 7.6, 7.7, 7.8, 8.8, 10.1, 11.4, 11.5, 12.4, 13.1, 13.2, 13.10 courtesy of Shutterstock

Figures 1.6a–c, 4.8, 8.4 courtesy of the Associated Press

Figure 2.3 courtesy of Eye of History, Wesleyan University

Figure 2.4 courtesy of Seminarioteorico01.blogspot.com

Figure 3.4 from Pryor, J. B., & Reeder, G. D. (1993). Collective and individual representations of HIV/AIDS stigma. In J. B. Pryor & G. D. Reeder (Eds.), *The social psychology of HIV infection* (p. 271). Hillsdale, NJ: Lawrence Erlbaum Associates

Figures 4.2a–b, 5.6, 5.8, 6.3, 6.4, 8.1a–d, 8.5, 8.7, 9.2, 9.3, 9.4, 9.5a–b, 11.2, 11.3, 12.5, 14.1a–c courtesy of Getty Images

Figure 4.3 with permission of The M. C. Escher Company–Holland

Figures 4.6, 5.1, 12.2, 13.3, 13.8, photographs by William C. Rieter

Figure 5.2 from Clary, E. G., Snyder, M., Ridge, R. D., Miene, P. K., & Haugen, J. A. (1994). Matching messages to motives in persuasion: A functional approach to promoting volunteerism. *Journal of Applied Social Psychology*, 24, 1129–1149

Figure 5.5 from Fishbein, M. & Ajzen, I. 2010. *Predicting and changing behavior: The reasoned action approach*. New York: Psychology Press

Figure 5.7 from Fazio, R. H., & Roskos-Ewoldsen, D. R. (1994). Acting as we feel: When and how attitudes guide behavior. In S. Shavitt & T. C. Brock (Eds.), *Persuasion: Psychological insights and perspectives* (pp. 71–93). Boston: Allyn and Bacon

Figure 6.1 adapted from Ostrom, T. M., Bond, C. F., Jr., Krosnick, J. A., & Sedikides, C. (1994). Attitude scales: How we measure the unmeasurable. In S. Shavitt & T. C. Brock (Eds.), *Persuasion: Psychological insights and perspectives* (pp. 15–42). Boston: Allyn and Bacon

Figure 7.4 adapted from Petty, R. E., & Wegener, D. T. (1999). The Elaboration Likelihood Model: Current status and controversies. In S. Chaiken & Y. Trope (Eds.), *Dual-process theories in social psychology* (pp. 41–72). New York: Guilford

Figure 7.5 from Petty, R. E., Cacioppo, J. T., & Goldman, R. (1981). Personal involvement as a determinant of argument-based persuasion. *Journal of Personality and Social Psychology*, 41, 847–855

Figure 8.3 courtesy of http://wikis.lib.ncsu.edu/index.php/Ethical_Concerns_in_ Experimental_Research

Figure 9.1, graph courtesy of Paul B. Shepson

Figure 10.2 courtesy of the Creative Advertising Archive

Figure 10.3 from Witte, K. (1998). Fear as motivator, fear as inhibitor: Using the Extended Parallel Process Model to explain fear appeal successes and failures. In P. A. Andersen & L. K. Guerrero (Eds.), *Handbook of communication and emotion: Research, theory, applications, and contexts* (pp. 423–450). San Diego: Academic Press

Figure 10.4 courtesy of Sodahead.com

Figure 11.1 courtesy of Columbia Pictures Corporation

Figure 13.4 image from Robert B. Zajonc, R. B. 1968. Attitudinal effects of mere exposure. *Journal of Personality and Social Psychology Monographs Supplement*, 9 (2, Pt. 2), 1–27

Figures 13.6a–c courtesy of Budweiser

Figure 13.9 based on the ELM, and Mitchell, A. A. (1986). Effects of visual and verbal components of advertisements on brand attitudes. *Journal of Consumer Research*, 13, 12–24

Images on pp. 384, 406 courtesy of Nike

Figure 14.2 courtesy of zdnet.com

Figure 14.3 reprinted with permission of the National Crime Prevention Council

Figure 14.4 from McGuire, W. J. (1989). Theoretical foundations of campaigns. In R. E. Rice & C. K. Atkin (Eds.), *Public communication campaigns* (2nd ed., pp. 43–65). Thousand Oaks, CA: Sage. Reprinted by permission of Sage

Figure 14.6 adapted from Maibach, E. W., Kreps, G. L., & Bonaguro, E. W. (1993). Developing strategic communication campaigns for HIV/AIDS prevention. In S. Ratzan (Ed.), *AIDS: Effective health communication for the 90s* (pp. 15–35). Washington, DC: Taylor & Francis

Figure 14.7 courtesy of Favors and Voices of Recovery—South Africa

Figure 14.8a–c courtesy of Tobacco News

Figure 14.9 from Pierce, J. P., Emery, S., & Gilpin, E. (2002). The California tobacco control program: A long-term health communication project. In R. Hornik (Ed.), *Public health communication: Evidence for behavior change* (pp. 97–114). Mahwah, NJ: Lawrence Erlbaum Associates

Figure 14.10 courtesy of the Penn State University Collegian

Part One **Foundations**

Chapter 1

Introduction to Persuasion

 Listen now to the author's chapter summary

When someone mentions persuasion, what leaps to mind? Advertising perhaps? Those sneaky subliminals your friend warned you about? Or maybe the annoying Internet ads that stalk you online based on your recent visits to commercial Web sites? Or perhaps it is something different: images of charismatic leaders who captivate an audience through the cadence of their speech? Or those slick politicians with perfectly coiffed hair, blow dried for television, always accompanied by a sinuous, insincere smile? That's persuasion, right? Powerful stuff—the kind of thing that wields strong effects on society and spells success for its purveyors. But what about you? What does persuasion mean to you personally? Can you think of times when the media or attractive communicators changed your mind about something? Anything come to mind? "Not really," you say. You've got the canny ability to see through what other people are trying to sell you.

Well, that's perhaps what we like to think. "It's everyone else who's influenced, not me or my friends—well, maybe my friends, but not me." But wait: What about those Levi's jeans, UGG boots, Juicy Couture sweater, or Nike sneakers you bought? Marketing had to play a role in that decision somehow. What about the book you purchased on Amazon after reading all the favorable customer reviews? You have to admit that other people's comments may have swayed you more than a smidgeon. And, if you search your mind, you probably can think of lots of times when you yielded to another's pushy persuasion, only to regret it later—the time you let yourself get talked into allowing a car repair that turned out to be unnecessary or agreed to loan a friend some money, only to discover she had no intention of paying you back.

But that's all negative. What of the positive side? Have you ever been helped by a persuasive communication—an antismoking ad or a reminder that it's not cool or safe to drink when you drive? Have you ever had a conversation with a friend who opened your eyes to new ways of seeing the world or a teacher who said you had potential you didn't know you had?

You see, this is persuasion too. Just about anything that involves molding or shaping attitudes involves persuasion. Now there's another term that may seem foreign at first: attitudes. Attitudes? There once was a rock group that called itself that. But we've got attitudes as surely as we have arms, legs, cell phones, or Facebook pages. We have attitudes about music, politics, money, sex, race, even God. We don't all share the same attitudes, and you may not care a whit about issues that intrigue your acquaintances. But we have attitudes and they shape our world in ways we don't always recognize. Persuasion is the study of attitudes and how to change them.

Persuasion calls to mind images of salespeople and manipulators, such as clever strategists on classic TV shows like *Survivor* and *The Apprentice.* It may also conjure up images of con artists, such as the swindlers who, just hours after the onset of Hurricane Katrina, created bogus Web sites soliciting donations for hurricane victims. Persuasion may bring to mind the unscrupulous bankers who lured prospective home buyers into purchasing mortgages they could not afford. It may also bring to mind those innumerable Web sites hoping to hoodwink people or offering questionable instruction on how to manage your money, fix your car, represent yourself in court, or live a happy life. (The British Web site VideoJug once had a link advising women to marry ugly men.) But there is another side too: persuasive communications have been used by good people to implement change. Social activists have used persuasion to change attitudes toward minorities and women. Consumer advocates have tirelessly warned people about dishonest business practices. Health communicators have launched countless campaigns to change people's thinking about cigarettes, alcohol, drugs, and unsafe sex. Political leaders have relied on persuasion when attempting to influence opinions toward policy issues or when trying to rally the country behind them during national crises. Some of our greatest leaders have been expert persuaders—Abraham Lincoln, Martin Luther King, Jr., and Franklin Delano Roosevelt come immediately to mind, as do the crop of current political persuaders, working in the thicket of the Internet age. (See Figure 1.1.)

Persuasion at once intrigues and repels us. We are fascinated by charisma, why some people have it and others don't. We are riveted by courtroom trials, both in television fiction and in real life. Many women waited in line to watch the trial of Casey Anthony, charged with killing her two-year-old daughter Caylee with chloroform and duct tape. Some curiosity-seekers longed to see if the prosecution could make the case that Casey killed her daughter because she grew frustrated with motherhood, which kept her away from the sybaritic life of cocktails and men. Others found themselves drawn in by the courtroom drama, intrigued by the strategies her lawyers ingeniously devised to poke holes in the prosecution's arguments. At the same time as we are piqued by persuasion in cases like the Anthony trial, we recoil when reading about its horrific excesses, such as its use by charismatic cult leaders and terrorists who lure vulnerable young people

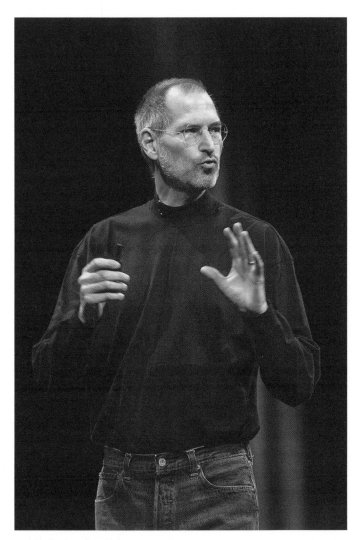

■ Figure 1.1 The late Steve Jobs, the computer and marketing guru, showcased the ways that persuasion could be harnessed for positive purposes. Jobs unleashed his communication skills to develop and promote Apple computers, the iPod, iPhone, and iPad.

Image courtesy of iStock photos.

into their lairs, only to later exploit their innocence in a deadly fashion. The power of persuasion—its ability to captivate and connive—fascinates people the world over.

This book explores these issues. It examines persuasive communication and the dynamics of attitudes that communicators hope to change. The text also examines applications of persuasion theories to a host of contexts, ranging from advertising to politics to physical health. On a more personal note, I try to show how you can use persuasion insights to become a more effective persuasive speaker and a more critical judge of social influence attempts.

PERSUASION: CONSTANCIES AND CHANGES

The study and practice of persuasion are not new. Persuasion can be found in the Old Testament—for example, in Jeremiah's attempts to convince his people to repent and establish a personal relationship with God. We come across persuasion when we read about John the Baptist's exhortations for Christ. John traveled the countryside, acting as Christ's "advance man," preaching that "Christ is coming, wait till you see him, when you look in his eyes you'll know that you've met Christ the Lord" (Whalen, 1996, p. 110).

Long before professional persuaders hoped to turn a profit from books on closing a deal, traveling educators known as the Sophists paraded through ancient Greece, charging money for lectures on public speaking and the art of political eloquence. Five centuries before political consultants advised presidential candidates how to package themselves on television, the Italian diplomat Niccolo Machiavelli rocked the Renaissance world with his how-to manual for political persuaders, entitled *The Prince*. Machiavelli believed in politics and respected crafty political leaders. He offered a litany of suggestions for how politicians could maintain power through cunning and deception.

In the United States, where persuasion has played an outsized role in politics and commercial sales, it should come as no surprise that communication campaigns are as American as media-advertised apple pie! The first crusade to change health behavior did not occur in 1970 or 1870, but in 1820. Nineteenth-century reformers expressed concern about increases in binge drinking and pushed for abstinence from alcohol. A few years later, activists committed to clean living tried to persuade Americans to quit using tobacco, exercise more, and adopt a vegetarian diet that included wheat bread, grains, fruits, and vegetables (Engs, 2000).

As they say in France: *Plus ça change, plus c'est la même chose* (the more things change, the more they remain the same). Yet, for all the similarities, there are important differences between our era of persuasion and those that preceded it. Each epoch has its own character, feeling, and rhythm. Contemporary persuasion differs from the past in the following six ways.

The Sheer Number of Persuasive Communications Has Grown Exponentially

Online advertising, public service announcements, negative political commercials, and those daily interruptions from telephone marketers are among the most salient indicators of this trend. Eons ago, you could go through a day with preciously little exposure to impersonal persuasive messages. This is no longer true during an epoch in which messages are conveyed through mediated channels, such as radio, television, the Internet, and cell phones. And it's not just Americans who are besieged by persuasion. The reach of mass persuasion extends to tiny villages thousands of miles away. A U.S. college student traveling in remote areas of China reported that, while stranded by winter weather, he came across a group of Tibetans. After sharing their food with the student, the Tibetans began to discuss an issue that touched on matters American. "Just how," one of the Tibetans asked the young American, "was Michael Jordan doing?" (LaFeber, 1999, p. 14). More recently, another basketball superstar—LeBron James of the Miami Heat—has become an international phenomenon. In an example of global persuasion's full-court press, James was a sensation in China, where National Basketball Association stores promoted his image, his Nike commercials were seen everywhere, and sports Web sites celebrated his accomplishments, at least until his brand elicited controversy in the wake of his decision to leave the Cleveland Cavaliers basketball team (Boyer, 2006; see Box 1.1).

Persuasive Messages Travel Faster Than Ever Before

Advertisements "move blindingly fast," one writer observes (Moore, 1993, p. B1). Ads quickly and seamlessly combine cultural celebrities (Beyoncé), symbols (success, fame, and athletic prowess), and commodity signs (the Nike swoosh). With the push of a button, political marketing specialists can send out a text message across the world. In August 2008, Barack Obama's presidential campaign spread the news that it planned to announce Obama's vice-presidential choice in a slick, contemporary fashion—via text message to supporters. The text message guaranteed favorable news coverage and provided a public relations bonanza.

Borrowing and adapting a technique from the political marketer's playbook, Google and Twitter organized a virtual protest in January, 2012 of Congressional online piracy legislation that could undermine freedom of expression on the Internet. Within hours after the protest captured attention, more than four million people had signed Google's online petition to convey their opposition to Congress, and more than two million posts on the topic had flowed through Twitter. Texts and short posts have become the signatures of instantaneous contemporary persuasion, characterized as much by their brevity as by their speed.

Persuasion Has Become Institutionalized

No longer can a Thomas Jefferson dash off a Declaration of Independence. In the 21st century, the Declaration would be edited by committees, test marketed in typical American communities, and checked with standards departments to make sure it did not offend potential constituents.

BOX 1.1 PERVASIVENESS OF PERSUASION

Persuasion is part of the fabric of everyday life, so much so that it is hard to escape its tentacles. One observer tried to count the number of direct attempts to influence his behavior over the course of a day. These included people asking him to do favors, countless requests to buy things, and assorted ideological appeals. "By the time I reached my office at mid-morning, I lost count somewhere around 500," he says (Rhoads, 1997).

From the Internet to television to salespeople selling . . . just about everything, our social environment is fraught with direct and indirect influence attempts. The development of an effective sales pitch is a key part of a business plan. But it's not just the commercial businesses that are after us. Consider these three very different examples of the pervasiveness of persuasion:

■ Pastor Lee McFarland is an evangelical Christian who is part marketer and part true believer. He quit a well-paying job at Microsoft to lead a church, splitting from Redmond, Washington, to a town with the unlikely name of Surprise, Arizona.

McFarland left before completing the correspondence classes he was taking to become an evangelical pastor. Knocking on doors, sending out fliers with the help of a direct mail company, and developing billboards that showed a smiling family next to the caption, "Isn't it time you laughed again?" McFarland plied his communication skills to attract people to a church he called Radiant. Recognizing that the young White residents of the Arizona exurbs were in search of a sense of community, McFarland built the church so that it would feel warm and inviting. The church foyer includes five plasma-screen TVs, 10 Xboxes for elementary school kids, a bookstore, and café. "We want the church to look like a mall," he says. "We want you to come in here and say, 'Dude, where's the cinema?'" (Mahler, 2005, p. 33). "If Oprah and Dr. Phil are doing it, why shouldn't we?" he adds. "We should be better at it because we have the power of God to offer" (Mahler, 2005, p. 35). Over the course of 8 years, weekly attendance at Radiant increased from 147 to 5,000, making it the fastest-growing of the city's 28 churches.

But questions remain. Some critics dismiss this new brand of religious persuasion as "Christianity lite." Scholar James B. Twitchell sees it as part of a new marketing phenomenon in which Christianity "went from in your heart to in your face." Describing a preacher who, like McFarland, aggressively markets his credo, Twitchell says, "He's not in the soul business, he's in the self business" (Blumenthal, 2006, p. B7).

■ The ad begins innocently enough, with the camera tracking a mother as she stands over a checkbook and calculator on her kitchen table. That's when her daughter, a young African-American woman, sits down and says, "Look Mom, if I decide I still want to be a doctor when I get out, I'll have had 4 years' experience as a nurse or an X-ray tech. That's why I want to enlist in the military; it'll be good for my career. What do you think?" The advertisement then fades and shows the address of the Defense Department's military recruitment Web site. A voiceover intones, "Make it a two-way conversation. Get the facts at *todaysmilitary.com*" (O'Brien, 2005, p. 1).

The Army spends close to $300 million annually on advertising, while at the same time pouring money into online video games geared to teenagers, leaflets (one brochure hyped the military's 30 days of annual paid vacation), and a battery of interpersonal influence techniques. Army recruiters spend several hours a day making cold calls to high school students. They show up at malls and high schools, doing whatever they can to entice young people to enlist (Cave, 2005a, 2005b). "The football team usually starts practicing in August," an Army recruiting handbook advises. "Contact the coach and volunteer to assist in leading calisthenics or calling cadence during team runs" (Herbert, 2005a, p. A29). One sergeant sounded more like a sales rep when he proclaimed to a campus group, "I mean, where else can you get paid to jump out of airplanes, shoot cool guns, blow stuff up and travel, seeing all kinds of different countries?" ("Leave No Sales Pitch Behind," 2005, p. A22).

Activities like these are perfectly legal. To many recruiters, it is a source of pride to recruit soldiers dedicated to fighting the nation's war on terrorism. But not everyone sees it this way. Columnist Bob Herbert, a relentless critic of the war in Iraq, points out that many recruiters exploit young people's vulnerabilities and present a false picture of what it is like to fight for your country. Although the Iraq war has ended, his observations remain pertinent. Herbert observed:

Continued

Recruiters desperate for warm bodies to be shipped to Iraq are prowling selected high schools and neighborhoods across the country with sales pitches that touch on everything but the possibility of being maimed or killed in combat . . . But war is not a game. Getting your face blown off is not fun . . . Potential recruits should be told the truth about what is expected of them, and what the risks are. And they should be told why it's a good idea for them to take those risks. If that results in too few people signing up for the military, the country is left with a couple of other options: Stop fighting unnecessary wars, or reinstate the draft.

(2005b, p. A17)

■ Lest you think that all persuasion today is ethically problematic, consider the truth-is-stranger-than-fiction case of Ashley Smith. On a Friday in mid-March, Brian Nichols, on trial in Atlanta for rape, seized the gun of a sheriff's deputy and fatally shot the judge in his case. On the run from police, Nichols accosted Ashley when she returned to her apartment from a late-night run to buy cigarettes. He bound her with masking tape and carried her to the bedroom, where he tied her up with more masking tape and an electrical cord.

Although most people would scream, panic, or fight back, Ashley turned the other cheek. She listened as Nichols told her what had happened in the Atlanta courthouse. She then explained that he had killed a man who was probably a father and a husband.

She asked Nichols if he would mind if she read from a book. He agreed. She read to him from a bestselling book, *The Purpose-Driven Life*, which claims that each person's life has a divinely inspired purpose. Ashley subsequently revealed aspects of her life to Nichols. She was married and had a 5-year-old daughter. But tragedy had struck when her husband was stabbed in a fight by old friends and died in her arms. The incident set in motion a dark period for Ashley, including arrests for drunken driving and assault. She had put her life in order, crediting her recovery to faith in God. "You need to turn yourself in. No one else needs to die and you're going to die if you don't," she told him.

She asked Nichols how he felt about what he had done and sensed a change in his demeanor. He was no longer the brazen warrior. They talked some more, she cooked him breakfast, and then called 911 on her cell phone. The police swarmed into the apartment and he surrendered. "I believe God brought him to my door so he couldn't hurt anyone else," Ashley said (Dewan & Goodstein, 2005; Rankin & Plummer, 2005, p. 2).

Numerous companies are in the persuasion business. Advertising agencies, public relations firms, marketing conglomerates, lobbying groups, social activists, pollsters, speech writers, image consultants—companies big and small—are involved with various facets of persuasion. The list is long and continues to grow.

Persuasion has become a critical weapon in the arsenal of powerful companies. Tobacco companies use public relations agents to massage their images in the face of broad public criticism. Political interest groups spend millions to influence the votes of members of Congress. Energy companies hire persuasion specialists to deflate the arguments of environmentalists concerned about global warming. Wealthy, powerful organizations have more resources to use persuasion effectively than do less politically connected groups. They can depend upon networks of connections spread across society's most influential institutions. While persuasive messages are prepared by entrepreneurial individuals working online, most persuasion activities occur in organizational settings, with high-powered companies playing an important role in the influence process.

Persuasive Communication Has Become More Subtle and Devious

We are long past the days in which brash salespeople knocked on your door to pitch encyclopedias or hawk Avon cosmetics directly. Nowadays, salespeople know all about flattery, empathy, nonverbal communication, and likeability appeals. Walk into a Nordstrom clothing store and you see a fashionably dressed man playing a piano. Nordstrom wants you to feel like you're in a special, elite place, one that not-so-incidentally sells brands of clothing that jibe with this image.

Advertising no longer relies only on hard-sell, "hammer it home" appeals, but also on soft-sell messages that play on emotions. Some years back, the United Colors of Benetton clothing company showed attention-grabbing pictures of a dying AIDS patient and a desperately poor Third World girl holding a White doll from a trash can. The pictures appeared with the tag line, "United Colors of Benetton." What do these images have to do with clothing? Nothing—and everything. Benetton was selling an image, not a product. It appealed to consumers' higher sensibilities, inviting them to recognize that "the world we live in is not neatly packaged and cleansed as most ads depict it . . . at Benetton we are not like others, we have vision" (Goldman & Papson, 1996, p. 52; see Figure 1.2).

You can also find examples of the subtlety and deceptiveness of persuasion in the news media. Some years ago the U.S. government produced a series of 90-second TV segments that looked like news, "smelled" like news, and were broadcast by local television stations in some of the nation's largest media markets, including New York City,

■ **Figure 1.2 Today's persuasive communications are characterized by the use of indirect and subtle appeals. What message do you think this ad for United Colors of Benetton, a clothing and fashion accessories company, is trying to convey?**

Image courtesy of Benetton.

Chicago, and Atlanta. One report described the Bush administration's program to strengthen aviation security, calling it "one of the most remarkable campaigns in aviation history." Another segment showed Bush signing into law legislation that gave prescription drug benefits to people with Medicare health insurance. The reporter, Karen Ryan, touted the advantages of the law, but failed to mention other aspects of the story, such as prominent criticism that it was a gift to the pharmaceutical industry. What the tens of millions of Americans who watched these reports did not know was that they were prepared by public relations experts hired by the federal government and "reporters" like Karen Ryan were actually PR consultants (Barstow & Stein, 2005).

Political and commercial messages like these have left an imprint on the public. They have made Americans more cynical about persuasion. Bombarded by communications promoted as truth but actually misleading, as well as by blogs that dissect institutional messages, consumers have grown wary of the truthfulness of persuaders' claims. They seem to recognize that this is an age of spin in which commercial and political communicators regard the truth as just another strategy in the persuasion armamentarium.

Persuasive Communication Is More Complex and Meditated

Once upon a time long ago, persuaders knew their clients. Everyone lived in the same small communities. When cities developed and industrialization spread, persuaders knew fewer of their customers, but could be reasonably confident that they understood their clients because they all shared the same cultural and ethnic background. As the United States has become more culturally and racially diverse, persuaders and consumers frequently come from different sociological places. A marketer cannot assume that her client thinks the same way that she does or approaches a communication encounter with the same assumptions. The intermingling of people from different cultural groups is a profoundly positive phenomenon, but it makes for more dicey and difficult interpersonal persuasion.

What's more, persuasive communication seems to bombard in multiple directions, from a plethora of media. Advertisements, political advertisements and even interpersonal appeals from Facebook friends to see this movie, join this cause, or reject another friend's manipulative stance are emblematic of the contemporary age. Technology increasingly mediates—comes between—the communicator and message recipient.

Persuasive Communication Has Gone Digital

Digital technology has changed the nature of persuasion in several key respects. It has increased complexity, blurring lines among information, entertainment, and influence. For example, a Web site intended to inform or amuse may capture the eye of a blogger, who combines it with imagery and sends the modification over the Internet. It's now a persuasive message, taking on a meaning the original communicator never intended. A classic example involves a song originally sung by the musical group Green Day, "Wake me up when September ends," a political song about war and romance. When a blogger known as Zadi linked the song with TV news coverage of Hurricane Katrina and posted it on her Web site in September 2005, it became a musically conveyed persuasive message about society's indifference to Katrina's victims (Boxer, 2005). The pairing of lyrics like "summer has come and passed, the innocent can never last" with images of devastation created an eerie, haunting message. When combined with suggestions that the Bush administration had been callous in its response to hurricane victims, the mélange conveyed a potent political message, one that might be at odds with the original Green Day song, with its more ambiguous stand toward the war in Iraq.

Over the ensuing decade, millions of people have routinely performed the same digital editing strategy on less storied persuasive messages. Contemporary technologies make it possible for people to alter the content of persuasive messages, giving messages meanings they did not have and that the original communicator did not intend. From a purist's perspective, this raises questions. How dare someone remix the Bible, or Shakespeare? To a purist, it seems almost . . . blasphemous. On the other hand, the freedom to modify the content of persuaders' messages empowers receivers, offering them opportunities to challenge powerful persuaders in innovative ways. And it is also fun, suggesting that the "p" in persuasion can also stand for playful.

Interactivity, for its part, allows endless two-way communication between senders and receivers, enabling receivers to transform the meaning of messages so they no longer comport with the original communication, producing a seemingly infinite potpourri of sender–receiver intersections. Thus, the Internet has democracized persuasive discourse, creating a mechanism by which "regular citizens, possessing nothing more than a cheap video camera (or just a cell phone or computer cam) can have a significant impact on an election, a public debate, a business controversy, or any other form of public issue" (Gurak & Antonijevic, 2009, p. 504).

Interactive technologies have eviscerated the boundary between persuader and per-suadee. As one writer notes, "the line between persuader and persuaded is becoming less like the one between labor and management and more like the one between driver and pedestrian—one we might cross over frequently in a single day" (Johnson, 2011, p. 18).

On the other hand, change is not without down sides. One of the negative aspects of online persuasion is that it allows individuals to hide behind the veil of a computer or anonymity. This can reduce psychological inhibitions, leading individuals to unleash vitriolic, virulently negative messages to communicators who have rubbed them the wrong way. (See Table 1.1 for a summary of persuasion changes).

■ **Table 1.1 Six ways today's persuasion differs from previous eras**

1. Number of messages
2. Speed
3. Conducted via institutions and organizations
4. Subtlety
5. Complexity and mediation
6. Digitization

FOUNDATIONS OF PERSUASION

Persuasion is celebrated as a quintessential human activity, but here's a subversive thought: Suppose we're not the only ones who do it? What if our friends in the higher animal kingdom also use a little homespun social influence? Frans de Waal painstakingly observed chimpanzees in a Dutch zoo and chronicled his observations in a book aptly called *Chimpanzee Politics* (1982). His conclusion: chimps use all sorts of techniques to get their way with peers. They frequently resort to violence, but not always. Chimps form coalitions, bluff each other, and even show some awareness of social reciprocity, as they seem to recognize that favors should be rewarded and disobedience punished.

Does this mean that chimpanzees are capable of persuasion? Some scientists would answer "yes" and cite as evidence chimps' subtle techniques to secure power. Indeed, there is growing evidence that apes can form images, use symbols, and employ deception (Angier, 2008; Miles, 1993). To some scientists, the difference between human and animal persuasion is one of degree, not kind.

Wait a minute. Do we really think that chimpanzees persuade their peers? Perhaps they persuade in the *Godfather* sense of making people an offer they can't refuse. However, this is not persuasion so much as it is coercion.

As we will see, persuasion involves the persuader's awareness that he or she is trying to influence someone else. It also requires that the "persuadee" make a conscious or unconscious decision to change his mind about something. With this definition in mind, chimpanzees' behavior is better described as social influence or coercion than persuasion. "Okay," you animal lovers say, "but let me tell you about my cat." "She sits sweetly in her favorite spot on my sofa when I return from school," one feline-loving student told me, "then curls up in my arms, and purrs softly until I go to the kitchen and fetch her some milk. Isn't that persuasion?" Well—no. Your cat may be trying to curry your favor, but she has not performed an act of persuasion. The cat is not cognizant that she is trying to "influence" you. What's more, she does not appreciate that you have a mental state—let alone a belief—that she wants to change. Some animals, like apes, do have cognitive abilities. For example, they are aware of themselves; they can recognize that a reflected image in a mirror is of them (Fountain, 2006). But there is no evidence that they have beliefs or attitudes; nor do their attempts to influence humans appear directed at changing human attitudes.

There is one other reason why it does not make sense to say that animals engage in persuasion. Persuasion has moral components; individuals choose to engage in morally beneficent or morally reprehensible actions. However, as philosopher Carl Cohen

(Cohen & Regan, 2001) points out, "with all the varied capacities of animals granted, it remains absolutely impossible for them to act *morally*, to be members of a moral community . . . A being subject to genuinely moral judgment must be capable of grasping the *maxim* of an act and capable, too, of grasping the *generality* of an ethical premise in a moral argument" (p. 38). Even granting that animals have mental and emotional capacities, they most assuredly cannot function as moral creatures who consciously make moral (or immoral) communicative decisions. (See Figure 1.3.)

At the same time, we need to remember that the difference between the capacity of humans and higher animals to persuade is frequently one of degree. In light of increasing evidence that monkeys have rudimentary abilities to read intentions, draw mental inferences and behave (if not think) in morally relevant ways (Hauser, 2006), we should remember that higher animals are capable of some social influence, but do not possess a full-blown ability to change attitudes in a manner that could be characterized as persuasion.

■ **Figure 1.3 Higher animals like apes and gorillas can coerce their peers. They can also engage in considerable social influence. However, they are not capable of persuasion, a human activity.**

Image courtesy of Shutterstock.

In sum, persuasion matters, and strikes to the core of our lives as human beings. This means that we must define what we mean by persuasion and differentiate it from related terms.

DEFINING PERSUASION

Scholars have defined persuasion in different ways. I list the following major definitions to show you how different researchers approach the topic. Persuasion, according to communication scholars, is:

- a communication process in which the communicator seeks to elicit a desired response from his receiver (Andersen, 1971, p. 6);
- a conscious attempt by one individual to change the attitudes, beliefs, or behavior of another individual or group of individuals through the transmission of some message (Bettinghaus & Cody, 1987, p. 3);
- a symbolic activity whose purpose is to effect the internalization or voluntary acceptance of new cognitive states or patterns of overt behavior through the exchange of messages (Smith, 1982, p. 7); and
- a successful intentional effort at influencing another's mental state through communication in a circumstance in which the persuadee has some measure of freedom (O'Keefe, 1990, p. 17).

All of these definitions have strengths. Boiling down the main components into one unified perspective (and adding a little of my own recipe), I define **persuasion** as a symbolic process in which communicators try to convince other people to change their own attitudes or behaviors regarding an issue through the transmission of a message in an atmosphere of free choice. There are five components of the definition.

Persuasion Is a Symbolic Process

Contrary to popular opinion, persuasion does not happen with the flick of a switch. You don't just change people's minds—snap, crackle, pop. On the contrary, persuasion takes time, consists of a number of steps, and actively involves the recipient of the message. As Mark Twain quipped, "Habit is habit, and not to be flung out of the window, but coaxed downstairs a step at a time" (cited in Prochaska et al., 1994, p. 471).

Many of us view persuasion in macho terms. Persuaders are seen as tough-talking salespeople, strongly stating their position, hitting people over the head with arguments, and pushing the deal to a close. But this oversimplifies matters. It assumes that persuasion is a boxing match, won by the fiercest competitor. In fact, persuasion is different.

It's more like teaching than boxing. Think of a persuader as a teacher, moving people step by step to a solution, helping them appreciate why the advocated position solves the problem best. Persuasion, in short, is a process.

Persuasion also involves the use of symbols. A **symbol** is a form of language in which one entity represents a concept or idea, communicating rich psychological and cultural meaning. Symbols include words like freedom, justice, and equality; nonverbal signs like the flag, Star of David, or Holy Cross; and images that are instantly recognized and processed like the Nike swoosh or McDonald's golden arches. Symbols are persuaders' tools, harnessed to change attitudes and mold opinions. Thus, persuasion frequently does not operate on a literal level. Language is subject to multiple interpretations. Meanings differ, depending on the way words and pictures pique audience members' imaginations, and the interpretations individuals apply to the same message. A rose is not always a rose. It may be a blossoming beauty to one audience and a thorn to another.

A message that uses the word "fetus" or "unborn child" has strikingly different meanings to pro-life and pro-choice audiences. To Jews, Christians, and Muslims who inhabit the Middle East, Jerusalem is not a neutral place, but calls up different religious meanings. It is a place of holiness to Jews, embedded in Jewish consciousness as the spiritual ancestral homeland of the Jewish people. For Christians, Jerusalem is the city where Jesus preached and healed, and prophetically sat at his Last Supper. For Muslims, Jerusalem is a sacred place, the site of the prophet Muhammad's ascent to heaven.

In political persuasive communications, you find that some of the most vociferous debates involve different symbols attached to material objects. To conservatives, guns are about the Second Amendment to the Constitution and freedom that cuts to the core of gun owners' identities. To liberals, guns connote killing, death of innocents, and a psychological insecurity cloaked in Second Amendment verbiage.

Meanings, multiple and shifting, inhabiting the rich tableau of the human mind: these are centerpieces of persuasion.

Persuasion Involves an Attempt to Influence

Persuasion does not automatically or inevitably succeed. Like companies that go out of business soon after they open, persuasive communications often fail to reach or influence their targets. However, persuasion does involve a deliberate attempt to influence another person. Persuaders must intend to change another individual's attitude or behavior and must be aware (at least at some level) that they are trying to accomplish this goal.

For this reason it does not make sense to say that chimpanzees persuade each other. As noted earlier, chimps, smart as they are, do not seem to possess high-level awareness that they are trying to change another primate, let alone modify a fellow chimp's mind. Indeed, it is unlikely that they can conceptualize that the other animal has a mind that they seek to change, let alone an attitude that they would like to modify.

In a similar fashion, we should not make the claim that very young children are capable of persuasion. True, a mother responds to an infant's cry for milk by dashing to the refrigerator (or lending her breast, if that's her feeding preference). Yes, we have all shopped in toy stores and watched as 2-year-olds point to toys seen on television and scream, "I want that." And we have been witness to the pitiful sight of parents, who pride themselves on being competent professionals, helplessly yielding to prevent any further embarrassment.

Yet the baby's cry for milk and the toddler's demand for toys do not qualify as persuasion. These youngsters have not reached the point where they are aware that they are trying to change another person's mental state. Their actions are better described as coercive social influence than persuasion. In order for children to practice persuasion, they must understand that other people can have desires and beliefs; recognize that the persuadee has a mental state that is susceptible to change; demonstrate a primitive awareness that they intend to influence another person; and realize that the persuadee has a perspective different from theirs, even if they cannot put all this into words (Bartsch & London, 2000). As children grow, they appreciate these things, rely less on coercive social influence attempts than on persuasion, and develop the ability to persuade others more effectively (Kline & Clinton, 1998).

The main point here is that persuasion represents a conscious attempt to influence the other party, along with an accompanying awareness that the persuadee has a mental state that is susceptible to change. It is a type of social influence. *Social influence* is the broad process in which the behavior of one person alters the thoughts or actions of another. Social influence can occur when receivers act on cues or messages that were not necessarily intended for their consumption (Dudczak, 2001). Persuasion occurs within a context of intentional messages that are initiated by a communicator in the hope of influencing the recipient. This is pretty heady stuff, but it is important because, if you include every possible influence attempt under the persuasion heading, you count every communication as persuasion. That would make for a very long book.

The larger question is whether persuasion should be defined from the perspective of the audience member or of the communicator. If you define it from the audience member's point of view, then every message that attempts to change someone's attitude gets counted as persuasion. This is democratic, but unwieldy. It means that communication and persuasion are identical. Yet people do a lot of communicating—talking, gossiping, disclosing things about themselves—that are not attempts to persuade. Some may be experienced as social influence, others less so. In any case, much everyday communication is not intended to change attitudes. For this reason, it is more useful to stipulate that persuasion involves some sort of deliberate effort to change another person's mind.

People Persuade Themselves

One of the great myths of persuasion is that persuaders convince us to do things we really don't want to do. They supposedly overwhelm us with so many arguments or such verbal ammunition that we acquiesce. They force us to give in. This overlooks an important point: people persuade themselves to change attitudes or behavior. Communicators provide the arguments. They set up the bait. We make the change, or refuse to yield. As D. Joel Whalen puts it:

> You can't force people to be persuaded—you can only activate their desire and show them the logic behind your ideas. You can't move a string by pushing it, you have to pull it. People are the same. Their devotion and total commitment to an idea come only when they fully understand and buy in with their total being.
>
> (1996, p. 5)

The observation of the legendary psychologist William James remains true today: "The greatest discovery of our generation is that human beings can alter their lives by altering their attitudes of mind. As you think, so shall you be" (quoted in Johnson & Boynton, 2010, p. 19).

You can understand the power of self-persuasion by considering an activity that does not at first blush seem to involve persuasive communication: therapy. Therapists undoubtedly help people make changes in their lives. But have you ever heard someone say, "My therapist persuaded me"? On the contrary, people who seek psychological help look into themselves, consider what ails them, and decide how best to cope. The therapist offers suggestions and provides an environment in which healing can take place (Kassan, 1999). But if progress occurs, it is the client who makes the change and the client who is responsible for making sure that there is no regression to the old ways of doing things. Of course, not every self-persuasion is therapeutic. Self-persuasion can be benevolent or malevolent. An ethical communicator will plant the seeds for healthy self-influence. A dishonest, evil persuader convinces a person to change her mind in a way that is personally or socially destructive. Note also that persuasion typically involves change. It does not focus on forming attitudes, but on inducing people to alter attitudes they already possess. This can involve shaping, molding, or reinforcing attitudes, as is discussed later in the chapter.

Persuasion Involves the Transmission of a Message

The message may be verbal or nonverbal. It can be relayed interpersonally, through mass media, or via the Internet. It may be reasonable or unreasonable, factual or emotional. The message can consist of arguments or simple cues, like music in an advertisement that brings pleasant memories to mind. Persuasion is a communicative activity; thus, there must be a message for persuasion, as opposed to other forms of social influence, to occur.

Life is packed with messages that change or influence attitudes. In addition to the usual contexts that come to mind when you think of persuasion—advertising, political campaigns, and interpersonal sales—there are other domains that contain attitude-altering messages. News unquestionably shapes attitudes and beliefs (McCombs & Reynolds, 2002). Talk to older Americans who watched TV coverage of White policemen beating Blacks in the South or chat with people who viewed television coverage of the Vietnam War, and you will gain firsthand evidence of how television news can shake up people's worldviews. News of more recent events—Hurricane Katrina, the tragedy of September 11, America's never-ending economic malaise—have left indelible impressions on people's views of politics and the world as a whole.

Art—books, movies, plays, and songs—also has a strong influence on how we think and feel about life. Artistic portrayals can transport people into different realities, changing the way they see life (Green & Brock, 2005). If you think for a moment, I'm sure you can call to mind books, movies, and songs that shook you up and pushed you to rethink your assumptions. Dostoyevsky's discussions of the human condition, a Picasso painting, movies like *The Help*, *The Color Purple*, *Schindler's List*, and *Inception*, *The Simpsons* television show, a folk melody or rap song—these can all influence and change people's worldviews.

Yet, although news and art contain messages that change attitudes, they are not pure exemplars of persuasion. Recall that persuasion is defined as an attempt to convince others to change their attitudes or behavior. In many cases, journalists are not trying to change people's attitudes toward a topic. They are describing events so as to provide people with information, offer new perspectives, or entice viewers to watch their programs. In the same fashion, most artists do not create art to change the world. They write, paint, or compose songs to express important personal concerns, articulate vexing problems of life, or soothe, uplift, or agitate people. In a sense, it demeans art to claim that artists attempt only to change our attitudes. Thus, art and news are best viewed as borderline cases of persuasion. Their messages can powerfully influence our worldviews, but because the intent of these communicators is broader and more complex than attitude change, news and art are best viewed as lying along the border of persuasion and the large domain of social influence.

For example, you can easily think of movies that have a clearly persuasive purpose. Michael Moore definitely hoped that *Fahrenheit 9/11* would convince Americans to change their attitudes toward former President Bush and the war in Iraq. Director Gus Van Sant seems to have hoped that *Milk*, the story of the first openly gay man to be elected to public office in California, would serve some educational functions, teaching people about the political plight of gay Americans. But other directors' motives are less clear cut. It seems unlikely that Paul Haggis wrote *Crash* some years back to promote a liberal or conservative agenda. Instead, he seems to have had grander, more complex purposes that in all likelihood centered on inducing viewers to think more deeply about the complex ways that prejudice insinuates its way into everyday American life. Was Haggis trying to persuade viewers, or, more likely, was he trying to nudge them to look at life through different lenses?

Persuasion Requires Free Choice

If, as noted earlier, self-persuasion is the key to successful influence, then an individual must be free to alter her own behavior or to do what he wishes in a communication setting. But what does it mean to be free? Philosophers have debated this question for centuries, and if you took a philosophy course, you may recall those famous debates about free will versus determinism.

There are more than 200 definitions of freedom, and, as we will see, it is hard to say precisely when coercion ends and persuasion begins. I suggest that a person is free when he has the ability to act otherwise—to do other than what the persuader suggests—or to reflect critically on his choices in a situation (Smythe, 1999). Even so, it is important to remember that people do not have absolute freedom, even in a democratic society like ours that enshrines human rights. Americans do not have the same access to international media, such as the Middle East television network Al Jazeera, that offer critical portraits of U.S. policies, as they do to American media that provide a more positive picture. Are Americans free to sample all media? Theoretically, yes, but practically, no. From an early age, American children are exposed to advertisements that tout the blessings of commercial products, but have virtually no exposure to communications that question the virtues of the capitalist system. Given the powers of socialization, how free are these individuals to reject the trappings of capitalism when they become adults? In America, girls and boys learn (partly through advertising) that diamond rings symbolize marital bliss and that marriage is a desirable life-pursuit. What is the likelihood that, as adults, these individuals could reject wedding rings and marriage after, say, reading articles that criticize the spiritual emptiness of material possessions and the rigidities of marital roles?

I ask these questions not to argue that wedding rings or marriage are without value, but to suggest that none of us is as free as we think—not in America or in any other culture, and that the concept of freedom that underlies persuasion is a relative, not an absolute, concept.

Summary

This section has offered a definition of persuasion, delineating its main features. Throughout the book, we will trace the ways in which these distinctive characteristics of persuasion play out in real life. The key attributes of persuasion are that it operates as a process, not a product; relies on symbols; involves the communicator's intent to influence; entails self-persuasion; requires the transmission of a message; and assumes free choice. Of all these attributes, the one that cuts to the core of persuasion is self-persuasion. *In the end, we persuade ourselves. We decide to change our own minds about issues, people, and ideas. Persuaders transmit messages, call on their most attractive features, play word games, and even manipulate verbal cues in hopes of convincing us to change our attitudes about an issue.*

Now that persuasion has been defined, it is important to differentiate it from related aspects of social influence. To truly understand the nature of persuasion, you have to appreciate how it overlaps with and diverges from coercion, propaganda, and manipulation.

PERSUASION VERSUS COERCION

How does persuasion differ from coercion? The answer may seem simple at first. Persuasion deals with reason and verbal appeals, while coercion employs force, you suggest. It's not a bad start, but there are subtle relationships between the terms—fascinating overlaps—that you might not ordinarily think of. Consider these scenarios:

- Tom works for a social service agency that receives some of its funding from United Way. At the end of each year, United Way asks employees to contribute to the charity. Tom would like to donate, but he needs every penny of his salary to support his family. One year, his boss, Anne, sends out a memo strongly urging employees to give to United Way. Anne doesn't threaten, but the implicit message is: I expect you to donate, and I'll know who did and who didn't. Tom opts to contribute money to United Way. Was he coerced or persuaded?
- Debbie, a college senior, makes an appointment with her favorite English professor, Dr. Stanley Hayes, to get advice on where to apply for graduate school. Hayes compliments Debbie on her writing style, tells her she is one of the best students he has had in 20 years of teaching, and reflects back on his own experiences as a youthful graduate student in American literature. The two chat for a bit, and Hayes

asks if she would mind dropping by his house for dessert and coffee to discuss this further. "Evening's best for me," Hayes adds. Debbie respects Professor Hayes and knows she needs his recommendation for graduate school, but she wonders about his intentions. She accepts the offer. Was she persuaded or coerced?

■ Elizabeth, a high school junior, has been a football fan since grade school and throughout middle school. Waiting eagerly for the homecoming game to start, she glances at the field, catching a glimpse of the senior class president as he strides out to the 50-yard line. Much to her surprise, the class president asks the crowd to stand and join him in prayer. Elizabeth is squeamish. She is not religious and suspects that she's an atheist. She notices that everyone around her is standing, nodding their heads, and reciting the Lord's Prayer. She glances to her left and sees four popular girls shooting nasty looks at her and shaking their heads. Without thinking, Elizabeth rises and nervously begins to speak the words herself. Was she coerced or persuaded?

Before we can answer these questions, we must know what is meant by coercion. Philosophers define coercion as a technique for forcing people to act as the coercer wants them to act—presumably contrary to their preferences. It usually employs a threat of some dire consequence if the actor does not do what the coercer demands (Feinberg, 1998, p. 387). Tom's boss, Debbie's professor, and Elizabeth's classmates pushed them to act in ways that were contrary to their preferences. The communicators employed a direct or veiled threat. It appears that they employed coercion.

Things get murkier when you look at scholarly definitions that compare coercion with persuasion. Mary J. Smith (1982) takes a relativist perspective, emphasizing the role of perception. According to this view, it's all a matter of how people perceive things. Smith argues that when people believe that they are free to reject the communicator's position, as a practical matter they are free, and the influence attempt falls under the persuasion umbrella. When individuals perceive that they have no choice but to comply, the influence attempt is better viewed as coercive.

Assume now that Tom, Debbie, and Elizabeth are all confident, strong-minded individuals. Tom feels that he can say no to his employer. Debbie, undaunted by Professor Hayes's flirtatiousness, believes that she is capable of rejecting his overtures. Elizabeth feels that she is free to do as she pleases at the football game. In this case, we would say that the influence agents persuaded the students to comply.

On the other hand, suppose Tom, Debbie, and Elizabeth lack confidence in themselves and don't believe that they can resist these communicators. In this case, we might say that these individuals perceived that they had little choice but to comply. We would conclude that coercion, not persuasion, had occurred.

You can now appreciate how difficult it is to differentiate persuasion and coercion. Scholars differ on where they draw the line between the two terms. Some would say that the three influence agents used a little bit of both. (My own view is that the first case is the clearest instance of coercion. The communicator employed a veiled threat. What's more, Tom's boss wielded power over him, leading to the reasonable perception that Tom had little choice but to comply. The other two scenarios are more ambiguous; arguably, they are more persuasion than coercion because most people would probably assume that they could resist the communicators' appeals. In addition, no direct threats of any kind were employed in these cases.) More generally, the point to remember here is that persuasion and coercion are not polar opposites but, rather, overlapping concepts.

PERSUASION AND COERCION OVERLAP ON THE INTERNATIONAL STAGE

Terrorism is unquestionably a coercive act: it employs threats of dire consequence and physical force to compel individuals to behave as the coercer wants them to behave. But terrorists also have persuasive goals. "The point of terrorism," Louise Richardson notes, "is not to defeat the enemy but to send a message . . . Victims are used as a means of altering the behavior of a larger audience" (2006, pp. 4–5). Terrorists commit violent acts to gain attention and sympathy for their cause. They may kill dozens of innocent people to influence millions of others. They attempt to provoke a reaction, hoping to scare people, convince them to change their lifestyles, or demonstrate that the terrorist organization remains capable of communicating a message. Persuasion and coercion are sometimes inextricable, more difficult to unravel than is commonly assumed.

One sees this all too clearly in the controversial abuses of Iraqi prisoners at the Abu Ghraib prison some years back (Zimbardo, 2007). During the war in Iraq, a handful of American soldiers humiliated and tortured Iraqi prisoners—for example, leaving a detainee naked in his cell and forcing him to bark like a dog and crawl on his stomach as soldiers urinated and spat on him. He was later sodomized by a police stick while two female military police officers threw a ball at his genitals. Even those who supported the war in Iraq and sympathized with the terrible pressures soldiers faced from attacks from insurgents acknowledged that the soldiers' behavior was unethical. Were the soldiers coerced or persuaded? It is hard to separate the two forms of social influence. Coercion clearly was at work. During the early phases of the war, senior military commanders made it clear that they wanted intelligence information about Iraqi pris-oners. This in turn placed pressure on lower-level officers to take whatever steps were necessary to obtain this information (Schmitt, 2004). The White House had declared that Al Qaeda and the Taliban were outside the purview of the Geneva Convention's restrictions on torture. Thus, it seems plausible that Pentagon officials implicitly conveyed acceptance of torture as a way to get information and that this attitude filtered down the chain of command.

By the same token, the soldiers who committed the abuses do not appear to have been ordered to perform these specific actions. Private Lynndie England—who held a leash around the neck of a naked Iraqi prisoner and gleefully posed next to naked Iraqi men who had been forced to simulate masturbation—told a military court she knew this was wrong. Pleading guilty to seven criminal counts, she admitted that she went along because her former lover, Sergeant Charles Graner, "asked me to." "Could you have chosen to walk away?" the judge asked her. "I could have," Private England said. "I was yielding to peer pressure" (Levy, 2005). Acknowledging her personal freedom, England sounds like she was acquiescing to a persuasive influence attempt.

It is easy to criticize England and Graner, but none of us knows what we would have done if we had faced the same pressures that these two soldiers experienced in Iraq. Social influence—coercion and persuasion—exerts powerful, not always positive, effects on human behavior. The line between persuasion and coercion is rarely clear and is even murkier in situations like Abu Ghraib (see Figures 1.4 and 1.5, and Box 1.2). Difficult as it is to make absolute demarcations, it is important to differentiate the terms clearly.

Those who say it all comes down to perception must wrestle with the ambiguity (unsatisfactory in a court of law) that an influence attempt can be persuasion for one person (if he claims to be free to reject the communicator's position), yet coercive for another (if she claims she has no choice but to comply). This means that two individuals could be influenced by the same message, but one (who claimed it was persuasion) would be held accountable for his actions, while the other (who perceived coercion) could be exonerated on the grounds that she lacked the freedom to reject the message. This is clearly unsatisfactory. Interesting as the perceptual approach is, it does not provide a clear boundary line between persuasion and coercion. A more concrete approach is needed.

Coercion and persuasion are not polar opposites. They are better viewed as lying along a continuum of social influence.

■ **Figure 1.4 Coercion and persuasion.**

■ **Figure 1.5 Understanding persuasion, coercion, and borderline cases of persuasion.**

Note that coercion can be negative, or positive (as in smoking bans and enforcement of seat belt laws). Borderline cases focus on persuasion rather than coercion. They lie just outside the boundary of persuasion because the intent of the communicator is not to explicitly change an individual's attitude toward the issue, but is, instead, broader and more complex (Gass & Seiter, 2011).

Based on contemporary approaches, we can say that **coercion** occurs when the influence agent: (a) delivers a believable threat of significant physical or emotional harm to those who refuse the directive, (b) deprives the individual of some measure of freedom or autonomy, and (c) attempts to induce the individual to act contrary to her preferences (Dahl, 1989; Feinberg, 1998; Rosenbaum, 1986). Persuasion, by contrast, occurs in an atmosphere of free choice: it assumes the individual is capable of resisting an influence attempt or of willingly persuading him or herself to alter an attitude about an issue.

THE BAD BOYS OF PERSUASION

We're not done yet! There are two additional terms that are bandied about when social influence and persuasion are discussed: *propaganda* and *manipulation*. Propaganda overlaps with persuasion, as both are invoked to describe powerful instances of social influence. **Propaganda** is defined as a form of communication in which the leaders of a ruling group have near or total control over the transmission of information, typically relying on mass media to reach target audience members, using language and symbols in a deceptive and manipulative fashion. There are several key differences between propaganda and persuasion.

First, propaganda refers to instances in which a group has total control over the transmission of information—for example, Hitler in Nazi Germany, the Chinese Communists during the Chinese Revolution, Saddam Hussein in Iraq, and violent religious cults. Persuasion can be slanted and one sided, but it ordinarily allows for a free flow of information; in persuasion situations, people can ordinarily question the persuader or offer contrasting opinions.

Second, propaganda is typically invoked to describe mass influence through mass media. Persuasion, by contrast, occurs in mediated settings, but also in interpersonal and organizational contexts.

Third, propaganda is deceptive and can be covert. Some years ago, the Pentagon planted articles in Iraqi newspapers. The articles put a positive spin on the Iraqi economy and the country's political future in an effort to win the hearts and minds of the Iraqi people (Gerth & Shane, 2005). Pentagon officials figured that Iraqis would be more persuaded if they perceived the stories to be bonafide news rather than what they were—stories written by an American public relations firm hired by the Defense Department. Neither the true source nor the intent of the communications could be discerned by audience members, pointing up another aspect of propaganda.

BOX 1.2 THE CULT OF PERSUASION

Edison Jessop, a resident of the Yearning for Zion Ranch in west Texas, had no complaints. "We've got 300 pounds of cabbage out of there already, and a couple hundred more coming," he said, as he drove by a garden (Kovach, 2008). Jessop regarded the ranch, home to followers of the Fundamentalist Church of Latter Day Saints, as a wonderful place to raise children. However, the church was also a polygamist community that followed the strict teachings of leader Rulon Jeffs and his son, Warren. Television and Internet were forbidden. Laughter was against the law. All the women wore old-fashioned "Little House on the Prairie Dresses." Some of the men had as many as five wives. Warren Jeffs is believed to have fathered more than 100 children (Atlas et al., 2008). Most disturbingly, there was evidence of possible sexual abuse. When a 16-year-old girl called a domestic abuse hotline, claiming she had been abused by her 50-year-old husband, state authorities raided the compound. Although there was disagreement about the merits—and legality—of the state's action, there was little doubt that the church bore the earmarks of a religious cult.

It was hardly the first time that a religious cult attracted national attention. In March 1997, the nation learned the tragic fate of the 39 members of Heaven's Gate Cult, all of whom committed suicide. Many wondered why 39 intelligent, committed men and women willingly took their own lives, joyfully announcing their decision in a farewell videotape and statement on their Web site. The suicide was timed to coincide with the arrival of the Hale–Bopp comet. Believing that a flying saucer was traveling behind the comet, members chose to leave their bodies behind to gain redemption in a Kingdom of Heaven (Robinson, 1997). To many people, this provided yet another example of the powerful, but mysterious, technique called brainwashing. The cult leader, Marshall Applewhite, known to his followers as "Do," supposedly brainwashed cult members into committing mass suicide in their home in Rancho Santa Fe, California. Although Heaven's Gate was the first Internet cult tragedy, one that drove millions of curiosity seekers to the group's Web site, it was only the most recent in a series of bizarre cult occurrences that observers could describe only as brainwashing. In one of the most famous of these tragic tales, over 900 members of the People's Temple followed leader Jim Jones's directive to drink cyanide-spiked Kool-Aid at the cult's home in Guyana, South America, back in 1978. (See Figure 1.6.) Other cases, including the violent story of David Koresh's Branch Davidians in Waco, Texas (circa 1993), continue to fascinate and disturb. Searching for a simple answer, people assume that charismatic leaders *brainwash* followers into submission.

Famous though it may be, brainwashing is not a satisfactory explanation for what happens in cults. It does not tell us why ordinary people choose to join and actively participate in cults. It does not explain how leaders wield influence or are able to induce followers to engage in self-destructive behavior. Instead, the brainwashing term condemns people and points fingers.

How can we explain the cult phenomenon? First, we need to define a cult. A **cult** is a group of individuals who are: (a) excessively devoted to a charismatic leader,

Continued

■ **Figure 1.6a–c The residues of cults:**
The dead at Jonestown, where more
than 900 individuals followed the
directive of cult leader Jim Jones
to drink cyanide-laced Kool-Aid at
the cult's home in Guyana, South
America in 1978. Some two decades
later, followers of Marshall
Applewhite, shown right, wore
identical clothing and displayed a
common group identity, as members
of the Heavens' Gate cult. Thirty-
nine cult members committed
suicide en masse, announcing their
decision in a farewell videotape on
the cult's Web site in March, 1997.

Images courtesy of the Associated Press.

himself or herself "the object of worship"; (b) effectively isolated from the rest of society; (c) denied access to alternative points of view; and (d) subjected to exploitative social influence techniques (see Lifton, 2003, p. xii). To appreciate how cults influence individuals, we need to consider the dynamics of persuasion and coercion. As an example, consider the case of one young person who fell into the Heaven's Gate cult and, by crook or the hook of social influence, could not get out. Her name was Gail Maeder, and she was one of the unlucky 39 who ended her life on that unhappy March day.

Gail, a soft-hearted soul, adored animals. The lanky 27-year-old also loved trees, so much so that she tried not to use much paper. Searching for something— maybe adventure, possibly herself—she left suburban New York for California. Traveling again, this time in the Southwest, she met some friendly folks in a van— members of Heaven's Gate, it turns out. Gail joined the group and told her parents not to worry. She was very happy.

If you look at Gail's picture in *People*, taken when she was 14, you see a bubbly all-American girl with braces, smiling as her brother touches her affectionately (Hewitt et al., 1997). Your heart breaks when you see the photo, knowing what will happen when she becomes an adult. People join cults—or sects, the less pejorative term—for many reasons. They are lonely and confused, and the cult provides a loving home. Simple religious answers beckon and offer a reason for living. Isolated from parents and friends, young people come to depend more on the cult for social rewards. The cult leader is charismatic and claims to have supernatural powers. He gains followers' trust and devotion. Purposelessness is relieved; order replaces chaos. The more people participate in the group's activities, the better they feel; the better they feel, the more committed they become; and the more committed they are, the more difficult it is to leave.

Initially, cult leaders employ persuasive appeals. Over time they rely increasingly on coercive techniques. Heaven's Gate leaders told followers that they must learn to deny their desires and defer to the group. At Heaven's Gate, it was considered an infraction if members put themselves first, expressed too much curiosity, showed sexual attraction, trusted their own judgment, or had private thoughts. Everyone woke at the same time to pray, ate the same food, wore short haircuts and nondescript clothing, and sported identical wedding rings on their fingers to symbolize marriage to each other. Individual identity was replaced by group

Continued

identity. Autonomy gave way, slowly replaced by the peacefulness of groupthink (Goodstein, 1997). Once this happens—and it occurs slowly—cult members no longer have free choice; they are psychologically unable to say no to leaders' demands. Coercion replaces persuasion. Conformity overtakes dissent. Persuasion and coercion coexist, shading into one another. Simple demarcations are hard to make.

Gail Maeder wasn't street smart, her father said. "She just got sucked in and couldn't get out" (Hewitt et al., 1997, p. 47).

Events like Heaven's Gate are deeply troubling. It is comforting to affix blame on charismatic cult leaders like Applewhite. It is easy to say that they brainwashed people into submission. But this ignores the powerful role that coercive social influence and persuasive communication play in cults. And it tragically underplays the psychological needs of people like Gail, folks who persuaded themselves that a doomsday cult provided the answer to their problems.

It would be a happy ending if Heaven's Gate were the last cult that exploited individuals' vulnerabilities. However, in recent years, we have witnessed the growth of cross-national terrorist cults composed of men who are convinced that America is the enemy of Islam and are willing to kill innocent people or themselves, if directed by their *maulanas* or masters (Goldberg, 2000). It is tempting to view these individuals as victims of terrorist brainwashing—automatons directed into action by receipt of an e-mail message. Once again, the brainwashing metaphor simplifies and distorts. These individuals have frequently joined Muslim religious schools out of their own volition. Bereft of meaning and purpose in a changing world, grasping for an outlet to express decades-long simmering hate, and seeking a way to exact revenge or seek recognition, they join terrorist cells. There they are groomed, influenced, even coerced by "teachers" and assorted leaders of an international political–religious cult (Zakaria, 2001).

"These are poor and impressionable boys kept entirely ignorant of the world and, for that matter, largely ignorant of all but one interpretation of Islam," notes journalist Jeffrey Goldberg (2000, p. 71). "They are the perfect jihad machines."

Individuals are hardly brainwashed into becoming suicide bombers. They are coerced or more likely persuaded, ultimately convincing themselves that their lives will take on grand meaning if they carry out an action on behalf of their brethren. Terrorist groups employ a host of persuasive techniques, not unlike those used by religious cults. Working in isolation, preying on young men's (and women's) vulnerabilities, and telling them that those who do not follow the extremist path are infidels, terrorists break down recruits' resistance. They convince individuals to commit suicide bombings in the name of Islam. As one recruit put it, "We were taught that . . . everyone else, including our families, was going to hell . . . And I wanted to be one of the select few who made it into heaven" (Ambah, 2006, C4).

A postscript: Not every Middle Eastern young man or woman who is isolated, feels vulnerable, or is tempted by self-sacrifice will become a suicide bomber. Far from it. Only an unusual handful will execute evil actions. As scholar Alan Wolfe notes, "political evil recruits those attracted to brutality, motivated by a burning sense of victimhood, anxious to right what they believe to be long-standing wrongs, and in extreme cases willing to die for their beliefs" (2011, pp. 78–79). Unfortunately, history is littered with examples of leaders harnessing coercion and manipulating the symbols of persuasion for destructive purposes.

The final difference between propaganda and persuasion lies in the connotation or meaning of the terms. Propaganda has a negative connotation; it is associated with bad things or evil forces. Persuasion, by contrast, is viewed as a more positive force, one that can produce beneficial outcomes. Subjectively, we use the term propaganda to refer to *a persuasive communication with which one disagrees and to which the individual attributes hostile intent.* Liberals claim that the news is unadulterated propaganda for Republicans; conservatives contend that the news is propaganda for the Left. Both use the propaganda term to disparage the news. When you hear people call a persuasive communication propaganda, beware. The speakers are using language to denounce a message with which they disagree.

A related term, frequently used synonymously with persuasion, is manipulation. People frequently use the term to criticize persuaders for employing underhanded techniques. "She's so manipulative," someone charges. "That's another example of media manipulation," a friend observes. Is manipulation the same as persuasion? Is all persuasion manipulative? Although the terms overlap, there are key differences. **Manipulation** is a persuasion technique that occurs when a communicator hides his or her true persuasive goals, hoping to mislead the recipient by delivering an overt message that disguises its true intent. Flattery, sweet talk, and false promises are manipulative techniques.

All persuasion is not manipulative. A persuader whose motives are honest and transparent is not employing manipulation. At the same time, message recipients can naively trust a communicator, failing to notice that the persuader is disguising more sinister intentions. A trusting receiver may fall prey to manipulative con artists, who run the gamut from sweet-talking salesmen promising infirmed elderly individuals "miracle" pain products at exorbitant prices to the celebrated case of financier Bernard Madoff, who bilked thousands of trusting clients of their life-savings in a $50 billion scam.

UNDERSTANDING PERSUASIVE COMMUNICATION EFFECTS

Up to this point, the discussion has emphasized the differences between persuasion and related terms. However, there are different kinds of persuasive communications, and they have different types of effects. Some messages dramatically influence attitudes; others exert smaller or more subtle impacts. Taking note of this, Miller (1980) proposed that communications exert three different persuasive effects: shaping, reinforcing, and changing responses.

Shaping. Today everyone has heard of the Nike "swoosh." You've seen it on hundreds of ads and on the clothing of celebrity athletes. It's a symbol that resonates and has helped make Nike a leader in the athletic shoe business. The now-classic ad campaigns featuring Michael Jordan and Bo Jackson helped mold attitudes toward Nike by linking Nike with movement, speed, and superhuman athletic achievement.

A nastier example is cigarette marketing. Tobacco companies spend millions to shape people's attitudes toward cigarettes, hoping they can entice young people to take a pleasurable, but deadly, puff. Marketers shape attitudes by associating cigarettes with beautiful women and virile men. They appeal to teenage girls searching for a way to rebel against boyfriends or parents by suggesting that smoking can make them appear defiant and strong willed. ("I always take the driver's seat. That way I'm never taken for a ride," said one Virginia Slims ad.)

On a more positive level, socialization can be regarded as an example of attitude shaping or formation. Influential social agents model a variety of pro-social values and attitudes, such as self-discipline, altruism, and religion.

Reinforcing. Contrary to popular opinion, many persuasive communications are not designed to convert people, but rather to reinforce a position they already hold. As will be discussed in Chapter 4, people have strong attitudes toward a variety of topics, and these attitudes are hard to change. Thus, persuaders try to join 'em, not beat 'em.

In political campaigns, candidates try to bolster party supporters' commitment to their cause. Democratic standard-bearers have made late-campaign appeals to African-American voters, the overwhelming majority of whom are registered Democrats. Republican candidates have won elections by appealing to religious conservatives. Increasingly, political consultants argue that elections are not solely about winning over undecided voters, but, rather, concentrate on appeals to the base.

In a similar fashion, health education experts try to reinforce individuals' decisions to quit smoking or to abstain from drinking in excess. Persuaders recognize that people can easily relapse under stress, and they design messages to help individuals maintain their commitment to giving up unhealthy substances.

Changing. This is perhaps the most important persuasive impact and the one that comes most frequently to mind when we think of persuasion. Communications can and do change attitudes. Just think how far this country has come in the last 50 years on the subject of race. In the 1950s and 1960s, Blacks were lynched for being in the wrong place at the wrong time, many southerners openly opposed school desegregation, and northern Whites steered clear of socializing with Black friends or colleagues. This changed as civil rights campaigns, heart-rending media stories, and increased dialogue between Blacks and Whites led Whites to rethink their prejudiced attitudes toward African-Americans (Thernstrom & Thernstrom, 1997). In 1948, 4 percent of Americans favored marriage between Blacks and Whites. Nearly a half century later, the percentage in agreement had increased 18-fold, to 72 percent (Grimes, 2005).

Negative attitudes toward gay marriage have also begun to crumble. In American cities where gay couples would have been flogged or killed decades ago, prejudice has given way to tolerance. Consider Jacksonville, Florida. A gay church was bombed there in the 1980s. Nowadays, eight churches accept gay parishioners and one seeks out couples who have children. In fact the city has one of the largest populations of gay parents in the U.S. A pastor who leads a program geared to children of gay parents likens the city's transformation to the metamorphosis of attitudes on civil rights. "Slowly but surely, all this will pass," she said. "I truly believe that" (Tavernise, 2011, A15).

Americans and people worldwide have changed their attitudes on a host of other topics, ranging from the environment to fatty fast food to exercise. Persuasive communications have had strong, desirable effects on these issues. They have influenced attitudes and behavior.

Important as these effects are, they rarely occur overnight. Persuasion is a process; change can be slow and painstaking. A bigot does not become more open minded after one persuasive encounter. It takes many years of exposure to people of color, rethinking of prejudices, and self-insight. Persuasion is a process. It happens over time, step by step, with each step counting as an instance of self-persuasion.

CONCLUSIONS

Persuasion is a ubiquitous part of contemporary life. If you search the term on the Web, you find hundreds of topics, ranging from "brainwashing controversies" to "marketing" to "how to get people to like you." The Internet is a persuader's paradise, with Web sites promoting millions of products and services. However, persuasion has more personal components. We can all think of times when we yielded to other people's influence attempts, tried to persuade friends to go along with us, or scratched our heads to figure out ways we could have done a better job of getting a colleague to accept our plan.

Persuasion is an ancient art. It dates back to the Bible and ancient Greece. Yet there are important aspects of contemporary persuasion that are unique to this era, notably the volume, speed, institutionalization, subtlety, complexity, and digitization of modern messages.

Persuasion is defined as a symbolic process in which communicators try to convince other people to change their own attitudes or behavior regarding an issue through the transmission of a message, in an atmosphere of free choice. A key aspect of persuasion is self-persuasion. Communicators do not change people's minds; people decide to alter their own attitudes or to resist persuasion. There is something liberating about self-persuasion. It says that we are free to change our lives in any way that we wish. We have the power to become what we want to become—to stop smoking, lose weight, modify dysfunctional behavior patterns, change career paths, or discover how to become a dynamic public speaker. Obviously, we can't do everything: there are limits set by both our cognitive skills and society. But in saying that people ultimately persuade themselves, I suggest that we are partly responsible if we let ourselves get conned by dishonest persuaders. I argue that people are capable of throwing off the shackles of dangerous messages and finding positive ways to live their lives.

Of course, this is not always easy. The tools of self-persuasion can be harnessed by both beneficent and malevolent communicators. Persuaders can be honest and truthful, appealing to the best angels in the message recipient. Or they can be dishonest and manipulative, trying to pull the wool over people's eyes. Trying to see the best in a persuader or hoping that a persuader's ministrations will bring them wealth, love, or happiness, people can coax themselves into accepting messages advanced by unsavory communicators. When this occurs, persuaders are ethically responsible for the choices they make.

Social influence is a powerful phenomenon. It can be viewed as a continuum, with coercion lying on one end and persuasion at the other. There are not always black-and-white differences between persuasion and coercion. They can overlap, as in situations involving authority, religious cults, and prisoner torture. Still, with clear definitions we can disentangle coercion and persuasion. Coercion occurs when the influence agent delivers a believable threat of some consequence, deprives the individual of some measure of freedom or autonomy, and attempts to induce the individual to act contrary to his or her preferences. Persuasion occurs in an atmosphere of free choice, where the individual is autonomous, capable of saying no, and able to change his or her mind about the issue.

Even in coercive situations, people "choose" to accept or reject the communicator's directive. But their choices and freedom are seriously compromised psychologically and philosophically, and they cannot be held ethically accountable for their behavior.

Persuasion overlaps with propaganda and manipulation. These terms carry negative connotations and differ in several ways from persuasion. In the main, propaganda occurs when leaders have near or total control over transmission of information, employ deception, and rely on media to target masses of individuals. Manipulation occurs when a persuader disguises his or her intent, hoping to mislead the message recipient with a charming or otherwise disingenuous message.

Persuasion, broadly defined, has a host of effects on individuals, including forming, reinforcing, and changing attitudes. Are these effects good or bad? Is persuasion a morally positive or pernicious force? Stay tuned. I take up these questions in the next chapter.

Test your knowledge now with interactive exercises

Chapter 2

Historical and Ethical Foundations

 Listen now to the author's chapter summary

Rhetoric has a bad name.

We say "that's just rhetoric" to indicate displeasure with a politician's attempt to puff up his or her record. Rhetoric is frequently linked with political double-talk. The term—if it is used at all—is synonymous with empty words and deliberately ambiguous statements.

It was not always thus. In ancient times, respected scholars viewed rhetoric through very different lenses. Rhetoric—what we now call persuasion—was an exalted component of civilization, one linked with eloquence, learning, and high moral character. Orators were lionized. Roman scholars proclaimed that society needed orators who had broad training in the liberal arts and ethics. As J. Michael Hogan (2013) thoughtfully observes, "a common thread ran through all of classical rhetoric: the need to educate for citizenship. Concerned with the practical and ethical requirements of civic life, the ancient rhetoricians aspired to equip young people with the skills and knowledge they would need to be citizens in a free society." This, of course, contrasts sharply with the contemporary emphasis on persuasion as a way of advancing self-interested goals and cynicism about those who harness oratory in the service of political change.

Calling on past as prologue, this chapter presents a historical and an ethical perspective on persuasion, introducing you to hallmarks in the scholarly study of persuasion over many centuries. After reviewing persuasion history, the chapter takes a contemporary turn, introducing the distinctive features of 21st-century scholarship on persuasion. In the final portion of the chapter, I call on time-honored perspectives on the philosophy of ethics, as I explore their implications for persuasion.

I begin with a historical overview for several reasons. First, historical overviews help us appreciate the origins of ideas. They remind us that we are not the first to ponder persuasion or to wrestle with persuasion dilemmas. Second, a historical approach helps us to glimpse continuities and changes. It demonstrates that dilemmas of today consumed the scholars of yore, while at the same time it calls attention to distinctive problems of contemporary life.

In a similar fashion, an ethical perspective helps us to appreciate how people have grappled with moral dimensions of persuasion over the course of many centuries. It offers insights on the moral issues that face persuaders and in this way can help you more thoughtfully to come to grips with the many ethical dilemmas that are at the heart of contemporary persuasion.

HISTORICAL REVIEW OF PERSUASION SCHOLARSHIP

Ancient Greece: "It's All Sophos to Me"

Rhetoric refers to the use of argumentation, language, and public address to influence audiences. "If any one group of people could be said to have invented rhetoric," James L. Golden and colleagues note, "it would be the ancient Greeks" (Golden, Berquist, & Coleman, 2000, p. 1). The Greeks loved public speech. Trophies were awarded for skill in oratory. Citizens frequently acted as prosecutors and defense attorneys in lawsuits that were daily occurrences in the Athenian city-state (Golden et al., 2000). Before long, citizens expressed interest in obtaining training in rhetoric, or the art of public persuasion.

To meet the demand, a group of teachers decided to offer courses in rhetoric, as well as in other academic areas. The teachers were called Sophists, after the Greek word, *sophos*, for knowledge. The Sophists traveled from city to city, peddling their intellectual wares for a fee; the Sophists were dedicated to their craft but needed to make a living. Two of the traveling teachers—Gorgias and Isocrates—taught classes on oratory, placing considerable emphasis on style.

The Sophists attracted a following, but not everyone who followed them liked what they saw. Plato, the great Greek philosopher, denounced their work in his dialogues. To Plato, truth was a supreme value. Yet the Sophists sacrificed truth at the altar of persuasion, in Plato's view. Thus, he lamented that "he who would be an orator has nothing to do with true justice, but only that which is likely to be approved by the many who sit in judgment" (Golden et al., 2000, p. 19). The Sophists, he charged, were not interested in discovering truth or advancing rational, "laborious, painstaking" arguments, but, rather, in "the quick, neat, and stylish argument that wins immediate approval—even if this argument has some hidden flaw" (Chappell, 1998, p. 516). To Plato, rhetoric was

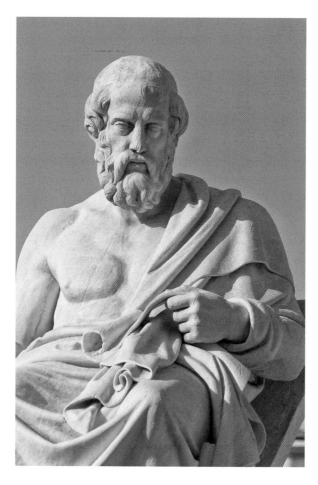

Figure 2.1 The great Greek philosopher Plato distrusted persuasion because it seemed to rely so frequently on style, not substance.

Image courtesy of Shutterstock.

like cosmetics or flattery: not philosophy and therefore not deserving of respect. (See Figure 2.1.)

The Sophists, for their part, saw persuasion differently. They surely believed that they were rocking the foundations of the educational establishment by giving people practical knowledge rather than "highfalutin" truth. They also were democrats, willing to teach any citizen who could afford their tuition.

Why do we care about the differences of opinion between Plato and the Sophists some 2,500 years later? We care because the same issues bedevil us today. Plato is the friend of all those who hate advertisements because they "lie" or stretch the truth. He is on the side of everyone who turns off the television during elections to stop the flow of "political speak," or candidates making any argument they can to win election. The Sophists address those practical persuaders—advertisers, politicians, salespeople—who have to make a living, need practical knowledge to promote their products, and are suspicious of "shadowy" abstract concepts like truth (Kennedy, 1963). The Sophists and Plato offer divergent, dueling perspectives on persuasive communication. Indeed, one of the themes of this book is that there are *dual approaches* to thinking about persuasion: one that emphasizes platonic thinking and cogent arguments and the other focusing on style, oratory, and simpler persuasive appeals that date back to some of the Sophist writers.

The First Persuasion Theorist

Plato's greatest contribution to persuasion—or rhetoric, as it was then called—may not have been the works he created but, rather, his intellectual offspring. His best student— a Renaissance person before there was a Renaissance, a theorist before "theories" gained

■ Figure 2.2 Aristotle developed the first systematic approach to persuasion effects and ethics.

Image courtesy of Shutterstock.

adherents—was Aristotle. Aristotle lived in the 4th century BC and wrote 170 works, including books on rhetoric. His treatise "Rhetoric" is regarded as "the most significant work on persuasion ever written" (Golden et al., 2000, p. 2; see Figure 2.2).

Aristotle's great insight was that both Plato and the Sophists had a point. Plato was right that truth was important, and the Sophists were correct that persuasive communication is a practical tool. Aristotle's great contribution was to recognize that rhetoric could be viewed in a more analytical fashion—as a phenomenon that could be described with precise concepts and by invoking probabilities (Golden et al., 2000; McCroskey, 1997). Drawing on his training in biology, Aristotle developed the first scientific approach to persuasion.

Rather than dismissing persuasion, as did Plato, the more practical Aristotle embraced it. "Aristotle said the goal of rhetoric wasn't so much finding the truth of a matter as convincing an audience to make the best decision about that matter," note Martha D. Cooper and William L. Nothstine (1998, p. 25). Aristotle proceeded to articulate a host of specific concepts on the nature of argumentation and the role of style in persuasion. He proposed methods by which persuasion occurred, described contexts in which it operated, and made ethics a centerpiece of his approach. During an era in which Plato was railing against the Sophists' pseudo-oratory, teachers were running around Greece offering short courses on rhetoric, and great orators made fortunes by serving as ghostwriters for the wealthy, Aristotle toiled tirelessly on the academic front, developing the first theories of persuasion.

Aristotle proposed that persuasion had three main ingredients: *ethos* (the nature of the communicator), *pathos* (emotional state of the audience), and *logos* (message arguments). Aristotle was also an early student of psychology, recognizing that speakers had to adapt to their audiences by considering in their speeches those factors that were most persuasive to an audience member. He valued the development of cogent arguments that could stimulate thoughtful debate in the civic sphere, an ideal that many find lacking in contemporary public life (see Box 2.1). Aristotle regarded ethics as an important component of persuasion, calling attention to the personal character of the orator and proclaiming that "we believe good men more fully and more readily than others."

Aristotle's Greece was a mecca for the study and practice of persuasion. Yet it was not always pretty or just. Women were assumed to be innately unfit for engaging in persuasive public speaking; they were denied citizenship and excluded from the teaching professions (Waggenspack, 2000). Although slaves outnumbered free men in ancient Athens, they could not participate in the vaunted democratic government. Aristotle, though he preached admirably and credibly about ethics, had blind spots that reflected the biases of the era in which he lived.

BOX 2.1 PERSONALITY AND ARGUMENTATION

"Early Sophists roamed ancient Greece fulfilling a great need in the city-states and fledgling democracies—they taught citizens how to argue effectively," Dominic A. Infante and Andrew S. Rancer observe. "Arguing," they note, "was an essential skill for success" (1996, p. 319). The art of argumentation, long prized in communication, has fallen on hard times. Debate classes are no longer required. Students receive preciously little training in developing cogent, logical arguments. The term "argument" has a negative connotation, calling to mind obstinate, unpleasant, even aggressive individuals. Yet skill in arguing is an important ability to cultivate. It can sharpen the mind and help people appreciate the value of sound, logical thinking. Skill in argumentation can also lead to professional success, as arguments and discussions are a critical aspect of just about any job you can think of. Argumentative skill can also help negotiators defuse interpersonal and ethnic conflicts.

Armed with these insights, contemporary scholars have approached argumentation from an empirical perspective, curious as to whether certain individuals are more enthusiastic about arguing than others. Infante and Rancer defined argumentativeness as "a generally stable trait which predisposes individuals in communication situations to advocate positions on controversial issues and to attack verbally the positions which other people hold on these issues" (Infante & Rancer, 1982, p. 72). Infante and Rancer (1982) developed a reliable, valid 20-item scale to tap argumentativeness. If you are an argumentative person (which ancient Greek rhetoricians would view as a positive trait), you would agree with items like these:

- I enjoy a good argument over a controversial issue.
- I have a pleasant, good feeling when I win a point in an argument.
- I consider an argument an exciting intellectual challenge.
- I enjoy defending my point of view on an issue.

Research shows that, contrary to stereotype, argumentativeness confers social benefits. Individuals high in argumentativeness are viewed as more credible persuaders than those low in this trait, and are more inclined to employ a greater range of influence strategies. They also encourage others to give their opinions on controversial matters and are judged as more capable communicators (Infante

Continued

& Rancer, 1996; Rancer, 1998). Interestingly, argumentative individuals are less apt to use their power to goad others into accepting their positions.

Argumentative individuals are not necessarily verbally aggressive, a point that scholars emphasize. "When individuals engage in argumentativeness, they attack the positions that others take or hold on controversial issues," Rancer notes. "When individuals engage in verbal aggressiveness they attack the self-concept of the other," he adds (1998, p. 152). Verbal aggressiveness includes insults, ridicule, and the universal put-down. It can be the province of the desperate communicator, the one who runs out of arguments and resorts to personal attacks. Do you know people who are verbally aggressive? They would be likely to agree with statements like these:

- When individuals are very stubborn, I use insults to soften the stubbornness.
- When I am not able to refute others' positions, I try to make them feel defensive in order to weaken their positions.
- If individuals I am trying to influence really deserve it, I attack their character.
- When people simply will not budge on a matter of importance, I lose my temper and say rather strong things to them.

(Infante & Wigley, 1986)

Verbal aggressiveness reduces the persuader's credibility and overall communication effectiveness (Infante & Rancer, 1996; Wigley, 1998). It produces destructive, rather than constructive, outcomes. Rather than helping or convincing people, one ends up hurting their feelings or feeling guilty oneself.

There are cautionary notes. Several researchers observe that argumentativeness and verbal aggressiveness scales may tap attitudes or self-concepts rather than personality traits per se (Kotowski et al., 2009). Other scholars point out that both argumentativeness and verbal aggressiveness are more likely to be activated in certain situations than in others, such as when the message concerns ego-involving issues. Noting the negative effects of verbal aggressiveness and the virtues of argumentativeness, researchers have developed training programs to teach individuals to argue constructively and to avoid getting enmeshed in destructive communication spirals (Rancer et al., 1997).

When Greek civilization gave way to Rome, the messengers were lost, but not the message. The practical Romans preserved much of Athenian civilization, adapting classic rhetorical works to Roman culture. Their rhetoricians also proclaimed that oratory was a virtue.

When in Rome, Speak as the Roman Rhetoricians

It was the Roman scholars who truly celebrated the art of eloquence. Lamenting the paucity of skilled orators in ancient Rome, Cicero extolled the virtue of public speech. He maintained that the ideal orator should be schooled in the psychology of emotional appeals and should be capable of controlling facial expressions, as well as physical gestures. But there was more to oration than oratorical skill. Cicero believed that the ideal orator should be an individual of high virtue who transcended his personal interests to serve the civic good. The Roman rhetorician Quintilian agreed, placing a premium on the development of moral principles as he integrated oratory and moral education with his aphorism that the ideal citizen is the "good man speaking well" (Hogan, 2013).

We need to be a little cautious in taking these statements at face value. Oratory undoubtedly had different—perhaps broader—meanings than it does today. The Romans' views of moral principles probably do not jibe with contemporary ethical precepts. Nonetheless, it is noteworthy that early rhetoricians so passionately celebrated the art of public address, perhaps launching a respect for great oratory that lives on in the adulation of political speakers encompassing Lincoln, Roosevelt, Churchill, Reagan, and Obama. Interestingly, the Roman rhetoricians' devotion to moral oratory presents a striking contrast to the savage moral culture prevalent in Rome at the time, suggesting that scholars may have developed their philosophy as an antidote to the vices that pervaded the Rome of their day.

Over the course of the ensuing centuries, a series of spectacular events occurred: the fall of the Roman empire, the growth of Christianity, the Black Death, the Italian Renaissance, and the European wars. Rhetorical thought paled in comparison to these events. Nonetheless, the work of the early rhetoricians survived and influenced the political philosophy of subsequent generations, including the founders of the United States.

Rhetorical Developments in the United States

Like Athens, 18th-century America was a persuader's paradise, with merchants, lawyers, politicians, and newspaper editors crafting arguments to mold public opinion. America's founding fathers grew up in a world in which an education in classical rhetoric was presumed to be a prerequisite for political leadership. It was expected that an aspiring political leader could deliver an effective, persuasive speech.

Great rhetorical works emerged in the eighteenth and nineteenth centuries, including the Declaration of Independence and Lincoln's Gettysburg Address. Yet, like ancient Greece, the public paradise was closed to slaves and women. But, unlike Greece, legal limits did not stifle protest voices. Frederick Douglass and, later, W. E. B. DuBois became eloquent spokesmen for disenfranchised African-Americans. Elizabeth Cady Stanton and Susan B. Anthony used rhetorical strategies derived from Cicero in their efforts to gain equality for women (Waggenspack, 2000).

Over the course of the 20th century, rhetoric took a different turn, as it emphasized the power of emotion, human psychology, and the increasingly pervasive mass media. Writing in the aftermath of the devastation of World War II, launched by the destructive rhetoric of Adolf Hitler, Kenneth Burke (1950) focused less on the classical traditions of Greece and Rome than on the enduring power of symbols and emotional identification. Drawing on philosophy and psychoanalysis, he showed how good and evil communicators could persuade people through identification with the audience. People were "symbol-using" creatures, Burke emphasized, and he suggested that audience members were not necessarily passive recipients of messages, but could play an active role in the persuasion process.

Importantly, as Hogan notes, Burkean theory turned rhetoric upside down. Rather than defending civility and the established order, as had been the time-honored practice of classical rhetoric, Burke's approach sympathetically suggested ways that social protest movements could harness rhetoric to challenge and upend the status quo. His theoretical approach anticipated the radical rhetoric of 1960s movements. Within academia, Burke helped to launch alternative perspectives that explored how rhetoric—and the symbols of persuasion—could be employed to challenge the Establishment.

In the years that followed, radical rhetorical critics went further than Burke, questioning rhetoric itself, suggesting that language and rhetoric are necessarily biased and inherently prop up the dominant groups in society. Michel Foucault questioned the notion that there is such a thing as true knowledge. Instead, he claimed, knowledge and truth are interwoven with power; those who rule a society define what is true and what counts as knowledge (Golden et al., 2000). Feminist critics like Karlyn Kohrs Campbell (1989) pointed out that rhetorical history has been dominated by men, and that women were barred from speaking in many supposedly great eras of rhetorical eloquence.

The latter approaches are valuable in that they point out biases in the hallowed tradition of classical rhetoric. At the same time, a number of contemporary scholars would question the postmodern views of Foucault, noting out that individuals are less susceptible to the rhetoric of dominant groups and government than Foucault suggested.

They would point to Internet blogs and Web pages as examples of how social movements develop their own strategies for challenging the status quo. The Occupy Wall Street movement, which popularized the slogan "We are the 99 percent," illustrates the ways protesters can use symbols and rhetorical devices to attract a following.

In our media-dominated age, it is appropriate that scholars have also examined the rhetorical components of mass communications. Marshall McLuhan (1967), using the catchy phrase "the medium is the message," startled and then captivated people by alerting them to the ways in which the medium—television, radio, print—was more important than the content of a communicator's speech. Others scholars followed suit, including Jamieson (1988), who explored "eloquence in an electronic age," as she titled an influential book. Eloquence, which in the past was associated with memorable oratory, now centers on the visual experience, sound bites, and dramatic stories. Beginning with Ronald Reagan and continuing through the present era, Jamieson noted, speakers are regarded as eloquent not when they employ arguments but when they emote and excel at telling folksy stories. Her thesis is engaging, although it was written during an era when television dominated the landscape. In our post-Web 2.0 era, new forms of political discourse that exquisitely fit the contours of interactive media are bound to develop, and they will take on distinctive rhetorical features.

From an academic perspective, rhetorical scholarship continues apace, but has been supplemented and to some degree replaced by social scientific approaches. Rhetorical approaches offer intriguing insights on the basic arguments employed in contemporary persuasion. However, they do not provide evidence about the effects that persuasive communications exert in everyday situations. Social science perspectives, by drawing on theories and scientific methods, yield a wealth of knowledge of the impact of persuasion and the processes by which it achieves its effects.

Origins of the Social Scientific Approach

Social scientific studies of persuasion were born in the 1930s with early research on attitudes (Allport, 1935). Psychologists were fascinated by the power of this new mental construct—*attitude*—and intrigued by the possibility of devising questionnaire methods to study social attitudes. For the first time, something mental and amorphous could be measured with the new techniques of social science. The heady excitement that greeted the development of new attitude measurement techniques was accompanied by a foreboding concern about the powers of propaganda and persuasion, evident in World War I government propaganda campaigns and the disturbing effects of a social movement in Germany that exploited communications for destructive purposes. Hitler's mastery of the new technologies of 20th-century media raised new questions about the ways persuasion could be harnessed for nefarious purposes. America needed to launch its own communication initiative to explore ways of using persuasive messages to mobilize soldiers and the Allied war effort.

Scholarship received a boost when the U.S. War Department commissioned a group of researchers to explore the effects of a series of documentary films. The movies were designed to educate Allied soldiers on the Nazi threat and to boost morale. The War Department asked Frank Capra, who had previously directed such classics as *Mr. Smith Goes to Washington*, to direct the films. They were called simply *Why We Fight*. (See Figure 2.3.)

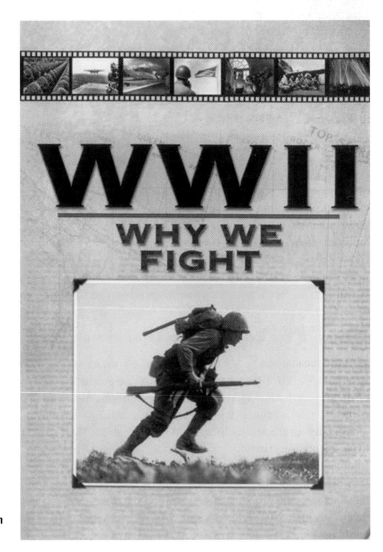

■ **Figure 2.3 The *Why We Fight* films offered an opportunity to test the psychological effects of morale-boosting war-time communications.**

Image courtesy of Eye of History, Wesleyan University.

■ **Figure 2.4 Carl Hovland conducted path-breaking experiments on the psychological effects of persuasive communications.**

Image courtesy of Seminarioteorico01.blogspot.com.

Asked to evaluate the effects of the wartime documentaries, the social scientists received the added benefit of working, albeit indirectly, with Capra. It must have been a heady experience, assessing the effects of a Hollywood director's films on beliefs and attitudes. The studies offered some of the first hard evidence that communications influenced attitudes, albeit complexly (Hovland, Lumsdaine, & Sheffield, 1949). The experiments showed that persuasion research could be harnessed by government for its own ends— in this case, beneficial ones, but certainly not value-neutral objectives.

Several of the researchers working on the *Why We Fight* research went on to do important research in the fields of psychology and communication. One of them, Carl Hovland, seized the moment, brilliantly combining experimental research methodology with the ideas of an old persuasion sage, the first scientist of persuasion, the A-man: Aristotle. Working in a university setting, Hovland painstakingly conducted a series of experiments on persuasive communication effects. (See Figure 2.4.) He and his colleagues took concepts invented by Aristotle—ethos, pathos, and logos—and systematically examined their effects, using newly refined techniques of scientific experimentation (Hovland, Janis, & Kelley, 1953). What the researchers discovered— for example, that credible sources influenced attitudes—was less important than how they went about their investigations. Hovland and colleagues devised hypotheses, developed elaborate procedures to test predictions, employed statistical procedures to determine whether predictions held true, and reported findings in scientific journals that could be scrutinized by critical observers.

Hovland died young, but his scientific approach to persuasion survived and proved to be an enduring legacy. A host of other social scientists, armed with theories, predictions, and questionnaires, began to follow suit. These included psychologists William J. McGuire and Milton Rokeach, and communication scholar Gerald R. Miller. The list of persuasion pioneers also includes Gordon Allport, the luminary psychologist who did so much to define and elaborate on the concept of attitude.

From a historical perspective, the distinctive element of the persuasion approach that began in the mid-20th century and continues today is its empirical foundation. Knowledge is gleaned from observation and evidence rather than armchair philosophizing. Researchers devise scientific theories, tease out hypotheses, and dream up ways of testing them in real-world settings. No one—not the Greeks, Romans, or 20th-century Western rhetorical theorists—had taken this approach. Capitalizing on the development of a scientific approach to behavior, new techniques for measuring attitudes, advances in statistics, and American pragmatism, early researchers were able to forge ahead, asking new questions and finding answers.

Scholarly activity continued apace from the 1960s onward, producing a wealth of persuasion concepts far surpassing those put forth by Aristotle and classical rhetoricians. These terms include attitude, belief, cognitive processing, cognitive dissonance, social judgments, and interpersonal compliance. We also have a body of knowledge—thousands of studies, books, and review pieces on persuasion. More articles and books on persuasion have been published over the past 50 years than in the previous 2,500 years.

What once was a small field that broke off from philosophy has blossomed into a multidisciplinary field of study. Different scholars carve out different parts of the pie. *Social psychologists* focus on the individual, exploring people's attitudes and susceptibility to persuasion. *Communication scholars* cast a broader net, looking at persuasion in two-person units, called dyads, and examining the influences of media on health and politics. *Marketing scholars* examine attitudes toward brands, advertising, and, more generally, the processes by which a society communicates valued products to masses of consumers. If you look up "persuasion" under PsycINFO or in Communication Abstracts, you will find thousands of studies, journal articles, and books.

What's more, research plays a critical role in everyday persuasion activities. Advertising agencies spend millions on research. When Nike plans campaigns geared to young people (with ads resembling music videos), company executives plug in facts gleaned from marketing research. Antismoking campaigns hire academic researchers to probe teenagers' attitudes toward smoking. Campaign specialists want to understand why kids smoke and which significant others are most apt to endorse smoking in order to design messages that change teens' attitudes. In the political sphere, presidential candidates poll voters constantly, trying to understand how they react to candidates' television performances and how candidates can adjust their styles so that they take voters' preferences into account.

Plato, the purist, would be horrified by these developments. Aristotle, the practical theorist, would be pleased that persuasion had become a respected field of academic study. But he would lament ethical shortcomings in the practice of persuasion: mean-spirited political debates and society's failure to insist that moral character serve as a prerequisite for a career in public office. Both would be amazed by the sheer volume of persuasion research and its numerous applications, pro and con, to everyday life. Who knows? Maybe they'll be talking about our age 500 years from now! So, sit back and enjoy. You're about to embark on an exciting intellectual journey, fraught with intriguing findings and complex applications to everyday life.

THE CONTEMPORARY STUDY OF PERSUASION

Contemporary scholars approach persuasion from a social science point of view. This may seem strange. After all, you may think of persuasion as an art. When someone mentions the word "persuasion," you may think of such things as "the gift of the gab," "manipulation," or "subliminal seduction." You may feel that by approaching persuasion from the vantage point of contemporary social science, we are reducing the area to something antiseptic. However, this is far from the truth. Social scientists are curious about the same phenomena that everybody else is: for example, what makes a person persuasive, what types of persuasive messages are most effective, and why people go along with the recommendations put forth by powerful persuaders. The difference between the scientist's approach and that of the layperson is that the scientist formulates theories about attitudes and persuasion, derives hypotheses from these theories, and puts the hypotheses to empirical test. By empirical test, I mean that hypotheses are evaluated on the basis of evidence and data collected from the real world.

Theory plays a major role in the social scientific enterprise. A *theory* is a large, umbrella conceptualization of a phenomenon that contains hypotheses, proposes linkages between variables, explains events, and offers predictions. It may seem strange to study something as dynamic as persuasion by focusing on abstract theories. But theories contain ideas that yield insights about communication effects. These ideas provide the impetus for change. They are the pen that is mightier than the sword.

In fact, we all have theories about human nature and about persuasion (Roskos-Ewoldsen, 1997a; Stiff, 1994). We may believe that people are basically good, parents have a major impact on kids' personalities, or men are more competitive than women. We also have theories about persuasion. Consider these propositions:

- *Advertising exploits people.*
- *You can't persuade people by scaring them.*
- *The key to being persuasive is physical appeal.*

At some level these are theoretical statements—propositions that contain interesting, testable ideas about persuasive communication. But there are problems with the statements from a scientific perspective. They are not bonafide theories of persuasion.

The first statement is problematic because it uses a value-laden term, *exploit*. Exploitation evokes negative images. Perhaps advertising doesn't exploit so much as guide consumers toward outcomes they sincerely want. The first rule of good theorizing is to state propositions in value-free language.

The second statement—you can't persuade people by merely scaring them—sounds reasonable until you start thinking about it from another point of view. One could argue that giving people a jolt of fear is just what is needed to get them to rethink dangerous behaviors like drug abuse or binge drinking. You could suggest that appeals to fear motivate people to take steps to protect themselves from dangerous outcomes.

The third statement—that physical appeal is the key to persuasion—can also be viewed with a critical eye. Perhaps attractive speakers turn audiences off because people resent their good looks or assume they made it because of their bodies, not their brains. I am sure you can think of communicators who are trustworthy and credible, but aren't so physically attractive.

Yet, at first blush, the three statements made sense. They could even be called intuitive "theories" of persuasion. But intuitive theories—our homegrown notions of what makes persuasion tick—are problematic. They lack objectivity. They are inextricably linked with our own biases of human nature (Stiff, 1994). What's more, they can't be scientifically tested or disconfirmed. By contrast, scientific theories are stated with sufficient precision that they can be empirically tested (through real-world research). They also contain formal explanations, hypotheses, and corollaries.

Researchers take formal theories, derive hypotheses, and test them in real-world experiments or surveys. If the hypotheses are supported over and over again, to a point of absolute confidence, we no longer call them theories but, rather, laws of human behavior. We have preciously few of these in social science. (Darwinian evolution counts as a theory whose hypotheses have been proven to the point that we can call it a law.)

At the same time, there are many useful social science theories that can forecast behavior, shed light on people's actions, and suggest strategies for social change.

The beauty of research is that it provides us with a yardstick for evaluating the truth value of ideas that at first blush seem intuitively correct. It lets us know whether our gut feelings about persuasion—for example, regarding fear or good looks—amount to a hill of beans in the real world. Moreover, research provides a mechanism for determining which notions of persuasion hold water, which ones leak water (are no good), and, in general, which ideas about persuasive communication are most accurate, compelling, and predictive of human action in everyday life.

Researchers study persuasion in primarily two ways. They conduct *experiments*, or controlled studies that take place in artificial settings. Experiments provide convincing evidence that one variable causes changes in another. Because experiments typically are conducted in university settings and primarily involve college students, they don't tell us about persuasion that occurs in everyday life among diverse population groups. For this reason, researchers conduct surveys. *Surveys* are questionnaire studies that examine the relationship between one factor (for example, exposure to a media antismoking campaign) and another (e.g., reduced smoking). Surveys do not provide unequivocal evidence of causation.

In the preceding example, it is possible that people may reduce smoking shortly after a media campaign, but the effects may have nothing to do with the campaign. Smokers may have decided to quit because friends bugged them or they wanted to save money on cigarette costs.

Most studies of persuasive communication effects are experiments. Studies of attitudes and media applications of persuasion are more likely to be surveys. Both experiments and surveys are useful, although they make different contributions (Hovland, 1959).

Research, the focus of this book, is important because it clarifies concepts, builds knowledge, and helps solve practical problems. One must not lose sight of the big picture: the role that persuasion plays in society and the fundamental ethics of persuasive communication. The final section of the chapter, building on the preceding discussion, examines these broader concerns.

SEEING THE BIG PICTURE

Persuasion is so pervasive that we often don't ask the question: What sort of world would it be if there were no persuasive communications? It would be a quieter world, that's for sure—one with less buzz, especially around dinnertime when telemarketers phone! But, without persuasion, people would have to resort to different means to get their way. Many would resort to verbal abuse, threats, and coercion to accomplish personal and political goals. Argument would be devalued or nonexistent. Force—either physical or psychological—would carry the day.

Persuasion, by contrast, is a profoundly civilizing influence. It prizes oratory and argument. It says that disagreements between people can be resolved through logic, empathy-based appeals, and the rough-and-tumble banter of group discussion. Persuasion provides us with a constructive mechanism for advancing our claims and trying to change institutions. It offers a way for disgruntled and disenfranchised people to influence society. Persuasion provides a mechanism for everybody—from kids promoting Web sites to Wall Street brokers selling stocks—to advance in life and achieve their goals.

Persuasion is not always pretty. It can be mean, vociferous, and ugly. Persuasion, as Winston Churchill might say, is the worst way to exert influence—except for all the others. Were there no persuasion, George W. Bush and Al Gore would have settled their dispute about the 2000 election vote not in the courtroom, but on the battlefield. Conversely, if persuasion were the accepted way to resolve problems among terrorist militia operating in the Middle East, peace, not deadly violence, would reign supreme.

Persuasion is not analogous to truth. As Aristotle recognized, persuasive communications are designed to influence, rather than uncover, universal truths (Cooper & Nothstine, 1998). In fact, persuaders sometimes hide truth, mislead, or lie outright in the service of their aims or clients. The field of ethics is concerned with determining when it is morally appropriate to deviate from truth and when such deviations are ethically indefensible.

Persuasion assumes without question that people have free choice—that they can do other than what the persuader suggests. This has an important consequence. It means that people are responsible for the decisions they make in response to persuasive messages. Naturally, people can't foresee every possible consequence of choices that they make. They cannot be held accountable for outcomes that could not reasonably have been foreseen.

But one of the essential aspects of life is choice—necessarily based on incomplete, and sometimes inaccurate, information. Provided that individuals have freedom of choice, a foundation of persuasion, they are responsible for the decisions they make. As religious scholar P. J. O'Rourke observed, "One of the annoying things about believing in free will and individual responsibility is the difficulty of finding somebody to blame your problems on. And when you do find somebody, it's remarkable how often his picture turns up on your driver's license" (quoted in Genzlinger, 2011, p. C6)!

At the same time, persuaders also make choices. They must decide how best to appeal to audiences. They necessarily must choose between ethical and unethical modes of persuasion. Persuaders who advance their claims in ethical ways deserve our respect. Those who employ unethical persuasion ploys should be held accountable for their choices. This raises an important question: Just what do we mean by ethical and unethical persuasion? The final portion of the chapter addresses this issue.

PERSUASION AND ETHICS

Is persuasion ethical? This simple question has engaged scholars and practitioners alike. Aristotle and Plato discussed it. Machiavelli touched on it. So have contemporary communication scholars and social psychologists. And you can bet that practitioners— Tommy Hilfiger, Nike's Phil Knight, and the late Steve Jobs—have mulled it over, some more than others, to be sure.

Yet persuasion ethics demand consideration. As human beings, we want to be treated with respect, and we value communications that treat others as an end, not a means, to use Immanuel Kant's famous phrase. At the same time, we are practical creatures, who want to achieve our goals, whether they be financial, social, emotional, or spiritual. The attainment of goals—money, prestige, love, or religious fulfillment—requires that we influence others in some fashion somewhere along the way. Is the need to influence *incompatible* with the ethical treatment of human beings?

Some scholars would say it invariably is. Plato, who regarded truth as "the only reality in life," was offended by persuasive communication (Golden et al., 2000, p. 17). As noted earlier, he regarded rhetoric as a form of flattery that appealed to people's worst instincts. Although Plato did believe in an ideal rhetoric admirably composed of truth and morality, he did not think that ordinary persuasion measured up to this standard.

The German philosopher Immanuel Kant would view persuasion as immoral for a different reason: in his view, it uses people, treating them as means to the persuader's end, not as valued ends in themselves (Borchert & Stewart, 1986). This violates Kant's ethical principles. As thoughtful as these perspectives are, they set up a rather high bar for human communication to reach. What's more, these authors tend to lump all persuasive communication together. Some communications are indeed false, designed to manipulate people by appealing to base emotions, or are in the interest of the sender and not the receiver. But others are not. Some messages make very intelligent appeals, based on logic and evidence. In addition, not all persuaders treat people as a means. Therapists and health professionals ordinarily accord clients a great deal of respect. Many people who do volunteer work—such as those who counsel teens in trouble or AIDS victims—do not receive great financial benefit from their work. Their communications can be very much in the best interest of those receiving the message.

On the other extreme are philosophers who argue that persuasion is fundamentally moral. Noting that people are free to accept or reject a communicator's message, conservative thinkers tend to embrace persuasion. Believing that people are sufficiently rational to distinguish between truth and falsehood, libertarian scholars argue that society is best served by diverse persuasive communications that run the gamut from entirely truthful to totally fallacious (Siebert, Peterson, & Schramm, 1956). Persuasion, they say, is better than coercion, and people are in any event free to accept or reject the communicator's message.

There is some wisdom in this perspective. However, to say that persuasion is inherently moral is an extreme, absolute statement. To assume that people are capable of maturely rejecting manipulative communicators' messages naively neglects cases in which trusted but evil people exploit others' vulnerability. What of men who trick or seduce women and then take advantage of their dependence to demand additional sexual and emotional favors? Perhaps we would argue that the women chose to get involved with the men— they're persuaded, not coerced—but it would be heartless to suggest that such persuasion is moral.

Consider also those nasty car salespeople who stretch the truth or lie outright to make a sale (Robin Williams skillfully played one of these some years back in the movie *Cadillac Man*). Don't forget history's legions of con men—the snake oil salesmen of the 19th century who promised that new nutritional cures would work magic on those who purchased them, and their modern counterparts, the hosts of infomercials that tell you that vitamin supplements will boost sales and sex. It defies credulity to argue that persuasion is inherently ethical.

This brings up a third viewpoint, which comes closest to truth. Persuasion can be used for good or bad purposes, with ethical and unethical intentions. Aristotle endorsed this view. He argued that persuasion could be used by anyone: "by a good person or a bad person, by a person seeking worthy ends or unworthy ends" (McCroskey, 1997, p. 9). Thus, charisma can be employed by a Hitler or a Martin Luther King, by a bin Laden or a Ghandi. Step-by-step persuasion techniques that begin with a small request and hook the person into larger and larger commitments have been used by North Korean captors of American soldiers during the Korean War and by religious cult leaders—but also by Alcoholics Anonymous.

What determines whether a particular persuasive act is ethical or unethical? How do we decide if a communicator has behaved in a moral or immoral fashion? In order to answer these questions, we must turn to moral philosophy. Philosophers have offered many perspectives on these issues, beginning with Plato and continuing to the present day.

Normative Theories of Ethics

A normative theory of ethics adopts a prescriptive approach. Social scientific theories describe and explain the world as it is. Normative theories prescribe, suggesting what people *ought* to do, in light of moral philosophy and a vision of the good life. Two classical normative perspectives with important implications for persuasion are utilitarianism and Kantian deontological thought.

Utilitarianism offers a series of common-sense solutions to moral dilemmas. It also contains an elaborate set of postulates that can help people to decide whether particular actions are morally justified. Developed by British philosophers Jeremy Bentham and John Stuart Mill and adapted by American thinkers over the years, utilitarianism emphasizes *utility* or *consequences*. Actions are judged based on whether they produce more positive than negative consequences. "In deciding what to do, we should, therefore, ask what course of conduct would promote the greatest amount of happiness for all those who will be affected," philosopher James Rachels (1986) notes (p. 81). To utilitarians, the moral act is the one that promotes the greatest good for the greatest number of people.

There is a certain elegant simplicity to utilitarianism. And while it may seem intuitively obvious, it is important to appreciate that when it was originally articulated in the 18th and 19th centuries, it represented a radical repudiation of contemporary ethical doctrines that emphasized fidelity to God. Rather than focusing on divine rules that came from the heavens, morality was intended to improve the happiness of human beings living on earth. Utilitarianism bespoke a compassion for mortal men and women.

Yet, as utilitarianism came under scrutiny, it became clear that it contained serious flaws. Consider this example. A guard is falsely accused of killing a prisoner in a maximum security prison. Prisoners begin to riot. The guard is innocent, but if he signs a confession and succumbs to arrest, the rioting will stop. The utilitarian would support this option. Although the confession and arrest might cause pain to the guard, it would forestall a riot, which would cause more harm to more people. But this solution seems unjust (Rachels, 1986).

Utilitarianism thus seems wrong because it places consequences ahead of other considerations, such as fairness and truth. It assumes that what is right is that which produces the most good. But there are instances in which something can be wrong, even though it leads to positive consequences. Utilitarianism gives short shrift to other values such as fairness and justice.

For example, in the persuasion arena, let's say that a tobacco company promotes an antismoking campaign solely to gain good public relations. It subscribes to the rule that companies should engage in actions that promote the corporate image. Utilitarianism would say that this campaign is morally equivalent to a similar campaign promoted by an anti-tobacco group that is motivated by a pro-social objective: convincing young people to kick the smoking habit. But it seems that a campaign launched selfishly by a tobacco company to preserve its brand image is morally suspect, in comparison to a campaign designed for the sole purpose of saving lives.

Kant's deontological theory. The great 18th-century German philosopher Immanuel Kant launched a devastating critique of utilitarianism that still makes sense today. (See Figure 2.5.)

According to Kantians, "just because something gives many people pleasure doesn't make it right. The mere fact that the majority, however big, favors a certain law, however intensely, does not make the law just" (Sandel, 2009, p. 106). A *deontological or*

■ Figure 2.5 Immanuel Kant's philosophy emphasized that the morality of persuasion should be based on intentions and moral duty, not simply the consequences of an action.

Image courtesy of Shutterstock.

Immanuel Kant.

duty-based theory emphasizes moral duties, universal obligations, and according respect to individuals as ends in and of themselves.

The deonotological approach argues that the moral value of an act derives not from the consequence it produces, but in the *intention* from which the act is performed (Sandel, 2009). Communication scholar James C. McCroskey is a proponent of intention-based morality. He argues, "If the communicator seeks to improve the well-being of his audience through his act of communication, he is committing a moral act. If he seeks to produce harm for his audience, the communicator is guilty of an immoral act" (1972, p. 270).

Deontological theory says that even if the tobacco company's antismoking campaign causes people to kick the habit, it is not a morally upright campaign. The company's intention is to improve its image, not save lives. An anti-tobacco group that launches a campaign for pro-social reasons has more morally praiseworthy intentions than the tobacco company. The anti-tobacco activists operate from honorable intentions. Therefore, their campaign is of high moral worth.

But how do we know what the communicator's intentions are? Perhaps the antismoking activists have selfish intentions. Maybe they hope to gain a little fame from their condemnation of tobacco companies. It can be difficult to pinpoint the content of another individual's intentions. Deontological theory assumes that, to the extent that we can appreciate another's true intentions, the morally right act is one that is performed for the right reason.

The classic statement of **deontological thought** is Kant's categorical imperative. Kant famously stated that: "Act in such a way that you always treat humanity, whether in your own person or in the person of any other, never simply as a means, but always at the same time as an end." His philosophical rule is nonnegotiable—it applies to all situations. It is an elegant statement, one worthy of emulation. However, it also raises difficult questions. Should a rule apply to all situations when different contexts contain complex quandaries that require moral flexibility? Kantians would say that lying is never permissible in persuasion, a worthwhile precept. Yet clearly, there are times when exceptions must be made to this rule. As Hauser (2006) notes, "If an adult sexually abuses a child and then tells the child to keep this a secret, it seems morally permissible, perhaps obligatory, for the child to report the abuse to an authority. Once again, a rigid deontological stance is problematic, because it is sometimes permissible to lie, breaking a promise to keep a secret" (pp. 269–270).

Importantly, deontological theory stipulates that to treat someone with respect and dignity means treating her as a responsible being, one who is accountable for her actions.

BOX 2.2 UNDERSTANDING PERSUASION ETHICS: PRIMER ON TWO PHILOSOPHICAL THEORIES

Utilitarianism judges ethics in terms of outcomes. The moral act is one that promotes the greatest good for the greatest number of people.

A shortcoming of utilitarianism is that it does not consider the communicator's intentions or moral obligations.

Deontological theory emphasizes moral duty, moral obligation, and according respect to individuals as ends in and of themselves. Actions are judged based on their adherence to obligations and universal moral rules.

A shortcoming of deontological thought is its rigidity. It does not allow for exceptions that ought to be made in particular situations.

Utilitarianism and deontological thought provide helpful yardsticks to judge the morality of persuasive communications.

People have autonomy, and freely decide what to do based on their beliefs. Thus, a persuader who delivers an uplifting, respectful message deserves praise. A communicator who chooses to mislead, lie, or distort in the service of persuasion deserves to be held accountable for his deeds (see Box 2.2 for a summary of key points in these theories).

Becoming an Ethical Persuader

What criteria do we employ to evaluate the ethics of a persuader's conduct? Utilitarianism urges that we examine the consequences of the action or underlying rule. Deontological thought steers us toward the intentions of the communicator, emphasizing that moral acts flow from our universal obligation to treat people with respect.

One choice people have is not to be ethical at all, to pursue self-interest at any cost. This is the emphasis of ethical egoism, a flawed approach to ethical decision making. In the end, philosophers cannot persuade people to make ethical judgments; they cannot convince unsavory characters to behave in humane ways or to use morally acceptable strategies to influence others. One can give many arguments on behalf of ethical persuasion, from the Golden Rule to moral duty to the Aristotelian notion that virtue is inextricably linked with a good life.

An ethical approach to persuasion emphasizes the development of thoughtful, humane arguments, advanced forcefully, but not aggressively. Ethical persuaders affirm the dignity of each person, treat audience members as free and autonomous agents, present facts and opinions fairly, and provide different perspectives on an issue to enable people to make the most thoughtful decision possible (e.g., Wallace, 1967). It is easy to be an ethical egoist, placing your self-interest of others. It is difficult to reflect on what constitutes the morally right thing to do and even harder to implement this in practice. But this is a worthwhile goal, a foundation of the good life.

THE PRESENT APPROACH

There are thousands of books on persuasion, hundreds of thousands of articles, probably more. "How to persuade" books, audios, and Web sites proliferate. No surprise here: a search for the keys to persuasion is surely among the most basic of human desires. Who among us has not entertained the thought that somewhere out there lies the secret to persuasion? Who has not dreamed that he or she might, with luck or perseverance, find the simple trick or magic elixir that contains the formula for social influence?

We may yet find the secret to persuasion or, failing that, we may someday understand perfectly why people need to believe that simple solutions exist. But you won't find a simple formula here. Instead, you will discover intriguing theories, bundles of evidence, creative methodologies, and rich applications of research to everyday life. This book, focusing on academic scholarship on persuasion, attempts to increase your knowledge of attitudes and persuasion.

The book is divided into four parts. The first part, which you have just completed, described the foundations of persuasion, defining terms, providing a historical overview, and introducing major theories of ethics (Chapters 1 and 2). The second part focuses on attitudes. Chapter 3 defines attitudes and discusses their complex structure. The fourth chapter follows this up with an examination of the power of strong attitudes. Chapter 5 discusses attitude functions and attitude–behavior consistency, using as a template functional theory and the classic theories of reasoned action and planned behavior, recently integrated into the Reasoned Action Model. Chapter 6 describes key approaches to attitude measurement.

The third part examines theories and research on persuasion and attitude change, using theory as a fulcrum to explain how communications change attitudes. Chapter 7 introduces cognitive processes and the influential dual theories of persuasion. Chapter 8 examines the communicator in persuasion, explaining the psychological effects that authority, credibility, and social attractiveness exert on attitudes. The next two chapters explore the persuasive message. Chapter 9 focuses on message structure, content factors, such as evidence and narrative, along with framing and language. Chapter 10 examines the impact of emotional message appeals, primarily fear. Chapter 11 is devoted to the granddaddy of attitude and persuasion approaches: cognitive dissonance theory. The varied counterintuitive, but fascinating, applications of dissonance to everyday persuasion are reviewed.

The final part explores persuasion contexts. Chapter 12 focuses on persuasion in interpersonal settings and everyday compliance. Chapter 13 (certainly not meant to be an unlucky chapter!) takes readers to the ubiquitous arena of marketing and advertising. The final chapter looks at communication campaigns and health, ending the book—appropriately, I think—with an examination of how persuasion has been and can be harnessed for pro-social purposes. Thus, I move from a general conceptual overview to a focus on the individual mind, expand the focus to the attitude-changing effects of sources and messages, and in the final section take an ever-broader perspective, exploring persuasion in interpersonal and societal contexts.

Throughout the book, I explore what it means to persuade and be persuaded, the contexts in which this occurs, and ethics of persuasive communications.

Certain themes predominate and run through the book:

■ the central role persuasion performs in contemporary life (from mass marketing to interpersonal compliance-gaining);
■ the important part that theory and research play in illuminating persuasive communication effects;
■ the centrality of self-persuasion, as we convince ourselves and change our own minds in response to persuasive messages;
■ the two very different ways people frequently process persuasive information, one effortful, the other more automatic;
■ the endless complexity of human behavior;
■ persuasion's capacity to manipulate but also soothe and comfort people; and
■ the importance of adopting an ethical approach to persuasion, particularly in an era of ever-subtle technological tricks.

CONCLUSIONS

Persuasive communications have been studied for thousands of years, beginning with the early Greeks. The Greeks grappled with some of the same issues we discuss today. The Sophists defended the art of persuasion, offering courses on oratory that usefully appealed to large numbers of citizens, but may have prized style over substance. Plato, an idealist, criticized the Sophists' philosophy, charging that it placed superficial arguments and appearance over truth. Thanks to Plato, we use the term sophistry to refer to persuasive arguments that are glib and favor style over more substantive concerns.

Aristotle, the first scholar of persuasion, argued that persuasion has virtues. He developed a series of principles to help shed light on the effects of rhetorical messages, as they were then known. Novel in his day, his principles called attention to source and message characteristics. Aristotle coupled his persuasion theorizing with a healthy respect for ethics. He emphasized that a broad education and development of moral character were essential characteristics in those who aspired to deliver compelling oratory. It was the Romans who elevated oratory to a higher plane. Cicero and Quintilian extolled the virtues of persuasion, emphasizing that the ideal citizen is the "good man speaking well." The emphasis on "man" was no accident. It would be centuries before women were brought into the realm of persuasion and public address.

Over the years, other rhetorical approaches were advanced, culminating in Kenneth Burke's influential mid-20th-century theory that emphasized the power of symbols and identification. Contemporary perspectives have adopted a more critical and self-reflective perspective on rhetoric.

Building on these perspectives and integrating them with scientific methods, the social science approach evolved, offering a framework to articulate principles about persuasion. It focuses on the development of theories, specific hypotheses, and research methods to test hypotheses in social settings.

Nowadays persuasion is so pervasive that we frequently forget to ask big questions like: What would society be like if there were no persuasion? Persuasion, at its best, offers a civilized means to solve human dilemmas, one that prizes language, argumentation, and the rough banter of verbal give and take. It assumes that people have free choice and are responsible for the persuasive messages they deliver.

At the heart of persuasion are ethical dilemmas. Persuasive communication can be used with great effectiveness by both moral and immoral persuaders. This does not mean that persuasion is amoral, as is sometimes believed. There is ethical and unethical persuasion.

To help adjudicate the ethics of persuasion, different normative or prescriptive theories have been developed. Utilitarianism emphasizes that we should judge actions based on their consequences. Utilitarianism offers a common-sense, explicit, and quantifiable series of principles to resolve moral problems. However, it gives moral duty, intentions, and universal obligations short shrift.

Kantian deontological theory emphasizes that the moral value of an act derives from the respect it accords individuals as ends in and of themselves. It also places a premium on duty and the persuader's intention, according weight to good intentions in the calculus of moral behavior. However, deontological theory can lead to rigid enforcement of obligations, underplaying instances where exceptions should be made to serve an uplifting moral end.

In the end, there are many reasons to practice ethical persuasion, not the least of which is that it is one of the requirements of being a good person and part of the curriculum of the good life. Calling on the respect for moral oratory that infused the writings of classical rhetorical theorists, J. Michael Hogan (2013) offers a ringing endorsement of how persuasion can be harnessed for positive purposes and to enhance the common good. "The challenge," he says, "lies in reviving the spirit of the classical rhetorical tradition—particularly its emphasis on the *ethics* of speech and the *responsibilities* of citizenship—in a culturally diverse and technologically advanced society." He calls for "a healthy politics of persuasion" in which "reasoned argument prevails over appeals to fears or prejudices, and diverse perspectives and opinions are encouraged and respected" (p. 16). It is a perspective that the classical rhetoricians, in their finest and most egalitarian moments, would passionately embrace.

Test your knowledge now with interactive exercises

Part Two

The Nature of Attitudes

Chapter 3

Attitudes: Definition and Structure

 Listen now to the author's chapter summary

Click onto a Web site for prayer in school, illegal immigration, gun control, or capital punishment. Or if you prefer cultural venues, check out sites for hip-hop music, body piercing, tattoos, NASCAR drivers, of women's fashion. If you prefer the older, traditional media, you can peruse books or letters to the editor, or you can tune in to a radio talk show. You will find them there.

What you will locate are attitudes—strong, deeply felt attitudes, as well as ambivalent, complex ones. You see, even today, when we communicate through Skype, cell phones, and Facebook, attitudes are ubiquitous. To illustrate the depth and strength of attitudes, I examined a topic that arouses strong feelings among some people: animal rights. (See Figure 3.1.)

By reading these views on the merits of conducting research on animals, you can appreciate the power of attitudes.

> Do you approve of the scientific experiments using animals that have in fact resulted in the protection of millions of human beings, probably including yourself and your children, from diphtheria, hepatitis, measles, rabies, rubella, and tetanus? Do you believe that the scientific studies now in progress to combat AIDS, lyme disease, Alzheimer's disease, heart disease, diabetes, and cancer—almost all of those studies relying essentially on the use of animals—are morally justifiable? Probably, you do. I surely do, with all my heart.
>
> (Cohen & Regan, 2001, p. 25)

> We humans kill billions of animals every year, just in the United States. Frequently what we do causes them intense physical pain; often they are made to live in deplorable conditions; in many, possibly the majority of cases, they go to their deaths without having had the opportunity to satisfy many of their most basic

■ **Figure 3.1 Research on animals elicits a variety of attitudes, highlighting the centrality of the attitude concept in everyday life.**

Image courtesy of Shutterstock.

desires . . . (Imagine) a mugger has pushed you to the ground and stolen your money; you are left with a number of cuts and bruises—minor to be sure, but still painful. Next, let us try to imagine the pain felt by the dogs who were vivisected by the scientists . . . the dogs who, without the benefit of anesthetic, had their four paws nailed to boards before being slit open. Are we to say that your minor pain is qualitatively worse than the much greater pain experienced by the dogs, because your pain is the pain of a human being, the dogs' pain not?

(Cohen & Regan, 2001, pp. 135, 291)

Animal research has contributed to 70% of the Nobel prizes for physiology or medicine; many award-winning scientists say they could not have made their discoveries without animals. Polio would still be claiming hundreds of lives a year in Britain if it wasn't for animal research by the Nobel laureate Albert Sabin. "There could have been no oral polio vaccine without the use of innumerable animals," he once said.

(Pigilito says . . . , 2006)

The small, shivering cat huddles against the corner of her tiny cage, trying to sleep but kept awake by the ever-present pain in her head and body. She has been awake for 43 hours now, undergoing experimental research . . . Sleep-deprived and dazed with pain, she is barely conscious . . . Worldwide, 100 to 300 million animals die each year in laboratory experiments, experiments whose methods are unnecessarily cruel and whose results are often inconclusive. Animal experimentation is unethical and impractical.

(Without-Feathers.com)

Attitudes—not always this strong or vitriolic, but indispensable parts of our psychological makeup—are the subject of this chapter and the ones that follow. Attitudes and their close cousins (beliefs and values) have been the focus of much research over the past 50 years. They are the stuff of persuasion—materials persuaders try to change, possessions we cling to tenaciously, badges that define us, categories that organize us, and constructs that marketers want to measure and manipulate. The first portion of the chapter defines attitude and discusses its main components. The second section focuses on the structure of attitudes, ambivalence, and how people cope with inconsistency. Chapter 4 follows this up with an exploration of the psychology of strong, deeply held attitudes.

THE CONCEPT OF ATTITUDE

"She's got an attitude problem," someone says, telegraphing familiarity with the term *attitude*. But being familiar with a term does not mean one can necessarily articulate a clear, comprehensive definition. This is a task that we look to scholars to perform, and social scientists have offered a litany of definitions of attitude, dating back to the 19th century. Darwin regarded attitude as a motor concept (a scowling face signifies a "hostile attitude"; see Petty, Ostrom, & Brock, 1981a). Freud, by contrast, "endowed [attitudes] with vitality, identifying them with longing, hatred and love, with passion and prejudice" (Allport, 1935, p. 801). Early 20th-century sociologists Thomas and Znaniecki placed attitude in a social context, defining it as a "state of mind of the individual toward a value" (Allport, 1935).

Their view resonated with a growing belief that the social environment influenced individuals, but then-contemporary terms like *custom* and *social force* were too vague and impersonal to capture the complex dynamics by which this occurred. *Attitude*, which referred to a force or quality of mind, seemed much more appropriate. By the 1930s, as researchers began to study the development of racial stereotypes, Gordon Allport (1935) declared that attitude was the most indispensable concept in contemporary social psychology.

Over the past century, attitude research has flourished. Social scientists have conducted surveys of people's attitudes, examining political, religious, and sex-role attitudes, to name but a few. They have explored the structure and functions of attitudes and documented relationships between attitudes and behavior. "A recent search for the term *attitude* in the American Psychological Association's comprehensive index to psychological and related literature (PsycINFO) yielded 180,910 references," Dolores Albarracín and her colleagues declared with perhaps a little bit of pride (Albarracín, Johnson, & Zanna, 2005, p. vii).

Attitude is a psychological construct. It is a mental and emotional entity that inheres in, or characterizes, the person. It has also been called a "hypothetical construct," a concept that cannot be observed directly but can only be inferred from people's actions. An exemplar of this approach is the Michigan psychology professor who ran through the halls of his department shouting (in jest), "I found it. I found it. I found the attitude." His comment illustrates that attitudes are different from the raw materials that other scientific disciplines examine—materials that can be touched or clearly seen, such as a rock, plant cell, or an organ in the human body.

Although in some sense we do infer a person's attitude from what he or she says or does, it would be a mistake to assume that for this reason attitudes are not real or are "mere mental constructs." This is a fallacy of behaviorism, the scientific theory that argues that all human activity can be reduced to behavioral units. Contemporary scholars reject this notion. They note that people have thoughts, cognitive structures, and a variety of emotions, all of which lose their essential qualities when viewed exclusively as behaviors. Moreover, they argue that an entity that is mental or emotional is no less real than a physical behavior. As Allport noted perceptively:

> Attitudes are never directly observed, but, unless they are admitted, through inference, as real and substantial ingredients in human nature, it becomes impossible to account satisfactorily either for the consistency of any individual's behavior, or for the stability of any society.
>
> (1935, p. 839)

Over the past century, numerous definitions of attitude have been proposed. The following views of attitude are representative of the population of definitions. According to scholars, an attitude is:

■ an association between a given object and a given evaluation (Fazio, 1989, p. 155);

■ a psychological tendency that is expressed by evaluating a particular entity with some degree of favor or disfavor (Eagly & Chaiken, 1993, p. 1);

- a learned predisposition to respond in a consistently favorable or unfavorable manner with respect to a given object (Fishbein & Ajzen, 1975, p. 6); or
- a more or less permanently enduring state of readiness of mental organization which predisposes an individual to react in a characteristic way to any object or situation with which it is related (Cantril, quoted in Allport, 1935, p. 804).

Notice that these definitions emphasize different aspects of the attitude concept. Fazio focuses simply on the mental association of an object and a feeling. Eagly and Chaiken stress that attitudes involve a person's evaluation of an issue. Fishbein and Ajzen, as well as Cantril, take a behavioral view, suggesting that attitudes predispose people to behave in a particular way. Which is right, you ask? Which definition is the correct one? There are no objective answers to these questions. As was the case with the definition of persuasion, scholars differ in how they view a particular phenomenon. You cannot say that one definition is more correct than another because defining terms is a logical, not empirical, exercise. If you find the lack of certainty frustrating, you're not alone. But take heart! Science has to start somewhere. Someone has to come up with a workable definition of a term before the empirical explorations can begin. Science requires a leap of faith. Yet this does not mean that one must settle with definitions that are inadequate or incomplete. Definitions are evaluated on the basis of their clarity, cogency, and comprehensiveness. The above definitions of attitude are erudite and perceptive. So which definition is correct? All are, in varying degrees. In this, a textbook that offers multiple approaches, I offer an integrative approach that combines these definitions and emphasizes commonalities.

Attitude is defined as: *a learned, global evaluation of an object (person, place, or issue) that influences thought and action*. Psychologically, an attitude is not a behavior, though it may consist of acquired patterns of reacting to social stimuli. It is not pure affect, though it is most assuredly emotional. It is a predisposition, a tendency, a state of readiness that guides and steers behavior in certain predictable, though not always rational, ways. The next section reviews the different components of the definition of attitude.

CHARACTERISTICS OF ATTITUDES

Attitudes Are Learned

People are not born with attitudes. They acquire attitudes over the course of socialization in childhood and adolescence. This has important implications. A critical one is this: No one is born prejudiced. Children don't naturally discriminate against kids with different skin color or religious preferences. Over time, kids acquire prejudiced attitudes. Or to be blunt, human beings learn to hate.

Fortunately, not all attitudes are so negative. Think about the rush you get when "The Star-Spangled Banner" is played after a U.S. victory at the Olympics. Sports fans across the world experience a similar thrill when their national anthem is performed at the Olympic Games. People have positive sentiments toward all sorts of things—hometown sports teams, teachers who lift our spirits, children, pets, cool cars—you get the drift. These are all learned.

Attitudes vary widely. They depend to a considerable degree on what individuals have learned in their course of cultural and social upbringing. Do you think abortion should be legal? Do you feel that homosexuality should be accepted or discouraged by society? Your attitude depends in part on your religious background. Twenty percent of Americans who belong to mainstream Protestant churches believe that abortion should be legal in all cases; however, only 8 percent of Mormons feel this way. Sixty-four percent of evangelical Christians believe that homosexuality should be discouraged by society, in contrast to 15 percent of Jews who espouse this position (Pew Forum on Religion and Public Life, 2008). Attitudes vary as a function of religion, social upbringing, even the cultural landscape in which an individual was raised. People tend to cluster with those who share their attitudes (Bishop, 2008). This is why they are frequently surprised to learn that people from different groups have vastly different outlooks on social issues from their own.

A Biological Basis of Attitudes?

For generations it was an article of faith that attitudes were entirely a product of the environment. Nurture, not nature, was assumed to be the foundation of attitudes. Over the past decades, with the explosion of research on biological determinants of behavior, psychologists have begun to rethink this thesis, wondering if genes might play some role in the development of our attitudes.

Some years back, Tesser (1993) explored this question. He acknowledged that there is not "a gene for attitudes toward jazz in the same way as there is a gene for eye color" (p. 139). But he argued that inherited physical differences in taste and hearing might influence attitudes toward food and loud rock music. Perhaps those who are born with higher activity levels gravitate to vigorous exercise or sports.

Others make a similar argument. There is a genetic basis for certain personality traits, like impulsivity (Albarracín & Vargas, 2010). If we find that impulsive people have more positive attitudes toward trying new experiences, we would have evidence that genes might play an indirect role in the formation of attitudes. At the same time, there is evidence that some political attitudes have a genetic basis (Alford, Funk, & Hibbing, 2005; Banaji & Heiphetz, 2010). Thus it is fair to say that nature—in the form of genes and heredity—shapes some attitudes, although considerably more research needs to be conducted before we can understand exactly the processes by which this occurs.

Even those who argue that genes play a role in attitude formation are quick to acknowledge that genes do not operate in isolation. Whatever influence they exert is in combination with the social environment. And culture exerts a mighty impact. There is no gene that causes attitudes toward sex roles, race, and religion. Whatever influence genes exert is critically filtered through environmentally experienced lenses. For example, a person might be genetically predisposed to like pineapple, but if pineapple is not available (or affordable), she cannot develop a positive attitude toward the fruit. In addition, if the first time she tastes pineapple she develops a rash or gets bitten by a dog, she is apt to evaluate pineapple more negatively.

Thus, even if attitudes have genetic antecedents, these inherited preferences are not equivalent to attitudes. Attitudes develop through encounters with social objects. "Individuals do not have an attitude until they first encounter the attitude object (or information about it) and respond evaluatively to it," Alice H. Eagly and Shelly Chaiken declare (1998, p. 270).

Attitudes Are Global, Typically Emotional, Evaluations

Attitudes are, first and foremost, evaluations. Having an attitude means that you have categorized something and made a judgment of its net value or worth. It means that you are no longer neutral about the topic. That doesn't mean you can't have mixed feelings, but your view on the issue is no longer bland or without color.

Attitudes invariably involve affect and emotions. "Attitudes express passions and hates, attractions and repulsions, likes and dislikes," note Eagly and Chaiken (1998, p. 269).

Affect usually plays an important part in how attitudes are formed or experienced. I say "usually" because some attitudes may develop more intellectually, by absorbing information, while others are acquired through reward and punishment of previous behavior (Dillard, 1993; Zanna & Rempel, 1988). Attitudes are complex. They have different components and are formed in different ways. A classic tripartite model emphasizes that attitudes can be expressed through thoughts, feelings, and behavior (Breckler, 1984). Our attitudes are not always internally consistent, and you may have contradictory attitudes toward the same issue.

Attitudes can be regarded as large summary evaluations of issues and people. (They are global, or macro, not micro.) Your attitude toward men's and women's roles is a large, complex entity composed of a number of beliefs and feelings. For this reason, researchers speak of "attitude systems" that consist of several subcomponents. Attitudes encompass beliefs, feelings, intentions to behave, and behavior itself.

Attitudes Influence Thought and Action

Attitudes (and values) organize our social world. They allow us to categorize people, places, and events quickly and to figure out what's going on. They are like notebook dividers or labels you use to categorize your collection of favorite books. Attitudes shape perceptions and influence judgments. If you're a Republican, you probably evaluate Republican political leaders favorably and have a negative, gut-level reaction to some Democratic politicians. And vice versa if you are a Democrat. On the other hand, if you hate politics and distrust politicians, you filter the political world through a skeptical set of lenses.

Attitudes also influence behavior. They guide our actions and steer us in the direction of doing what we believe. In our society, consistency between attitude and behavior is valued, so people try hard to "practice what they preach." As will be discussed, people usually translate attitudes into behavior, but not always.

Attitudes come in different shapes and sizes. Some attitudes are strong; others are weaker and susceptible to influence. Still others contain inconsistent elements. Some attitudes exert a stronger impact on thought and behavior than others. In sum: attitudes are complex, dynamic entities—like people. Persuasion scholar Muzafer Sherif put it best:

> When we talk about attitudes, we are talking about what a person has learned in the process of becoming a member of a family, a member of a group, and of society that makes him react to his social world in a *consistent and characteristic* way, instead of a transitory and haphazard way. We are talking about the fact that he is no longer neutral in sizing up the world around him; he is *attracted* or *repelled*, *for* or *against*, *favorable* or *unfavorable*.
>
> (1967, p. 2)

VALUES AND BELIEFS

What do you value? What do you believe about life and society? To answer these questions, it helps to define value and belief clearly. Both concepts play an important role in persuasion. Like attitudes, values and beliefs are learned and shape the ways we interpret information.

Values are ideals, *"guiding principles in one's life,"* or *overarching goals that people strive to obtain* (Maio & Olson, 1998). They are *our "conceptions of the desirable means and ends of action"* (Kluckhohn, 1951). More comprehensively, values are *"desirable end states or behaviors that transcend specific situations, guide selection or evaluation of behavior and events, and are ordered by relative importance"* (see Schwartz & Bilsky, 1987, p. 551). Values can either transcend or celebrate selfish concerns. Freedom, equality, and a world of beauty are universal values that extend beyond individual interests (Rokeach, 1973; Schwartz, 1996). Self-fulfillment, excitement, and recognition express strong desires to enrich our own lives. Power and achievement are self-enhancement values. Warm relationships with others and a sense of belonging emphasize love and security (Kahle, 1996).

In everyday life, values conflict and collide. "Difficult choices are unavoidable," observe Philip E. Tetlock and colleagues (Tetlock, Peterson, & Lerner, 1996, p. 25). Values are large macro constructs that underlie attitudes. Recall the divergent attitudes people hold toward research on animals. Those who support scientific research on animals place a greater value on human life, arguing that we owe humans obligations that we do not owe to animals. Those who strenuously oppose animal research retort that this reeks of "specism." They accord equal value to all living sentient beings, whether animals or humans. Your attitude toward animal research derives from your more general values.

In contrast to values, beliefs are more specific and cognitive. Freedom encompasses attitudes toward censorship, entrepreneurship, political correctness, and smoking in public. People have hundreds of attitudes, but dozens of values (e.g., Rokeach, 1973). Even more than attitudes, values strike to the core of our self-concepts. Values are more global and abstract than attitudes. In contrast, beliefs are more specific and cognitive. You can think of values as the broad macro term that encompasses attitudes. Attitudes in turn consist of specific beliefs (see Figure 3.2).

Beliefs number in the hundreds, perhaps thousands! These are typical:

- Girls talk more about relationships than do guys.
- Maintaining a vegetarian diet improves your state of mind.
- Video games are addictive.
- College students drink too much.
- A daily dose of religion uplifts the spirits.

Beliefs are more cognitive than values or attitudes. Beliefs are *cognitions about the world—subjective probabilities that an object has a particular attribute or that an action will lead to a particular outcome* (Fishbein & Ajzen, 1975).

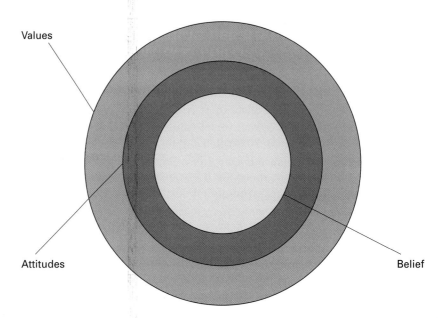

Values

Attitudes

Belief

■ **Figure 3.2 Schematic diagram of values, attitudes, and beliefs.**

People frequently confuse beliefs with facts. Just because we fervently believe something to be true does not make it so. Almost half of the American public does not accept the theory of evolution, believing instead that God created human beings in their present form (Collins, 2006). Yet more than a century's worth of scientific studies offers incontrovertible support for evolution and principles such as natural selection and adaptation (Dennett, 2005; Scott, 2004).

Beliefs can be patently and unequivocally false. A Taliban leader from Afghanistan claimed that in America, parents do not show love to their children and the only good thing to come out of the United States is candy (Goldberg, 2000). Unfortunately, beliefs like these are tenaciously held and highly resistant to change.

Other beliefs can be strongly held, but impossible to verify. You probably did not know that 68 percent of Americans believe in life after death, 62 percent believe in hell, and 59 percent believe in the devil (Schott, 2008). Try verifying these beliefs and then convincing believers they are wrong!

Beliefs can also be categorized into different subtypes. *Descriptive beliefs*, such as those previously discussed, are perceptions or hypotheses about the world that people carry around in their heads. *Prescriptive beliefs* are "ought" or "should" statements that express conceptions of preferred end-states. Prescriptive beliefs, such as "Prostitution should be legal" or "Capital punishment should be banned," cannot be tested by empirical research. They are part of people's worldviews. Some scholars regard prescriptive beliefs as components of values.

Certain beliefs can appear rational to the believer but, in fact, may be highly irrational and even delusional. Other beliefs may seem irrational, but have a strong rational foundation. After Hurricane Katrina hit New Orleans, some Blacks suspected that the levees had been deliberately blown (Remnick, 2005). While recognizing the dubious nature of the proposition, they nonetheless harbored the belief because it resonated so powerfully with racist historical events: Whites' refusal to rescue African-Americans during a terrible 1927 New Orleans flood; an engineer's proposal at the time to order several hundred Blacks to lie on top of a levee to prevent further overflow of water; and, of course, the notorious Tuskegee experiments that used Black men as guinea pigs in a study of syphilis. "Perception is reality, and their reality is terrible," explained Jim Amoss, the editor of a New Orleans newspaper. "We are talking about people who are very poor and have a precondition to accept this belief . . . They are isolated in shelters and they know a thing or two about victimization. It fits well into a system of belief" (Remnick, 2005, p. 56). Thus, beliefs that seemed uncanny to many Whites had a rational foundation to many African-Americans, one that squared with actual historical events.

Beliefs and values are fascinating and important. Yet they have been the focus of somewhat less empirical research study than attitudes. This is because, historically, the attitude concept helped bridge behaviorist and cognitive approaches to psychology. It explained how people could be influenced by society, yet also internalize what they learned. It articulated a process by which social forces could affect behavior and not merely stamp their response on the organism.

STRUCTURE OF ATTITUDES

Suppose we could glimpse an attitude up close. Let's say we could handle it, feel its shape and texture, and then inspect it carefully. What would we see?

We cannot observe attitudes with the same exactitude that scientists employ when examining molecules under electron microscopes. We lack the attitudinal equivalent to the human genome, the long strand of DNA that contains our 23 critical chromosome pairs. Instead, we infer attitudes from what people do or say, and what they report on carefully constructed survey instruments. This does not make attitudes any less real than chemical elements on the periodic table, the 30,000 human genes, rocks, plants, or any other material that scientists scrutinize. It simply makes our job of uncovering their basic content more challenging and perhaps more subject to human fallibility.

Just as the human genome and physical substances have structure, attitudes also possess a certain organization. How are attitudes organized? What are their major components? Social scientists have proposed several models to help answer these questions.

Expectancy–Value Approach

The **expectancy–value approach** asserts that attitudes have two components: cognition and affect (or head and heart). Your attitude is a combination of what you believe or expect of a certain object and how you feel about (evaluate) these expectations. The theory was developed by Martin Fishbein and Icek Ajzen in 1975 and is still going strong today! According to Fishbein and Ajzen, attitude is a multiplicative combination of (a) strength of beliefs that an object has certain attributes, and (b) evaluations of these attributes (see Figure 3.3). The prediction is represented by the following mathematical formula:

$$A = \text{sum } b(i) \times e(i)$$

where $b(i)$ = each belief and $e(i)$ = each evaluation.

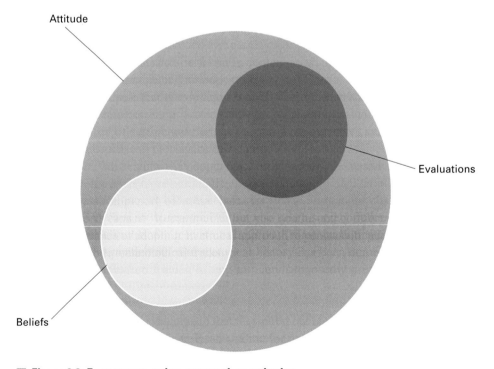

■ **Figure 3.3 Expectancy–value approach to attitudes.**

Formulas like these are helpful because they allow for more precise tests of hypotheses. There is abundant evidence that attitudes can be accurately estimated by combining beliefs and evaluations. Fishbein and Ajzen showed that beliefs (particularly personally important ones) and evaluations accurately estimate attitudes toward a host of topics, ranging from politics to sex roles (Fishbein & Ajzen, 1975; Ajzen & Fishbein, 2008). Beliefs are the centerpiece of attitude and have provided researchers with rich insights into the dynamics of attitudes and behaviors.

Diane M. Morrison and her colleagues (1996) systematically examined beliefs about smoking in an elaborate study of elementary school children's decisions to smoke cigarettes. They measured *beliefs* about smoking by asking kids whether they thought that smoking cigarettes would:

- hurt your lungs;
- give you bad breath;
- make your friends like you better;
- make you feel more grown up; or
- taste good.

The researchers assessed *evaluations* by asking children if they felt that these attributes (e.g., hurting your lungs, making your friends like you better) were good or bad. An evaluation was measured in this general fashion:

> Do you think that making your friends like you better is: *very good, good, not good or bad, bad,* or *very bad*?

Morrison and colleagues gained rich insights into the dynamics of children's attitudes toward smoking. Had they just measured attitude, they would have discovered only how kids evaluated cigarette smoking. By focusing on beliefs, they identified specific reasons why some children felt positively toward smoking. By assessing evaluations, the researchers tapped into the affect associated with these attributes. Their analysis indicated that two children could hold different attitudes about smoking because they had different beliefs about smoking's consequences or because they held the same beliefs but evaluated the consequences differently.

Some children evaluate smoking favorably because they believe that their friends will like them better if they smoke or that smoking makes them feel grown up. Kids who value these outcomes may be particularly inclined to start smoking before they hit adolescence. This information is clearly useful to health educators who design anti-smoking information campaigns.

Affect, Symbols, and Ideologies

A second perspective on attitude structure places emotion and symbols at center stage. According to the symbolic approach, attitudes—particularly political ones—are characterized by emotional reactions, sweeping sentiments, and powerful prejudices. These, rather than molecular beliefs, are believed to lie at the core of people's evaluations of social issues.

Consider racism, sexism, or attitudes toward abortion. These evaluations are rife with symbols and charged with affect. According to David O. Sears, people acquire affective responses to symbols early in life from parents, peers, and mass media (Sears & Funk, 1991). Symbols include the flag, religious ornaments, and code words associated with minority groups.

As a result of early learning experiences, people develop strong attitudes toward their country, as well as religious values, ethnic loyalties, and racial prejudices. These "symbolic predispositions," as they are called, lie at the core of people's attitudes toward social issues. Two examples may be helpful here.

Back in the 1970s, many Whites opposed school busing to achieve racial integration. Some observers suggested that one reason Whites reacted this way was because they were personally affected by busing. Their kids would have to be bused, perhaps taking the bus for a considerable distance. But this turned out not to be the case. In fact, the best predictor of Whites' opposition to busing was racial prejudice, a symbolic predisposition (Sears, Henry, & Kosterman, 2000; Sears et al., 1980).

A more recent example involves AIDS. Although Americans have become more empathic toward the plight of AIDS victims in recent years, many still harbor prejudice toward those who have contracted the AIDS virus. John Pryor and Glenn Reeder offer the following explanation:

> HIV/AIDS may have acquired a symbolic meaning in our culture. As a symbol or a metaphor, it represents things like homosexual promiscuity, moral decadence, and the wrath of God for moral transgressions . . . So, when people react negatively to someone with AIDS (or HIV), they may be expressing their feelings about the symbol. This analysis could explain why those strongly opposed to homosexuality react negatively to nonhomosexuals with HIV. Even the infected child bears the symbol of homosexual promiscuity.
>
> (1993, p. 279)

Pryor and Reeder argue that we cognitively represent people and ideas in certain ways. A person with AIDS (called a person node) is not a neutral entity, but is connected with all sorts of other ideas and emotions that come to mind when we think about AIDS.

STRUCTURE OF ATTITUDES

■ **Figure 3.4 A symbolic view of attitudes toward HIV/AIDS.**

From Pryor, J. B., & Reeder, G. D. (1993). Collective and individual representations of HIV/AIDS stigma. In J. B. Pryor & G. D. Reeder (Eds.), *The social psychology of HIV infection* (p. 271). Hillsdale, NJ: Lawrence Erlbaum Associates.

AIDS (or HIV) may be associated in an individual's mind with homosexuals, drug users, minorities, promiscuous sex, even death. All of these entities are charged with emotion or affect. These emotions become powerfully associated with a person with AIDS (see Figure 3.4).

The symbolic attitude perspective goes a long way toward helping us to deconstruct people's views on contemporary issues. It calls attention to the role that associations play in attitude structure (as well as the effect of more elaborated beliefs; Sears et al., 2000).

The Role of Ideology

A third view of attitude organization emphasizes ideology, or worldview. Some people's attitudes are guided by broad ideological principles. These individuals typically forge stronger connections among diverse political attitudes than do those who don't think much about ideology. For example, conservatives, whose worldviews emphasize self-reliance, responsibility, and reward for hard work, typically oppose welfare because it gives money to those who don't hold down jobs. Conservatives support across-the-board tax cuts because they reward with tax refunds those who have earned the most money (Lakoff, 1996). Attitudes toward welfare and taxes, flowing from a conservative ideology, are therefore interrelated.

By contrast, liberals—who value nurturance, fairness, and compassion for the disadvantaged—favor welfare because it helps indigent individuals who have been left behind by society. Liberal thinkers also oppose across-the-board tax cuts because (in their view) these tax reductions favor the rich; liberals prefer targeted tax cuts that redistribute money to low- and middle-income people. Attitudes toward welfare and tax cuts go together—are correlated—in liberals' minds (see Figure 3.5).

As a general rule, individuals with strong ideological positions view social and political issues differently from the way ordinary citizens do. Unlike many people, who respond to political issues primarily on the basis of simple symbolic predispositions, those who hold a strong ideological viewpoint begin with an ideology, and their attitudes flow from this (see Lavine, Thomsen, & Gonzales, 1997).

The **ideological approach to attitudes** asserts that attitudes are organized "top-down." That is, attitudes flow from the hierarchy of principles (or predispositions) that individuals have acquired and developed.

A shortcoming with this approach is that it assumes that people operate on the basis of one set of ideological beliefs. In fact, individuals frequently call on a variety of prescriptive beliefs when thinking about social issues (Conover & Feldman, 1984). For instance, a student might be a social liberal, believing affirmative action is needed to redress societal wrongs. She could also be an economic conservative, believing that government should not excessively regulate private companies. The student might also have strong religious convictions and a deep belief in a Supreme Being. Her social attitudes are thus structured by a variety of belief systems (sometimes called schema), rather than by one singular ideological set of principles.

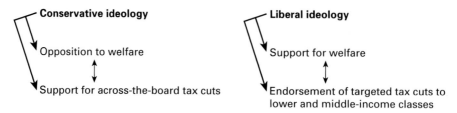

■ **Figure 3.5 Large arrow depicts influence of ideology on attitudes. Smaller arrow denotes association between two attitudes.**

ATTITUDE STRUCTURE AND PERSUASION

These perspectives on attitude structure contain insights about the underlying dynamics of people's attitudes. They also are of interest to communicators who hope to change attitudes. For example, suppose you were asked to develop a campaign to increase Americans' support for gay marriage, still a contentious issue for some Americans. The expectancy–value approach suggests you should first explore beliefs about gay marriage, such as biased perceptions that gay people who want to have children would be bad parents. You would then find information to counteract these beliefs.

The symbolic approach would focus on the affective basis of attitudes—chiefly the negative feelings some Americans experience when linking the storied institution of marriage with gay men and women. Communications might warmly depict a gay parent frolicking in loving ways with his or her children. This could produce a more positive association between marriage and gay individuals.

The ideological approach would locate the bedrock principle underlying a particular ideological perspective. For instance, when targeting conservatives, who appropriately put a premium on self-reliance and responsibility, the campaign might emphasize that gay parents are just as apt as heterosexual parents to demand independence, discipline, and personal responsibility from their kids.

ARE ATTITUDES INTERNALLY CONSISTENT?

As we have seen, expectations, symbols, and ideology influence attitudes and persuasion. This raises a new question, one filled with intriguing dimensions. Given that attitudes are complex macromolecules with so many different components, are they in harmony or in disarray? Are attitudes at peace or ready to ignite, due to the combustible combination of cognitions, affect, and behavior? In other words, when we have an attitude toward an issue, are we all of one mind, consistent in our thoughts and feelings, or are we divided and ambivalent? These are questions that many of us have probably asked in one way or another. We have heard people say, "Intellectually, I agree, but emotionally I don't," or "You're a hypocrite; you say one thing and do another."

Intra-Attitudinal Consistency

It is pleasant when we are all of one mind on an issue—when our general attitude is in sync with specific beliefs about the topic or has the same "electrical charge" as our feelings. However, life does not always grant us this pleasure. We are ambivalent about many issues. Ambivalence occurs when we feel both positively and negatively about a person or issue (Thompson, Zanna, & Griffin, 1995). Ambivalence is characterized by uncertainty or conflict among attitude elements.

One type of ambivalence occurs when we hold seemingly incompatible beliefs. Many people evaluate their own doctor positively, but view the health system negatively. They believe their family is healthy, but American families are in trouble. And they frequently have kind things to say about their own representative to Congress, but disparage "the bums in Washington" (Perloff, 1996). One source for this discrepancy is the mass media, which typically focus on the seamy side of political life. An effect is an ambivalence about the issue in question.

Perhaps the most common type of ambivalence is the head-versus-heart variety—our cognitions take us one way, but our feelings pull us somewhere else. Expectancy–value theory deals with this when it stipulates that people can have strong beliefs about two or more outcomes, but evaluate the outcomes very differently. For example, a student may believe that her professor taught her a lot about physiology, but at the same time kept her waiting in his office. She evaluates knowledge gain positively, but time misspent negatively. A more dramatic example involves the ambivalent attitudes many young women harbor toward safer sex. For example, many women (correctly) believe that using condoms can prevent AIDS, and they evaluate AIDS prevention positively. Some also believe that requesting condoms will upset their boyfriends, and worry about this. "My boyfriend hates them," one young woman said, adding, "Frankly, I can't blame him. For me it certainly puts a crimp on what I would like to do to satisfy him" (Perloff, 2001, p. 13). Persuaders face a challenge in cases like this one. To change this woman's attitude toward safer sex, they must help her rethink her fear of offending her boyfriend.

Ambivalence can frequently be found among young women who love the power and responsibility that comes with high-powered jobs, yet also worry that their commitment to a career will compromise their chances of raising a family when they reach their 30s. Writer Peggy Orenstein (2000) documented this, interviewing scores of women across the country, asking them to share their feelings about careers, relationships, and future plans to become a mom and raise a family. Some of the 20-something women Orenstein interviewed worried that "having a child 'too soon' would be a disaster: it would cut short their quest for identity and destroy their career prospects" (pp. 33–34). At the same time, these women felt pressure not to have kids too late, noting that women have more difficulty conceiving a child when they reach their late 30s. On the other side of the career track, educated women who "mommy-tracked" their aspirations to raise families also experienced mixed feelings. These women found enormous gratification in being a mom, yet at the same time lamented, as one woman put it, that "I don't really have a career and I feel crummy about that" (p. 224). "Ambivalence may be the only sane response to motherhood at this juncture in history, to the schism it creates in women's lives," Orenstein concluded (p. 141).

Ambivalence is also a reasonable response to the complex issues women face in another arena: abortion. In contrast to the us-versus-them and pro-life versus pro-choice polarities that characterize the media debate, in reality, most women find themselves on shakier ground, balancing moral values against practical realities, "weighing religious, ethical, practical, sentimental and financial imperatives that [are] often in conflict" (Leland, 2005, p. 29). Women who learn that a child has a strong chance of having Down syndrome must balance their fear of raising a child with this condition against a religious belief in the sanctity of life. Poor women who received abortions at an Arkansas medical clinic readily admitted their ambivalence and pain. "I know it's against God," said Tammy, who works in a coffee shop in Tennessee:

> But you have three kids, you want to raise them good. My friends and sister-in-law say, "You care about money problems but don't care about what God will do," I believe it's wrong. I pray to God to forgive me. This will be the last one. Never, never again.
>
> (Leland, 2005, p. 29)

Balancing Things Out

Ambivalence drives some people berserk. They will do anything to resolve it. More generally, psychologists argue that individuals dislike inconsistency among cognitive elements and are motivated to reconfigure things mentally so as to achieve a harmonious state of mind. Fritz Heider (1958) proposed an algebraic model of attitudes, called **balance theory**. Heider's model involves a triad of relationships: a person or perceiver (P), another person (O), and an issue (X). Heider argued that people prefer a balanced relationship among P, O, and X.

Borrowing from chemistry, Heider suggested that cognitive elements have a positive or negative valence (or charge). A positive relationship, in which P likes O or X, is symbolized with a plus sign. A negative relationship, in which P dislikes O or X, is assigned a minus sign. A visual thinker, Heider diagrammed his model with a series of triangles. Each of the three relationships (P,O; P,X; and O,X) is assigned a plus or minus. Attitudes are in harmony when the signs multiplied together yield a plus. If you remember your elementary arithmetic, you recall that a plus × a plus is a plus, a minus × a minus is a plus, and a plus × a minus yields a minus. Let's see how this works in real life to understand how people cope with inconsistency among attitudinal elements.

Consider for a moment the contemporary quandary of an individual—let's call him Sam—who believes in evolution. A religious friend, Samantha, a devotee of intelligent design, believes God created human beings in their present form. She questions the validity of Darwinian evolution. Sam's belief in evolution is symbolized by a + in the model. Sam's liking of Samantha is conveyed by a +. Samantha's disagreement with evolution is symbolized by a −. Multiplying the three terms, one gets a minus, suggesting that Sam's attitude is imbalanced, or not entirely consistent (Figure 3.6a). Presumably,

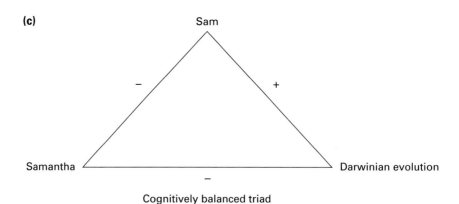

■ **Figure 3.6 Balance theory analysis of Sam's attitudes toward Darwinian evolution and those of a friend who does not believe in evolution ("+" indicates positive sentiments; "–" shows negative ones).**

Sam would find the inconsistency uncomfortable and would feel impelled to restore mental harmony. Balance theory says that he has several options. He could change his attitude toward evolution and question the notion that human beings evolved from earlier species of animals (Figure 3.6b). Or he could alter his attitude toward Samantha, deciding that he can't be friendly with someone who harbors such opinions (Figure 3.6c).

Balance theory helps us understand many situations in which people face cognitive inconsistency. For example, one anti-abortion activist told a researcher that she could not be a friend with somebody who disagreed with her on abortion (Granberg, 1993). Unfortunately, balance theory does not describe many subtleties in people's judgments. It also fails to describe those situations in which people manage to like people with whom they disagree (Milburn, 1991). Thus, we need another approach to explain how people grapple with inconsistency. A model proposed by Robert P. Abelson (1959) is more helpful. Abelson suggested that people resolve cognitive conflict in four ways: (a) denial, (b) bolstering, (c) differentiation, and (d) transcendence, or what could also be called integration.

Consider how this could work in the earlier example:

Denial. Sam could try to forget about the fact that he and Samantha disagree about evolution.

Bolstering. Sam could add mental elements to his attitude, noting that there is strong empirical support for the idea of natural selection and no scientific challenge to the notion that human beings evolved from earlier species of animals. In this way, he might feel more strongly about the belief, thereby reducing cognitive imbalance.

Differentiation. He might differentiate his liking of Samantha from her disbelief in evolution. In effect, Sam could agree to disagree with Samantha, noting they have been long-time friends and agree about other issues.

Integration. Sam could try to integrate his views with those of Samantha in a way that suggests both can peacefully coexist. He could acknowledge that there is no contradiction between his belief in evolution and her belief in God. Integrating his beliefs with hers, he could conclude that science explains *how* human beings evolve, while religion explains *why* humans developed in the first place. By combining the views in a way that allows him to see good in both perspectives, he might reconcile his belief in evolution with Samantha's theist principles.

As this example suggests, people regularly struggle with inconsistencies among different elements of their attitudes. Mental inconsistencies are part of life. Balance theory and the modification discussed above suggest that people try to find ways to reduce cognitive imbalance. They do not always succeed. Finding ambiguity uncomfortable, many people prefer to deny or derogate a position that conflicts with an aspect of an attitude. On the other hand, there are times when the strain to achieve cognitive balance can produce changes in attitude. A good example involves attitudes toward same-sex marriage.

Although attitudes have changed in recent years, many Americans continue to be affectively uncomfortable with gay marriage. Yet they care deeply for their gay close friends and family members. These individuals favorably evaluate same-sex marriage. In balance theory terms, we have an unbalanced triad. Washington State representative Maureen Walsh faced just this quandary. She supported domestic partnerships for gay couples, but drew a line when it came to same-sex marriage. Then she began thinking about her 26-year-old daughter, who had recently announced she was gay. "In some selfish way I did think what an affront to my beautiful daughter, who deserves something everybody else has in this country," she said. She then explained her change in attitude by stating, "It's selfishness, but it's motivated by love. And I'd rather err on the side of love, wouldn't you?" (Cooper & Peters, 2012, p. A16). Interesting, isn't it? Walsh's need to restore cognitive balance among her attitude toward same-sex marriage, her daughter's view, and her love of her daughter led to a change of heart.

CONCLUSIONS

Attitudes—emotional, evaluative, frequently formed at a young age—are a core dimension of persuasion. Attitudes, after all, are the entities that communicators seek to shape, reinforce, mold, and change. An attitude is defined as a learned, global evaluation of an object (person, place, or issue) that influences thought and action.

Values underlie or shape attitudes. Values are guiding principles in an individual's life. They include universal values, like freedom, and self-enhancing values, such as achievement. Beliefs, defined as cognitions about the world, in turn are viewed as components of attitudes. People cling tenaciously to beliefs, sometimes assuming their beliefs are facts. (They're not.) There are two types of beliefs: descriptive beliefs, the perceptions of the world that people carry in their heads, and prescriptive beliefs, or mental prescriptions of what should or ought to happen in life.

One of the interesting questions about attitudes concerns their structure or organization. Expectancy–value theory says that attitudes are composed of expectations (beliefs) and evaluations of these beliefs. It emphasizes the role that salient, or psychologically relevant, beliefs play in shaping attitudes. Expectancy–value theory helps break down the macro-concept of attitude into component parts, yielding rich information about the human mind. The **symbolic attitude approach** argues that symbolic predispositions, like prejudice and deep-seated values, lie at the heart of attitudes. It calls attention to the many affective attributes that are associated with the attitude object. An ideological perspective contends that attitudes are organized around ideological principles, like liberalism–conservatism.

Because people are complex, attitudes are not always internally consistent. Individuals frequently experience ambivalence, feeling both positively and negatively about a person or issue. Preferring harmony to discord, people strive to reduce inconsistency among cognitive elements. Balance theory and other cognitive consistency models describe ways that individuals can restore mental harmony. We don't always succeed in this endeavor, and inconsistency is inevitably a fact of life.

Persuaders can change attitudes by gaining insights into their complex structure. They could focus on changing beliefs, altering the symbolic affect associated with beliefs, or target messages at bedrock moral principles. They can also encourage individuals to alter elements of their attitudes so as to gain cognitive harmony. In some cases, these persuasion attempts can fail, but in other instances, guided by a deft persuader who combines the science and art of persuasion, the appeals can prove stunningly successful.

Test your knowledge now with interactive exercises

Chapter 4

The Power of Our Passions: Theory and Research on Strong Attitudes

 Listen now to the author's chapter summary

What is it about a player, wearing the uniform of his nation, dribbling, kicking, and pummeling a funny-looking spherical ball that drives Europeans berserk? Why does the emotional temperature of so many ordinarily tame and sober Europeans skyrocket as World Cup fever draws closer? What causes a handful of European men to access their inner hooligan when the start of a fierce cross-national soccer rivalry commences? Why did a qualifying match between Italy and Serbia have to be cancelled after just 7 minutes of play in Genoa? You want to know why. It's football, baby! Football! It's athletic greats Pele, Cristiano Ronaldo, Petr Cech, and—yes him too—David Beckham. It's 11 players, a field of grass, a fake, quick pass, a game-winning boot that vanquishes the hopes of the rivals and swells the pride of a nation.

Football, as it is known in Europe, and soccer in the American parlance, is one of many topics that elicits **strong attitudes**. A host of social issues—including gender roles, prayer in school, and contentious topics like gun control and abortion—also arouse powerful passions. Why do people hold attitudes with such tenacity? What is the nature of these attitudes? Why are some partisans frequently so dogmatic and impervious to argument? These are some of the topics discussed in this chapter, as I continue the exploration of attitude dynamics and implications for persuasion. (See Figure 4.1.)

Guided by academic research and theory, the first section of the chapter examines the nature of strong attitudes, while the second and third portions apply two major theoretical approaches: social judgment theory and accessibility. The final part of the chapter examines contemporary perspectives on strong attitudes that emphasize implicit attitudes and neuroscience.

■ **Figure 4.1 European soccer or football, as played here in a competitive match in the Ukraine, elicits strong attitudes, swelling national pride and sometimes causing outbreaks of violence.**

Image courtesy of Shutterstock.

WHAT ARE STRONG ATTITUDES?

From the French Revolution to violence perpetrated against doctors who perform abortion, "the incidents that attract our attention are often those associated with strong sentiments," Jon A. Krosnick and Richard E. Petty observed (1995, p. 1; see Figure 4.2). Intrigued by the dynamics of such attitudes, social psychologists have embarked on a series of studies exploring strong attitude characteristics and effects.

This might all seem obvious at first blush. People with strong attitudes have lots of passion and care a lot; isn't that what one would expect? Yes—but remember that persuasion scholars take a scientific approach. They want to understand what a strong

■ **Figure 4.2a–b Abortion is one of many issues that evokes strong passions. Could part of its power stem from its linkage with strong values, such as freedom and religion?**

Images courtesy of Getty Images.

attitude looks like, what it means psychologically to feel deeply about an issue, and how strong attitudes differ from weaker or more ambivalent ones. Remember also that people have acted brutally in the name of strong attitudes. They have killed innocent people and destroyed themselves. The more we can understand such attitudes, the more likely it is that we can devise ways to convince troubled or violent people to rethink their approaches to life.

Attitudes, by definition, influence thought and action. But strong attitudes are particularly likely to: (a) persist over time, (b) affect judgments, (c) guide behavior, and (d) prove resistant to change (Krosnick & Petty, 1995). Why is this so? Why are strong attitudes stable? According to Maureen Wang Erber and her colleagues:

> First, strong attitudes are probably anchored by other beliefs and values, making them more resistant to change. If people were to change their basic religious beliefs, for example, many other attitudes and values linked to these beliefs would have to be changed as well. Second, people are likely to know more about issues they feel strongly about, making them more resistant to counterarguments. Third, people are likely to associate with others who feel similarly on important issues, and these people help maintain and support these attitudes. Fourth, strong attitudes are often more elaborated and accessible, making it more likely that they will be at the tip of the tongue when people are asked how they feel on different occasions. Fifth,

people with strong attitudes are likely to attend to and seek out information relevant to the topic, arming them with still more arguments with which to resist attempts to change their minds.

(Wang Erber, Hodges, & Wilson, 1995, pp. 437–438)

The symbolic approach discussed in Chapter 3 suggests that people acquire strong attitudes at an early age. They are learned, rehearsed, and associated with positive aspects of a child's upbringing. Attitudes are also formed through observation of role models and reinforced when models, such as parents or peers, reward children for displaying the attitude (Bandura, 1971). Consider the example of a sportsman who has a staunchly favorable (yet complicated) attitude toward hunting. Hunter Steve Tuttle explained how he acquired his attitude:

> I remember the first time I ever killed something. It was a rabbit, and I was about 12 years old. I put my gun to my shoulder and aimed—taking care to lead the target—and pulled the trigger. The animal seemed to tumble end over end in slow motion . . . My father . . . looked up at me and said, "Good shot, boy!" and handed me the rabbit. I was proud and devastated all at once . . . The other men in the hunting party came over and slapped me on the back. Little did they know that I would have given anything to bring that rabbit back to life. I would feel sad about it for weeks . . . I went on to shoot a lot more game over the years, but none ever had the same emotional impact, nor did I ever get teary-eyed at the moment of the kill. In my culture, in the rural America of western Virginia, that was the day I began to change from boy to man.
>
> (2006, pp. 50–51)

Notice that during this pivotal experience the boy was rewarded for shooting the rabbit by a role model, his father ("Good shot, boy"), as well as by the other men in the hunting party, who slapped him on the back. In this way the positive aspects of an attitude toward guns were formed.

The ideological approach takes another tack, emphasizing that strong attitudes are likely to be organized around principles and values. For example, pro-gun partisans anchor their support of gun owners' rights in fidelity to values like freedom and self-reliance. Anti-gun activists support gun control, based on an equally heart-felt concern with the terrible effects of gun violence.

Social psychologists who study strong attitudes offer additional insights. They emphasize that strong attitudes, such as support for and opposition to gun control, possess different attributes from weak attitudes (Holbrook et al., 2005). Strong attitudes are characterized by:

- importance (we care deeply about the issue);
- ego-involvement (the attitude is linked to core values or the self);
- extremity (the attitude deviates significantly from neutrality);
- certainty (we are convinced that our attitude is correct);
- accessibility (the attitude comes quickly to mind);
- knowledge (we are highly informed about the topic); and
- hierarchical organization (the attitude is internally consistent and embedded in an elaborate attitudinal structure).

ATTITUDES AND INFORMATION PROCESSING

Strong attitudes influence message evaluations and judgments of communications. Two theories—social judgment theory and the attitude accessibility approach—shed light on how this occurs. Both are theories about attitudes in general, but they offer insights into the dynamics of strong attitudes.

Social Judgment Theory

On the eve of a Subway Series between the New York Yankees and New York Mets a few years back, a reporter filed this tongue-in-cheek report on how Yankee and Mets fans saw each other, based on interviews with New York baseball fans. It is a case study in how partisans on opposite sides of an issue perceive their antagonists:

> "Yankee fans are much more highly educated," [Allen Sherman, a Yankee fan] said. ". . . We have to be. It's harder to spell Yankees than Mets. And we can curse in so many different languages. We earn more, so when we throw a beer can it's those high-priced beer cans . . ." Fred Sayed, 26, a technical support manager from Queens and an ardent Mets fan, was able to be pretty explicit himself in defining Yankee fans: "All Yankee fans are just flat-out stupid."
>
> (Kleinfield, 2000, p. A1)

Or consider how differently those natural enemies of the baseball diamond—pitchers and hitters—perceive the increase in balls swatted out of the park:

> Ask a baseball pitcher why so many home runs are hit these days and you will hear an impassioned speech from a member of an oppressed minority. You will hear how umpires are calling a fist-size strike zone (*They're sticking it to us!*), . . . the mounds are lower (*They won't give us any edge!*) and, of course, the baseball is different . . . (*We're throwing golf balls out there!*). Ask an infielder, an outfielder or any player except a pitcher about the inordinate increase in home runs and a royal smirk

often precedes the response. (*The answers are pretty obvious, aren't they?*) You are informed the hitters are stronger than they used to be . . . , train daily (*I am a machine!*) and capitalize on modern technology (*We study videotape between at-bats and recognize the weaknesses in all pitchers*).

(Olney, 2000, p. 38)

Lest we ignore partisanship in other sports, I invite you to consider LeBron James, just about the most hated person in Cleveland, Ohio because he dissed the city's beloved Cleveland Cavaliers professional basketball team by joining the Miami Heat. Frustrated by his inability to win a championship ring as a Cavalier, James announced, in a nationally televised announcement that followed a much-publicized series of interviews with other NBA team executives who courted the talented athlete, that he was taking "his talents to South Beach." While Miami fans applauded the decision and others credited James with having the entrepreneurial guts to break the umbilical cord that had locked him into a contract with the Cavaliers since he joined the team at the age of 19, Cleveland fans were furious, to the point of violence. Longing for a national championship that had eluded the city for more than four decades, Clevelanders felt betrayed, first by James's decision and then by the way he announced it, teasing them for weeks by raising hopes that (in the eyes of fans) he knew would be dashed. Fans called him "narcissistic" and said they felt their "hearts been ripped out." One long-time fan called him the "the whore of Akron" (Sandomir, 2011). Others burned replicas of his jersey or threw rocks at a downtown billboard that featured James. Police had to be called out to stem the riots.

These anecdotes show that some people have very strong—actually extremely strong—attitudes toward sports. But the examples tell us more than this. They speak to the biases individuals have when they harbor strong feelings about a topic, and, in this way, illustrate the social judgment approach to attitudes. Pioneered by Muzafer Sherif and Carolyn Sherif (1967), social judgment theory emphasizes that people evaluate issues based on where they stand on the topic. As Sherif and Sherif noted:

> The basic information for predicting a person's reaction to a communication is *where* he places its position and the communicator relative to himself. The way that a person appraises a communication and perceives its position relative to his own stand affects his reaction to it and what he will do as a result.

(p. 129)

Social judgment theory emphasizes that receivers do not evaluate a message purely on the merits of the arguments. Instead, the theory stipulates that people compare the advocated position with their attitude and then determine whether they should accept the position advocated in the message. Like Narcissus preoccupied with his reflection

■ **Figure 4.3** **This painting,** *Hand with Reflecting Globe,* **by the artist M. C. Escher, illustrates a central principle of social judgment theory. It highlights the notion that people are consumed by their own attitudes toward a topic. They cannot escape their own perspectives on the issue.**

From M. C. Escher's *Hand with Reflecting Sphere* © 2007 The M. C. Escher Company—Holland. www. mescher.com. With permission.

in the water, receivers are consumed with their own attitudes toward the topic. They can never escape their own points of view (see Figure 4.3).

Social judgment theory, so named because it emphasizes people's subjective judgments about social issues, articulates several core concepts. These are: (a) latitudes of acceptance, rejection, and noncommitment; (b) assimilation and contrast; and (c) ego-involvement.

Latitudes. Attitudes consist of a continuum of evaluations—a range of acceptable and unacceptable positions, as well as positions toward which the individual has no strong commitment. The *latitude of acceptance* consists of all those positions on an issue that an individual finds acceptable, including the most acceptable position. The *latitude of rejection* includes those positions that the individual finds objectionable, including the most objectionable position. Lying between these two regions is the *latitude of non-commitment*, which consists of those positions on which the individual has preferred to remain noncommittal. This is the arena of the "don't know," "not sure," and "haven't made up my mind" responses (see Figure 4.4).

Early research focused on the relationship between extreme attitudes and size of the latitudes. Studies indicated that extremity of position influenced the size of the latitudes of rejection and acceptance (Sherif, Sherif, & Nebergall, 1965). Individuals with strong —in particular, extreme—views on a topic have large latitudes of rejection. They reject nearly all opposing arguments and accept only statements that are adjacent to their own stands on the issue. This is one reason why it is hard to change these folks' minds.

Assimilation/contrast. One way to appreciate these terms is to focus on an entirely different issue for a moment: the weather. For example, if the weather is unseasonably warm in Chicago one January afternoon (say, 45°), Chicagoans will excitedly talk about the temperature, remarking on how warm it is outside. Expecting the temperature to

(a)

(b)

■ Figure 4.4 Latitude of rejection (LOR), latitude of non-commitment (LON), and latitude of acceptance (LOA) of individuals with strong and moderate attitudes on an issue. Panel (a) illustrates latitudes of an individual with a strong attitude. Note the large size of the latitude of rejection and the small size of the latitude of acceptance. Panel (b) shows latitudes of an individual with a moderate attitude. This individual's latitudes of acceptance and non-commitment are larger and the latitude of rejection is smaller, signifying greater openness to alternative points of view. The hypothetical scale goes from 0 to 100, where 100 indicates a message in total agreement with an individual's position and 0 a position in total disagreement.

register 25° or below, they are pleasantly surprised, so much so that some giddy Chicago residents will slip on shorts, take a long jog around Lake Michigan—and a day later get really sick because, for most people, 45° is still too cold for a long run in shorts! This is a *contrast effect*, in which we focus on how different reality is from expectation.

On the other hand, if the Chicago thermometer reads 32° during the frigid days of January, people think nothing of it. Expecting the temperature to be in the 20s, they are hardly surprised. They *assimilate* the temperature to what they expected, neglecting the fact that 32° is somewhat warmer than average for the Windy City in January.

Assimilation and contrast are perceptual mistakes, distortions that result from the tendency to perceive phenomena from the standpoint of a personal reference point or anchor. People judge message positions not objectively but, rather, subjectively. Their initial attitude serves as the reference point. In **assimilation**, people pull a somewhat congenial message toward their own attitude, assuming that the message is more similar to their attitude than it really is. They overestimate the similarity between a speaker's attitude and their own. In the case of **contrast**, individuals push a somewhat disagreeable message away from their attitude, assuming that it is more different than it really is. They overestimate the difference between the communicator's attitude and their own (Granberg, 1993).

Thus, we assimilate our friends' attitudes toward our own, assuming that their views are more similar to ours than they really are. This is one reason why people who fall in love are so shocked at their first disagreement. At the same time, we contrast our foes, exaggerating the degree to which their attitudes are different from ours. "You mean, we actually agree," we jokingly say to an opponent at the office.

Assimilation and contrast are natural human biases that occur because we perceive events through our own frames of reference, not objectively. Both processes can help people cope with everyday persuasion events. However, they have psychological costs as well. When we assimilate, we assume everyone shares our attitudes and thereby close our eyes to instances where others have intriguingly different perspectives. When we contrast, we automatically assume that others with whom we disagree on an issue are "bad people" or disagree with us about everything. This blinds us to areas of potential agreement. Assimilation and contrast allow us to maintain our own view of the world, which provides stability. But they can perpetuate dogmatic perspectives on issues and an unwillingness to look at matters from alternative points of view. Such is the power of strong attitudes, social judgment theory emphasizes.

Messages. Social judgment theory has interesting implications for persuasion. In the main, it suggests that persuaders have a tough road to hoe. People's existing attitudes serve as anchors, serving as filters through which individuals evaluate incoming messages. Messages that land within the latitude of acceptance are assimilated or assumed to be closer to the individual's own position than they actually are (Eagly & Chaiken, 1993). A communication that resonates with the individual's initial attitude, but advocates a stronger position, can actually persuade the individual—so long as it lands in the latitude of acceptance. The person will assimilate the message, figure that it's something he or she pretty much agrees with, and accept the advocated position. The same holds true for a message that lands in the latitude of noncommitment, provided the message is ambiguous. (This is a reason why sometimes it's good to be vague and hedge your bets.)

But it's a very different scenario when the persuader delivers a message with which the person disagrees. Once the message ends up in the latitude of rejection, it's "Goodbye Charlie." The message recipient will contrast the message, perceiving it is to be more disagreeable than it actually is. The more discrepant the message, the less the attitude change. (See Box 4.1 for a summary of main aspects of social judgment theory.)

Ego-involvement. If you had to say which concept from social judgment theory exerted the greatest influence on research, it would be involvement. Social scientists have found involvement fascinating because it seems to have such a strong impact on latitudes and assimilation/contrast. Practitioners have been intrigued because of its many implications for intractable conflict on social and political issues.

Ego-involvement is "the arousal, singly or in combination, of the individual's commitments or stands in the context of appropriate situations" (Sherif et al., 1965, p. 65). People are ego-involved when they perceive that the issue touches on their self-concepts or core values. Highly involved individuals differ from less involved persons in two ways. First, when people are involved in or care deeply about a social issue, they have larger latitudes of rejection relative to their latitudes of acceptance and noncommitment. This means that they reject just about any position that is not in sync with their own. Second, when concerned deeply about an issue, people are apt to assimilate ambiguous messages only when the arguments are generally consistent with their preconceived attitudes (Sherif et al., 1965). Individuals with ego-involved stands are hard to persuade: they are stubborn or resilient, depending on your point of view (see Figure 4.4).

There has been much research exploring the psychology of ego-involved attitudes. Studies have shown that when individuals are ego-involved in an issue (as people frequently are with the environment, religion, or animal rights), they engage in what is known as *selective perception*. They perceive events so that they fit their preconceived beliefs and attitudes (e.g., Edwards & Smith, 1996; Hastorf & Cantril, 1954; Hovland, Harvey, and Sherif, 1957). An intriguing study by Charles G. Lord, Lee Ross, and Mark

---

BOX 4.1 UNDERSTANDING THEORY: PRIMER ON SOCIAL JUDGMENT THEORY

1. Social judgment theory emphasizes that individuals do not assess a message based on its objective qualities, but compare the message to their own attitudes.
2. People assimilate congruent messages to their own attitude, presuming the message is more consonant with their attitude than it actually is. They contrast discrepant messages from their attitude, presuming the message differs more sharply from their attitude than it actually does.
3. There are three layers of an attitude: latitude of acceptance, or the positions an individual finds acceptable, latitude of rejection, those that are seen as intolerable or absolutely unacceptable, and the latitude of noncommitment, the area where the person has preferred to remain noncommittal, an area of potential attitude change.
4. When people are high in ego-involvement or have strong views on the issue, they are especially resistant to persuasion.
5. Persuasion requires a match between the message and the individual's existing attitude. Persuaders cannot veer too far from the individual's preexisting position if they hope to nudge the individual to change his or her attitude on the issue.
6. The theory is vague on where you shoot the message arrow so it persuades individuals. It does not tell you how to frame your arguments to maximize success.
7. Social judgment theory says that persuading people to make sweeping changes in their attitudes is difficult and unlikely to occur.

R. Lepper (1979) provides a snapshot of current thinking on this issue. The study was conducted more than 30 years ago, but is regarded as a classic in the field.

Partisanship and Capital Punishment. Lord and his colleagues sought out individuals with strong views on the contentious topic of the death penalty. One group favored the death penalty, believing it to be an effective deterrent against crime. The second group opposed it, maintaining that capital punishment was inhumane or an ineffective deterrent. Individuals from each group read brief descriptions of two purported investigations of the death penalty's deterrent effects. One study always reported evidence that the death penalty was effective (e.g., "in 11 of the 14 states, murder rates were *lower* after adoption of the death penalty"). The other study used similar statistics to make the opposite point—that the death penalty was an ineffective deterrent against crime (e.g., in 8 of the 10 states, "murder rates were *higher* in the state *with* capital punishment").

Thus, students read one study that supported and one study that opposed their position on the death penalty. The evidence in support of the death penalty's deterrent effect was virtually the same as the evidence that questioned its impact.

If people were objective and fair, they would acknowledge that the evidence for both sides was equally strong. But that is not how these ego-involved partisans responded. Proponents of capital punishment found the pro-death-penalty study more convincing, and opponents found the anti-death-penalty study more persuasive. For example, *a supporter of capital punishment* said this about a study supporting the individual's position on the death penalty:

> "The experiment was well thought out, the data collected was valid, and they were able to come up with responses to all criticisms."

The same person reacted to the anti-capital-punishment study by remarking that:

> "There were too many flaws in the picking of the states and too many variables involved in the experiment as a whole to change my opinion."

An *opponent of capital punishment* said this of a sympathetic study that opposed the death penalty:

> "The states were chosen at random, so the results show the average effect capital punishment has across the nation. The fact that 8 out of 10 states show a rise in murders stands as good evidence."

The opponent reacted in this way to the pro-capital-punishment study:

> "The study was taken only 1 year before and 1 year after capital punishment was reinstated. To be a more effective study they should have taken data from at least 10 years before and as many years as possible after."
>
> (Lord et al., 1979, p. 2103)

You can appreciate what happened. Individuals liked studies that supported their position on capital punishment and managed to find fault with studies that opposed their position. They processed information very selectively, exhibiting what the authors called *biased assimilation*. They assimilated ambiguous information to their point of view, believing that it was consistent with their position on capital punishment. What's more, proponents and opponents managed to feel even more strongly about the issue by the study's conclusion. Proponents reported that they were more in favor of the death penalty than they had been at the study's start. Opponents indicated that they were more opposed than they had been at the beginning of the experiment. Reading the arguments did not reduce biased perceptions; it caused partisans to become even *more* polarized, *more* convinced that they were right! (See Figure 4.5.)

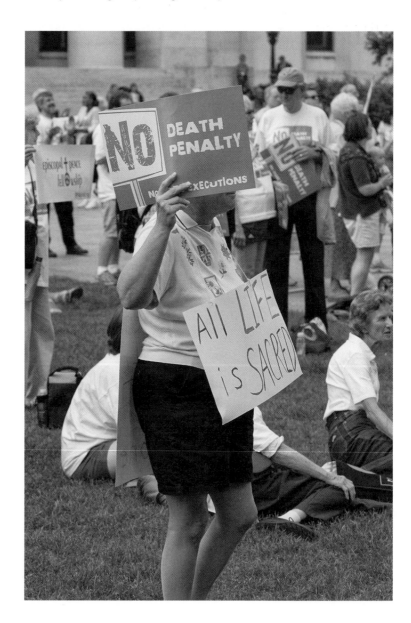

Figure 4.5 Supporters and opponents of capital punishment have such strong attitudes that they hold steadfastly to their positions, even when the evidence appears to support the other side.

Image courtesy of Shutterstock.

Social psychologists have been fascinated by the cognitive underpinnings of attitude polarization and the dynamics of selective perception. They have tried to piece together what happens inside an individual's mind when he or she is faced with conflicting evidence on an issue. They have suggested that people with strong attitudes have no intention of mentally searching for information that might prove their position wrong. On the contrary, they engage in a "biased memory search" at the get-go; convinced that their position is correct, they search memory for facts that support their view of the world, conveniently overlooking or rejecting evidence on the other side that might call their ideas into question (Edwards & Smith, 1996).

These findings help explain many events in everyday life. For example, if you did not know about biased assimilation, you might think that the tragic Arizona shooting spree that left six dead and seriously injured Congresswoman Gabrielle Giffords in January, 2011 would give advocates and opponents of gun control pause, the horrific event perhaps symbolizing the need for both sides to lay down verbal arms and look for areas of mutual agreement. On the contrary, the violence seemed to have exerted precisely the opposite effect, hardening positions. Gun control advocates maintained that the wild abundance of guns in Arizona made it easy for the mentally unstable shooter, Jared Loughner, to purchase a Glock handgun. But to pro-gun partisans, the truth was precisely the opposite. "To point any fingers at the gun industry is ignorant," said Anthony Scherer, owner of a shooting supplies company. "That's like pointing a finger at Ford and blaming them for car deaths," he said (Nagourney, 2011, p. A19). A similar chain of selective perceptions occurred after the Newtown, Connecticut massacre, with many gun control and gun rights advocates hardening their positions. This illustrates the findings of Lord, Ross, and Lepper's study to a tee: Tragic, complex events were selectively perceived by partisans of different stripes, perhaps leading to increased polarization of attitudes (see also Box 4.2).

One final point: it may seem as if this discussion applies only to those strong-minded, ego-involved partisans out there—individuals driven to protest and agitate. Nothing could be farther from the truth. Everybody—me, you, our friends—has strong attitudes on certain topics. It may not be global warming or animal research or electoral politics. It could be fashion, Facebook, football, or video games. There are certain issues on which we all are biased and psychologically intransigent. Social judgment research leaves no doubt that when we encounter messages on these topics, we will selectively perceive information, reject viewpoints that actually might be congenial to our own, even assume the communicator harbors hostile intentions. Such is the power of strong social attitudes. Once one recognizes this, one can take steps to counteract selective biases—for example, by considering that the other individual has a legitimate point of view and that one's own perspective may blind one to the cogent arguments in the other's position.

BOX 4.2 ON STRONG ATTITUDES AND POLITICAL SEGREGATION

It was November 2000. Democratic nominee Al Gore led Republican George W. Bush in Electoral College votes, but Bush held a 1,784-vote lead in Florida. If Bush won Florida, he would gain enough electoral votes to win the presidency. Gore's supporters challenged the outcome, citing the time-honored rule that when an election is in doubt, you count the votes by hand. Republican partisans filed a lawsuit, arguing that manual recounts are notoriously subjective.

An automatic voting-machine-conducted recount, more objective in the Bush team's eyes, had reduced Bush's margin, but still showed him the victor. Hordes of celebrity lawyers, politicians, public relations specialists, and activists streamed into Florida, trying to win the battle for public opinion.

Strong attitudes reigned supreme. Eighty-nine percent of Bush voters believed the results that proclaimed Bush the winner were a fair and accurate count. Democrats saw a different verdict: 83 percent of Gore voters perceived that the results were neither a fair nor an accurate rendering of the vote (Berke & Elder, 2000).

Political biases are so strong that they can even manifest themselves in brain activity. A group of psychologists asked supporters of President Bush and Democratic opponent John Kerry in 2004 to consider dissonant or consonant information about the candidates. Partisans processed the information while being monitored by magnetic resonance imaging. The reasoning arenas of their brains "shut down" when they were considering information inconsistent with their political positions, and the emotional areas lit up brightly when processing consonant information (Westen et al., 2006; see also Tavris & Aronson, 2007). We do not know how pervasive these tendencies are or the causal connection between the brain and mental processing. However, the findings suggest that selective perception is a fundamental aspect of human psychology.

Selective exposure is also pervasive. Selective exposure is the tendency to seek out communications that embrace one's worldview. To be sure, there are situations in which people deliberately look for information that contradicts their position, as when they are trying to make an important financial or medical decision and realize that they need both sides to make an informed choice (Frey, 1986). However, in subtle ways, selective exposure is a norm. People select social worlds—neighborhoods, friends, even Web sites and blogs—that reinforce their preexisting viewpoints (Iyengar & Hahn, 2009). Many of us grew up in neighborhoods peopled by individuals who shared our social attitudes and lifestyles. People tend to cluster or segregate by attitudes, so that voters are most likely to live and talk with those who share their political points of view (Bishop, 2008; Mutz, 2006). This selectivity even extends to preference for movies that aroused controversy some years back.

In 2004, Mel Gibson's *The Passion of the Christ* and Michael Moore's *Fahrenheit 9/11* grossed hundreds of millions at the box office. But there was a striking political schism.

The top theaters for *Passion* were typically located in Republican strongholds: suburbs and in the West, Southwest, and South. The highest grossing theaters for *Fahrenheit* were located in urban, traditionally Democratic areas, such as New York City, Los Angeles, and San Francisco (Waxman, 2004; see Stroud, 2007 for more empirical support). This exemplifies what one writer called "political segregation"—people's tendency to prefer media that support their side and live with people like themselves.

As columnist David Brooks (2004) observed:

> Once you've joined a side, the information age makes it easier for you to surround yourself with people like yourself. And if there is one thing we have learned over the past generation, it's that we are really into self-validation. We don't only want radio programs and Web sites from members of our side—we want to live near people like ourselves . . . The information age was supposed to make distance dead, but because of clustering, geography becomes more important. The political result is that Republican places become more Republican and Democratic places become more Democratic . . . When we find ourselves in such communities, our views shift even further in the dominant direction.
>
> (p. A27)

Attitude Accessibility

The event happened years ago, but we still remember it. On September 11, 2001, Americans received a massive, tragic jolt from their quiescence. The terrorist attacks on the World Trade Center and Pentagon had an enormous impact on the country. A particularly dramatic—and ironically positive—effect was the outpouring of patriotism that the events unleashed. Flags flew everywhere. They could be seen on houses, cars, clothing, book bags, even tattoos. People sang the national anthem and "America the Beautiful" proudly and with feeling, not mumbling the words in private embarrassment.

In 2011, the tenth anniversary of 9/11 brought out some of these same feelings. For many, the affect was unbearably sad. A woman who lost her son-in-law recalled the day's "visuals, the smells, the sounds of human misery . . . the heartbreak as bagpipes played 'Amazing Grace,' and you knew exactly why, as families tried to bury their dead" (Duff-Adlum, 2011, p. G-1).

Tragically, for many people the events of September 11 accessed emotion-packed attitudes—toward loved ones, the United States, and the preciousness of human life. They thus provide a poignant introduction to the concept of attitude accessibility, a helpful approach to attitude dynamics developed by Russell H. Fazio. Fazio (1995) views attitude as an association between an object (person, place, or issue) and an evaluation. It's a linkage between a country (United States) and a great feeling; an ethnic identity (Black, Hispanic, Asian) and feelings of pride; or a product (Nike tennis shoes) and exhilaration. Prejudiced attitudes, by contrast, are associations between the object and feelings of disgust or hatred.

Attitudes vary along a continuum of strength. Weak attitudes are characterized by a familiarity with the object, but a lukewarm evaluation of its net worth. Your attitudes toward Denmark, Eskimos, or an infrequently advertised brand of sneakers probably fall under the weak label. You have heard of the entities, but don't have particularly positive or negative feelings toward them. You can retrieve your attitude toward these objects, but not automatically or without effort. Strong attitudes—toward country, an ethnic group, a celebrity, or favorite product—are characterized by well-learned associations between the object and your evaluation. These attitudes are so strong and enduring that we can activate them automatically from memory. Simply reading the name of the object in print will trigger the association and call the attitude to mind. (Thought experiment: look at the word "Denmark" and observe what comes to mind. Now try "U.S.A." or a religious group with which you identify. What thoughts leap to mind? What emotions do you feel? According to accessibility theory, a global feeling about America, or your religion, should come to mind when you see the word on the page; see Figure 4.6.)

The key constructs of the theory are accessibility and association. **Accessibility** refers to the degree to which attitude is automatically activated from memory. If you want a simple colloquial phrase, think of accessibility as "getting in touch with your feelings." Associations are links among different components of the attitude. The stronger the

■ **Figure 4.6** The American flag evokes strong sentiments, typically pride and reverence for country. What comes to mind when you see these flags?

Photograph by William C. Rieter.

linkages are, the stronger is the attitude. Accessibility theory calls on a cognitive model of associative networks to explain attitude strength (see Roskos-Ewoldsen, Roskos-Ewoldsen, & Carpentier, 2009). It's a complex model, so an example may help you to appreciate the associative notion.

Consider attitude toward America, mentioned previously. Imagine the attitude is located somewhere in your mind, with "pathways" or "roads" connecting different components of the attitude. Each component is linked with a positive or negative evaluation. Fourth of July is associated with positive affect, which radiates out (in red, white, and blue) to fireworks and hot dogs, also evaluated positively. Other components of the America concept could be freedom of speech, Thomas Jefferson, the "Star-Spangled Banner," baseball, land of opportunity, and rock 'n' roll. Many people have good feelings about these concepts. The stronger the association between the overall concept, America, and a positive evaluation is, the more likely it is that a strong, favorable attitude will come quickly to mind when people see the word "America."

Needless to say, not everyone loves America. Some Americans have a negative attitude toward their country. Racial prejudice, school violence, and poverty might be images of the United States that these individuals have conjured up many times. Having learned to strongly associate America with negative feelings, they have a strongly unfavorable attitude that would come automatically to mind when they encounter the name of their country (see Figure 4.7).

Stimulated by the accessibility notion, researchers have conducted numerous experiments over the past couple of decades. They have examined factors that make it more likely that we are "in touch with" our attitudes. They also have explored the influence of accessibility on processing information (Fazio, 1990, 2000; Roskos-Ewoldsen, 1997b; Roskos-Ewoldsen, Arpan-Ralstin, & St. Pierre, 2002). In order to measure this deep-seated construct, researchers have used reaction time procedures. Participants in the study view the name or picture of an attitude object on a computer screen and indicate whether they like or dislike the object. The speed with which they push a button on the computer indexes accessibility. The quicker their **response time**, the more accessible the attitude. Guided by this and related procedures, psychologists have learned a great deal about attitude accessibility. Key findings include:

- *The more frequently that people mentally rehearse the association between an object and evaluation, the stronger the connection will be.* For example, hatred of terrorist groups, on the negative side, and love of country, on the positive side, are strong attitudes. People have come over time to frequently associate terrorists with horrific outcomes and commonly link one's country with good feelings. These attitudes have increased in strength over time and can influence our behavior, sometimes without our being aware of it.
- *Objects toward which we have accessible attitudes are more likely to capture attention* (Roskos-Ewoldsen & Fazio, 1992). Objects that are strongly associated in memory with good or bad feelings are more likely to get noticed. This has interesting implications for advertising, as is discussed in Chapter 13.
- *Accessible attitudes serve as filters for processing information.* Attitudes that people can call up quickly from their minds influence how they interpret incoming information. An attitude cannot influence thinking if people cannot call it to mind, and attitudes based on strong linkages between the issue and feelings are more apt to be activated when people encounter the issue in real life. These attitudes should serve as filters that influence how people interpret messages.

Attitude accessibility, pioneered over 20 years ago, has become such a popular staple in social psychology that it has generated criticism as well as praise. Although intrigued

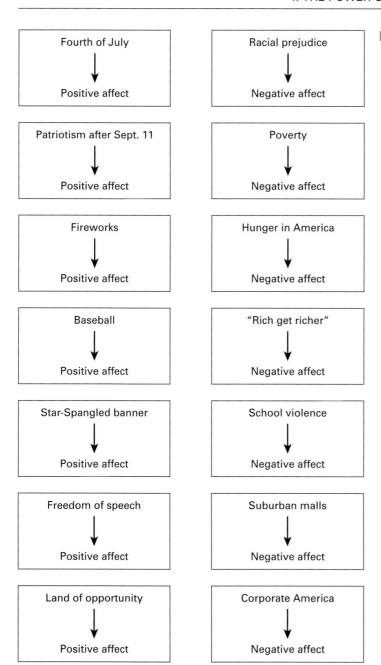

Fourth of July → Positive affect

Patriotism after Sept. 11 → Positive affect

Fireworks → Positive affect

Baseball → Positive affect

Star-Spangled banner → Positive affect

Freedom of speech → Positive affect

Land of opportunity → Positive affect

Racial prejudice → Negative affect

Poverty → Negative affect

Hunger in America → Negative affect

"Rich get richer" → Negative affect

School violence → Negative affect

Suburban malls → Negative affect

Corporate America → Negative affect

Figure 4.7 Associations and accessibility. Associative networks for an individual with a positive attitude toward America (left) and for an individual with a negative attitude toward America (right). When attitudes are strong, they can be accessed immediately—in this case, as soon as individuals see the word "America." Of course, associative networks about one's country are not limited to Americans. We could chart positive and negative associative networks for individuals from a host of other countries—for example, the United Kingdom, the Netherlands, Germany, Russia, and China. The stronger the associations between country and evaluations, the more likely the attitude should come quickly to mind.

by the concept, some researchers question whether accessibility has the strong effects Fazio attributes to it (Doll & Ajzen, 1992). Others have suggested that accessibility is less important than other aspects of attitude strength, such as the ways in which attitudes are mentally structured (Eagly & Chaiken, 1995). These are complex issues. Some researchers, like Fazio, believe that accessibility is the key aspect of attitude strength. Other researchers maintain that personal importance of the attitude is what differentiates strong from weak attitudes; still other scholars believe that ego-involvement is critical. (And you thought strong attitudes were simple!) Despite their differences, social psychologists agree that accessibility is an intriguing construct, with fascinating implications for information processing and persuasion.

IMPLICIT ATTITUDES

Some strong attitudes are characterized by a feature not discussed thus far in the book: they are outside conscious awareness. In other words, we are not consciously aware that we harbor certain feelings about the person or issue. Consider prejudiced attitudes— instances in which people blindly hate other people from different racial, ethnic, or religious groups. Prejudiced persons do not give the despised group member much chance; the mere thought or sight of the other elicits a volcanically negative response. Consider the case of Amadou Diallo. (See Figure 4.8.)

■ Figure 4.8 Amadou Diallo, a dark-skinned immigrant, may have automatically evoked implicit stereotyped attitudes on a February night in Manhattan, leading to tragic consequences.

Image courtesy of the Associated Press.

Diallo, born in Guinea, worked in 1999 as a peddler selling videotapes on a sidewalk in lower Manhattan. While he was standing on the steps of his apartment building one February night, his behavior aroused the suspicion of four White plainclothes police officers wearing sweatshirts and baseball caps.

Convinced that Diallo fit the description of a serial rapist who had stalked the neighborhood a year ago, one of the policemen confronted Diallo and asked to have a word with him. Frightened, Diallo ran into a nearby building. The police followed, demanding that he take his hands out of his pockets. His hand on the door knob, Diallo began slowly pulling an object from his pocket, an object that looked unmistakably to the officers like the slide of a black gun. Fearing for their lives, the officers opened fire. It was only when they examined Diallo's dead body and looked at his open palm that they could see the object up-close. It was a wallet. Diallo, the dark-skinned immigrant, perhaps thinking the police wanted to see his ID, had reached for a wallet.

Had the policemen, in that split second when impressions are formed and attitudes jell, misperceived Diallo based on stereotypes of his race? Had they categorized him as Black and therefore, at lightning-quick speed, accessed a negative attitude that led them to infer he was a criminal ready to gun them down? Perhaps.

This tragic case points up the potential power of implicit attitudes. **Implicit attitudes** are defined as:

> evaluations that (a) have an unknown origin (i.e., people are unaware of the basis of their evaluation); (b) are activated automatically; and (c) influence implicit responses, namely uncontrollable responses and ones that people do not view as an expression of their attitude and thus do not attempt to control.
>
> (Wilson, Lindsey, & Schooler, 2000, p. 104)

Implicit attitudes are habitual; they emerge automatically, in the absence of conscious thought. Such attitudes may be formed at an early age. As early as 6 years of age, White children display a pro-White, anti-Black evaluation (Baron & Banaji, 2006). In fairness, as children grow up, they learn about the prejudice African-Americans faced in this country and are exposed to egalitarian role models. This encourages the development of favorable attitudes toward people of different racial groups. What happens to the implicit, negative evaluation acquired at an early age? Some psychologists argue that it persists, even coexists, with a positive attitude toward the ethnic group.

Timothy D. Wilson and colleagues (2000) argue that people have *dual attitudes*: an explicit attitude that operates on a conscious level and guides much everyday behavior, and an implicit attitude that influences nonverbal behaviors and other responses over which we lack total control. The implicit attitude can be activated automatically, perhaps in highly charged emotional situations in which the individual is not able to keep feelings at bay. This may have happened to the police officers who confronted Amadou Diallo that cold February night.

There is much discussion about these issues in the academic journals. Critics note that all attitudes may not have dual components; a moderately held pro-environmental attitude may operate only on the conscious level. It may lack the preconscious primitive dimension. It is also possible that people don't have dual attitudes at all, but instead have one rather complex attitude that contains aspects they are aware of and others that elude conscious awareness. In addition, there are instances in which people are fully and proudly conscious that they hold virulently negative attitudes. One thinks of bigots who get drunk and brag about their racist, anti-Semitic, or homophobic attitudes. Finally, an implicit attitude need not always be negative; it can be positive, as are attitudes toward one's country, religion, or God.

There is much that we need to know about implicit attitudes and how dual attitudes operate. For now, these new approaches provide new insights on strong attitudes. They suggest that when people harbor highly prejudiced attitudes, the negative, gut-level feelings acquired at a young age can overwhelm or override social norms or positive attitudes acquired later. Hateful attitudes may be impervious to influence because they are so much a part of the individual or because the person is not aware of the depths of prejudice. This raises troubling questions for those of us who believe in persuasion. To what degree can prejudice be unlearned? Can a positive attitude override the negative feelings learned at a young age? Can an individual learn to focus on higher ideals and cultivate the tolerant attitudes that are part of a more mature self? Or, when stereotypes turn to prejudice and prejudice morphs into hate, is argumentation powerless? Can people who hate ever change their minds?

A NEUROSCIENCE APPROACH

Building on the foregoing research, which emphasizes the powerful (sometimes non-conscious) impact of attitudes, is the **neuroscience perspective** on social behavior. Neuroscientists emphasize that attitudes have biological, as well as psychological, foundations. Articulating its core assumption, Myers (2008) explains that "everything psychological—every idea, every mood, every urge—is simultaneously biological. We find it convenient to talk separately of biological and psychological influences, but we need to remember: To think, feel, or act without a body would be like running without legs" (p. 35).

Neuroscience research has become a pervasive part of the cognitive and behavioral sciences over the past couple of decades. It has intriguing implications for attitudes and persuasion, and particularly interesting applications to the underpinnings of strong attitudes. It is important to first define several key terms. A *neuron* is a nerve cell, the foundation of the nervous system. Extensions of the nerve cell receive information and conduct it toward the body of the cell. The information is subsequently passed on to other neurons, glands, or muscles in an elaborate neural communication system. Chemical stimulation is fired across a synaptic junction or small gap between a sending and receiving neuron. Neurons in essence talk with each other at these synaptic gaps, facilitating information processing.

At the foundation of all mental activity is the brain, the bundle of neurons that makes possible the human mind. The brain has numerous components, including a network of nerves called the reticular formation that helps control arousal; the cerebellum, which coordinates processing of sensory information and movement; and the amygdala, associated with emotions.

Neuroscientists look into the brain by magnetic resonance imaging (MRI). An MRI scan offers detailed information about soft tissues in the brain (and body), revealing structures inside the brain. **Functional magnetic resonance imaging** or fMRI reveals blood flow, and thus brain activity, offering a snapshot of the brain's functioning and structure. Comparisons of successive MRI scans allow researchers to see the brain essentially light up as an individual engages in different mental tasks (Myers, 2008). This offers insight into the biological basis of what we commonly call the mind, as well as our attitudes.

Using techniques like these, researchers have gleaned new information about a variety of attitudes. Using fMRI techniques, researchers uncovered a positive relationship between a type of strong attitude—racial prejudice (as assessed by implicit attitude measures)—and activity in the portion of the brain involved in processing threatening information, the amygdala. White Americans who had prejudiced scores on an implicit attitude test displayed heightened brain activity in response to photographs of unfamiliar African-American faces, but not to faces of positive Black role models like Martin Luther King (see Ward, 2010). Do individuals unconsciously engage in racist behavior? Or do the findings more benignly reflect growing up in all-White neighborhoods and lack of comfort with unfamiliar faces of individuals from a different racial group?

The neuroscience data provide a valuable a snapshot of the biological underpinnings of prejudiced racial attitudes. But, given current knowledge of brain processes, they cannot tell us which of these two above interpretations is correct. That requires knowledge of the more elusive, ineffable human mind.

At the same time, other research has tied brain activity more directly to persuasive messages (Falk et al., 2010). In one study, 20 young adults read persuasive messages about the importance of wearing sunscreen to protect against skin cancer. They viewed the text and images on the slides while in an fMRI scanner. Researchers assessed neural activities in regions of the brain that have been linked with psychological processes. They also obtained self-report measures of sunscreen use before and after the scanning session.

The persuasive message increased subsequent sunscreen use. Importantly, use of sunscreen was significantly associated with brain activity. Neural activity in key regions of the brain was correlated with persuasion-produced behavior change.

The findings do not indicate that the brain caused people to change their sunscreen use in response to the persuasive message. It could be that attitudes led to the behavioral change and brain activity reflected this. The causal relationship between the mind and brain activity is very complex.

It is easy to become enamored of the neuroscience approach and conclude that every-thing boils down to the brain, and we are wired to obey our neurons. This does not reflect an accurate understanding of the neuroscience perspective. Its insight is that persuasive message effects and attitudes have biological, brain-based underpinnings. These can offer fascinating new clues about the dynamics of complex, multifaceted attitudes, particularly strong attitudes rooted in prejudice. Armed with these insights, we can gain a more comprehensive understanding of linkages between the gray matter of the brain and the emotionally rich images, passions, and convictions that animate everyday life (e.g., Harmon-Jones & Winkielman, 2007).

CONCLUSIONS

Strong attitudes are part of what make us human. They enrich, empower, and enlighten. They showcase the willingness of people to put themselves on the line for issues that cut to the core of their convictions. Strong attitudes also exemplify the darker side of human beings: their biases, closed-mindedness, and refusal to consider alternative points of view.

Strong attitudes have a number of characteristics, including personal importance, extremity, and certainty. Social judgment theory provides many insights into the nature of strong attitudes. The social judgment approach emphasizes the ways in which people use preexisting attitudes to filter incoming messages, interpreting persuasive arguments in light of what they already believe. It calls attention to ways that ego-involved partisans assimilate and contrast messages so as to maintain their original perspective on the issue. Social judgment theory suggests that strong attitudes are exceedingly hard to change. Messages can influence attitudes only if they fall within the latitude of acceptance or within areas of susceptibility in the latitude of noncommitment. Messages that fall within the latitude of rejection are contrasted, assumed to be more discrepant from the individual's own attitude than they actually are, and are typically rejected. So much for human objectivity!

Fazio's accessibility approach also sheds light on the nature of strong attitudes. Strong attitudes—toward religion, ethnicity, and even a favorite sports team—are characterized by well-learned associations between the object and an evaluation. These attitudes are usually so strong and enduring—or chronically accessible—that people can call them up automatically from memory. The more frequently people rehearse linkages between an object and a positive association—for example, between chocolate and memories of delicacy—the stronger one's love of chocolate. Conversely, the more frequently one repeats negative associations—between chicken gizzards and disgust—the stronger the negative attitude. In this way, positive attitudes—from adoration of food to love of country—as well as negative attitudes—to both food and my country's "enemies"—inexorably develop.

Biased thinking is also likely when people harbor strong implicit attitudes, or those excluded from total awareness. Some prejudiced attitudes may operate at this level, making them resistant to persuasion. Illuminating the biological basis of these attitudes, neuroscience studies suggest that strong attitudes may have a different neurological foundation from weaker attitudes (Westen et al., 2006). A neuroscience approach has shed light on attitudes, identifying the biological underpinnings of strong affective evaluations, including activation in the portion of the brain involved in processing threatening information.

Theory and research on strong attitudes have many practical applications. They can shed light on why partisans disagree so vehemently about contemporary social issues. Partisans size up the problem differently, perceive matters in a biased manner, and tend to be resistant to persuasive communication. Ethicists suggest that if we could just supply people with the facts, they would put aside opinions and act rationally (Frankena, 1963). Unfortunately, there are no such things as pure facts. Partisans come to the table with different interpretations of the facts. Just bringing people from different sides together cannot guarantee that they will reach agreement. This is why negotiations on issues ranging from labor–management disputes to the Middle East frequently fail.

This fact—that objective facts frequently elude us and biased perceptions are the order of the day—has become a ubiquitous part of contemporary culture. Comedian Stephen

Colbert famously calls it "truthiness." "I'm not a fan of facts," he remarked satirically. "You see, facts can change, but my opinion will never change, no matter what the facts are" (Peyser, 2006).

All this raises the specter that one can never change strong attitudes. And, to be sure, people with strong attitudes are loath to change them, as a result of selective perception and the host of social judgment biases discussed in this chapter. But pessimists do not always have the last word. Communications have changed strongly held attitudes on a host of topics, from high-cholesterol junk food to ethnic prejudice. Persuasion research holds out a key. Persuaders may be able to nudge people into changing their attitudes if they understand the structure, functions, and underlying dynamics of these attitudes. There is no guarantee that change will occur, but it is certainly more likely if communicators appreciate the psychology of the individuals they hope to influence.

Test your knowledge now with interactive exercises

Chapter 5

Attitudes: Functions and Consequences

 Listen now to the author's chapter summary

Leslie Maltz regards herself as a California housewife, "virtually a byword for conventionality," as a magazine reporter put it (Adler, 1999, p. 76). But a while back she ventured outside her comfort zone. She had her navel pierced and put "a diamond-studded horseshoe through it." As a result, she no longer regards herself as a housewife. "I feel like a sex symbol," she says (Adler, 1999, p. 76).

Leslie's bodacious decision illustrates a theme of this chapter: attitudes serve functions for people, and people must decide how to translate their attitudes into action. As we will see, the issues of attitude functions and attitude–behavior consistency are intricate, complicated, and filled with implications for persuasion. This chapter continues the exploration of attitudes launched in the previous chapters, focusing first on attitude function theory and research. The second section examines the venerable issue of attitude–behavior consistency, more colloquially expressed as: Do people practice what they preach?

FUNCTIONS OF ATTITUDES

Functional theories of attitude examine why people hold the attitudes they do. These approaches explore the needs that attitudes fulfill and the motives they serve. Functional approaches turn attitudes on their head. Instead of taking attitudes as a given and looking at their structure, they ask: "Just what benefits do attitudes provide? What if people did not have attitudes? What then?" Bombarded by numerous stimuli and faced with countless choices about issues and products, individuals would be forced to painstakingly assess the costs and benefits of each particular choice in each of hundreds of daily decisions (Fazio, 2000). Deprived of general attitudes to help structure the environment and position individuals in certain directions, human beings would find daily life arduous. Noting that this is not the case, theorists conclude that attitudes help people manage and cope with life. In a word, attitudes are functional.

The beauty of functional theory is that it helps us understand why people hold attitudes. This not only is interesting to theorists, but also appeals to the people watcher in us all. Ever wonder why certain people are driven to dedicate their lives to helping others, why other individuals buy fancy sports cars at the zenith of their midlives, or why younger folks, in a carefree moment, decide to get themselves tattooed? Attitude function theories shed light on these decisions.

Researchers have catalogued the main functions of attitudes or the primary *benefits* that attitudes provide (Katz, 1960; Maio & Olson, 2000a; Smith, Bruner, & White, 1956; see also Carpenter, Boster, & Andrews, 2013). Main attitude functions include:

Knowledge. Attitudes help people make sense of the world and explain baffling events. They provide an overarching framework, one that assists individuals in cognitively coming to terms with the array of ambiguous and sometimes scary stimuli they face in everyday life. Religious attitudes fulfill this function for many people, particularly those who have experienced personal tragedies. For example, relatives of people who were killed in the September 11 attacks found comfort in "religious certainty of a hereafter. 'A plan of exultation, a plan of salvation: they both are in a better place,'" said Margaret Wahlstrom, whose mother-in-law died at the World Trade Center (Clines, 2001, p. B8).

Utilitarian. On a more material level, attitudes help people obtain rewards and avoid punishments. Smart but mathematically challenged students say that it is functional to develop a positive attitude toward statistics courses. They figure that if they show enthusiasm, the professor will like them more. They also recognize that if they look on the bright side of the course, they can more easily muster the motivation to study. On the other hand, if they decide at the outset to blow off the course because it's too hard, they will deprive themselves of the chance to prove themselves up to the task. In a similar vein, athletes find it functional to develop a positive—rather than hostile—attitude toward a tough coach. A positive attitude can help them get along with the "drill sergeant type," thereby minimizing the chances they will earn the coach's wrath.

Social adjustive. We all like to be accepted by others. Attitudes help us "adjust to" reference groups. People sometimes adopt attitudes not because they truly agree with the advocated position, but rather because they believe they will be more accepted by others if they take this side. For example, a student who wants to get along with a musically hip group of friends may find it functional to adopt a more favorable attitude toward alternative bands. During the Vietnam War protest era of 1960s and early 1970s, political attitudes served a social adjustive function for some students. Although many young people marched in rallies to express strong political attitudes, not all participated for this reason. Some students attended rallies for social adjustive purposes—to prove to others or themselves that they were "with it," or meshed with the prevailing groove of the time. Similarly, some of those who participated in the anti-capitalism Occupy Wall Street protests of 2011 may have joined to gain social approval from friends playing an active role in the protest.

Social identity. People hold attitudes to communicate who they are and what that they aspire to be (Shavitt & Nelson, 2000). This is one reason people buy certain products; they hope that by displaying the product in their homes (or on their bodies), they will communicate something special about themselves. Women wear perfumes like Obsession and men don Polo cologne to communicate that they have money and brains (Twitchell, 1999). Others buy T-shirts with the names of brand-name stores (Hard Rock Café) or dates of rock band tours to tell passersby something of their identity ("I'm not just an ordinary student; I'm with the band. See my shirt?").

Other people get tattooed to express a social identity. Patriotic symbols, mythological creatures, animals, arm bands, and flowers are among the many designs people have inked on their bodies to express a group identity or enhance their sense of uniqueness. As one woman said,

> I see tattooing as crafting your body into a piece of moving art. Look at my arms . . . what is naturally attractive about a blank arm? Place a beautiful piece of art on your arm and it becomes something unique . . . Tattooing might be our generation's call to be aware of artistic bodies.
>
> (Atkinson, 2004, p. 133)

Products other than tattoos, T-shirts, and perfume can fulfill social identity functions. Electronic products can do this too. One study found that men use cell phones "to advertise to females their worth, status and desirability" (Angier, 2000a, p. D5). On our campus I have observed women holding cell phones like they are prized possessions, objects that lift these students from the pedestrian realm of test taking to the lofty arena of transacting deals or settling interpersonal dilemmas. For some men and women, attitudes toward cell phones serve a social identity function. In one study, young Australians maintained that their cell phones "were part of them" (Paul, 2011).

Value-expressive. Another important reason people hold attitudes is to express core values and cherished beliefs. According to Maio and Olson,

> [Some individuals] claim that they favor capital punishment because they value law and order; they support affirmative action programs as a means of promoting equality; they support recycling programs because they value the environment . . . and they frown on cheating because it is dishonest.
>
> (2000b, p. 249)

The value-expressive function is pervasive. Some young people pierce their noses, tongues, belly buttons, or . . . well, other body parts to express a variety of values, including autonomy and independence from parents (see Figure 5.1).

Ego-defensive. Attitudes can serve as a "defense" against unpleasant emotions people do not want to consciously acknowledge. People adopt attitudes to shield them from psychologically uncomfortable truths. Let's say a young woman decides to break up with her boyfriend, realizing that the relationship is not going anywhere and fearing he will dump her when they go their separate ways after college. She still has feelings for her soon-to-be-ex, but to defend against these feelings and to make her position known to him clearly and with conviction, she declares in no uncertain terms that their relationship is over, kaput. Adopting a hostile attitude toward her boyfriend is functional because it helps her muster the strength she needs to call off the romance.

ATTITUDES AND PERSUASION

A central principle of functional theory is that the same attitudes can serve different functions for different people. In other words, different people can hold the same attitude toward a person, product, or issue; however, they may harbor this view for very different reasons.

Consider attitudes toward shopping. Some people shop for utilitarian reasons. They trek to the mall to happily purchase presents for loved ones and go home once the presents are paid for. Others shop for ego-defensive reasons, to help them forget about their problems or relieve stress. Recent immigrants to America sometimes shop to satisfy value-expressive needs. To these folks, America symbolizes the freedom to do as they wish. For those who grew up in economically and socially impoverished dictatorships, the notion that you can "buy what you want when and where you want it" is one of the great appeals of the United States (Twitchell, 1999, p. 23).

For American teenagers, shopping fulfills entirely different functions. Some teens shop to reinforce a social identity. Stores like the Apple Store, Abercrombie, and American Eagle are like "countries for the young." They offer teens a territory in which they are king and queen and can rule the roost. Malls provide adolescents with space to strut about and to shop for products that define them as distinctive and important. (Of course, critics view this somewhat differently. James B. Twitchell (1999) says that "the mall approaches a totalitarian Eden into which the innocent and the oppressed enter eagerly, lured by the dream of riches" (p. 299).)

It's not just attitudes toward products that serve diverse psychological functions. People can be deeply religious for different reasons, become active in politics to satisfy different

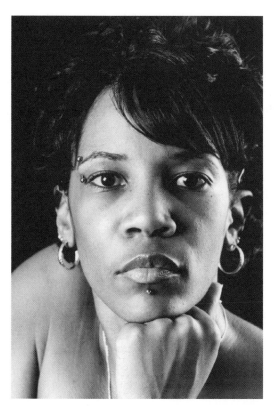

Figure 5.1 Body piercing is popular among young people. It does different things for different people, or fulfills diverse psychological functions.

Photograph by William C. Rieter.

needs, even pursue identical career paths for vastly different motivations. It's fascinating to discover just how different individuals can be once you peel away the superficial attribute of attitude similarity. Such an insight emerges with particular clarity in research on the psychology of volunteerism.

Attitude Functions and Persuasion

Millions of Americans—as many as 89 million—annually volunteer their time and services to help sick, needy, homeless, and psychologically troubled individuals (Snyder, Clary, & Stukas, 2000). They work in soup kitchens on weekends, participate in AIDS walkathons, offer counseling to depressed youth, aid victims of disasters, and try mightily to cheer the spirits of kids who have incurable cancer. A functional theorist, moved by people's willingness to help others in need, asks why. Why do people give so generously of themselves? Do different people have different motives? Mark Snyder and his colleagues found that people volunteer for very different reasons. Their reasons include:

- expressing values related to altruistic and humanitarian concern for others;
- satisfying intellectual curiosity about the world, learning about people different from themselves;
- coping with inner conflicts (reducing guilt about being more fortunate than other people);
- providing opportunities to participate in activities valued by important others; and
- providing career-related benefits, such as new skills and professional contacts. (Snyder et al., 2000, pp. 370–371)

These functions are intriguing. They also suggest ideas for how to promote pro-volunteering attitudes and behavior. **Functional theory** suggests that *a persuasive message is most likely to change an individual's attitude when the message is directed at the underlying function the attitude serves. Messages that match the function served by an attitude should be more compelling than those that are not relevant to the function addressed by the attitude.* The more that a persuasive appeal can explain how the advocated position satisfies needs important to the individual, the greater its impact is.

Thus, if you want to recruit volunteers or persuade people to continue engaging in volunteer activities, you must appreciate why individuals chose to volunteer in the first place. One message will not fit all. The message must match the motivational function served by volunteering. E. Gil Clary, Mark Snyder, and their colleagues dreamed up a study to test this hypothesis. They asked students to rate the importance of a series of reasons for volunteering. Reasons or functions included knowledge ("I can learn useful skills"), utilitarian ("I can gain prestige at school or work"), and value-expressive ("I believe someone would help me if I were ever in a similar situation") (Clary et al., 1994, p. 1133). The researchers then computed each student's responses to identify the volunteering function that was most and least important to him or her. Armed with this information, Clary and colleagues assigned individuals to watch a videotaped message that recommended involvement in volunteer activities. The message targeted a student's most important volunteer function (*matched* condition) or his or her least important function (*mismatched* condition). Each student watched either a matched or mismatched videotape.

For example, if a student said that volunteering mostly served a utilitarian function, he would watch a matched videotape that contained a utilitarian appeal: "You know, what I really like about all this is that I can make myself more marketable to employers and be a volunteer at the same time." If another student indicated that volunteering primarily fulfilled a value-expressive need, she would view a matched value-expressive video that noted: "By volunteering I get to turn my concerns into actions and make a difference in someone else's life" (Clary et al., 1994, pp. 1147–1148). Other students received *mismatched* videos (e.g., a student who volunteered for value-expressive reasons watched the utilitarian video).

Students then rated the effectiveness of the videotape. The results showed that matched messages were more persuasive than mismatched ones. Videotapes that targeted students' most important volunteering functions were more appealing than those that were directed at less important functions (see Figure 5.2). The implications are intriguing: they suggest that if we know the motives that volunteering fulfills, we can promote positive attitudes toward helping others. For a person who volunteers for value-expressive reasons, the message should emphasize how volunteering can relieve suffering or contribute to the social good. But a message like this will not cut it with an individual who pursues utilitarian goals. For this person, the message should emphasize how volunteering can enhance career skills. Idealists would find it heartless that a utilitarian message is more persuasive than an altruistic appeal. They may have a point, but such is the nature of human attitudes. To change an attitude, one must understand the function it serves and direct the message to the underlying function. This works for volunteering and other attitudes as well (Hullett, 2004, 2006; Julka & Marsh, 2005). (See Box 5.1: Understanding Theory: Primer on Functional Theory.)

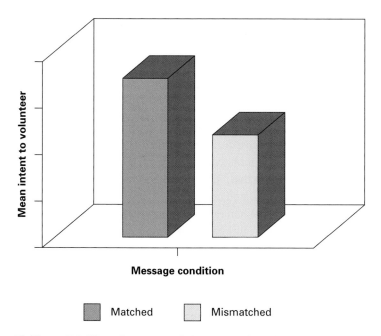

Message condition

☐ Matched   ☐ Mismatched

■ **Figure 5.2 Mean intent to volunteer as a function of match of message with personal motivations.**

From Clary, E. G., Snyder, M., Ridge, R. D., Miene, P. K., & Haugen, J. A. (1994). Matching messages to motives in persuasion: A functional approach to promoting volunteerism. *Journal of Applied Social Psychology*, 24, 1129–1149.

BOX 5.1 UNDERSTANDING THEORY: PRIMER ON FUNCTIONAL THEORY

1. People hold attitudes to help them cope with life.
2. Attitudes serve diverse functions, including knowledge, utilitarian, social adjustive, social identity, value-expressive, and ego-defensive functions.
3. Two people can hold the same attitude for very different reasons.
4. An attitude can have negative or dysfunctional effects on the individual who holds the attitude, as well as on others.
5. A persuasive message is most likely to alter an attitude when the message targets the underlying function the attitude serves.
6. Functional theory offers many insights. However, it sometimes can be difficult to clearly identify the particular function an attitude serves for an individual.

Attitude dysfunctions. There is, unfortunately, a dark side to attitude functions. An attitude that helps an individual satisfy certain needs can be detrimental in another respect. An attitude can assist the person in coping with one problem, while exerting a more harmful or dysfunctional effect in another area of the person's life.

Consider attitudes toward body piercing. *The New York Times* reported the story of a 15-year-old named David, who had his tongue pierced over the objections of his father (Brody, 2000). The tongue-pierce may have fulfilled a value-expressive function for David, a way to stake out his autonomy from his dad. But the stud in the tongue quickly became dysfunctional when David found that "for more than a week, he could hardly talk and could eat little other than mush." David now warns: "Think of the consequences and things that might happen afterward. When one says that the first five or six days is close to hell, you won't fully understand it until you get a tongue-pierce" (Brody, p. D8).

An additional complication of the functional approach is that attitudes can be functional for one person, but dysfunctional for others. Yakking on a cell phone while one walks can serve social identity needs for a phone buff, but try listening to someone rant and rave over the phone while you wait in line at the drugstore! Harboring prejudiced attitudes may serve an ego-defensive function for a bigot. ("It's not my fault. It's them—those blankety blank others.") However, prejudice is not exactly functional for those at the other end of the hate-monger's stick.

The foregoing discussion alerts us to several problems with the functional approach. It is hard to know whether an attitude is primarily functional or dysfunctional. If it helps the individual satisfy a need, do we call it functional, even if it has adverse consequences in other areas of the individual's life? How do we precisely weigh the benefits that the attitude provides to the individual with the negative consequences on others? It can also be difficult to identify clearly the function that an attitude serves. People may not know why they hold an attitude or may not want to admit the truth. However, no theory is perfect, and on balance the functional approach is more functional than dysfunctional for persuasion scholarship! It contains hypotheses for study and generates useful insights for everyday life. These include the following nuggets:

- *People are deep and complicated creatures.* We often do things that appear inexplicable or strange, until we probe deeper and understand the needs they satisfy.
- *We should extend tolerance to others.* People have many reasons for holding an attitude. These may not be our motivations, but they can be subjectively important to that particular person.
- *Persuaders must be acutely sensitive to the functions attitudes serve.* "What warms one ego, chills another," Gordon Allport observed (1945, p. 127). A message can change attitudes only if it connects with people's needs. One may totally disagree with a person's attitude, believing it to be immoral. However, condemning the other may be less useful than probing why the individual feels the way he or she does and gently nudging the individual toward change.

ATTITUDES AND BEHAVIOR

- Kelly has strong values, but you wouldn't guess this by observing her in everyday situations. She is charming, likeable, and adept at getting along with different kinds of people. Her friends sometimes call her a chameleon. Yet Kelly has strong views on certain issues, notably the environment and protecting endangered species. At a party, conversation turns to politics and several people advocate drilling for oil in the Arctic National Wildlife Refuge. Will Kelly take issue with their position?
- Susan is an agnostic, a skeptic who has doubts about the existence of God, and believes religion is of little use in today's society. She is a strong believer in Darwinian evolution, a forceful critic of creationist philosophy. At the same time, Susan has a soft spot for religion because it means a lot to her dad. An old friend of her dad's calls one day. He's been teaching Sunday school, but will be out of town next week when the class is scheduled to discuss the beauty of God's creation of the universe. He asks whether Susan would mind filling in for him just this once. Will Susan agree?

What is your best guess? Do these anecdotes remind you of people you know or conflicts you've experienced? These two examples are fictitious, but are based on factors studied in actual psychological experiments. They also focus on a central issue in attitude research—the connection between attitudes and behavior. The question is of theoretical and practical importance.

Theoretically, attitudes are assumed to predispose people to behave in certain ways. For example, suppose we found that attitudes had no impact on behavior. There would be less reason to study attitudes in depth. We would be better advised to spend our time exploring behavior. From a practitioner's perspective, attitudes are important only if they predict behavior. Who cares what consumers think about fast food or fast cars if their attitudes don't forecast what they buy? On the other hand, if attitudes do forecast behavior, it becomes useful for marketers to understand people's attitudes toward commercial products. Then there's us. The people watcher—intuitive psychologist—in us all is intrigued by the attitude–behavior relationship. We can all think of times when we did not practice what we preached. You probably know people who frequently say one thing and do another. The research discussed in this section sheds light on these issues.

The discussion that follows examines conditions under which people are likely to display attitude–behavior consistency. A subsequent section introduces theories of the attitude–behavior relationship. The final part of the chapter views consistency in a larger perspective.

Historical Background

It is morning in America, 1933. President Roosevelt is hard at work in Washington, DC, trying to harness the forces of government to get the country moving again. It's a daunting task. Depression and frustration are adrift in the land. People are unemployed, and some take out their anger on minorities. A psychologist, Richard LaPiere, is aware of the prejudice that one ethnic group, located in his home state of California, faces. He decides to examine the relationship between behavior and attitudes toward the Chinese.

Accompanied by a personable Chinese couple, LaPiere stops at restaurants and hotels across America. Much to his surprise, the group is served at all but one of the restaurants or hotels. But when he sends out questionnaires asking if owners would accept members of the Chinese race as guests in their establishments, over 91 percent of those surveyed reply, "No" (LaPiere, 1934).

The findings surprise LaPiere and attract the attention of scholars. It appears as if behavior (serving the Chinese) is out of whack with attitude (questionnaire responses). For years, LaPiere's findings dominate the field. Researchers conclude that attitudes do not predict behavior, and some researchers recommend that we discard the term attitude entirely (Wicker, 1969).

But hold the cell phone! It turns out that LaPiere's study had a number of problems. First, the people who waited on the Chinese couple were not those who filled out the questionnaires. Second, the survey probed intention to serve a Chinese couple, but the behavioral measure involved serving a personable Chinese couple accompanied by an educated Caucasian man.

What is more, when researchers systematically examined the relationship between attitude and behavior over the ensuing decades, they found that LaPiere's study was an anomaly. Most surveys reported significant correlations between attitudes and behavior (Fishbein & Ajzen, 1975, 2010; Kim & Hunter, 1993).

But give the early scholars their due. They correctly observed that attitudes do not *always* predict behavior. They called attention to the fact that attitudes do not forecast action nearly as well as one might assume on the basis of common sense. But they threw out the attitudinal baby with the dirty behavioral bath water! Sure, attitudes do not always predict what we will do. But that does not mean they aren't useful guides or reasonable predictors, given the incredible complexity of everyday life. The consensus of opinion today is that attitudes do influence action; they predispose people toward certain behavioral choices, but not all the time. Under some conditions, attitudes forecast behavior; in other circumstances they do not. The relationship between attitude and behavior is exquisitely complex.

Now here's the good news: we can identify the factors that moderate the attitude–behavior relationship. Key variables are: (a) aspects of the situation, (b) characteristics of the person, and (c) qualities of the attitude (Fazio & Roskos-Ewoldsen, 1994; Zanna & Fazio, 1982).

Situational Factors

The context—the situation we're in—exerts a powerful impact on behavior. We are not always aware of how our behavior is subtly constrained by norms, roles, and a desire to do the socially correct thing. A **norm** is an individual's belief about the appropriate behavior in a situation. Roles are parts we perform in everyday life, socially prescribed functions like professor, student, parent, child, and friend.

Norms and roles. Individuals may hold an attitude, but choose not to express the attitude because it would violate a social norm. You may not like an acquaintance at work, but realize that it violates conventional norms to criticize the person to his face.

Someone may harbor prejudice toward co-workers, but be savvy enough to know that she had better hold her tongue lest she get in trouble on the job (Kiesler, Collins, & Miller, 1969).

Norms vary across cultures. In traditional Middle Eastern societies, friendly, outgoing behavior can be held in low repute. Gregarious behavior that is regarded positively in the United States ("Hey, how ya' doin'?") may be viewed negatively in some Middle Eastern countries. Instead, the norm is to be serious, even somber in public (Yousef, 1982). Thus, a person may hide her affection for a colleague when seeing him at work. Attitude fails to predict behavior because the public display of attitude runs counter to cultural norms.

Roles also influence the attitude–behavior relationship. When people take on professional roles, they have to act the part, putting their biases aside. This helps explain why reporters, who have strong political beliefs, rarely display biases in their professional activity at newspapers or television stations. For example, many Washington reporters are liberal Democrats, but their news stories go right down the middle, offering criticism of Democrat and Republican politicians (Perloff, 1998). One of the requirements of news is that it show no favoritism to either side—that it be perceived as fair and objective. Journalists know that if they write biased news stories, they will quickly lose their jobs or will be viewed as unprofessional by colleagues. Thus, liberal political attitudes do not reliably predict reporters' public behavior.

Scripts. To illustrate the concept of script, I ask that you imagine you face a term paper deadline and are hard at work at your word processor. A phone rings; it's a telemarketer, the tenth to call this week. She's asking for money for injured war veterans, a cause you normally support because a relative got hurt while serving in the Iraq war. Not thinking and mindlessly putting on your "I'm busy, leave me alone" hat, you cut the volunteer off, telling her in no uncertain terms that you have work to do.

Your attitude obviously didn't come into play here. If it had, you would have promised a donation. Instead, you invoked a script: an "organized bundle of expectations about an event sequence" or an activity (Abelson, 1982, p. 134). Like an actor who has memorized his lines and says them on cue, you call on well-learned rules about how to handle pushy telemarketers interrupting your day. Your expectations of how the transaction with the telemarketer is going to proceed—the overly pleasant intro, follow-up for money, plea to keep you on the phone—set the tone for the conversation, and you mindlessly follow the script rather than taking the time to consult your attitude toward veterans.

Characteristics of the Person

Individuals differ in the extent to which they display consistency between attitudes and behavior. Some people are remarkably consistent; others are more variable. Social psychological research has helped pinpoint the ways in which personal factors moderate the attitude–behavior relationship. Two moderating factors are self-monitoring and direct experience.

Self-monitoring. Social psychologist Mark Snyder, whose research we glimpsed before, confidently believes people can be divided into two categories. A first group consists of individuals who are concerned with displaying appropriate behavior in social situations. Adept at reading situational cues and figuring out the expected behavior at a given place and time, these individuals adjust their behavior to fit the situation. When filling out Snyder's (1974) scale, they agree that "in different situations and with different people, I often act like very different persons." These individuals are called high self-monitors because they "*monitor* the public appearances of self they display in social situations" (Snyder, 1987, pp. 4–5).

A second group is less concerned with fitting into a situation or displaying socially correct behavior. Rather than looking to the situation to figure out how to behave, they consult their inner feelings and attitudes. "My behavior is usually an expression of my true inner feelings, attitudes, and beliefs," they proudly declare, strongly agreeing with this item in the self-monitoring scale. These individuals are called low self-monitors.

High self-monitors exhibit less attitude–behavior consistency than do low self-monitors (Snyder & Kendzierski, 1982; Snyder & Tanke, 1976). High self-monitors look to the situation to decide how to act. As "actor types" who enjoy doing the socially correct thing, they don't view each and every situation in life as a test of character. If a situation requires that they put their attitudes aside for a moment, they happily do so. Low self-monitors strongly disagree. Living by the credo, "To thine own self be true," low self-monitors place value on practicing what they preach and maintaining congruence between attitude and behavior. Not to do so would violate a personal canon for low self-monitors.

In the example given earlier, Kelly—the outgoing, chameleon-like young woman who has strong attitudes toward wildlife preservation—would be in a pickle if acquaintances at a party began taking an anti-environmental stand. Her personality description suggests she is a high self-monitor. If so, she would be unlikely to challenge her acquaintances. Instead, she might smile sweetly, nod her head, and resolve to talk up the environmental issue in situations where she could make a difference. Needless to say, a low self-monitor who shared Kelly's values would be foaming at the mouth when her friends began saying that we should drill for oil in the National Wildlife Refuge. She probably would not hesitate to tell them how she felt.

Direct experience. Experience also moderates the attitude–behavior relationship. Some of our attitudes are based on direct experience with an issue; we have encountered the problem in real life, it has evoked strong feelings, or led us to think through the implications of behaving in a certain way. Other attitudes are formed indirectly—from listening to parents or peers, reading books, watching television, or skimming Facebook posts. Attitudes formed through direct experience "are more clearly defined, held with greater certainty, more stable over time, and more resistant to counter influence" than attitudes formed through indirect experience (Fazio & Zanna, 1981, p. 185; see also Millar & Millar, 1996). Attitudes produced by direct experience also come more quickly to mind than attitudes acquired through indirect experiences. For these reasons, people are more apt to translate attitude into behavior when the attitude has been formed through direct experiences in real-world situations (Fazio & Zanna, 1978).

■ **Figure 5.3 A young man with a negative attitude toward drugs may not translate attitude into behavior if tempted by peers and if he has little direct experience with drugs to guide him.**

Image courtesy of Shutterstock.

Consider a contemporary example: adolescent drug abuse. Two teenagers may both have negative attitudes toward drug use. One formed her attitude through direct experience: She smoked a lot of marijuana, tried Ecstasy as a high school sophomore, got sick, and found the experience psychologically scary. A teenage guy formed his attitude indirectly, from reading lots of articles warning of harmful effects of drugs and getting the drug rap from parents. During the last week of high school each is tempted to try some drugs at a pulsating pre-graduation party. As she contemplates her decision, the young woman accesses and recalls the negative experiences she had a couple of years back, leading her to reject the offer. Although the guy initially says no, he finds the offer to smoke some weed tempting, his negative attitude less strongly felt, less accessible, and not sufficiently powerful to overcome the allure of a marijuana high. (See Figure 5.3.)

Attitudes based on direct experience are more likely to predict behavior than those formed indirectly. Thus, persuaders can take advantage of people—persuading them to cast their better judgments to the wind—when individuals are uncertain about what they believe or have not thought through their attitudes and beliefs.

Characteristics of the Attitude

As noted in Chapters 3 and 4, attitudes differ in their structure and strength. The nature of an attitude moderates the relationship between attitudes and behavior.

General versus specific attitudes. Ajzen and Fishbein (1977) distinguished between *general* and *highly specific* attitudes. A general attitude, the focus of discussion up to this point, is the global evaluation that cuts across different situations. A specific attitude, called *attitude toward a behavior*, is evaluation of a single act, or specific behavior that takes place in a particular context at a particular time. For example, consider the issue of predicting religious behavior from religious attitudes. The general attitude is the individual's attitude toward religion. This is the sum total of the person's evaluations of many religious behaviors, such as praying, attending religious services, partaking in holiday rituals, talking about religion in everyday life, and donating money to religious causes. The specific attitude is the attitude toward one of these behaviors at a particular place and time.

A general attitude, sometimes called *attitude toward the object*, will not predict each and every religious behavior. A Ph.D. student who is deeply religious may attend only a handful of religious services over the course of 6 months—not because he has abandoned religion, but because he is immersed in doctoral comprehensive exams and realizes he must forsake this part of his religious identity for a time. (To compensate, the student may regularly devote time to reading inspirational portions of the Bible.)

The student harbors a favorable attitude toward religion, but rarely, it seems, translates attitude into behavior.

But here's the rub: if you take the dozens of other religious behaviors in which the student could (and does) partake (from praying to Bible reading), and include them in your equation, you will discover that attitude predicts behavior rather handsomely.

This is the conclusion that Fishbein and Ajzen reached in an exhaustive review of this topic. In a 1974 study—old but still good—the investigators asked people to indicate their general religious attitude, as well as how frequently they participated in each of 100 specific religious behaviors. The correlation, or association, between general attitude toward religion and any specific action was 0.15. This is a very small correlation; it means that attitude toward religion is not closely related to a particular behavior in a given situation. But when Fishbein and Ajzen (1974) looked at the overall behavior pattern, focusing not on one situation but rather on the sum total, they discovered that the relationship between attitude toward religion and religious behavior was substantial. The correlation was 0.71, approaching 1 (the latter a perfect correlation).

Other researchers, focusing on different behaviors, have obtained similar findings. For example, Weigel and Newman (1976) found that individuals who had favorable attitudes toward environmental preservation were more likely than those with less positive attitudes to participate in a variety of environmental protection projects. The projects included signing petitions opposing construction of nuclear power plants, distributing petitions to family members and friends, and taking part in a roadside litter pickup. The more positive individuals' environmental attitudes were, the more likely they were to engage in a broad range of pro-environmental activities.

However, harboring a positive attitude toward the environment did not lead people to participate in each and every environmental cause. For example, one woman who scored high on the environmental attitude scale declined to participate in a litter pickup project. Her husband asked her not to do so. Apparently, the man was also an environmentalist and, as luck would have it, planned to organize a local Boy Scout troop in a similar project. He feared that his wife's litter pickup project might interfere with his plans. His wife, either because she agreed with him or chose to be deferent, opted not to participate in the pickup project.

Again, it was not that the woman had displayed marked inconsistency between attitude and behavior, for she apparently translated her environmental attitude into action across most other domains (signing petitions, distributing them, and so forth). It was that, as often happens in life, something else came up. If you wished to predict the woman's behavior in particular circumstances, you would be better advised, Fishbein and Ajzen say, to consider her *specific attitude* toward participating in the environmental project in question.

These ideas are an outgrowth of what Ajzen and Fishbein (1977) call the **compatibility principle**. *A strong relationship between attitude and behavior is possible only if the attitudinal predictor corresponds with the behavioral criteria.* "Corresponds with" means that the attitudinal and behavioral entities are measured at the same level of specificity. Thus, specific attitudes toward a behavior predict highly specific acts. General attitudes predict broad classes of behavior that cut across different situations (see Figure 5.4).

Attitude strength. Another moderator of the attitude–behavior relationship is the strength of the individual's attitude. Strong attitudes are particularly likely to forecast behavior (Lord, Lepper, & Mackie, 1984). This makes sense psychologically and resonates with ordinary experience. Those with strong convictions on issues ranging from abortion to immigration are the ones who are out there on the picket lines or are lobbying Congress to pass legislation favorable to their groups.

It gets more complicated when you consider those instances when we're ambivalent about issues. When people have strong feelings on both sides of an issue or are torn between head and heart, they are less apt to translate attitude into behavior (Armitage & Conner, 2000; Lavine et al. 1998). Different feelings push people in different behavioral directions. The affective aspect of an attitude (feelings) can propel people toward one choice, while the cognitive dimension (beliefs) can push them in a different direction. Faced with these cross-pressures, individuals may behave in accord with their attitude in one situation, but not so much in another.

Consider the case of Susan, the agnostic mentioned earlier who believes strongly in evolution, but has a soft spot for religion because it means a lot to her dad. Asked to

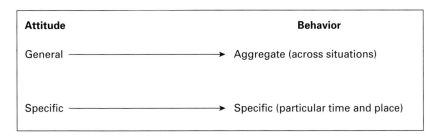

■ **Figure 5.4 Compatibility principle. Arrows denote strong relationships between attitude and behavior. General attitude will not predict specific behavior, and a specific attitude will not forecast behavior in the aggregate.**

teach a Sunday school class in which she has to take a creationist position on evolution, Susan is likely to have mixed feelings. Her negative views toward religion should propel her to reject the request. (Fishbein and Ajzen's model suggests that her specific negative evaluation of teaching creationism should also push her in that direction.) However, cognition clashes with affect: Susan's relationship with her dad means a lot, and the call from an old friend of her father evokes fond memories. If heart governs head and feelings overpower thoughts, she is likely to agree to teach the class. If she opts to base her decision on logic, she will politely decline. Much depends on what information comes to mind at the moment of decision, and how she goes about deciding which course to take (Wang Erber, Hodges, & Wilson, 1995).

MODELS OF ATTITUDE–BEHAVIOR RELATIONS

As we have seen, people are complex. They can be consistent, practicing what they preach, or they can surprise you, doing things that you would not expect based on their attitudes. Research sheds light on these phenomena. We know that attitudes frequently guide behavior, though the effects are stronger under certain circumstances, for some individuals, and with some attitudes more than others. The studies offer a patchwork—a pastiche—of conditions under which attitudes are more or less likely to influence action. Social scientists prefer more organized frameworks, such as models that explain and predict behavior. Two major theories of attitude–behavior relations have been proposed: the reasoned action and accessibility models.

The Reasoned Action Model

Fishbein and Ajzen, who brought you the precision of the compatibility principle, also formulated a major approach to attitude–behavior relations: the **Reasoned Action Model** (Fishbein & Ajzen 2010). Originally proposed by Fishbein and Ajzen in 1975, the approach was extended by Ajzen in 1991 in his planned behavior approach. In 2010, the model was given a face-lift; it was streamlined, clarified, and modified to take into account new ideas.

Reasoned action offers the most systematic explanation in the field of the processes by which beliefs influence behavior. It offers a roadmap for the journey that thoughts in a person's head must travel before they can affect the actions he or she performs. In so doing, it generates a series of specific strategies that persuaders should employ to craft communications on any topic you can imagine.

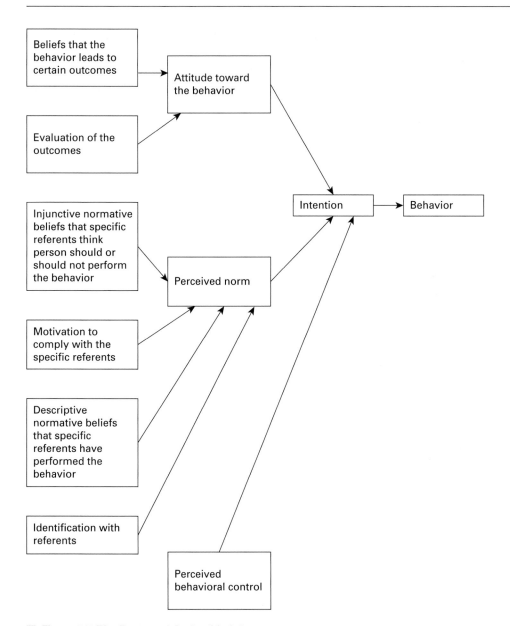

■ **Figure 5.5 The Reasoned Action Model.**

From Fishbein, M. & Ajzen, I. 2010. *Predicting and changing behavior: The reasoned action approach.*
New York: Psychology Press.

First, a word about the name. The term *reasoned action* implies that people are rational and deliberate in how they go about deciding whether to perform a particular behavior. Fishbein and Ajzen (2010) are quick to acknowledge that people do not always think their decisions through mindfully. Instead, they argue that once people form a set of beliefs, they proceed to act on these beliefs in a predictable and consistent fashion. Their beliefs provide the cognitive basis from which attitudes, intentions, and behavior subsequently follow. Beliefs, scholar Marco Yzer (2013) emphasizes, are not always rational. However, they are powerful. For example, he explains:

> Someone suffering from paranoid personality disorder may lock the door of his office because he believes that his colleagues are conspiring against him. This person acts in a reasoned manner on a belief, even though others would deem his belief irrational. Regardless whether beliefs are irrational, incorrect (because based on false information), or motivationally biased, once beliefs are formed they are the cognitive basis from which behavior reasonably follows (p. 121).

There are five components of the theory: *attitude toward the behavior*, the individual's judgment that performing the action is good or bad; *perceived norm*, perceived social pressure to perform the action; *perceived behavioral control*, the degree to which individuals believe they are capable of performing a particular behavior; *behavioral intention*, the intent or plan to perform a particular behavior; and *behavior* itself, the action in a particular situation (see Figure 5.5, p. 135).

As an example, suppose you are doing volunteer work for a local high school, impelled by a recent near-fatal accident a high school friend sustained when he veered off the road, his attention diverted by an urgent text message he was sending to his girlfriend about a party later that evening. Propelled by knowledge that reckless driving is a major cause of lethal injuries in young adults (Fischer et al., 2011), you agree to help devise persuasive appeals to convince teenagers not to text when they drive. You decide to employ the reasoned action approach, launching your research by trying to understand why teens like to text when they drive. (See Figure 5.6.)

Attitude. Attitude toward the behavior is a highly specific attitude. It consists of two subcomponents: behavioral beliefs (beliefs about consequences of the behavior) and outcome evaluations (evaluations of the consequences). These two elements are combined as they were in the simple expectancy–value model described in Chapter 3. Each behavioral belief is multiplied by the corresponding evaluation, and results are summed across items. Beliefs and evaluations about texting while driving could be measured in this way:

■ **Figure 5.6 Texting while driving can increase the chances of traffic fatalities. The Reasoned Action Model suggests strategies to persuade people not to engage in this risky behavior by shedding light on the psychological elements that underlie the behavior.**

Image courtesy of Getty Images.

Behavioral beliefs

Texting while driving on my way to school:

1. Helps me stay in touch with friends

   (Likely)   1   2   3   4   5   6   7   (Unlikely)

2. Keeps me from getting bored

   (Likely)   1   2   3   4   5   6   7   (Unlikely)

3. Makes me feel less lonely when I drive

   (Likely)   1   2   3   4   5   6   7   (Unlikely)

4. Reduces my ability to drive safely

   (Likely)   1   2   3   4   5   6   7   (Unlikely)

Outcome evaluations

1. Staying in touch with friends

   (Good)　1　2　3　4　5　6　7　　(Bad)

2. Getting bored

   (Good)　1　2　3　4　5　6　7　　(Bad)

3. Feeling lonely when I drive

   (Good)　1　2　3　4　5　6　7　　(Bad)

4. Driving safely

   (Good)　1　2　3　4　5　6　7　　(Bad)

Perceived norm. Norms refer to acceptable, recommended behavior in a society. A perceived norm is perceived social pressure to perform a particular action. The perceived norm has two components: *injunctive norms*, or perceptions of what other people think we *should* do, and *descriptive norms*, perceptions of what others have done, are doing, or are likely to do in the future (Fishbein & Ajzen, 2010, p. 151).

Each consists of two sub-components, which are multiplied together.

Injunctive norms consist of: (a) injunctive normative beliefs, or beliefs that individuals who are important to endorse the behavior; and (b) motivation to comply, the person's motivation to go along with these significant others.

Descriptive norms are composed of: (a) descriptive normative beliefs, or beliefs about how frequently important others engage in the behavior; and (b) identification, the degree to which an individual identifies with these significant others.

Injunctive normative beliefs

1. My mom thinks that:

   (I should)　1　2　3　4　5　6　7　　(I should not text when I drive to school)

2. My dad thinks that:

   (I should)　1　2　3　4　5　6　7　　(I should not text when I drive to school)

3. My best friend thinks that:

   (I should)　1　2　3　4　5　6　7　　(I should not text when I drive to school)

Motivation to comply

1. When it comes to matters of safety, I want to do what my mom thinks I should do.

    (Strongly agree)   1   2   3   4   5   6   7   (Strongly disagree)

2. When it comes to matters of safety, I want to do what my dad thinks I should do.

    (Strongly agree)   1   2   3   4   5   6   7   (Strongly disagree)

3. When it comes to matters of safety, I want to do what my best friend thinks I should do.

    (Strongly agree)   1   2   3   4   5   6   7   (Strongly disagree)

Descriptive Normative Beliefs

1. My mom texts when she drives me to school.

    (All of the time)   1   2   3   4   5   6   7   (Never)

2. My dad texts when he drives me to school.

    (All of the time)   1   2   3   4   5   6   7   (Never)

3. My best friend texts when (s)he drives me to school.

    (All of the time)   1   2   3   4   5   6   7   (Never)

Identification

1. When it comes to matters of safety, how much do you want to be like your mom?

    (A lot)   1   2   3   4   5   6   7   (Not at all)

2. When it comes to matters of safety, how much do you want to be like your dad?

    (A lot)   1   2   3   4   5   6   7   (Not at all)

3. When it comes to matters of safety, how much do you want to be like your best friend?

    (A lot)   1   2   3   4   5   6   7   (Not at all)

Descriptive and injunctive norms are then combined to produce an item measuring perceived norms.

Perceived behavioral control. This concept was proposed by Ajzen (1991) in his work on planned behavior. It is fascinating, but complicated. Thus, it requires a little more explanation.

Let's say that a young woman harbors a favorable attitude toward a behavior, *and* believes that important others endorse the behavior and perform it themselves. You would think that she would then perform the action. However, she might be *unable* to perform the behavior because she lacks either the necessary skills or confidence that she can enact the behavior in a particular situation.

For example: A woman may feel positively toward losing weight and perceive social pressure to drop 10 pounds. But she just can't muster the self-control to stay on a diet. A young man may harbor a positive attitude toward quitting smoking and recognize that his friends all want him to quit. But every time he feels nervous, he takes a smoke. He lacks the cognitive skills or self-discipline to quit the habit. So, attitudes and norms will not predict intention or behavior in these cases. But if we add a perceived behavioral control to the mix, we increase the odds of predicting behavior. Among individuals who feel they have the psychological capacity to say no to food and cigarettes, attitude and norm will forecast the intention to lose weight and quit smoking. Among individuals who don't think they can resist the lure of food and cigarettes, attitude and norm will not predict intention. No matter how positively they feel and how much they seek their friends' approval, they don't have the strength to implement the intention or to carry out their plans.

Thus, by adding perceived control to the model, we can come up with more accurate predictions about when attitudes predict intentions and behavior.

Okay, let's get back to the problem at hand: measuring the degree to which teens plan to text when they drive. Simplifying Fishbein and Ajzen's measurement strategy just a bit, you might come up with these two questionnaire items to measure perceived behavioral control.

Perceived behavioral control

1. How much control do you feel you have over whether you text when you drive to school?

   (No control)   1   2   3   4   5   6   7 (Complete control)

2. How much do you feel that texting while driving to school is under your control?

   (A lot)   1   2   3   4   5   6   7   (Not at all)

Behavioral intention. As the name suggests, behavioral intention is the intention to perform a particular action, a plan to put behavior into effect. Intention can be predicted quite accurately from attitude toward the behavior, perceived norm, and perceived behavioral control. Intention is most likely to predict behavior when it corresponds with—is identical to—the behavior in key ways. If you want to predict whether people will text when they drive to school, you should ask them if they intend to do just that. Asking them if they intend to text when they drive around the neighborhood or when they go on a family vacation would not predict texting while driving to school.

The model uses a mathematical formula to determine the impact that each of the three factors exerts on intentions.

Intention to text when driving, measured as specifically as possible, could be assessed in this way:

I intend to text when I drive to school.

(Definitely)   1   2   3   4   5   6   7 (Definitely do not)

Behavior. In general, intention to perform a particular behavior should predict the actual performance of the act. Thus, to provide an accurate measurement of behavior, you could ask respondents this question:

Over the past month, how often have you texted when you drove to school?

(Never)   1   2   3   4   5   6   7   (Almost always)

The model says that intention to text while driving—determined by attitude, norm, and perceived behavioral control—should do a pretty good job of predicting behavior.

Predicting behavior from attitude. Recall the question guiding this section: Do attitudes predict behavior? The reasoned action approach allows us to specify the precise impact that attitudes exert on behavior. In the present case, young people who strongly *believe* that texting while driving leads to positive outcomes should be especially likely to intend to text when they drive.

In some cases, though, attitudes will not forecast action. Instead, norms dictate what people do. An adolescent might positively evaluate texting, but refrain because his mom does not think it is a good idea or because it is frowned on in the peer group.

Thus, the theory offers a framework for predicting behavior from attitude. Fishbein and Ajzen caution that behavior can be predicted, but you need to consider likes and dislikes (attitudes), people's natural propensity to please others (norms), and individuals' confidence that they can carry out their plans (perceived behavioral control). When strong social pressures are present, attitudes do not accurately forecast behavior (Wallace et al., 2005). When people do not have the skills or lack the confidence to execute their plans, attitudes may not predict intentions and intentions will not predict behavior. Reasoned action theory emphasizes that attitudes are a reasonably accurate indicator of what people will do, provided certain conditions are met. There will always be circumstances in which people, being complex, will behave on the basis of factors other than attitude.

The Facts on the Ground

Reasoned action has an outstanding track record in predicting behavior. More than 1,000 published studies have tested the model (Fishbein & Ajzen, 2010). Think about this for a moment: a thousand studies! Each study occurred in a different setting, surveyed different individuals, and yet was carefully executed. The fact that so many empirical studies have confirmed the model should give us pause—and confidence (see model summary in Box 5.2). Some 35 years after the theory was introduced, we know that attitudes, perceived norms, and perceived behavioral control forecast intentions, and intentions help predict behavior (Ajzen & Fishbein, 2005; Albaracín et al., 2001; Sheeran, Abraham, & Orbell, 1999; Sutton, 1998). There is a long, diverse list of behavioral correlates that the model has illuminated and usefully predicted. They include:

- women's occupational orientations (Sperber, Fishbein, & Ajzen, 1980);
- voting in a national election;
- grabbing meals in fast-food restaurants (Brinberg & Durand, 1983);
- eating a healthy diet (see Booth-Butterfield & Reger, 2004);
- condom use among high-risk heterosexual and homosexual adults in the U.S. and abroad (see Ajzen, Albarracín, & Hornik, 2007 and Morrison, Gillmore, & Baker, 1995);
- breast-feeding and bottle-feeding infants (Manstead, Proffitt, & Smart, 1983); and
- drug use.

Shortcomings. If models could walk, this one looks like it walks on water! Well walk, for sure, but maybe only on land! As good as the model is, like all approaches, it has limitations. Some scholars protest that attitude and behavioral intention measures are virtually the same, making predictions obvious and not so interesting. Others note that, contrary to the assumption that the impact of attitudes on behavior is mediated by intentions, attitudes exert a direct impact on behavior (Bentler & Speckhart, 1979; Fazio, Powell, & Williams, 1989). A number of critics lament that the model assumes that

---

BOX 5.2 UNDERSTANDING THEORY: PRIMER ON THE REASONED ACTION MODEL

1. The Reasoned Action Model offers a wide-ranging guide to attitudes and behavior.
2. There are five components of the theory: *attitude toward the behavior, perceived norm, perceived behavioral control, behavioral intention*, and *behavior*.
3. Attitude toward the behavior consists of behavioral beliefs and outcome evaluations.
4. Perceived norm has two components: an injunctive norm, or motivation to comply with what significant others think one should do in a particular situation; and a descriptive norm, beliefs about how frequently significant others have performed the targeted behavior and identification with these others.
5. These constructs, with their subcomponents, can forecast intention to behave in a particular situation. The degree to which attitude, norm, and perceived behavioral control predict intention depends on the particular context.
6. Perceived behavioral control, or perception of whether one is psychologically capable of performing the behavior, helps determine whether attitude or norm predicts behavioral intention.
7. Behavioral intention predicts behavior, with prediction more accurate the closer and more specifically that intention corresponds to behavior.

---

human beings are logical, when much behavior is spontaneous and even impulsive. They note that when people hold a strong implicit prejudice, their conscious expression of the attitude on the survey will *not* predict negative body language toward a member of the disliked group (Ajzen & Fishbein, 2005).

There has been a lively debate about these issues over the past decades, with Fishbein and Ajzen emphasizing that their model *can* predict a wide variety of behaviors, including spontaneous and seemingly irrational behavior, like exceeding the legal speed limit and performing sex without a condom. Critics, for their part, argue that the model provides an unwieldy explanation of irrational behaviors and, in any event, not all behavior is preceded by an intention. In order to appreciate an alternative perspective based on these criticisms, the next section describes another approach to attitude–behavior relations.

Accessibility Theory

It's a humid summer day, and you feel like a cold one. Glancing over the usual suspects—Miller Lite, Coors, Michelob, Bud Lite—your mouth watering, you want to make a quick choice of which six-pack to buy at the convenience store. Suddenly, the expression "Whazzup?" from an advertisement of some years back leaps into your mind. You smile, and reach for the Budweiser.

According to Fazio's accessibility-focused model (see Chapter 4), your attitude toward Budweiser is accessible, or capable of being quickly activated from memory. Your favorable attitude toward Bud Lite predicts your purchase behavior. Now, if we wanted, we could measure your behavioral beliefs, normative beliefs, perceptions of behavioral control, and other variables from the Reasoned Action Model. However, all this would be beside the point and far too laborious a process, according to accessibility theory. *The core notion of accessibility theory is that attitudes will predict behavior if they can be activated from memory at the time of a decision.* If a person is in touch with her attitudes, she will act on them. If not, she will be swayed by salient aspects of the situation.

This captures the gist of the model, but the core notions are more complicated. In reality, two things must transpire for an attitude to influence behavior. First, the attitude must come spontaneously to mind in a situation. That is, it must be activated from memory. Second, the attitude must influence perceptions of an issue or person, serving as a filter through which the issue or person is viewed (Fazio & Roskos-Ewoldsen, 1994, p. 85). These perceptions should then color the way people define the situation, pushing them to behave in sync with their attitude. (If people do not call up their attitude from memory, they will be susceptible to influence from other factors in the situation, such as norms or eye-catching stimuli; see Figure 5.7).

In short: you can harbor an attitude toward a person or issue, but unless the attitude comes to mind when you encounter the other person or issue, you cannot act on the attitude in a particular situation. This is one reason why it's good to be in touch with your attitudes: you can act on them when important issues come up in life.

Fazio's approach extends knowledge of attitude–behavior relations by calling attention to the role accessibility plays in the process. The model suggests that attitudes guide behavior if people automatically call up attitudes from memory at the time of decision. But here is where it gets a little complicated.

Fazio argues that under some conditions people behave like Fishbein and Ajzen suggest: they consider the consequences of behaving in a particular fashion and may deliberate about pros and cons of doing x or y. But when people lack the motivation or opportunity

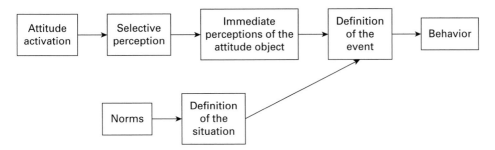

Figure 5.7 Fazio's attitude-to-behavior process model.

From Fazio, R. H., & Roskos-Ewoldsen, D. R. (1994). Acting as we feel: When and how attitudes guide behavior. In S. Shavitt & T. C. Brock (Eds.), *Persuasion: Psychological insights and perspectives* (pp. 71–93). Boston: Allyn and Bacon.

to deliberate in this fashion, they act more spontaneously. In such situations, attitude can guide behavior if people automatically call up attitudes from memory.

Research supports these propositions (Kraus, 1995). One study found that individuals who were "in touch" with attitudes toward then-President Reagan were more likely to vote for Reagan than those who could not quickly access their favorable assessment of Reagan (Fazio & Williams, 1986; see also Bassili, 1995). In a similar vein, students who could immediately call to mind a favorable attitude toward food products were more inclined to select these products as a free gift than those with less accessible attitudes (Fazio et al., 1989). Interestingly, two students might have equally favorable attitudes toward Snickers candy bar. The student who was more "in touch" with her feelings about Snickers—who could say immediately that she liked Snickers—was more likely to select Snickers than a fellow student who had to think a little before recognizing how much she enjoyed Snickers (see Box 5.3 for a summary of accessibility theory).

Implications for Persuasion

Reasoned action and accessibility both offer intriguing insights about the attitude–behavior issue. As of now, reasoned action has more facts on its side, making it the most comprehensive model of beliefs, attitudes, and behavior.

What do the models suggest about persuasion? They both offer concrete ideas, demonstrating that communicators need to understand the dynamics of the mind before crafting a message. But what part of the mind do they need to change? Let's examine this question by returning to the hypothetical challenge that initiated this section: You are trying to devise a persuasive message to convince teenagers not to text when they drive.

BOX 5.3 UNDERSTANDING THEORY: PRIMER ON ACCESSIBILITY THEORY

1. Accessibility is a general term used to describe the degree to which an attitude is automatically activated from memory.
2. Objects toward which we have accessible attitudes are more likely to capture attention.
3. For an attitude to influence behavior, it must: (a) come spontaneously to mind in a situation; and (b) influence perceptions of the attitude object, serving as a filter through which the object is viewed.
4. We can harbor an attitude toward a person or issue, but unless the attitude comes to mind in the situation, we are not likely to translate it to behavior.
5. In contrast to the Reasoned Action Model, the accessibility approach can help account for attitude–behavior relations in cases where a behavior is enacted spontaneously, rather than deliberately, and with minimal cognitive awareness (Rhodes and Ewoldsen, 2013).

Here are some persuasive strategies derived from the attitude–behavior approaches. The first four are based on the Reasoned Action Model; the next two are adapted from Fazio's accessibility approach.

1. *Target relevant beliefs.* You should probe teens' salient or relevant beliefs to discover why they text while driving. Don't assume reasons that apply to you also apply to high school students. If students say they text because they like to keep in touch with friends, develop a message that explains there are safer ways to stay in the loop. If they think they can maintain control of the car while they punch letters to write a message, show them evidence that this is not true. Offer vivid examples.

2. *Target outcome evaluations.* If teens say they text while driving because they don't like to feel lonely or bored, help them appreciate that loneliness and boredom aren't terrible things to experience while driving. Suggest that they try to alleviate these feelings in other ways.

3. *Appeal to social norms.* Based on the Reasoned Action Model and research on social norms (Goldstein & Cialdini, 2007; Park & Smith, 2007) you should call attention to the behavior of influential individuals in their social network. You could highlight injunctive norms by emphasizing that close friends think it is dangerous to text while one drives. You might target descriptive norms by noting that many teen drivers have stopped texting when they drive, suggesting that the message recipient is behind the times.

4. *Target perceived behavioral control.* A message could suggest that it isn't hard to avoid texting once you get in the habit. After all, they learned to drive without constantly texting. It can be done!

5. *Change attitudes through association techniques.* Research (Olson & Fazio, 2006) suggests that if campaign specialists repeatedly paired texting-while-driving with gruesome images, they could cause individuals to develop more unfavorable attitudes toward this practice. Since attitudes have a strong affective component, communications directed at the affective aspect could be effective.

6. *Put people in touch with their feelings.* Research suggests that when an attitude has been recently activated or reflected on, it is relatively accessible, at least for a short amount of time (Arpan, Rhodes, & Roskos-Ewoldsen, 2007). Thus, you could encourage teens to attach to their dashboard a picture of a banged-up car driven by a friend who was injured when he lost control of his car while texting. This might push drivers to access the sad feelings the incident evokes, perhaps deterring them from texting while they drive.

Will these techniques work? As discussed in Chapter 4, they won't change the attitudes of adolescents with strong attitudes, those who are determined to text when they drive, no matter what. The messages will also run up against the psychological functions that texting serves. But these six strategies are derived from research and, if packaged effectively, should appeal to receptive members of the audience. They may also induce teens to think twice about their behavior, ushering in questions that could instigate attitude change.

JUDGING CONSISTENCY: GRAY AREAS AND ETHICAL ISSUES

The term "hypocrisy" frequently gets bandied about when people observe inconsistencies between attitudes and behavior. It reflects an ethical concern, the belief that an individual is not living up to prescribed standards. Now that you have an appreciation for the complex underpinnings of attitude–behavior consistency, we can proceed to this more controversial aspect of the consistency issue.

Every day, it seems, we hear of famous men or women behaving badly and subsequently earning the wrath of observers, who call them hypocrites. Thomas Jefferson is the classic example. The egalitarian author of the Declaration of Independence, who penned that "all men are created equal," owned more than 100 slaves and believed that Blacks were inferior in mind and body to Whites. Was Jefferson a hypocrite, or a complicated man who harbored both revolutionary and prejudiced attitudes?

A more recent example of alleged hypocrisy in a president involves Bill Clinton's relationship with Monica Lewinsky. During his first term and while running for

■ **Figure 5.8 President Bill Clinton championed family values as president, but had an extramarital affair with a White House intern, Monica Lewinsky. Did this constitute hypocrisy or an understandable inconsistency between attitude and behavior?**

Image courtesy of Getty Images.

re-election in 1996, Clinton championed family values, telegraphing what appeared to be a positive attitude toward marriage and monogamy. Yet he behaved quite differently, cheating on his wife and engaging in a long, sordid affair with Lewinsky. Critics pointed to the blatant contradictions between Clinton's words and actions (Bennett, 1998; see Figure 5.8).

Others viewed the situation differently. We should be wary of "judging a complex being by a simple standard," one psychoanalyst said of the Clinton quandary. "To equate consistency with moral (and political) virtue, and then to demand consistency of people," wrote Adam Phillips, "can only cultivate people's sense of personal failure" (1998, p. A27). In other words, we should not ask people to be consistent. To do so is to set people up for failure, as none of us is perfect in this regard.

Consider the case of Reverend Jesse Jackson, who preached religious values, commitment to Biblical commandments like "Thou shalt not commit adultery," and counseled President Clinton regarding his sexual sins. In early 2001, the public learned that

Jackson fathered a child out of wedlock. Was Jackson a hypocrite? He would seem to be, if one consults the Webster's dictionary definition. A hypocrite, the dictionary tells us, is one who pretends to be what he or she is not, or harbors principles or beliefs that he or she does not have. However, critic Michael Eric Dyson, taking a different view of hypocrisy, viewed Jackson differently. Dyson argued:

> It is not hypocritical to fail to achieve the moral standards that one believes are correct. Hypocrisy comes when leaders conjure moral standards that they refuse to apply to themselves and when they do not accept the same consequences they imagine for others who offend moral standards.
>
> (2001, p. A23)

Noting that Jackson accepted responsibility for his behavior, Dyson said he was not a hypocrite.

More recently, critics accused Governor Sarah Palin, the 2008 Republican vice-presidential candidate, of hypocrisy. As a family-values conservative, she publicly supported abstinence-until-marriage education in schools. However, her unmarried 17-year-old daughter, Bristol, became pregnant, suggesting to some that Palin had not practiced what she preached when it came to her own family. Others were more tolerant. "The media is already trying to spin this as evidence that Governor Palin is a hypocrite," noted James Dobson, the founder of Focus on the Family. "But all it really means is that she and her family are human" (Nagourney, 2008, p. A18).

Thus, the term "hypocrite" is subject to different readings and different points of view. In trying to decide if someone behaved in a hypocritical fashion, a variety of issues emerge. What criteria do we use to say that someone is a hypocrite? Is it hypocritical if the individual displays a single inconsistency between attitude and behavior? Or is that too strict a criterion? How many inconsistencies must the person commit before the hypocrite label fits? Do certain inconsistencies get more weight than others? Does a blatant violation of an individual's deeply held values cut more to the heart of hypocrisy than other inconsistencies? Are certain kinds of attitude–behavior inconsistencies (e.g., violations of marital oaths) more ethically problematic and therefore more deserving of the hypocrite label than others? Is hypocrisy culturally relative, with certain kinds of inconsistencies more apt to be regarded as hypocritical in one culture than in another? Does application of the label "hypocrite" tell us more about the observer than the person being judged?

These strike me as valid questions, reflective of the enduring complexity of human behavior. And yet one can take this nonjudgmental, relativist view too far. There are times when individuals do not practice what they have long preached. From an ethical perspective, people should be held accountable for instances in which their behavior flouts attitudes that they profess to harbor. Dictionaries tell us that hypocrisy involves pretense—pretending to have moral principles to which one's own behaviors do not conform. Such pretense violates deontological principles. Not every attitude–behavior inconsistency counts as hypocrisy. However, when an individual professes to harbor strongly held beliefs and then behaves in ways that are palpably incongruent, we can count these as instances of hypocrisy. Behaving hypocritically is not the end of the world; we all do it from time to time. When we do it, we should be held accountable.

CONCLUSIONS

Attitude research sheds light on the reasons why people hold the attitudes they do and the degree to which attitudes predict behavior.

Functional theory stipulates that people would not hold attitudes unless they satisfied core human needs. Attitudes help people cope, serving knowledge, utilitarian, social adjustive, social identity, value-expressive, and ego-defense functions. Two people can hold the same attitude for different reasons, and an attitude that is functional for one person may be dysfunctional for someone else. An attitude can help a person function nicely in one part of his or her life, while leading to negative consequences in another domain. Attitude function research also suggests strategies for attitude change. It emphasizes that persuaders should probe the function a particular attitude serves for an individual and design the message so that it matches this need.

The bottom-line question for attitude researchers is whether attitudes forecast behavior. Decades of research have made it abundantly clear that attitudes do not always predict behavior and people are not entirely consistent. People are especially unlikely to translate attitude into behavior when norms and scripts operate, they are ambivalent about the issue, or they regard themselves as high self-monitors. Under a variety of other conditions, attitudes predict behavior handsomely. When attitudes and behavior are measured at the same level of specificity, attitudes forecast behavior. Attitudes guide and influence behavior, but not in every life situation.

The Reasoned Action Model, updated in 2010, offers rich insights into attitude–behavior relations. It emphasizes that once individuals develop a set of beliefs, they proceed to act on these beliefs in a predictable and consistent fashion. Beliefs are not always rational, but they can powerfully influence behavior. The model has three components: attitude, norm, and perceived behavioral control, with each helping determine when intention predicts behavior. With its postulates tested in more than 1,000 studies, the Reasoned Action Model has shown that attitudes, if carefully measured, can predict behavior in a vast array of contexts. Critics have argued that the model's weakness is that it can only usefully predict behaviors preceded by rational deliberation, when much behavior is impulsive and spontaneous.

Accessibility theory sheds light on the latter behaviors. It argues that for an attitude to affect action, it must come spontaneously to mind in a particular context and influence key perceptions of the issue or person. Fazio notes that in some circumstances people behave like Fishbein and Ajzen suggest: they consider the utilitarian consequences of acting in a particular fashion and may deliberate about pros and cons of doing x or y. However, when people lack the motivation or opportunity to deliberate in this fashion, they behave more spontaneously. In such situations, attitude can guide behavior if people automatically call up an attitude from memory. There is less empirical evidence supporting the accessibility approach's predictions on attitude–behavior consistency than there is for reasoned action theory. However, it offers a useful counterpoint.

Both theories have implications for persuasion, though they focus on different factors. Stylistically and metaphorically, reasoned action is heavy and sturdy, like an engine, while accessibility is lithe and free form, resembling a youthful, somewhat impulsive dancer. This illustrates the dual nature of persuasion that sometimes manifests itself in everyday life: one system of our mind is geared to cognitive, effortful thinking; the other emphasizes simpler, automatic processes (Kahneman, 2011).

Attitude–behavior theories offer an excellent guide to predicting behavior. However, they cannot forecast behavior in every situation in life. There is a tension between the predictions derived from social science theory and the ultimate unpredictability of humans in everyday life. An individual may recognize the benefits of staying calm in the heat of an argument with an acquaintance, yet lash out physically against the other person. You may positively evaluate safe sex but, in the passion of the moment, conveniently forget about the condom sitting on the dresser. A co-worker may feel that it is important to complete assignments on time. However, feeling lonely and frustrated, she gets drunk the night before and fails to turn in the assignment until after the deadline has passed. People are not always consistent. Theories strive to capture the complexity of human behavior, but do not always succeed because of the many factors that come into play. Still, attitude–behavior models have done much to help shed light on the circumstances under which attitudes forecast behavior. They remind us that, even if you can't predict all the people all the time, you can do a much better job of accounting for human behavior if you take attitudes, norms, and intentions into account.

Consistency between attitude and behavior—or practicing what you preach—remains a core aspect of human character, the essence of integrity. But because we are human beings, the promise of rewards or desire to fit in can thwart attempts of the best of us to act on what we know to be our attitude or moral values. As the noted military leader Norman Schwarzkopf said, "The truth of the matter is that you always know the right thing to do. The hard part is doing it" (Dowd, 2006a, p. A23).

Test your knowledge now with interactive exercises

Chapter 6

Attitude Measurement

 Listen now to the author's chapter summary

Pollsters do it with precision. Theorists do it with conceptual flair. Survey researchers do it for a living. "It," of course, is designing questionnaires to measure attitudes!

Puns and double entendres aside, attitude measurement plays a critical role in the study and practice of persuasion. It is the practical side of the field, the down-to-earth domain that provides the instrumentation to test hypotheses and to track changes in attitudes and beliefs. If there were no reliable scientific techniques to measure attitudes, we would not know how people evaluated social and political issues. We would not know the impact that persuasive communications had on people's feelings and thoughts. Documenting the effects of large-scale media campaigns would permanently elude us.

This chapter explores the main themes in attitude measurement. It describes scales used to tap attitudes, as well as the pitfalls and challenges researchers face when trying to assess attitudes empirically. After reading this chapter, you should know more about how to write good attitude questions and how to locate valid scales that measure specific attitudes.

OVERVIEW

Attitude questionnaires date back to 1928. It was in this year that psychologist Louis Thurstone published an article titled "Attitudes Can Be Measured." Thurstone proposed an elaborate procedure to assess people's views on social issues. Although measurement techniques have been streamlined over the years, Thurstone "started the fire." We now have established methodologies for assessing attitudes. What's more, thousands of questionnaires have been developed to tap beliefs and attitudes on countless issues.

Are you interested in attitudes toward race or affirmative action? You can find dozens of surveys, such as those developed by McConahay (1986) and Schmermund and colleagues (2001). Do you want to explore attitudes toward the homeless? Aberson and McVean (2008) developed a scale to measure biases toward homeless individuals. Did a recent trip to Las Vegas whet your intellectual appetite toward gambling? If so, you can find a valid scale tapping gambling passion in an article by Rousseau and associates (2002). Are you curious to know if people find it easier to reveal personal information online than face-to-face? Well, then you can click onto an intriguing scale that measures online communication attitudes by Ledbetter (2009). There are questionnaires tapping attitudes on hundreds of issues, including environmental pollution, prejudice against fat people, adulation of thin models, sex, sex roles, basking in the glory of sports teams, political activism, even cloning human beings.

It is not easy to write good attitude questions. You can appreciate this if you have ever tried to dream up questions assessing views on one or another issue. Administering your survey to others, you may have found respondents scratching their heads and asking, "What do you mean by this question?" Devising reliable attitude items is not as easy as it looks.

There are people who do this for a living—folks who are so proficient at devising questions that they work for professional research centers or advertising firms. There is a science to writing attitude questions, one that calls on principles of measurement, statistics, and cognitive psychology (Hippler, Schwarz, & Sudman, 1987; Tourangeau & Rasinski, 1988). It all flows from an underlying belief—core assumption—that one can measure phenomena by assigning numbers to objects on the basis of rules or guidelines (Stevens, 1950; see Figure 6.1).

Perhaps the simplest way to assess attitudes is to ask people if they like or dislike the attitude object. National opinion polls tap Americans' attitudes toward the president by asking if they approve or disapprove of the way the chief executive is handling the economy. However, there are two problems with this procedure. First, the agree–disagree scale offers people only two choices. It does not allow for shades of gray. Second, it measures attitudes with only one item. This puts all the researcher's eggs in one basket. If the item is ambiguous or the respondent misunderstands the question, then all hope of accurately measuring the attitude disappears. In addition, by relying on only one item, the researcher misses the opportunity to tap complex, even contradictory, components of the attitude.

For these reasons, researchers prefer to include many survey items and to assess attitudes along a numerical continuum. Questionnaires that employ these procedures are called scales. There are three standard attitude scales: (a) Likert, (b) Guttman, and (c) the semantic differential.

QUESTIONNAIRE MEASURES OF ATTITUDE

Likert Scale

The nice thing about being the first to do something is that they name it after you.

A psychologist named Rensis Likert (pronounced Lickert) refined Thurstone's procedures in 1932 (Likert, 1932). Thurstone had asked as many as several hundred individuals to serve as judges. These individuals then sort attitude items into different evaluative categories. Although the procedure is elegant, it is cumbersome and assumes judges are objective. Likert recommended that researchers devise items, thereby simplifying the Thurstone procedure and offering the template for the modern attitude scale.

A **Likert scale** contains a series of opinion statements. Respondents read each item and indicate their agreement or disagreement with each statement along a numerical scale. A Likert scale assumes that each item taps the same underlying attitude and there are significant interrelationships among items. It also presumes that there are equal intervals among categories. For example, on a 5-point (*strongly agree, somewhat agree, neutral, somewhat disagree, strongly disagree*) scale, researchers assume that the psychological difference between strongly agree and somewhat agree is the same as that between strongly disagree and somewhat disagree.

Likert scales are commonplace today. No doubt you've completed dozens of these strongly agree–strongly disagree surveys. An example is the course evaluation questionnaire students complete on the last day of class. (You know, the day your professor acts oh-so-nice to you and bakes those fudge brownies!) Students indicate how much they agree or disagree with statements regarding the prof's teaching abilities and the course content.

Likert scales can proceed from 1 to 5, as noted previously. They can also include other numerical options, such as 1 to 7, 1 to 9, or 1 to 100. Most researchers prefer 5- or 7-point scales because they allow respondents to indicate shades of gray in their opinions, but do not provide so many categories that people feel overwhelmed by choices.

To help you appreciate how researchers measure attitudes with Likert and other scales, an example is provided, using the ever-popular issue of attitudes toward sex roles (see Figure 6.2). A sample Likert scale, focused on sex-role attitudes, appears in Table 6.1. You might enjoy completing it to see how you feel about this issue.

Panel A: Stair-step scale

Question: What is your attitude toward the Republican Party?
Instructions: Place a check mark on the stairstep that best describes your attitude.

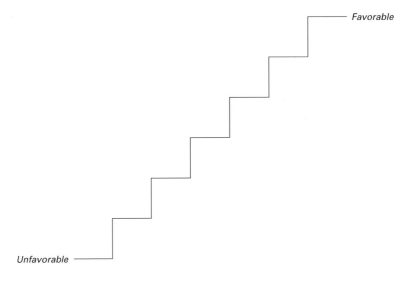

Panel B: Opinion thermometer

Question: How do you feel about Barack Obama?
Instructions: Circle the number on the thermometer scale that best describes your feelings.

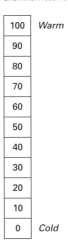

■ **Figure 6.1 Two different types of numerical attitude scales.**

Adapted from Ostrom, T. M., Bond, C. F., Jr., Krosnick, J. A., & Sedikides, C. (1994). Attitude scales: How we measure the unmeasurable. In S. Shavitt & T. C. Brock (Eds.), *Persuasion: Psychological insights and perspectives* (pp. 15–42). Boston: Allyn and Bacon.

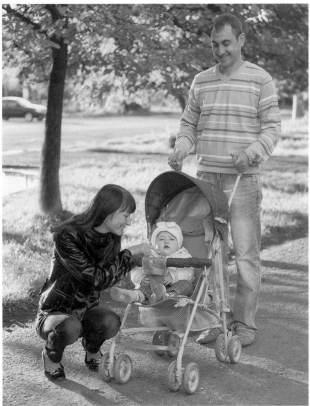

■ **Figure 6.2a–c** **Attitudes toward sex roles have different aspects, including dating, work, and child-rearing. Scales to measure attitudes should ideally take these different aspects into account.**

Images courtesy of Shutterstock.

■ **Table 6.1 Likert scale for sex role attitudes**

Please indicate whether you Strongly Agree (SA), Agree (A), are Neutral (N), Disagree (D), or Strongly Disagree (SD) with each of these statements.

	SA	A	N	D	SD
1. Women are more emotional than men	1	2	3	4	5
2. Swearing and obscenity are more repulsive in the speech of a woman than of a man	1	2	3	4	5
3. When two people go out on a date, the man should be the one to pay the check	1	2	3	4	5
4. When a couple is going somewhere by car, it's better for the man to do most of the driving	1	2	3	4	5
5. If both husband and wife work full-time, her career should be just as important as his in determining where the family lives	1	2	3	4	5
6. Most women interpret innocent remarks or acts as being sexist	1	2	3	4	5
7. Society has reached the point where women and men have equal opportunities for achievement	1	2	3	4	5
8. Many women have a quality of purity that few men possess	1	2	3	4	5
9. Women should be cherished and protected by men	1	2	3	4	5

Sources: Statement 2 is from Spence, J. T., Helmreich, R., & Stapp, J. (1973), *Bulletin of the Psychonomic Society, 2*, 219–220. Statements 4 and 5 are from Peplau, L. A., Hill, C. T., & Rubin, Z. (1993), *Journal of Social Issues, 49*(*3*), 31–52. Items 6, 8, and 9 are from Glick, P. & Fiske, S. T. (1996). *Journal of Personality and Social Psychology, 70*, 491–512. Statement 7 is from Swim, J. K., Aikin, K. J., Hall, W. S., & Hunter, B. A. (1995), *Journal of Personality and Social Psychology, 68*, 199–214. Note: Items 1, 2, 6, 7, and 8 can be regarded as descriptive beliefs; statements 3, 4, 5, and 9 are prescriptive beliefs.

Guttman Scale

Sometimes it seems that the person with the strongest attitude toward a topic is the one willing to take the most difficult stands, those that require the greatest gumption. One may not agree with these positions, but one is hard pressed to deny that these are difficult positions to endorse. A **Guttman scale** (named after Louis Guttman) takes this approach to measuring attitudes (Guttman, 1944).

The scale progresses from items easiest to accept to those most difficult to endorse. Those who get the highest score on a Guttman scale agree with all items. Those with

■ **Table 6.2 Guttman scale for sex roles**

Least difficult to accept	1	Fathers should spend some of their leisure time helping to care for the children
	2	Fathers should share in infant care responsibilities, such as getting up when the baby cries at night and changing diapers
	3	If both parents work, the father and mother should divide up equally the task of staying at home when children get sick
Most difficult to accept	4	If both parents work, the father and mother should divide up equally the task of raising the children

moderate attitudes agree with questions that are easy and moderately difficult to endorse, and those with mildly positive attitudes agree only with items that are easy to accept. A Guttman scale for sex roles appears in Table 6.2.

Guttman scales are hard to construct. They are not as easy to administer as Likert scales. However, they can be useful in tapping attitudes on sensitive topics like abortion. Opposition to abortion could be scaled by examining whether respondents believe it would be acceptable for a woman to have an abortion under increasingly difficult circumstances. Many people would agree that an abortion is wrong if performed primarily because the woman has low income and cannot afford to have any more children. However, fewer would agree that abortion is wrong if the pregnancy has resulted from rape. Respondents with an extremely strong pro-life attitude would endorse the strongest, absolutist option: abortion is wrong in all circumstances, even when the pregnancy endangers the mother's life.

Semantic Differential

Charles Osgood and colleagues do not have a scale that bears their name. But they succeeded in developing one of the most frequently used scales in the attitude business. Osgood, Suci, and Tannenbaum (1957) chose not to assess beliefs or agreement with opinion statements. Instead, they explored the meanings that people attach to social objects, focusing on the emotional aspect of attitude. The term *semantic* is used because their instrument asks people to indicate feelings about an object on a pair of bipolar, adjective scales. The term *differential* comes from the fact that the scale assesses the different meanings people ascribe to a person or issue.

Participants rate a concept using bipolar adjectives: one adjective lies at one end of the scale; its opposite is at the other end. Osgood and colleagues discovered that people

▓ **Table 6.3 Semantic differential for sex roles**

FEMINISM

Good	—	—	—	—	—	—	—	Bad
Pleasant	—	—	—	—	—	—	—	Unpleasant
Strong	—	—	—	—	—	—	—	Weak
Heavy	—	—	—	—	—	—	—	Light
Active	—	—	—	—	—	—	—	Passive
Wholesome	—	—	—	—	—	—	—	Unhealthy
Valuable	—	—	—	—	—	—	—	Worthless

Note: Numbers do not appear underneath the dashes. For each item, a response is assigned a score from 3 to 3, with a 3 assigned to the blank closest to the positive pole and a 3 to the blank nearest the negative pole.

typically employ three dimensions to rate concepts: evaluation (Is it good or bad for me?), potency (Is it strong or weak?), and activity (Is it active or passive?) (Osgood, 1974). A semantic differential scale for sex roles appears in Table 6.3. You could also use this scale to tap attitudes toward female politicians, corporate leaders, or rock stars. Any come to mind?

PITFALLS IN ATTITUDE MEASUREMENT

There is no perfect attitude scale. Even the best scales can fail to measure attitudes accurately. Inaccuracies result from such factors as: (a) respondent carelessness in answering the questions, (b) people's desire to say the socially appropriate thing rather than what they truly believe, and (c) a tendency to agree with items regardless of their content (Dawes & Smith, 1985). Although these problems can be reduced through adroit survey measurement techniques (see next section), some inaccuracy in responses to attitude scales is inevitable.

A particularly gnawing problem in survey research involves the format and wording of questions. The way the researcher words the question and designs the questionnaire can elicit from the respondent answers that may not reflect the individual's true attitude (Schuman & Presser, 1981; Schwarz, 1999). The manner in which the question is asked can influence the response that the researcher receives. It reminds one of what writer Gertrude Stein reportedly said on her death bed. With death near, she asked her long-time romantic partner, "What is the answer?" When her partner did not reply, Stein said, "In that case, what is the question?"

Two key survey design factors that can influence—or bias—attitude responses are survey context and wording.

Context. Survey questions appear one after another on a piece of paper, computer screen, or in an interview administered over the telephone. Questions occurring early in the survey can influence responses to later questions. This is because thoughts triggered by earlier questions can shape subsequent responses. The answers that individuals supply may thus be artifacts of the "context" of the survey instrument rather than reflections of their actual attitudes.

For instance, respondents asked to evaluate the morality of American business leaders might respond differently if they heard Bernard Madoff's name at the beginning rather than at the end of a list (e.g., Schwarz & Bless, 1992). Some years back, Madoff bilked thousands of investors of their fortunes and life savings in a $50 billion scam. With Madoff as an anchor or standard of comparison, respondents might give other business leaders favorable ratings, noting that they had at least not cheated people out of their hard-earned money. But if Madoff's name did not appear until the end of the list, respondents would have no reason to base evaluations of other business leaders on comparisons with Madoff's morally unscrupulous behavior. As a result, business leaders might receive comparatively less positive ratings.

Howard Schuman and Stanley Presser (1981) documented question-order effects in a classic study of Americans' attitudes toward abortion. Naturally, abortion attitudes were complex, but a majority supported legalized abortion. When asked, "Do you think it should be possible for a pregnant woman to obtain a legal abortion if she is married and does not want any more children?" over 60 percent said "Yes." However, support dropped when the following question was asked first: *Do you think it should be possible for a pregnant woman to obtain a legal abortion if there is a strong chance of serious defect in the baby?*

In this case, only 48 percent agreed that a married woman should be able to obtain a legal abortion if she did not want any more children. To be sure, these attitudes are controversial and would outrage those who oppose abortion in all instances. But the point here is methodological, not ideological. The order of questions influenced evaluations of abortion. Something of a contrast effect appears to have emerged.

In the first case, respondents had no other anchor than abortion in the case of a married woman who does not want any more children. A substantial majority came out in favor of abortion in this case. But after considering the gut-wrenching issue of aborting a fetus with a medical defect and deciding in favor of this option, a second group of respondents now mulled over the question of abortion for married women who did not want any more children. In comparison to the birth-defect choice, this seemed relatively unsubstantial, perhaps trivial. Using the birth-defect case as the standard for comparison, the idea that a woman should get a legal abortion if she did not want any more children seemed not to measure up to these individuals' moral criterion for abortion. Not surprisingly, fewer individuals supported abortion in this case.

It is also possible that, in light of the ambivalence many neutral or pro-choice supporters feel toward abortion, those who supported abortion in the case of a serious defect in the baby felt guilty. To reduce guilt, some may have shifted their position on abortion for married women, saying they opposed abortion in this less taxing situation. Whatever the explanation, it seems clear that the order in which the questions appeared influenced respondents' reports of their attitudes.

Another example involves measurement of happiness and dating. When students are asked first to say how happy they are and then to indicate how often they are dating, there is no relationship between happiness and dating. However, when the questions are reversed something interesting happens. When the first question is "How often are you dating?" and the second is, "How happy are you?" responses to the questions are highly correlated. Students who date a lot say they are happy and those who do not date very much claim they are unhappy. Presumably, the daters think to themselves, "I have been dating a lot. I have been going out with lots of different guys (girls). That must make me pretty happy about my life this semester." Non-daters ruminate that, "Gosh, I haven't gone on a date for months now. No one has asked me out and I have not tried to hook up with anyone. No wonder I'm depressed!" Both daters and non-daters infer their happiness from how often they have been dating (Thaler & Sunstein, 2008; see also self-perception theory, Chapter 11). The results have everything to do with the order in which questions were asked.

Wording. As writers have long known, language is full of meaning, capable of conveying powerful sentiments. It should, therefore, come as no surprise that the way a question is worded can influence respondents' evaluations of the issue.

This has become abundantly clear on the topic of affirmative action (Kinder & Sanders, 1990). A *New York Times*/CBS News poll probed Americans' attitudes toward racial diversity, using a variety of questions to tap beliefs. When asked their opinion of programs that "*give preferential treatment to racial minorities*," just 26 percent of respondents indicated they would favor such programs. But when asked their views of programs that "*make special efforts to help minorities get ahead*," significantly more Americans (55 percent) expressed approval (Verhovek, 1997).

A more recent example emerged during polling about health reform in late 2009. While just about everybody agreed that the nation's health-care system needed overhaul, there were sharp disagreements among political leaders about just what type of health plan was best for America. In such a situation, public opinion exerted a pivotal influence on the debate, and the way opinion poll questions were phrased produced vastly different results. When a national poll asked respondents whether they would favor or oppose "*creating a public health care plan administered by the federal government that would compete directly with private health insurance companies*," only 48 percent indicated they would support such a plan. However, when individuals were asked how important they felt it was "*to give people a choice of both a public plan administered by the federal government and a private plan for their health insurance*," 72 percent said they believed this was very important (Connelly, 2009, p. A17). The wording in the first question emphasizes competition with private health insurance companies, while the second focuses on choice, a positive value to Americans.

Perhaps the most striking example of wording effects came from polls probing an even more emotional issue: Americans' belief that the Holocaust actually occurred. (See Figure 6.3.)

■ **Figure 6.3 During World War II, the Nazis exterminated 6 million European Jews. In this heart-rending image, people await possible deportation or death. Some 50 years later, pollsters measured attitudes toward the Holocaust, discovering that the wording of the question influenced responses on this profoundly disturbing issue.**

Image courtesy of Getty Images.

With some anti-Semitic groups arguing that the Holocaust had never happened and was a figment of Jews' imagination, the Roper polling organization launched a national survey to see how many Americans actually bought into this false belief. In 1992, Roper probed Americans' attitudes toward the Holocaust, tapping beliefs with this key question:

> The term Holocaust usually refers to the killing of millions of Jews in Nazi death camps during World War II. Does it seem possible or does it seem impossible to you that the Nazi extermination of the Jews never happened?

Amazingly, 22 percent of respondents said it was "possible" that the mass executions never happened, about 12 percent claimed they "didn't know," and 65 percent said it was "impossible" that the event had not happened. "The fact that nearly one fourth of U.S. adults denied that the Holocaust had happened . . . raised serious questions about the quality of knowledge about recent history," observed Carroll J. Glynn and colleagues (Glynn et al., 1999, p. 76). It also raised the possibility that large numbers of Americans consciously or unconsciously subscribed to an anti-Semitic ideology.

Public opinion researchers suspected that the problem, once again, was not ideological, but methodological. They suggested that the Roper question was misleading and the double negative had confused people. Several polling organizations, including Roper, conducted new surveys, this time with clearer questions like: *"Does it seem possible to you that the Nazi extermination of the Jews never happened, or do you feel certain that it happened?"*

This time, 91 percent said they were certain it happened. Just 1 percent of the public said it was possible the Holocaust never happened, and 8 percent did not know (Smith, 1995).

The results restored faith in the public's knowledge and good sense. They also revealed the strong influence that question wording has on reports of attitudes.

POLICY IMPLICATIONS

Question wording is not just of interest to academic researchers. It is of considerable importance to policymakers, who recognize that the way a question is worded or framed can shape the contours of policy debates. Consider the case of polling on embryonic stem cell research. (See Figure 6.4.)

This research is controversial because initiating a line of stem cells typically involves destruction of the human embryo. Opponents argue that this is morally wrong and it is

■ **Figure 6.4 A scientist conducts medical tests on stem cells, an important but ethically controversial issue. Differences in question wording on items measuring attitudes toward embryonic stem cell research can have policy implications.**

Image courtesy of Getty Images.

immoral to use embryos for research purposes. Supporters say the embryos would be discarded anyway and the stem cells have the potential to produce life-saving cures for a host of medical conditions, such as spinal cord injuries and Parkinson's disease. With the White House weighing ethical and political dimensions, opinion polls have been a factor in policy decisions.

Polls have obtained strikingly different results, depending on the way questions have been framed. A partisan poll sponsored by a national Catholic organization stated that *"live embryos would be destroyed in their first week of development to obtain these cells."* When the question was worded this way, 70 percent of the public opposed using federal tax dollars for stem cell experiments. The results gratified the Catholic group, which opposes stem cell research on religious grounds. But when nonpartisan polls conducted by news and professional opinion research organizations framed the issue in terms of utilitarian benefits of such research, the results were dramatically different.

For example, an NBC News/*Wall Street Journal* poll gave opponents' side and supporters' position, noting that the research "*could lead to breakthrough cures for many diseases, such as cancer, Alzheimer's, Parkinson's, and spinal cord injuries, and this research uses only embryos that otherwise would be discarded.*" When the question was worded this way, 69 percent of respondents favored stem cell research (Bishop, 2005, pp. 42–44).

Partisan lobbyists seize upon supportive findings such as these and distribute them to lawmakers. Manipulation of statistical information is a routine and accepted way of doing the business of political persuasion in a democracy. Yet it can be troublesome when the goals of persuasion clash with larger interests of the country.

An example that resonates with those concerned with America's long-term energy policies concerns beliefs about a gasoline tax. Experts argue that U.S. dependence on foreign oil is self-defeating because oil profits go to countries (like Iran and Saudi Arabia) that support terrorist groups determined to attack this country. The only way to solve the problem, some say, is to raise the gasoline tax. This would discourage consumers from driving cars as frequently, which in turn would encourage Detroit to develop more fuel-efficient hybrid automobiles (Friedman, 2006). As a consequence, over the long haul, despots in the Middle East would have less oil money and would need to broker deals with Western powers.

Enter opinion poll findings. When Americans are asked simply if they favor a gasoline tax, 85 percent say they do not. However, when pollsters frame the gas tax issue in more specific terms—such as a way to reduce the country's dependence on foreign oil—55 percent favor it. Even more Americans (59 percent) support the tax when it is described as a way to reduce global warming (Friedman, 2006). "Sadly," columnist Thomas L. Friedman notes, "both sides fear the other will smear them if they run on this issue. O.K., say you're running for Congress and you propose a gas tax, but your opponent denounces you as a wimpy, tree-hugging, girlie-man, a tax-and-spender" (p. A25). Fearing such silly but politically consequential labels, politicians are apt to run for cover. A simple way to justify their refusal to support a gas tax is to point to polls showing that 85 percent of the public oppose the tax. In this way, political leaders can use polls to rationalize a reluctance to embrace bold measures for social change.

Psychological issues. Wording and context effects have stimulated much discussion among researchers. In addition to raising questions about political manipulation of poll findings, researchers have elucidated more scholarly concerns. Some theorists have suggested that the reason why question wording exerts such strong effects is not just that people are sensitive to subtle variations in language, but because in many cases they don't have full-blown attitudes at all. Instead, these researchers suggest, individuals construct their attitudes on the spot, based on what happens to be on their minds at the time or on thoughts triggered by survey questions (Bishop, 2005; Wilson, LaFleur, & Anderson, 1996; Zaller, 1992). In support of this position, research has found that large numbers of people volunteer opinions on fictitious issues, those that the pollster has invented for the purposes of the survey. For example, over 50 percent of respondents gave their opinion of the Monetary Control Bill, legislation dreamed up by survey researchers (Bishop, Tuchfarber, & Oldendick, 1986)!

People *do* construct attitudes on the spot in response to pollsters' questions. We should not assume that this is the norm, however. It pushes the envelope to argue that people lack attitudes; clearly, people harbor attitudes when the issue touches on strong values, is the product of socialization, or has been mentally worked through. At the same time, there are plenty of policy issues in which people lack firm beliefs or opinions. In such cases, their attitudes can be swayed by pollsters' questions, a fact that has not been lost on savvy marketers hoping to manipulate public opinion (see Box 6.1).

BOX 6.1 SKEWING THE SURVEY RESULTS

You have probably heard television advertisements that claim that "a majority of people interviewed in a major survey" said such-and-such about the product. The results make it sound like a scientific study proved that people prefer Crest to Colgate, Coke to Pepsi, Burger King to McDonald's, or Google to its competitors. As you listened, you no doubt thought to yourself, "Is this research real, or what?"

"Or what" is the appropriate answer. Some of the research that companies cite on their behalf is based on questionable methods. It is a powerful example of how marketing researchers can cook the data to fit the client, or design surveys that assure that companies will receive the answers they desire. Reporter Cynthia Crossen (1991) discussed this trend in the *Wall Street Journal*. She reported that:

■ When Levi Strauss & Co. asked students which clothes would be most popular this year, 90 percent said Levi's 501 jeans. They were the only jeans on the list.
■ A survey for Black Flag said: "A roach disk . . . poisons a roach slowly. The dying roach returns to the nest and after it dies is eaten by other roaches. In turn these roaches become poisoned and die. How effective do you think this

Continued

type of product would be in killing roaches?" Not surprisingly, 79 percent said effective.

■ An obviously-dated Chrysler study showing its cars were preferred to Toyota's included just 100 people in each of two tests. But more important, none of the people surveyed owned a foreign car, so they may well have been predisposed to U.S.-made vehicles.

(pp. A1, A7)

Summarizing her report on the use of marketing research, Crossen acknowledged that some studies use valid measurement techniques. But many surveys are filled with loaded questions and are designed to prove a point rather than investigate one. "There's been a slow sliding in ethics," said Eric Miller, who reviewed thousands of marketing studies as editor of a research newsletter. "The scary part is, people make decisions based on this stuff. It may be an invisible crime, but it's not a victimless one" (Crossen, 1999, p. A1).

ASKING GOOD QUESTIONS

As long as surveys are constructed by human beings and administered to human beings, we will never totally eliminate order or wording effects. You have to put your questions in a certain order and use particular words to communicate meaning. These are bound to influence respondents. Nonetheless, we can minimize the impact of context factors by taking precautions when designing the survey. More generally, there are many things researchers can do to improve the quality of attitude questions (Sudman & Bradburn, 1982). The next time you are asked to develop a self-report survey, you might consider these suggestions:

1. Use words that all respondents can comprehend.
2. Write specific and unambiguous items.
3. Avoid double negatives.
4. Pretest items to make sure people understand your questions.
5. If you think order of questions will influence respondents, ask questions in different sequences to check out order effects.
6. Avoid politically correct phrases that encourage socially desirable responses.
7. Write items so that they take both the positive and negative sides of an issue (to reduce respondents' tendency to always agree).
8. Consider whether your questions deal with sensitive, threatening issues (sex, drugs, antisocial behavior). If so, ask these questions at the end of the survey, once trust has been established.

9. Allow people to say "I don't know." This will eliminate responses based on guesses or a desire to please the interviewer.
10. Include many questions to tap different aspects of the attitude.

You can also save yourself some time—and improve the quality of your questionnaire—by turning to established attitude scales. You don't have to reinvent the wheel if someone else has developed a scale on the topic you're researching. To paraphrase the lyrics of an old folk song, "You can get anything you want at Alice's Restaurant"—you can get pretty much any scale you want, if you do a thorough search.

There are many standardized scales out there that tap attitudes very effectively. The advantage of using someone else's scale (other than that it frees you up to relax!) is that the scale has passed scientific muster—it is reliable, valid, and comprehensible to respondents. You can find scales from computerized databases, such as PsycINFO, Health and Psychosocial Instruments, and Communication Abstracts, or in specialized books (for example, Robinson, Shaver, & Wrightsman, 1999; Rubin, Palmgreen, & Sypher, 1994). Of course, if you're researching a new issue or want to cook up your own questions, you will have to devise your own questionnaire.

As you construct your survey, just remember that people are complex and that you will need good questions to tap their attitudes.

Focus Groups and Open-Ended Measures

The main advantage of attitude scales—that they offer an efficient way to measure social attitudes accurately—is their main drawback. Scales do not always shed light on the underlying dynamics of attitudes—the rich underbelly of cognitions and emotions. These components can be measured through focus groups and open-ended techniques.

You undoubtedly have heard of focus groups. Sometimes it seems that every marketing or political consultant is a focus group guru, magically divining the attitudes of participants from what they say in a group interview. Focus group participants' responses in turn are heralded and put forward as prescient predictors of the latest trend in Android phones, reality show preferences, or voters' attitudes. The political consultant and Fox News executive Roger Ailes captured this when he humorously said "when I die, I want to come back with real power. I want to come back as a member of a focus group" (quoted in Jarvis, 2011, p. 283).

A focus group is essentially a structured, systematic method to solicit collective information about attitudes toward a person, product, or issue. More specifically, a **focus group** is defined as "a qualitative research method in which a trained moderator conducts a collective interview of a set of participants" (Jarvis, 2011, p. 283). Focus groups have been employed to probe a host of topics, including attitudes toward presidential candidates, beliefs about nuclear risks, young people's reluctance to follow the news, and peer pressure among girls. The strength of a focus group is the rich dialogue-based information it provides about the meanings people attach to social issues. Its limitation is that, as a qualitative method, it can yield subjective conclusions that hinge on the personal interpretations of the analyst. However, in recent years, computer software programs have been created to analyze responses, yielding more reliable results.

Open-ended measures are another strategy to measure attitudes. These are employed in more structured measurement settings, complementing the three attitude scales discussed earlier. One well-known open-ended technique involves assessing cognitive responses to communications (Petty, Ostrom, & Brock, 1981b). Individuals typically read or view a message and list their cognitive reactions (i.e., thoughts). For example, if you wanted to measure people's cognitive responses regarding sex roles, you might have them view a sexist advertisement and ask them to write down the first ideas that come to mind. These responses could be subsequently categorized by researchers according to specific criteria (Cacioppo, Harkins, & Petty, 1981).

Affect can also be assessed in an open-ended way. People can be asked to write down 10 emotions that they ordinarily feel toward members of a group, organization, or nation (Eagly, Mladinic, & Otto, 1994; see also Crites, Fabrigar, & Petty, 1994).

Combining open-ended measures with traditional attitude scales increases the odds that researchers will tap attitudes accurately and completely. Of course, this does not guarantee success. Even the best survey researchers err. Some years ago pollster Richard Morin listed "the worst of the worst"—the most terrible questions ever asked in a poll. One of them appeared in a 1953 Gallup Poll: "*If you were taking a new job and had your choice of a boss, would you prefer to work under a man or a woman?*" (1997, p. 35).

INDIRECT METHODS TO MEASURE ATTITUDES

In light of such doozies (the question just cited) and the methodological problems noted earlier, some researchers recommend measuring attitude through ways other than questionnaires. They advocate the use of a variety of indirect techniques to assess attitudes. Although not without their problems, indirect measures can be useful when it is physically difficult to administer attitude scales or when people are reluctant to acknowledge what they really believe on a questionnaire. Key indirect measures include the following:

Unobtrusive measures. Researchers can observe individuals unobtrusively or without their knowledge. Behavior is used as a surrogate for attitude.

Unobtrusive measures can be useful in cases where it is not possible to administer self-report scales or one fears individuals will not accurately report attitudes (Webb et al., 1966). They also can be employed to document the impact of a major event on attitudes. For example, suppose researchers wanted to assess the effects of media publicity about a pop music star's death (e.g., Michael Jackson or Whitney Houston) on the singer's popularity. They might compare the number of hits on their YouTube videos before and at several time-points after their deaths. Useful as these techniques could be, the obvious problem is that they might not tap liking of the music so much as interest or idle curiosity.

Physiological measurements. Did you ever sweat a little when you asked someone out for a date? Do you know anyone whose pupils seem to get bigger when they are talking about something they really care about? Have you ever noticed how some people's facial muscles—eyebrows and cheeks—can telegraph what they are feeling? If so, you are intimately aware of the physiology of attitudes. Physiological measures can provide useful indirect assessments of attitudes.

A physiological approach to attitudes has gained adherents in recent years as researchers have recognized that attitudes have a motor or bodily component (Cacioppo, Priester, & Berntson, 1993). There is a host of ways of tapping attitudes through physiological techniques. These include (a) *galvanic skin response*, a change in the electrical resistance of the skin (e.g., measurements of sweating); (b) *pupil dilation* (precise assessments of expansion of the pupils); and (c) *facial electromyographic (EMG) techniques* that tap movements of facial muscles, particularly in the brow, cheek, and eye regions. The latter can provide a particularly sensitive reading of attitudes. In one study, students imagined they were reading an editorial with which they agreed or disagreed. Findings showed that students displayed more EMG activity over the brow region when imagining they were reading an article they disliked than one they liked (Cacioppo, Petty, & Marshall-Goodell, 1984).

Physiological measures can be useful in tapping feelings people are not aware they have, or which they might choose to disguise on a questionnaire. Marketing firms have used galvanic skin response measures to test advertising copy (LaBarbera & Tucciarone, 1995). Advertising researchers have found that facial EMG techniques can provide a more sensitive measure of emotional responses to ads than self-reports (Hazlett & Hazlett, 1999). Pupil dilation measures can shed light on abnormal sexual attitudes (Atwood & Howell, 1971).

Useful as these devices are, they can, unfortunately, tap responses other than attitudes. Sweating, pupil dilation, and facial muscle activity can occur because people are interested in or perplexed about the attitude object. Physiological reactions do not always provide a sensitive indication of the directionality (pro vs. con) of people's feelings. It is also frequently impractical or expensive to use physiological techniques.

On a more optimistic note, the development of neuroscience techniques, such as fMRI, supplement traditional physiological measures. Neuroscience measures offer information about attitudes that can be difficult if not impossible to detect through conventional measurement strategies. These methods can offer insight into deep-seated prejudiced attitudes.

Implicit Association Test. A variety of measures assess the latency or length of time it takes people to indicate if they agree or disagree with a statement. For example, individuals may sit before a computer screen and read a question (e.g., "Do you favor capital punishment?"). They are instructed to hit a button to indicate whether they do or do not favor capital punishment. Researchers do not focus on whether individuals are pro or con, or favorable or unfavorable to the attitude object. Their primary interest is in how long it takes individuals to make their selection (Fazio, 1995). The assumption is that the longer it takes people to access their attitude, the less well developed or strong the attitude is. Conversely, the more quickly people punch a button to indicate their attitude, the stronger the attitude is presumed to be.

The most popular response-time-based measure is the **Implicit Association Test (IAT)**, developed by Anthony Greenwald and colleagues (Greenwald, McGhee, & Schwartz, 1998). The IAT has been a godsend to researchers seeking to measure deep-seated attitudes, particularly implicit attitudes that operate unconsciously. Such attitudes, especially when they involve prejudices, are notoriously hard to uncover on paper-and-pencil questionnaires. People do not like to admit they harbor prejudices or may not be conscious of their biases. The IAT can tap such prejudices because it involves a less obtrusive methodology.

For example, in a study conducted back in the election campaign of 2008, researchers deliberately darkened Barack Obama's image to highlight racial cues. Some students saw the darkened version of Obama's photograph, and others viewed a lighter version. Conservative and liberal students looked at both pictures, responding with the subtle IAT measure of prejudice. Conservative and liberal students did not differ in their reactions to Obama when viewing the lightened photograph. However, conservatives displayed more negative responses to the darker images (Nevid & McClelland, 2010). The findings suggested that the IAT picked up on conservatives' hidden prejudices in a way standard questionnaires might not.

Here is how the IAT works: Researchers present individuals with a series of items. If the item belongs to a category in the left-hand column, they might push the letter *e*. If it belongs to the category in the right-hand column, they might push the letter *i*.

In the race IAT, the category White American could appear on the left and African-American on the right. The practice rounds are easy. When you see a photograph of a White person, you push the letter *e* and when you view a Black person, you push *i*. The test begins when the racial category appears along with a label, either "good" or "bad." Here is where it gets a little tricky. The labels could be: (a) White American or good; (b) African-American or bad; (c) White American or bad; and (d) African-American or good. You then see pictures of Whites and Blacks again. How long does it take to classify the photograph of a White person when the category is "White American or good," and how long to classify a Black when the category is "African-American or bad?" Now the counter-stereotypic case: *How long does it take to classify the photograph of the White person when the category is "White American or bad" and a Black when the category is "African-American or good?"* Writer Malcolm Gladwell described what happened when the latter scenario occurred:

> Immediately, something strange happened to me. The task of putting the . . . faces in the right categories suddenly became more difficult. I found myself slowing down. I had to think. Sometimes I assigned something to one category when I really meant to assign it to the other category.
>
> (2005, pp. 82–83)

The IAT provides a measure of the strength of association between an attribute, such as race, and positive or negative feelings. It assumes that the less time it takes a respondent to punch the appropriate key, the stronger the attitude. Presumably, if the attitude is strong and well learned, the individual should push a key (or letter on the keyboard) immediately without having to think about the issue. For example, someone with a very positive attitude toward Whites as a category should take less time to push the key when the photograph of a White appears with "White American or good" than with "White American or bad." An individual harboring a prejudice toward African-Americans should also should take less time to push the key when the photograph of a Black appears with "African-American or bad" than with "African-American or good."

"When there's a strong prior association, people answer in between four hundred and six hundred milliseconds," researcher Greenwald says. "When there isn't, they might take two hundred to three hundred milliseconds longer than that—which in the realm of these kinds of effects is huge" (Gladwell, 2005, p. 81).

Criticisms. There is fierce debate about the validity of the IAT (Arkes & Tetlock, 2004; Olson & Fazio, 2004). Critics argue that the test does not measure individuals' attitudes so much as the cultural associations they have learned. I may have learned that White is linked with "good" in our culture, but this does not mean I personally harbor a pro-White/anti-Black attitude. For example, two psychologists note, "in early Western movies, Hopalong Cassidy, Gene Autry, and Roy Rogers always wore white hats whereas villains always wore black. Thus, when people taking the IAT respond faster to 'white/good' and 'black/bad' combinations than to 'white/bad' and 'black/good' combinations, it is not at all clear that this is truly an indication of a prejudicial attitude toward African Americans" (Fishbein & Ajzen, 2010, p. 272). In addition, it is not clear that responding to certain words on a computer test means that an individual harbors latent prejudices or deep-seated hostility toward members of minority groups. Critics worry that unfairly labeling individuals as prejudiced, based on a computerized test, can itself have dysfunctional, harmful effects on race relations (Tetlock & Arkes, 2004).

CONCLUSIONS

Attitude measurement plays a critical role in persuasion research. Persuasion is a science, as well as an art, and we need valid instruments to assess attitudes. Three venerable scales are typically employed: Likert, Guttman, and the semantic differential. A Likert scale taps agreement or disagreement with a series of opinion statements. The Guttman scale focuses on items that vary in their degree of psychological difficulty. The **semantic differential** uses bipolar adjectives to measure the meaning associated with attitude objects. It took real ingenuity to devise these scales and they remain useful decades after they were originally developed. The Likert scale is used most frequently because it offers a viable method to tap attitudes, can be constructed easily, and its validity and reliability can be effectively documented.

Open-ended measures, such as cognitive responses, can supplement closed-ended, structured scales. Focus groups offer a more dynamic way to explore attitudes about a contemporary issue.

There are a variety of problems in measuring attitudes through traditional self-reports, including survey context and wording effects. To minimize these problems, researchers have devised strategies to improve questionnaire quality that focus on asking questions clearly and thoughtfully. Supplementing self-report surveys are several indirect techniques to assess attitudes, such as unobtrusive, physiological, and response-time measures. Indirect techniques such as the IAT can shed light on attitudes that people are reluctant to reveal on self-report questionnaires, lest they look bad in the eyes of the researcher. The IAT, as well as neuroscience techniques such as the fMRI, can illuminate attitudes that elude conscious awareness and are difficult to accurately detect through conventional scales.

The IAT, for its part, is not without problems. Critics note that responses may reflect well-learned cultural associations rather than attitudes. However, there is evidence that substantiates its validity, and it offers a creative way to tap into prejudice and other socially sensitive attitudes that people would rather not or cannot acknowledge on a questionnaire.

In the end, as Jon Krosnick and his colleagues thoughtfully point out, "Both traditional self-report and more indirect attitude measures will continue to be used. The goal is not to come up with a single 'best' attitude measure, but rather to measure attitudes in all their complexity and all their manifestations" (Krosnick, Judd, & Wittenbrink, 2005, p. 63). Given the complexity of attitudes, and the pervasive part they play in our lives, we need every valid measurement technique we can develop and perfect.

Test your knowledge now with interactive exercises

Part Three **Changing Attitudes and Behavior**

Chapter 7

Processing Persuasive Communications

 Listen now to the author's chapter summary

Kate and Ben, recently married, delightfully employed, and happy to be on their own after 4 long years of college, are embarking on a major decision—a happy one, but an important one. They're buying a car. They have some money saved up from the wedding and have decided that, the way the stock market has been going, they'd be better off spending it than losing cash on some risky Internet investment.

Sitting in their living room one Thursday night watching TV, they find that they are tuning in more closely to the car commercials than the sitcoms. "That's a sign we're an old married couple," Kate jokes. Ben nods in agreement.

The next day after work, at Kate's request they click onto the *Consumer Reports* Web site and print out information about compact cars. On Saturday they brave the car dealerships, get the lowdown from car salesmen, and take spins in the cars. Kate, armed with her incredible memory for detail and ten 3 × 5 cards, hurls questions at the car salesmen, while Ben, shirt hanging out, eyes glazed, looks dreamily at the sports cars he knows he can't afford.

By early the next week, they have narrowed down the choices to a Honda Accord and a Hyundai Sonata. Her desk covered with papers, printouts, and stacks of warranties and brochures from the dealerships, Kate is thinking at a feverish pace; she pauses, then shares her conclusions with her husband: "Okay, this is it. The Honda gets more miles per gallon and handles great on the highway. But *Consumer Reports* gives the new Sonata better ratings on safety on account of their anti-lock brakes and traction control, which is important. The Sonata also has a better repair record than the Accord. But the big thing is we get a stronger warranty with the Hyundai dealer and, Ben, the Sonata is a thousand bucks cheaper. Soooo . . . what do you think?"

Ben looks up. "Well, you know, I'm not into all this technical stuff like you are. I say if the Sonata gets better ratings from *Consumer Reports*, go for it. I also think the Sonata salesman made a lot of good points—real nice guy. The Honda guy basically blew us off when we told him we needed the weekend to think it over."

"There's also the other thing," says Kate, sporting a grin. "What?"

"The name."

"It's true," says Ben a bit sheepishly. "The name 'Sonata' is cool. I like it." "What am I going to do with you?" Kate asks, with a smile and a deliberately exaggerated sigh.

"How about, take me to the Hyundai dealer, so we can buy our new car?" Ben says, gently running his hands through the 3 × 5 cards as he walks out the front door.

The story is fiction—but perhaps not too far from everyday experience. It is based on interviews with consumers and observations of people buying cars. The example illustrates two very different styles of processing information: careful consideration of message arguments (Kate) and superficial examination of information and a focus on simple cues (Ben). These two ways of processing information are the main elements of contemporary theories of persuasion and form the centerpiece of the present chapter.

This chapter launches the third part of the book, which examines theory and research on the effects of persuasive communication. The chapter describes guiding models of attitude and behavior change—approaches that underlie much of the research and applications that follow. The cornerstone of these theoretical approaches is a focus on *process.* Scholars believe that if they can understand *how* people cognitively process messages, they can better explicate the impact that communications have on attitudes. They believe that the better they comprehend individuals' modes of processing information, the more accurately they can explain the diverse effects messages have on attitudes. This is what scholars mean when they say you cannot understand the effects of communications on people without knowing how people process the message.

Contemporary models evolved from earlier perspectives on persuasion—notably Hovland's pathbreaking work and research conducted in the 1960s. It is important to describe these programs of research because they contributed helpful insights and also laid the groundwork for current theorizing. The first section of the chapter provides an overview of these approaches. The second portion of the chapter describes dual-process models of persuasion, focusing on a major cognitive processing model, the Elaboration Likelihood Model. Subsequent sections focus on real-life applications, fine points of the model, intellectual criticisms, and the model's contributions to persuasion.

HISTORICAL FOUNDATIONS

Yale Attitude Change Approach

As noted in Chapter 2, Carl Hovland and colleagues at Yale University conducted the first detailed, empirical research on the effects of persuasive communications. The **Yale attitude change approach** was distinctive because it provided facts about the effects on attitudes of the communicator's credibility, message appeals, and audience members' personality traits. Convinced by theory and their generation's experience with World War II persuasion campaigns that communications had strong effects on attitudes, the researchers set out to examine who says what to whom with what effect (Hovland, Janis, & Kelley, 1953; Smith, Lasswell, & Casey, 1946).

Although Hovland and colleagues' findings were interesting, it was their theory-driven approach and commitment to testing hypotheses that proved enduring. The Yale researchers were also interested in understanding why messages changed attitudes. Working in an era dominated by reward-based learning theories and research on rats' mastery of mazes, Hovland naturally gravitated to explanations that focused on learning and motivation. He emphasized that persuasion entailed learning message arguments and noted that attitude change occurred in a series of steps. To be persuaded, individuals had to attend to, comprehend, learn, accept, and retain the message (see Figure 7.1).

It sounds logical enough. Indeed there is considerable evidence that learning is a component of persuasion—the more people learn and comprehend message arguments, the more likely they are to accept the advocated positions (Chaiken, Wood, & Eagly, 1996). However, the thesis misses the mark in an important respect. It assumes that people are

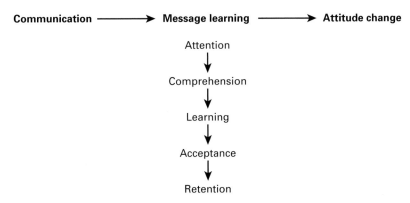

■ **Figure 7.1 The Hovland/Yale model of persuasion.**

sponge-like creatures who passively take in information they receive. In fact, as Leon Festinger and Nathan Maccoby noted, an audience member:

> does not sit there listening and absorbing what is said without any counteraction on his part. Indeed, it is more likely that under such circumstances, while he is listening to the persuasive communication, he is very actively, inside his own mind, counterarguing, derogating the points the communicator makes and derogating the communicator himself.
>
> (1964, p. 360)

Think of how you react to a persuasive message. Do you sit there, taking in everything the speaker says? Are you so mesmerized by the communicator that you stifle any thoughts or mental arguments? Hardly. You actively think about the speaker, message, or persuasion context. You may remember message arguments, yet probably recall with greater accuracy your own criticisms of the speaker's point of view. This view of persuasion developed in the years that followed the publication of Hovland's research and is known as the **cognitive response approach to persuasion**.

Cognitive Response Approach

The cognitive response perspective asserts that people's own mental reactions to a message play a critical role in the persuasion process, typically a more important role than the message itself (Brock, 1967; Greenwald, 1968; Petty, Ostrom, & Brock, 1981b). Cognitive responses include thoughts that are favorable to the position advocated in the message (*proarguments*) and those that criticize the message (*counterarguments*). Persuasion occurs if the communicator induces the audience member to generate favorable cognitive responses regarding the communicator or message.

The cognitive response view says that people play an active role in the persuasion process. It emphasizes that people's *own* thoughts about a message are more important

■ **Figure 7.2 The Cognitive Response Model of Persuasion.**

factors in persuasion than memory of message arguments (Perloff & Brock, 1980; see Figure 7.2). There is a good deal of evidence to substantiate this view. In fact, it may seem obvious that thoughts matter in persuasion. But remember that what is obvious at one point in time is not always apparent in an earlier era. During the 1950s and early 1960s, animal learning models of human behavior dominated psychology, and, on a broader level, Americans were assumed to follow lock, stock, and barrel the dictates of government and free-enterprise capitalism. It seemed only natural to theorize that persuasion was primarily a passive process of learning and reinforcement.

With the advent of the 1960s, all this changed. Cognitive models emphasizing active thought processes gained adherents. It became clear that older views, while useful, needed to be supplemented by approaches that afforded more respect to the individual and assigned more emphasis to dynamics of the gray matter inside the brain.

"Feed your head," the rock group Jefferson Airplane belted out during this decade. The cognitive response approach echoed the refrain. It stimulated research, bottled old scholarly wine in new explanations, and helped pave the way for new theories of attitude change. By calling attention to the role that thoughts play in persuasion, the cognitive response approach illuminated scholarly understanding of persuasion. Consider the following examples.

The first involves **forewarning**, which occurs when a persuader warns people that they will soon be exposed to a persuasive communication. This is a common occurrence in life, and research has explored what happens when people are warned that they are going to receive a message with which they will staunchly disagree. Cognitive response studies have clarified just what happens inside people's minds when this occurs. Individuals generate a large number of counterarguments, strengthening their opposition to the advocated position (Petty & Cacioppo, 1977). An old expression, "Forewarned is forearmed," describes this phenomenon, but sheds no light on why it occurs. Cognitive response analysis helps us understand it better.

When a close friend marches out of the house in the middle of an argument, vowing, "We'll talk about this when I get home," you are likely to intensify your resolve not to give in. Generating arguments on your behalf and persuading yourself that you are right, you arm yourself with a battering ram of justifications that you invoke when your friend returns. In fact, as cognitive response research predicts, forewarning someone in this general fashion significantly reduces the likelihood that a subsequent persuasive communication will succeed. "Forewarning an audience to expect a persuasive message tends to make that message less persuasive," William L. Benoit concludes after studying this issue (1998, p. 146).

Another way of saying this is that forewarnings stiffen resistance to persuasion. Arming individuals to resist harmful communications is important, given that people are frequently tempted to yield to peers' requests that they smoke, drink when they drive, or take drugs (Quinn & Wood, 2004). Forewarnings typically can instill resistance, provided they get people to consider the issue and the arguments contained in the message.

Cognitive responses also help explain an off-beat persuasion effect called **distraction**. Sometimes people are distracted from paying attention to a communication with which they disagree. Other people may be talking, or music may be blaring at a party at precisely the moment when someone chooses to explain why she disagrees with a position one holds on an issue. In other cases, communicators intentionally distract receivers from paying attention to a message. Advertisers do this all the time, using humor, music, and sex to take people's attention away from the message. In such circumstances, people can be highly susceptible to persuasion. The distraction hypothesis holds that distraction facilitates persuasion by blocking the dominant cognitive response to a message (Petty, Wells, & Brock, 1976). If I listen to a message with which I disagree, my normal response is probably to counterargue with the communicator in my head. But if my mind is elsewhere—I'm grooving to the music or am laughing at a joke—I am not able to formulate arguments against the message. I, therefore, have fewer mental objections to the advocated position. As a result, I end up moving somewhat closer to the communicator's point of view than I would have if I had not been distracted in this way.

Notice what is going on here. It's not the distraction from the message that counts; rather, it's the distraction from our own arguments regarding the message (Osterhouse & Brock, 1970). Recognizing that people are primed to contest advertisements in their own minds, advertisers resort to all sorts of clever distractions (see Chapter 13). Sometimes they even seem to be aware that we mentally take issue with ads that appear on television, as they try to tease us into not taking the ad so seriously. This too can be distracting and can facilitate persuasion. Mind you—distraction does not always succeed, and it does not always work by inhibiting counterargument production. Indeed, David B. Buller and John R. Hall (1998) present an array of evidence that challenges the counterargument disruption thesis. However, the distraction research caught researchers' eyes by raising the possibility that cognitive responses could influence attitude change. This in turn stimulated scholarship and suggested new ideas for everyday persuasion.

In general, the cognitive response research has called attention to the subtle and powerful role thinking plays in the persuasion process. Thinking—and especially mentally counterarguing with persuasive messages—can stiffen resistance to persuasion, as a classic persuasion effect known as inoculation highlights (see Box 7.1).

BOX 7.1 INOCULATION THEORY

Persuasion not only involves changing attitudes. It also centers on convincing people not to fall prey to unethical or undesirable influence attempts. Communicators frequently attempt to persuade individuals to resist social and political messages that are regarded as unhealthy or unwise. For example, health campaigns urge young people to "say no" to drugs, smoking, drinking when driving, and unsafe sex. In the political domain, candidates attempt to persuade wavering voters to resist the temptation to bolt their party and vote for the opposing party candidate or a third-party contender.

A variety of techniques have been developed to strengthen resistance to persuasion. The techniques work by triggering counterarguments that, along with other factors, help individuals resist persuasive appeals. One of the most famous strategies evolved from a biological analogy and is known as inoculation theory. The theory is an ingenious effort to draw a comparison between the body's mechanisms to ward off disease and the mind's ways of defending itself against verbal onslaughts. In his statement of the theory, William McGuire noted that doctors increase resistance to disease by injecting the person with a small dose of the attacking virus, as in a flu shot (McGuire & Papageorgis, 1961; see Figure 7.3). Pre-exposure to the virus in a weakened form stimulates the body's defenses: it leads to production of antibodies, which help the body fight off disease. In the same fashion, exposure to a weak dose of opposition arguments, "strong enough to stimulate his defenses, but not strong enough to overwhelm him," should produce the mental equivalent of antibodies—counterarguments (McGuire, 1970, p. 37). Counterarguing the oppositional message in one's own mind should lead to strengthening of initial attitude and increased resistance to persuasion.

One of the hallmarks of inoculation research is the creativity with which it has been tested. McGuire and colleagues chose to expose people to attacks against attitudes that had been rarely if ever criticized: cultural truisms, or beliefs individuals learn through socialization. Cultural truisms include: "You should brush your teeth three times a day" and "People should get a yearly checkup." In essence, participants in the experiments received either a supportive defense— arguments defending the truism—or an inoculation defense (for example, arguments against the notion that you should brush your teeth three times a

Continued

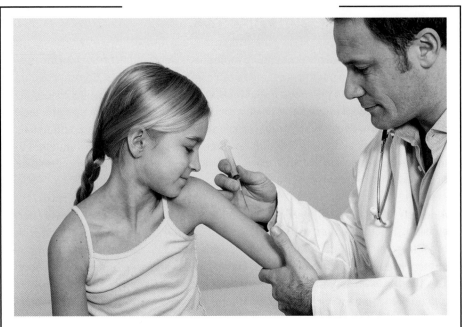

■ **Figure 7.3 The inoculation perspective draws an analogy between the ability of a flu shot to increase resistance to disease and the ways in which weak doses of opposition arguments can stiffen resistance to persuasion.**

Image courtesy of Shutterstock.

day, along with refutation of these arguments). Individuals who received the inoculation defense were more likely to resist subsequent attacks on a brush-your-teeth-three-times-a-day type truism than those who just received supportive arguments (McGuire & Papageorgis, 1961). Presumably, the attack and refutation stimulated individuals to formulate arguments why the truism was indeed correct. They were apparently more motivated than those who heard the usual "rah-rah, it's true" supportive arguments.

These findings provided the first support for **inoculation** theory. The theory fundamentally stipulates that resistance to persuasion can be induced by exposing individuals to a small dose of arguments against a particular idea, coupled with appropriate criticism of these arguments. In essence, inoculation works by introducing a threat to a person's belief system and then providing a way for individuals to cope with the threat (that is, by refuting the counterattitudinal message). As Michael Pfau noted, "By motivating receivers, and then preemptively refuting one or more potential counterarguments, inoculation spreads a broad blanket of protection both against specific counterarguments raised in refutational preemption and against those counterarguments not raised" (1997, pp. 137–138).

Other explanations of inoculation have also been advanced. Some researchers suggest that inoculation confers resistance to persuasion by providing the persuader with an opportunity to reframe the arguments before the opposition gets to them (Williams & Dolnik, 2001). Pfau and colleagues (2003) have shown that inoculations make attitudes more accessible and stronger, and therefore more resistant to attack. Although there is healthy debate about just which processes account best for inoculation effects, there is little doubt that inoculation provides a useful way to encourage resistance to persuasive communications (Banas & Rains, 2010; Benoit, 1991; Lim & Ki, 2007; Pfau, 1997; Szabo & Pfau, 2002).

Indeed, inoculation theory has stimulated considerable research over the years, usefully transcending its initial focus on cultural truisms, explored exclusively in laboratory settings. Communication scholars have taken the concept to the real world, examining its applications to commercial advertising, political campaigns, and health (Compton, 2013). A number of practical conclusions have emerged from this research. They include the following:

1. **Inoculation can be a potent weapon in politics and the law.** Politicians can anticipate the opposition's attacks and preempt them by using inoculation techniques (Pfau & Burgoon, 1988; Pfau & Kenski, 1990). Barack Obama used the technique in the 2008 election, trying to build voter resistance to Republican opponent John McCain. Obama first acknowledged McCain's service to his country. "Now let there be no doubt. The Republican nominee, John McCain, has worn the uniform of our country with bravery and distinction, and for that we owe him our gratitude and respect. And we'll also hear about those occasions when he's broken with his party as evidence that he can deliver the change that we need." He then proffered the counterargument. "But the record's clear: John McCain has voted with George Bush 90 percent of the time. Senator McCain likes to talk about judgment, but, really, what does it say about your judgment when you think George Bush was right more than 90 percent of the time? I don't know about you, but I'm not ready to take a 10 percent change on change." The crowd roared. Obama's staffers undoubtedly hoped that their candidate had successfully inoculated Americans who heard snippets of the speech on television at home.

Continued

Lawyers also exploit inoculation to their advantage. A now-classic example of inoculation in the courtroom came in the trial of Casey Anthony, charged with the murder of her 2-year-old daughter. In his closing arguments, defense attorney Jose Baez acknowledged that Casey was "a liar and a slut" and made some stupid decisions. But, he quickly added, she was not a murderer and should not pay with her life. By acknowledging the obvious—Casey had blatantly lied in the aftermath of her daughter's death—Baez helped the jury get beyond her prevarications to focus on problems with the prosecution's case.

2. **In a world filled with unethical persuaders, inoculation offers a technique to help people resist unwanted influence attempts.** The theory says that the best way to induce resistance to unethical persuasion is to provide people with a small dose of the dangerous information and then help them refute it. This offers a useful counterpoint to those who say that parents should shield children from the world's evils or shelter them from unpleasant realities. As Pratkanis and Aronson note, "We cannot resist propaganda by burying our heads in the sand. The person who is easiest to persuade is the person whose beliefs are based on slogans that have never been seriously challenged" (1992, p. 215).

ELABORATION LIKELIHOOD MODEL

Without a doubt, the cognitive response approach advanced knowledge of persuasion. It placed thinking at the center of the persuasion process. It also provided a method to measure cognitive aspects of attitudes creatively. After a time, though, researchers realized that the approach had two limitations. First, it assumed that people think carefully about messages. Yet there are many times when people turn their minds off to persuasive communications, making decisions based on mental shortcuts. Second, the cognitive response approach failed to shed much light on the ways that messages influence people. It did not explain how we can utilize cognitive responses so as to devise messages to change attitudes or behavior. In order to rectify these problems, scholars proceeded to develop process-based models of persuasion.

Two models currently dominate the field. The first, devised by Shelly Chaiken and Alice H. Eagly, is called the Heuristic-Systematic Model (HSM) (Chaiken, Liberman, & Eagly, 1989; Todorov, Chaiken, & Henderson, 2002). The second, formulated by Richard E. Petty and John T. Cacioppo, is the Elaboration Likelihood Model (ELM) (Petty & Cacioppo, 1986; Petty & Wegener, 1999; Petty, Wheeler, & Tormala, 2003). Both approaches emphasize that you cannot understand communication effects without appreciating the underlying processes by which messages influence attitudes. Both are *dual-process models* in that they claim that there are two different mechanisms by which communications affect attitudes.

Each model has strengths. The **Heuristic-Systematic Model** offers a compelling explanation of message processing when people opt to expend relatively little effort and devote few resources to the task. Its emphasis on heuristics—a term that will be subsequently discussed—represented a substantive contribution to the academic literature on persuasion.

The **Elaboration Likelihood Model** provides a comprehensive framework for understanding the effects of a host of source, message, and receiver factors on persuasion. It also has provided a useful integration of a wealth of empirical data. This chapter focuses on the ELM because it has generated more interdisciplinary research on persuasive communication and has been applied to more communication contexts.

ELM Principles

The first question students may have when reading about an Elaboration Likelihood Model of persuasion is: "Just what does the term 'Elaboration Likelihood' mean?" This is a reasonable question. *Elaboration* refers to the extent to which the individual thinks about or mentally modifies arguments contained in the communication. *Likelihood*, referring to the probability that an event will occur, is used to point out the fact that elaboration can be either likely or unlikely. Elaboration is assumed to fall along a continuum, with one end characterized by considerable rumination on the central merits of an issue and the other by relatively little mental activity. The model tells us when people should be particularly likely to elaborate, or not elaborate, on persuasive messages.

The ELM stipulates that there are two distinct ways people process communications. These are called routes, suggesting that two different highways crisscross the mind, transporting thoughts and reactions to messages. The term *route* is a metaphor: we do not know for sure that these routes exist (any more than we know with absolute certainty that any mental construct exists in precisely the way theorists use it). Social scientists employ terms like "processing route" (or attitude) to describe complex cognitive and behavioral phenomena. As with attitude, the term "processing route" makes eminent sense and is supported by a great deal of empirical evidence. The ELM refers to the two routes to persuasion as the *central and peripheral routes*, or central and peripheral processes.

The **central route** is characterized by considerable cognitive elaboration. When people process information centrally, they carefully evaluate message arguments, ponder implications of the communicator's ideas, and relate information to their own knowledge and values. This is the thinking person's route to persuasion.

The **peripheral route** is entirely different. Rather than examining issue-relevant arguments, people examine the message quickly or focus on simple cues to help them decide whether to accept the position advocated in the message. Factors that are peripheral to message arguments carry the day. These can include a communicator's physical appeal, glib speaking style, or pleasant association between the message and music playing in the background.

When processing peripherally, people invariably rely on simple decision-making rules or **heuristics**. For example, an individual may invoke the heuristic that "experts are to be believed" and, for this reason (and this reason only), accept the speaker's recommendation. In a similar fashion, people employ a "bandwagon heuristic," illustrated by the belief that "if other people think this is good, then it probably is." You see this all the time on social networking sites, as when one infers an individual's popularity from the number of friends she has on Facebook, judges a song to be desirable based on song download rankings, or decides to purchase a book based on a listing of their friends' favorite books via a connection to their Facebook account on Amazon.com (Schmierbach et al., 2009).

Thus, the ELM says that people can be simple information processors—"cognitive misers" as they are sometimes called (Taylor, 1981)—or deep, detailed thinkers. Under some conditions (when processing superperipherally), they are susceptible to slick persuaders—and can be thus characterized by the saying attributed to P. T. Barnum: "There's a sucker born every minute!" In other circumstances (when processing centrally), individuals are akin to Plato's ideal students—seeking truth and dutifully considering logical arguments—or to Aristotelian thinkers, persuaded only by cogent arguments (logos). The model says people are neither suckers nor deep thinkers. Complex creatures that we are, we are both peripheral and central, heuristic and systematic, processors. The critical questions are when people process centrally, when they prefer the peripheral pathway, and the implications for persuasion. The nifty thing about the ELM is that it answers these questions, laying out conditions under which central or peripheral processing is most likely, and the effects of such processing on attitude change.

The key factors that determine processing strategy are *motivation* and *ability*. When people are motivated to consider the message seriously, they process centrally. They also pursue the central route when they are cognitively able to ponder message arguments. Situations can limit or enhance people's ability to process centrally, and so too can personal characteristics. On the other hand, when people lack the motivation or ability to process a message carefully, they opt for a simpler strategy. They process superficially.

It is frequently neither possible nor functional to process every message carefully. "Just imagine if you thought carefully about every television or radio commercial you heard or ad you came across in newspapers or magazines," note Richard Petty and colleagues. "If you ever made it out of the house in the morning, you probably would be too mentally exhausted to do anything else!" (Petty et al., 1994, p. 118). Contemporary society, with its multiple stimuli, unfathomably complex issues, and relentless social change, makes it inevitable that people will rely on mental shortcuts much of the time.

In addition to spelling out factors that make peripheral processing most likely, the ELM contains hypotheses about the impact that such processing exerts on persuasion. Different persuasive appeals are effective, depending on the processing route. These appeals also differ in their long-term effects on attitudes (see Figure 7.4).

MOTIVATION TO PROCESS

Involvement. Can you think of an issue that has important implications for your own life? Perhaps it is a university proposal to raise tuition, a plan to change requirements in your major, or even a proposal to ban cell phoning while driving. Now think of an issue that has little impact on your day-to-day routines. This could be a proposal to strengthen the graduation requirements at local high schools or a plan to use a different weed spray in farming communities. You will certainly process the first issues differently from the second. Different persuasive appeals are likely to be effective in these two circumstances as well.

The topics just cited differ in their level of personal involvement, or the degree to which they are perceived to be personally relevant to individuals. *Individuals are high in involvement when they perceive that an issue is personally relevant or bears directly on their own lives. They are low in involvement when they believe that an issue has little or no impact on their own lives.*

ELM Predictions and a Classic Experiment

The ELM stipulates that when individuals are high in involvement, they will be motivated to engage in issue-relevant thinking. They will recognize that it is in their best interest to consider the arguments in the message carefully. Even if they oppose the position advocated in the message, they may change their attitudes if the arguments are sufficiently compelling to persuade them that they will benefit by adopting the advocated

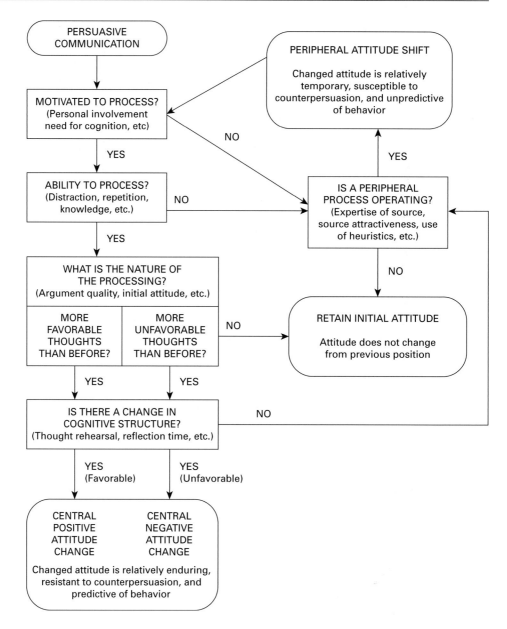

Figure 7.4 The Elaboration Likelihood Model of persuasion.

Adapted from Petty, R. E., & Wegener, D. T. (1999). The Elaboration Likelihood Model: Current status and controversies. In S. Chaiken & Y. Trope (Eds.), *Dual-process theories in social psychology* (pp. 41–72). New York: Guilford.

position. Under high involvement, people should process messages through the central route, systematically scrutinizing message arguments.

By contrast, under low involvement, people have little motivation to focus on message arguments. The issue is of little personal consequence; therefore, it doesn't pay to spend much time thinking about the message. As a result, people look for mental shortcuts to help them decide whether to accept the communicator's position. They process the message peripherally, unconcerned with the substance of the communication.

These predictions are intriguing, but how do we know if they hold water in the real world? In order to discover if hypotheses are correct, researchers test them empirically. Petty, Cacioppo, and Goldman (1981) examined these hypotheses in a now-classic study. To help you appreciate the procedures, I ask that you imagine that the experiment was being conducted again today using equivalent methods and materials. Here is how it would work:

You first enter a small room in a university building, take a seat, and wait for the experimenter. When the experimenter arrives, she tells you that the university is currently reevaluating its academic programs and is soliciting feedback about possible changes in policy. One proposal concerns a requirement that seniors take a comprehensive exam in their major area of study.

If randomly assigned to the high-involvement condition, you would be told that the comprehensive exam requirement could begin next year. That's clearly involving as it bears directly on your educational plans. How would you feel if you learned that you might have to take a big exam in your major—communication, psychology, marketing, or whatever it happened to be? You would probably feel nervous, angry, worried, or curious. Whichever emotion you felt, you clearly would be concerned about the issue.

If, on the other hand, you had been assigned to the low-involvement condition, you would be told that the exam requirement would not take effect for 10 years. That clearly is low involvement. Even if you're on the laid-back, two-classes-a-semester plan, you do not envision being in college 10 years from now! Realizing the message is of little personal consequence, you would gently switch gears from high energy to autopilot.

Regardless of involvement level, you would be asked now to listen to one of two messages delivered by one of two communicators. The particular message and source would be determined by lot, or random assignment.

You would listen to either strong or weak arguments on behalf of the exam. Strong arguments employ statistics and evidence ("Institution of the exams had led to a reversal in the declining scores on standardized achievement tests at other universities"). They offer cogent arguments on behalf of the exam requirement. Weak arguments are shoddy and unpersuasive (for example, "A friend of the author's had to take a comprehensive exam and now has a prestigious academic position").

Lastly, you would be led to believe that the comprehensive exam proposal had been prepared by a communicator either high or low in expertise. If assigned to the high-expertise group, you would be told that the report had been developed by the Carnegie Commission on Higher Education, which had been chaired by an education professor at Princeton University. If randomly assigned to the low-expertise communicator, you would be informed that the proposal had been prepared by a class at a local high school. You would then indicate your overall evaluation of the exam.

This constituted the basic design of the study. In formal terms, there were three conditions: involvement (high or low), argument quality (strong or weak), and expertise (high or low). Petty and colleagues found that the impact of arguments and expertise depended to a considerable degree on level of involvement.

Under high involvement, argument quality exerted a significant impact on attitudes toward the comprehensive exam. Regardless of whether a high school class or Princeton professor was the source of the message, strong arguments led to more attitude change than did weak arguments. Under low involvement, the opposite pattern of results emerged. A highly expert source induced more attitude change than did a low-expert source, regardless of whether the arguments were strong or weak (see Figure 7.5).

The ELM provides a parsimonious explanation of the findings. Under high involvement, students believed that the senior exam would affect them directly. This heightened motivation to pay careful attention to the quality of the arguments. Processing the arguments carefully through the central route, students naturally were more swayed by strong than by weak arguments.

Imagine how you would react if you had been in this condition. Although you would hardly be overjoyed at the prospect of an exam in your major area of study, the idea would grab your attention, and you would think carefully about the arguments. After reading them, you would not be 100 percent in favor of the comprehensive exam—but having thought through the ideas and noted the benefits the exam provided, you might be more sympathetic to the idea than you would have been at the outset, and certainly more favorable than if you had listened to weak arguments on behalf of the exam.

Now imagine you had been assigned to the low-involvement and high-expertise group. You'd be on autopilot because the exam would not take place until long after you had

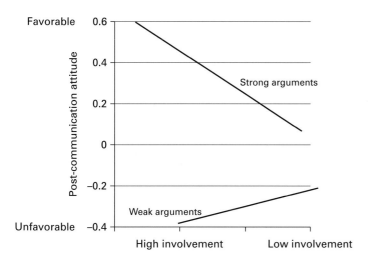

■ **Figure 7.5 Effects of involvement, source expertise, and argument quality on attitudes.**

From Petty, R. E., Cacioppo, J. T., & Goldman, R. (1981). Personal involvement as a determinant of argument-based persuasion. *Journal of Personality and Social Psychology*, 41, 847–855.

graduated. Blasé about the whole thing, feeling little motivation to think carefully about the issue, you would understandably have little incentive to pay close attention to the quality of arguments.

You would focus on one salient cue—a factor that might help you decide what to do about this issue so that you could complete the assignment and get on with your day.

The fact that the communicator was from Princeton might capture your attention and offer a compelling reason to go along with the message. "If this Princeton prof. thinks it's a good idea, it's fine with me," you might think. Click-whirr—just like that, you would go along with the message (Cialdini, 2009).

As we will see, these findings have intriguing implications for everyday persuasion. Looking back on the study findings, it may seem as if the main principle is that under high involvement, "what is said" is most important, and under low involvement, "who says it" is the key. There is some truth to this, but it greatly oversimplifies matters.

The key point is not that message appeals are more effective under high involvement and communicator appeals are more compelling under low involvement. Instead, the core issue is that people engage in issue-relevant thinking under high involvement, but under low involvement, they focus on simple cues that are peripheral to the main issues. In fact, there are times when a peripheral aspect of the message can carry the day under low involvement.

Case in point: number of message arguments. This attribute is absolutely irrelevant, or peripheral, to the quality of the message. A speaker can have nine shoddy arguments or one extremely cogent appeal. However, the number of arguments can signify quality of argumentation in the minds of perceivers. If people would rather not think too deeply about an issue, they may fall into the trap of assuming that the more arguments a message has, the more convincing it is. This is exactly what Petty and Cacioppo (1984) discovered. When students were evaluating a proposal to institute senior comprehensive exams at their own school 10 years in the future, they were more influenced by a message that had nine arguments. It didn't matter if all of them were weak. However, when contemplating a senior exam policy that would take place next year, they were naturally more motivated to devote energy to thinking about the issue. They processed arguments centrally, seeing through the shoddy ones and accepting the message only if arguments were strong.

NEED FOR COGNITION

Do you enjoy thinking? Or do you think only as hard as you have to? Do you prefer complex to simple problems? Or do you gravitate to tasks that are important, but don't require much thought?

These questions focus on another motivational factor that influences processing: a personality trait called the need for cognition. **Need for cognition (NFC)** is "a stable individual difference in people's tendency to engage in and enjoy effortful cognitive activity" (Cacioppo et al., 1996, p. 198). NFC is a need to understand the world and to employ thinking to accomplish this goal.

People high in NFC enjoy thinking abstractly. They will tell you that they "end up deliberating about issues even when they do not affect (them) personally." Ask them if they "would prefer a task that is intellectual, difficult and important to one that is somewhat important but does not require much thought," and they will readily agree.

Those on the other end of the continuum—those low in need for cognition—will tell you that, frankly, "thinking is not (their) idea of fun" and they think only as hard as they have to. They do not enjoy deliberating about issues that do not affect them personally, do not gravitate to intellectually demanding tasks, and "feel relief rather than satisfaction after completing a task that required a lot of mental effort" (see Cacioppo, Petty, & Kao, 1984). John T. Cacioppo and his colleagues developed a scale to assess NFC and they demonstrated that the scale reliably and validly taps the concept.

Need for cognition is not the same as intelligence. The two are related: you have to be somewhat intelligent to enjoy contemplating issues; thus, there is a modest relationship between verbal intelligence and need for cognition. However, two people could score high on verbal intelligence tests, yet one individual could find abstract thinking appealing, while the other could find it monotonous.

What does need for cognition have to do with persuasion? Plenty. Individuals high in NFC recall more message arguments, generate a greater number of issue-relevant thoughts, and seek more information about complex issues than those low in NFC (Briñol & Petty, 2005; Cacioppo et al., 1996). Given that people high in NFC like to think, they should be more influenced by quality-of-message arguments than those low in NFC. And in fact cogent issue arguments do carry more weight with high-NFC individuals. By contrast, those low in NFC are more influenced by cues that save them from effortful thought. They are frequently swayed more by a variety of simple cues, such as source credibility, communicator attractiveness, and celebrity endorsements (Cacioppo et al., 1996; Green et al., 2008; Haugtvedt, Petty, & Cacioppo, 1992; Kaufman, Stasson, & Hart, 1999; Priester & Petty, 1995).

Even the enthusiastic endorsement of a message by others can sway low-NFC individuals. For example, in a study conducted by Axsom, Yates, and Chaiken (1987), the experimenters manipulated—or experimentally varied—involvement, argument quality, and audience response, a peripheral cue. The peripheral cue is most relevant for the present discussion. In a key aspect of the study, both high- and low-NFC participants listened to a tape-recorded segment from a low-involvement debate on the merits of replacing probation with imprisonment. In one condition, the audience reacted with "five enthusiastic bursts of clapping and cheers of approval," while in another condition, the speech was greeted with occasional derision and the speaker's "concluding statement was met with an indifferent, barely polite smattering of applause" (Axsom et al., p. 33). Research participants were then asked to indicate their attitude toward the message recommendation. Even though an audience's enthusiastic endorsement does not mean a speech has merit, low-NFC individuals grabbed at a simple way to make a decision on the message. They supported the message recommendation when the audience enthusiastically supported the speaker, and rejected it when the audience was critical of the speaker's ideas. Click-whirr, as Cialdini (2009) would say!

To be sure, there are times when low-NFC individuals will pay close attention to the message. When the issue bears directly on their personal lives, people low in NFC will process arguments centrally. Otherwise, they gravitate to the peripheral path.

Collectively, these findings have interesting practical implications. When persuaders direct messages to individuals who they know are high in NFC, they should make certain that they employ strong arguments or make cogent appeals to respondents' values. If, on the other hand, the message is directed at low-NFC respondents, persuaders should develop appeals that don't tax these folks' mental capacities. Simple, clear appeals— the simpler, the better—are probably advisable. For example, Bakker (1999), in a study of AIDS-prevention messages, found that simple, visual safer-sex messages were highly effective for low-NFC individuals. Similar findings in different health contexts have also been reported (Braverman, 2008; Vidrine, Simmons, & Brandon, 2007; Williams-Piehota et al., 2003).

What is more, even a subtle cue can unleash differences in NFC. *The mere perception that a message is complex can produce intriguing differences* (See, Petty, & Evans, 2009.) High-NFC individuals applied mental effort when they expected a communication to be complex, but not when they thought it would be simple. Expecting the message would pleasantly engage their thought processes, they threw themselves into the task. By contrast, individuals low in need for cognition exerted cognitive energy when they thought the message would be simple, but not when they anticipated that it would be complex. Noting that the message suited their preference for simple intellectual tasks, they expended mental effort. But when they expected it would be complex, they shied away, reluctant to devote energy to a message with undue complexity.

One cautionary note: it is easy to breeze through this and (on a personal level) conclude that it is better to be high than low in NFC. That is not necessarily so. You can be high in NFC, enjoy thinking abstractly, but puzzle so long about a simple issue that you lose the forest for the trees. One could be low in NFC and get straight to the heart of the issue, without getting bogged down in excessive detail. The key for persuaders is to accept individuals for what and who they are. Communicators are more apt to be successful if they match messages to individuals' personality styles. Individuals who enjoy thinking are more likely to change their minds when they receive cogent messages that stimulate central processing. By contrast, people who make decisions based on intuition and gut feelings may be more swayed by messages that sketch a vision or tug at the heartstrings (Aune & Reynolds, 1994; Smith, 1993).

This underscores an important contribution that the ELM makes to knowledge of personality and persuasion. For many years, scholars hypothesized that certain individuals—for example, those with low self-esteem or low intelligence—were more gullible and susceptible to persuasion than others. Research indicated that this was not the case. There is not a gullible personality type, or if there is, researchers have had difficulty empirically identifying its contours. A more reasonable way to unravel the relationship between personality and personality is to follow the directives of the ELM: Take into account the different ways that individuals who are high or low in a particular personality characteristic process persuasive messages and tailor communications to fit their processing style.

ABILITY

A second determinant of processing strategy (besides motivation) is the person's ability to process the message. Situations can enhance or hamper individuals' ability to process a message. For example, people are less able to process a message when they are distracted, resulting in persuasive effects discussed earlier. More interestingly, we centrally or peripherally process messages depending on our cognitive ability, or knowledge. When individuals possess the ability to elaborate on a message, everything being equal, they gravitate to the central route. When they lack the ability to understand message arguments, they rely on heuristics and look to those slippery peripheral cues.

Consider knowledge as an example of ability. When people know a lot about an issue, they process information carefully and skillfully. They are better able to separate the rhetorical wheat from the chaff than are those with little knowledge of the issue. They are more capable of evaluating the cogency of information and are adept at identifying shortcomings in message arguments. It doesn't matter what the issue is: it could be nuclear physics, baseball, or roof repair. Knowledgeable people process information centrally and are ordinarily tough nuts for persuaders to crack (Wood, Rhodes, & Biek, 1995). By contrast, people with minimal knowledge on a topic lack the background to differentiate strong from weak arguments. They also may lack confidence in their opinions. They are the peripheral processors, frequently susceptible to peripheral cues on messages about these topics.

As an example, think of an issue you know a lot about—let's say, contemporary movies. Now conjure up a topic about which you know little—let's say, computer scanners. The ELM says that you will process persuasive messages on these topics very differently and that persuaders should use different techniques to change your mind on these topics. Given your expertise on modern films (you know all about different film techniques and the strengths and weaknesses of famous directors), there is every reason to believe you would centrally process a message that claims 1960s movies are superior to those of today. The message would grab your attention and could change your attitudes—provided it contained strong, compelling arguments.

A "rational" approach like this would be stunningly ineffective on the subject of scanners that digitize photos and convert words on a printed page into word-processing files. Given your ignorance of scanners, you would have difficulty processing technical arguments about optical character recognition, driver software, or high-resolution scans. On the other hand, the salesperson who used a peripheral approach might be highly effective. A salesperson who said she had been in the business 10 years or who furnished 10 arguments why Canon was superior to Epson might easily connect with you, perhaps changing your attitude or inducing you to buy a Canon scanner. Consistent with this logic, Wood, Kallgren, and Preisler (1985) found that argument quality had a stronger impact on attitudes among individuals with a great deal of knowledge on an issue. However, a peripheral cue, message length, exerted a stronger influence on those with little knowledge of the issue.

PERIPHERAL PROCESSING IN REAL LIFE

There is nothing as practical as a good theory, Kurt Lewin famously said. This is abundantly apparent in the case of the ELM. Once you appreciate the model, you begin to find all sorts of examples of how it is employed in everyday life. Four examples of peripheral processing follow, with an application to online persuasion offered in Box 7.2.

The Oprah Book Club Effect

For 25 years, millions of Americans watched "Oprah's Book Club," a monthly segment of *The Oprah Winfrey Show* that featured engaging discussions of recently published novels. Book club shows involved a discussion among Winfrey, the author, and several viewers, who discuss the book and its relationship to their own lives. "The show receives

BOX 7.2 ONLINE BAMBOOZLING

Your older brother's 21st birthday is a week away and you haven't bought him a gift. It is not the first time you have procrastinated. He is a computer geek, a nerd's nerd, and a devotee of the television program, *The Big Bang Theory*, because he would fit right in. You never know what to get him. You could not be more different: You are an extrovert, a people person who loves the art of conversation. So here you are sitting before your computer, cruising the web—well, careening would be a more apt description, given the speed at which your fingers are moving. How do you decide what gift to purchase? What factors convince you to choose one laptop bag over another? An engaging study by Miriam J.

◼ **Figure 7.6 People frequently shop online, purchasing products as they sit in front of their personal computers. The ELM reminds us that when people lack motivation or ability, they will make purchase decisions based on a host of heuristics and peripheral cues. In some cases, this makes them easy prey for unscrupulous online persuaders.**

Image courtesy of Shutterstock.

Continued

Metzger, Andrew J. Flanagin, and Ryan B. Medders (2010) offers some clues. The study is important because it demonstrates that the ELM has intriguing implications for self-persuasion via the Internet, thereby enlarging its explanatory scope (see Figure 7.6).

In ELM terms, you are a computer-searching shopper who is low in computer ability (at least compared with Einstein, your older sib). The ELM predicts that under conditions of low ability, consumers will base their product decisions on peripheral cues, relying on trusted heuristics to help them decide which products to purchase. In their study of 109 focus group participants from across the U.S., Metzger, Flanagin, and Medders (2010) found that individuals relied on several key heuristics when seeking product information online. Notice that each of these represents reasonable, quite rational strategies for making a choice. At the same time, as we will see, they are short-circuited rules of thumb that leave people vulnerable to commercial manipulation. The key heuristics include:

Reputation. Focus group respondents frequently indicated that they relied on the reputation of a Web site. When low in involvement and ability, people may base judgments on the perceived credibility of a brand rather than on conscientious thinking about the content of the site. As one San Antonio, Texas respondent explained, "if it's a government Web site or if it's a big company like CNN, they've already established their credibility and so . . . you're gonna be more trusting of it" (p. 426).

Endorsement. Participants trust Internet sources that are recommended by others or have garnered a great deal of favorable feedback. One Cleveland respondent noted that when looking for toys for children, "I just look and see which ones got five stars and I buy it for them . . . If 200,000 people buy that game, it must be a good game" (p. 427).

Consistency. Consumers may also superficially evaluate the consistency of information across Web sites as a way of making decisions. A Boston consumer disclosed that, "you go to so many different Web sites for the same thing, that if you find they're all basically saying the same thing then you tend to believe that they're credible and what they're saying is the truth" (p. 428).

The catch is this: Just because a site has a strong reputation, ringing endorsements, or is consistent with other sites does not mean the information it contains is true or valid. People can be fooled by the patina of credibility and illusion of social proof (Cialdini, 2009). What's more, companies sometimes use computer tricks to elevate themselves to the top of a search engine, a procedure called "black hat optimization." They may buy links for terms they want to associate with their product. Observers suspected that J. C. Penney had employed these tactics, as the store appeared regularly at the Number One spot when people searched Google for dresses, bedding, and area rugs, products that are not ordinarily associated with Penney's (Segal, 2011). By gaming the system, Penney's may have elevated its prestige, encouraging people to think of the store when turning to time-honored heuristics.

It is not just Penney's that employs these kinds of strategies. Conniving entrepreneurs regularly sell five-star reviews to companies. "For $5, I will submit two great reviews for your business," one poster wrote on a help-for-hire site (Streitfeld, 2011).

As a consequence of such techniques, you, who are looking with great speed but little knowledge for a gift for your brother, may end up buying a clunker of a computer product from a company which has successfully manipulated the psychology of peripheral cues.

as many as 10,000 letters each month from people eager to participate," a reporter related,

> By the time the segment appears, 500,000 viewers have read at least part of the novel. Nearly as many buy the book in the weeks that follow . . . Oprah's Book Club has been responsible for 28 consecutive best sellers. It has sold more than 20 million books and made many of its authors millionaires.
>
> (Max, 1999, pp. 36–37)

"Oprah's Book Club" has been a great thing for books and publishing. It is also an example of peripheral processing in action. What convinces hundreds of thousands of people to buy these novels? What persuades them to purchase Wally Lamb's *She's Come Undone*, the story of an intelligent, overweight woman who overcomes problems stemming from sexual abuse, rather than an equally compelling novel about abuse and redemption? The answer, in a word, is Oprah. Her credibility, warmth, and celebrity status suggest to viewers that the book is worth a try. It is not that audience members are meticulously comparing one book with another, opting to integrate Oprah's advice with their literary assessments of the plot and character development. They lack motivation and perhaps ability. So, they rely on Oprah's advice and purchase the book, much to the delight of the publishing house and struggling novelist. (See Figure 7.7.)

■ **Figure 7.7 Oprah Winfrey is a charismatic, credible communicator. Her endorsement of a book on "Oprah's Book Club" can serve as a powerful peripheral cue, persuading some consumers to buy the book just on the basis of her say-so.**

Image courtesy of Shutterstock.

Oprah as peripheral cue can also work to the detriment of an author. When she criticizes an author, as she did after discovering that James Frey had fabricated much of *A Million Little Pieces*—a book once touted on her book club—sales of the book plummet. As one critic put it, "Fool millions, make millions. Fool Oprah, lord help you" (Carr, 2006, p. C1). With the book club now a regular program on her new network, the stage is set for the continued impact of peripheral cues.

The Electoral Road Show

To many Americans, politics is like a traveling road show, a circus that the media cover every four years, complete with clowns, midgets, and daredevils who will do just about anything to win the crowd's approval. Politics does not affect them personally—or so many believe. About half of the electorate votes in presidential elections, and many are cynical about the political process (Doppelt & Shearer, 1999).

Feeling cynical about politics and blasé about their participation, large numbers of voters put little mental energy into the vote decision. Instead, they process politics peripherally, if at all. When it comes time to cast their vote, low-involved voters frequently consider such peripheral cues as:

- *Candidate appearance.* Although people hate to admit it, they are influenced by candidates' physical appeal (Budesheim & DePaola, 1994; Rosenberg & McCafferty, 1987). In some cases, low-involved voters watch a physically attractive candidate, feel positively, and connect their positive affect with the candidate when it comes time to cast their vote. Or they may decide that the attractive candidate just looks presidential.

- *Endorsements.* Political ads frequently contain long lists of endorsements. Names of well-known groups—for example, the American Bar Association, Fraternal Order of Police, and National Organization for Women—as well as not-so-famous organizations appear on a television screen, while the voice-over praises the candidate. The list serves as a peripheral cue, inviting the inference that "if all these groups give their endorsement, that candidate has got to be qualified."

- *Names.* In low-involving elections, the name of the candidate can make a difference. Voters prefer candidates whose names they have heard many times, in part because such names have positive associations (Grush, McKeough, & Ahlering, 1978). In an Illinois primary election, two candidates with relatively smooth-sounding names (Fairchild and Hart) defeated candidates with less pleasant-sounding names (Sangmeister and Pucinksi). Many voters were probably shocked to discover that Mark Fairchild and Janice Hart were followers of the extremist and unconventional political candidate Lyndon LaRouche (O'Sullivan et al. 1988)! How, voters must have wondered, could candidates with such nice names like *Fairchild* and *Hart* be members of such an unfriendly, weird political group? But they were!

What do attractiveness, slogans, endorsements, and name sound have to do with a candidate's qualifications for office? Not too much: they are peripheral to the main issues of the campaign. Yet low-involved voters often rely on these cues and can be swayed by superficial appeals. This in turn raises troubling questions about the role communications play in contemporary democracy.

Jargon

Has this ever happened to you? Your car engine is on the blink; you take the auto to the mechanic; he (they're usually guys) looks at you with an expression that says, "You're clueless about cars, aren't you?" and then puts his hands to his hips and begins to talk in tongues—invoking the most complicated car jargon you have ever heard. Impressed by the verbiage and afraid to admit you don't know much about cars, you acquiesce to his appeal (see Figure 7.8).

Tom and Ray Magliozzi, hosts of the National Public Radio show *Car Talk*, echoed this point in a humorous but telling article. Asked by an interviewer how someone could fake being a car mechanic, they recommend a heavy use of jargon (Nitze, 2001). Use

■ Figure 7.8 **A car mechanic can try to persuade a customer to make a much-needed car repair, using many different arguments. When the customer lacks involvement in the decision or does not know much about cars, the mechanic may pull the wool over the customer's eyes by using fancy-sounding car jargon or words like "negative torque."**

Image courtesy of Shutterstock.

words like "the torque wrench and torquing," Tom says. Ray replies, "Torquing always sounds good." Tom adds, "I'll bet you, you could walk into some party and mention the expression 'negative torque,' there would be nobody who would have the guts to ask you what that meant. A pro included" (p. 38).

This fits right in with the ELM. Individuals with little knowledge about car mechanics have trouble following explanations involving torque or car computer systems. When a mechanic begins using the jargon, they invoke the heuristic, "Mechanics who talk this way know their stuff; if they say this, it must be so." And, just like that, the mechanic persuades these customers to make the purchase. (A similar example comes from the movie *My Cousin Vinny*, when the character played by Marisa Tomei wows a judge and jury, using jargon comprehensible only to car experts to prove that a getaway car could not possibly have been driven by the two men accused of the crime.)

Seduced by a Quick Fix

How were countless Americans lured into purchasing mortgages they could not afford? Over the course of a decade—from about 1998 to 2008—home buyers across the country signed their names on legally binding documents, committing themselves to purchase homes at prices that were too good to be true. With details complicated and technical terms (like variable rate loans and adjustable rate mortgages) reeling in their minds, many buyers put their trust in lenders. Big mistake.

The ELM reminds us that when individuals lack ability on an issue, they resort to the peripheral route, accepting a message because a credible source recommends it. Unfortunately, some credible bank loan officers were all too eager to pitch crooked messages. Under pressure from their bosses to approve mortgages so that the bank could amass huge profits, the lending agents frequently pulled out all stops, offering loans to buyers who they knew could not afford the monthly payments. Executives at one bank, Washington Mutual, were particularly eager to exploit (they would say "convince") borrowers who lacked adequate credit.

Washington Mutual relied heavily on adjustable rate mortgages that functioned as the financial equivalent of smoke and mirrors. Unschooled in the fine points of adjustable mortgages, home buyers were enticed by the promise that they could decide how much their house payment would cost each month. There was a catch: borrowers who chose to make small monthly payments were underpaying interest due on the loan, while adding to the principal—the actual amount of money lent by the bank. In the long run, this caused loan payments to skyrocket (Goodman & Morgenson, 2008, p. A21). One elderly couple found their housing costs rose from about $1,000 to $3,000 a month, leading them to fall behind in their monthly payments.

On the other hand, no one put a gun to borrowers' heads. They freely chose to accept the terms of the loan, relying on peripheral credibility cues, while discounting their responsibility to study payment arrangements. Yet bank executives knew they were making shaky loans and encouraged loan officers to ignore their fiduciary responsibilities.

"If you were alive, they would give you a loan. Actually, I think if you were dead, they would still give you a loan," one banking expert said (Goodman & Morgenson, 2008).

The upshot of all this is that peripheral persuasion can be harnessed for a variety of ethically nefarious purposes. There are a host of issues and conundrums that come up. Although there are no easy answers, the problems are worth pondering. Box 7.3 offers some perspectives.

BOX 7.3 ETHICS OF PERIPHERAL CUES

Peripheral persuasion raises ethical questions. Is it ethical to employ glib appeals, the trappings of slick jargon, and computer gimmicks? Is it even more ethically problematic to use these techniques when people lack involvement or ability?

From a Kantian perspective, the use of such peripheral cues is immoral. They are lies that disrespect individuals, treating them as a means to the persuader's goal, not dignified ends in and of themselves. Utilitarians would adopt a more measured perspective. They would weigh the good that comes from allowing marketers to develop self-interested appeals that promote useful products against the bad that flows from deception. The Federal Trade Commission, which regulates advertising, has specific rules about **advertising deception**. If an ad contains a misleading claim that could influence the consumer's product decision, it may be deceptive. A message must be stated so that a reasonable person can appreciate the marketer's intent (see discussion in Chapter 13).

You could argue that low-involved, even low-ability, consumers understand that advertising uses a host of sly gimmicks to sell products and they can reasonably appreciate the persuader's intent. But you could also assert that marketing messages prey on their vulnerability, inducing them to form false beliefs about the product. Although peripheral appeals are hardly illegal, they are frequently manipulative, designed, if not to deceive consumers, to trick them into ignoring certain features of the product in favor of others, hoping to goad them to accept the message based on promises that the product or service cannot fulfill.

More devious issues have arisen with the Internet. As critic Eli Pariser (2011a) notes:

> Today, most recommendations and targeting systems focus on the products: Commerce sites analyze our consumption patterns and use that info to figure out that, say, viewers of *Iron Man* also watch *The Dark Knight* . . . But new work . . . suggests that there's another factor that can be brought into play. Retailers could not only personalize which products are shown, they could personalize the way they're pitched too.

Pariser suggests that online persuaders can now direct different persuasive appeals to customers until they find the individual's particular vulnerabilities. For example, they could examine whether an individual falls prey to pitches that hype the credibility of the source, ones that appeal to peer pressure, or ELM-type strategies that emphasize message processing. Once online marketers determine the particular type of appeal to which the customer succumbs, they could pitch similar online appeals to the individual in the future. Now, in fairness we do not know how common these techniques are and if they actually work. Besides, consumers might figure them out—perhaps tipped off by online blogs that revealed them—and adopt appropriate defenses. As Pariser notes, "the first line of defense is to know that persuasion profiling is on the way, keep an eye out for it, and view marketing arguments with the skepticism they deserve."

CENTRAL PROCESSING

Peripheral processing is a persuader's paradise. It allows communicators to devise simplistic—sometimes deceptive—appeals to influence individuals. Tempting as it is to conclude that this is the basis for all contemporary persuasion, the fact is that much persuasion also involves careful, thoughtful consideration of message arguments. As discussed earlier, when people are motivated or able to process messages, they do not rely exclusively on peripheral cues or necessarily fall for a persuader's ploys. Instead, they attend closely to the communicator's arguments. In these situations, persuasion flows through the central route, and appeals are necessarily crafted at a higher intellectual level.

Attitudes changed through deep, central-route thinking are more likely to persist over time than those formed through short-circuited thinking or peripheral cues (Petty, Haugtvedt, & Smith, 1995). Integrated into the individual's overall cognitive structure, linked with a person's self-concept, and relatively accessible from memory, centrally processed attitudes tend to be resistant to change. This is an important point. It suggests that, once formed through central processing, attitudes endure. This is bad when the attitude is prejudice, and good when the attitude is tolerance toward different groups.

On an everyday level, central processing is ordinarily in operation when people buy big-ticket, high-involvement products like wedding rings, cars, and, of course, houses: They respond to cogent arguments in support of the particular product in question. In politics, when voters are out of work or concerned about the economy, they listen closely to candidates' plans to revitalize the nation's finances. For example, way back in the dark ages of 1980, with the U.S. reeling from double-digit inflation, Ronald Reagan made the economy a centerpiece of his campaign against then-president Jimmy Carter. "Are you better off than you were 4 years ago?" he asked Americans in a presidential debate. Reagan went on to suggest that many folks were worse off than they had been prior to Carter's taking office. In posing the question this way, Reagan induced people to think seriously about their own economic situations and at the same time to give his challenge to an incumbent president dutiful consideration. His appeals apparently worked, for Reagan handily defeated Carter in the November election (Ritter & Henry, 1994).

Arguments, however, do not always carry the day in persuasion. Cogent arguments can fall on deaf ears when they run counter to an individual's strong attitudes or values. Recall the discussion in Chapter 4 of how passionate supporters and opponents of the death penalty reacted to evidence that questioned their position. They did not alter their attitudes. On the contrary, they criticized data that disputed their point of view, praised evidence that supported their position, and emerged with renewed confidence that their view on capital punishment was correct. How could this be, one wonders, if people are supposed to consider arguments rationally when they are interested in the issue in question?

The answer points to a complexity in the ELM. All central-route processing is not rational and free of bias. Human beings are not objective thinkers. The key is the degree to which the issue touches on an individual's strong attitudes, values, or ego-entrenched positions. It is useful to distinguish between issues that are of interest because they bear on important outcomes in the individual's life—comprehensive exams, tuition increases, the economy—and those that bear on values or deep-seated attitudes. When the message focuses on a personally relevant outcome, people process arguments rationally, putting aside their biases as best they can, focusing on the merits of issue arguments. However, when the issue touches on core values or *ego-involved* schema, individuals can be extremely biased and selective in how they approach the issue.

Make no mistake: in both cases, they process centrally, engaging in considerable thinking and evaluating the basic ideas contained in the message. However, when thinking about outcomes (a comprehensive exam), they are open to cogent arguments. When considering a message that touches on core values (capital punishment, abortion), they attend to the opponent's arguments, but usually reject them (Johnson & Eagly, 1989; Wood et al., 1985, though see Park et al., 2007). Highly knowledgeable people with strong attitudes will muster all sorts of sophisticated reasons why the opponent's plan is a bad one. They will impress you with their ability to remember the other side's arguments, but in the end they will prove to be just as biased as anyone else. In these situations, people behave like ostriches, stubbornly rejecting ideas that are inconsistent with their attitude and sticking only with communications with which they already agree.

Central Processing and Persuasion

What does this suggest for persuasion? It tells us that when individuals are considering a personally relevant outcome, persuaders should direct them through the central route, harnessing arguments and cogent appeals. When the message touches on core values, persuaders must be careful, cognizant of the psychological mine-fields that could explode in their face. When individuals have strong attitudes, they engage in biased processing. In this arena, social judgment theory, described in Chapter 4, offers useful suggestions. Persuaders must be political, mindful that a strident message could land them in the latitude of rejection. They need to avoid hot-button issues. Instead, they want to encourage recipients to assimilate their arguments and view them as a friend, not a foe. They want to offer strong arguments that fall within audience members' latitudes of acceptance.

In politics, when addressing high-involvement voters with strong attitudes, a candidate does not try to change attitudes so much as convince voters that he or she shares voters' positions on the issues. In general elections, politicians frequently moderate their stands to attract a heterogeneous block of voters. This, of course, is one of the things people do not like about politics. They feel that politicians equivocate, never take positions on issues, and take poll-driven positions. Unfortunately, such moderation is necessary if a candidate would rather, to paraphrase the 19th-century American politician Henry Clay, be president than right.

Complexities, Complexities: The Multiple Functions Postulate

This section examines a particularly tricky, but intriguing, aspect of the ELM. Petty and Cacioppo introduced the ELM more than a quarter-century ago. The theory has been lavishly praised, but it has also stimulated considerable discussion, debate, criticism, and, yes, elaborations.

A key issue involves the ability of a particular variable to do different things or serve diverse functions. Consider physical attractiveness. If you had to describe the role physical attractiveness plays in persuasion, based on the earlier discussions, you might suggest that it serves as a peripheral cue. You might speculate that when people do not care much about an issue or lack ability to process the message, they fall back on the physical appeal of the speaker. Opting not to process the message carefully, they let themselves get carried away a bit by the speaker's good looks. This analysis of attractiveness is indeed in sync with the ELM as it has been discussed thus far. Attractiveness frequently has just this effect, serving as a cue for peripheral processing.

Unfortunately, matters become more complicated when we examine other persuasion settings. For example, suppose a young woman is systematically searching for a beauty product, flips through the pages of *Glamour* magazine, and sees models promoting L'Oréal and Cover Girl lipcolors. The models' good looks represent key selling points for the products. Isn't a model's attractiveness central to the decision regarding the product, not peripheral? Couldn't the physical appeal of the model—the fact that she is beautiful and uses this product—serve as a compelling reason to purchase the particular facial cream, lipcolor, or makeup? Didn't endorsements by Jessica Simpson and Katy Perry constitute central arguments that buttressed the case for purchasing the acne medicine, Proactiv? The answer to these questions is "Yes."

The ELM argues that, theoretically, a particular variable can serve in one of a variety of capacities. For someone conscientiously comparing two beauty products, the communicator's attractiveness can serve as an *argument* for one of the products (Kahle & Homer, 1985).

In another context—electoral politics—attractiveness can function as a *peripheral cue*, as when a low-involved voter decides to vote for a candidate because she likes his facial features and he is taller than his opponent.

Consider a third situation involving a different aspect of politics. Let's say a person has mixed feelings on environmental and energy issues. He believes that the United States needs to locate alternative sources of fuel, but also feels it is important to preserve breathtakingly beautiful wildlife refuges. When an attractive source like actor Robert Redford (2001) criticizes policies to drill for oil in the Arctic National Wildlife Refuge, he may find himself *devoting more cognitive energy* to the communicator's arguments. He may picture Redford in his mind, link up his attractive appearance with the beauty of the wilderness, and therefore give his arguments more thought than if a less attractive communicator had advanced these positions.

Similarly, when a beautiful actress like Cate Blanchett lends her name to environmental causes, such as conservation, individuals who are ambivalent about the issue may wonder why Blanchett has signed on to environmental issues. They may picture her, think about her movies, and, impelled by curiosity or enchantment, consider arguments on behalf of the environment just a little more thoughtfully.

Thus, attractiveness can serve as a cue, a persuasive argument, and a catalyst to thinking. There is a fourth role that a source factor like attractiveness can play too. It can enhance or reduce message receivers' confidence in the quality of their thoughts about a persuasive message. Petty and his colleagues showed that when a message produces primarily positive thoughts, increasing confidence in these thoughts enhances persuasion (Petty, Brinol, & Tormala, 2002). This suggests that when people have mostly positive thoughts about a message *and* they are confident in the quality of those thoughts, they are especially likely to change their attitudes. A confident, charismatic, attractive persuader may be particularly effective in convincing receivers to change their minds because she subtly induces audience members to feel good about themselves, thereby inducing them to have confidence in their own thoughts about the message. A less attractive persuader may fail to change attitudes because he causes message recipients to doubt the quality of their thoughts. The first persuader therefore changes attitudes, while the second increases resistance.

Consider another example of multiple functions, focusing on a different environmental issue: global warming. Some Americans are unaware of evidence that the world is hotter now than it has been at any point in the last 2,000 years. Suppose a reputable Web site called "Feeling the Heat" presents a list of credible scientists who declare that there is incontrovertible evidence that significant global warming is occurring (Easterbrook, 2006). The Web site has the imprimatur of the National Academy of Sciences. The opinions of scientists on this issue can be influential. What does the ELM say about the role played by credibility here?

The model says credibility will perform multiple functions, depending on elaboration likelihood.

The scientists' expertise can serve as a *peripheral cue* for people low in concern or knowledge about environmental issues. These folks may say to themselves, "Who knows what's going on with the environment these days? It's beyond me. I'll go with what the scientists say. If they say this, it must be right."

For those with considerable knowledge and concern about the environment, the scientists' views may actually function as an *argument*. These highly involved individuals may think:

> I know the scientific community had been reluctant to declare that temperatures are artificially rising or that carbon dioxide emissions are responsible for global warming. If scientists have changed their tune now, it must be that there is strong evidence that global warming effects are real.

To other individuals, with moderate knowledge or involvement, the scientists' proclamations about global warming may *stimulate issue-relevant thinking*. They may consider the issue more carefully now that the National Academy of Sciences, as well as scientific academies across the world, have concluded that significant global warming is occurring across the planet. They may not change their minds, especially if they have strong views on this issue. However, the highly credible-source endorsement might catalyze their thinking, leading them to develop more detailed arguments on global warming.

In addition, expert scientists speaking on the global warming issue could affect higher-involved audience members' attitudes by *bolstering their confidence in their own thoughts about the message.* After hearing the expert scientists speak in favor of global warming, people might come to evaluate their own cognitive responses more favorably. They might think: "Gee, the speaker made really good arguments. The more I think about this, the more confident I feel that that global warming is a serious problem."

In this way, a particular variable can serve multiple functions. Source, message, and receiver factors are not one-dimensional, but multi-faceted. Just as an attitude can serve different functions for different people, so too a persuasion factor can play different roles in different situations.

In sum, the multiple functions postulate states that a particular factor can play different roles, such as serving as: (1) a peripheral cue under low elaboration likelihood (low motivation and ability) circumstances; (2) a persuasive argument when elaboration likelihood is high; (3) a catalyst to thinking when ability or motivation is moderate; and (4) a determinant of confidence in one's thoughts about the message, when there is greater likelihood of elaboration.

The ELM is complicated because people are complex. (For a summary of its main theoretical emphases, see Box 7.4.)

CRITICISMS AND RECONCILIATIONS

Any academic model that has been around for a while will stimulate ideas—and controversy. This is as it should be: theories are meant to be criticized and subjected to empirical scrutiny. Knowledge advances from the dueling of conflicting scholarly guns. New ideas emerge from the critical exchange of points of view.

The ELM has elicited its share of criticism, with bullets targeted at the multiple functions notion previously discussed. Critics have lamented the lack of clarity of this notion. They have argued that the ELM position permits it "to explain all possible outcomes," making it impossible in principle to prove the model wrong (Stiff & Boster, 1987, p. 251). "A persuader can conduct a post mortem to find out what happened but cannot forecast the impact of a particular message," Allen and Preiss contend (1997a, pp. 117–118).

Proponents of the ELM have thundered back, arguing that critics fail to appreciate the model's strengths (Petty et al., 1987; Petty et al., 1993). As a general rule, proponents note, individuals will be more likely to elaborate on messages when they are high in

BOX 7.4 UNDERSTANDING THEORY: PRIMER ON THE ELM

1. The Elaboration Likelihood Model (ELM) argues that you cannot appreciate persuasion without understanding the underlying processes by which messages affect attitudes.
2. The model stipulates that the likelihood of elaborating on, or thinking carefully about, a message depends on individuals' motivation and ability.
3. As a dual-process model, the ELM asserts that there are two routes to persuasion: central, characterized by careful thinking about the message, and peripheral, exemplified by a focus on simple cues and simple decision-making rules or heuristics that are irrelevant to the main arguments in the message.
4. Attitude changes that result from central processing persist longer and are more likely to predict behavior than peripherally induced attitude changes.
5. There is evidence that under low motivation—such as when people lack involvement in the issue—peripheral cues are persuasive. Under high motivational conditions—for example, when individuals are high in involvement—central processing occurs, with strong arguments significantly influencing attitudes. Similar findings have occurred under low- and high-ability conditions.
6. A particular persuasion factor can serve in different capacities. It can function as a peripheral cue, argument, catalyst to thinking, or a factor that enhances or reduces confidence in one's cognitive responses to a message. This is the multiple functions postulate that showcases the complexity and flexibility of the model.
7. A shortcoming of the ELM is its inability to specify the type of message that will be maximally effective under high involvement, or high elaboration likelihood.
8. The model's strength is its process-oriented approach, which sheds light on persuasion. The ELM, with the Heuristic-Systematic Model, offers a unified, integrative framework to guide persuasion.

motivation or ability, and more inclined to focus on peripheral cues when they are lower in ability or motivation. What's more, they say, if you understand the particular variable under investigation and the situation in which it operates, you can make clear predictions about the influences of persuasion factors on attitudes (Haugtvedt & Wegener, 1994; Petty & Wegener, 1998). Persuasion and human behavior are so complex, ELM proponents assert, that it is not possible to make precise predictions for every variable in each and every situation. On balance, they maintain, the ELM offers a highly useful framework for understanding how persuasion works in the panoply of situations in which it occurs in everyday life.

Both sides have a point. The multiple functions notion discussed earlier is intriguing, but it points to a problematic ambiguity in the model: the ELM is so all inclusive that it is difficult to prove the model incorrect. We want hypotheses to be capable of being proven right—and wrong.

The ELM has other limitations. It does not clearly specify the type of message that persuaders should employ under high involvement. The only advice the model offers is that communicators should induce audience members to generate positive thoughts on behalf of the message. But what type of message should you employ? How should you frame your message to get people thinking positively? Just what constitutes a high-quality, strong argument in the ELM? The model is silent on these matters, as Frymier and Nadler (2011) helpfully point out. The model has other shortcomings. It lumps a variety of peripheral processes under the same umbrella, when one might plausibly argue that certain cues are more effective than others.

Nevertheless, no theory is perfect, and the ELM has done a great deal for the field of persuasion research. It has illuminated the psychological reasons why communications can powerfully influence attitudes. It has linked cognitive processes to communication effects in a coherent way. These are important contributions, ones that should not be minimized. Before the ELM (and the Heuristic-Systematic Model, see Box 7.5) was formulated, there were few in-depth approaches to understanding cognitive processing and persuasive communication. There was a hodgepodge of results—findings about this type of communicator, that type of message, and this kind of message recipient. It was like a jigsaw puzzle that didn't quite fit together. The ELM has helped provide us with a coherent perspective to understand the blooming, buzzing confusion of persuasion, offering a framework for understanding the psychology of persuasive communication. It has helped explain why different messages are effective in different circumstances, while also debunking the simple notion that a particular factor can affect attitudes through one path (O'Keefe, 2013). More than 25 years after it was introduced, the model continues to offer insights, adapting its predictions to new areas, such as implicit attitudes, while also offering guidance to practitioners in areas ranging from marketing to health promotion (Petty, Barden, & Wheeler, 2009).

BOX 7.5 THE HEURISTIC-SYSTEMATIC MODEL

The Heuristic-Systematic Model (HSM) complements the Elaboration Likelihood Model. It too has generated a great deal of research. No discussion on persuasion would be complete without discussing its main features.

Like the ELM, the HSM says that motivation and ability determine processing strategy. But while the ELM says the main purpose of message processing is to develop an accurate attitude in tune with reality, the HSM takes a broader approach (Dillard, 2010). It emphasizes that people can be motivated by a need to hold accurate attitudes, but also by defensive needs to maintain attitudes that bear on the self-concept, or desire to make a positive impression on others (Chen & Chaiken, 1999).

Like the ELM, the HSM emphasizes that there are two processes by which persuasion occurs. Instead of calling the routes central and peripheral, it speaks of systematic and heuristic processing. Systematic processing entails comprehensive consideration of issue-relevant arguments. Heuristic processing, discussed earlier in this chapter, involves the use of cognitive shortcuts.

A major contribution of the HSM is its suggestion that simple decision rules or heuristics play an important role in attitude change. People are viewed as "minimalist information processors" who are unwilling to devote much effort to processing persuasive arguments (Stiff, 1994). They like their shortcuts and they use them frequently in everyday life. Even so, there are some conditions under which people will gravitate to a systematic processing mode, and individuals seek a balance between relying on shortcuts and carefully processing a message.

The HSM, interestingly, emphasizes that heuristic and systematic processes are not mutually exclusive. Instead, it says that, under certain circumstances, people can rely on heuristics and systematically process a message (Eagly & Chaiken, 1993; Todorov et al., 2002).

The HSM stipulates that two principles govern cognitive processing of persuasive messages. The first is the *least effort principle*, which stipulates that "people prefer less effortful to more effortful modes of information processing" (Eagly & Chaiken, 1993, p. 330). They frequently reject systematic processing in favor of heuristic decision making.

Continued

The second principle is an outgrowth of the recognition that people seek to balance their desire to minimize thinking, on the one hand, with a need to satisfy various situational objectives, such as holding accurate attitudes, defending important opinions, and conveying socially acceptable beliefs. The *sufficiency principle* stipulates that "people will exert whatever effort is required to attain a 'sufficient' degree of confidence that they have satisfactorily accomplished their processing goals" (Eagly & Chaiken, 1993, p. 330). However, once they are confident that they have developed an attitude that advances their goals, they typically quit processing the message and move on to another task.

Despite their differences, both models emphasize that there are two fundamentally different ways to process a persuasive message. They maintain that people use one of these two routes, depending on how much they care about the issue and how capable they are of understanding the topic at hand.

Although most researchers like the idea of two different routes to persuasion, there are dissenters. Arie W. Kruglanski and Erik P. Thompson (1999) have argued that it is easier to think of just one pathway to persuasion; the key is how extensively people process information. However, these researchers also emphasize that you can't appreciate the effects of persuasion without understanding the process. Or you can't understand the message without appreciating the mind.

CONCLUSIONS

Early persuasion research tested some of the ideas about sources and messages that Aristotle developed centuries before. The Yale Attitude Change approach offered some of the first hard-nosed experimental tests of persuasion hypotheses. The cognitive response approach refined the Yale studies by calling attention to the role that cognitive responses play in persuasion, particularly in forewarning, distraction, and, later, inoculation. These studies paved the way for dual-process models of persuasion.

We can trace dual-process models to ancient Greece. Plato's ideal thinkers epitomized systematic, deep processing of persuasive messages; some of the Sophist writers (at least as depicted by Plato) embodied the colorful, stylistic appeals we associate with the peripheral route. Contemporary models, attempting to explain a very different world of persuasion than that which bedeviled the Greeks, hark back to the duality that preoccupied Plato in the 4th century BC.

Contemporary models stipulate that there are two routes to persuasion—one thoughtful, focusing on the main arguments in the message, the other superficial and short circuited, characterized by an attempt to make a quick choice, an easy fix. The ELM and HSM, building on the Yale Attitude Change and Cognitive Response approaches, offer insights about how people process messages in many situations. Motivation and ability determine processing strategy. Processing route, in turn, determines the type of message appeal that is maximally effective in a particular context, as well as the long-term effects of the message on attitudes. In other words, if you understand the factors impinging on someone and how he or she thinks about a persuasive message, you have a good chance of devising a message that will target the individual's attitudes.

Complications arise when we consider that persuasion factors perform multiple functions. A particular factor can serve as a cue, an argument, a catalyst to thought, or a stimulus that bolsters confidence in one's mental reactions to a persuasive message. The multiple functions notion helps explain a variety of persuasion effects; however, its ambiguity can frustrate attempts to derive clear applications of the ELM to real-life situations. Like other psychological approaches, the model does not always clearly explain how an understanding of people's thought processes can help persuaders to generate specific messages.

Yet there is much to praise in the ELM's approach. Viewed broadly, it provides an integrative framework for understanding persuasion and provides practitioners with ideas for designing effective appeals (see Box 7.6). In essence, the model tells persuaders—in areas ranging from politics to health—to understand how their audiences approach and process messages. The ELM cautions against confrontation. Instead, it instructs communicators to tailor their arguments to audience members' motives and abilities.

From an ethical perspective, the model is value neutral. Use of heuristics can help people make efficient decisions when they lack time or resources. But peripheral cues can also mislead individuals, tricking them into buying products they do not need. Centrally processing arguments can lead to more thoughtful, reasoned decisions. However, when individuals have strong biases, such processing can reinforce prejudices, reducing openness to different points of view.

As a psychological theory, rather than a normative approach, the model does not tell us whether the motivation to carefully consider message arguments under high personal involvement balances out the drawbacks of biased, dogmatic processing or susceptibility to manipulation under low involvement. It would seem as if the most pragmatic way to resolve these conundrums is to hold persuaders responsible for their violations of ethical principles, but also remember that we are responsible for persuasive decisions we make.

BOX 7.6 PERSUASION TIPS

One of the nifty things about the ELM is that it contains practical, as well as theoretical, suggestions. Here are several suggestions for everyday persuasion, gleaned from the model:

1. As you prepare a presentation, ask yourself if the topic is one that engages the audience or is one of little consequence. Does the audience care a lot about the issue? Or is it of little personal relevance? If it is a high-involvement issue, you should make sure you prepare strong arguments and get the audience thinking. If it is a low-involvement matter, you should emphasize peripheral cues, simple strategies, and ways to bolster the audience's confidence that you know your stuff. But in either case, make sure you deliver your message ethically and with respect for moral values.

2. Next time you are trying to convince someone of something, you should ask yourself: What is central, or most critical, to my attempt to change the other's mind? What type of appeal will serve my goal best? For example, people are frequently scared of giving a public speech and assume that the most important thing is to look nice—buy fancy clothes, put on lots of makeup, and so forth. This can be an important aspect of persuasion, but it may be peripheral to the task. If you are trying to make a sale, you need compelling arguments that the purchase is in the client's interest. If you are trying to convince people to get more exercise, you must show them that exercise can help them achieve their goals.

By the same token, remember that something that appears peripheral to you may be of considerable importance to the person you are trying to convince (Soldat, Sinclair, & Mark, 1997). You may spend a lot of time coming up with great arguments to convince neighbors to sign a petition against McDonald's building a new franchise near a beautiful park located down the block. But if your memo has a couple of typos or your Web site containing the message is overloaded with information, people may think a little less of you. They may jump to the conclusion that your arguments are flawed. To you, the typos or abundance of information are of much less consequence than the cogency of your arguments. And you may be right. But what is peripheral to you can be central to someone else. Put yourself in the minds of those receiving your message, and consider how they will react to what you say and how you package your message.

It is our responsibility to recognize that we take mental shortcuts when we care or know little about an issue and persuaders may exploit this tendency. In the end, it is our responsibility to protect ourselves from the peripheral persuaders of the world.

Test your knowledge now with interactive exercises

Chapter 8

"Who Says It": Source Factors in Persuasion

 Listen now to the author's chapter summary

Charisma. It is a word that comes to mind frequently when people speak of persuasion. You probably think of great speakers, a certain magnetic quality, or perhaps people you know who seem to embody this trait. Charisma is also one of those "god-terms" in persuasion (Weaver, 1953)—concepts that have positive connotations, but have been used for good and evil purposes. We can glimpse this in the tumultuous events of the 20th century, events that were shaped in no small measure by the power of charismatic leaders. We can also observe this in speeches delivered by orators in the 21st century, speeches that influenced political history. For example:

On July 27, 2004, a little-known state senator from Illinois, Barack Obama, rocked the Democratic national convention in Boston, delivering a keynote speech that propelled him to his party's nomination four years later and sent ripples of change through the system. He spoke forcefully and with poise. His syntax, sentence structure, and clever turns of a phrase captured the delegates' attention. "His height, his prominent sober head, (and) his long arms" lent him "a commanding aura." His voice, "with its oratorical cadences," boomed (Messud, 2008, p. 49). Calling on time-honored myths rooted deeply in the American experience and harnessing the power of language, Obama transported the audience to a higher place. After paying tribute to American individualism, he spoke of "another ingredient in the American saga, a belief that we are all connected as one people." Offering up several emotional examples, he intoned:

> Now even as we speak, there are those who are preparing to divide us, the spin masters and negative ad peddlers who embrace the politics of anything goes. Well, I say to them tonight, there's not a liberal America and a conservative America; there's the United States of America. There's not a Black America and White America and Latino America and Asian America; there's the United States of America. The pundits, the pundits like to slice and dice our country into red states and blue states; red states for Republicans, blue states for Democrats. But I've got

news for them, too. We worship an awesome God in the blue states, and we don't like federal agents poking around our libraries in the red states. We coach Little League in the blue states and, yes, we've got some gay friends in the red states. There are patriots who opposed the war in Iraq, and there are patriots who supported the war in Iraq. We are one people, all of us pledging allegiance to the stars and stripes, all of us defending the United States of America (see http://www.washingtonpost.com/wp-dyn/articles/A19751-2004Jul27.html).

As president, Obama returned to this theme. Faced with the daunting demands of governing, his words did not always change attitudes. However, even his opponents acknowledged his ability to move audiences with his oratorical skills.

Obama followed in the footsteps of another charismatic orator, Reverend Martin Luther King, Jr., whose words had inspired a movement. On August 28, 1963, King delivered his most famous address.

On that day, hundreds of thousands of people converged on Washington, DC, protesting racial prejudice and hoping to place pressure on Congress to pass a civil rights bill. The protesters marched from the Washington Monument to the Lincoln Memorial, listening to a litany of distinguished speakers, but waiting patiently for King to address the crowd. King had worked all night on his speech, a sermonic address that would prove to be among the most moving of all delivered on American soil. He alluded to Abraham Lincoln, called on Old Testament prophets, and presented "an entire inventory of patriotic themes and images typical of Fourth of July oratory," captivating the audience with his exclamation, repeated time and again, that "I have a dream" (Miller, 1992, p. 143). King's wife, Coretta Scott King, recalls the pantheon:

> Two hundred and fifty thousand people applauded thunderously, and voiced in a sort of chant, Martin Luther King . . . He started out with the written speech, delivering it with great eloquence . . . When he got to the rhythmic part of demanding freedom now, and wanting jobs now, the crowd caught the timing and shouted now in a cadence. Their response lifted Martin in a surge of emotion to new heights of inspiration. Abandoning his written speech, forgetting time, he spoke from his heart, his voice soaring magnificently out over that great crowd and over to all the world. It seemed to all of us there that day that his words flowed from some higher place, through Martin, to the weary people before him. Yea—Heaven itself opened up and we all seemed transformed.
>
> (1969, pp. 238–239)

Charisma also was in force some 60 years earlier, at a different place, during a different time. In cities like Nuremberg and Berlin, to audiences of Germans—young, old, educated, uneducated, cultured, and uncultured—Adolf Hitler spoke, using words and exploiting symbols, bringing audiences to their feet "with his overwhelming, hysterical passion, shouting the same message they had heard over and over again, that they had been done in by traitors, by conspirators . . . , by Communists, plutocrats, and Jews" (Davidson, 1977, p. 183). Like King's, Hitler's oratory moved people and appealed to their hopes and dreams. But his speeches malevolently twisted hope into some gnarled ghastly entity and appealed to Germans' latent, darkest prejudices. Here is how a journalist who carefully observed Hitler described the Führer's charismatic skill:

> With unerring sureness, Hitler expressed the speechless panic of the masses faced by an invisible enemy and gave the nameless specter a name. He was a pure fragment of the modern mass soul, unclouded by any personal qualities. One scarcely need ask with what arts he conquered the masses; he did not conquer them, he portrayed and represented them. His speeches are daydreams of this mass soul; they are chaotic, full of contradictions, if their words are taken literally, often senseless as dreams are, and yet charged with deeper meaning . . . The speeches always begin with deep pessimism, and end in overjoyed redemption, a triumphant, happy ending, often they can be refuted by reason, but they follow the far mightier logic of the subconscious, which no refutation can touch. Hitler has given speech to the speechless terror of the modern mass, and to the nameless fear he has given a name. That makes him the greatest mass orator of the mass age.
>
> (Quoted in Burleigh, 2000, pp. 100–101)

Charisma—exploited for evil purposes by Hitler, used to lift human spirits by Martin Luther King—describes the power of so many forceful speakers, including (in the political realm), American presidents John F. Kennedy, Ronald Reagan, and Bill Clinton, ex-British prime minister Tony Blair, and Silvio Berlusconi, the colorful former prime minister of Italy. Charisma aptly describes the magnetism of Malcolm X and Jesse Jackson in the domain of civil rights, Nelson Mandela and Mahatma Ghandi in the international domain of human rights, and Bono, the rock musician and tireless champion for Africans afflicted with AIDS (see Figure 8.1).

Regrettably, it also describes a legion of cult leaders, who enchanted, then deceived, dozens, even hundreds, of starry-eyed followers. The list of charismatic cult leaders includes Charles Manson; Jim Jones, who induced 900 people to commit suicide in Guyana; David Koresh, leader of the ill-fated Branch Davidians in Waco, Texas; Marshall Applewhite, who led 38 members of the Heaven's Gate cult to commit suicide in 1997; and, most recently, Osama bin Laden, who masterminded the September 11 attacks and, to many, was the personification of evil.

Charismatic sociopaths such as these fascinate people. "Everything that deceives," Plato declared, "may be said to enchant."

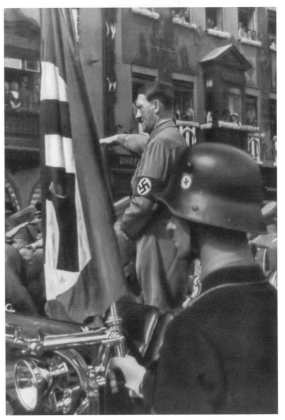

■ Figure 8.1a–d Charisma has been harnessed in profoundly positive ways by political leaders, such as former British prime minister Tony Blair, the American civil rights leader Martin Luther King, and Bono, the Irish rock star who raised awareness of AIDS and poverty in Africa.
Charismatic leaders like Adolf Hitler wielded their persuasive powers in destructive ways, using words and language to deceive and pulverize.

Images courtesy of Getty Images.

What is charisma? How is it defined? A term coined over a century ago by German sociologist Max Weber (1968), **charisma** is "a certain quality of the individual personality by virtue of which he is set apart from ordinary men and treated as endowed with supernatural, superhuman, or at least exceptional powers and qualities" (p. 241). Scholars who have studied charisma acknowledge the powerful influence it can have over ordinary people. Yet they also are quick to identify more subtle features. There are two factors that complicate charisma effects.

First, charisma interacts with audience factors. Followers influence the self-perception of leaders. As Ronald E. Riggio notes, "The charismatic leader inspires the crowd, but he also becomes charged by the emotions of the followers. Thus, there is an interplay between leader and followers that helps to build a strong union between them" (1987, p. 76).

Second, charisma is constrained by historical factors. A person who has charisma in one era might not wield the same influences on audiences in another historical period. The chemistry between speaker and audience is a product of a particular set of circumstances, psychological needs, and social conditions. For example, Martin Luther King might not be charismatic in today's more complex multicultural era, which involves increased tolerance for racial diversity but also wariness of the costs of worthy social experiments like affirmative action. Franklin Delano Roosevelt, a grand and majestic speaker on radio, might not move millions of television viewers, who would watch a crippled president clutch his wheelchair for support. Even John F. Kennedy, who was captivating on television, might be charismatically challenged on YouTube, a medium that prizes technological manipulations—elegantly designed videos, cutaways, exquisite cinematography—that were unheard of in his era.

Charisma, a powerful force in the 20th century, is not likely to disappear. People need to believe in the power of myth, and charismatic leaders feed—and can exploit—this motivation. Charismatic leaders in the 21st century will exude qualities different from those of orators of previous eras. They will adapt their styles to the conditions and media of their times.

What more can be said of charisma? What role does it play in everyday persuasion? These questions are more difficult to answer. Charisma is an intriguing factor in persuasion, but an elusive one, to be sure. Granted, charisma involves a persuader's ability to command and compel an audience, but what specific traits are involved? The communicator's sociability? Attractiveness? Power? Or does it involve a host of characteristics, including charm, empathy, and involvement (Levine, Muenchen, & Brooks, 2010)? Alternatively, does charisma have more to do with the audience—individuals' own vulnerability and need to believe that a communicator has certain qualities they yearn for in life? These questions point to the difficulty of defining charisma with sufficient precision that it can be studied in social scientific settings. There is no question that charisma exists and has been a powerful force in persuasion. On a practical level, it is difficult to study the concept and to determine just how it works and why.

Thus, those who wish to understand why the Martin Luther Kings and Hitlers of the world have profoundly affected audiences must take a different tack. They must either study political history or take a more finely tuned, social scientific approach to examining communicator effects.

More generally, those of us who want to comprehend how persuaders persuade are advised to chip away at the question by examining the different pieces of the puzzle. A key piece of the puzzle—a core aspect of charisma—is the communicator. His or her qualities, and the ways in which these characteristics interact with the audience, can strongly influence attitudes. This chapter continues with an overview of communicator (or source) factors. It then discusses key factors in depth, applying them to contemporary life, and harnessing concepts to shed light on the power—and limits—of communicator attributes.

UNDERSTANDING THE COMMUNICATOR

Just as there is not one type of charismatic leader (Barack Obama differs vastly from Martin Luther King), there is not one defining characteristic of effective communicators. Communicators have different attributes and influence audiences through different processes. There are three fundamental communicator characteristics: authority, credibility, and social attractiveness. Authorities, credible communicators, and attractive ones produce attitude change through different mechanisms (Kelman, 1958).

Authorities frequently influence others through compliance. Individuals adopt a particular behavior not because they agree with its content but, rather, because they expect "to gain specific rewards or approval and avoid specific punishments or disapproval by conforming" (Kelman, 1958, p. 53). In other words, people go along with authority figures because they hope to obtain rewards or avoid punishment.

Credible communicators, by contrast, influence attitudes through internalization. We accept recommendations advanced by credible communicators because they are congruent with our values or attitudes.

Attractive communicators—likeable and physically appealing ones—seem to achieve influence through more affective processes, such as identification. People go along with

▪ **Figure 8.2 Communicators and the influence process.**

attractive speakers because they identify with them, or want to establish a positive relationship with the communicators (Kelman, 1958). Figure 8.2 illustrates the different processes by which sources influence attitudes.

Authority

It was an amazing study—unique in its time, bold, yet controversial, an attempt to create a laboratory analogue for the worst conformity in 20th-century history and one of the most graphic cases of criminal obedience in the history of humankind. Legendary psychologist Gordon W. Allport called the program of research "the Eichmann experiment" because it attempted to explain the subhuman behavior of Nazis like Adolf Eichmann: after ordering the slaughter of 6 million Jews, Eichmann said, "It was unthinkable that I would not follow orders" (Cohen, 1999, p. A1). More generally, the research was designed to shed light on the power that authorities hold over ordinary people, and how they are able to induce individuals to obey their directives, sometimes in ways that violate human decency.

You may have heard of the research program called the Milgram experiments after psychologist Stanley Milgram, who conceptualized and directed them. They are described in social psychology and social influence texts. A documentary film depicting the studies has been shown in thousands of college classrooms (you may have seen it). Milgram's 1974 book, *Obedience to Authority*, has been translated into 11 languages. A rock musician of the 1980s, Peter Gabriel, called on the research in his song, "We Do What We're Told—Milgram's 37."

Experimental Procedures and Results

Milgram conducted his research—it was actually not one study, but a series of experiments—from 1960 to 1963 at Yale University and nearby Bridgeport, Connecticut. The basic procedure is described below.

On reporting to the experiment, each individual receives $4.50 for participating in the experiment, billed as a study of memory and learning. At the laboratory, participants are joined by a man introduced as a fellow subject in the study, who is actually working for the researcher.

At this point the participants are told that they will draw slips of paper to determine who will serve as the "teacher" and who will take the "learner" role. The drawing is rigged so that the naive subject is always selected to be the teacher.

The experimenter tells teacher and learner that the study concerns the effects of punishment on learning. The teacher watches as an experimenter escorts the learner to a room, seats him in a chair, straps his arms to prevent too much movement, and attaches an electrode to his wrist. The learner is told that he must learn a list of word pairs. When he makes a mistake, he will receive electric shocks, the intensity increasing with each error committed.

The teacher then is seated before a shock generator that contains a horizontal line of 30 switches varying from 15 to 450 volts and descriptions ranging from SLIGHT SHOCK to DANGER—SEVERE SHOCK. The experimenter instructs the teacher to read the word pairs to the learner, located in the next room. When the learner responds incorrectly, the teacher is to administer an electric shock, starting at the mildest level (15 volts) and increasing in 15-volt increments. After a series of shocks have been administered, the learner begins to express pain, grunting, complaining, screaming at 285 volts, and then remaining silent. Each time the teacher expresses misgivings about administering a shock, the experimenter orders him or her to continue, saying, "It is absolutely essential that you continue."

In reality, of course, the learner is not getting shocked. The experiment does not concern the effect of punishment on learning, but instead is designed to determine how far people will go in obeying an authority's directives to inflict harm on a protesting victim (Milgram, 1974). Although the shocks are not real, they seem quite authentic to individuals participating in the study. Participants frequently experience considerable tension, torn between sympathy for a suffering compatriot and perceived duty to comply with authority. As Milgram notes:

> I observed a mature and initially poised businessman enter the laboratory smiling and confident. Within 20 minutes he was reduced to a twitching, stuttering wreck, who was rapidly approaching a point of nervous collapse . . . At one point he pushed his fist into his forehead and muttered: "Oh God, let's stop it." And yet he continued to respond to every word of the experimenter, and obeyed to the end.
>
> (1963, p. 377)

The businessman was the norm, not the exception. Although a group of psychiatrists predicted that about only 1 in 1,000 individuals would administer the highest shock on

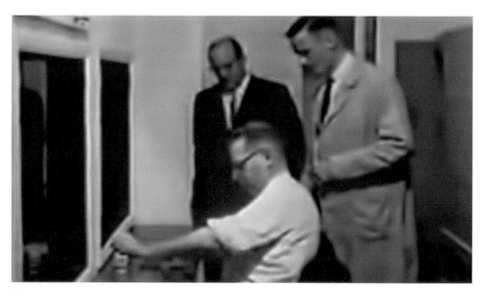

■ **Figure 8.3 In the classic Milgram experiments, many participants, such as the man pictured here, followed the experimenter's orders to administer electric shocks, with some going to dangerous extremes.**

Image courtesy of http://wikis.lib.ncsu.edu/index.php/Ethical_Concerns_in_Experimental_Research.

the shock generator, more than 65 percent went this far. Large numbers of individuals were perfectly content to go along with the experimenter's orders (see Figure 8.3).

The Milgram studies are one of many investigations of the effects of authority on behavior. There is an entire research literature on this topic (Kelman & Hamilton, 1989). The Milgram research provides a useful framework for understanding these effects— it is a window on the role authority plays in persuading individuals to comply with diverse requests.

Milgram's interest was in obedience, but not typical obedience in everyday life, like obeying traffic signs or laws prohibiting shoplifting. This obedience is not objectionable. Milgram's focus was obedience to malevolent authority, obedience that violates moral judgments, what Kelman and Hamilton call "crimes of obedience." Authority—the concept that preoccupied Milgram—is assumed to emanate not from personal qualities, *"but from (the person's) perceived position in a social structure"* (Milgram, 1974, p. 139). A legitimate authority is someone who is presumed to have "the right to prescribe behavior" for others (Milgram, 1974, pp. 142–143). In the experimental drama of the Milgram studies, the experimenter exploited his authority and led many people to administer shocks to a helpless victim.

Explanations

Why? Why would normal, upstanding human beings ignore their consciences and administer what they thought were electric shocks to a middle-aged learner? The explanation must lie in part with the power that situations can exert on human behavior, particularly the effects of the aura—or trappings—of authority. Interpretations of the Milgram findings include:

■ *Early socialization.* People are socialized to obey authority, and they get rewarded for doing so. Success in school, on sports teams, in corporate organizations, and even in Hollywood movies requires complying with the requests of authorities. "We learn to value obedience, even if what ensues in its name is unpleasant," Arthur G. Miller and colleagues note. "We also trust the legitimacy of the many authorities in our lives," they remark (Miller, Collins, & Brief, 1995, p. 9).

■ *Trappings of authority.* Various aspects of the experimental situation contributed to its majesty, or "aura of legitimacy" (Kelman & Hamilton, 1989, p. 151). These included: (a) status of the institution, Yale University; (b) complex, expensive scientific equipment in the room; (c) the experimenter's clothing (his lab coat served as a symbol of scientific expertise); and (d) the experimenter's gender—men are accorded more prestige "simply by virtue of being male" (Rudman & Kilianski, 2000, p. 1315). These trappings of authority could have served as peripheral cues, calling up the rule of thumb that "you do what authorities ask."

■ *Binding forces.* The experiment set in motion powerful psychological forces that "locked" participants into compliance. Participants did not want to harm the learner and probably harbored doubts about the necessity of administering severe electric shocks to advance scientific knowledge of memory. Still, they were reluctant to mention these concerns. Believing they lacked the knowledge or expertise to challenge the experimenter's requests, afraid of what would happen if they confronted the experimenter, concerned that he might implicitly indict them for failing to serve the noble goals of science and Yale University, they knuckled under. "To refuse to go on meant to challenge the experimenter's authority," Kelman and Hamilton note (1989, p. 153). While some people were willing to undertake this challenge, most did not. They did not perceive that they had the right or ability to question the experimenter, and thus opted to accept his view of the situation.

The Milgram experiments illustrate the powerful impact that social influence can exert on behavior. To some degree, the experiments straddle the line between coercion and persuasion. There is a coercive aspect to the studies in that the experimenter was pushing individuals to act contrary to their preferences, and participants may have experienced the authority's directives as a threat. But the bottom line is that no one was holding a gun to participants' heads; they were free to stop the shocks whenever they wanted, and some individuals did. The experimenter set up the bait, but individuals persuaded themselves to go along with his commands.

Additional Issues

Milgram conducted a variety of studies of obedience, varying aspects of the experimental situation. He found that obedience was more likely to occur under certain conditions than others. For example, substantially more individuals obeyed when the experimenter sat a few feet from the teacher than when he left the room and relayed orders by telephone. In one experiment, three individuals served as teachers. Unbeknownst to the subject, two worked for the experimenter. When the two individuals refused to shock the learner, obedience dropped sharply. This is the most hopeful aspect of the research. It suggests that authorities lose their grip if enough people resist.

Over the years, Milgram's studies have generated considerable discussion in the academic community. It would be ironic if academics accepted Milgram's findings lock, stock, and barrel—if they marched to Milgram's music in unison, just as his subjects followed the experimenter's order. I am happy to report that this is not what has occurred. Milgram's studies have been endlessly debated, criticized, and praised (Miller, 1986; Orne & Holland, 1968).

Critics have pointed out that the study involved the use of archaic, physical violence; yet much violence involves verbal or psychological abuse (Meeus & Raaijmakers, 1986). Scholars have also suggested that individuals' obedience was not as nasty as Milgram suggested. "Subjects take it for granted that the experimenter is familiar with the shock generator and that he knows that the shocks are not fatal," two researchers contended (Meeus & Raaijmakers, 1986, p. 312). In response, Milgram has noted that research participants—the teachers—perceived that the experimental situation was very real—not a game. They believed that the shocks had inflicted pain.

Others have objected to the experiments on ethical grounds, arguing that Milgram had no right to play God. They suggest that it was immoral to leave participants with knowledge that they could be cruel, slavishly obedient creatures (Baumrind, 1964). The ethical critique has stimulated much discussion, with Milgram (1974) pointing out that participants in his studies had been debriefed, had not suffered harm, and actually viewed the experiment as enlightening. Yet even if one shares Milgram's positive assessment of the research, there is still something unsettling—and, at some level, wrong—about deceiving people in the name of science.

Granting these deontological objections, there are strong utilitarian reasons to evaluate the experiment positively. It has generated rich insights about human behavior, illuminating dark sides of persuasion that continue to intrigue students and scholars today. What's more, knowledge of the findings can help people take steps to protect themselves against engaging in unethical obedience.

Revisiting Milgram: The 2009 Replication Article

For decades, persuasion students have wondered if Milgram's findings would be obtained today. Some scholars argued that obedience is a universal feature of the human condition. Others countered that the obedience experiments were period pieces, studies conducted a half century ago in a profoundly different time when authorities were revered and citizens compliant. The debate has raged over the years, with some researchers contending the findings would not hold up in our more irreverent era and others pointing to recent studies that report disturbing evidence of contemporary obedience, albeit to orders that were milder than those administered by Milgram's experimenter (see Blass, 1992; Meeus & Raaijmakers, 1986). Researchers have been unable to replicate Milgram's study, in light of strong ethical proscriptions—guidelines to protect human subjects from harm—that were implemented as a result of concerns about Milgram's research.

In January 2009, the flagship journal of the American Psychological Association published a major article by Jerry M. Burger that caught the attention of persuasion scholars and others across the world who were familiar with Milgram's classic study. Burger had done what thousands of researchers had dreamed of doing. He had conducted a study that employed many of the same procedures Milgram had used, but took necessary ethical precautions. He had convinced the institutional review board at his university that the experiment satisfied guidelines designed to protect human subjects from stress and psychological harm. Burger had designed an experiment that allowed researchers to answer the time-honored question: "Would people still obey today?" (Burger, 2009).

In order to protect individuals' welfare, Burger informed participants that they could leave the experiment at any juncture and still keep the money they had been paid for participating in the experiment. They were told the confederate (the learner) had been given the same assurance. Berger also screened participants prior to the study, eliminating those who reported that they suffered from anxiety or depression. Moreover, Burger stopped the experiment when subjects administered a shock of 150 volts, rather than allowing them to continue to the stressful 450-volt level.

Did participants behave as their counterparts had some 40 years earlier? Or did they choose to disobey?

Burger found that the rate of obedience paralleled that obtained in Milgram's experiments. Seventy percent of participants in Burger's replication delivered 150-volt shocks, compared to 82.5 percent in a comparable condition in Milgram's study. Although there was more obedience a half-century ago, the difference between the proportions that obeyed was not statistically significant. Obedience seems not to have meaningfully decreased over the span of four decades.

Questions remain, of course: Would the same findings emerge with different ethnic groups? (A majority of Burger's participants were White, and, in line with Milgram's study, the learner was also Caucasian.) Non-White racial groups might have different norms governing conformity. Suppose the teacher was White and the learner of a different race? Would this attenuate or increase obedience? These questions remain interesting issues to pursue and are worthwhile topics for scholarly investigation. They do not reduce the significance of Burger's findings. His replication (supported as it is by conceptually similar work over the years) showed that Milgram's experiment stands the test of time. Participants in a laboratory study of obedience readily comply with the unethical directives of an authority figure.

Applications

The Milgram experiments are classic studies in the psychology of persuasion. They have emerged, as one scholar put it, as "one of the most singular, most penetrating, and most disturbing inquiries into human conduct that modern psychology has produced" (quoted in Blass, 1999, p. 957). They provide an explanation—not the only one, but a powerful one—for the Holocaust of the Jews. Many German soldiers and civilians slavishly conformed to the orders of Nazi authorities. (To be sure, decades of virulent anti-Semitism laid the groundwork for German conformity; see Lipstadt, 2011). The Milgram findings also illuminate more recent wartime atrocities, such as in Korea, Vietnam, and Iraq, as when U.S. soldiers—responding to orders by higher-ups and peer pressure—tortured prisoners at the Abu Ghraib, Iraq prison.

Consider Private Lynndie England, who was photographed holding a naked prisoner with a strap around his neck, like it was a leash (see Figure 8.4).

Lynndie grew up in a trailer park in a small town in West Virginia. As a girl, she wore her hair short, played softball, and participated in Future Farmers of America. She quit her job at a chicken-processing plant because she objected to the management's decision to send unhealthy chicken parts down the factory line (McKelvey, 2007). It was therefore ironic that she ended up doing the bidding of her commanders at Abu Ghraib, particularly Sergeant Charles A. Graner, Jr., the crude and violent man with whom she was infatuated. Brigadier General Janis L. Karpinski, who supervised detainee operations at Abu Ghraib, ventured an explanation:

■ **Figure 8.4 A photo obtained by The Washington Post and released May 6, 2004, shows U.S. Army Private Lynndie England, of the 372nd Military Police Company, with a naked detainee at the Abu Ghraib prison in Baghdad.**

Image courtesy of the Associated Press.

"You have to understand that it builds into a crescendo . . . You're being mortared every night. You are breathing dust and broken concrete. It's hot. You feel dehumanized. You're drained of every bit of compassion you have. She did it because she wanted to come back from this godforsaken war and say, 'We did this for the government.' . . . She was made to believe this was of such importance to national security. It was, you know, 'You stick with me, kid, and you might even win a medal.'"

(McKelvey, 2007, pp. 238–239)

Thus do ordinary people, who are not cruel by nature, find themselves engaged in extraordinarily violent acts. England and others were justly punished for their actions, justly, as they chose to perform them. Yet the higher-ups who created the conditions under which these behaviors were normative emerged scot free. No high-ranking Army officer or general served prison time. No Defense Department or administration official was charged with torture or war crimes. England and others succumbed to the pressure of authorities and were punished for their compliance.

The Milgram findings shed light not only on compliance to authorities during wartime, but on conformity in a variety of political and organizational contexts. They help us understand why White House aides have followed presidents' commands to cover up illegal acts, lie about them, or stonewall the press. Events such as these occurred during Watergate (Kelman & Hamilton, 1989) and, to some degree, during the Clinton–Lewinsky scandal.

The results can be applied to the Penn State child abuse scandal. Former Penn State University assistant football coach Jerry Sandusky sexually abused boys for years, and university employees were afraid to take action, for fear of crossing revered head coach Joe Paterno, a Sandusky ally. In 2000, a university janitor watched as Sandusky performed oral sex on a boy in the showers. He told his co-workers, but none went to the police. "I know Paterno has so much power, if he wanted to get rid of someone, I would have been gone," one janitor said, poignantly adding that reporting the assault "would have been like going against the president of the United States in my eyes" (Mulvihill, Armas & Scolforo, 2012, p. A-12). Like a subject in the original shock-machine studies who feared challenging the august image of Yale University, the janitor felt he had no choice but to comply.

There are other applications. The studies also explain actions taken in health maintenance organizations (HMOs), as when doctors slavishly follow HMO authorities' orders to have special medical procedures performed only at the HMO. Some years back, a physician found that a patient's appendix was inflamed, but told her she would have to wait over a week to have an exam performed by the HMO staff. While she was waiting for her appointment, the patient's appendix burst, leading to a complicated medical situation (Greenhouse, 1999). Had the physician not followed orders, she might have found a way out of the logjam.

The Milgram study also helps explain a much different, but no less stressful, situation: the distress many professional secretaries experience when their bosses ask them to commit unethical acts. Eighty-eight percent of administrative professionals admitted they had told a "little white lie" for a supervisor (Romano, 1998). Some have done worse, like the secretary for a school district who routinely complied with her boss's requests to inflate grades of college-bound students. "What am I supposed to do?" the 48-year-old woman, a single mother of two children, said to reporter Lois Romano. "I have to put food on the table. I need the benefits and so I am forced to do things I know are not correct. I have nowhere to go" (Romano, 1998, p. 29).

The woman's comments illustrate the tension people feel when faced with having to carry out orders they know are wrong. The secretary is frank about her problem, but mistaken in one respect, I maintain.

She says she has nowhere to go. Yet people always have places to go. There are always choices in life, and people can usually find a way to reconcile conscience with survival needs. The secretary may not have been able to quit her job, but she could have blown the whistle on the boss by asking a newspaper reporter to investigate the issue. Failing that, she could have kept a diary, and at a later time in life—when she could afford to leave the job or had retired—could reveal all. Or, realizing she had to put bread on the table, she might have thought through her predicament, redefined the situation as one in which her compliance was required but did not reflect her true personality, and resolved to do morally upstanding things in other aspects of her life.

The point is: there is always a way to respect conscience and resist exploitive authorities, in some way, shape, or form. If ever you are faced with a situation in which you must choose between your morals and the tempting desire to follow the crowd or a boss, remember the Milgram results.

Ask yourself: What do I believe? Is this something I really want to do? How will I feel tomorrow when I realize I could have respected my own beliefs? If you ask these questions, you will be less likely to acquiesce to authority and more inclined to do something that will sit well with your inner convictions.

Credibility

Take a deep breath. We're about to shift gears now, moving from the transcendental moral issues of authority to everyday questions of credibility. Credibility is one of the "big 3" communicator factors—along with authority and social attractiveness. It dates back to Aristotle, who coined the term *ethos* to describe qualities of the source that facilitated persuasion. Hovland explored it in his early research, communication researchers deconstructed credibility in the 1960s and 1970s, and the concept continues to fascinate scholars today. Of course, corporate managers, salespeople, and politicians are very interested in what makes someone credible. Nowadays, consultants offer pointers to clients who want to improve the credibility of their commercial Web sites. D. Joel Whalen, in a book on persuasive business communication, says that credibility is "the single biggest variable under the speaker's control during the presentation" (1996, p. 97). Jay A. Conger, writing about the role persuasion plays in business, observes that "credibility is the cornerstone of effective persuading; without it, a persuader won't be given the time of day" (1998, p. 90).

So, what is credibility? First, let's say what it is *not*. It is not the same as authority, although the two are frequently confused. **Authority** emanates from a person's position in a social structure. It involves the ability to dispense rewards and punishments. Credibility is a psychological or interpersonal communication construct. You can be an authority, but lack credibility. Parents can be authority figures to their kids, but have zero credibility in their children's eyes due to their hypocrisy or indifference. In politics, a president is the nation's commander-in-chief—the top political authority. However, a president can lack credibility in the nation's eyes if he (or she) ignores the nation's economic problems or gets embroiled in a scandal. Dictators can do as they please; they have total, supreme authority. But ask their citizens in private what they think of these people and you will quickly discover that authority does not translate into credibility.

Credibility is defined as "the attitude toward a source of communication held at a given time by a receiver" (McCroskey, 1997, p. 87). It is an audience member's perceptions of the communicator's qualities. Although we commonly think of credibility as something a communicator has, it is more complex. As Roderick Hart and colleagues note:

"Credibility is *not a thing*. It is not some sort of overcoat that we put on and take off at will. Rather, it is a perception of us that lies inside of the people to whom we talk" (Hart, Friedrich, & Brummett, 1983, p. 204).

Credibility is more than a psychological characteristic. It is also a communication variable. It is part of the two-way interaction between communicator and message recipients—a dynamic entity that emerges from the transaction between source and audience member. This means that communicators are not guaranteed credibility by virtue of who they are, their title, or academic pedigree. As Hart reminds us, credibility "is not something we can be assured of keeping once gotten. Credibility can only be earned by paying the price of effective communication" (Hart et al., 1983, pp. 204–205). There is something democratic about credibility. It says that communicators have to enter the rough-and-tumble realm of persuasion. They must meet and greet—either interpersonally or electronically—those they seek to influence. They must earn an audience's respect and win its credibility. We observe this in many spheres of life, of which one of the most salient is public relations. Companies have engaged in splendid public relations, enhancing their credibility. Yet they also have bombed, their spokespersons making statements that have eroded corporate credibility (see Box 8.1). In addition, it is important to remember that, like all persuasion attributes, credibility can be used for both good and nefarious purposes (see Box 8.2).

BOX 8.1 PUBLIC RELATIONS 101

Credibility is of central importance in public relations. "Receivers must have confidence in the sender and high regard for the source's competence on the subject," noted Cutlip, Center, and Broom (2006) in their public relations text (p. 358). Companies have garnered considerable goodwill by visibly demonstrating that they place the highest priority on consumer health and well-being. The classic case is Johnson & Johnson, the makers of Tylenol. When seven people died in Chicago from ingesting cyanide-laced Tylenol in 1982, the company acted immediately. Placing people ahead of profits and implementing deontological ethical principles (Cutlip et al., 2006), the company halted production of Tylenol capsules, pulled Tylenol packages from store shelves, and designed tamper-resistant packages. Polls showed that 9 out of 10 Americans did not blame the company for the poisonings. In fact, Johnson & Johnson garnered positive press for its handling of the crisis.

On the other end of the credibility spectrum sits the energy behemoth BP, which caused the worst oil spill in U.S. history in 2010. In addition to killing 11 people, the spill in the Gulf of Mexico, near the Mississippi River Delta, released nearly 5 million barrels of crude oil over a 3-month period, extensively damaging wildlife. In contrast to Johnson & Johnson, BP eschewed personal responsibility, focusing instead on damage control and spinning excuses. Initially the company estimated that only 1,000 barrels a day spilled into the water. In fact, close to 60,000 barrels a day reached the water.

Then came the *incredible* public appearances and statements from BP CEO Tony Hayward. Hayward's pinstriped suits contrasted sharply with the coveralls worn by fishermen in the Gulf, and his British accent called up images of British royalty. Although Hayward was not born to the purple or educated at elite schools, his accent, coupled with an air of indifference, telegraphed corporate contempt.

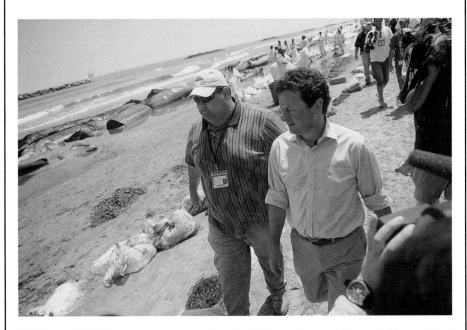

■ **Figure 8.5 BP faced serious moral and public relations problems in the wake of the 2010 oil spill in the Gulf of Mexico. CEO Tony Hayward, shown here (at right) touring the damage, made a number of public relations mistakes, further eroding BP's credibility.**

Image courtesy of Getty Images.

Continued

His comments were worse. "The Gulf of Mexico is a very big ocean," he said, noting that the volume of oil "we are putting into it is tiny in relation to the total water volume." Several days later, he opined: "The environmental impact of this disaster is likely to have been very, very modest." And then, in the verbal *coup de grâce*, after apologizing to those whose lives had been torn asunder, he added, "There's no one who wants this thing over more than I do. I'd like my life back." Television happily conveyed images of his life: wealth and attendance at a yacht race with his family. His "tin-eared utterances" suggested to many that he lacked goodwill and was disingenuous in his apologetic remarks (Goodman, 2010, p. 1; see Figure 8.5).

In the realm of public relations, Hayward was wayward.

To be sure, the scope of the damage, along with BP's previous environmental mishaps, presented strong indictments of the corporate energy giant. But BP might have mitigated some of the perceptual damage by implementing more adept—and consumer-centered—public relations. "It was one of the worst P.R. approaches that I've seen in my 56 years of business," said public relations expert Howard Rubinstein. "They basically thought they could spin their way out of catastrophe. It doesn't work that way." "Once you lose credibility, that's the kiss of death," added another PR specialist (Goodman, 2010, p. 6).

BOX 8.2 THE CON IN CON MAN STANDS FOR . . .

How do con men connive? (And, while we're on the topic, why don't we ever talk about con women?)

The answer to the first question is confidence. Con men pull the persuasive wool over gullible individuals' eyes by projecting confidence and credibility. Cunning persuaders exploit peripheral credibility cues, speaking quickly to enhance expertise (see Chapter 9), exploiting smiles to convey goodwill, and projecting confidence to gain the trust of potential prey. "Confidence convinces," writer Dan Gardner (2011, p. 153) concluded, attributing its effects to a confidence heuristic. "If someone's confidence is high, we believe they are probably right; if they are less certain, we feel they are less reliable" (pp. 153–154). In a way, this is unfair, because an intelligent person who appreciates the complexity of events and fallibility of prediction should be uncertain, even humble. But we're talking persuasion—and in the world of persuasion, confidence convinces.

Empirical studies substantiate this notion. In a well-known study, three psychologists hired an actor to play the role of a distinguished faculty member whom they called Dr. Myron Fox, devised a lecture on an erudite topic, "mathematical game theory as applied to physician education," and placed the fictitious Dr. Fox in front of an audience of psychologists, psychiatrists, and social work educators. His speech was absolute nonsense: double talk, non sequiturs and contradictory assertions. But because he spoke confidently and projected authority, an audience of professional mental health experts offered glowing evaluations, even giving him a perfect score in response to the question, "Did he stimulate your thinking?" (Naftulin, Ware, & Donnelly, 1973).

In a more quantitative demonstration, Zarnoth and Sniezek (1997) asked students to grapple with several cognitive tasks: math problems, a temperature forecast, and verbal analogies. Students indicated the degree to which they were confident that their answers were correct. Subsequently, students were assigned to a group and offered a collective judgment regarding the correct answer to the problems. Individuals who had displayed greater confidence exerted more impact on group judgments, even when their answers were objectively wrong!

So, the "con" in con man stands, at least in part, for confidence. But it's not just con *men* who can dupe gullible receivers. A New York City psychic, Sylvia Mitchell, is currently on the lam, wanted by law enforcement authorities for swindling an unsuspecting client. One day in July, 2008, a middle-aged woman entered Mitchell's Manhattan parlor, with its lanterns and hanging plants, had her palm read, and was told that there was "very important information that could help her change and better her life, but it would cost her $1,000." Feeling vulnerable because of a romantic breakup and desperate for positive news, the woman plunked down a thousand bucks. Who would succumb to such a silly scam? Explained a seasoned New York City lieutenant, the secret lies in the psychic's ability to locate a psychologically vulnerable client with money to spare. "They gain your confidence," he said. "And then you're scammed" (Wilson, 2011, p. A15).

Core Characteristics

What are the main attributes of credibility? What does it mean to be a credible speaker?

Communication researchers have explored these time-honored questions, using empirical methodologies and survey research. Scholars asked people to evaluate the believability of famous people, giving speeches on various topics, and to rate friends or supervisors on semantic differential scales. They found that credibility is not a simple, unitary concept: it has more than one dimension, more than a single layer. Credible communicators are perceived as having expertise, trustworthiness, goodwill, dynamism, extroversion, sociability, and composure (e.g., Berlo, Lemert, & Mertz, 1969; McCroskey & Young, 1981).

By far the most important characteristics—the ones that have emerged in study after study or generated the greatest theoretical interest—are (a) *expertise*, (b) *trustworthiness*, and (c) *goodwill*.

Expertise and trustworthiness have emerged with greatest regularity, and goodwill has been uncovered in systematic research by James McCroskey (McCroskey & Teven, 1999). Based on the studies as a whole, one can say that a credible communicator is one who is seen as an expert, is regarded as trustworthy, and displays goodwill toward audience members. Each quality is important and deserves brief discussion.

Expertise is the knowledge or ability ascribed to the communicator. It is the belief that the communicator has special skills or know-how. You see experts used all the time in commercials. Lawyers pay for experts to testify for their side in courtroom trials. There is abundant evidence that experts are perceived as credible and can influence attitudes (Petty & Wegener, 1998). However, expertise has limits. For instance, if you are trying to reach inner-city drug abusers, you might think twice about calling on the Surgeon General. True, the Surgeon General is a recognized expert on health, but the doctor also is seen as a member of the ruling elite. It would be better to employ a former drug user who has seen the error of his or her ways and can communicate on the same wavelength as the inner-city audience (Levine & Valle, 1975). The former drug user also inspires trust, which is an important attribute of credibility.

Trustworthiness, the next core credibility component, refers to the communicator's perceived honesty, character, and safety. A speaker may lack expertise, but can be seen as an individual of integrity and character. This can work wonders in persuasion. Some years ago, Ross Perot, the billionaire businessman-turned-politician, declared on a television talk show that he would be willing to run for president if citizens worked steadfastly in his behalf. His declaration stimulated a flood of support from ordinary Americans who liked his persona and plans to reduce the deficit. Within months he had an army of loyal campaign workers. Legions of reporters trailed him everywhere, and he became a major force in the 1992 election campaign. Perot was no political expert; he had never held political office, although he was widely known to the public for his committed political stances. Many Americans perceived Perot as a man of integrity, someone who said what he meant and meant what he said. Finding this refreshing, they supported Perot—and he led the polls for a time, in mid-June (Abramson, Aldrich, & Rohde, 1994). A similar phenomenon occurred in 2012 when Congressman Ron Paul attracted a legion of loyal supporters in his campaign for the Republican presidential nomination. Paul's honesty and willingness to take unpopular positions on foreign policy earned him high marks on the trustworthiness scale.

Goodwill or perceived caring, is the final core communicator factor. Communicators who display goodwill convey that they have listeners' interests at heart, show understanding of others' ideas, and are empathic toward their audiences' problems (McCroskey & Teven, 1999). You can probably think of a doctor who knows her stuff and is honest, but seems preoccupied or uninterested in you when you complain about medical problems. The physician undoubtedly gets low marks on your credibility scale, and her advice probably has little impact on you.

On the positive side, communicators who show us they care can gain our trust and inspire us. Goodwill is an element of charisma, as embodied by leaders like Gandhi and Martin Luther King. It is also a quality that can help persuaders achieve practical goals. Salespeople who understand their clients' needs can tailor their appeals to suit particular clients. This can help them achieve day-to-day success on the job (McBane, 1995). Goodwill also has important implications for medical communication, particularly between physicians and patients. Doctors who convey empathy with patients' needs can enhance patients' satisfaction and compliance with medical recommendations (Kim, Kaplowitz, & Johnston, 2004).

Role of Context

Expertise, trustworthiness, and goodwill are the primary attributes of credibility. Communicators who are credible have all or at least one of these qualities. There is a complicating factor, however: context. As anyone who has worked in telemarketing, politics, or community organizing can tell you, the situation you are in can potently influence persuasion. This means that different facets of credibility will be influential in different social situations. This conclusion emerged from early academic studies of credibility, which found that results varied, depending on the ways in which researchers probed credibility and circumstances in which the speeches were delivered (Cronkhite & Liska, 1976). Critical situational factors include audience size, communicator role, and cultural dynamics.

Audience size. Do you remember those big lecture classes where no one knows anyone else and you have to listen to a professor talk or present material via PowerPoint for an hour? It's hard to impart information in these contexts, and if I were in charge of American universities, I'd get rid of them immediately! Unfortunately, mass lectures are here to stay because they allow universities to educate thousands of students efficiently and at low cost. And, in fairness, some lecture classes can be pretty interesting, even entertaining. That brings me to the point. If a prof. hopes to gain credibility in a large lecture, he or she must be dynamic and extroverted. These qualities are necessary to capture students' attention.

Now consider a small seminar. A professor who is bold and talkative, hams it up, and booms out lecture material in a loud voice may be perceived as insensitive or "incredible" in a small seminar. In this context, students want a teacher to listen, share information, and help them relate personally to the course. A more empathic, caring style of communicating may be perceived as more credible in this situation.

Communicator role. In a similar vein, the role a communicator plays—or functions he or she performs for the individual—can determine the particular aspect of credibility that is most important. In the case of a therapist, credibility involves composure, poise, character, and goodwill.

Yet, if a communicator is addressing cognitive aspects of attitudes—for example, beliefs about a far-reaching issue—he or she is better advised to dramatize a different aspect of credibility. A scientist speaking to an audience about global warming should convey expertise—that is, intelligence and knowledge of the technical aspects of this subject.

Culture and political context. National and political culture can play an important role in credibility judgments. American students evaluate political leaders on the basis of competence and character, while Japanese students sometimes employ two additional attributes: consideration and appearance (King, Minami, & Samovar, 1985). What's more, the particular type of credibility that is important can depend on the particular time and political place. In some national elections, expertise can be the key attribute that Americans value in a president.

A long time ago, in 1972, Richard Nixon emphasized his political experience. Realizing that he was not a particularly likeable guy but had vastly more expertise than his opponent, his consultants urged Nixon to stress his qualifications and experience. Nixon defeated George McGovern by a landslide in 1972.

What a difference four years makes! After Nixon's blatant lies to the public during the Watergate affair, the nation yearned for a more honest political leader. Along came

Jimmy Carter riding on a white horse and striking many as a "John Boy Walton" character (after the popular television show of the 1970s). Carter promised he would never lie to the American people, thereby stressing trustworthiness and integrity. Carter defeated incumbent Gerald Ford in a close election.

Fast-forward to the 1990s, and you find candidate Bill Clinton exuding compassion and sensitivity, trying to distance himself from the incumbent president, George H. Bush. Many Americans perceived Bush as out of touch with their problems and insufficiently concerned with the economic recession (Denton, 1994). Showing goodwill and empathy toward the plight of ordinary Americans, Clinton gained in stature and credibility. This helped him defeat Bush in the 1992 election.

Trustworthiness was in vogue again in 2000, especially among voters displeased with Clinton's sexual shenanigans and lies under oath during the Lewinsky scandal. Democratic candidate Al Gore and Republican nominee George W. Bush tripped over themselves to show that they could be trusted not to violate family values that Americans held dear.

Four years later, in 2008, with the economy in tailspin and voters concerned about their pocketbooks, candidates' credibility on economic issues became a salient factor in voters' decisions. Republican candidate John McCain had enormous credibility on foreign affairs, but, unfortunately for McCain, this was not relevant to voters in 2008. Instead, the economy was the main issue in the campaign, and Democrat Barack Obama conveyed goodwill by empathizing with American's financial woes. In 2012, with more than 8 percent unemployment and the deficit growing, the economy was a nettlesome noose around Obama's neck. His *expertise* in running the country came under attack.

In sum, candidate credibility plays a prominent role in presidential campaigns, with voters attending to credibility cues. The lesson for persuasion students is that the particular type of credibility that communicators emphasize depends on the time and political place. Certain components are more consequential, with effects varying as a function of economic, political, and psychological circumstances.

If there is an overarching lesson in this, it is that we need to adopt a flexible approach to credibility. If credibility were a key, it would have to be adapted to fit the particular persuasion door in question. If credibility were a recipe, chefs would have to take the main ingredients and season them to suit the tastes of the folks at the restaurant. Smart persuaders know how to adapt their traits to fit the situation. They apply persuasion knowledge to the context in question, selecting the particular style of expertise, trustworthiness, and goodwill that best suits the audience and circumstances. In politics, as in so many other contexts, there is an ineffable quality to the ways in which these features are combined in situations. Credible, and especially charismatic, political leaders have a way of connecting with voters, making contact with gut-level values and pressing human concerns. Obama did this in 2008, as did Clinton in the 1990s and Reagan in the 1980s. It is a cardinal feature of persuasion.

A Theoretical Account

As noted earlier in the book, social scientists attempt to develop theories to explain and predict events. In the case of credibility, researchers have devised a model that assumes people are canny, skeptical observers of persuaders. Eagly, Wood, and Chaiken (1978) argue that people figure persuaders have their own motives for saying what they do. What's more, audience members attribute persuaders' statements to various factors. The attribution that individuals make can exert an important influence on credibility judgments and persuasion.

Eagly and colleagues point out that individuals make predictions—or develop expectations—about what a particular communicator will say, based on what they know about him or her, and the situation. For instance, if you were told that a member of the college track team was going to talk about exercise, you probably would assume he was going to explain why running is healthy. Or, to take a political example, if informed that a candidate was speaking to a pro-environmental group, you might assume he or she was going to sing the praises of conservation.

Expectations can be confirmed—it turns out you are correct—or disconfirmed—you end up being wrong. When a speaker disconfirms your expectation, you scratch your head and want to figure out why this occurred. In such cases, you may (as we will see) conclude that the communicator is a credible source. The underpinnings for this lie in two psychological concepts: *knowledge bias* and *reporting bias*.

Knowledge bias. Suppose you were told that a young female professor was scheduled to give a lecture on affirmative action. If you ventured a prediction about what she was going to say, you might guess that, being young and a professor (and, therefore you assume, liberal), she would advocate affirmative action programs for women. If the speaker confirmed your prediction, you might conclude that she possessed what is called a knowledge bias. A **knowledge bias** is the presumption that a communicator has a biased view of an issue. It is an audience member's belief that the speaker's background—gender, ethnicity, religion, or age—has prevented him or her from looking objectively at the various sides of the issue. The audience member concludes that the communicator has a limited base of knowledge, produced by a need to view an issue in accord with the dominant views of her social group. "Oh, she's a modern woman; of course she'd see things that way," you might say, meaning no disrespect. Communicators who are perceived to harbor knowledge biases lack credibility and do not change attitudes (Eagly et al., 1978).

Now suppose that the speaker took the unexpected position and spoke out against affirmative action programs for women. The theory says that individuals might be taken aback by this and would feel a need to explain why the communicator defied expectation. Unable to attribute her position to gender or background, they would have to conclude that something else was operating. They might reasonably infer that the arguments against affirmative action were so compelling that they persuaded the young professor to go against the grain and take an unpopular stand. Or they might conclude that the communicator was a bit of an iconoclast, someone who defied the norm. Both these interpretations could enhance the speaker's credibility and increase the odds that she would change audience attitudes. As a general rule, when communicators are perceived to violate the knowledge bias, they gain in credibility (see Figure 8.6a).

Knowledge bias is admittedly a different way of looking at communicators and so it takes some getting used to. But once you appreciate the idea, it becomes an appealing way to explain seemingly paradoxical situations in everyday life. Consider the following examples:

■ African-American lawyer David P. Baugh defended Barry E. Black, a White member of the Ku Klux Klan accused of burning a cross. The case was intriguing because of "the paradox of an African-American defending a white supremacist, who, if he had his way, would oppress his lawyer because of his race" (Holmes, 1998, p. A14). Arguing that the principle of free speech overwhelmed any discomfort he had about the defendant's actions, the lawyer violated the knowledge bias and may have enhanced his credibility in the case.

■ At the 50th anniversary of the *Brown* v. *Board of Education* school desegregation decision, Bill Cosby lambasted African-Americans who don't speak proper English, saying, "You can't land a plane with 'why you ain't' . . . You can't be a doctor with that kind of crap coming out of your mouth." He blamed Black parents for failing to take responsibility for their children's moral transgressions, criticizing those who buy their kids $500 sneakers, but refuse to "spend $250 on Hooked on Phonics" (Dyson, 2005, pp. 57–58). Cosby's comments seemed to have resonated with a number of African-American adults. Defying expectation, they were precisely the opposite of what one expected to hear on this occasion from a trailblazing Black entertainer who had been a tireless fighter for racial justice. If Bill Cosby is so outraged by the parenting styles of some Black parents, people likely thought to themselves, then perhaps there is merit in his criticisms (see Figure 8.7).

■ Some of the country's wealthiest Americans, including Warren Buffet and David Rockefeller, Jr., urged Congress not to repeal federal taxes on estates. Although they would benefit from repeal of the tax, since they own lavish estates, Buffet, Rockefeller, and other billionaires said repealing the tax "would enrich the heirs of America's millionaires and billionaires while hurting families who struggle to make ends meet" (Johnston, 2001, p. A1). This is not what you would expect ultra-rich individuals to say and, for this reason, their statements may enhance the credibility of their claims.

Reporting bias. When judging communicators, audience members also examine the extent to which speakers are taking the position merely to make points with the audience. If they believe the communicator is brownnosing the group, they assume that the speech reflects a situational pressure to say the socially correct thing. They conclude that the communicator has withheld—or chosen not to report—facts that would upset the group. This is the **reporting bias**, the perception that the communicator has opted not to report or disclose certain facts or points of view.

When individuals believe that speakers are guilty of a reporting bias, they downgrade their credibility. Upon hearing that a candidate tailors her statements to fit the ideology of the group she is addressing, voters frequently doubt the sincerity of the candidate. "A typical politician," voters think to themselves.

On the other hand, when audience members' expectations are violated—the communicator says something that is inconsistent with group values—the speaker is seen as credible and convincing. Individuals figure that anyone who has the courage to go against the grain must truly believe what he or she is saying. They figure that the position must be so compelling and cogent that it led the speaker to ignore social conventions and adopt the position as her own (see Eagly et al., 1978; see Figure 8.6b). The reporting bias helps us understand why voters like maverick candidates, such as Ron Paul, Ross Perot, and Ralph Nader. These candidates violate the reporting bias and are seen as having the guts to challenge the status quo.

There is an important exception to the reporting bias. When a speaker violates the bias, but takes a position that a group finds objectionable and offensive, the communicator will be seen as incredible, the advocated position landing in the latitude of rejection. The speaker gets points for honesty, but loses more for taking a position that is strongly inconsistent with audience members' values. People are happy to respect an unconventional communicator who seems to defy pressures to tell groups what they want to hear—until the communicator stumbles on their own group and tramples on their own attitude, particularly a strong one, such as gun rights or abortion. When it comes to strong attitudes, people seem to prefer a mildly insincere communicator who shares their values to a sincere speaker who opposes a position they believe, in their heart of hearts, to be correct.

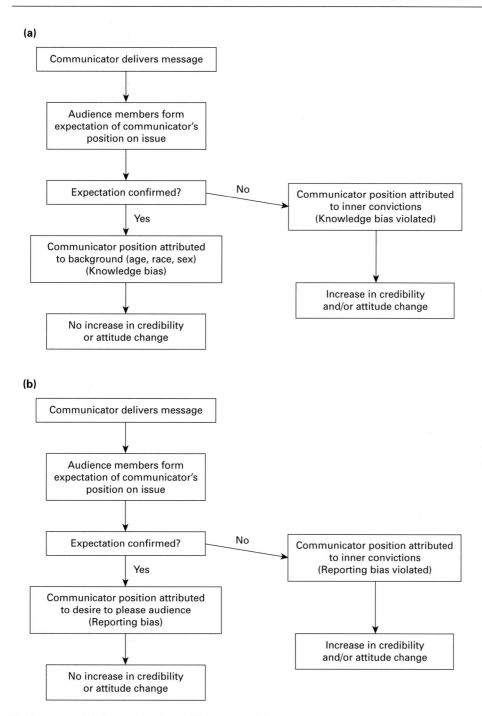

Figure 8.6 (a) Knowledge bias; (b) reporting bias.

■ **Figure 8.7** The comedian and celebrity Bill Cosby may have gained credibility when he defied expectations, blaming African-American parents who bought their children expensive sneakers but refused to spend money on an educational phonics package. Do you think Cosby was persuasive, or instead irritated those he hoped to convert?

Image courtesy of Getty Images.

Social Attractiveness

Credibility is an important factor in persuasion. But it is not the only communicator characteristic that influences attitudes. Socially attractive communicators—those who are likeable, similar to message recipients, and physically appealing—can also induce attitude change. Let's see how.

Likeability

Do you know someone who is just so nice and appealing you can't reject what he says? This person may score high on likeability. There is evidence that likeable communicators can change attitudes (Rhoads & Cialdini, 2002; Sharma, 1999). There are several reasons for this. First, a likeable person makes you feel good, and the positive feelings become transferred to the message. Second, a likeable persuader puts you in a good mood, which helps you access positive thoughts about the product the persuader is peddling. Third, a likeable speaker may convey that she has your interest at heart, which communicates goodwill.

Likeability effects appear in a variety of public arenas, from politics to corporate consulting. One context in which likeability matters is one that probably would not occur to you initially: tipping waiters and waitresses. Restaurant servers who are likeable get bigger tips (e.g. Rind & Bordia, 1995). What's more, there are several techniques that waiters and waitresses can use to make themselves more likeable; these, in turn, have been found to increase the amount of money customers leave on the table. If anyone reading this book is currently waiting tables, he or she may find these strategies lucrative, or at least useful! Research indicates that the following techniques increase tip size (suggestions culled from Crusco & Wetzel, 1984; Leodoro & Lynn, 2007; Lynn & Mynier, 1993; and Rind & Bordia, 1995, 1996):

■ writing "thank you" on the back of the check;
■ drawing a happy, smiling face on the back of checks before giving them to customers;
■ squatting down next to tables; and
■ touching the diner's palm or shoulder (waitresses only; sorry, guys).

As this discussion suggests, a communicator's *nonverbal behaviors* can enhance liking. For example, a persuader who touches a message recipient lightly on the upper arm or shoulder while making a request is more likely to gain compliance than a communicator who does not touch the target (Segrin, 1993). Making eye contact and standing closer to a target can also enhance persuasion. As you might expect, a host of contextual factors come into play, such as the nature of the touch or gaze, the relationship between communicator and recipient, and gender.

Similarity

Is a communicator who shares your values or perspective or dresses like you do more apt to change attitudes than one who does not? The answer is yes, especially under some conditions.

Similarity between source and receiver can facilitate persuasion in business (Brock, 1965), on social issues (Berscheid, 1966), and for health problems. For example, research indicates that African-American women are more likely to feel positively toward performing a breast self-exam and to getting tested for HIV when the message is delivered by an African-American female (Anderson & McMillion, 1995; Kalichman & Coley, 1995).

There is also anecdotal support for the influences of similarity on attitudes. Think back to Ashley Smith, the Atlanta woman kidnapped by an accused rapist, who talked the man into turning himself in (see Box 1.1). Ashley called on her own hard-scrabble background, her own arrests for drunk driving, and redemption through discovery of God. "She felt the sadness and she felt the aloneness—she could relate," her aunt said later. "I don't think a socialite or a squeaky clean could have done that," she said (Dewan & Goodstein, 2005, p. A11).

Political organizers also place a premium on similarity. In September, 2001 a grassroots group that organized protests near Wall Street to protest economic inequality paraded a series of pictures of ordinary people on its Web site, using them as spokespersons for the campaign. Calling itself "We are the 99 percent" to differentiate the group from the wealthiest 1 percent of Americans who had advanced their fortunes during the recession, the ragtag organization unabashedly appealed to communicator–receiver similarity. In one picture a man held up a sign that said, "I am a 50 year-old owner of a local moving company. My business has dropped 75% since 2008. I have sole custody of my 11 year-old daughter. I declared bankruptcy in February 2011. I am the 99%." A young woman, looking visibly frustrated, was pictured near a sign that said, "I am a college senior paying for school myself. I am thousands of dollars in debt . . . I just had to give up grad school because I can't pay. I am the 99%."

Similarity works for some of the same reasons that likeability succeeds. It induces positive affect and promotes favorable cognitive responses. In addition, people compare themselves to similar others. I may infer that if someone who is similar to me endorses a position, it is a good bet that the proposal will work for me as well.

Similarity is particularly likely to succeed if the similarity is relevant to the message (Berscheid, 1966). Salespeople selling running shoes to high school cross-country participants are more likely to make a sale if they explain that they ran 5K races in high school than if they play up the fact that they grew up in the same community as the teenager. However, similarity may fail if the persuader suggests to a message receiver that he is just like the recipient—and is therefore no expert. In this case, the communicator is believed to lack credibility and the recommendation is rejected.

Similarity versus Expertise: "Just Like Me" versus "Too Much Like Me"

The foregoing discussion raises the knotty question of when communicators should stress similarity and when they should emphasize expertise. There are no quick and easy answers. Research suggests that similarity is more effective when people must make personal and emotional decisions (Goethals & Nelson, 1973). In these cases we feel a kinship with the similar other and assume that the similar communicator is more apt to empathize with our concerns than a dissimilar speaker. By contrast, when the issue concerns factual matters, experts' intellectual knowledge may carry the day.

The question of whether a communicator should emphasize expertise or similarity comes up in many real-life persuasion situations. Politicians, advertisers, and sales-people are often faced with deciding whether to emphasize their experience or the fact that they are "just plain folks." Increasingly, it seems, companies are putting a premium on similarity, particularly similarity in appearance. Many businesses, finding that formal attire can turn off clients dressed in jeans or simple pants suits, are telling employees to dress like their clients (Puente, 1999). Indeed, it would seem as if the buttoned-down business announcement has gone out of style. Few who watched the two casually dressed, youthful founders of YouTube announce in a video clip that they had sold their company to Google for $1.65 billion thought twice about the young geeks' informal attire.

Steve Constanides, an owner of a computer graphics firm, exemplifies this trend. "When you went on a sales call, you definitely got a cooler reaction if you showed up in a nice suit, because the clients would see you as just a salesman," Constanides related. "If I came in more casual attire, all of a sudden I'm like them. And it's easier to get a project," he said (Puente, 1999, p. 2D).

On the other hand, if his computer graphics sales staff abandoned expertise entirely and talked just like the clients—saying, "Hey, what's up dude?" or "Man, that's awesome!"— they would probably not sell much high-tech equipment!

Back in 2008, Republican vice-presidential candidate Sarah Palin played on similarity, as she emphasized that she was just "your average hockey mom," married to her high school sweetheart, and raising four children, including an infant son with Down syn-drome. This appealed to many voters until Palin stumbled in her campaign appearances, leading one New York woman, Donna Davis, to observe that she could understand how women felt that Palin could understand their experiences. "The question for them," Davis asked, is: "'Am I ready to be vice-president of the United States?'" (Davis, 2008, p. A28). In Palin's case, her lack of expertise trumped perceived similarity.

Thus, similarity can enhance persuasion until it reduces perceptions of expertise and competence.

Physical Attractiveness

It is something we covet, even if we don't like to admit it. At some level, everyone wants to be physically attractive. Even people who are widely acknowledged to be sexually alluring are never quite satisfied with this or that aspect of their physique. Besides the obvious advantages it bestows in capturing mates, attractiveness attracts for other reasons. We assume that physical appeal can catapult us to success, helping us land the job or deal that we privately covet. A casual glance at celebrities reveals their stunning physical features. Advertisers obviously believe that attractiveness sells. Why else would they employ the sensationally attractive to champion products?

Hold on. Celebrities are not representative of the population as a whole. The fact that advertisers assume attractiveness works does not mean it actually does. This brings up the question: Does attractiveness enhance persuasion? You could argue that it works because physical appeal is a supremely valued commodity in America. Or you could say it doesn't because people resent extremely attractive people, or assume they're dumb. To determine the role physical attractiveness plays in persuasion, researchers conduct experiments pitting communicators who vary in attractiveness against one another, examining who exerts the greatest impact on attitudes. Many studies find that attractiveness enhances persuasion.

In a nifty study, Chaiken (1979) recruited individuals who were high and low in physical appeal and instructed them to approach students on a university campus. Attractive and not-so-attractive communicators gave a spiel, advocating that the university stop serving meat at breakfast and lunch at the campus dining hall. Students who heard the message from the attractive speakers were more inclined to agree that meat should not be served than were students exposed to the less-attractive communicators. The arguments that both sets of speakers gave were exactly the same; the only difference was that one group of communicators was nicer looking than the other. Yet this peripheral factor carried the day, inducing students to change their minds on the topic.

Why does attractiveness influence attitudes? First, people are more likely to pay attention to an attractive speaker, and this can increase the odds that they will remember message arguments. Second, attractiveness becomes associated with the message. The pleasant affect one feels when gazing at a pretty woman or handsome guy gets merged with the message, resulting in an overall favorable evaluation of the topic. Third, people like and identify with attractive communicators. At some level, perhaps unconscious, we feel we can improve our own standing in life if we do what attractive people suggest. Fourth, attractive individuals may simply be better public speakers. As psychologist Susan Fiske explains, "if you're beautiful or handsome, people laugh at your jokes and interact with you in such a way that it's easy to be socially skilled" (Belluck, 2009, p. 8).

Contextual factors. A communicator's physical appeal can add sweetness and value to a product or person. Most of us, scholar Daniel S. Hamermesh (2011) notes, "prefer as customers to buy from better-looking salespeople, as jurors to listen to better-looking attorneys, as voters to be led by better-looking politicians, as students to learn from better-looking professors" (p. 12; see also Figure 8.8).

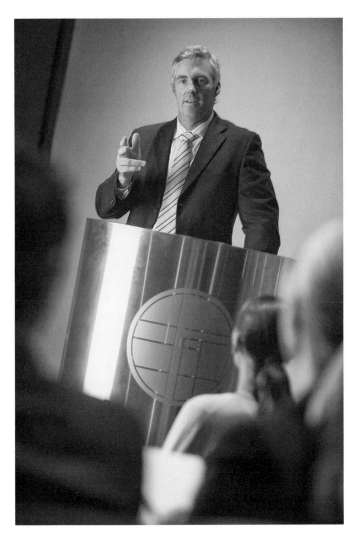

■ **Figure 8.8 Physical attractiveness can enhance persuasion in a variety of situations. The interesting questions are why attractiveness influences attitudes and when it is most likely to be effective.**

Image courtesy of Shutterstock.

Attractive communicators seem to be more effective than their less attractive counterparts, everything else being equal. But everything else is never totally equal. Attractiveness influences attitudes more under certain conditions than under others.

First, attractiveness can help form attitudes. One reason people begin buying certain perfumes or toothpastes is that they link the product with attractive models, and develop a favorable attitude toward the product. Unfortunately, the same process can work with unhealthy products like cigarettes, which is one reason why cigarette advertisements feature physically attractive smokers.

Second, attractiveness can be effective when the communicator's goal is to capture attention. This is one reason why advertisers use drop-dead gorgeous models. They want to break through the clutter and get people to notice the product. Once that is accomplished, they rely on other strategies to convince people to purchase the good or service.

Third, attractiveness can be effective under low involvement, as when people are trying to decide which of two advertised convenience store products to buy or for whom to vote in a low-level election. In these cases, physical appeal acts as a peripheral cue.

Fourth, on the other extreme, attractiveness can be a deciding factor when the communicator's physical appeal is relevant to the product. In cases of beauty products or expensive clothing lines, a model's or salesperson's good looks can swing the sale. Physical appeal serves as an argument for the product, as the ELM suggests. Interestingly, attractiveness is particularly helpful in selling an appearance-related product when people are high in involvement (Trampe et al., 2010). If you are hunting for the right outfit for a job interview and are attending closely to online apparel advertisements, the ad with the nice-looking model can provide a strong argument that this is the outfit you should buy. Notice how powerful attractiveness is: It works under low and high involvement, but for different reasons.

Fifth, attractiveness can influence opinions when it violates expectations. Consider the true story of Rebekka Armstrong, former *Playboy* playmate who contracted HIV from intercourse with a male model. After years of suffering, denial, and drug abuse, Armstrong went public with her story, trying to teach young people the dangers of unprotected sex. She has spoken to capacity university crowds and has her own Web site (Perloff, 2001). Why might she be effective?

Your image—or schema—of a *Playboy* model does not include contracting HIV. This disconfirms your expectation, and you have to think about it to put things back together mentally. As one listens to an attractive model like Armstrong talk, one discovers that she is arguing for these positions not because of a knowledge or reporting bias—but because she truly believes people must take precautions against AIDS. Thus, when attractive communicators say or do unexpected things that seem out of sync with their good looks and these events can be attributed to inner convictions, these speakers can influence attitudes.

When doesn't attractiveness make a difference?

Physical appeal cannot change deeply felt attitudes. Listening to an attractive speaker explain why abortion is necessary is not going to change the mind of a staunch pro-life advocate. Attractiveness is rarely enough to close a deal when the issue is personally consequential or stimulates considerable thinking.

Just as attractiveness can work when it positively violates expectations, it can fail when it negatively violates expectations of what is appropriate for a particular job or role (Burgoon, 1989). You would not expect your family doctor to be sensationally attractive. If the doctor accentuates his or her physical attributes, this could interfere with processing the message or lead you to derogate the doctor. "Patients and colleagues may dismiss a young doctor's skills and knowledge or feel their concerns aren't being taken seriously when the doctor is dressed in a manner more suitable for the gym or a night on the town," one medical expert noted (Marcus, 2006, p. D5). (On the other hand, some might argue that patients display a subtle prejudice when they reject an expert *because* she is good looking.)

Finally, attractiveness effects tend to be rather short lived. As a primarily peripheral cue, attractiveness tends not to be integrated with the person's overall attitude. The person may feel positively toward the communicator, but fail to do the cognitive work necessary to develop a strong, lasting attitude toward the issue.

Beauty, in sum, has always fascinated us. It always will. Attractiveness is commonly assumed to weave a magical spell on people. Its effects are more psychological than astrological, and are inevitably due to individuals letting themselves be bowled over by an attractive person or allowing themselves to fantasize about what will happen if they go along with the communicator's recommendations.

Real-world persuaders have long recognized that attractiveness sells, even if they are less familiar with the psychological trappings of attractiveness effects. Advertisers use physical appeal as a peripheral cue to sell many products and as a central argument for beauty products. Drug companies hire former college cheerleaders to sell pharmaceutical products to doctors. In an article headlined, "Gimme an Rx! Cheerleaders Pep Up Drug Sales," a *New York Times* reporter describes how ex-cheerleaders, including a former Miss Florida USA, traipse into physicians' offices promoting pharmaceutical products. They combine physical appeal, charm, and likeability to influence the nation's doctors, who are mostly men. "There's a saying that you'll never meet an ugly drug rep," one physician said (Saul, 2005, p. A1).

Discriminating *in favor* of physically attractive women is not against the law in the United States. And handsome, athletic men are also apt to be hired as pharmaceutical reps and lobbyists. Attractiveness raises ethical issues when individuals are hired solely on the basis of their physical appeal or someone less attractive is fired, as has happened with older female newscasters. The pursuit of beauty also raises ethical issues when advertisements featuring unrealistically thin models tempt adolescent girls to starve themselves and adopt dangerously unhealthy diets (see Box 8.3).

BOX 8.3 PHYSICAL ATTRACTIVENESS AND CULTURE

Is attractiveness relative?

Is physical beauty culturally relative, or are standards of beauty universal phenomena? It's an interesting question, with relevance for attractiveness effects in persuasion.

Some scholars argue that signs of youth, such as cleanliness, clear skin, and absence of disease, are universally perceived as attractive. They note that there is consensus across cultures that symmetrical faces are attractive (Buss & Kenrick, 1998). Evolutionary psychologists consistently find that across different societies men like full lips, long glistening hair, symmetrical features, a small distance between the mouth and chin, and a waist-to-hip ratio of approximately .7 (Brooks, 2011). Fair enough—but culture leaves its imprint in a host of other ways.

In the United States, thin is in. Lean, ever-skinnier female models define the culture's standard for beauty in women. There has been a significant reduction in body measurements of *Playboy* centerfolds and beauty pageant contestants over time (see Harrison & Cantor, 1997). Cosmetic plastic surgery has increased dramatically, with tummy tucks up by over 140 percent since 1997 (Kuczynski, 2006). Yet thinness in women—propelled by the fashion industry, advertising, and young girls' desire to emulate sometimes dangerously thin models—is a relatively new cultural invention. In earlier eras, voluptuous body shapes were regarded as sexy. "The concept of beauty has never been static," researcher April Fallon reports (1990, p. 84).

Going a long, long way back in time, one finds that, between 1400 and 1700, "fat was considered both erotic and fashionable . . . Women were desired for their procreative value and were often either pregnant or nursing. The beautiful woman was portrayed as a plump matron with full, nurturant breasts" (Fallon, 1990, p. 85). The art of Botticelli and Rubens reflects this ideal.

There are also subcultural variations in what is regarded as beautiful in the United States. Research shows that African-American women are less likely than White women to be preoccupied with body weight (Angier, 2000b). "It's a cultural thing," observed Roneice Weaver, a coauthor of *Slim Down Sister*, a weight-loss book for Black women. She said that Black men don't judge women's physical appeal by their waist size (Angier, 2000b, p. D2).

The attractiveness of other body features also varies with culture. In America, breast size is linked with beauty, as indicated by the popularity of bras that pad and surgical breast implants. Yet in Brazil, large breasts are viewed as déclassé, "a libido killer," and in Japan bosoms are less enchanting than the nape of the neck, which is seen as an erotic zone (Kaufman, 2000, p. 3). In Peru, big ears are considered beautiful, and Mexican women regard low foreheads as an indication of beauty (de Botton, 2000).

Standards for male attractiveness also vary across cultures and historical periods. Macho guys like Humphrey Bogart and Marlon Brando have been replaced by softer-looking icons of attractiveness, like Leonardo DiCaprio, Justin Timberlake, Robert Pattinson, Bruno Mars, and other music stars just breaking into the mainstream (Fitzpatrick, 2000).

To be sure, there are some universals in physical appeal. Yet culture still powerfully influences standards of physical appeal. Increasingly, the American emphasis on hourglass Barbie-like figures has insinuated itself into other cultures, which historically valued plumper physiques (Rohter, 2007). As Fallon notes, "Culturally bound and consensually validated definitions of what is desirable and attractive play an important part in the development of body image" (1990, p. 80). Our standards for what is beautiful are acquired and molded through culture, with the mass media playing an influential role in transmitting and shaping cultural norms. Technological innovations exert insidious influences. "On the covers of magazines, all the beautiful women are photoshopped, their skin is cleaned up. Everybody does it," notes a beauty specialist at a San Francisco advertising firm (Williams, 2008, p. 12). In this way young women acquire unrealistic and false notions of attractiveness. Thus, culture leaves a strong imprint on conceptions of physical attractiveness, and we apply these—consciously and unconsciously—in evaluating everyday persuaders.

CONCLUSIONS

This chapter has focused on the communicator—a key feature of persuasion. The concept of charisma comes to mind when we think about the communicator, and for good reason: charismatic speakers captivate audiences, influencing attitudes in benevolent and malevolent ways. Charisma involves a host of characteristics, not well understood, and for this reason scholars have tried to break down the term into constituent parts. Preferring a scientific approach to this topic, researchers have focused painstakingly on three core communicator qualities: authority, credibility, and social attractiveness.

Authority, epitomized by the Milgram study of obedience, can influence behaviors through a process of compliance. Participants in the Milgram study obeyed a legitimate authority significantly more than experts predicted—a testament to the role of early socialization, authority's trappings, and binding psychological forces. Although Milgram's experiments raised questions about the ethics of deception in research, they nonetheless shed light on continuing crimes of obedience in society.

Credibility, a distant cousin of authority, is a critical communicator factor, the cornerstone of effective persuasion. Research suggests that expertise, trustworthiness, and goodwill are the three core dimensions of credibility. (Expertise and trustworthiness have emerged with greater regularity, and goodwill has been uncovered in more recent research.)

Each of these factors is important in its own right, and can interact with contextual factors, such as audience size, communicator role, and historical epoch.

Major theoretical approaches to credibility include the ELM and an expectancy-violation model. The latter assumes that communicators gain in credibility to the degree that they take unexpected positions on issues—stands that audiences cannot attribute to their background or situation.

Social attractiveness consists of three elements: likeability, similarity, and physical appeal. All three factors can influence attitudes under particular conditions and have intriguing implications for everyday persuasive communication (see Box 8.4).

Interestingly, credibility and social attractiveness translate easily to the interactive environment.

You have probably come across Web sites that convey credibility or lack thereof. Undoubtedly you have glimpsed visually attractive sites that invite exploration and lead you to positively evaluate the sponsoring organization. Research shows that expertise is conveyed by comprehensiveness of information listed on the site, as well as by sponsor credentials (Dutta-Bergman, 2004; Fogg, 2003; Metzger, Flanagin, & Medders, 2010). Trustworthiness is enhanced by including explicit policy statements and by lack of advertising. Social attractiveness is conveyed by layout, colorful pictures, and perceived beauty. These features can also be used to mislead or bamboozle consumers. But once again, we see that "who says it" and the nature of the source are fundamental facets of persuasion, as critical to effective persuasion today as they were in Aristotle's age of oral communication. Messages and channels have changed, but, as the song from *Casablanca* puts it, the fundamental things apply.

BOX 8.4 COMMUNICATOR TIPS

Can research and theory offer practical suggestions on how to be a more effective communicator? You bet! Here are five ideas, gleaned from persuasion concepts and experiments:

1. If you are delivering a speech and have technical knowledge about the topic, you should let your audience know this at the outset. Don't blow your horn too much or you will come off as obnoxious. Instead, discreetly note your credentials. If, on the other hand, you are new on the job and have not accumulated much technical knowledge, don't mention this before you give the talk. There is some evidence that this could reduce your credibility in the audience's eyes (Greenberg & Miller, 1966). Instead, demonstrate your qualifications as you discuss your ideas (Whalen, 1996).

2. Show your audience you care about both the topic and your role as a persuader. Goodwill counts for a great deal in persuasion, as discussed earlier. People forgive a lot if they believe you have their interests at heart. You should be true to yourself here: don't fake deep caring if you don't feel it. Instead, identify one or two issues that you are legitimately interested in imparting, and focus on these.

3. Try to get the audience to like you. Likeability can enhance persuasion (Sharma, 1999), so you should find a feature of your personality that you are comfortable with and let this shine through during your talk. It may be your serenity, sensitivity, gregariousness, or sense of humor. Use this as a way to connect with the audience.

Continued

4. Find out as much as you can about your audience's tastes, attitudes, and familiarity with the issues under discussion. The ELM emphasizes that persuasion works best when it is attuned to the processing style of the audience. If working in an organization, "you should make a concerted effort to meet one-on-one with all the key people you plan to persuade," Conger advises (1998, p. 89). This will provide you with the range of viewpoints on the issue and help you gear your presentation accordingly.

Test your knowledge now with interactive exercises

Chapter 9

Fundamentals of the Message

 Listen now to the author's chapter summary

How should you say it? Just how should you mold your message? Should you insert the florid phrase or the dull, but venerable, adjective? Should you hit the audience over the head with the argument or hedge your bets? Is it better to wow them with fancy stats or tug at their heartstrings by telling a tale of woe? If you want to convince smokers to quit, should you scare the bejeebers out of them or just frighten them a little? These questions center on the message, a time-honored factor in persuasion research and the focus of the next two chapters.

The message has endlessly fascinated persuasion scholars. Aristotle delineated different message factors, emphasizing that deductive syllogisms are the centerpiece of strong rhetorical arguments. Twentieth-century rhetoricians, building on Aristotle's foundations, identified key components of valid, cogent arguments (Toulmin, 1958). Contemporary scholars assume as a first principle that messages cannot be understood without appreciating the psychology of the audience. They have explored the influences of different message factors on receivers, trying to understand which components have the most impact and why. This chapter focuses on the structure, content, and style of the persuasive message. Chapter 10 explores the psychology of emotional messages, primarily fear appeals.

UNDERSTANDING THE MESSAGE

It seems pretty obvious.

The message—what you say and how you say it—influences people. Uh-huh, an intelligent person impatient with intellectual theories might think; now can we move on? Persuasion scholars would like to move on too—they have books to write, students to teach, and families to feed. But they—and you too, no doubt—recognize that the message construct is so big and unwieldy that it needs to be broken down, decomposed, and analyzed in terms of content and process.

This chapter explores four categories of message factor (see Table 9.1). The first concerns the structure of the message—how it is prepared and organized. The second is the specific content of the communication. The third factor is framing; and the fourth focuses on a related factor, language—how communicators use words and symbols to persuade an audience. Emotional appears are discussed in the next chapter.

■ **Table 9.1 Key message factors**

Message structure

1. Message sidedness
2. Conclusion drawing
3. Order of presentation (primacy vs. recency)*

Message content

1. Evidence
2. Narrative

Framing

1. Frames that define the problem and recommend a solution

Language

1. Speed of speech
2. Powerless versus powerful language
3. Intense language
4. Political language

Emotional appeals

1. Fear-arousing messages
2. Guilt appeals

* Primacy occurs when an argument presented early in a message, or the first of two opposing messages, is most persuasive. Recency occurs when an argument presented later in a message, or the second of two opposing messages, is most compelling. There is no conclusive evidence in favor of either primacy or recency. Effects depend on situational factors, such as amount of time that elapses between messages, and audience involvement.

MESSAGE STRUCTURE

How should you package your message? What is the best way to organize your arguments? These are practical questions, ones that have attracted research interest since Hovland's path-breaking studies of the 1950s. There are two particularly interesting issues here. The first concerns whether communicators should present both sides of the issue or just their own. The second focuses on the most persuasive way to conclude the message.

One or Two Sides?

A *one-sided message* presents one perspective on the issue. A *two-sided message* offers arguments on behalf of both the persuader's position and the opposition. Which is more persuasive?

You might argue that it is best to ignore the other side and hammer home your perspective. After all, this lets you spend precious time detailing reasons why your side is correct. On the other hand, if you overlook opposition arguments with which everyone is familiar, you look like you have something to hide. For example, returning to an example discussed in Chapter 5, let's say you are one of those individuals who is fed up with people who text and yak on the cell phone when they drive. You have decided, after years of frustration, to take this issue to the city council. Should you present one or both sides of this issue to council members?

A review of **message sidedness** research provides an answer to this question. Two communication scholars conducted *meta-analyses* of research on one- and two-sided messages. A meta-analysis is a study of other studies. A researcher locates all the investigations of a phenomenon and uses statistical procedures to determine the strength of the findings. After exhaustively reviewing the many studies in this area, researchers Mike Allen (1998) and Daniel J. O'Keefe (1999) reached the same conclusion, something that does not always happen in social science research! Researchers O'Keefe and Allen concluded that *two-sided messages influence attitudes more than one-sided messages, provided one very important condition is met: the message refutes opposition arguments.* When the communication mentions, but not does demolish, an opponent's viewpoint, a two-sided message is actually less compelling than a one-sided message.

Refutational two-sided messages, as they are called, gain their persuasive advantage by: (a) enhancing the credibility of the speaker (he or she is perceived as honest enough to discuss both sides of the coin); and (b) providing cogent reasons why opposing arguments are wrong.

This has obvious implications for your speech urging a ban on talking on a cell phone while driving. You should present arguments for your side (texting or talking on a handheld cell phone while driving is a dangerous distractor) and the other position (there are other distractors, like putting a CD in the disc player or applying makeup, which should also be banned if local government is planning to restrict cell phone use). You should then refute the other side, citing evidence that texting while driving has caused large numbers of automobile accidents; cell phone use causes more serious accidents than other distractors because it interferes with visual processing skills; and talking on the phone is a prolonged, not temporary, distraction from the road.

You could end on a quantitative crescendo by citing evidence, such as a National Safety Council estimate that some 1.6 million crashes that occur each year—28 percent of the total—are caused by drivers who are texting or using cell phones (Brody, 2011). Armed with two-sided arguments, you should have a better chance of convincing your city council to adopt a more safety-conscious policy on cell phone use.

On a more philosophical level, the sidedness research leaves us with a reassuring finding about human nature. It tells us that communicators can change attitudes when they are fair, mention both sides, and offer cogent arguments in support of their position. The results celebrate values most of us would affirm: honesty and intellectual rigor.

Conclusion Drawing

Should persuaders *explicitly* draw the conclusion? Should they wrap things up for listeners in an unambiguous, forceful fashion, making it 100 percent clear which path they want audience members to pursue? Or should they be more circumspect and indirect, letting audience members put things together for themselves? These questions point to the question of explicit versus implicit conclusion drawing. Arguments can be made for both sides. Perhaps, since audience attention wanders, it is best to present a detailed and forceful conclusion. On the other hand, people might prefer that persuaders not tell them explicitly what to do, but instead allow them to arrive at the conclusion on their own.

A meta-analysis of research provides us with an answer to this dilemma. O'Keefe (1997) found that messages clearly or explicitly articulating an overall conclusion are more persuasive than those that omit a conclusion. As McGuire bluntly observed: "In communication, it appears, it is not sufficient to lead the horse to the water; one must also push his head underneath to get him to drink" (1969, p. 209). Making the conclusion explicit minimizes the chances that individuals will be confused about where the communicator stands. It also helps people to comprehend the message, which in turn enhances source evaluations and persuasion (Cruz, 1998).

MESSAGE CONTENT

Evidence

- American adolescents are steering clear of risky behaviors. Teenagers' use of tobacco, alcohol, and most illegal drugs is significantly lower than it was three decades ago. In 1980, more than 30 percent of high school seniors had smoked cigarettes in the past month; by 2011, that number had dropped to less than 1 in 5 (Parker-Pope, 2012).
- Passive smoking is a major cause of lung cancer. A husband or wife who has never smoked has an approximately 16 percent increased chance of contracting lung cancer if he or she lives with a smoker.
- Median earnings for college graduates are more than $21,000 higher than median salary and wages for high school graduates in a given year and nearly twice as much over the course of a lifetime.
- There was no forensic evidence linking Casey Anthony to the murder of her 2-year-old-daughter Caylee. The prosecution could not supply concrete evidence that proved Casey had murdered her daughter by administering chloroform and applying duct tape.

These diverse arguments have one thing in common: they use evidence to substantiate their claims. Evidence is employed by persuaders working in a variety of settings, including advertising, health, and politics. Evidence, John C. Reinard notes, is a classic "building block of arguments," or "information used as proof" (1991, p. 102). **Evidence** is a broad term, McCroskey observes. He defines it as: "factual statements originating from a source other than the speaker, objects not created by the speaker, and opinions of persons other than the speaker that are offered in support of the speaker's claims" (1969, p. 170).

Evidence consists of factual assertions, quantitative information (like statistics; see Figure 9.1), eyewitness statements, testimonials, or opinions advanced by credible sources. We are all familiar with evidence and have witnessed its use many times. Communication researchers, also intrigued by evidence, have conducted numerous studies over a 50-year period, probing the effects of evidence on attitudes. Does evidence change attitudes?

You bet.

"The use of evidence produces more attitude change than the use of no evidence," Rodney A. Reynolds and J. Lynn Reynolds declare after reviewing the many studies in the area (2002, p. 428). Reinard goes further, observing that "there actually may be more consistency in evidence research than can be found in almost any other area of

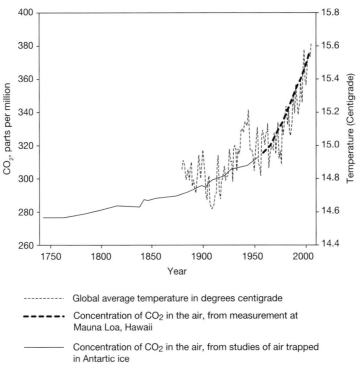

---------- Global average temperature in degrees centigrade

▬ ▬ ▬ ▬ ▪ Concentration of CO₂ in the air, from measurement at
Mauna Loa, Hawaii

─────── Concentration of CO₂ in the air, from studies of air trapped
in Antartic ice

■ **Figure 9.1 This graph illustrates the ways evidence can be harnessed in persuasion. The figure shows that the amount of carbon dioxide in the air has risen about 35 percent since the beginning of the Industrial Revolution in the 1700s. During this same period, the global average temperature has risen about 0.7°C. Scientists attribute this to human activities, like the burning of fossil fuels. The use of evidence can bolster the case for global warming, a controversial social issue.**

Data from Carbon Dioxide Information Analysis Center, Oakridge National Laboratory, and the National Climatic Data Center, National Oceanographic & Atmospheric Administration. Graph supplied courtesy of Paul B. Shepson.

persuasion. Evidence appears to produce general persuasive effects that appear surprisingly stable" (1988, p. 46).

When Evidence Persuades

Evidence is especially persuasive when attributed to a highly credible source—an outgrowth of principles discussed in the previous two chapters. Evidence is also more apt to change attitudes, the more plausible and novel it is (Morley & Walker, 1987).

Persuaders must do more than simply mention evidence: audience members must recognize that evidence has been offered in support of a proposition and perceive the evidence to be legitimate (Parrott et al., 2005; Reynolds & Reynolds, 2002). If individuals are dozing off and don't hear the evidence, or they dispute the legitimacy of the factual assertions, the evidence presented has less impact on attitudes.

Evidence, in short, must be processed. The ELM reminds us that the ways in which evidence is elaborated determine its effect on persuasion. When people are highly involved in or knowledgeable about the issue, evidence will be processed centrally. Under these circumstances, quality of evidence matters. Cogent evidence can change people's minds. But remember: even the most compelling evidence is unlikely to change strong attitudes—those that touch on the self-concept or core values.

Evidence can have striking effects under low involvement, but it works through different processes. When people lack motivation or ability to decipher the issue, they rely on peripheral cues. They may go along with arguments that sound impressive because the communicator cites many facts, uses highfalutin statistics, or throws in testimonial statements. The trappings of evidence are more important than the legal or statistical quality of the facts. Evidence operates more as a cue than an argument when people are not motivated or knowledgeable about the issue. In such cases, communicators can use evidence truthfully, or they can lie with statistics (Huff, 1954). This highlights once again the ways persuasion can be used for morally positive, as well as more questionable, purposes.

The next section continues the discussion of the persuasive message, focusing on an attribute that works through very different psychological processes from evidence.

Narrative

A movie plot spins around in your head for days as you mull over the moral courage the main character displayed in the face of personal danger. A short story presents a compelling portrait of a teenage girl brimming with pride, but also feeling anxious, as she delivers a baby she had once considered aborting. You are moved by a television drama that tells the tale of a young man who joins the Peace Corps and matriculates to South Africa to escape his family, only to find himself caught up in the daily suffering experienced by children with HIV. The program offers a nuanced portrait of the kids— their innocence in the face of a global pandemic, but also their street-wise antics as they pick the Peace Corps activist's pockets as he sleeps. The program movingly depicts the stark realities of AIDS in Africa, along with the personal challenges the characters face as they deal with the brutal challenges of everyday life.

The examples—hypothetical, but similar to current media fare—exemplify narrative persuasion (Bilandzic & Busselle, 2013). We are familiar with communications that harness stories in the service of persuasion. They are all around us: on television, in movie theaters, on our Kindles, and sometimes, in glorified form, in video games. As discussed in Chapter 1, these communications fall into the category of borderline persuasion because the communicator typically does not intend to change attitudes so much as to enlighten or agitate. And yet, as Timothy C. Brock and his colleagues note, "*Public narratives*—the stories we hear everyday in the news media and the stories that we consume in books, films, plays, soap operas, and so forth—command a large share of our waking attention" (Brock, Strange, & Green, 2002, p. 1). What's more, social narratives in books and movies have profoundly affected society. Charles Dickens' descriptions of life in 19th-century England awakened people to the plight of children working in dangerous factories. Novels about race (Harriet Beecher Stowe's *Uncle Tom's Cabin*, James Baldwin's *The Fire Next Time*) helped build social movements that led to the Civil War in the 19th century and the civil rights protests of the 1960s. The list of movies that have influenced beliefs and attitudes is seemingly endless. One thinks of *Schlindler's List*, *Saving Private Ryan*, *Milk*, *The Help*, *The Adjustment Bureau*, even *Super Size Me*. You can probably think of other movies that affected your outlook toward social issues (see Figure 9.2).

For years the academic literature on persuasion neglected the impact of public narratives on attitudes, emphasizing instead the effects of advocacy (e.g., messages deliberately designed to change attitudes). Over the past decade, researchers have discovered narrative and have explored the impact of a multitude of entertainment stories on attitudes and intentions. Researchers have probed effects of narratives on such issues as cancer, unplanned teenage pregnancy, obesity, HIV/AIDS, and the death penalty (e.g., Dunlop, Wakefield, & Kashima, 2010; Moyer-Guse & Nabi, 2010; Murphy et al., 2011; Niederdeppe, Shapiro, & Porticella, 2011; Slater, Rouner, & Long, 2006; Smith, Downs, & Witte, 2007).

What exactly is a narrative? It is a "symbolic representation of events" that employs elements that typically are not used in persuasive messages (Bilandzic & Busselle, 2013). These include characters, plotlines, and dramatic devices that draw more on the features of fiction than on explicit advocacy. Specifically, **narrative** is defined as "any cohesive and coherent story with an identifiable beginning, middle, and end that provides information about scene, characters, and conflict; raises unanswered questions or unresolved conflict; and provides resolution" (Hinyard & Kreuter, 2007, p. 778).

Narrative seems to work through different psychological processes from advocacy messages that employ standard argumentative fare, such as speeches, public service announcements, and blogs. Advocacy communications influence attitudes by evoking

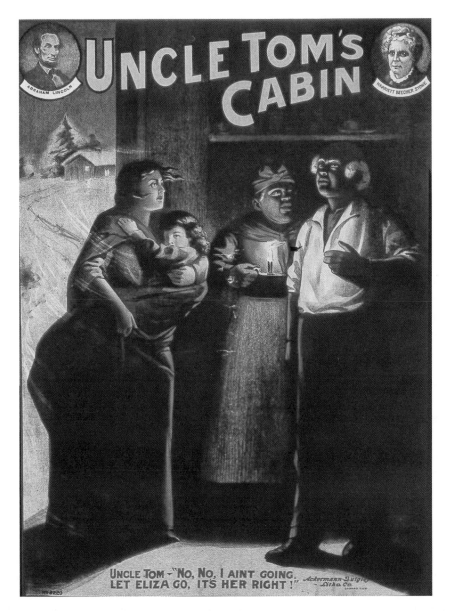

■ Figure 9.2 Narrative persuasion—the telling of stories—can powerfully influence
attitudes. The 19th-century novel *Uncle Tom's Cabin* is widely believed to have stirred
the conscience of Northerners in the United States, helping lay the groundwork for the
Civil War. Narratives depicted in movies can also change beliefs and attitudes.
Research is shedding light on the processes and effects of narrative messages.

Image courtesy of Getty Images.

central and peripheral processing, calling on social norms, and arousing inconsistencies. Narrative is different.

Transporting Us to Different Places

Transportation, articulated by Melanie C. Green and Timothy C. Brock (2000, 2002), offers an engaging view of narrative impact. Great novels and artistic works transport people to different mental arenas—the world of the author's imagination. "The traveler returns to the world of origin, somewhat changed by the journey" (Gerrig, 1993, p. 11). Psychologically transported or immersed in a story, individuals generate mental images of events that, while literally untrue, play out figuratively in their minds, inducing questioning of existing beliefs. While transfixed by the artist's creation of an imaginary world, individuals may be more open to questioning their ideas than when they are focusing on an ordinary persuasive message. The narrative may inhibit the normal process of counterarguing with a persuasive message, in part because it can be psychologically difficult to offer logical arguments to a panorama of mental images that a story stimulates (Bilandzic & Busselle, 2013; see also Mazzocco & Brock, 2006; Skalski et al., 2009).

Transportation captures the experience a lot of us have when we become immersed in a story. In research you have to test your ideas in the real world, and Green and Brock (2000) devised a nifty way to study these issues empirically. They developed a scale to measure the tendency to become transported to the narrative world created by the artist. Their scale includes items like: "I was mentally involved in the narrative while reading it" and "I could picture myself in the scene of the events described in the narrative." Focusing on the reading experience, Green and Brock asked research participants to read an evocative story, "Murder at the Mall," that concerned a college student whose younger sister is brutally murdered by a psychiatric patient at the mall. The researchers then asked participants a series of questions about the story and characters.

Eager to determine the impact of being transported into a narrative world, Green and Brock examined participants' responses to questions, such as those above. Individuals who strongly agreed that transportation scale items described them to a tee were classified as high in transportation. Those who said these statements did not describe their personalities particularly well were classified as low in transportation. Highly transported individuals were more influenced by the story, reporting more beliefs consistent with the narrative. After reading the story, they were more likely than low-transported participants to believe that the world was less just and psychiatric patients' freedoms should be curtailed. They were less inclined to doubt the story, viewing it as more authentic than those low in transportation.

Emboldened by this perspective and intrigued about its applications to television entertainment, four University of Southern California researchers, located not far from the world's television and movie entertainment capital, explored whether a lymphoma storyline in a Hollywood television drama could transport viewers, helping them to develop more healthy attitudes toward social support for cancer. A series of six episodes in the TV program *Desperate Housewives* centered on how one of the major female characters, Lynette Scavo, played by Felicity Huffman, had been diagnosed with lymphoma, was subsequently treated with chemotherapy, and became completely bald. She wore a wig, even making love with the wig on. In the end, Lynette began to feel better and was declared cancer free. The California researchers found that transportation mattered and had salutary effects. Viewers who were psychologically transported by the program were particularly likely to feel positively about the importance of social support during cancer and to talk to family and friends about cancer (Murphy et al., 2011).

Besides transporting people, narratives can change attitudes by encouraging identification with characters and facilitating the perception of similarity between oneself and the protagonist (Moyer-Guse & Nabi, 2010; Moyer-Guse, Chung & Jain, 2011).

When Are Narratives Influential?

Narratives do not always carry the day in persuasion. One of the issues that intrigues researchers is whether narratives, with their emphasis on personalized, emotionally engaging stories, have a greater impact on attitudes than does evidence, which emphasizes hard facts and cold numbers.

Some scholars argue that narratives are more effective than evidence. They observe that persuaders—running the gamut from attorneys to advocacy groups to health practitioners—frequently call on vivid, personalized stories, hoping these will hug at our heartstrings and influence beliefs (see Box 9.1). Never mind that these stories sometimes are based on the experience of just one person, and statistics derive from the experiences of hundreds, maybe thousands. Vivid case histories evoke stronger mental images than abstractly presented information, are easier to access from memory, and are therefore more likely to influence attitudes when the individual is trying to decide whether to accept message recommendations (Rook, 1987). Narratives and graphic images are— let's face it—more interesting than statistical evidence (Green & Brock, 2000). As stories, they engage the imagination and are "intuitively appealing to humans, as we are all essentially storytellers and avid story recipients" (Kopfman et al., 1998, p. 281).

An alternative view, put forth by other scholars, is that narratives can be so distracting that they interfere with reception of the message. When this occurs, people fail to process message arguments or overlook the merits of the position advocated in the

BOX 9.1 A VIVID NARRATIVE ON DRINKING AND DRIVING

Mothers Against Drunk Driving and Students Against Drug Driving frequently rely on vivid anecdotes—commonly a part of narratives—to convey their arguments. They undoubtedly regard these as more persuasive than gray statistics about the number of deaths caused by drunk drivers. Here is one particularly gripping example, supplied by a student. She read it during high school prom week, the narrative poem made an indelible impression, and she kept it over the years. As you read it over, ask yourself if you find this persuasive—and if so, why?

> I went to a party, Mom, I remembered what you said.
> You told me not to drink, Mom, so I drank a coke instead . . .
> I know I did the right thing, Mom, I know you're always right.
> Now the party is finally ending, Mom, as everyone drives out of sight . . .
> I started to drive away, Mom, but as I pulled onto the road,
> The other car didn't see me, Mom, it hit me like a load.
> As I lay here on the pavement, Mom, I hear the policeman say
> The other guy is drunk, Mom, and I'm the one who'll pay.
> I'm lying here dying, Mom, I wish you'd get here soon.
> How come this happened to me, Mom? My life burst like a balloon . . .
> The guy who hit me, Mom, is walking. I don't think that's fair.
> I'm lying here dying, Mom, while all he can do is stare . . .
> Someone should have told him, Mom, not to drink and drive.
> If only they would have taken the time, Mom, I would still be alive.
> My breath is getting shorter, Mom. I'm becoming very scared . . .
> Please don't cry for me Mom, because when I needed you, you were always there.
> I have one last question, Mom, before I say goodbye,
> I didn't ever drink, Mom, so why am I to die?

communication (e.g., Frey & Eagly, 1993). According to this view, statistical evidence, dull though it may be, has the upper hand in persuasion. Evidence, as discussed in the previous section and by the ELM, is demonstrably effective, serving multiple functions in the persuasion process.

With such strong logic on the sides of both narratives and statistical evidence, it should come as no surprise that both have been found to influence attitudes (Allen et al., 2000; Kazoleas, 1993). Evidence seems to carry more weight when persuaders are trying to influence cognitions or when people are sufficiently high in involvement that they are motivated to process more informative, evidence-based messages (Braverman, 2008; Kopfman et al., 1998). Narratives may be more impactful when communicators are trying to shake up people who strongly disagree with the message (Slater & Rouner, 1996). Truth be told, we do not yet know the precise circumstances under which narrative outguns evidence and evidence overpowers stories (Bilandzic & Busselle, 2013). Narrative is a relatively new area of scholarly study, compared with evidence, which has generated considerable research.

In the long run, the differential effectiveness of narrative and evidence is of less consequence than the psychology underlying their effects. Evidence works by influencing the likelihood of cognitive elaboration. Narrative operates through more affective processes: transportation, identification with characters, and processes ordinarily associated with reading fiction. A narrative—a story with an educational message—can elide the usual resistance people put up in the face of persuasive messages. However, it will influence individuals only if it is believable and succeeds in immersing individuals in the lives of fictional characters. There is a delicious irony that lies at the heart of narrative persuasion. Sometimes communicators may find that the most effective way to change attitudes about issues steeped in everyday life is to conjure up a universe that exists solely in the spiritual figment known as the human imagination.

Framing

Several decades ago, just when researchers thought they knew all there was to know about human thought processes, a couple of Israeli psychologists conducted an array of studies that transformed the conventional wisdom. At the time, scholars believed that people were rational information processors who made decisions based exclusively on what would maximize their self-interest. Amos Tversky and Daniel Kahneman turned this assumption on its head, showing that people are susceptible to breathtaking biases in intuition. Even the most intelligent and erudite individuals fell prey to cognitive biases and mental traps, frequently induced by how a message is framed. Consider:

In one study, physicians at the Harvard University Medical School read statistics attesting to the success of two different treatments for lung cancer: surgery and radiation. They were then asked to indicate whether they preferred surgery or radiation. Although survival rates over five years favored the surgical option, in the short run, surgery has more risks than radiation. Half of the doctors read this statistic about the short-term consequences of surgery:

The one-month survival rate is 90%.

The other half read this statistic about the outcomes of surgery:

There is 10% mortality in the first month.

Reread the two outcomes. Which would you choose?

Now note that the outcomes are logically the same. Rational thinkers should make the same decision, regardless of which statement they read. But, defying predictions of rationality, the results showed that 84% of the physicians who read the first option chose surgery, compared to just 50% in the second group. The way the outcomes were phrased made all the difference. "Ninety percent survival sounds encouraging whereas 10% mortality is frightening," Kahneman (2011) notes (p. 367).

This illustrates the power of a **frame**, or the overarching way an idea is communicated, or phrased. A frame is the slant, focal point, or frame of reference. To frame, communication researcher Robert Entman (1993), explained:

> is to select some aspects of a perceived reality and make them more salient in a communicating text in such a way as to promote a particular problem definition, causal interpretation, moral evaluation, and/or treatment recommendation.
>
> (p. 52)

Research has documented that simply varying the way a message is framed can strongly influence attitudes. Different versions contain the same facts, but they communicate the information through different frames of reference.

Kahneman and Tversky's research has been criticized for posing artificial, brain-teasing problems that produce results that would not occur in the real world. It is a reasonable criticism. However, in the main this criticism falls short, because their findings have been obtained consistently and over the course of several decades with different populations and in different experimental tests. Their results have done much to enhance understanding of the automatic, not-so-rational processes that underly decision making and attitude change. In 2002, Kahneman and the late Tversky received the Nobel Prize for their work on decision making.

Message framing effects capitalize on subtle but psychologically important variations in message wording (O'Keefe & Jensen, 2006; Simon & Jerit, 2007; Tewksbury & Scheufele, 2009). Frames work by accessing a particular perspective on an issue. Frames can activate mental frameworks, and when the mental frameworks differ in their implications for decision making, the results can be dramatic.

More than a decade ago, Europeans learned of a disturbing difference among four countries in the rate of organ donation connected with accidental death. The organ donation rate was almost 100% in Austria, and 86% in Sweden. But in Germany it was 12% and in Denmark a mere 4%. There is no compelling reason to think that citizens of Austria and Sweden are more inherently compassionate on this issue than their counterparts in Germany and Denmark. So what gives?

Austria and Sweden employ an "opt-out form," in which individuals who prefer not to donate must check a box on a form. Unless they take this step, they are regarded as organ donors. But Germany and Denmark use an "opt-in" form, where individuals have to check a box if they want to donate organs. The first frame makes it difficult for people to say no. They have to expend effort and make a conscious decision to opt out in a context in which peripheral, low-involvement processing may be the norm. The second frame makes it more difficult to opt in. Because many people are ambivalent about organ donation, they may be reluctant to expend the effort necessary to put a checkmark in a box. There may be a variety of other reasons why these countries differ in organ donation rates. However, framing offers a compelling interpretation (Kahneman, 2011; see Figure 9.3).

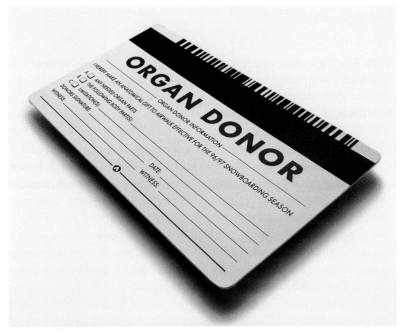

■ **Figure 9.3 How should a communicator frame requests for organ donation? Research in Europe finds that the manner in which organ donation requests are framed, such as the one shown above, can strongly influence donation rates.**

Image courtesy of Getty Images.

Framing has other intriguing implications for persuasion, as will be subsequently discussed. The next section continues this venue by focusing on another area in which words and verbal frameworks matter.

LANGUAGE

Great persuaders have long known that how you say it can be as important as what you say. Persuasion scholars and speakers alike recognize that the words persuaders choose can influence attitudes. But just what impact does language have? How can we get beyond the generalities to hone in on the specific features of language that matter most? How can you use language more effectively yourself in your efforts to convince people to go along with what you recommend?

These are social scientific questions—specific inquiries that allow us to explore theories and see how they play out in everyday life.

Speed of Speech

Ever since America mythologized the fast-talking salesman, people have assumed that fast speakers are more compelling than slow ones. The character Harold Hill in the American classic *The Music Man* epitomizes our stereotype of the fast-talking peddler of wares. Since then, movies, videos, and songs have rhapsodized about the supposed persuasive effects of fast-talking persuaders.

Leave it to social scientists to study the phenomenon! Does speed of speech enhance persuasion? Early studies suggested it did (Miller et al., 1976; Street & Brady, 1982). However, more recent studies have cast doubt on this glib conclusion. Researchers have discovered that speech rate does not inevitably change attitudes and, under some conditions, may not exert a particularly strong impact on attitudes or beliefs (Buller et al., 1992). Just as you can hypothesize that faster speech should be persuasive because it acts as a credibility cue, you can also reason that it should reduce persuasion if it interferes with message processing or annoys the audience ("Don't y'all know we don't speak as fast as you Yankees down here in ol' Alabama?").

Thus, there are both theoretical and practical reasons to argue that speech rate does not have a uniformly positive or negative effect on persuasion. Instead, the most reasonable conclusion is that effects depend on the context. Several contextual factors are important.

First, speech rate may enhance persuasion when the goal of the persuader is to capture attention. Second, it also can be effective when the persuader's goal is to be perceived as competent. Speaking quickly can suggest that the communicator is credible, knowledgeable, or possesses expertise. Moderately fast and fast speakers are seen as more intelligent, confident, and effective than their slower-speaking counterparts.

Third, speech rate can be effective when audience members are low in involvement (Smith & Shaffer, 1995). Under low involvement, speech rate can serve as a peripheral cue. Invoking the heuristic or cultural stereotype that "fast talkers know their stuff," audience members may go along with fast speakers because they assume they are credible or correct. Fast speech may be a facade, employed to disguise a lack of knowledge, but by the time message recipients discover this, they may have already plunked down their money to purchase the product.

Fourth, speech rate can also enhance persuasion when it is relevant to the message topic. A now-famous advertisement for Federal Express depicted a harried businessman, facing an urgent deadline. The man barked out orders to a subordinate and both spoke quickly.

A more recent ad you may have seen on TV or on YouTube harnessed the FedEx fast-speaking technique. It applied it to a business that, like FedEx, values speed of speech: Jimmy John's Sandwich Shop. The ad goes like this, with each person speaking in a staccato voice at lightning-quick speed:

Employer: What's on your mind, kid? Make it fast.
Young man: I'd like to work here at Jimmy John's World's Greatest Gourmet Sandwich Shop, sir.
Employer: Why do you want to work at Jimmy John's, kid?
Young man: I'm perfect for Jimmy John's.
Employer: Doing what?
Young man: Delivery.
Employer: Delivery?
Young man: Delivery.
Employer: We deliver pretty fast here at Jimmy John's.
Young man: That's what I heard.
Employer: What'd you hear?
Young man: You deliver pretty fast here at Jimmy John's.
Employer: Then you heard right.
Young man: I'm a fast study, sir.
Employer: You know the Jimmy John's slogan?
Young man: The Jimmy John's slogan?
Employer: The Jimmy John's slogan is said so fast you'll freak.
Young man: Said so fast you'll freak is a swell slogan, sir.

Employer: When people call for a Jimmy John's sandwich, they want it fast.
Young man: Then I'm your man, sir . . .
Employer: Okay, give me some time to think it over.
Young man: Okay.
Employer: Okay, I've thought it over. When can you start?
Young man: Now.
Employer: Now's good. What's your name, kid?
Young man: Stephanopolopodopolous.
Employer: Too long.
Young man: How about Ed?
Employer: Ed's fine. Welcome aboard, Ed.

The fast-talker ad may have contributed to the success of the Jimmy John's franchise. The symmetry between the theme of the ad—speed of speech—and a business that hyped fast service may have helped promote the restaurant with consumers.

Under other conditions, fast speech is not so likely to enhance credibility or persuasion. When the message concerns sensitive or intimate issues, a faster speaker may communicate insensitivity or coldness (Giles & Street, 1994; Ray, Ray, & Zahn, 1991). When a message focuses on medical problems, safer sex, or a personal dilemma, slow speech may be preferable. In these situations, slow speech may convey communicator concern, empathy, and goodwill.

This plays out on a national political level as well. When citizens are experiencing a national crisis, they may respond more positively to a slower speaker, whose slower pace conveys calm and reassurance. During the 1930s and 1940s, when Americans faced the Depression and World War II, they found solace in the slow speech—and melodious voice—of President Franklin Delano Roosevelt (Winfield, 1994). Had FDR spoken quickly, he might have made people nervous; his pace might have reminded them of the succession of problems that faced them on a daily basis.

Thus, one of the intriguing lessons of speech-rate research is that faster speech is not inherently more effective than slow speech. Instead, persuaders must appreciate context, and the audience's motivation and ability to process the message. It would be nice if we could offer a simple prescription, like one your doctor gives the pharmacist. The reality is that speech-rate effects are more complex. For researchers, complexity is not a throw-up-your-hands stopping point, but a sign that more penetrating perspectives are needed to pull together diverse strands in the research area.

Perhaps the most useful framework to help integrate the different issues in speech-rate research is an interpersonal communication perspective called **communication**

accommodation theory (McGlone & Giles, 2011). The theory is guided by the insight that communicators sometimes adapt their behavior toward others, as when a speaker slows down when talking to an older person. The accommodation perspective looks at when individuals adapt their communication behavior toward others—or accommodate them—and when they diverge from others, or speak in a style that differs from the majority of audience members.

A fast-talking speaker who finds that he is addressing a slower-speaking audience might want to accommodate the audience by slowing his speech rate down. Audience members would appreciate the effort and would also affirm the similarity between the speaker and their own speech style. On the other hand, a speaker could misjudge the situation. For example, she might be talking to an older audience, assume they are slow speakers and reduce her speech rate, only to find the majority are quick-thinking, fast-talking retired neuroscientists, who resent her attempt to pander to them!

From an academic perspective, the communication accommodation framework reminds us that the effects of speech rate on persuasion depend on a host of contextual factors, including: (a) the similarity between the speech rate of the communicator and the audience; (b) the communicator's perceptions of how quickly audience members speak; (c) the audience's perceptions of how quickly the communicator is talking; (d) stereotypes of speech rate that both communicator and audience members bring to bear; and (e) the topic of the message. Complicated stuff, but, as you now appreciate, persuasion is a complicated business.

Powerless versus Powerful Speech

Has this ever happened to you? You're sitting in class when a student raises his hand and says, "I know this sounds like a stupid question, but . . ." and proceeds to ask the professor his question. You cringe as you hear him introduce his query in this manner; you feel embarrassed for your classmate and bothered that someone is about to waste your time with a dumb question. Something interesting has just happened. The student has deliberately undercut his own credibility by suggesting to the class that a query that may be perfectly intelligent is somehow less than adequate. The words preceding the question—not the question itself—have produced these effects, providing another example of the subtle role language plays in communication.

The linguistic form at work here is **powerless speech**. It is a constellation of characteristics that may suggest to a message receiver that the communicator is less than powerful or is not so confident. In contrast, **powerful speech** is marked by the conspicuous absence of these features.

The primary components of powerless speech are:

Hesitation forms. "Uh" and "well, you know" communicate lack of certainty or confidence.

Hedges. "Sort of," "kinda," and "I guess" are phrases that reduce the definitiveness of a persuader's assertion.

Tag questions. The communicator "tags" a declarative statement with a question, as in, "That plan will cost us too much, don't you think?" A tag is "a declarative statement without the assumption that the statement will be believed by the receiver" (Bradley, 1981, p. 77).

Disclaimers. "This may sound a little out of the ordinary, but" or "I'm no expert, of course" are introductory expressions that ask the listener to show understanding or to make allowances.

Researchers have examined the effects of powerless and powerful speech on persuasion. Studies overwhelmingly show that powerless speech is perceived as less persuasive and credible than powerful speech (Burrell & Koper, 1998; Hosman, 2002). Communicators who use powerless speech are perceived to be less competent, dynamic, and attractive than those who speak in a powerful fashion (e.g., Adkins & Brashers, 1995; Erickson et al., 1978; Haleta, 1996; Holtgraves & Lasky, 1999; Hosman, 1989). There are several reasons why powerless communicators are downgraded. Their use of hedges, hesitations, and qualifiers communicates uncertainty or lack of confidence. Powerless speech may also serve as a low-credibility cue, a culturally learned heuristic that suggests the speaker is not intelligent or knowledgeable (Sparks & Areni, 2008). In addition, powerless speech distracts audience members, which reduces their ability to attend to message arguments.

This research has abundant practical applications. It suggests that, when giving a talk or preparing a written address, communicators should speak concisely and directly. They should avoid qualifiers, hedges, tag questions, and hesitations. Instead, they should emphasize assertive speech (see Box 9.2).

Another application of powerless speech research has been to courtroom presentations. Two experts in the psychology of law argue, based on research evidence, that "the attorney should, whenever possible, come directly to the point and not hedge his points with extensive qualifications" (Linz & Penrod, 1984, pp. 44–45). Witnesses, they add, should be encouraged to answer attorneys' questions as directly and with as few hesitations and qualifiers as possible.

Although powerful speech is usually more persuasive than powerless language, there is one context in which powerless speech can be effective. When communicators wish to generate goodwill rather than project expertise, certain types of unassertive speech can work to their advantage.

Let's say that an authority figure wants to humanize herself and appear more down-to-earth in message recipients' eyes. She may find it useful to end some statements with a question. Physicians and therapists frequently use tags to gain rapport with clients. Tag questions such as "That must have made you feel angry, right?," can show empathy with patients' concerns (Harres, 1998). As researcher Annette Harres observed, after studying physicians' use of language devices, "Affective tag questions were a very effective way of showing that the doctor was genuinely concerned about the patient's physical and psychological well-being . . . They can indicate to patients that their concerns are taken seriously" (Harres, 1998, pp. 122–123).

BOX 9.2 LANGUAGE TIPS

How can you use language to spruce up your persuasive communications? Here are several suggestions, based on research and theory:

1. Avoid "uh," "um," and other non-fluencies.
2. Don't use disclaimers ("I'm no expert, but . . ."). Just make your point.
3. If you are nervous, think through the reasons you feel that way and try to increase your confidence. You may feel better by sharing your uncertainty with your audience, but the powerlessness you convey will reduce your persuasiveness.
4. Vary your pitch as much as possible. Avoid the boring monotone.
5. Accommodate your speech to listeners' language style. If your audience speaks quickly (and your talk does not concern intimate issues), speak at a faster clip.
6. Accommodate to audience language style, but don't pander. One African-American student related a story of a White speaker who addressed her high school class. Trying to be hip, he infused his talk with Black lingo (using phrases of the "yo, what's poppin'?" variety). The students laughed, seeing through his insincere attempt to appeal to them.
7. Be careful about using intense, obscene speech. Intense language can work, particularly when the communicator is credible and the topic is of low ego-

Continued

> involvement. Obscenities can be effective, if listeners expect the speaker to use four-letter words. In his heyday, radio DJ Howard Stern's fans expected him to use obscene speech, and when he used it, he may have positively influenced attitudes. Obscenity can be the norm in certain neighborhoods; thus, if speakers don't swear, they will be disregarded. But in most instances, obscene speech is risky; it violates audience expectations of what is appropriate and can offend key constituents.
>
> 8. Be aware of your nonverbal expressions. About 65 percent of the meaning in an interpersonal interaction is communicated nonverbally (Burgoon, 1994). Thus, you may know your stuff, but if you look like you're not happy to be speaking—because you're frowning or clenching your fists—you can trump the positive effects of expertise. Use facial expressions and a posture that you're comfortable with. And unless you're communicating bad news, smile.

Language Intensity

This is the aspect of language that most people think of when they free-associate about language effects. Language intensity includes metaphors, strong and vivid language, and emotionally charged words. It is the province of political rhetoric, social activism, hate speech, and eloquent public address.

One prominent feature of language intensity is the metaphor. A *metaphor* is "a linguistic phrase of the form 'A is B,' such that a comparison is suggested between the two terms leading to a transfer of attributes associated with B to A" (Sopory & Dillard, 2002, p. 407). For example, former president Ronald Reagan liked to describe America as "a torch shedding light to all the hopeless of the world." The metaphor consists of two parts: A (America) and B ("torch shedding light to all the hopeless of the world"). It suggests a comparison between A and B, such that the properties associated with a torch shedding light to the world's hopeless are transferred to America.

Persuaders in all walks of life employ metaphor as a technique to alter attitudes. Do they work? Researchers Pradeep Sopory and James P. Dillard (2002) conducted a meta-analytic review of the empirical research on metaphor and persuasion. They concluded that messages containing metaphors produce somewhat greater attitude change than do communications without metaphors. Metaphors are effective because they evoke strong semantic associations; these in turn produce a tighter mental organization of the persuasive arguments, helping people to access the arguments more efficiently.

Powerful as metaphors are, they are not the only component of intense language (Bowers, 1964; Hamilton & Hunter, 1998; Hosman, 2002). **Intense language** includes specific, graphic language. It also encompasses emotion-laden words like "freedom" and "beauty," as well as "suffering" and "death." Intense language can also reflect the extremity of the communicator's issue position. A communicator who describes efforts to clone human beings as "disgusting" is using more intense language than one who calls such research "inappropriate." The first speaker's language also points up a more extreme position on the cloning issue.

What impact does such language have on attitudes? Should persuaders deploy vivid, graphic terms? The answer depends on the persuader's goal, his or her credibility, and the audience's involvement in the issue. If the goal is to enhance your dynamism—to convince the audience you are a dynamic speaker—intense language can help you achieve this goal. But intense language will not change the minds of audience members who oppose your position and are ego-involved in the issue (Hamilton & Hunter, 1998; Hosman, 2002). They are too stuck in their ways, too committed to the position for mere word choice to change their minds.

By contrast, if the audience disagrees with your position, but is less personally involved in the issue, it is likely to respond to intense language. The only hitch is that you need to be perceived as credible by those who hear or read your speech. Based on research, one can conclude that *intense language can goad audience members into changing their attitudes toward an issue, provided they are not terribly ego-involved in the matter, the communicator possesses considerable credibility, and the speaker's use of such language is seen as appropriate or suitable in the particular context.* Under these conditions, graphic, emotional language can cause people to pay more attention to the message, which in turn can produce more favorable evaluations of the persuader's position (see Hamilton & Hunter, 1998, for more complex discussions of these issues).

Application: Language and Abortion

Social activists are adept at choosing metaphors that can galvanize support for their cause. They recognize that the way they frame the issue—and the linguistic terms they select—can strongly influence attitudes. Case in point: the appeals made by opponents and supporters of abortion (see Figure 9.4).

Abortion foes chose the metaphor "pro-life" to describe their heartfelt opposition to abortion in the United States. Just about everyone loves life. By linking a fetus with life, activists succeeded in making a powerful symbolic statement. It placed those who did not believe that a fetus constituted a full, living human being on the defensive. What's more, pro-life activists deployed vivid visual metaphors to make their case. They

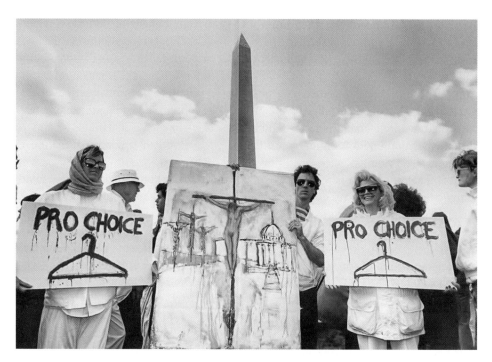

■ **Figure 9.4 Intense language, notably metaphors and vivid language, has characterized persuasive battles on the issue of abortion. Such language can arouse supporters to action, but it can also polarize people. In some cases it may have helped spark violent confrontations.**

Image courtesy of Getty Images.

developed brochures and movies that depicted powerful images—for example, "a fetus floating in amniotic fluid, tiny fetal feet dangled by a pair of adult hands, [and] a mutilated, bloodied, aborted fetus with a misshapen head and a missing arm" (Lavin, 2001, p. 144). These visual images became the centerpiece of a national anti-abortion campaign that began in the 1960s and 1970s.

Over the ensuing decades, the language became more intense, the rhetoric fiercer. Pro-life activists spent much linguistic energy condemning a specific late-term abortion procedure, called partial-birth abortion. The procedure is unpleasant and controversial, and pro-life supporters have gained rhetorical punch by promoting the name "partial-birth abortion" rather than employing a formal medical term, intact dilation and evacuation.

Appreciating the power of language, pro-life advocates have been adept at describing the entity that is removed from the womb as a "baby" rather than a "fetus." The linguistic frame matters. In one study, individuals who read an article on a ban on partial-birth abortion that used the term "baby" registered more opposition to legalizing partial-birth abortion than those who read the same article with the term "fetus" (Simon & Jerit, 2007).

On the other side of the abortion divide, women's groups that favor abortion rights have also exploited the symbolic power of language and pictures. They used a coat hanger dripping blood as a metaphor for "the horrid means and consequences of the illegal abortions that occur when legal abortion is banned" (Condit, 1990, p. 92). They argued that the fetus should be characterized as a lump of tissues rather than a baby. Pro-choice activists went to lengths to frame the issue around favoring choice rather than supporting abortion.

One popular pro-choice pamphlet presented the Statue of Liberty, with the line that "there are no pictures in this pamphlet, because you can't take a picture of liberty." Condit notes that "the statue—as a woman, a symbol of the downtrodden, and a symbol of Freedom, Liberty, and home—embodied the ideal American representation of Choice or Reproductive Freedom" (1990, pp. 93–94).

Although pro-choice appeals to values like freedom helped to shift the focus of the abortion debate, it did not eliminate the rhetorical power of visual images, like mangled fetuses. The coat hanger packs less rhetorical punch than a bloody fetus, and the choice metaphor loses out in the language-intensity war when pitted against graphic images of "aborted babies." As one abortion advocate conceded, "When someone holds up a model of a 6-month-old fetus and a pair of surgical scissors, we say 'choice,' and we lose" (Klusendorf, 2001). One can acknowledge that some pro-life activists have nothing but pure motives in using this imagery, while also lamenting that it has led to a "visualization of the abortion debate" that has polarized both sides, made compromise more difficult, and in some cases sparked violent and deadly confrontation (Lavin, 2001).

Intense language has also been a persuasive weapon in other issues as well. Proponents and opponents are battling for public opinion. They are trying to change people's attitudes. This is a complex issue. There are many facets, angles, scientific layers, and moral perspectives. As you read about this topic over the coming years, you might take note of the ways in which activists frame the issue. Listen to the words they use. Be cognizant of the words you select to describe the issue to others. Words matter. They can subtly influence the way we think about social issues.

Language and Electoral Politics

> When Aeschines spoke, they said, "How well he speaks." But when Demosthenes spoke, they said, "Let us march . . .".

As this legendary quote illustrates, political oratory has been prized for centuries. In this country, some of the most gifted persuaders have been political leaders. One thinks of Abraham Lincoln's speeches during the Civil War and Franklin D. Roosevelt's fireside chats in the 1930s. During the late 20th century, Ronald Reagan became known as "the great communicator" for his ability to speak simply and persuasively. Political language includes linguistic features discussed earlier: powerful speech, metaphors, and intensity. Its goal is to influence public attitudes and shape political agendas. In an era of mediated communication, the most effective way that leaders can reach citizens is through the media and Internet. What leaders say and how well they say it is a fundamental ingredient of contemporary political leadership.

One important aspect of political speech is *simplicity*. As an example, consider the contrast between presidents Jimmy Carter and Ronald Reagan (see Figure 9.5).

As a thinker, strategist, and peacemaker, Carter was brilliant, a gifted politician who could think outside normal political boundaries. But Carter failed to inspire the American public. He was a dreary, lugubrious speaker whose language confused and dispirited the public. Roderick Hart notes:

> Only a person intent on political suicide would, on national television and radio, use a sentence like the following: "To help curtail the excessive uses of credit and by dampening inflation, they [his new policies] should, along with the budget measures that I have described, speed prospects for reducing the strains which presently exist in our financial markets."
>
> (1984, p. 180)

The rhetorical opposite of Carter, Reagan spoke plainly and clearly. He adapted his language to the demands of television, speaking in short sentences not loaded down by modifying structures. A cabdriver said, "He's the only politician I can understand." In addition, Reagan spoke positively. Drawing shamelessly on American values, he delivered a simple, optimistic message (Perloff, 1998). Consider the following, typical of Reagan's speech:

> We have every right to dream heroic dreams. Those who say that we're in a time when there are no heroes, they just don't know where to look. You can see heroes every day, going in and out of factory gates. Others, a handful in number, produce enough food to feed all of us and then the world beyond. You meet heroes across a

counter. And they're on both sides of that counter . . . Their patriotism is deep. Their values sustain our national life.

(Hart, 1984, p. 228)

The same words would come off as schmaltzy and trite in another speaker.

In Reagan, they played well because he believed what he said and felt what he believed. They also fit the rhetorical demands of the 1980s, an era in which most Americans sought a leader who could restore their faith that America could tackle any problem, whatever its complexity and wherever its geographic origin.

■ **Figure 9.5a–b Presidents Ronald Reagan and Jimmy Carter used political language very differently. Reagan spoke plainly, clearly, and optimistically, colorfully adapting his message to the demands of television. Carter employed more complicated phrases, and his speeches could sometimes confuse and dispirit the public.**

Images courtesy of Getty Images.

As an actor, Reagan had another card to play. He persuasively conveyed political emotions. Through compelling use of his facial expressions, Reagan communicated anger and happiness in ways that resonated with the public.

Bill Clinton displayed a similar skill, moving audiences to laughter and tears in ways that even his opponents had to admire. "He's unpredictable," noted Republican consultant Frank Luntz. "When he drapes his hands over the podium and looks at you, there's this aw-shucks demeanor. He's completely unpredictable, and so you listen. I say this to Republicans all the time, and they nod their heads" (Hernandez, 2006, p. A19).

Both Clinton and Reagan, when at their best, used language and nonverbal cues to connect with the public. They communicated emotion persuasively and they did so in ways that were appropriate to the particular situations. In this way they conveyed leadership through communication.

Framing and Politics

In addition to effectively conveying verbal and nonverbal information, politicians manipulate another dimension of language, one touched on earlier: the frame. By framing an issue in one way rather than another, candidates make certain aspects of an issue salient or promote one way of looking at a problem rather than another.

Consider the issue of cutting taxes. For years Republicans framed the issue as lowering the tax burden and Democrats counterargued that tax cuts reduce the money government has available to provide needed social services. Both views were plausible; thus, the debate produced no political winners. Then the Republicans got the bright idea of framing the issue not as tax cuts, but as tax relief. Linguist George Lakoff explains why this was persuasive:

> Think of the framing for *relief*. For there to be relief there must be an affliction, an afflicted party, and a reliever who removes the affliction and is therefore a hero. And if people try to stop the hero, those people are villains for trying to prevent relief.
>
> When the word *tax* is added to *relief*, the result is a metaphor: Taxation is an affliction. And the person who takes it away is a hero, and anyone who tries to stop him is a bad guy.
>
> (2004, pp. 3–4)

Framing is at the heart of the persuasive battles played out in political campaigns. In the 2012 American presidential campaign, Republicans framed the election around Obama, arguing that the fundamental issue was Obama's failure to solve the nation's economic woes. Democrats framed the election as a choice between Obama, who, in their view, had eased many Americans' financial strains, and his Republican opponent, who they argued would make things worse for his countrymen's pocketbooks. Similarly, Europeans framed the continent's economic crisis resulting from high debts and outsized spending, in different ways. For example, in Italy several years back, the Italian government framed the issue as one of shared sacrifice to return the country to economic normalcy. By contrast, Italy's young people focused on whether the austerity measures would be administered fairly, so that budget-tightening pain was felt by the rich and privileged, as well as the working class.

Political framing has both adherents and critics. Supporters say that frames are useful devices that derive from a coherent political philosophy. When Democrats frame issues in terms of caring or community and Republicans emphasize strength and discipline, they are calling on core values. By emphasizing one frame over another, a candidate employs language to convey ideas. Critics retort that frames are word games. Rather than developing a coherent message, politicians use catch phrases, test-marketing their language so that it sounds authentic, employing words that resonate with voters, in hopes of snaring their votes.

CONCLUSIONS

The message is the heart of persuasion—the rhetorical artery of the persuasion process. Scholars from Aristotle to contemporary communication researchers have theorized about the most effective ways to harness messages so as to change attitudes. A hallmark of today's scholarship is the recognition that messages do not have simple influences. Instead, their effects hinge on: (a) the particular facet of the message communicators employ and (b) the ways that receivers think about what they have seen or heard. This chapter has introduced you to different categories of the message: structure, content, framing, and language.

Focusing first on message structure, research indicates that: (a) two-sided messages are more persuasive than one-sided messages, provided they refute the opposing side; and (b) explicit **conclusion drawing** is usually more effective than implicit drawing of the conclusion.

Two core message content factors are evidence and narrative. Evidence is defined as factual statements that originate from a source other than the communicator that are offered to verify the communicator's claims. It typically consists of quantitative information, like statistics. Research finds that evidence changes attitudes. Psychologically, evidence works through processes laid out by the ELM. Under conditions of low involvement and ability, evidence serves as a peripheral cue. Under higher involvement and ability, it serves as an argument, catalyst to thought, or factor that bolsters confidence in a receiver's assessment of the message.

Narrative operates very differently. It straddles the line between entertainment and pure persuasion. Narratives are coherent stories that provide information about characters and conflict, raise questions, and offer a resolution to the problem. Unlike advocacy messages, which work primarily through central and peripheral processes or social norms, narratives transport individuals to different psychological realms. In so doing, they immerse audiences in an imaginative domain that reduces counterarguing and increases receptivity to new ideas about an issue. Narratives can also deflect the usual resistance that accompanies reception of a persuasive message.

Framing and language focus on the strong influence that verbal frameworks and words have on attitudes. Attitudes can be steered by subtle changes in emphasis in how problems are defined and phrased. Frames highlight certain concepts and encourage people to interpret the facts in a particular way.

In a similar fashion, words and linguistic features of a message can sway feelings and thoughts. Key language components are speed of speech, powerless/powerful speech, and language intensity. Fast speech can influence attitudes by conveying credibility and distracting audience members from counterarguing with the message. Speech-rate effects on persuasion are complex, with impact depending on the topic and the similarity between the speech rate of the communicator and the audience.

Powerful speech, characterized by the absence of hesitation, hedges, disclaimers, and other unassertive speech forms, can convey credibility and influence attitudes. Audiences may ignore the content of what the speaker is saying and focus instead on how he or she says it, forming an evaluation of the speaker and message based on whether he hedges, hesitates or qualifies. Thus, a speaker who really knows her stuff may be dismissed if she speaks in a manner that conveys uncertainty.

Intense language is the feature of language that comes to mind when many of us think about the power of words. We think of charismatic speakers who use language colorfully and metaphorically. Indeed, intense language, notably metaphors, can influence attitudes, increasing motivation and evoking positive mental images. Like all message variables, language intensity works under particular conditions and has been harnessed for good and bad ends.

The structure, content, and language of a message are weapons in the persuader's arsenal. They are not magical. They work through psychological processes that offer insights into the dynamics of persuasion. Sometimes message effects occur immediately after receipt of the communication. In other cases, effects do not emerge until later, a phenomenon known as the sleeper effect (see Box 9.3).

Knowledge of the persuasive message can help us appreciate the ways messages are employed in contemporary persuasive communication. It can also provide a few nuggets of personal wisdom, offering tips on how we can better use language to accomplish our own persuasive goals. Alas, more than 2,000 years after Aristotle first called attention to the potential impact of the persuasive message, thanks to communication research, we have a deeper appreciation of how messages influence audiences and why.

BOX 9.3 THE SLEEPER EFFECT

McDonald's hamburgers have ground worms.
Girl Scout cookies have been mixed with hashish.
A subliminal message is embedded on the pack of Camel cigarettes.

These statements have been bandied about for years, and some people (more than you would think) assume they are true. But these assertions are false. How do people come to develop false beliefs? There are many explanations, but one, relevant to this chapter, is this: these messages were relayed by communicators who initially inspired little trust or respect. As time elapsed, people forgot the source of the message, but continued to remember—and believe—the message itself.

This illustrates the **sleeper effect**: the notion that the effects of a persuasive communication increase with the passage of time. As Allen and Stiff note, "The term 'sleeper' derives from an expectation that the long-term effect is larger than the short-term effect in some manner (the effect is asleep but awakes to be effective later)" (1998, p. 176).

The core thesis is that a message initially discounted by message receivers comes to be accepted over time. The message is initially accompanied by a discounting cue that leads individuals to question or reject the advocated position. At Time 1, individuals believe that the message is persuasive, but are bowled over by the discounting cue, such as information that the source is not an expert (Gruder

Continued

et al., 1978). They therefore reject the message. Over time the cue (low-credibility source) becomes disassociated from the message. Individuals forget the source of the message, but remember the message arguments, perhaps because the arguments are more extensively processed and more accessible in memory than the source cue (Hannah & Sternthal, 1984).

A vexing part of the sleeper effect is that a message delivered by a highly credible source becomes less persuasive over time, while the same message transmitted by a low-credibility source becomes more convincing. How can this be? What may occur is that message recipients agree with the message initially because the source is credible. The credibility of the source sells them on the message. Over time, source and message become disassociated, and people forget the key selling proposition—the source's credibility. Because this was what sold them on the message, its disappearance from memory reduces the persuasiveness of the message. By contrast, a message delivered by a low-credibility communicator can gain in acceptance over time, having never been accepted exclusively on the basis of the credibility of the source.

Keep in mind that sleeper effects are not the norm in persuasion. Highly credible sources are invariably more effective, particularly in the short term. It is certainly better for persuaders to strive to have high rather than low credibility. Nonetheless, sleeper effects occur in various contexts (Kumkale & Albarracín, 2004). Both conventional persuasion and fictional narratives can fail to influence receivers immediately, but exert a striking impact over the longer haul (Jensen et al., 2011). These effects have intriguing implications for politics and marketing. Unfortunately, these applications have not been lost on unsavory marketing specialists.

False messages disseminated by low-credibility communicators can come to be viewed as true over time, particularly if they are memorable. Opportunistic political consultants exploit the sleeper effect when they try to implant misleading or negative information about their opponents into the public mind. They attempt to do this through push-polls, or telephone surveys in which an interviewer working for a political candidate (Candidate A) slips false and negative infor- mation about Candidate B into the poll, and asks respondents whether that would change their opinion of Candidate B. The questions are designed to push voters away from one candidate and *pull* them toward the candidate financing the poll (Sabato & Simpson, 1996).

In some cases, pollsters have deliberately exploited voter prejudices, hoping this would push individuals away from their preferred candidates. Interviewers have fabricated information, in one case claiming that an Alaska Democrat supported gay marriage when he had never endorsed marriage between homosexuals. In another case, an unmarried Democratic Congressman from Ohio kept receiving reports about push-polls that would ask his supporters, "Would you still vote for him if you knew he was gay?" The candidate noted that he was not gay, but acknowledged the tactic placed him in a "catch-22." "What do you do?" he asked. "Do you hold a press conference and say, 'I'm not gay!'?" (Sabato & Simpson, 1996, p. 265).

The candidate did not hold a press conference. He also did not get reelected to Congress.

The sleeper effect provides one explanation for those outcomes. The push-pollsters' negative messages about opposing candidates were persuasive, encouraging cognitive elaboration (Priester et al., 1999). The pollster was a low-credibility source, a discounting cue. Over time, the cue became disassociated from the message. The message was deeply processed and memorable. At a later point in time, the message awoke and influenced attitudes toward the candidates.

A sleeper effect may also underlie the widely reported perception during the 2008 presidential campaign that Barack Obama was a Muslim. Thirteen percent of registered voters insisted that Obama was a Muslim. Some of these voters asked columnist Nicholas Kristof questions like *That Obama—is he really a Christian? Isn't he a Muslim or something?*" (Kristof, 2008, p. 9). In fact, Obama is a Christian and this was widely pointed out. These beliefs had a variety of sources, but one source may have been viral attacks—vicious Internet messages claiming Obama was a Muslim. A sleeper effect may have been operating, with people remembering the negative message but forgetting the low-credibility source that conveyed it.

In fairness, other election-year Web sites also spread rumors on the other candidates, such as those suggesting in 2008 that Republican vice-presidential nominee Sarah Palin had faked her pregnancy, or one in 2012 that claimed that Mitt Romney's first act as president would be to allow polygamy in the U.S. Although these claims were so incredible that they undoubtedly did not get to first base with most Republican voters, they may have exerted sleeper effects on individuals sympathetic with the claims.

Test your knowledge now with interactive exercises

(Q)

Chapter 10

Emotional Message Appeals: Fear and Guilt

 Listen now to the author's chapter summary

Fear. It's that gyrating feeling you have in the pit of your stomach, the dizziness you feel when the doctor tells you he is not sure why your arm hurts and will need to conduct some tests to evaluate the problem. Fear is the emotion we experience when we learn that our dependence on something or someone could be bad for our health. It's the sinking sensation you have when you suddenly realize that the careening out-of-control car you are driving is going to smash another car and probably injure you and the other driver. Fear. It is part of being human, but it is not pleasant and, except maybe when you are riding a roller coaster you know will return safely to the hub, it is aversive and almost never fun.

Fear is a powerful emotion. For this reason it has been a source of fascination to persuasion researchers, who have sought to understand how it can be harnessed in the service of attitude change. This chapter examines the processes and effects of two emotional persuasive appeals: fear and guilt. The first section, the thrust of the chapter, explores fear appeals, while the second portion examines guilt.

Emotions are complex critters. An emotion involves a cognitive assessment of a situation, physiological arousal, a subjective set of feelings, motivation to behave in a certain way, and a motor or facial expression (Nabi, 2009). Given the emotional underpinnings of attitudes, emotions invariably come into play in the conceptualization of communications designed to change attitudes. Unlike positive emotions, like pride or warmth, which are characterized by satisfaction with a mood state, fear motivates people to take action. Unlike anger, which can have destructive and debilitating effects, fear may be harnessed to change attitudes in a constructive fashion. Let's turn now to the fear factor, the name of a reality television show and also the concept that has stimulated thousands of persuasion studies across social science disciplines.

FEAR APPEALS

Some years back, Maureen Coyne, a college senior enrolled in a persuasion class, rumi-nated about a question her professor asked: Think of a time when you tried to change someone's attitude about an issue. How did you go about accomplishing this task? After thinking for a few moments, Maureen recalled a series of events from her childhood, salient incidents in which she mightily tried to influence loved ones' attitudes. "My entire life," she related, "I have been trying to persuade my lovely parents to quit smoking. It started with the smell of smoke," she said, recollecting:

> I would go to school and kids could smell it on me to the extent that they would ask me if my parents smoked. It was humiliating. Then the lessons began from the teachers. They vehemently expressed how unhealthy this habit was through videos, books, and even puppet shows. In my head, the case against smoking was building. From my perspective, smoking was hurting my parents, my younger brothers, and me. With this in mind, it is understandable that a young, energetic, opinionated child would try and do something to rid her life of this nasty habit. Well, try I did. I educated them constantly about the dangers of first- and second-hand smoke, with help from class assignments. I would tell them about the cancers, carbon monoxide, etc., and remind them every time I saw something on TV or in the paper about smoking statistics. I begged and begged and begged (and then cried a little). I explained how much it hurt my brothers and me. I reminded them that they should practice what they preach (they told us not to smoke).
>
> (Coyne, 2000)

Although Maureen's valiant persuasive efforts ultimately failed (her parents disregarded her loving advice), she showed a knack for devising a compelling fear appeal to influence attitudes toward smoking. Maureen is hardly alone in trying to scare people into changing a dysfunctional attitude or behavior. Fear appeals are ubiquitous. Consider the following:

- Hoping to deter juvenile criminals from a life of crime, a New Jersey prison adopted a novel approach in the late 1970s. Teenagers who had been arrested for crimes like robbery were carted off to Rahway State Prison to participate in a communication experiment. The teens were seated before a group of lifers, men who had been sentenced to life imprisonment for murder and armed robbery. The men, bruising, brawling criminals, intimidated the youngsters, swearing at them and threatening to hurt them. At the same time, they used obscene and intense language to scare the youngsters into changing their ways. The program, *Scared Straight*, was videotaped and broadcast on national television numerous times over the ensuing decades. Although there is mixed evidence regarding its actual effects in deterring juvenile crime (Finckenauer, 1982), it has become part of popular culture, excerpted on YouTube and parodied on *The Office*.

- Public service announcements (PSAs) in magazines, on television, and on Web sites regularly arouse fear in hopes of convincing young people to stop smoking, quit using dangerous drugs like methamphetamine, and avoid binge-drinking episodes. Some PSAs have become world famous, like the Partnership for a Drug-Free America's "brain on drugs" ad. ("This is your brain. This is drugs. This is your brain on drugs. Any questions?")

- Advertisers, who exploited fears long before public-health specialists devised health PSAs, continue to arouse fear in television spots. Toothpaste and deodorant ads suggest that if you don't buy their products, you will be shunned by friends who smell your bad breath or body odor. Liquid bleach commercials warn that a baby's clothing can breed germs that cause diaper rash or other skin irritations. To avoid these consequences—and the larger humiliation of being viewed as a bad parent—you only need plunk down some money to buy Clorox or another liquid bleach.

Fear appeals evoke different reactions in people. They remind some individuals of the worst moments of adolescence, when parents warned them that every pleasurable activity would end up haunting them in later life. Others, noting that life is full of dangers, approve of and appreciate these communications. Still other observers wonder why we must resort to fear; why can't we just give people the facts?

Appealing to people's fears is, to a considerable degree, a negative communication strategy. The communicator must arouse a little pain in the individual, hoping it will produce gain. The persuader may have to go further than the facts of the situation warrant, raising specters and scenarios that may be rather unlikely to occur even if the individual continues to engage in the dysfunctional behavior. In an ideal world, it would not be necessary to arouse fear. Communicators could simply present the facts, and logic would carry the day. But this is not an ideal world; people are emotional, as well as cognitive, creatures, and they do not always do what is best for them. People are tempted by all sorts of demons—objects, choices, and substances that seem appealing but actually can cause quite a bit of harm. Thus, fear appeals are a necessary persuasive strategy, useful in a variety of arenas of life (see Figure 10.1).

The Psychology of Fear

Before discussing the role that fear plays in persuasion, it is instructive to define our terms. What is fear? What is a fear appeal? Social scientists define the terms in the following ways:

■ **Figure 10.1 People engage in lots of risky behaviors. Fear appeals are a way to persuade them to change their attitudes toward these problems and adopt a healthier behavioral regimen. However, fear is a dicey weapon in the persuasion arsenal and works only if it is used deftly and sensitively.**

Image courtesy of Shutterstock.

- *Fear*: an internal emotional reaction composed of psychological and physiological dimensions that may be aroused when a serious and personally relevant threat is perceived (Witte, Meyer, & Martell, 2001, p. 20).
- **Fear appeal**: a persuasive communication that tries to scare people into changing their attitudes by conjuring up negative consequences that will occur if they do not comply with the message recommendations.

Over the past half-century, researchers have conducted numerous studies of fear-arousing messages. As a result of this research, we know a great deal about the psychology of fear and the impact of fear appeals on attitudes. The research has also done much to clarify common-sense notions—in some cases misconceptions—of fear message effects.

At first glance, it probably seems like it is very easy to scare people. According to popular belief, all persuaders need do is conjure up really terrible outcomes, get the person feeling jittery and anxious, and wait as fear drives the individual to follow the recommended action. There are two misconceptions here: first, that fear appeals invariably work, and second, that fear acts as a simple drive. Let's see how these notions oversimplify matters.

Contrary to what you may have heard, it is not easy to scare people successfully. Arousing fear does not always produce attitude change. After reviewing the research in this area, Franklin J. Boster and Paul Mongeau concluded that "manipulating fear does not appear to be an easy task. What appears to be a highly-arousing persuasive message to the experimenter may not induce much fear into the recipient of the persuasive message" (1984, p. 375).

More generally, persuaders frequently assume that a message scares audience members. However, they may be surprised to discover that individuals either are not frightened or did not tune in to the message because they perceived that it was irrelevant to their needs. This has been a recurring problem with automobile safety videos—those designed to persuade people to wear seat belts or not drink when they drive. Message designers undoubtedly have the best of intentions, but their persuasive videos are often seen by audience members as hokey, far-fetched, or just plain silly (Robertson et al., 1974).

Not only can fear appeals fail because they arouse too little fear, but they can also backfire if they scare individuals too much (Morris & Swann, 1996). Fear messages invariably suggest that bad things will happen if individuals continue engaging in dangerous behaviors, like smoking or excessive drinking. None of us likes to admit that these outcomes will happen to us, so we deny or defensively distort the communicator's message. There is considerable evidence that people perceive that bad things are less likely to happen to them than to others (Weinstein, 1980, 1993). In a classic study, Neil D. Weinstein (1980) asked college students to estimate how much their own chances of experiencing negative life events differed from the chances of their peers. Students perceived that they were significantly less likely than others to experience a host of outcomes, including:

- dropping out of college;
- getting divorced a few years after getting married;
- being fired from a job;
- having a drinking problem;
- getting lung cancer; and
- contracting venereal disease.

Think of it this way: Remember high school when a friend wanted to be cool and hip, showed up at a party once, drank too much, and embarrassed herself. In her mind, there was zero chance that negative consequences would befall her. Unfortunately, it does not always work that way. Teenagers will boast on Facebook about their social or sexual exploits, only to regret it afterwards or discover that school officials read their messages. Some teens do outlandish pranks, hoping to gain notoriety by videotaping and posting them on YouTube. One New Jersey teen loaded his bathtub with fireworks, layered himself in protective clothing, and turned on a video camera to record the spectacle. The explosion, which the boy said he hoped to place on YouTube, produced a fireball that left the youngster with burns on more than 10 percent of his body (Parker-Pope, 2010).

The belief that one is less likely to experience negative life events than others is known as *unrealistic optimism* or the **illusion of invulnerability**. People harbor such illusions for three reasons.

First, they do not want to admit that life's misfortunes can befall them. For instance, many young people routinely accept medications like Ritalin from friends, switch from Paxil to Prozac based on the recommendation of an e-mail acquaintance, or trade Ativan for Ambien (Harmon, 2005). Youthful, assured, and confident of their knowledge, they minimize the risks involved in taking drugs for which they do not have a prescription.

A second reason people harbor an illusion of invulnerability is that they maintain a stereotype of the typical victim of negative events and blithely maintain that they do not fit the mold. For example, in the case of cigarette smoking, they may assume that the typical smoker who gets lung cancer is a thin, nervous, jittery, middle-aged man who smokes like a chimney. Noting that they smoke but do not fit the prototype, individuals conclude they are not at risk. This overlooks the fact that few of those who get cancer from smoking actually match the stereotype.

A third reason is that people, enjoying the pleasures of risky choices, decide to offload the costs of these pleasures to the more mature adults they will become in the future (Holt, 2006). In essence, an individual separates out his present and future selves, then rationalizes pursuit of a risky behavior in the here and now, "making the future self suffer for the pleasure of the moment" (Holt, 2006, pp. 16–17). In so doing the individual minimizes the long-term consequences that he will endure as an adult (see Box 10.1).

The illusion of invulnerability is a major barrier to fear appeals' success. If I don't believe or don't want to believe that I am susceptible to danger, then I am unlikely to accept the persuader's advice.

A second misconception of fear appeals follows from this tendency. Fear is commonly thought to be a simple drive that propels people to do as the persuader requests. According to this notion (popularized by early theorists), fear is an unpleasant psychological state, one that people are motivated to reduce. Supposedly, when the message provides recommendations that alleviate fear, people accept the recommendations and change their behavior (Hovland, Janis, & Kelley, 1953). To be sure, fear is an unpleasant emotional state, but, contrary to early theorists, people do not behave in a simple, animal-like manner to rid themselves of painful sensations. Fear is more complicated.

A message can scare someone, but fail to change attitudes because it does not connect with the person's beliefs about the problem, or neglects to provide a solution to the difficulty that ails the individual. The drive model puts a premium on fear. However, we now know that persuaders must do more than arouse fear so as to change an individual's attitude or behavior. They must convince message recipients that they are susceptible to negative outcomes and that the recommended response will alleviate the threat. Messages must work on a cognitive, as well as affective, level. They must help individuals appreciate the problem and, through the power of words and suggestions, encourage people to come to grips with the danger at hand.

BOX 10.1 ILLUSIONS OF INVULNERABILITY

"I never thought I needed to worry about AIDS," confessed Jana. "I thought it only happened to big-city people, not people like me who are tucked away in the Midwest. But 18 months ago, I was diagnosed with the virus that causes AIDS. Now I live in fear of this deadly illness every single day of my life," she told a writer from *Cosmopolitan* (Ziv, 1998).

Born in a small Midwestern town, Jana had an unhappy childhood: broken home, deadbeat dad, life in foster homes. After moving to a city and completing vocational training, Jana met a good-looking 22-year-old man, who flattered her with compliments, told her he loved her, and seemed like the answer to her prayers. They soon became sexually intimate. "We had sex, on average, four times a week," Jana recalled. "We didn't talk about using condoms or getting tested, and I wasn't worried about using protection. We used condoms only when we had any lying around." Fearing Jana might get pregnant, her boyfriend coaxed her into having anal sex, which they performed 10 times, never with a condom.

One day in July, Jana decided to get an AIDS test. The test confirmed her worst fears: she was HIV-positive and had been infected by her boyfriend. He had tested positive years earlier, but never bothered to tell Jana. Although she knew the dangers of unprotected sex, Jana felt invulnerable. "I was one of those girls who thought, *AIDS won't happen to me*," Jana said (Ziv, 1998, p. 241).

What crosses your mind when you read this story? That it is sad and tragic? That Jana took risks, ones your friends or you wouldn't take? That she's not like you, with her checkered past and desperate need for companionship? Perhaps you didn't have such thoughts at all—but if you did, if you tried to psychologically distance yourself from Jana or told yourself her situation is much different from yours or silently whispered, "This couldn't happen to me because . . .," you've revealed something important. You've shown yourself a mite susceptible to what psychologists call the illusion of invulnerability.

How forcefully the illusion of invulnerability operates in the arena of HIV and AIDS! The rate of HIV infection has risen sharply among young people (DiClemente, 1992). Sexually transmitted diseases (STDs) are common among adolescents, and the presence of STDs increases susceptibility to HIV. Yet college students may underestimate their own susceptibility to HIV, while overestimating other students' risks.

What's more, although students know that condom use helps prevent HIV, they frequently engage in unprotected sex. Sexually active college students frequently report that they used condoms less than 50 percent of the time when they had sex over the past year (Thompson et al., 1996). But wait a minute. The overwhelming number of AIDS cases in America have been found among gay men and injecting drug users. "Heterosexual AIDS in North America and Europe is, and will remain, rare," Robert Root-Bernstein notes, observing that "the chances that a healthy, drug-free heterosexual will contract AIDS from another heterosexual are so small they are hardly worth worrying about" (1993, pp. 312– 313). Experts across the scientific and political spectrum agree with this analysis.

And yet, bad things do happen to innocent people: healthy individuals like you and me get cancer or contract viruses we never heard of (the odds of this happening are one in a million, but I bet you can think of someone, one person, you know personally who suddenly got very sick or died young). Although middle-class, heterosexual high school and college students are not at high risk for HIV infection, handfuls of young people from these backgrounds will fall prey to HIV in the coming years. Some may get HIV by contracting STDs that produce lesions, offering the HIV convenient access to the bloodstream. Although sexually transmitted infections do not cause HIV infection, they can increase the odds that a person will contract the AIDS virus (adapted from Perloff, 2001; see Figure 10.2).

Continued

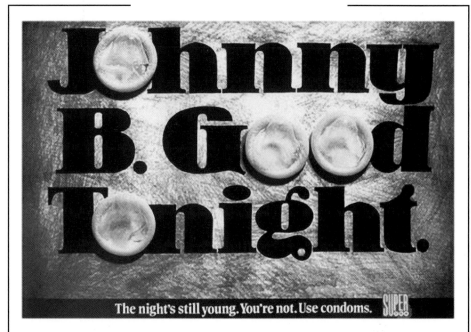

Figure 10.2 Condoms can offer protection against sexually transmitted diseases, notably HIV/AIDS. Yet many people, harboring illusions of invulnerability, do not practice safer sex. The message here is designed to influence attitudes on this topic. Do you think it is effective? What are its pros and cons?

Image courtesy of the Creative Advertising Archive.

A Theory of Fear Appeals

Devising an effective fear appeal is, to some extent, an art, but it is an art that requires a scientist's appreciation of the intricacies of human behavior. For this reason, theoretical approaches to fear messages are particularly important to develop, and there has been no shortage of these over the years (Dillard, 1994; Rogers, 1975). The most comprehensive is Kim Witte's **Extended Parallel Process Model (EPPM)**. As the name suggests, the model extends previous work on fear appeals, synthesizing different research strands and sharpening predictions. It also emphasizes two parallel processes, or two different mechanisms by which fear appeals can influence attitudes. Like the ELM, the EPPM is a process model, one that calls attention to the ways in which people think and feel about persuasive messages. Reasoning that fear is a complex emotion, Witte (1998) invokes specific terms. She talks about fear, but recognizes that we need to consider other subtle aspects of fear-arousing messages if we are to understand their effects on attitudes.

A fear-arousing message contains two basic elements: *threat* and *efficacy information*, or a problem and solution. A message must first threaten the individual, convincing him or her that dangers lurk in the environment. To do this, a message must contain the following threat-oriented elements:

1. *Severity information*: information about the seriousness or magnitude of the threat ("Consumption of fatty food can lead to heart disease.").
2. *Susceptibility information*: information about the likelihood that the threatening outcomes will occur ("People who eat a junk-food diet put themselves at risk for getting a heart attack before the age of 40.").

After threatening or scaring the person, the message must provide a recommended response—a way the individual can avert the threat. It must contain efficacy information or facts about effective ways to cope with the danger at hand. Efficacy consists of two components, which result in two additional elements of a fear appeal:

3. *Response efficacy*: information about the effectiveness of the recommended action ("Maintaining a diet high in fruits and vegetables, but low in saturated fat, can reduce the incidence of heart disease.").
4. *Self-efficacy information*: arguments that the individual is capable of performing the recommended action ("You can change your diet. Millions have.").

Each of these message components theoretically triggers a cognitive reaction in the person. Severity and susceptibility information should convince the individual that the threat is serious and likely to occur, provided no change is made in the problematic behavior. Response efficacy and self-efficacy information should persuade the individual that these outcomes can be avoided if the recommended actions are internalized and believed.

The operative word is *should*. There is no guarantee a fear appeal will work in exactly this way. Much depends on which of the two parallel processes the message unleashes. The two cognitive processes at the core of the model are danger control and fear control (see Figure 10.3).

Danger control occurs when people perceive that they are capable of averting the threat by undertaking the recommended action. When in danger control mode, people turn their attention outward, appraise the external danger, and adopt strategies to cope with the problem.

By contrast, **fear control** occurs when people face a serious threat but focus inwardly on the fear, rather than on the problem at hand. They concentrate on ways of containing

Figure 10.3 Extended Parallel Process Model.

From Witte, K. (1998). Fear as motivator, fear as inhibitor: Using the Extended Parallel Process Model to explain fear appeal successes and failures. In P. A. Andersen & L. K. Guerrero (Eds.), *Handbook of communication and emotion: Research, theory, applications, and contexts* (pp. 423–450). San Diego: Academic Press.

their fear and keeping it at bay, rather than on developing strategies to ward off the danger. Witte and colleagues invite us to consider how the processes might work:

> Think of a situation in which you were faced with a grave threat. Sometimes, you may have tried to control the danger by thinking about your risk of experiencing the threat and ways to avoid it. If you did this, you engaged in the danger control process. Now, think of times when your fear was so overwhelming that you didn't even think of the threat. Instead, you focused on ways to calm down your racing heart, your sweaty palms, and your nervousness. You may have taken some deep breaths, drunk some water, or smoked a cigarette. These all are fear control strategies. You were controlling your fear, but without any thought of the actual danger facing you.
>
> (2001, pp. 14–15)

In essence, a fear appeal works if it nudges the person into danger control. It fails if it pushes the individual into fear control. If the message convinces people that they can cope, it can change attitudes. If people are bowled over by their fear and paralyzed by the severity of the threat, the message backfires. Indeed, when people possess unusually high levels of fear, scaring them can be counterproductive. When individuals are terrified about a social problem, scaring them can increase anxiety and render fear appeals ineffective (Muthusamy, Levine, & Weber, 2009).

Scholars, attempting to develop a more precise formulation to help theorists and practitioners, emphasize that when threat and efficacy are high, people are motivated to consider changing their attitude (Mongeau, 2013). When perceived efficacy exceeds perceived threat, individuals engage in danger control and adopt recommendations to avert the danger (Witte et al., 2001). They feel motivated to protect themselves from danger (protection motivation in the model) and take necessary steps to deal with the problem at hand. However, if perceived threat exceeds perceived efficacy, people shift into fear control mode, obsess about the fear, defensively process the message, and do nothing to alter their behavior. For example, an antismoking campaign succeeds if it convinces the smoker that the risk of cancer can be averted if he quits smoking now and begins chewing Nicorette gum instead of smoking Camels. The campaign fails if it gets the individual so worried that he will get cancer that he begins smoking cigarettes just to calm down!

What role does fear play in all this? Fear is probably a necessary condition for messages to succeed. People have to be scared, and messages that arouse high levels of fear can produce significant attitude change (Boster & Mongeau, 1984; Mongeau, 1998). But fear is not enough. In order to change attitudes, a message must harness fear and channel it into a constructive (danger control) direction. This entails "pushing all the right buttons" or, more precisely, convincing people that the threat is severe and real, but that there is something they can do to ward off the danger (see Box 10.2).

Applying Theory to the Real World

Fear appeal theories like Witte's have generated many studies, mostly experiments. Researchers have randomly assigned one group of subjects to watch a video or DVD that contains a very threatening message. They have exposed an equivalent group to a message that raises milder threats. Experimenters have also varied other aspects of the message, such as the effectiveness of the recommended response or self-efficacy. A variety of studies support the EPPM. For example, in one study smokers who were led to believe that there was a high probability that smoking causes cancer indicated an intention to quit only if they believed that the recommended practice (quitting smoking) was highly effective (Rogers & Mewborn, 1976).

Research Support: Gun Control in Michigan

Particularly compelling support for the model was offered in an experiment on gun safety. Firearms are a leading cause of fatal injury in the United States, even surpassing car accidents in several states to become the primary cause of fatal injuries. Concerned about this problem, researcher Anthony J. Roberto and colleagues developed a graphic videotape to influence attitudes toward gun safety (Roberto et al., 2000). Guided by the

---

BOX 10.2 UNDERSTANDING THEORY: PRIMER ON THE EXTENDED PARALLEL PROCESS MODEL

1. The model *extends* other research and emphasizes *processes* that mediate the effects of fear-arousing messages on attitudes.
2. A first set of parallel processes is fear control and danger control. Messages that drive receivers into fear control fail, as individuals focus on the inward fear, not the danger. Messages can succeed when they push individuals into danger control, where they process the danger at hand.
3. A second set of processes is perceived efficacy and perceived threat. When perceived efficacy exceeds perceived threat—when the message convinces individuals that recommendations can avert the danger more than it induces them to worry about the threat—the message can change attitudes toward the problem.
4. The four components of a fear appeal are severity, susceptibility, response efficacy and self-efficacy.
5. Messages must arouse fear in order to influence attitudes. But they also need to tap into cognitions, convincing people that the message can alleviate the threat.
6. The model does not offer a precise recipe for how to combine the various elements so as to influence attitudes.
7. On balance, the EPPM offers a helpful model, shedding light on the processes and effects of fear appeals.

EPPM, they organized the videotape so that it presented susceptibility, severity, response efficacy, and self-efficacy information.

The video presents heart-rending statements by young men whose physical and emotional lives were shattered by gun accidents. For example, Andy, a 29-year-old Michigan native, relates that one night he was cleaning his gun and accidentally shot himself in the leg. Severely wounded, Andy crawled about 50 feet to his home to get help. Although doctors saved Andy's life, his leg was amputated below the knee.

In the video you are introduced to other young people who were severely injured by gun accidents. They talk openly about what happened and how the accident could have been prevented.

Severity information is persuasively communicated by comments like this one: "If you get shot in the head, there is an 80 percent chance you will die. If you get shot in the body, there is a 90 percent chance you will need surgery."

Susceptibility is displayed through comments like this one, spoken by Andy: "I've been around guns all my life. I knew gun safety. I was always careful. I never thought that I could have an accident with a gun."

Response efficacy is relayed by statements like: "If I just had a trigger lock on the gun, none of this would have happened." Self-efficacy information is relayed by statements like: "A gun safety class takes only a few hours to complete."

In Michigan, 175 individuals enrolled in hunter safety classes participated in the experiment. Participants in the experimental group watched the video and filled out a survey probing perceptions of gun safety. Individuals in the control group answered the gun safety questions first and then watched the video. In dramatic support of the EPPM, experimental group participants (a) perceived that gun injuries resulted in more severe consequences, (b) believed that they were more susceptible to accidental gun injuries, and (c) listed more recommended gun safety practices, such as always using a trigger lock, than individuals in the control group (Roberto et al., 2000).

Harnessing the EPPM

As we have seen with other models, the EPPM is not perfect. There remain important questions about what happens psychologically when perceived threat exceeds perceived efficacy. The ways in which mental, emotional, and physiological processes combine and collide when fear is aroused are not entirely understood (e.g., Dillard & Anderson, 2004; Mongeau, 2013; Nabi, 2002; Rimal & Real, 2003). The model also does not provide a precise recipe for how to design the optimum fear appeal (O'Keefe, 2003). Nevertheless, the EPPM has shed considerable light on the psychology of fear appeals and the ways that fear messages change attitudes. It helps explain diverse findings on fear message effects (Lewis, Watson, & White, 2013; Roberto, 2013; Witte, 2013; Witte & Allen, 2000; Wong & Cappella, 2009), offering a framework for discussing fear appeals. The model also offers general guidelines for designing health risk communications. Listed below are five practical suggestions that emerge from theory and research.

1. *Communicators must scare the heck out of recipients.* We are frequently tempted to go easy on others, trying not to hurt their feelings. Research suggests that fear enhances persuasion and that high-fear appeals are more effective than low-fear appeals (Boster & Mongeau, 1984). "Adding additional fear-arousing content to a persuasive message is likely to generate greater levels of persuasion," Paul A. Mongeau concluded after reviewing the research in the area (1998, p. 64).

2. *Persuaders must shatter the illusion of invulnerability.* To persuade people, we must convince them that bad things can happen to them. Individuals can consider the

possibility of change only when they acknowledge that their behavior is part of the problem. Communicators can help people appreciate that negative outcomes can befall them by developing appeals that vividly describe consequences of engaging in risky behavior. For example, if you wanted to convince people not to drink when they drive, you might write a message like the one in Box 10.3.

BOX 10.3 AN ANTI DUI APPEAL

Here's what can happen: You attend a small dinner party at your brother's house with your 80-year-old mother, your visiting 74-year-old second cousin from Holland and assorted other family members. As per family custom, you enjoy hors d'oeuvres and several glasses of wine over a lovely meal full of conversation and laughter.

Around 9 o'clock, after a couple of small cups of coffee, and a little more wine, a thimble's worth of Scotch, you prepare to leave, and do so. Ten minutes later, on a quiet country road near a small town, you notice flashing blue lights behind you; you stop, and you are spoken to by a young officer who asks if you have been drinking.

"Yes," you say, "I had a couple of glasses of wine at a family dinner."

You are asked to step out of the car for some "field sobriety tests" . . . The officer asks if you are willing to take a Breathalyzer; if you refuse, you will receive an automatic six-month suspended license. You agree, somewhat hopefully: you blow into the tube—very well, and slowly. He repeats the process. There is a pause, and the young man says, rather abruptly: "Put your hands behind your back. You have the right to remain silent . . ." You feel the cold hardness of your new manacles, and the hardness of the back seat of the police cruiser, which is made of plastic.

You arrive at the police station, where you are processed and re-Breathalyzed twice—"point 08," you hear the officer say. In your state it's the lowest measurable illegal amount.

It used to be .10. Your license is taken away.

You pay your own bail, $40, and call your brother, who agrees to pick you up. While you wait, you are put in a jail cell, and you lie on a shiny aluminum "bed" under a bright yellow light, feeling dumb and criminal, in the company of a gleaming metal toilet. You use it . . .

Two weeks later, you are back in court with your brother-in-law lawyer to learn your fate. He negotiates . . . and the judge reads you your sentence: 45 (more) days' suspended license; one year's probation; 16 weekly alcohol-education classes, including two A.A. meetings and a "victim-impact movie" . . .

By August, you have completed all 16 classes, and have only seven more monthly checks of $65 to send to your probation officer. In November, a note from your car-insurance company informs you that your policy has been canceled; you call, and they say you can reapply with a subsidiary. Your premium more than doubles.

This is what can happen. And while all this is happening, you find yourself thinking more and more about something else that could have: you could have crashed and killed someone, including yourself (Updike, 2010, p. 74).

3. *Persuaders must discuss solutions, as well as problems.* Communicators must offer hope, telling individuals that they can avert the dangers graphically laid out earlier in the message. Communications must "get 'em well" after they "get 'em sick." They must teach, as well as scare, placing people in touch with their attitude toward the issue (Roskos-Ewoldsen, Yu, & Rhodes, 2004).

In short, as Aristotle wrote years ago, people cannot overcome the "anguish of uncertainty" without "some lurking hope of deliverance." After all, "no one deliberates about things that are hopeless" (see Witte & Roberto, 2009, p. 605). A fear appeal must leave the receiver with the prospect of hope and a belief that adversity can be overcome.

4. *Efficacy recommendations should emphasize costs of not taking precautionary actions, as well as benefits of undertaking the activity.* This suggestion draws on framing research. Persuaders frequently must decide whether to frame the message so that it emphasizes *benefits* of adopting a behavior ("a diet high in fruits and vegetables, but low in fat, can keep you healthy") or *costs* of not performing the requested action ("a diet low in fruits and vegetables, but high in fat, can lead to cancer") (Salovey & Wegener, 2002). Messages that emphasize benefits of adopting a behavior are **gain-framed**; those that present the costs of not adopting the behavior are **loss-framed**.

Traditionally, fear messages were couched in terms of gain. However, they also can be framed on the basis of losses. It may seem strange to emphasize what people lose from not performing a behavior, until you consider that negative information—losses linked with inaction—can be more memorable than benefits associated with action. Beth E. Meyerowitz and Shelly Chaiken (1987) demonstrated this in a study of persuasive communication and breast self-examination, a simple behavior that can help women diagnose breast cancer but that is not performed nearly as often as it should be.

One group of undergraduate female subjects in the study read gain-framed arguments ("by doing breast self-examination now, you can learn what your normal, healthy breasts feel like so that you will be better prepared to notice any small, abnormal changes that might occur as you get older"). Others read loss-oriented arguments ("by not doing breast self-examination now, you will not learn what your normal, healthy breasts feel like, so you will be ill prepared to notice any small, abnormal changes that might occur as you get older"; Meyerowitz & Chaiken, 1987, p. 506). Women who read the loss-framed arguments held more positive attitudes toward breast self-exams and were more likely than gain-oriented subjects to report performing this behavior at a four-month follow-up.

Behavior being complex, there are also cases in which gain-framed arguments are more compelling. Alexander J. Rothman and colleagues (Rothman et al., 1993) compared the effects of gain- and loss-framed pamphlets regarding skin cancer prevention. The gain-framed message emphasized benefits rather than costs, and focused on positive aspects of displaying concern about skin cancer ("regular use of sunscreen products can protect you against the sun's harmful rays"). The loss-framed message stressed risks, rather than benefits ("If you don't use sunscreen products regularly, you won't be protected against the sun's harmful rays"). Of those who read the positive, gain-framed message, 71 percent requested sunscreen with an appropriate sun protection factor. Only 46 percent of those who read the loss-framed pamphlet asked for sunscreen with an appropriate sun-protection level (see also Reinhart et al., 2007).

Gain-framed messages are more effective in promoting *health-affirming (disease prevention) behaviors*. These are behaviors where gains or benefits are obvious, such as sunscreen use or physical exercise. Emphasizing the positive—what one gains from compliance—is persuasive. Loss-framed message effects are more complex (O'Keefe & Jensen, 2006; see also O'Keefe & Jensen, 2009). However, loss-framed messages may be particularly effective when individuals feel vulnerable. In these situations, people focus on negative aspects of the issue, leading them to be more susceptible to the negatively oriented, loss-framed communications.

Hyunyi Cho and Franklin J. Boster (2008) obtained evidence consistent with this view. They reported that loss-framed antidrug ads that emphasized the *disadvantages* of doing drugs exerted a stronger impact on teenagers who reported their friends used drugs than did gain-framed ads that focused on the *benefits* of not doing drugs. If your friends do drugs, you will probably feel anxious or nervous about doing drugs yourself, but worried that your friends may reject you if you don't partake. With negative issues salient in adolescents' minds, loss-framed messages carried greater weight (though see O'Keefe, 2012).

Well, there is little doubt that this is a complex area! If you are faced with a health-persuasion task, the research suggests that you should frame the message in terms of benefits when you want to encourage individuals to take positive, proactive steps, like engaging in disease prevention. If there is negativity associated with the situation, risks attached to the recommended action, or the individual habitually focuses more on costs than benefits, a loss-framed message may provide a better fit between the message and the person (Cesario, Grant, & Higgins, 2004; Nan, 2007, 2012; and Yan, Dillard, & Shen, 2010; see also Shen & Bigsby, 2013).

5. Finally, and in a related fashion, *threats and recommendations should be salient— or relevant—to the target audience.* You cannot assume that what scares you also terrifies your target audience. Different fears are salient to different groups (Crano, 2010). If you want to scare middle-class high school girls into practicing safer sex, you should stress that they might get pregnant. These teens don't want to have a baby; pregnancy represents a serious threat. However, if your target audience is poor ethnic women, you should rethink this appeal. To some low-income women, pregnancy is a positive, rather than negative, consequence of sexual intercourse. It produces a human being who depends on them and loves them to bits; it also, at least in the best of worlds, shows that they have a loving, trusting relationship with a man, which provides status and emotional fulfillment (Sobo, 1995; Witte et al., 2001).

Surprisingly, perhaps, the main drawback of getting pregnant, in the view of inner-city teenage girls, is that you get fat and lose your friends (Witte et al., 2001). Thus, a campaign to promote abstinence or safer sex among inner-city teenagers might emphasize how much weight you gain when you're pregnant. It should also explain that you can lose your friends if you have to spend time taking care of a baby rather than hanging with them (Witte et al., 2001).

Summary

Fear appeals are among the diciest weapons in the persuader's arsenal. This is because they evoke fear, a strong emotion with physiological correlates, touch on ego-involved issues, and attempt to change dysfunctional behaviors that are difficult to extinguish. To succeed, fear-arousing messages must trigger the right emotional reaction, lest they push the message recipient into fear control mode. Kathryn A. Morris and William B.

Swann aptly observed that health risk communications must "walk the whisker-thin line between too little and too much—between making targets of persuasive communications care enough to attend to the message but not dismiss the message through denial processes" (1996, p. 70). The campaign communication floor is littered with examples of fear appeals that failed because they did not maintain the proper balance between fear and danger, or threat and efficacy.

GUILT APPEALS

Charitable organizations frequently depict graphic appeals of deprived children, portraying them as abused, undernourished, and in desperate need of attention (see Figure 10.4).

■ Figure 10.4 Graphic appeals to help deprived, hungry children tug at our heart strings, arousing guilt. Yet, sadly, they face many obstacles to success. How do you think we can increase the persuasive power of appeals like these?

Image courtesy of Sodahead.com.

The pictures haunt you—the child's gaunt face, sad eyes, mournful expression. These televised messages—you have watched them many times—are unabashed guilt appeals, attempts to arouse guilt in an effort to induce people to donate money to charitable groups. Do these appeals work?

Like fear, guilt is a negative emotional response, one that has affective and cognitive components. Guilt, however, involves "ought" and "should" dimensions. *Guilt* "occurs when an individual notes with remorse that s/he failed to do what s/he 'ought to' or 'should' do—for example, when s/he violates some social custom, ethical or moral principle, or legal regulation," explain Debra Basil and her colleagues (Basil, Ridgway, & Basil, 2008, p. 3).

Basil and colleagues proposed a model of guilt and giving derived from the EPPM. They argue that the two key processes are empathy and efficacy. Just as a fear appeal contains a threat to motivate people to act, a guilt appeal arouses empathy so as to induce individuals to perform a particular helping behavior. Empathizing with the plight of deprived children should remind people of a cultural norm to assist the less fortunate. This in turn should arouse guilt, an unpleasant feeling that people are motivated to reduce—ideally, by donating to charity. Guilt is not a sufficient condition. Basil's model stipulates that people will donate to a charitable organization only if guilt is combined with efficacy, the perception that one can effectively engage in the advocated action. Televised messages frequently contain self-efficacy messages, such as "for less than a $1 a day you can save a child's life."

In experiments to examine guilt appeal effects, Basil and colleagues devised messages to prod individuals to donate to charity. Research participants were randomly assigned to read messages high or low in guilt, empathy, and efficacy. For example, the following message was designed to induce both empathy and guilt:

> *You are Lilia*. You are eight, and curious about books and pens, things that you knew for a few months in your school before it burned. Before your mother became sick, and lost the resources within her care to care adequately for a child. And before you reached the point where you stopped drawing pictures in the dirt with sticks, because you are so tired from doing your mother's job.

> As a citizen of the most privileged country in the world, your life couldn't be more different from Lilia's. Not only do you live in America, you also get to go to college. So not having access to elementary education is difficult to imagine. But it's frighteningly common. Please help. Childreach needs your donation.
>
> (Basil, Ridgway, & Basil, 2006, p. 1052)

There is evidence that guilt appeals like these have positive effects. In line with their model, Basil and colleagues (2008) found that a message promoting empathy with deprived children induced guilt, which in turn led to an increase in intent to donate to a charitable organization. Self-efficacy also spurred donation intentions.

Many of us have viewed heart-rending televised messages such as the one above, yet have not donated a dime. How could this be, if experiments demonstrate that guilt appeals work? There are many reasons. First, the televised appeals may be less impactful than the laboratory messages; the television messages may fail to induce empathy or guilt. Second, research shows only that people intend to donate; many factors determine whether people actually make good on their intentions, such as external constraints and availability of significant others who endorse the norm of giving (Fishbein & Ajzen, 2010). Third, people may distrust charitable organizations, suspecting that they are inefficient or corrupt. Fourth, individuals may not believe it is their responsibility to improve the lives of these needy children.

Like fear appeals, guilt communications are effective only if certain conditions are met. Basil's research suggests that charitable appeals can work if the message induces empathy, reminds individuals that inaction is inconsistent with their moral standards, and convinces them that a donation can reduce feelings of guilt. However, guilt is a complex emotion, and there have been only a handful of studies of its effects on persuasion (O'Keefe, 2002). We know that people frequently employ guilt appeals in interpersonal conversations, particularly when relationships are close. But guilt messages do not always persuade message recipients to change their attitude or comply with a request. They can backfire when recipients perceive that the speaker is applying inappropriate interpersonal pressure to induce them to comply. Nonetheless, when used appropriately, guilt has salutary effects. It can promote helping behavior and enhance maturity. Appeals to guilt—frequently referred to as the "sinking feeling in the stomach"—can build character (Tierney, 2009, p. D1).

CONCLUSIONS

This chapter has examined the effects of two message factors designed to arouse emotions. Research on both fear and guilt has been guided by ideas generated by the Extended Parallel Process Model.

Fear appeals are defined as persuasive communications that try to arouse fear and conjure up negative consequences that will occur if people do not comply with message recommendations. They play on fear, an internal emotion composed of psychological and physiological elements that can be evoked when threats are perceived. Fear is a tricky emotion. It can trigger anxiety, worry, and paralysis. It can also be harnessed for constructive purposes, leading to acceptance of pro-social messages. An influential model, the EPPM, stipulates that fear messages influence attitudes when they convince individuals to rethink the problem and recognize that they are capable of averting the threat by accepting recommendations contained in the message. The EPPM stipulates that a fear message succeeds when it moves people into the zone of danger control. In order for this to happen, the model says, persuaders should devise a message that contains severity, susceptibility, response efficacy, and self-efficacy information. When perceived efficacy exceeds perceived threat, the message can push people into a danger control mode.

Framing research suggests that persuaders should consider whether to frame the message so it emphasizes benefits of adopting a recommended behavior (gain-framing) or focuses on costs of not performing the recommended action (lost-framing). The literature is complicated (no surprise, right!). However, it yields insights, suggesting that gain-framed messages are more influential than loss-framed appeals when you want someone to adopt a health-affirming, illness-prevention behavior. If there are negativity or serious emotional risks associated with the situation, a loss-framed message may be worth pursuing.

The EPPM has generated a number of studies and helps us appreciate diverse findings in this decades-long area of research. The model is not without problems. For example, it does not offer a precise recipe as to how to design an optimum fear message.

Persuasion research also has explored the impact of guilt, also a multifaceted emotion. Unlike fear, guilt contains "should' or "ought" dimensions. Moralistic parents, stern preachers, and Jewish mothers are among those who have invoked guilt in the service of persuasion! And, of course, the many PSAs calling attention to the plight of abused or impoverished children abroad and in the U.S. also call on guilt. Does guilt persuade?

Several investigations, combining EPPM concepts with a focus on empathy, have found that guilt appeals can influence attitudes. Messages designed to arouse guilt, such as PSAs urging viewers to save a poor child from dying of hunger, can backfire by failing to convince individuals that their behavior will make a difference, or even to arouse guilt. This is one reason why all tug-on-the-heartstrings televised appeals don't propel us to donate money.

Persuasive messages can employ other emotions besides fear and guilt. Messages can evoke positive feelings like pride and warmth, along with negative emotions, such as anger and sadness. Research tells us that when people experience a positive emotion or are in a good mood, they often think in rather simple terms, and avoid heavy details, not wanting anything to put them out of their blissful state (Nabi, 2007). However, invariably, negative emotions motivate more serious attention to a message. When we are scared, worried, or even angry, we can attend more closely to a persuader's arguments, recognizing that a serious problem demands our consideration.

Persuading people when they have strong emotions is a challenge. But it is also important, given that emotions like anxiety and fear can lead to irrational resistance to communications urging people to take steps that are important for their health. This is where persuasion comes into the picture. Hopefully, after reading this chapter you have a better appreciation of the barriers to persuasion, along with ways to convince people to take better care of their health. Success requires appreciation of theory and an artful combination of cognition and emotion. As communication researcher Robin L. Nabi (2007) notes, a consideration of both thoughts and feelings is "essential for progress to be made, and whereas the right combination can motivate effective behavior, the wrong combination will most assuredly backfire. Finding the most effective blending of cognitive and emotional persuasive elements, then, should be both our challenge and our goal" (p. 394).

Test your knowledge now with interactive exercises

Chapter 11

Cognitive Dissonance Theory

 Listen now to the author's chapter summary

■ When Litesa Wallace packed her bags for college at Western Illinois University some years back, she never harbored any doubt that she would pledge a sorority. The initiation rites for Delta Sigma Theta turned out to be a tad more severe than Litesa expected: doing 3,000 sit-ups, drinking hot sauce and vinegar, and swallowing her own vomit. While some might have quit at this point, Litesa endured the hardship. "She wanted to be in the sorority very badly. It's very prestigious, and she believed that it would be beneficial to her life," her attorney explained. Attorney? That's right: Ms. Wallace sued the sorority for hazing after she was hospitalized for injuries sustained during the initiation period. Yet, even as she awaited the outcome of her suit, Litesa remained a Delta, apparently feeling considerable loyalty to the sorority (Pharnor, 1999).

■ Movies strike resonant chords in many people, and the following conversation from the 1982 movie *The Big Chill* sheds light on a phenomenon that many have probably experienced in everyday life:

Sam: Why is it what you just said strikes me as a mass of rationalizations?

Michael: Don't knock rationalizations. Where would we be without it? I don't know anyone who could get through the day without two or three juicy rationalizations. They're more important than sex.

Sam: Ah, come on. Nothin's more important than sex.

Michael: Oh yeah? You ever gone a week without a rationalization? (Steele, 1988; see Figure 11.1).

■ A week after the 9/11 attacks, a strange development occurred. Five anthrax-laced envelopes were mailed to major media outlets in New York City. Three weeks later, two anthrax-laden envelopes were sent to the offices of two U.S. senators. The anthrax-laden materials ultimately killed five people, caused 17 others to become sick, and led to widespread national panic.

Over a 7-year period, FBI investigators conducted more than 9,000 interviews and close to 100 searches, in the most intricate criminal investigation in FBI history. But the emotional costs were high. Federal officials pegged Dr. Kenneth Berry, an emergency room doctor concerned about bioterrorism problems, as a suspect. Although Berry turned out not to be the culprit, the stress took a toll on his career and marriage.

Dr. Steven Hatfill, a physician and former Army researcher, became the focus of the FBI investigation in 2002. FBI agents informed the woman he was living with that he was a murderer, threatening her if she did not talk. Although Hatfill claimed he was innocent, the FBI trailed him for a year and raided his home. Prominent news articles associated him with the case. He sued the U.S. Department of Justice and *The New York Times*. He was subsequently cleared and received $4.6 million from the U.S. government.

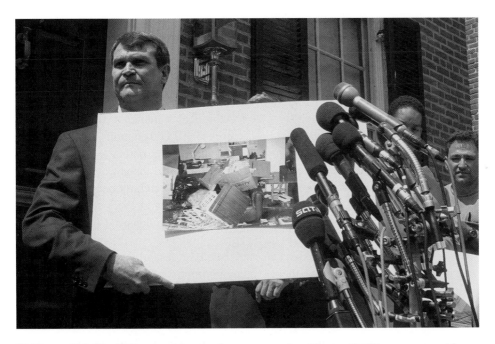

■ **Figure 11.2 The FBI pegged former Army researcher Steven Hatfill as a suspect in an investigation of the deaths of five people from anthrax-laden materials in 2001. Hatfill, pictured above, holds a photograph that depicts the inside of his girlfriend's apartment after an FBI search. Although Hatfill was subsequently cleared of wrongdoing, the authorities strongly denied that they had made mistakes, a classic, if dysfunctional, example of dissonance reduction.**

Image courtesy of Getty Images.

Despite all this, authorities steadfastly denied they did anything wrong. Federal officials rejected criticisms from government colleagues, voicing neither regret nor remorse. "I do not apologize for any aspect of the investigation," FBI director Robert Mueller III said. It is incorrect to "say there were mistakes" (Broad & Shane, 2008, p. 17; see Figure 11.2).

What do these different examples have in common? They illustrate the powerful role that a phenomenon called cognitive dissonance plays in everyday life. You may have heard the term "cognitive dissonance." No surprise: it has become part of the popular lexicon. Writers, politicians, therapists, and people like you and me use the term to describe conflict or negative feelings about issues. But what exactly does dissonance mean? Why did one psychologist call it the greatest achievement of social psychology? (See Aron & Aron, 1989.) How can dissonance principles be harnessed in the service of persuasion? And what insights can cognitive dissonance theory contribute to everyday life? This chapter examines these issues.

FOUNDATIONS

Cognitive dissonance is a bona fide theory, one of the oldies but goodies. It contains definitions, hypotheses, explanations, and theoretical statements. It has generated numerous studies; indeed, the concept boasts more than 2,000 citations (Crano, Cooper & Forgas, 2010). Yet it has provoked profound disagreements among scholars as to just why a particular finding has emerged. It is a psychological theory, one of a wave of 1950s-style approaches that assumed people have an overarching need for cognitive consistency or balance. Leon Festinger developed the theory in 1957, conducted some of the major experiments on dissonance effects, and then departed from the social psychology scene to pursue studies of human perception. That was dissonant—or inconsistent—with what you would expect an established, successful theorist to do. But in a way it was typical of dissonance theory: a counterintuitive "reverse psychology" sort of approach that turned ideas on their head, but in a fashion that stimulated and intrigued scholars across the world.

So what do we mean by cognitive dissonance? Dissonance means discord, incongruity, or strife. Thus, cognitive dissonance means incongruity among thoughts or mental elements. Two cognitions are in a dissonant relationship when the opposite of one cognitive element follows from the other. For example, the idea that "eating junk food is bad for your heart" is ordinarily dissonant with the cognition that "I love junk food." The cognition "I just plunked down $20,000 for a car" is dissonant with the observation that "I just found out you can't accelerate past 60 on the highway in this piece of junk." The cognitions "My boyfriend gets abusive when he's mad" and "I love him and want to stay with him always" are also dissonant. Finally, and most gravely, the cognition "The world is a beautiful and wonderful place" is dissonant with the realization that "evil people can kill thousands of innocent people in a single day."

Dissonance, as these examples suggest, cuts across contexts. It is specifically and formally defined as *"a negative, unpleasant state that occurs whenever a person holds two cognitions that are psychologically inconsistent"* (Aronson, 1968, p. 6). Notice that I say "psychologically inconsistent." Two thoughts can be psychologically—but not logically—inconsistent. The cognition "I love junk food" is not logically inconsistent with the belief that "eating junk food is bad for your heart." Knowing that a junk-food diet increases the risk of heart disease does not make it illogical to eat burgers, fries, and nuggets. However, the two cognitions arouse dissonance because, psychologically, it does not make sense—at least for most people—to engage in a behavior that increases the risk of disease. Dissonance is a complex theory with many hypotheses. It has been refined many times over the years. Its core components remain the following:

1. Dissonance is psychologically uncomfortable, physiologically arousing, and drives individuals to take steps to reduce it.
2. Dissonance occurs when an individual: (a) holds two clearly incongruent thoughts, (b) makes a decision that rules out a desirable alternative, (c) expends effort to participate in what turns out to be a less than ideal activity, or (d) in general is unable to find sufficient psychological justification for an attitude or behavior he or she adopts.
3. The magnitude of dissonance depends on a host of factors, including the number of dissonant elements and the importance of the issue.
4. People are motivated to take steps to reduce dissonance, including changing their attitude in response to a persuasive message.
5. For dissonance arousal to lead to attitude change, the individual must have freely decided to perform the advocated behavior.
6. People may not always succeed in alleviating dissonance, but they are motivated to try.

Dissonance theory is intriguing in an important respect. The theories discussed up to this point have suggested that changes in attitude can produce changes in behavior. Dissonance theory suggests that the opposite can occur—changes in behavior can produce changes in attitude (Cooper & Scher, 1994). For this to happen, a critical requirement of persuasion must be satisfied: people must persuade themselves to adopt a new attitude on the topic. Dissonance theory, as one would expect from a theory of persuasion, assigns central importance to the power of self-persuasion.

DISSONANCE AND DECISION MAKING

Life is filled with decisions, and decisions (as a general rule) arouse dissonance. For example, suppose you had to decide whether to accept a job in a stunningly beautiful area of the country or to turn down the job so that you could be near friends and family. Either way, you would experience dissonance. If you took the job, you would miss loved ones; if you turned down the job, you would long wistfully for the breathtaking mountains, luscious waterfalls, and lovely evening sunsets. Both alternatives have their good and bad points. The rub is that making a decision cuts off the possibility that you can enjoy the advantages of the unchosen alternative. It also ensures that you must accept the negative elements of the choice you make.

The writer Adam Ross captures the feeling aptly in the ending of a story about Sara, a beleaguered 39-year-old mother of two, whose husband still arouses warmth in her, but not sexual ardor. For this reason, she contemplates flying to L.A. for a rendezvous with Thom, with whom she had a romantic relationship while in college but whom she has not seen until she decides on a lark to meet him again. She meets up with him in Nashville, where they are both doing professional work; they kiss briefly, make plans to meet at 11 that night, but Thom, claiming to be consumed by unexpected professional business, texts her, inviting her to meet him in L.A. tomorrow. Flying from Nashville to L.A., with an intermediary stop in St. Louis, she sits and, as the plane lands in St. Louis, she contemplates whether she should hook up with Thom, knowing whatever she decides will bring about cognitive dissonance:

> Then, with uncanny synchronicity, a call came from Thom. Unknown Number, her screen said, with two choices given below: Answer. Ignore. She pressed the latter and remained seated. Group A was just boarding. She could get off here, in St. Louis, catch a flight to LaGuardia, and be home. She could forgive herself for Thom, for the kiss, for all of it. No harm, no foul. Yet it was the possible regrets that troubled her most, no matter what choice she made, the ones that would come to her later, in the night, and gnawed at her even now—starting with what you didn't take versus what you did. Not to mention the stories she might tell a future stranger about this moment, and what she'd decided before she was airborne again.
>
> (Ross, 2011, p. 241)

This mirrors choices we all face in real life. In actual situations, people behave like Sara, experiencing conflicts when making a decision and anticipating regrets about whatever choice that they make.

It is only after the decision is made that they experience the particular stress known as dissonance (Aronson, 1968). At this point, they truly are faced with two incompatible cognitions: I chose Alternative A, but this means I must forego the benefits of Alternative B. We do not experience dissonance after each and every decision. It's the ones that are the most important and least amenable to change that seem to trigger the greatest amount of cognitive dissonance (Simon, Greenberg, & Brehm, 1995; Wicklund & Brehm, 1976). Thus, choosing between two equally desirable paper towels should ordinarily produce less dissonance than selecting between two attractive and similarly priced apartments. In addition, if you can revise your decision—take it back, so to speak— you should have less dissonance than if you have signed the deal on the dotted line and cannot revisit your choice, except with considerable psychological or financial pain. If you suddenly discover, after you signed your lease, that the apartment you're renting is located in a dwelling built with asbestos, you're apt to experience a good deal of cognitive dissonance.

Just how this would feel would depend on you and how you deal with decisional stress. But there is little doubt that it wouldn't feel good! Scholars have actually studied how dissonance "feels," and they conclude it's a complex amalgamation of physiological arousal, negative affect, and mental anguish (Cooper & Fazio, 1984; Elkin & Leippe, 1986; Elliot & Devine, 1994).

So how do people cope with this discomfort we call dissonance? Theorists argue that they employ a variety of different techniques. To illustrate, consider this example: you invite a close friend to a movie that has garnered favorable reviews. The movie, obligatory popcorn, and soft drinks are expensive, so you hope the film will pan out. It doesn't; the movie turns out to be a real loser, and you find yourself sitting there, hoping it will get better. Hope springs eternal; nevertheless, the movie stinks.

You are in a state of cognitive dissonance. The cognition "I spent a lot of money on this movie" is dissonant with the knowledge that the movie is no good. Or, the thought that "I'm personally responsible for ruining my friend's evening" is dissonant with your positive self-concept or your desire to look good in your friend's eyes. How can you reduce dissonance? Research suggests you will try one or several of these techniques:

1. *Change your attitude.* Convince yourself it's a great flick, on balance—this may be hard if the movie is really bad.
2. *Add consonant cognitions.* Note how cool the cinematography is or decide that one of the actors delivered an especially convincing portrayal.
3. *Derogate the unchosen alternative.* Tell yourself that going to a movie beats sitting at home, shuffling endlessly through your iPod.
4. *Alter the importance of the cognitive elements.* Trivialize the decision by telling yourself that it's only a movie, just 2 hours of your life.

5. *Suppress thoughts.* Deny the problem and just try to get into the movie as much as you can.
6. *Communicate.* Talk up the movie with your friend, using the conversation to convince yourself it was a good decision.
7. *Alter the behavior.* Leave.

It is amazing how few people seem to avail themselves of the last option. Don't we frequently sit through a bad movie, spending our valuable cognitive energy justifying and rationalizing instead of saving ourselves the hardship by walking out? Yet this is consistent with dissonance theory. Dissonance theorists emphasize that people prefer easier to harder ways of changing cognitive elements (Simon et al., 1995). It is hard to alter behavior. Behavior is well learned and can be costly to modify. Walking out could prove embarrassing. To be sure, sticking through a lemon of a movie is not necessarily rational; it is an example of what psychologists call a sunk cost (Garland, 1990). You are not going to get the money back, no matter how much you convince yourself that it was a great film. However, as dissonance theorists are fond of reminding us, human beings are not *rational* animals, but, rather, rationalizing animals, seeking "to appear rational, both to others and [themselves]" (Aronson, 1968, p. 6). Rather than admit they are wrong, people rationalize. They deny and distort reality, refusing to acknowledge that they made a mistake. As Carol Tavris and Elliott Aronson (2007) note, "most people, when directly confronted by evidence that they are wrong, do not change their point of view or course of action but justify it even more tenaciously" (p. 2).

How apt a description of human decision making! Immediately after people make up their minds to embark on one course rather than another, they bear an uncanny resemblance to the proverbial ostrich, sticking their heads in the sand to avoid perspectives that might conflict with the option they chose, doing all they can to reaffirm the wisdom of their decision. For example, let's say a friend of yours smokes a pack a day. If you asked her why she smokes, you would hear a long list of rationalizations speaking to the power of dissonance reduction. Her reasons might include: "I know I should quit, but I've got too much stress right now to go through quitting again"; "I guess I'd rather smoke than pig out and end up looking like a blimp"; and "Hey, we're all going to die anyway. I'd rather do what I enjoy." All these reasons make great sense to your friend; they help restore consonance, but they prevent her from taking the steps needed to preserve her health. Such is the power of cognitive dissonance.

DISSONANCE AND EXPENDITURE OF EFFORT

Have you ever wondered why fraternity pledges come to like a fraternity more after they have undergone a severe initiation procedure? Ever been curious why law students who have survived the torturous experience of being asked to cite legal precedent before a class of hundreds come to think positively of their law school professors? Or why medical interns who work 30-hour shifts, with barely any sleep, vigorously defend the system, sometimes viewing it as a grand way to learn the practice of medicine (Kleinfield, 1999)? An explanation of these phenomena can be found in the application of dissonance theory to the expenditure of effort.

The core notion here is quite simple, as Aronson and Mills explained:

> No matter how attractive a group is to a person it is rarely completely positive; i.e., usually there are some aspects of the group that the individual does not like. If he has undergone an unpleasant initiation to gain admission to the group, his cognition that he has gone through an unpleasant experience for the sake of membership is dissonant with the cognition that there are things about the group that he does not like.
>
> (1959, p. 177)

One way to reduce dissonance is to convince oneself that the group has many positive characteristics that justify the expenditure of effort.

Elliot Aronson and Judson Mills tested this hypothesis long ago—in 1959. Yet their findings have been replicated by other experimenters, and continue to shed light on events occurring today. Like many researchers of their era, they preferred to set up a contrived procedure to study dissonance and effort. Believing that they needed to provide a pure test of the hypothesis, they devised an experiment in which female college students were told they would be participating in several group discussions on the psychology of sex. Informed that the group had been meeting for several weeks and they would be replacing a woman who had dropped out due to scheduling conflicts, women in the experimental condition were told they would be screened before gaining formal admission to the group. (The experimenters deliberately chose women, perhaps because they felt that the sexual words they would ask women to read would have a stronger effect on these 1950s coeds than on male students. Researchers conducting the study in today's savvy college environment would no doubt employ a different procedure.)

Students assigned to the severe initiation condition read aloud twelve obscene words and two graphic descriptions of sexual activity from contemporary novels. Women in the mild initiation condition read five sex-related words that were not obscene. Subjects in both conditions were then informed they had performed satisfactorily and had been admitted into the group. All the women subsequently listened to a tape-recorded discussion of a group meeting. The discussion was made to seem dull and banal, with group members speaking dryly and contradicting each other.

The discussion was set up this way to arouse dissonance. Female participants in the study had to confront the fact that they had undergone a humiliating experience, reading sexual words in front of some guy they had never met, for the sake of membership in a group that seemed boring and dull.

You might think that women in the severe initiation condition would dislike the group. Indeed, simple learning models would suggest that the unpleasant experience these women underwent would increase antipathy to the group. However, dissonance theory made the opposite prediction. It predicted that women in the severe initiation treatment would evaluate the group most positively. They had the most dissonance, and one way to reduce it would be to rationalize the unpleasant initiation by convincing themselves that the group discussion was not as bad as it seemed and was, in some sense, worth the pain they endured. This is what happened: women in the severe initiation condition gave the group discussion higher ratings than other subjects did.

Although Aronson and Mills' study was intriguing, it did not convince all researchers. Some suggested that perhaps the severe initiation procedure did not embarrass the women at all, but aroused them sexually! If this were true, women in the severe initiation condition would have liked the group more because they associated the pleasant arousal with the group experience (Chapanis & Chapanis, 1964). To rule out this and other alternative explanations, researchers conducted a different test of the effort justification hypothesis, one that involved not a sexual embarrassment test but, rather, different initiation procedures. Using these operationalizations, experimenters found additional support for the Aronson and Mills findings (Cooper & Axsom, 1982; Gerard & Mathewson, 1966).

Applications

We must be careful not to apply these findings glibly to the real world. People do not always rationalize effort by changing their attitude toward the group; they may reduce dissonance in other ways—for example, by trivializing the initiation rite. In some cases, the effort expended is so enormous and the initiation ceremony so humiliating that people cannot convince themselves that the group is worth it. This helps explain why Litesa Wallace, the young woman mentioned at the beginning of the chapter, sued her sorority (while still remaining a Delta). Nevertheless, effort justification sheds light on real-life situations. And, like all persuasion techniques, it exerts both positive and negative effects.

Jewish children spend much time at synagogue learning Hebrew and reciting the Torah in preparation for their Bar and Bat Mitzvahs. The time spent is dissonant with the knowledge that they could be having more fun doing other things, but in the end the need to reduce dissonance pushes them to evaluate the experience positively. This enables the ritual—and religion—to get passed on to future generations, thus preserving time-honored traditions.

The use of effort justification in other contexts is more controversial. On the one hand, initiation rituals at many college fraternities and sororities, while mildly stressful, are not harmful. Through a process of dissonance reduction, students forge bonds and form a strong commitment to a valued social group. Rites of passage employed by college sports teams and the military can serve similar positive functions. However, when groups initiate new members through physical abuse, verbal harassment, or humiliation, they cross an ethical line, engaging in hazing. Over the years, young people have been seriously injured and died as a result of hazing rituals at colleges and universities. In 2011, a Cornell University sophomore died while partaking in a fraternity hazing incident that included a mock kidnapping and forced drinking. Although hazing is illegal in most states, unfortunately it still occurs. Dissonance theory helps us understand its allure. Seniors who underwent the initiation procedure as freshmen rationalize the effort expended, develop a favorable attitude to the group, and derive gratification from passing on this tradition to new recruits (Marklein, 2000; see Figure 11.3).

■ **Figure 11.3 Although fraternity and sorority initiations rarely involve hazing (illustrated by the activity shown here), extreme hazing does occur. Cognitive dissonance theory offers a novel explanation for why these practices continue and can, paradoxically, lead initiates to develop a favorable attitude toward the group.**

Image courtesy of Getty Images.

INDUCED COMPLIANCE

What happens if a person is coaxed to argue publicly for a position he or she does not privately accept? Further, what if the individual is paid a paltry sum to take this position? Suppose you gave a speech that advocated banning cell phone use in cars, although you privately disagreed with this position? Let's say someone paid you a dollar to take this stand. Dissonance theory makes the unusual prediction that, under these circumstances, you would actually come to evaluate the proposal favorably.

This prediction is part of a phenomenon known as **induced compliance**. The name comes from the fact that a person has been induced—gently persuaded—to comply with a persuader's request. The person freely chooses to perform an action that is inconsistent with his or her beliefs or attitude. Such actions are called counterattitudinal. When individuals perform a counterattitudinal behavior and cannot rationalize the act—as they could if they had received a large reward—they are in a state of dissonance. One way to reduce dissonance is to change one's attitude so that it is consistent with the behavior—that is, convince oneself that one really agrees with the discrepant message.

This hypothesis was elegantly tested and supported by Leon Festinger and J. Merrill Carlsmith in 1959. Students were asked to perform two tasks that were phenomenally boring: (1) placing spools on a tray, emptying the tray, and refilling it with spools; and (2) turning each of 48 pegs on a peg board a quarter turn clockwise, then another quarter turn, and so on for half an hour. In what could have been an episode from the old TV show *Spy TV*, the experimenter then asked students to do him a favor: tell the next participant in the study that this monotonous experiment had been enjoyable, exciting, and a lot of fun. You see, the experimenter suggested, the person who usually does this couldn't do it today, and we're looking for someone we could hire to do it for us. The whole thing was a ruse: there was no other person who usually performed the task. The intent was to induce students to say that a boring task was enjoyable—a dissonant act. There was also a twist.

Some students were paid $20 for telling the lie that they enjoyed the task. Others were paid $1, and those in a control condition did not tell a lie at all. Participants then rated the enjoyableness of the tasks. As it turned out, those paid $1 said they liked the tasks more and displayed greater willingness to participate in similar experiments in the future than did other students (see Table 11.1).

How can we explain the findings? According to theory, the cognition that "the spool-removing and peg-turning tasks were really boring" was dissonant with the cognition that "I just told someone it was lots of fun." The $20 provided students with external justification for telling the lie. It helped them justify why they said one thing (the tasks

Table 11.1 Results of Festinger and Carlsmith study

Question	Experimental condition		
	$1	$20	Control
How enjoyable were tasks? (rated from −5 to +5)	1.35	−.05	−.45
Were tasks scientifically important? (rated from 0 to 10)	6.45	5.18	5.60
Are you willing to participate in similar experiments? (rated from −5 to +5)	1.20	−.25	−.62

Source: Festinger, L. & Carlsmith, J. M., 1959, *Journal of Abnormal and Social Psychology*, 58, 203–210.

were exciting), yet believed another (they were really boring). They received $20; that helped them feel good about the whole thing, and they had no need to change their attitude so as to restore consonance. Like a stiff drink that helps people forget their sorrows, the $20 helped to erase the dissonance, or sufficiently so that students didn't feel any need to change their attitude toward the tasks.

For students paid $1, it was a different matter. Lacking a sufficient external justification for the inconsistency, they had to turn inward to get one. They needed to bring their private attitude in line with their public behavior. One way to do this was to change their attitude toward the tasks. By convincing themselves that "the thing with the spools wasn't so bad; it gave me a chance to do something, perfect my hand–eye coordination—yeah, that's the ticket," they could comfortably believe that the statement they made to a fellow student ("I had a lot of fun") actually reflected their inner feelings. Dissonance was thus resolved; they had restored cognitive harmony (see Figure 11.4).

Note that these findings are exactly the opposite of what you might expect based on common sense and classic learning theory. Both would suggest that people paid more money would like something more. Reward leads to liking, right? Not according to dissonance theory. Indeed, the negative relationship between reward and liking, consistent with cognitive dissonance theory, has held up in other studies conceptually replicating the Festinger and Carlsmith experiment (Harmon-Jones, 2002; Preiss & Allen, 1998).

The early research had exciting theoretical implications. As researcher Elliot Aronson observed:

> As a community we have yet to recover from the impact of this research—fortunately! . . . Because the finding departed from the general orientation accepted

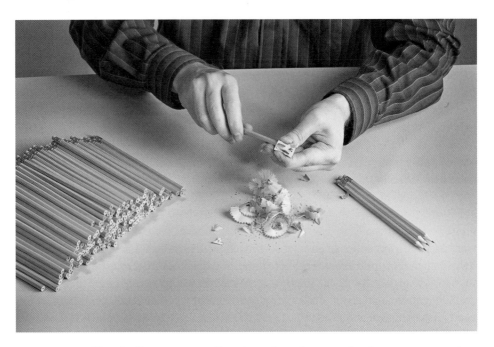

■ **Figure 11.4 Classic dissonance studies show that when people choose to engage in a boring task—such as carefully sharpening a large number of pencils with a small pencil sharpener—and receive a meager reward, they can change their attitude toward the task. To reduce dissonance, they justify their behavior and convince themselves the task was enjoyable.**

Image courtesy of Shutterstock.

either tacitly or explicitly by most social psychologists in the 1950s: [that] high reward—never low reward—is accompanied by greater learning, greater conformity, greater performance, greater satisfaction, greater persuasion . . . [But in Festinger and Carlsmith] either reward theory made no prediction at all or the opposite prediction. These results represented a striking and convincing act of liberation from the dominance of a general reward-reinforcement theory.

(Quoted in Aron & Aron, 1989, p. 116)

More generally, the results of this strange—but elegantly conducted—experiment suggested that people could not be counted on to slavishly do as experts predicted. They were not mere automatons whose thoughts could be controlled by behavioral engineering or psychologists' rewards. Like Dostoyevsky's underground man, who celebrated his emotion and spontaneity, dissonance researchers rejoiced in the study's findings, for they spoke to the subjectivity and inner-directedness of human beings.

Applications

The great contribution of induced compliance research is theoretical, in suggesting new ways to think about human attitudes and persuasion. However, the research does have practical applications. The negative incentive effect—paying people less changes their attitudes more—can be applied to the problem of motivating individuals to engage in positive, healthy acts they would rather not perform. For example, consider the case of a parent who wants to convince a couch-potato child to exercise more. Should the parent pay the kid each time she or he jogs, plays tennis, or swims laps? Dissonance theory says no. It stipulates that children frequently face dissonance after engaging in vigorous physical exercise—for example, "*I just ran a mile, but, geez, did that hurt*"; "*I just ran five laps, but I could have been on Facebook.*" By paying sons or daughters money for exercising, parents undermine children's motivation to change their attitudes. The money provides strong external justification, erasing the dissonance: the child no longer feels a need to change an anti-exercise attitude so that it is compatible with behavior (jogging a mile a day). Instead, the money bridges thought and action and becomes the main thing the child gets out of the event. Thus, the same old negative attitude toward exercise persists.

By contrast, if parents don't pay their children a hefty sum (or give them only a paltry reward), children must reduce the dissonance on their own. To be sure, kids may not restore consonance by developing a positive attitude toward exercise (they could blame their parents for "forcing" them to work up a sweat or just complain about how sore their bodies feel). But it is entirely possible—and I've seen examples of this with parents in my neighborhood, to say nothing of research that backs it up (Deci, 1975)—that children will change their attitude to fit their behavior. They develop a positive attitude toward exercise to justify their behavior. Exercise becomes a positive, not a negative, force in their lives; it becomes associated with pleasant activities; and the attitude motivates, then triggers behavior. The child begins to exercise spontaneously, on his or her own, without parental prodding (see Figure 11.5).

EXPLANATIONS AND CONTROVERSIES

When a theory is developed, researchers test it to determine if it holds water. If hypotheses generated from the theory are empirically supported, researchers are elated: they have come upon a concept that yields new insights, and they have landed a way to publish studies that enhance their professional reputations. But once all this happens, the question "What have you done for me lately?" comes to mind. The ideas become rather familiar. What's more, scholars begin wondering just why the theory works

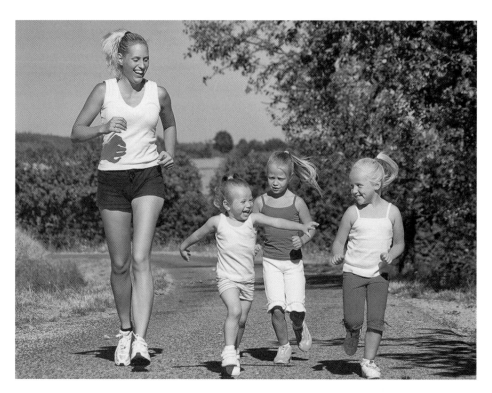

■ Figure 11.5 How can parents convince their children to get off the couch or put away their electronic devices and hit the jogging trail? Dissonance theory suggests that they should create a situation of insufficient justification: encouraging children to agree to get some exercise, while not dispensing any reward. The resultant dissonance may lead children to develop a more positive attitude toward exercising, and they may come to enjoy running with their mom or dad, or by themselves.

Image courtesy of Shutterstock.

and come to recognize that it may hold only under particular conditions. These new questions lead to revisions of the theory and advance science. They also help to "keep the theory young" by forcing tests in new eras, with new generations of scholars and different social values.

Dissonance theory fits this trajectory. After the studies of the 1950s and 1960s were completed (yes, they were conducted that long ago!), scholars began asking deeper questions about dissonance theory. They began to wonder just why dissonance leads to attitude change and whether there weren't other reasons why individuals seek to restore dissonance than those Festinger posited. Many theorists proposed alternative accounts of dissonance and tested their ideas.

The catalyst for this research was the Festinger and Carlsmith boring-task study previously discussed. Like a Rorschach projection test, it has been interpreted in different ways by different scholars. Their research suggests that when people engage in counterattitudinal behavior, there is more going on than you might think. Four explanations of the study have been advanced. Each offers a different perspective on human nature and persuasion. Yet all four agree on one point: Festinger's thesis—people are driven by an overarching need to reduce inconsistency—is not the only psychological engine that leads to attitude change. Students in the boring-task study may have been bothered by the inconsistency between attitude toward the task and behavior (telling others it was enjoyable). However, there were other reasons why they changed their attitude than the mere discomfort that inconsistency causes. Let's review these four perspectives on cognitive dissonance.

Unpleasant Consequences + Responsibility = Dissonance

What really bothered students in Festinger and Carlsmith's experiment, researcher Joel Cooper has suggested, is that they might be personally responsible for having caused unpleasant consequences (Scher & Cooper, 1989). By leading an innocent person to believe that a monotonous study was enjoyable, they had, arguably, caused a fellow student to develop an expectation that would not be met by reality. This realization caused them discomfort. To alleviate the pain, they convinced themselves that the task was really interesting. Thus, it was not inconsistency per se but, rather, "the desire to avoid feeling personally responsible for producing the aversive consequence of having harmed the other participant" that motivated attitude change (Harmon-Jones & Mills, 1999, p. 14).

Dissonance Occurs When You Are Concerned That You Look Bad in Front of Others

This view emphasizes people's need to manage impressions or present themselves positively in front of other people (Tedeschi, Schlenker, & Bonoma, 1971). Theorists argue that students in Festinger and Carlsmith's study did not really change their attitudes, but marked down on the questionnaire that they liked the task only to avoid being viewed negatively by the experimenter. Concerned that the experimenter would look down on them for being willing to breach their ethics for the reward of $1, students in the $1 condition strategically changed their attitude so that it looked as if they really liked the task. Thus, they could not be accused of selling their souls for a trivial sum of money (Cooper & Fazio, 1984).

Dissonance Involves a Threat to Self-Esteem

The self-concept is at the center of this interpretation. In Aronson's (1968) view, students in Festinger and Carlsmith's study experienced dissonance between the cognition "I am a good and moral person" and the knowledge that "I just lied to someone, and I won't have a chance to 'set him straight' because I probably won't see him again" (p. 24). Students were not bothered by the mere inconsistency between thoughts but, rather, by the fact that their behavior was inconsistent with—or violated—their positive self-concept. Of course, lying is not dissonant to a pathological liar; yet it was assumed that for most people, telling a fib would be moderately dissonant with their views of themselves as honest individuals. The self-concept is at the center of other contemporary views of dissonance reduction, such as Steele's theory (1988), which takes a slightly different approach to the issue.

It's not Dissonance, but Self-Perception

Daryl J. Bem (1970) argued that effects observed in experiments like Festinger and Carlsmith's had nothing to do with cognitive dissonance, but were due to an entirely different psychological process. Unlike the three explanations just discussed, Bem's theory dismisses dissonance entirely. Arguing that people aren't so much neurotic rationalizers as dispassionate, cool observers of their own behavior, Bem suggests that people look to their own behavior when they want to understand their attitudes. Behavior leads to attitude, Bem (1972) argues, but not because people want to bring attitude in line with behavior so as to gain consistency. Instead, behavior causes attitude because people infer their attitudes from observing their behavior. For example, according to Bem, a young woman forms her attitude toward vegetarian food by observing her behavior: "I'm always eating pasta and vegetables. I never order meat from restaurants anymore. I must really like veggie food." Or a guy decides he likes a girl, not on the basis of his positive thoughts but, rather, because he observes that "I'm always texting her and get excited when she texts back. I must really like her."

Applying this analysis to Festinger and Carlsmith's classic experiment, Bem argued that students paid $20 to say a boring task was interesting quickly looked to the situation, asked themselves why they would do this, and observed that they had just been paid $20 to make the statement. "Oh, I must have done it for the money," they concluded. Having reached this judgment, there was not the slightest reason for them to assume that their behavior reflected an attitude.

Subjects paid $1 looked dispassionately at their behavior to help decide why they told the other student the task was fun. Noting that they had received only a buck to lie, they concluded, "I sure didn't do this for the money." Seeking to further understand why they behaved as they did, the $1 subjects then asked themselves, "Now why would I have told the experimenter the tasks were interesting? I didn't get any big external reward for saying this." Then came the explanation, obvious and plausible: "I must have really liked those tasks. Why else would I have agreed to make the statements?" These inferences—rather than rationalizations—led to the $1 students' forming a favorable attitude toward the tasks.

RESOLUTIONS

Who's right? Who's wrong? Which view has the most support or the most adherents? What's the right answer?

These questions probably occur to you as you read the different views of dissonance. However, there is usually not one correct interpretation of a complex phenomenon, but many. Thus, there are various reasons why low reward or counterattitudinal advocacy leads to attitude change. Inconsistency between cognitions, feeling responsible for producing negative consequences, discomfort at looking bad in front of others, perceiving that one has engaged in behavior that is incongruent with one's sense of self, and subsequent self-perceptions all motivate individuals to change attitudes to fit behavior. For a number of years, researchers tried to tease out which explanation explained the $1 vs. $20 findings best. It became so difficult to disentangle the different psychological processes that researchers moved on, concluding that each perspective contributed different insights.

Of the different approaches advanced above, the two that have generated the most knowledge of persuasion have been the self-concept and self-perception theories. Self-concept perspectives, such as Steele's (1988) **self-affirmation theory**, have intriguing implications for persuasion and health (see Box 11.1). **Self-perception theory** has helped explain an important interpersonal compliance phenomenon known as foot-in-the-door (see Chapter 12).

BOX 11.1 DISSONANCE AND MENTAL HEALTH

One of the great things about dissonance theory is that over half a century after it was formulated, it continues to contain enlightening ideas about everyday life. Some of these ideas have interesting implications for mental health. Here are five suggestions, culled from theory and research, for how to harness dissonance in the service of a happier, healthier life:

Continued

1. *Expect to experience dissonance after a decision.* Don't expect life to be clean and free of stress. If you choose one product or side of the issue instead of another and the selection was difficult, there is bound to be discomfort.

2. *Don't feel you have to eliminate the dissonance immediately.* Some people, uncomfortable with dissonance, mentally decree that no unpleasant thoughts about the decision should enter their mind. But sometimes the more we try to suppress something, the more apt it is to return to consciousness (Wegner et al., 1987). Dissonance can present us with a learning experience; it can help us come to grips with aspects of decisions we didn't like or positions that have more of a gray area than we believed at the outset. The thinking that dissonance stimulates can help us make better decisions, or deliver more compelling persuasive communication next time around. Of course, it is perfectly natural to want to reduce dissonance that follows a decision or performance of a behavior. However, we should also be open to the possibility that dissonance can be a teaching tool, as well as an annoyance—a phenomenon that can deepen our understanding of human experience.

3. *Don't feel bound to each and every commitment you make.* Dissonance research indicates that once people make a public commitment, they are loath to change their minds, for fear of looking bad or having to confront the fact that they made a mistake, and so on. But there are times—such as undergoing a cruel initiation rite to join a sorority—when backing out of a commitment may be the healthy thing to do. Naturally, we should try to honor our commitments as much as possible, but we also should not feel obligated to do something unhealthy or unethical just because we sunk a lot of time into the project.

4. *Admit your mistakes.* Most of us are loath to admit we made a mistake. Fearing that the mistake would reflect negatively on their self-concept or arouse other dissonant elements, people cling tenaciously to their original decision. But this is not always a mature or helpful response. Understanding why a decision caused dissonance and learning from mistakes can help us grow and avoid similar errors in the future. The Chinese philosopher Lao Tzu said: "A great nation is like a great man: when he makes a mistake, he realizes it. Having realized it, he admits it. Having admitted it, he corrects it. He considers those who point out his faults as his most benevolent teachers" (Tavris & Aronson, 2007).

5. *Be creative in your attempts to reduce dissonance.* You may not be able to reduce all the dissonance that results from a decision or performance of behavior. A young woman who smokes, quits for a while, and then starts up again is apt to feel dissonance. A deadbeat dad may finally feel guilt or

discomfort after years of leaving and neglecting his kids. According to Claude M. Steele and colleagues, these individuals feel dissonant because they have performed actions that call into question their self-worth or sense of themselves as competent, good people (Aronson, Cohen, & Nail, 1999; Steele, 1988). Given that this is the root of dissonance, these folks can alleviate dissonance by doing things that help them look good in their own eyes, Steele argues. Although the smoker cannot reduce all the dissonance aroused by her failure to quit smoking, she might restore a sense of self-competence by completing important projects at work or doing other things that show she can follow up on personal promises she makes. Realistically, the deadbeat dad may have alienated his kids so much that he can't do much to regain their trust. However, he might be able to restore a positive sense of self by at least celebrating their major accomplishments, or by taking the radically different step of spending time with other children in need.

In sum, more than half a century since Festinger invented the concept, cognitive dissonance continues to stimulate scholarly discussion and theorizing about persuasion. There is no question that dissonance produces genuine, abiding changes in attitudes, beliefs, and behavior. However, for dissonance to produce attitude change, the individual must have freely chosen to perform the advocated behavior. Dissonance does not produce attitude change when behavior is coerced; in such situations, the person feels no internal need to rationalize the behavior (for a summary of the theory, see Box 11.2).

This brings us to the final issue in this chapter—an important one for this book: implications of dissonance theory for attitude change. The next section explores ways in which communication experts can use dissonance theory to influence attitudes in a variety of real-life settings.

DISSONANCE AND PERSUASION

Dissonance theorists take a decidedly different approach to persuasion from approaches reviewed in earlier chapters. Rather than trying to accommodate the other person's thinking or speech style, like the ELM or speech accommodation, dissonance theory has a confrontational streak. It says that persuaders should deliberately arouse cognitive dissonance and then let psychology do its work. Once dissonance is evoked, individuals should be motivated to reduce the discomfort. One way they can do this is to change their attitude in the direction the persuader recommends.

BOX 11.2 UNDERSTANDING THEORY: PRIMER ON COGNITIVE DISSONANCE THEORY

1. Cognitive dissonance occurs when an individual holds two psychologically inconsistent cognitions.
2. Dissonance is psychologically uncomfortable, physiologically arousing, and drives individuals to take steps to reduce this uncomfortable state.
3. Dissonance occurs under several conditions, such as when an individual: (a) is faced with a psychologically difficult decision; (b) expends effort to participate in what turns out to be a less-than-ideal task; and (c) in general freely performs a behavior that is inconsistent with an attitude. Individuals are motivated to take steps to reduce dissonance.
4. One method to rid oneself of dissonance is to change the problematic attitude after receiving a persuasive message.
5. The classic $1 vs. $20 induced compliance study found that when individuals freely choose to perform an unpleasant task, they are more likely to feel positively toward the task when they are paid a small amount of money than when they are paid a lot of money.
6. There are a variety of psychological explanations for this finding and for dissonance effects in general. These include an emphasis on aversive consequences, self-presentation, self-esteem, and self-perception.
7. Cognitive dissonance theory emphasizes the power of self-persuasion. We persuade ourselves that a decision or action is justified.
8. Persuaders can harness dissonance theory to help individuals change attitudes. They can call on the power of commitments, effects of hypocrisy inducement, and self-affirmation.

Calling on the major implications of the approaches previously discussed, we can suggest some concrete ways that dissonance theory can be employed in the service of persuasion.

Make a commitment public. When we commit ourselves publicly to an action, something interesting happens. We put pressure on ourselves to translate intention into action. If we fail to make good on a promise that others expect us to keep, we face opprobrium from strangers or friends; we also risk a very public blow to our self-esteem. In order to forestall such negative consequences, dissonant as they are, people find it psychologically easier to make good on their commitments. Research indicates that the strategy works. Women who made a long-term *public* commitment to losing weight were especially likely to achieve their goal, losing more weight than women who did not make any commitment (Nyer & Dellande, 2010).

In contemporary life, individuals frequently make commitments by posting details on Web sites and blogs.

More than 63,000 public commitments have been posted on a Web site called stickK (Rosenbloom, 2011). The name conjures up the desire to "stick" to your promises, and the capital K is legal shorthand symbol for the term "contract." Meander through the site and you will see familiar promises to lose weight, exercise, and avoid junk food. But you also will find more idiosyncratic resolutions like practicing perfect pitch daily, quitting "reading and writing fiction until I'm done with med school applying," only using Facebook "once a week for 30 minutes at most," never being mean to my girlfriend, and not eating meat or fish "with the exception of chicken wings in Buffalo" (stickK, 2011)!

Here is how it works: People publicly resolve to accomplish a goal, make a financial commitment (giving a credit card number, but money is charged only in the case of failure), and indicate where the funds should be allocated if they do not follow through on their commitment. An individual might select a charitable organization she likes, or, to offer additional motivation to succeed, a charity she dislikes. People also choose others to serve as online supporters to cheer them on. Does it work? We can't know for sure. Some people swear by it; others no doubt failed to implement their plans. Public commitment does not guarantee that dissonance will produce attitude change. However, under the right circumstances, commitment can nudge the process along.

Encourage people to publicly advocate a position with which they disagree. How can we nudge people into reducing a prejudiced attitude? One way is to call on the power of public behavior. If individuals who harbor a prejudiced attitude toward minorities or gays can be coaxed into making a tolerant statement in public, they may feel cognitive dissonance. They privately do not like the particular group, but now, lo and behold, they have delivered a favorable speech in public. This may heighten the dissonance and, in some instances, motivate the individuals to bring attitude in line with public behavior. In a study that tested this hypothesis, Michael R. Leippe and Donna Eisenstadt (1994) gave White students an opportunity to write essays endorsing a scholarship policy that would significantly increase money available to Blacks, presumably at the expense of Whites. White students who believed their essays could be made public became more favorable toward both the policy and African-Americans (see also Eisenstadt et al., 2005).

Interestingly, a judge used a variant of this procedure on a bigot who burned a Black doll and a cross in Black residents' yards. In addition to using coercive punishments—such as sentencing him to jail—the judge ordered the man to go to the library to research the impact of cross burnings (Martin, 2001). Studying the issue could help the man think through his misguided sentiments. In addition, researching the topic in a public setting might lead the man to come to grips with his racist attitudes, perhaps inducing attitude change.

Confront people with their own hypocrisy. This strategy places dissonance front and center in the individual's mind. A communicator directly confronts the person, letting him know that he has performed a behavior that violates a personal belief. The inconsistency is psychologically disturbing, propelling the individual to alter the attitude.

Stone and his colleagues employed this procedure in an engaging study of safe sex. They recognized that most students believe they should use condoms to prevent the spread of AIDS, but do not always practice what they preach. Stone and colleagues argued that, if they reminded individuals of this fact, "the resulting inconsistency between [students'] public commitment and the increased awareness of their current risky sexual behavior should cause dissonance" (Stone et al., 1994, p. 117). To alleviate dissonance, students might begin to practice safer sex.

Participants in the study were led to believe they were helping to design an AIDS prevention program for use at the high school level. Experimental group subjects wrote a persuasive speech about safer sex and delivered it in front of a video camera. They read about circumstances that made it difficult for people to use condoms and listed the circumstances that surrounded their own previous failures to practice safe sex. This was designed to provoke inconsistency or induce hypocrisy. (Control group subjects did not list these reasons or make the safer-sex speech before a video camera.)

All students were given an opportunity to buy condoms, using the $4 they had earned for participating in the study. As predicted, more students in the hypocrisy condition purchased condoms and bought more condoms than students in the control conditions. Their behavior was apparently motivated by the discomfort and guilt they experienced when they recognized they did not always practice what they preached (O'Keefe, 2000).

As intriguing as Stone and colleagues' findings are, we need to be cautious about glibly endorsing **hypocrisy induction** as a method for safer-sex induction. First, making people feel hypocritical may make them angry and that may cause the treatment to boomerang. Second, safer-sex requests in real-world situations meet up against a variety of roadblocks, including the pleasures of sex, reluctance to offend a partner by proposing condom use, and even anxiety about being physically assaulted if one suggests using a condom. Hypocrisy induction may change attitudes in an experimental context, but persuasion is apt to be more difficult in actual sexual situations.

At the same time, the strategy has intriguing possibilities. Letting people know that a behavior they perform or position they endorse is incompatible with an important component of their self-concepts can make them feel uncomfortable (Takaku, 2006). Telling someone straight out that she has made a prejudiced remark can reduce the likelihood that this person will behave in a stereotyped way in the future (Czopp, Monteith, & Mark, 2006). Confronting individuals with an instance of their prejudice or self-incongruent behavior can be just the right psychological medicine to goad them into changing their attitudes (see Box 11.3).

BOX 11.3 90210 DISSONANCE

This story is about a father and teenage son who lived in the 90210 zip code region of the United States. You may know where that is. It's Beverly Hills, California. All too ordinary in some respects, the story concerns a high school student who was heavily dependent on drugs, and a dad who found out and tried to do something about it. The story, originally broadcast on the National Public Radio program *This American Life* on January 16, 1998, would not be relevant to this chapter except for one small but important fact: the father used dissonance theory to try to convince his son to quit doing drugs. His dad probably had never heard of cognitive dissonance, but his persuasive effort is a moving testament to the ways that dissonance can be used in family crisis situations. Here is what happened:

Joshua, a student at plush Beverly Hills High School, got involved with drugs in a big way. "I failed English. I failed P.E. even, which is difficult to do, unless, you're, you know, running off getting stoned whenever you're supposed to be running around the track. And I just, you know, I just did whatever I wanted to do whenever I wanted to do it," he told an interviewer. He stole money from his parents regularly to finance his drug habit.

Joshua had no reason to suspect his parents knew. But strange things began to happen. His dad started to punish him, grounding him on the eve of a weekend he planned to do LSD, offering no reason for the punishment. Claiming there was going to be a drug bust at Beverly Hills High, Josh's dad revealed the names of students who were doing drugs. How could his father know this? Josh wondered.

About a month later, Josh and a buddy were hanging out in his backyard. The night before, there had been a big wind storm. It ripped off a panel from the side

Continued

of the house. He and his friend were smoking a joint, like they did every day after school, when his buddy, noticing the downed panel, suddenly said, "Dude, what is this? Come here, dude. Come here, dude. Look at this." Josh saw only a strange piece of machinery inside a wall, when his buddy shocked him. "Dude, your parents are taping your calls."

Suddenly, Josh understood. That explained his dad's punishments and knowledge of the high school drug group. At this point, the radio program switched to Josh's dad, who revealed what had happened. He said he became upset when Josh's grades plunged and his son "started acting like a complete fool." Concerned and noticing that Josh spent a lot of time on the phone, he decided to tape-record Josh's phone calls. The ethical aspects of this appeared not to bother the father.

Aware his dad was taping him, Josh made a decision. He would not quit drugs—that was too great a change—but would tell his friends that he was going straight when they talked on the phone. This worked for a while, until Josh felt guilty about lying to his father. He valued his relationship with his dad and decided to talk to him. He cornered his dad at a party and told him that he knew he had been taping his phone calls.

In a dramatic admission, his father conceded he had been tape-recording Josh's conversations and said he was not going to do it anymore. He then told his son that there was something he didn't know yet, and perhaps would not understand. "Josh," he said, "you think that because I'm your father and I am in this role of the disciplinarian, that it's between you and me. What you haven't realized yet is that your actions have far more impact on your own life than they will on mine." He told Josh that he was going to take out the tape recorder the following day. At this point, Josh was waiting for a punishment—a severe punitive action, he assumed, perhaps military school. "I'll take the tape recorder out tomorrow," his dad said, "and there is only one thing I want you to do. I have about 40 tapes. I am going to give them to you, and I want you to listen to them, and that's all I ask."

With this statement, Josh's father hoped to unleash cognitive dissonance in his son. He wanted Josh to hear how he sounded on the tapes—his redundant, frequently incoherent conversations, non sequiturs, his cruel treatment of others. Clearly, his dad wanted to provoke an inconsistency between Josh's self-concept and his behavior on the tapes. And this was exactly what occurred. Josh was embarrassed—appalled—by the conversations that he heard. He listened to a call from his girlfriend, upset that he had ignored her and that he treated her coldly and with indifference. He showed the same indifference with his friends.

"I had no idea what I sounded like and I didn't like what I sounded like at all," Josh said. "I was very self-centered and egotistical and uncaring of other people. It was about me. I was the star of my own stage and everybody else could basically, you know, go to hell as far as I was concerned. I had never realized that aspect of my personality. I didn't know how mean in that sense I had gotten."

After listening to the tapes, over time, Josh changed his attitudes toward drugs, stopped lying, and altered his life's course. His father—who instigated the radical plan—was amazed. "He understood the entire thing that he was doing," he said proudly.

Affirm people. People frequently reject messages not just because they are inconsistent with an attitude, but because they threaten a core sense of self. Gun owners dislike gun control because guns are connected in their minds with a valued belief in freedom. Gun opponents reject pro-gun arguments because these undermine an abiding commitment to nonviolence. People also resist changing unhealthy habits because addictions to cigarettes, drugs, and gambling have become important parts of their social identities. Self-affirmation, which evolved out of cognitive dissonance theory, suggests an intriguing way to change these attitudes. According to the self-affirmation view, people reject threatening social and health information to preserve a positive sense of self. But if one's self-concept can be elevated in some other fashion, the impulse to react defensively to threatening messages can be diminished (Sherman, Nelson, & Steele, 2000, p. 1048; Steele, 1988).

In a series of studies, researchers induced self-affirmation by asking students to describe experiences in which they implemented values that were personally important. For example, a student who valued a sense of humor discussed an incident where her sense of humor took on importance and led her to feel positively about herself. Control group participants engaged in a neutral activity, listing everything they had eaten or drunk over the past two days. Everyone then read a scientific report that presented arguments critical of their attitude toward capital punishment. Participants who supported the death penalty read an anti-capital punishment scientific report. Those opposed to the death penalty read a pro-capital punishment article. Now here is where self-affirmation kicked in: Students who had earlier affirmed an important value like humor were more open to evidence that opposed their capital punishment position than were those in the control group. Affirmed students actually *changed* their attitudes toward capital punishment— an issue they felt strongly about—more than non-affirmed subjects (Cohen, Aronson, & Steele, 2000).

"Shoring up global self-worth," the researchers concluded, "takes the sting out of new ideas, making them less painful to accept as true" (Cohen et al., 2000, p. 1161). But if our global self-worth has been validated, we are a tad less defensive and more open to giving the other side another look (see also Sherman & Cohen, 2006).

Thus, if persuaders want to reduce defensiveness to information that threatens a strongly held attitude, they should engage in a little jujitsu. They should affirm people's self-concepts and help them feel good about their values. This will open psychological receptors and give people the strength they need to consider information that questions a habit of mind. But there are limits to how robustly this can work in everyday life. If people are extraordinarily wedded to an attitude, such as abortion, or are psychologically dependent upon a behavior, like drugs, or distrust the persuader, it will take more than simple praise to change their attitude. Self-affirmation provides us with clues on how to change deep-seated attitudes, but the trick is how to make it work in dicey everyday situations.

CONCLUSIONS

Cognitive dissonance remains an important, intriguing psychological theory with numerous implications for persuasion. Dissonance is an uncomfortable state that arises when individuals hold psychologically inconsistent cognitions. As revised and reconceptualized over the years, dissonance also refers to feeling personally responsible for unpleasant consequences, and experiencing stress over actions that reflect negatively on the self. There are different views of dissonance and diverse explanations as to why it exerts the impact that it does on attitudes.

There is little doubt that dissonance influences attitudes and cognitions. Its effects fan out to influence decision making, justification of effort, compliance under low reward, and advocating a position with which one disagrees. The theory also helps us understand why people commit themselves to causes—both good and bad ones. It offers suggestions for how to help people remain committed to good causes and how to aid individuals in quitting dysfunctional groups. The theory also has intriguing implications for persuasion. Departing from conventional strategies that emphasize accommodating people or meeting them halfway, dissonance theory recommends that persuaders (either overtly or subtly) provoke inconsistencies in individuals. Dissonance then serves as the engine that motivates attitude change. In this sense, dissonance is a powerful theory of persuasive communication, emphasizing, as it does, the central role that self-persuasion plays in attitude change.

Test your knowledge now with interactive exercises

Part Four | # Persuasive Communication Contexts

Chapter 12

Interpersonal Persuasion

 Listen now to the author's chapter summary

Bernae Gunderson, a paralegal specialist from St. Paul, has no difficulty deciphering the fine print of legal documents. Still, she was puzzled by materials she received from her mortgage company. They didn't jibe with the home equity loan she and her husband had been promised. Mrs. Gunderson called the company, First Alliance Corporation, asked questions about monthly payments and fees, and was promptly reassured that her understanding of the loan was indeed correct. What Mrs. Gunderson was not told—but soon would discover—was that First Alliance had tacked on $13,000 in fees to the loan, and the interest rate rose a full percentage point every 6 months (Henriques & Bergman, 2000).

First Alliance, it turned out, used deceptive sales procedures to promote its services. Sued by regulators in five states, the company recruited unsuspecting borrowers using a high-level con game and elaborate sales pitch that was designed to snooker people into paying higher fees and interest rates than were justified by market factors. The company's loan officers were required to memorize a 27-page selling routine that included the following gambits:

■ Establish rapport and a common bond. Initiate a conversation about jobs, children, or pets. Say something funny to get them laughing.
■ To soften the financial blow, when talking about dollar amounts, say "merely," "simply," or "only."
■ If the customer asks questions about fees, just reply, "May I ignore your concern about the rate and costs if I can show you that these are minor issues in a loan?"
■ If all else fails and the sale appears to be lost, say, "I want to apologize for being so inept a loan officer. I want you to know that it's all my fault, and I'm truly sorry. Just so I don't make the same mistake again, would you mind telling me what I did that was wrong? Didn't I cover that?" (And get right back into it.)

(Henriques & Bergman, 2000, p. C12).

There is nothing wrong with using persuasion techniques to make a sale. The problem is that First Alliance trained its loan officers to deceive customers about its services. They lied about the terms of home equity loans and refused to come clean when people like Bernae Gunderson raised questions. They were experts in using strategies of interpersonal persuasion. Unfortunately, they exploited their knowledge, manipulating individuals into signing off on deals that were unduly expensive and unfair.

Interpersonal persuasion, the centerpiece of First Alliance's promotional campaign and subject of this chapter, offers a glimpse into a realm of persuasion that is somewhat different from those discussed so far in the book. Unlike purely psychological approaches, it focuses on the dyad, or two-person unit (persuader and persuadee). In contrast to attitude-based research, it centers on changing behavior—on inducing people to comply with the persuader's requests. Unlike message-oriented persuasion research, which focuses on modifying views about political or social issues, it explores techniques people employ to accomplish interpersonal objectives—for example, how they "sell themselves" to others.

Drawing on the fields of interpersonal communication and social psychology, interpersonal persuasion research examines the strategies people use to gain compliance. It looks at how individuals try to get their way with others (something we all want to do). It examines techniques businesses use to convince customers to sign on the dotted line, strategies charities employ to gain donations, and methods that health practitioners use to convince people to take better care of their health. To gain insight into these practical issues, interpersonal persuasion scholars develop theories and conduct empirical studies—both experiments and surveys. In some ways, this is the most practical, down-to-earth chapter in the book; in other ways, it is the most complicated because it calls on taxonomies and cognitive concepts applied to the dynamic dance of interpersonal communication.

The first portion of the chapter looks at a variety of techniques that have amusing sales pitch names like foot-in-the-door and door-in-the-face. These persuasive tactics are known as **sequential influence techniques**, in which persuasive communications follow one another in a step-by-step fashion. Influence in such cases "often proceeds in stages, each of which establishes the foundation for further changes in beliefs or behavior. Individuals slowly come to embrace new opinions, and actors often induce others to gradually comply with target requests" (Seibold, Cantrill, & Meyers, 1994, p. 560). The second section of the chapter focuses more directly on the communication aspect of interpersonal persuasion. It looks at the strategies that people—you, me, our friends, and parents—use to gain compliance, how researchers study this, and the many factors that influence compliance-gaining.

FOOT-IN-THE-DOOR

This classic persuasion strategy dates back to the days when salespeople knocked on doors and plied tricks of the trade to maneuver their way into residents' homes. If they could just overcome initial resistance—get a "foot in the door" of the domicile—they felt they could surmount subsequent obstacles and make the sale of an Avon perfume, a vacuum cleaner, or a set of encyclopedias. Going door to door is out of date, but starting small and moving to a larger request is still in vogue. The **foot-in-the-door** technique stipulates that an individual is more likely to comply with a second, larger request if he or she has agreed to perform a small initial request.

Many studies have found support for the foot-in-the-door (FITD) procedure. Researchers typically ask individuals in an experimental group to perform a small favor, one to which almost everyone agrees. Experimenters next ask these folks to comply with a second, larger request, the one in which the experimenter is actually interested. Participants in the control condition receive only the second request. Experimental group participants are typically more likely than control subjects to comply with the second request. For example:

- In a classic study, Freedman and Fraser (1966) arranged for experimenters working for a local traffic safety committee to ask California residents if they would mind putting a 3-inch "Be a safe driver" sign in their cars. Two weeks later, residents were asked if they would place a large, unattractive "Drive Carefully" sign on their front lawns. Homeowners in a control condition were asked only the second request. Seventeen percent of control group residents agreed to put the large sign on their lawns. However, 76 percent of those who agreed to the initial request or had been approached the first time complied with the second request.
- Participants were more willing to volunteer to construct a hiking trail if they had agreed to address envelopes for an environmental group than if they had not acceded to the initial request (Dillard, 1990a).
- Individuals were more likely to volunteer a large amount of time for a children's social skill project if they had initially assisted a child with a small request—helping an 8-year-old get candy from a candy machine (Rittle, 1981).

Emboldened by results like these, researchers have conducted over 100 studies of the FITD strategy. Meta-analytic, statistically based reviews of the research show that the effect is reliable and occurs more frequently than would be expected by chance (e.g., Dillard, Hunter, & Burgoon, 1984). Given its utility, professional persuaders—ranging from telemarketers to university alumni fundraisers—frequently employ FITD.

Why Does It Work?

There are three reasons why the foot-in-the-door technique produces compliance. The first explanation calls on Bem's self-perception theory, described in Chapter 11. According to this view, individuals who perform a small favor for someone look at their behavior and infer that they are helpful, cooperative people. They become, in their own eyes, the kinds of people who do these sorts of things, go along with requests made by strangers, and cooperate with worthwhile causes (Freedman & Fraser, 1966, p. 201). Having formed this self-perception, they naturally accede to the second, larger request.

A second interpretation emphasizes consistency needs. Recalling that they agreed to the first request, individuals find it dissonant to reject the second, target request. Perhaps having formed the perception that they are helpful people, they feel motivated to behave in a way that is consistent with their newly formed view of themselves. In a sense, they may feel more committed to the requester or to the goal of helping others.

A third explanation places emphasis on social norms. "Being asked to perform an initial small request makes people more aware of the norm of social responsibility, a norm that prescribes that one should help those who are in need," William DeJong explains (1979, p. 2236).

When Does It Work?

The FITD technique does not always produce compliance. It is particularly likely to work when the request concerns a pro-social issue, such as asking for a donation to charity or requesting favors from strangers. Self-perceptions, consistency needs, and social norms are likely to kick in under these circumstances. Foot-in-the-door is also more apt to succeed when the second query is "a continuation," or logical outgrowth, of the initial request, and when people actually perform the requested behavior (Burger, 1999; Dillard et al., 1984).

FITD is not so likely to succeed if the same persuader asks for a second favor immediately after having hit up people for a first request. The bang-bang, request-upon-request approach may create resentment, leading people to say no just to reassert their independence (Chartrand, Pinckert, & Burger, 1999).

Next time you do a favor for someone and are tempted to accede to a second, larger request, check to see if the facilitating factors operating in the situation match those just described. If they do, you may be more apt to go along with the request, and it may be one that you would rather decline.

DOOR-IN-THE-FACE

This technique undoubtedly gets the award for the most memorable name in the Persuasion Tactics Hall of Fame. It occurs when a persuader makes a large request that is almost certain to be denied. After being turned down, the persuader returns with a smaller request, the target request the communicator had in mind at the beginning. **Door-in-the-face** (DITF) is exactly the opposite of foot-in-the-door. Foot-in-the-door starts with a small request and moves to a larger one. DITF begins with a large request and scales down to an appropriately modest request. Researchers study the technique by asking experimental group participants to comply with a large request, one certain to be denied. When they refuse, participants are asked if they would mind going along with a smaller, second request. Control group subjects receive only the second request.

The DITF technique has been tested in dozens of studies. It emerges reliably and dependably, meta-analytic studies tell us (Feeley, Anker, & Aloe, 2012; O'Keefe & Hale, 1998). Consider the following supportive findings:

- A volunteer, supposedly working for a local blood services organization, asked students if they would donate a unit of blood once every 2 months for a period of at least 3 years. Everyone declined this outlandish request. The volunteer then asked experimental group subjects if they would donate just one unit of blood between 8:00 a.m. and 3:30 p.m. the next day. Control group participants were asked the same question. Of those who rejected the first request, 49 percent agreed to donate blood, compared with 32 percent of those in the control group (Cialdini & Ascani, 1976).
- An experimenter working with a boys and girls club asked students if they would mind spending about 15 hours a week tutoring children. When this request was declined, the experimenter asked if students would be willing to spend an afternoon taking kids to a museum or the movies. Students who turned down the initial request were more likely to agree to spend an afternoon with children than those who only heard the second request (O'Keefe & Figgé, 1999).
- An individual claiming to represent a Californian company asked respondents if they would be willing to spend 2 hours answering survey questions on home or dorm safety. After the request was declined, the experimenter asked if individuals would mind taking 15 minutes to complete a small portion of the survey. Control group participants were asked only the second request. Of those who refused the first request, 44 percent agreed to participate in the shorter survey. By contrast, only 25 percent of control group subjects complied with the second request (Mowen & Cialdini, 1980).

Why Does It Work?

Four rather interesting explanations for the DITF strategy have been advanced. One view emphasizes a powerful psychological factor akin to dissonance but more emotion packed: guilt. Individuals feel guilty about turning down the first request. To reduce guilt, an unpleasant feeling, they go along with the second request (O'Keefe & Figgé, 1999). There is some evidence that guilt helps explain DITF effects.

A second view emphasizes reciprocal concessions. As a persuader (deliberately) scales down his request, he is seen as having made a concession. This leads the persuadee to invoke the social rule that "you should make concessions to those who make concessions to you" or "you should meet the other fellow halfway." As a result, the persuadee yields and goes along with the second request (Cialdini et al., 1975; Rhoads & Cialdini, 2002; Turner et al., 2007).

Third, social judgment processes also operate in the DITF situation. The extreme first request functions as an anchor against which the second request is compared. After the outrageous initial request, the second request seems less costly and severe. However, control group participants who are asked to comply only with the smaller request do not have this anchor available to them. Thus, experimental group participants are more apt than control group subjects to go along with the target request.

Fourth, self-presentation concerns may also intervene. People fear that the persuader will evaluate them negatively for turning down the first request. Not realizing that the whole gambit has been staged, they accede to the second request to make themselves look good in the persuader's eyes.

When Does It Work?

Like other persuasion factors discussed, the DITF technique is sensitive to contextual factors (Fern, Monroe, & Avila, 1986; O'Keefe & Hale, 1998). DITF works particularly well when the request concerns pro-social issues. People may feel guilty about turning down a charitable organization's request for a large donation or time expenditure. They can make things right by agreeing to the second request.

DITF effects also emerge when the same individual makes both requests. People may feel an obligation to reciprocate a concession if they note that the person who asked for too much is scaling down her request. If two different people make the requests, the feeling that "you should make concessions to those who make concessions to you" may not kick in.

The DITF strategy is also more apt to work if there is only a short delay between the first and second requests. If too long a time passes between requests, the persuadee's guilt might possibly dissipate. In addition, the more time that passes between requests, the less salient is the contrast between the extreme first request and the seemingly more reasonable second request.

APPLICATIONS

The FITD and DITF techniques are regularly used by compliance professionals. Noting that you gave $25 to a charity last year, a volunteer asks if you might increase your gift to $50. A representative from the local newspaper calls and asks if you would like to take out a daily subscription. When you tell her you don't have time to read the paper every day, she asks, "How about Sunday?" Or the bank loan officer wonders if you can afford a $100 monthly payment on your student loan. When you decline, he asks if you can pay $50 each month, exactly the amount he had in mind from the beginning.

FITD and DITF, like all persuasion techniques, can be used for unethical, as well as morally acceptable, purposes. Unsavory telemarketers or front organizations posing as charities can manipulate people into donating money through adroit use of these tactics. At the same time, pro-social groups can employ these techniques to achieve worthwhile goals. For example, a volunteer from Mothers Against Drunk Driving might use FITD to induce bar patrons to sign a petition against drunk driving. Sometime later in the evening, the volunteer could ask patrons if they would agree to let a taxi take them home (Taylor & Booth-Butterfield, 1993). In the same fashion, charitable organizations such as the Red Cross or Purple Heart might employ DITF gently to arouse guilt that inevitably follows refusal of the initial request.

The FITD and DITF strategies have generated the most research, and we know the most about when they work and why. A number of other compliance techniques have been described. Reviewing key compliance strategies offers insights into the canny ways that persuaders use communication to achieve their goals (e.g., Pratkanis, 2007).

PRE-GIVING

As the name suggests, the persuader who employs this technique gives the target a reward or gift, or does the individual a favor. Subsequently, our persuader asks for help or presents a message that requires the target to return the favor. Like DITF, **pre-giving** assumes that the recipient will feel pressured by the reciprocity norm that emphasizes reciprocal concessions. People feel socially obligated to return a favor that someone has bestowed upon them (Cialdini, 2009). They also do not like to feel indebted to others, as this imposes a psychological burden to reciprocate at a cost that may not be comfortable. However, a gnawing sense of indebtedness is *not* the only reason why pre-giving works. There are also two positive reasons: gratitude and liking. People feel grateful to someone who does them a favor, and they understandably like the favor-giver. These good feelings lead individuals to want to do something kind to the persuader in return (Goei et al., 2003, 2007; see Figure 12.1).

There is evidence that pre-giving enhances compliance. Robert A. Bell and his colleagues (1996) solicited money for the Sacramento AIDS Foundation, arranging for their assistants to knock on doors in the state's capital city. For half of the households, the solicitor performed a favor of sorts, explaining the organization's mission and handing the individual a pamphlet describing how HIV spreads, along with places to

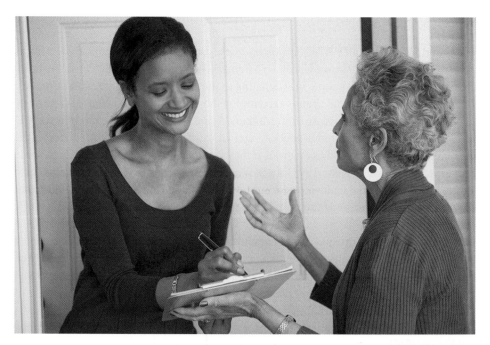

■ Figure 12.1 People may comply with an interpersonal request, such as signing a petition for a pro-social cause, if the persuader employs foot-in-the-door, door-in-the-face, pre-giving, and other interpersonal persuasion strategies. The trick is knowing when, for example, a strategy like foot-in-the-door or door-in-the-face is particularly likely to work.

Image courtesy of iStock.

seek medical information. The other half of the households served as the control and received no pre-giving treatment. Individuals who received the pamphlet were almost twice as likely to give as controls. They gave more money ($1.29 on average, compared with 77 cents).

For pre-giving to succeed, it is necessary that targets accept the favor. If they reject it cold, they feel no obligation to reciprocate (Dillard & Knobloch, 2011). (Unlike DITF, the persuader does not return with a smaller request.) In addition, pre-giving works better when the persuader and target are strangers rather than friends. The norm of reciprocity is less likely to operate between friends, close friends, or family members. When one is close or intimate with another, it is expected that one extends help because one cares for the other, not out of picayune concern that a favor be reciprocated. Interestingly, pre-giving is regularly harnessed by businesses, sometimes in nefarious ways (see Box 12.1).

BOX 12.1 YOU SCRATCH MY WALLET AND I'LL FATTEN YOURS

Compliance professionals regularly employ pre-giving. Also called social exchange, the concept works like this: Person A provides Person B with a tangible, material, or psychological reward. In exchange, when Person A approaches B with a request, B complies (see also Homans, 1961; West & Turner, 2010).

Although the technique can be employed for pro-social purposes, it can also be harnessed for selfish, sometimes exploitative, ends. Consider these troubling examples in medical marketing:

■ Since 2009, a dozen big drug companies have paid doctors and other medical representatives more than $755 million for promotional speaking, consulting, and medical research. Although pharmaceutical firms claim the payments can benefit patients, others worry about a quid pro quo derived from social exchange. As a reporter covering the problem notes, "a growing number of critics say the payments show the extent of the influence drug makers have on doctors. They [critics] are most critical about the speaking payments because the talks, most of which are carefully scripted by drug companies, essentially turn physicians into drug company employees, casting doubt on

Continued

whether the doctors are placing the interests of the drug companies above patients" (Davis, 2011, p. A8). "You should know that many of these speakers bureaus require the physicians to use slides developed by the company to have just exactly the right sales message," one leading physician said (p. A8). Noted another medical ethics expert, "drug and device companies are very shrewd and very sophisticated. If they did not think this kind of gifting mattered, they wouldn't do it."

- Drug companies fork over money to doctors. This "persuades" a small—but disturbing—minority of mercenary physicians to recommend a drug from which they stand to benefit. As one critic sarcastically observed, "you're not being bribed. You're being gifted" (p. A8)!

- The drug maker Scheering-Plough paid doctors large sums of money to prescribe the company's drug for hepatitis C. Schering threatened to remove any doctor from its consulting program if the physician wrote prescriptions for competing drugs or spoke favorably about competitors' treatments. Schering's tactics attracted the interest of federal prosecutors, who suspected that it was using payoffs to convince doctors to prescribe drugs that patients did not need (Harris, 2004).

- Some companies prefer the carrot to the stick. The drug companies Merck, Novartis, and Sankyo gave $700,000 to a medical society that used the money on a series of dinner lectures at Ruth's Chris Steak House. The main theme of the lectures was an expanded notion of high blood pressure that could increase the number of patients buying the companies' drugs. The lecturers argued for a new category of Stage 1 hypertension or incipient high blood pressure that could require the prescription of medications not uncoincidentally produced by the drug companies. A number of doctors saw through the drug companies' ploys and said so publicly. Yet the companies clearly hoped that both the dinner lectures and revised definition of high blood pressure (developed by doctors who received grants from the firms) would expand the market for their medications (Saul, 2006).

- The pharmaceutical firm Merck developed an elaborate plan to train salespeople in their interactions with physicians. The company used military metaphors to describe sales of therapeutic drugs, calling physicians "targets" and sales goals "triggers." They suggested that competitors' claims—like saying the drug Vioxx was dangerous—were outrageous, although about 60,000 people died while taking the drug during a 4-year period. There was detailed instruction on how to shake doctors' hands with a proper positioning of the thumb joint, and appropriate etiquette when treating doctors to dinner, such as how to dexterously break up small pieces of bread. (Lyon & Mirivel, 2011).

■ "It's not quite brainwashing, but they have a way of influencing your think-ing," a doctor said of drug companies' attempts to promote new drugs in another area of medicine (Santora, 2006, p. A13). "You're making [a doctor] money in several ways," explained one former sales manager at Merck. "You're paying him for the talk. You're increasing his referral base so he's getting more patients. And you're helping to develop his name. The hope in all this is that a silent quid quo pro is created. I've done so much for you, the only thing I need from you is that you write more of my products" (Harris & Roberts, 2007, p. A18).

You may ask, "What is wrong with a little quid pro quo, or the old I'll scratch your back if you scratch mine?" However, the unsavory relationship between doctors and drug manufacturers usurps the trust that underlies a relationship between a doctor and patient. Patients trust that doctors will prescribe medications based solely on their medical needs. If physicians, albeit a minority, base pharma-ceutical recommendations on their own financial self-interest, they are acting unethically. The social exchange between drug reps and doctors amounts to bribery, potentially putting patients at serious risk.

LOW-BALLING

This strategy earns its name from the observation that persuaders—most famously, car salespeople—try to secure compliance by "throwing the customer a low ball." In persuasion scholarship, **low-balling** has a precise meaning. It occurs when a persuader induces someone to comply with a request and then "ups the ante" by increasing the cost of compliance. Having made the initial decision to comply, individuals experience dissonance at the thought that they may have to back away from their commitment. Once individuals have committed themselves to a decision, they are loath to change their minds, even when the cost of a decision is raised significantly and unfairly (Cialdini et al., 1978).

Low-balling is similar to FITD in that the persuader begins with a small request and follows it up with a more grandiose alternative. In low-balling, though, the action initially requested is the target behavior; what changes is the cost associated with performing the target action. In the case of FITD, the behavior that the persuader asks the person to initially perform is a setup to induce the individual to comply with the larger, critical request.

Robert B. Cialdini and colleagues have conducted experiments demonstrating that low-balling can increase compliance. Their findings shed light on sales practices in the ever colorful, always controversial, business of selling cars. As the authors explain:

> The critical component of the procedure is for the salesperson to induce the customer to make an *active decision* to buy one of the dealership's cars by offering an extremely good price, perhaps as much as $300 below competitors' prices. Once the customer has made the decision for a specific car (and has even begun completing the appropriate forms), the salesperson removes the price advantage in one of a variety of ways . . . In each instance, the result is the same: the reason that the customer made a favorable purchase decision is removed, and the performance of the target behavior (i.e., buying that specific automobile) is rendered more costly. The increased cost is such that the final price is equivalent to, or sometimes slightly above, that of the dealer's competitors. Yet, car dealership lore has it that more customers will remain with their decision to purchase the automobile, even at the adjusted figure, than would have bought it had the full price been revealed before a purchase decision had been obtained.
>
> (1978, p. 464; see Figure 12.2)

■ **Figure 12.2 Car salesmen famously employ the low-balling persuasion tactic to make a sale.**

Photograph by William C. Rieter.

"THAT'S NOT ALL"

Another tactic that borrows from persuasion practitioners is the "that's-not-all" technique. You have probably heard TV announcers make claims like, "And that's not all—if you call now and place an order for this one-time only collection of '60s oldies, we'll throw in an extra rock and roll CD—so call right away!" Researcher Jerry M. Burger capitalized on such real-life observations. He conceptualized and tested the effectiveness of the **that's-not-all technique**. In theory, Burger explained:

> The salesperson presents a product and a price but does not allow the buyer to respond immediately. Instead, after a few seconds of mulling over the price, the buyer is told "that's not all"; that is, there is an additional small product that goes along with the larger item, or that "just for you" or perhaps "today only" the price is lower than that originally cited. The seller, of course, had planned to sell the items together or at the lower price all along but allows the buyer to think about the possibility of buying the single item or the higher priced item first. Supposedly, this approach is more effective than presenting the eventual deal to the customer in the beginning.
>
> (1986, p. 277)

Burger demonstrated that the that's-not-all tactic can influence compliance. In one experiment, two researchers sat at tables that had a sign promoting the university psychology club's bake sale. Cupcakes were featured at the table. Individuals who wandered by sometimes expressed interest in the cupcakes, curious how much they cost. Those assigned to the experimental group were told that cupcakes cost 75 cents each. After listening to a seemingly impromptu conversation between the two experimenters, these individuals were told that the price included two medium-sized cookies. By contrast, subjects in the control group were shown the cookies when they inquired about the cost of the cupcakes. They were told that the package cost 75 cents. Even though people got the same products for the identical cost in both conditions, more experimental group subjects purchased sweets (73 percent) than did control group subjects (40 percent).

That's-not-all relies on a semantic ploy, the suggestion that the buyer is getting something for nothing. In addition, like DITF, the technique plays on the reciprocity norm. Thus, participants in Burger's experimental group naively assumed the persuader had done them a favor by throwing in two cookies. Not knowing that this was part of the gambit, they acquiesced.

FEAR-THEN-RELIEF

This is somewhat different from the other techniques in that the persuader deliberately places the recipient in a state of fear. Suddenly and abruptly, the persuader eliminates the threat, replaces fear with kind words, and asks the recipient to comply with a request. The ensuing relief pushes the persuadee to acquiesce.

Dolinski and Nawrat (1998) demonstrated **fear-then-relief** in several clever experiments. In one study, the researchers placed a piece of paper that resembled a parking ticket behind a car's windshield wiper. When drivers arrived at their cars, they experienced that telltale feeling of fear on noticing what looked to be a parking ticket. In fact, the paper was a leaflet that contained an appeal for blood donations. As drivers' anxiety was replaced with reassurance, an experimenter asked them if they would mind taking 15 minutes to complete a questionnaire. Sixty-eight percent of experimental group subjects complied with the request, compared with 36 percent of control group participants.

Fear-then-relief works for two reasons. First, the relief experienced when the threat is removed is reinforcing. It becomes associated with the second request, leading to more compliance. Second, the ensuing relief places people in a state of "temporary mind-lessness." Preoccupied with the danger that could have snared them, and their own supposed carelessness, individuals are distracted. They are less attentive, and more susceptible to the persuader's request.

The technique has interesting implications for a powerful domain of persuasion, yet one infrequently discussed—interrogation of prisoners. We often think that compliance with captors results from the induction of terror and fear. Fear-then-relief suggests that a more subtle, self-persuasion dynamic is in operation. Captors initially scream at a prisoner, threaten him or her with torture, and begin to hurt the prisoner physically. Suddenly, the abuse ends and is replaced by a softer tone and a nice voice. In some cases, "the sudden withdrawal of the source of anxiety intensifies compliance" (Dolinski & Nawrat, 1998, p. 27; Schein, 1961).

Fear-then-relief is used in peacetime situations too—by parents, teachers, and other authority figures who replace the stick quickly with a carrot. Like other tactics (e.g., Aune & Basil, 1994), it capitalizes on the element of surprise, which succeeds in disrupting people's normal defenses.

PIQUE AND DISRUPT-THEN-REFRAME

Surprise is the key in a couple of other techniques that psychologists have studied, ones no doubt used by compliance professionals. The first is known as the **pique technique**. It involves "making the request in an unusual and atypical manner so that the target's interest is piqued, the refusal script is disrupted, and the target is induced to think positively about compliance" (Santos, Leve, & Pratkanis, 1994, p. 756). In an experimental demonstration of the technique, Santos and colleagues reported that students posing as panhandlers received more money from passersby when they asked, "Can you spare 17 cents (or 37 cents)?" than when they asked if the people could spare a quarter or any change. When was the last time that a panhandler asked you for 37 cents? Never happened, right? Therein lies the ingenuity—and potential lure—of the pique technique.

The pique procedure works because it disrupts our normal routine. It engages and consumes the conscious mind, thereby diverting it from the resistance that typically follows a persuader's request.

Disruption of conscious modes of thought plays a critical role in acquiescence to persuasion, in the view of Eric S. Knowles and his colleagues (2001). Knowles emphasizes that persuaders succeed when they devise clever ways to break down our resistance. He and his colleagues have shown that persuaders can disrupt resistance by subtly changing the wording of requests. Employing what they call the **disrupt-then-reframe** technique, Knowles and his colleagues have shown that they can dramatically increase compliance by first mildly disrupting "the ongoing script of a persuasive request" and then reframing the request or encouraging the listener to "understand the issue in a new way" (Knowles, Butler, & Linn, 2001, p. 50).

In the bold tradition of interpersonal persuasion research, the researchers went door to door selling Christmas cards. They explained that money from the sales would go—as indeed it did—to a nonprofit center that helps developmentally disabled children and adults. The experimenters told some residents that the price of a Christmas card package was $3. They informed others that the price was $3 and then added, "It's a bargain." In the key disrupt-then-reframe condition, the experimenter stated, "This package of cards sells for 300 pennies" (thereby shaking up the normal script for a door-to-door request). She then added, after pausing, "That's $3. It's a bargain" (reframe). Of respondents who purchased cards, 65 percent were in the disrupt-then-reframe treatment, compared with 35 percent in the other groups. Other experiments obtained similar findings, demonstrating that a small, but subtle, variation in a persuasive request can produce dramatic differences in compliance (Davis & Knowles, 1999).

Application

Con artists have long known how to disrupt and reframe, harnessing the technique to disarm and then exploit vulnerable targets. Twelve-year-old Glenn Sparks fell prey to a thief's cunning persuasion as a youngster working in his dad's doughnut shop. Sparks, now a successful professor of communication at Purdue University, relates the incident, based loosely on disrupt-then-reframe, in an enjoyable book aptly called *Rolling in Dough*:

> One man bought two coffee rolls and paid the 70 cent sale with a $20 bill. I gave him some coins and 19 single bills and prepared to move on to another customer. But, before I could do so, the man asked me if he could have two $10 bills for the $20 in singles that he was now briskly counting out on the counter between us. He asked me to count it to make sure there was $20. He had pulled a $1 bill from his pocket and added it to the $19 in bills that I had just given him. I am not sure what in the world I was thinking (that was part of the flimflam art), but instead of taking the $20 to the register, depositing it, and getting the two tens, I went to the register first and retrieved the two tens and came back to the counter.
>
> The man was quick. He added the two $10 bills I had given him to the small pile of $20 that was sitting between us. He quickly picked it up and counted it out. Forty dollars. Then, he asked me to count it out to see if there was $40 in the pile. There was. Somehow, the fact that I was able to agree with him about this helped me ignore my feeling that something wasn't going right about this transaction. He asked me if he could have eight $5 bills for the pile of $40. Again, I went to the register to retrieve the money, leaving the pile on the counter. And once again, the man took the bills that I gave him with one hand and scooped up the pile of cash sitting between us with the other, counting furiously. He asked me for another transaction and we repeated the ritual. One more transaction later, and on my way down the counter to the second register to get more cash (because there were no bills left in the first register), I realized that something was very wrong . . . When I turned around to challenge the man, he was gone . . . I had been flimflammed.
>
> (Sparks, 2010, pp. 29–30)

The con artist first disrupted, distracting Sparks by counting bills and then asking him to count them too. He then implicitly reframed his request, asking for eight $5 bills. Only later did Sparks appreciate the con that had been perpetrated!

A meta-analysis of empirical studies of disrupt-then-reframe documents the success of the technique (Carpenter & Boster, 2009). Once again, we see the power of framing in persuasion. Disrupt-then-reframe, after all, works in part because of the subtle influence exerted by an alteration in the persuader's framework.

Summary

All the techniques discussed in this section play on what Freedman and Fraser called "compliance without pressure." They are soft-sell, not hard-ball, tactics that worm their way through consumers' defenses, capitalizing on social norms, emotions, and sly disruption of ordinary routines. Used adroitly by canny professionals, they can be remarkably effective. They also work because people respond automatically to many such requests, employing heuristics that persuaders exploit for their own advantage.

Although the psychological research on sequential influence techniques is clever and has advanced knowledge, it is primarily experimental in nature. We do not know the real-life parameters that increase or decrease the likelihood that individuals will comply with strategies such as FITD, DITF, and disrupt-then-reframe. The next section describes another arena of interpersonal persuasion that probes compliance in more real-life venues.

COMPLIANCE-GAINING

> You want to dine out with someone, but you disagree about which restaurant it is going to be; someone in the department must do an unpleasant job, but you want to make sure that in any case it will not be you; you want to make new work arrangements, but you are afraid your boss will not agree; you want to get your partner to come with you to that tedious family party, but you suspect that he or she does not want to come along.
>
> (van Knippenberg et al., 1999, p. 806)

Add to these more serious requests for compliance: an effort to convince a close friend to return to school after having dropped out for a couple of years, a doctor's attempt to persuade a seriously overweight patient to pursue an exercise program, a husband's effort to persuade his wife to quit hitting the bottle. Such requests are pervasive in everyday life. They speak to the strong interest human beings have in getting their way—that is, in persuading others to comply with their requests and pleas. This section of the chapter moves from an exploration of how professional persuaders achieve their goals to an examination of us—how we try to gain compliance in everyday life. The area of research is appropriately called compliance-gaining.

Compliance-gaining is defined as "any interaction in which a message source attempts to induce a target individual to perform some desired behavior that the target otherwise might not perform" (Wilson, 2002, p. 4). Notice that the focus of compliance-gaining is on communication. It examines not only the psychology of the individual's request for compliance, but also the broader interaction, the dyadic (one-on-one) conversation between people, or among individuals. This is important because it calls attention to the dynamic interpersonal dance that characterizes so much of everyday persuasion. Interpersonal communication scholars, who have pioneered research in this area, have sought to understand how individuals try to get others to go along with their requests in social situations. They have probed the strategies people use, the impact of context on compliance-gaining strategies, and the goals individuals pursue to gain compliance from others.

How We Study Compliance-Gaining

One of the daunting issues researchers face is how to empirically study a broad area, like compliance-gaining. They could devise experiments of the sort conducted by psychologists researching FITD and DITF. Although these would allow researchers to test hypotheses, they would not tell them how compliance-gaining works in the real world that lies outside the experimenter's laboratory. Scholars could observe people trying to gain compliance—on the job, at school, or in social settings like bars (that might be fun!). However, this would provide an endless amount of data, too much to code meaningfully. Dissatisfied with these methodologies, scholars hit on the idea of conducting surveys that ask people how they would gain compliance, either in situations suggested by the researcher or in an open-ended manner, in the individuals' own words.

The first survey method is *closed-ended* in that it provides individuals with hypothetical situations and asks them to choose among various strategies for compliance. For example, researchers have asked participants to imagine that they have been carrying on a close relationship with a person of the opposite sex for 2 years. Unexpectedly, an old acquaintance happens to be in town one evening. Desirous of getting together with their old friend, but mindful that their current boyfriend or girlfriend is counting on getting together that night, respondents are asked to indicate how they would try to convince their current steady to let them visit their former acquaintance (Miller et al., 1977).

Subjects have also been asked to imagine that their neighbors, whom they do not know very well, own a dog that barks almost all night. This in turn incites the other local canines to do the same. Students are asked how they would attempt to convince the neighbors to curb their dog's nighttime antics (Cody, McLaughlin, & Jordan, 1980). Individuals are provided with a list of strategies, such as friendly appeals, moral arguments, manipulative tactics, and threats. They are asked to indicate on a Likert scale how likely they would be to use these techniques. (See Box 12.2 for a practical example of a closed-ended compliance-gaining measurement technique.)

BOX 12.2   COMPLIANCE-GAINING AT THE HEALTH CLUB

What techniques do salespersons at a health club use to induce customers to join? (See Figure 12.3.)

Some years back, one of my students, Karen Karp, visited a local health club and talked to salespeople in search of an answer to this question. Karp pretended she was interested in joining and listened as the salesperson made his spiel. She then categorized his responses using a classic scheme devised by Marwell and Schmitt (1967). Based on what the salesman had said and her extrapolations from the interview, she and I developed an example of each of the 16 Marwell and Schmitt tactics.

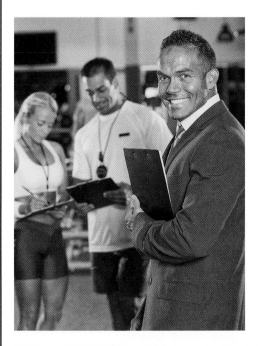

■ **Figure 12.3 Thinking of joining a health club to shed some pounds? Be prepared for the health club's sales representative to employ some "friendly persuasion"! He or she will try to hook you by pitching a variety of classic compliance-gaining strategies—direct and indirect, rational and nonrational, and external and internal.**

Image courtesy of iStock.

Continued

Tactic Example

1. Promise (If you comply, I will reward you)

   "If you begin your membership today, you'll receive a bonus of three free months."

2. Threat (If you do not comply I will punish you)

   "If you do not join today, you may find that people are kind of mean to you when you do join."

3. Expertise (If you comply, you will be rewarded because of "the nature of (positive) things")

   "Joining will guarantee that you'll maintain your health and that you'll get all the benefits of a healthy, totally in-shape body."

4. Expertise (If you do not comply, you will be punished because of "the nature of (negative) things")

   "If you do not join you'll end up looking fat."

5. Liking (Actor is friendly and helpful to get target in "good frame of mind" so that he will comply with request)

   "I think it's great that you've decided to begin an exercise program. The staff is here to help you reach your fitness goals."

6. Pre-giving (Actor rewards target before requesting compliance)

   "I'll give you a $50 bonus for coming in today; now, let's talk about how I can help you slim down."

7. Aversive stimulation (Actor continually punishes target, making cessation contingent upon compliance)

   "I won't let you leave this little room until you agree to join."

8. Debt (You owe me compliance because of past favors)

   "I've spent an hour showing you the club and demonstrating the machines; now I'm sure that you are ready to join."

9. Moral appeal (You are immoral if you do not comply)

   "Fitness is so important. I think it's almost immoral not to take good care of your health."

10. Self-feeling (You will feel better about yourself if you comply)

    (positive) "Why don't you sign up right now? You'll feel so good about yourself once you begin a workout program."

11. Self-feeling (You will feel worse about yourself if you do not comply)

    (negative) "You know how important regular exercise is. You'll feel bad about yourself if you do not take out a membership today."

12. Altercasting (A person with "good" qualities would comply)

    (positive) "I can tell that you're committed to looking and feeling healthy and fit. You're the kind of person who would really benefit from this club."

13. Altercasting (Only a person with "bad" qualities would not comply)

    (negative) "It's only laziness that keeps people from joining, but that's not you, is it?"

14. Altruism (I need your compliance very badly, so do it for me)

    (whispering) "I need to sign one more member this week."

15. Esteem (People you value will think better of you if you comply)

    (positive) "Begin a membership. Your family is going to be so proud of you when you start a fitness program."

16. Esteem (People you value will think worse of you if you do not comply)

    (negative) "Do not disappoint your family. Didn't you promise them that you would start taking better care of yourself?"

A second way to tap compliance-gaining is to use *open-ended* survey techniques. If a researcher wanted to employ an open-ended strategy, he or she might hand each respondent a sheet of paper. On the top of the page would appear the words:

On this page, write a paragraph about "How I Get My Way." Please be frank and honest (Falbo, 1977).

What would you say? How *do* you get your way? Are you rational, arguing incessantly like one of the nerds on the television program "The Big Bang Theory?" Are you a charmer, acting "sweety-sweet" until you get what you want? What *do* you do to get what you want? Researchers would classify the open-ended responses, placing them into a smaller number of categories that cut across different respondents' answers.

Closed- and open-ended techniques each have advantages and drawbacks. The closed-ended selection technique provides an efficient way to gather information. It also provides insights on how people try to gain compliance in representative life situations. Its drawback is that people frequently give socially desirable responses to closed-ended surveys. They are reluctant to admit that they sometimes use brutish, socially inappropriate tactics to get their way (Burleson et al., 1988).

The strength of the open-ended method is that it allows people to indicate, in their own words, how they get compliance. There is no speculation about hypothetical behavior in artificial situations. A drawback is that researchers must make sense of—and categorize—subjects' responses. This can be difficult and time consuming. Scholars may not fully capture or appreciate an individual's thought processes.

What We Know about Compliance-Gaining

Despite their limitations, when taken together, open- and closed-ended questionnaires have provided useful insights about compliance-gaining. Researchers, using both types of procedures, have devised a variety of typologies to map out the techniques people use to gain compliance. These typologies have yielded insights about the major strategies individuals (at least on American college campuses) use to influence others. Strategies can be classified according to whether they are:

1. *Direct versus indirect.* Direct techniques include assertion (voicing one's wishes loudly) and persistence (reiterating one's point). Indirect tactics include "emotion-target" (putting the other person in a good mood) and thought manipulation (trying to get your way by making the other person feel it is his idea) (Falbo, 1977; see also Dillard, Kinney, & Cruz, 1996).
2. *Rational versus nonrational.* Rational techniques include reason (arguing logically) and doing favors. Non-rational tactics include deceit (fast talking and lying) and threat (telling her I will never speak to her again if she doesn't do what I want) (Falbo, 1977).
3. *Hard-sell versus soft-sell.* Hard-sell tactics include yelling, demanding, and verbal aggression. Soft-sell techniques include kindness, flattery, and flirting (Kipnis & Schmidt, 1996).
4. *Dominance-based versus non-dominance-based.* Dominance-oriented strategies emphasize the power the communicator has over the target, while the latter employ a more egalitarian, conciliatory approach (Dillard et al., 1997).
5. *External versus internal.* Tactics can be externally focused, such as rewards or punishments. To motivate a child to study, a parent could use a carrot, like promise ("I'll raise your allowance if you study more"), or a stick, like aversive stimulation ("You're banned from driving until you hit the books"). Techniques can also be

internally focused—that is, self-persuasion-type appeals designed to engage the recipient. These include positive self-feeling ("You'll feel good about yourself if you study a lot") and negative self-feeling ("You'll be disappointed with yourself in the long run if you don't study more"; see Marwell & Schmitt, 1967; Miller & Parks, 1982).

Notice that the same techniques can be categorized in several ways. Threat could be direct, nonrational, hard-ball, and external. Positive self-feeling could be indirect, rational, and soft-sell, as well as internal. This cross-categorization occurs because there is not one but a variety of compliance-gaining taxonomies, constructed by different scholars, for different purposes. Nonetheless, these five sets of labels provide a useful way of categorizing compliance-gaining behavior.

Contextual Influences

People are complex creatures. They use different techniques to gain compliance, depending on the situation. In one situation, a person may use reason; in another she may scream and yell, employing verbal aggression. We are all chameleons, to a degree. Which situations are the most critical determinants of compliance-gaining? Scholars have studied this issue, delineating a host of important contextual influences on strategy selection. The following factors are especially important.

Intimacy. Contexts differ in the degree to which they involve intimate associations between persuader and persuadee. As you move along the continuum from stranger to acquaintance to friend to lover or family member, you find that the same individual can behave very differently, depending on which of these "others" the person is trying to influence. In an old but still engaging study, Fitzpatrick and Winke (1979) reported that level of intimacy predicted use of conflict-reducing strategies. Focusing on people casually involved in romantic relationships, those in serious relationships, and married partners, the investigators found that married persons were especially likely to employ emotional appeals or personal rejections ("withholding affection and acting cold until he or she gives in") to resolve differences. "You always hurt the one you love," Fitzpatrick and Winke observed. They explained:

> Individuals in a more committed relationship generally have less concern about the strengths of the relational bonds. Consequently, they employ more spontaneous and emotionally toned strategies in their relational conflicts . . . In the less committed relationships, the cohesiveness of the partners is still being negotiated . . . Undoubtedly, it would be too risky for them to employ the more open conflict strategies of the firmly committed.
>
> (1979, p. 10)

This is not to say that everyone uses more emotional or highly manipulative tactics in intimate settings than in everyday interpersonal encounters. These findings emerged from one study, conducted at one point in time. However, research indicates that intimacy can exert an important impact on compliance-gaining behavior (Cody & McLaughlin, 1980).

Dependency. We use different strategies to gain compliance, depending on whether we are dependent on the person we are trying to influence. People are more reluctant to use hard-ball tactics when the other has control over important outcomes in their lives (van Knippenberg et al., 1999). Graduate teaching assistants who say they "dominate arguments" and "argue insistently" with disgruntled undergraduate students acknowledge that they prefer to use nonconfrontational techniques, even sidestepping disagreements, when discussing job-related conflicts with the professor (Putnam & Wilson, 1982). It is only natural to be more careful when trying to gain compliance from those who have control over important outcomes in your life. Thus, when people lack power, they are more likely to employ rational and indirect tactics "because no other power base is available to them" (Cody & McLaughlin, 1985).

Rights. People employ different tactics to get their way, depending on whether they believe they have the right to pursue a particular option. If they do not feel they have the moral right to make a request, they may use softer tactics. However, if they believe they have the right to make a request, or if they feel they have been treated unfairly, they are more apt to employ hard rather than soft techniques (van Knippenberg et al., 1999). Consider the marked change in tactics employed by people trying to convince smokers to quit smoking in public places. Decades ago, individuals who objected to smokers polluting public space said little, afraid they would offend smokers. Nowadays, nonsmokers, redefining the meaning of public space and feeling they have the right to insist that smokers not puff in public, frequently use uncompromising, even nonrational, tactics to induce smokers to put out a cigarette. This change in compliance-gaining strategies resulted from years of social protest against smoking. Protests against problematic social norms, and subsequent changes in the law, can empower ordinary people, encouraging them to use feistier techniques to get their way.

Cultural and Individual Differences

Individuals differ dramatically in how they go about trying to get their way. Some people are direct; others are shy. Some individuals worry a great deal about hurting others' feelings; other individuals care not a whit. Some people respect social conventions; other people disregard them.

If individuals differ in their compliance-gaining strategies, can research elucidate or specify the differences? You bet! Scholars have focused on two factors that influence compliance-gaining choices: the macro factor, culture, and a micro variable: the personality factor, self-monitoring.

One important aspect of culture is the degree to which the society emphasizes individualism or collectivism. Individualism stresses independence, self-determination, and pursuit of one's self-interest. Collectivism emphasizes concern with group harmony, maintaining positive interpersonal relationships, and a "we" rather than "I" identification. On a cultural level, Western nations like the United States are individualistic, while Asian societies, such as South Korea and Japan, tend to be more collectivist.

In intriguing studies, Min-Sun Kim and colleagues have found that culture influences choice of compliance-gaining strategies. When asked to identify the most important determinants of whether a request is effective, South Korean students emphasized the degree to which the request is sensitive to the other individual's feelings and does not create disapproval. By contrast, U.S. students maintained that a request is more effective when it is made as clearly and directly as possible. South Korean students regard an indirect strategy like hinting as relatively effective for gaining compliance, while American students put a higher premium on direct statements (Kim & Bresnahan, 1994; Kim & Wilson, 1994). Naturally, there are additional differences within Western and Asian cultures that complicate matters. Regardless of country of origin, students whose self-concepts revolve around independence place more emphasis on being direct. Students whose self-concepts center on group harmony put a higher premium on not hurting the other individual's feelings (Kim & Sharkey, 1995).

A second factor that influences compliance-gaining is the personality factor, self-monitoring. High self-monitors, attuned as they are to the requirements of the situation, tend to adapt their strategy to fit the person they are trying to influence (Caldwell & Burger, 1997). Low self-monitors are more apt to use the same technique with different people. High self-monitors are more likely to develop elaborate strategic plans prior to the actual influence attempt (Jordan & Roloff, 1997). In keeping with their concern with image management, high self-monitors are more apt than low self-monitors to include in their plans a consideration of how they could manipulate their personal impression so as to achieve their goals.

Do you use the same techniques with different people and across different situations? If so, you may be a low self-monitor. Do you vary your strategies to fit the constraints of the situation? In this case, you could be a high self-monitor. Research provides facts about compliance-gaining in everyday life and can also offer insights into our own behavior.

Application

Compliance-gaining richly explains people's choice of behavioral persuasion techniques in a variety of situations, ranging from the amusing—how individuals try to convince people not to give them traffic tickets (see Box 12.3)—to the serious: communication that occurs in medical settings. Compliance-gaining research has particularly enriching implications for health. It offers guidelines to doctors on how they can improve their style of communicating medical information, provides clues on how young adults can convince their partners to practice safe sex, and suggests ways that pre-teens can, say, turn down shady requests to experiment with drugs (Burgoon et al., 1989; Perloff, 2001).

To appreciate the ways this research can shed light on social problems, I invite you to consider another issue that has become so commonplace we have become desensitized to its serious effects. The problem is child abuse. Child abuse and neglect are important problems both in the United States and abroad. Parents can abuse their children through physical, sexual, and verbal aggression, as well as through outright neglect. Abusive parents employ a battery of cruel and aggressive strategies to induce their children to comply with their requests. Lynn Oldershaw and colleagues (1986) conducted an observational study to examine whether abusive mothers differed from non-abusive moms in their compliance-gaining strategies.

The researchers compared 10 physically abusive mothers and 10 non-abusive moms, watching them interact for 45 minutes with one of their children, a 2- to 4-year-old. They carefully classified the mothers' ways of seeking compliance from their toddlers, categorizing them into power-assertive techniques, such as threat, humiliation, and negative physical touch, and positive pro-social strategies like modeling, reasoning, and bargaining. There were stark and disturbing differences between abusive and comparison moms.

For abusive mothers, the interaction was all about their power over the child. They employed power-assertive strategies, like those used above, or were more likely than comparison mothers to command their children to engage in a particular behavior. They tended to issue their commands without offering any rationale and without conveying a favorable vocal tone. Not only were the abusive mothers' techniques cruel, they were ineffective. Abused children were less likely to comply with their mothers' requests for compliance than non-abused children. Even when their kids did comply, abusive mothers were as likely to respond with criticism, such as "It's about time you did that," as with compliments. Comparison mothers typically complimented their kids when they complied (see Wilson, 2010).

The study leaves a powerful imprint. One feels terrible for the kids: 2- to 4-year-old toddlers. But the implications are as important as the findings are heart-rending. If

■ **Figure 12.4 Compliance-gaining research offers clues about how parents can gain compliance from their children without resorting to power-assertive techniques like threat or physical aggression.**

Image courtesy of Shutterstock.

mothers could be taught to seek compliance in more humane ways, perhaps future abuse could be halted. We need to persuade moms to seek compliance in different ways. This is not an easy task. But, thanks to Oldershaw and his associates' study, we have some clues as to where to begin (see Figure 12.4).

BOX 12.3 COMPLIANCE AND THE COPS

You're driving home one evening, speeding a little because you've got to get ready for a party later that night. The radio's blaring and you're feeling good as you tap your fingers and sing the words of a song you've heard many times before. Out of the corner of your eye you see a couple of lights, but ignore them until you see them again—the telltale flashing light of a police car. Your heart

Continued

skips a beat as you realize the police car is following you. The siren is sounding now and you get that terrible sinking feeling and agonizing fear that something bad is going to happen.

At this point, many of us faced with the impending possibility of a speeding ticket search our minds ferociously for an excuse, an extenuating reason, a white or black lie, a rhetorical rabbit we can pull out of the hat to convince the officer not to give us a ticket (see Figure 12.5). Of course, in an ideal world, if one ran afoul of the law, he or she would admit it and graciously take responsibility for the mistake. But this is not an ideal world, and many individuals are probably more willing to shade the truth a little than to come clean and suffer the indemnity of

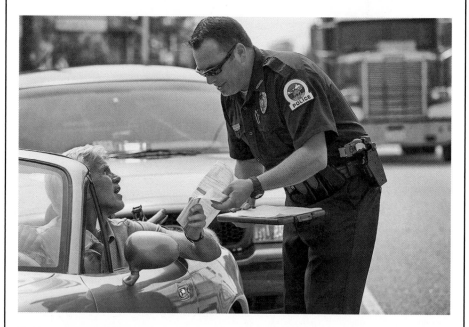

■ Figure 12.5 When a police officer turns on the flashing light and signals for a driver to pull over, people frequently dream up lots of reasons—some based in fact, others much less so—to persuade the officer not to give them a ticket. Individuals differ in the compliance-gaining techniques they employ (and their success in avoiding the ticket). Understandable as it is to try to persuade your way out of a ticket, the more prudent and safety-conscious approach is to acknowledge the error and try to be a better driver.

Image courtesy of Getty Images.

a fine and points on their record. Thus, many people try to persuade the police officer not to ticket them, relying on a variety of compliance-gaining techniques.

How do people try to secure compliance from a police officer when they are stopped for traffic violations? Jennifer Preisler and Todd Pinetti, students in a communication class some years back, explored this issue by talking with many young people who had found themselves in this predicament.

Their research, along with my own explorations, uncovered some interesting findings, including the following responses from young people regarding how they have tried to persuade a police officer not to ticket them:

- "I will be extra nice and respectful to the officer. I will apologize for my negligence and error. I tell them about the police officers I know."
- "I flirt my way out of it, smile a lot. [Or I say] 'My speedometer is broken. Honestly, it hasn't worked since August.'"
- "When I am stopped for speeding, I usually do not try to persuade the officer to not give me a ticket. He has the proof that I was speeding, so I don't try to insult his intelligence by making up some stupid excuse. I do try to look very pathetic and innocent, hoping maybe he will feel bad for me and not give me a ticket."
- "I turn on the dome light and turn off the ignition, roll down the window no matter how cold it is outside. I put my keys, driver's license, and proof of insurance on the dashboard, and put my hands at 10 and 2 on the wheel. I do all this before the officer gets to the window. I am honest and hope for the best. I have tried three times and all three were successful."
- "The officer said, 'I've been waiting for an idiot like you [who he could pull over for speeding] all night.' I told him, 'Yeah, I got here as fast as I could.' He laughed for about two minutes straight and let us go."
- "I gain compliance by smiling [big] and saying, 'Officer, what seems to be the problem?'"
- "I'm on my way to church.'"
- "The line that I have used to get out of a ticket is 'My wife's in labor.'"
- "My technique is when I am getting pulled over, I reach into my glove compartment and spray a dab of hair spray onto my finger. Then I put it in my eyes and I start to cry. I have gotten pulled over about 15 to 20 times and I have only gotten one ticket."

Continued

Many people suspect that gender intervenes—that is, male police officers are more forgiving of females than of males who violate a traffic law. Research bears this out. Male police officers issued a greater percentage of citations to male drivers than did female police officers. In a similar fashion, female police officers issued a greater percentage of their traffic citations to female drivers than did male officers (Koehler & Willis, 1994). Police officers may be more lenient with opposite-sex than same-sex offenders; they may find the arguments provided by opposite-sex individuals to be more persuasive because they are attracted sexually to the drivers. Or they may be less apt to believe excuses offered by members of their own gender.

BEYOND COMPLIANCE-GAINING

Compliance-gaining research has richly informed our knowledge of interpersonal persuasion. Unfortunately, the area reached an impasse because of a series of procedural problems. For all the advantages that compliance-gaining typologies offer practitioners, they are filled with methodological problems. Strategies are frequently defined ambiguously, inconsistently, or so specifically that it is difficult to know what the strategies mean (Kellermann & Cole, 1994; see also Wilson, 2002). Critics have also noted that much of the research involves responses to hypothetical situations, rather than actual compliance-gaining behavior.

The good news is that the intuitive strength of the area—a down-to-earth explanation of how people go about gaining compliance—has generated new research perspectives. An important framework focuses on the persuasion objectives individuals seek to attain in interpersonal situations.

Interpersonal Persuasion Goals

The research begins with the insight that people do not approach compliance-gaining with a blank slate. Instead, they define a situation in a particular way, pursuing goals and enacting plans. People have primary and secondary goals (Dillard, Segrin, & Harden, 1989; Wilson, 2010). A primary goal structures the interaction, propelling individuals to seek a particular behavior from the target. Primary or key influence goals include:

- Asking a favor ("Can you drive me to the airport?")
- Giving advice ("I think you should quit drinking")

- Obtaining permission ("Professor, can I get an extension on my paper?")
- Sharing activity ("Let's see a movie"); and
- Enforcing obligations ("You promised to clean the kitchen. Come on, it's not fair if you don't do your part.")

(Dillard & Knobloch, 2011)

These are everyday, down-to-earth influence objectives. So too are secondary goals. Secondary goals determine how people approach their primary goal. Focusing on the interpersonal dynamics of the situation, secondary goals influence individuals as they pursue their primary objectives. Secondary goals include:

- maintaining a positive public impression, or face;
- avoiding behaviors that would tarnish another person's image or face;
- maintaining interpersonal relationships; and
- avoiding resource risks, such as wasting time or money.

It is a complex dance. People have multiple, sometimes conflicting, goals they want to accomplish in a particular situation (Dillard, 1990b). What's more, people are always balancing intrapersonal and interpersonal needs. They want to maintain their autonomy, yet need approval from others (Brown & Levinson, 1987). They want to get their way, but recognize that this can threaten another's image, autonomy, or "face" (Wilson, Aleman, & Leatham, 1998). They don't want to hurt the other's feelings, but recognize that if they are too nice they may kill the clarity of their request with politeness and ambiguity.

People frequently must balance their desire to achieve a *primary goal*—influencing the target's behavior—with an attempt to meet a *secondary goal* also, such as maintaining a good public impression, not damaging a friendship, or doing the morally right thing (Dillard, et al., 1989; Meyer, 2007; Wilson, 2002). There is a yin and yang between primary goals, which push the persuader toward action, and secondary goals, which pull or constrain the individual from going too far. We all have been in situations where we want to get our way, but realize that if we are too argumentative or dismissive of the other person's feelings, we will destroy a valued relationship.

Scholars have studied how people process these matters and go about balancing conflicting needs. Their models emphasize that people have elaborate cognitive structures regarding compliance-gaining and ways to achieve their goals (Wilson, 1999). This is fascinating because we all go about the business of trying to get our way, but rarely give any thought to how we think about trying to gain compliance or how we process, in our own minds, "all that stuff going on in the situation." Interpersonal communication models and research shed light on such issues.

Theoretical frameworks have focused on communicators' face or interpersonal presentation needs. People want to gain important others' approval of their interpersonal behavior (positive face), while not wanting to lose their autonomy or have their actions restricted without reason (negative face; see Brown & Levinson, 1987).

A core model that offers an integrative perspective to goals and interpersonal interaction is James P. Dillard's (1990b) goal-driven approach. According to a goals approach, when persuaders are more concerned with achieving primary than secondary goals, they will interpersonally engage the target, generating and editing plans to help implement the goal. When the primary and secondary goals are equally important, persuaders will choose an influence strategy that takes into account their concern about not thwarting secondary goals. In these cases, the dynamics of influence are more complex. Seeking a strategy that will not interfere with secondary goals, they may mentally consider or reformulate their plans before confronting the other person.

Application

To appreciate how all this works in real life, consider the following example:

Professors sometimes require group projects, in which students work together on a task and complete a group paper. While opinions are divided on group projects—some students find them unfair, others like group interaction—they have been a consistent part of university classes for a long time. The primary goal is successful completion of the project. A secondary goal arises when one student in the group fails to pull his weight and other students must decide how to communicate their dissatisfaction to the slacker in a way that preserves their reputation, does not unduly threaten the slacker's face, and does not destroy the relationship. If the primary goal is paramount, other students may tell the slacker off, demanding he put in his fair share of the work, with little concern about offending him. If primary and secondary goals are weighed equally—perhaps because the slacker is a friend—then the other students will tread more carefully, mentally mulling over strategies before they act, balancing bluntness with politeness, and perhaps avoiding a strategy that would totally embarrass their friend.

It is a dicey situation. Researchers find that when people possess incompatible goals—such as trying to convince a target to do something she most definitely does not want to do, while at the same time not hurting her feelings in the slightest—they pause more and don't communicate as effectively (Greene et al., 1993). The incongruity of goals puts stress on the mental system. Thus, the best advice in this situation may be not to beat around the bush. Persuaders may be most effective when they honestly and unambiguously share their objection to the slacker, in a way that respects their friend's autonomy, but also communicates the importance of the primary goal.

Of course, as any of us who have valiantly embarked on this strategy only to be ignored or criticized by our slacker friend will attest, this technique is not guaranteed to work. Much depends on the content of the request, the manner in which it is implemented, and the personality of the persuader and target. The nature of the relationship also matters. Strategies will vary, depending on so-called intimacy (how well you know the slacker and nature of the interpersonal relationship), dominance (whether one of you has power over the other), and the benefits that the paper and the relationship offer both parties.

If this strikes you as interesting, but vague, you are right! The strength of interpersonal persuasion research has been in articulating the cognitive and situational dynamics of interpersonal influence contexts. Its shortcoming has been in laying out predictions or hypotheses about optimum strategies to achieve persuasion goals. Nevertheless, the interpersonal goals approach helpfully advances knowledge by shedding light on the cognitive and interpersonal dynamics of everyday compliance-gaining situations. It underscores the emotional messiness of everyday persuasion. By articulating goals and the mental activities in which persuaders engage, it helps to clarify the nature of interpersonal persuasion.

ETHICAL ISSUES

"Communication is founded on a presumption of truth," two scholars aptly note (Buller & Burgoon, 1996, p. 203). Yet persuasion commonly involves some shading of truth, a tinting that is rationalized by persuaders and lamented by message receivers. Interpersonal persuasion—from the sequential influence techniques discussed earlier in the chapter to the endless variety of compliance-gaining tactics just described— sometimes seems to put a premium on distorting communication in the service of social influence. Distorting communication in the service of social influence? A blunter, more accurate way to describe this is "lying."

Lying is remarkably common in everyday life. In two diary studies, college students reported that they told two lies a day. They admitted they lied in one of every three of their social interactions (DePaulo et al., 1996). To be sure, some of these lies were told to protect other people from embarrassment, loss of face, or having their feelings hurt. However, other lies were told to enhance the psychological state of the liars—for example, to make the liars appear better than they were, to protect them from looking bad, or to protect their privacy. Many of these were white lies that we have told ourselves; others were darker distortions, outright falsehoods (DePaulo et al., 1996).

Persuasion—from sequential influence tactics to compliance gaining—is fraught with lies. Even flattery involves a certain amount of shading of truth, a convention that many people admittedly enjoy and cherish (Stengel, 2000). All this has stimulated considerable debate among philosophers over the years. As discussed in Chapter 2, utilitarians argue that a lie must be evaluated in terms of its consequences. Deontological thinkers tend to disapprove of lies in principle because they distort truth. Related approaches emphasize that what matters is the motivation of the liar—a lie told for a good, virtuous end may be permissible under some circumstances (Gass & Seiter, 2011).

We cannot resolve this debate. In my view, social discourse—and the warp and woof of social influence—contain much truth, shading of truth, and lies. They also contain certain corrective mechanisms. Those who lie habitually run the risk of earning others' disapproval, or finding that even their truthful statements are disbelieved. Social norms operate to discourage chronic lying. So too do psychodynamic mechanisms that have evolved over human history. Guilt and internalized ethical rules help regulate people's desire to regularly stretch the truth.

However, a certain amount of lying is inevitable, indeed permissible, in everyday interpersonal communication. Social influence—and persuasive communication—are human endeavors, part of the drama of everyday life, in which people are free to pursue their own ends, restrained by internalized moral values and social conventions (Scheibe, 2000). Democratic, civilized society enshrines people's freedom to pursue their own interests and celebrates those who can exert influence over others. The "downside" of this is that some people will abuse their freedom and seek to manipulate others, distorting truth and using deceitful tactics. Human evolution has not yet evolved to the point that ethics totally trumps (or at least restrains) self-interest, and perhaps it never will. The best hope is education: increased self-understanding, development of humane values, and (trite as it may sound) application of the time-honored, but always relevant, Golden Rule.

CONCLUSIONS

This chapter has examined interpersonal persuasion—the many techniques individuals use to influence one another in dyadic or one-on-one interactions. Social psychological research has documented that gambits like foot-in-the-door and door-in-the-face can be especially effective in securing compliance. Make no mistake: these tactics do not always work, and many consumers have learned to resist them. However, they are used regularly in sales and pro-social charity work; under certain conditions, for various psychological reasons, they can work handily. Other tactics employed by professional persuaders—pre-giving exchange, low-balling, "that's-not-all," fear-then-relief, pique, and disrupt-then-reframe—can also influence compliance.

In everyday life, we employ a variety of tactics to get our way. Interpersonal communication scholars have developed typologies to categorize these techniques. Strategies vary in their directness, rationality, and emphasis on self-persuasion. Different strategies are used in different situations, and the same person may use a direct approach in one setting and a cautious, indirect technique in another. Culture and personality factors like self-monitoring also place limits on compliance-gaining choices. Compliance-gaining research has illuminated knowledge of interpersonal persuasion. Its strength is its rich exploration of dyadic interactions. Its shortcomings include absence of theory and lack of precision in strategy measurement.

Other approaches have extended interpersonal persuasion research, notably, those that explore the nature of primary and secondary goals. A primary goal structures an interaction between people, while a secondary objective focuses on the interpersonal dynamics of the situation. In some instances, what began as a secondary goal—maintaining a positive public face or not hurting someone's feelings—can become the preeminent goal in the situation.

Everyday interpersonal persuasion is complex and dynamic. Persuaders are constantly editing and reformulating plans so that they can balance primary and secondary goals. Compliance choices vary as a function of whether a primary or secondary goal is paramount, the nature of the situation, and the feelings that the compliance-gaining elicits. Research, focusing on ever-more cognitive aspects of individuals' strategic choices, is shedding light on the dynamics of everyday interpersonal persuasion.

Given the central role that interpersonal persuasion plays in everyday life and in business transactions, it behooves us to understand and master it. A practical strategy that experts suggest is to look to the behavior of highly effective persuaders. Successful persuaders recognize that persuasion requires give and take, flexibility, and ability to see things from the other party's point of view (Cody & Seiter, 2001; Delia, Kline, & Burleson, 1979; Waldron & Applegate, 1998). "Effective persuaders have a strong and accurate sense of their audience's emotional state, and they adjust the tone of their arguments accordingly," observes Jay A. Conger (1998, p. 93). He notes that they plan arguments and self-presentational strategies in advance and "enter the persuasion process prepared to adjust their viewpoints and incorporate others' ideas. That approach to persuasion is, interestingly, highly persuasive in itself" (p. 87).

Test your knowledge now with interactive exercises

Chapter 13

Advertising, Marketing, and Persuasion

▷ **Listen now to the author's chapter summary**

You have seen it in hundreds of commercials and on all types of clothing—shirts, jackets, and hats. It is an oversized check mark, a smoker's pipe that juts outward, a "curvy, speedy-looking blur" (Hartley, 2000). Take a look below. It's the Nike "swoosh"—the symbol of Nike products, promoted by celebrity athletes; an emblem of Nike's television advertising campaigns; and, to many, the embodiment of speed, grace, mobility, and cool. The swoosh is a major reason why Nike is the major player in the sneaker market, and a testament to the success of commercial advertising (Goldman & Papson, 1996).

 Image courtesy of Nike.

Advertising. That's a topic we know something about, though if you asked, we would probably politely suggest that it's everyone else who's influenced. Yet if each of us is immune to advertising's impact, how come so many people can correctly match the following slogans with the advertised products?

- Just do it
- Good to the last drop
- I'm lovin' it
- Got ____?
- Be all that you can be
- Where's the beef?
- Do the Dew
- There are some things money can't buy. For everything else, there's _____.

Answers: Nike; Maxwell House Coffee; McDonald's; milk; U.S. Army; Wendy's; Mountain Dew; MasterCard.

Advertising—the genre we love to hate, the ultimate symbol of American society—is showcased every day on television and each time you log onto Internet Web sites and catch banner spots. It's on buses and billboards, elementary school classrooms, YouTube, and increasingly on cell phones. It is on subway turnstiles, which bear messages for Geico car insurance; Chinese food cartons that advertise Continental Airlines; in bus shelters, where "Got milk?" billboards emit the smell of chocolate chip cookies; and even in major league baseball stadiums, where, in a deal concocted by the New York Life Insurance Company, a player who is called safe at home plate triggers the appearance of the company's logo on the TV screen and the announcer must state, "Safe at home. Safe and secure. New York Life" (Story, 2007; Sandel, 2012). As if this were not enough, marketers are pervasively present on social media, with promoted brand tweets on Twitter and ads based on products that people like on Facebook.

It's the most real of communications, for it promotes tangible objects—things, stuff, and goods. It's also the most surrealistic, most unreal of mass communications. It shows us "a world where normal social and physical arrangements simply do not hold," critic Sut Jhally (1998) observes. "A simple shampoo brings intense sexual pleasure, nerdy young men on the beach, through the wonders of video rewind, can constantly call up beautiful women walking by, old women become magically young, offering both sex and beer to young men," he notes.

Advertising has been universally praised and condemned. It has been cheered by those who view it as emblematic of the American Dream—the notion that anyone with money and moxie can promote a product to masses of consumers, along with the promise, cherished by immigrants, that an escape from brutal poverty can be found through purchase of products and services not available in more oppressive economies. Advertising has been roundly condemned by those who despise its attack on our senses; its appropriation of language for use in a misty world located somewhere between truth and falsehood; and its relentless, shameless exploitation of cultural icons to sell goods and services (Cross, 1996, p. 2; Schudson, 1986; see Figure 13.1).

Advertising, the focus of this chapter, is a complex, colorful arena. It is paid materialist speech—messages for which companies pay in order to shape, reinforce, and change attitudes. (And they pay handsomely for these messages, to the tune of $3.7 million per 30-second ad during the Super Bowl.) Advertising operates on a micro level, subtly influencing consumer behavior. It also works on the macro level, serving as the vehicle by which capitalist society communicates and promotes goods to masses of consumers. To appreciate advertising's effects, we need to look at both micro-level effects on individuals and macro-level cultural issues.

Increasingly, advertising has given way to **marketing**, the broader term that refers to the activities and processes by which a society communicates products and services of

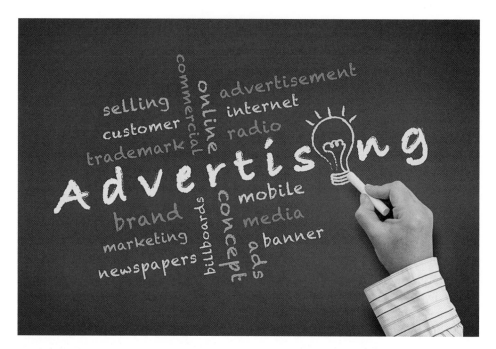

■ **Figure 13.1 Advertising, which has been widely praised for its ingenuity and condemned for its attack on our sensibilities, works by exploiting a sophisticated understanding of the social psychology of the mind.**

Image courtesy of Shutterstock.

value to masses of consumers. With the proliferation of media and reliance on appeals that transcend commercials, marketing has become the preeminent way by which mass societies promote and distribute products. Advertising involves paid promotion of a product or service. It is a critical part of marketing, but not the only one. Marketing also involves market research, media planning, and distribution; it is the overall strategy to connect a seller and buyer around a brand. Persuasion is the psychological and communicative foundation of both these areas.

This chapter covers a lot of territory. I begin by debunking a common myth of advertising; move on to discuss the key psychological effects of advertising and marketing on attitudes, applying theories described earlier in the book; and conclude with a look at the complex ethical and legal aspects of contemporary advertising and marketing. Given the colorful and controversial aspects of contemporary marketing, laced with applications to social media, the chapter will illustrate concepts with examples drawn from everyday life.

THE SUBLIMINAL MYTH

It began, appropriately enough, in the 1950s, a decade in which post-World War II Americans were bewildered by all manner of things, ranging from reports of flying saucers to the successful Soviet launching of a space satellite. In 1957, the same year the Soviets sent up Sputnik, an enterprising marketer named James Vicary reported an equally jarring set of facts. He arranged for a drive-in movie theater in Fort Lee, New Jersey, a suburb of New York City, to beam the words "Drink Coca-Cola" and "Eat popcorn" for less than a millisecond during the romantic movie *Picnic*. Vicary immediately proclaimed success. He claimed an 18 percent rise in Coke sales and a 58 percent increase in popcorn purchases, compared with an earlier period.

The nation's media were shocked, *shocked*. Minds have been "broken and entered," *The New Yorker* declared on September 21, 1957. The National Association of Broadcasters forbade its members from using subliminal ads. One writer, convinced that subliminal messages had dangerous effects, wrote several best-selling books on the subject. Wilson

■ **Figure 13.2 Advertising images that play up sexuality are commonly assumed to contain embedded subliminal messages. They almost never do. In fact, advertised sexual appeals influence consumers not through "subliminal seduction," but because they psychologically connect with individuals in a number of ways.**

Image courtesy of Shutterstock.

Bryan Key claimed that subliminal stimuli were everywhere! "You cannot pick up a newspaper, magazine, or pamphlet, hear radio, or view television anywhere in North America without being assaulted subliminally," Key announced (1974, p. 5). He claimed that advertisements for cigarettes, liquor, and perfume contained embedded erotic pictures that caused people to march off and buy these products, like brainwashed automatons from the old film *Coma*. (See Figure 13.2.)

You yourself may have heard the term *subliminal* or *subliminal advertising*. It's easy to locate the words on the Web. There are dozens of Web sites with names like "Subliminal Ads—Brainwashing Consumers?" and "The Top 13 Subliminal Messages in Presidential Campaign Ads." Reflecting this belief in the power of subliminal ads, over 70 percent of respondents in scientific surveys maintain that subliminal advertisements are widely used and are successful in promoting products (Rogers & Smith, 1993; Zanot, Pincus, & Lamp, 1983). In a similar fashion, many people believe that subliminal messages in rock songs manipulate listeners. Some years back, parents of two men who committed suicide charged that the rock group Judas Priest had induced their sons to kill themselves. The parents claimed that Judas Priest had subliminally inserted the words "Do it, do it" underneath the lyrics in a morbid song called "Beyond the Realms of Death." (The parents lost the case.)

Beliefs are powerful entities. In the case of subliminal advertising, they can drive fears and influence emotions. Researchers, curious about subliminal message effects, have long studied the impact of subliminally embedded words and pictures. Their conclusion: *there is little evidence to support the claim that subliminal ads influence attitudes or behavior*. To appreciate how scholars arrived at this judgment and what it tells us about the psychology of advertising, we need to examine the research on this issue.

Definition

In the popular view, subliminal advertising means powerful advertising that appeals to emotional, even unconscious, needs. Given this broad definition, it is not surprising that many people believe advertising is subliminal. Scholars define "subliminal" differently—and far more precisely. **Subliminal perception** occurs when stimuli are "discriminated by the senses," yet are transmitted in such a way "that they cannot reach conscious awareness, even if attention is directed to them" (Dijksterhuis, Aarts, & Smith, 2005, pp. 80–81).

More simply, subliminal perception is perception without awareness of the object being perceived. It is "sublimen," or below the "limen" or threshold of conscious awareness. Making matters more complicated, the limen is a hypothetical construct, not one that is always easy to pinpoint.

Applying this perceptual concept to advertising is not a simple matter and is far more complicated than glib commentators like Key assume. But if one struggles to apply it to advertising, in order to put popular ideas to the test, we could say that a **subliminal advertisement** is one that includes a brief, specific message (picture, words, or sounds) that cannot be perceived at a normal level of conscious awareness. This definition excludes many appeals commonly associated with subliminal ads. Commercials that contain sexy models, erotic images, vibrant colors, haunting images, or throbbing music are not, in themselves, subliminal. Why? Because the erotic or colorful image appeal is right there—you see it or hear it and, if someone asks, you could tell her what you saw or heard. Product images that have been strategically placed in movies are not necessarily or inherently subliminal (see Box 13.1). A subliminal ad—or, more precisely, one that contains a message that eludes conscious awareness—is a very different animal.

Subliminally embedded messages exist, though. The key question is: How common are they? A study of advertising executives found that few, if any, advertising agencies strive to develop subliminal ads (Rogers & Seiler, 1994). In view of the powerful impact that ordinary ads exert, it doesn't make much sense for advertisers to rack their brains to embed subliminal messages in commercials. Besides, if the news media ever found out that an agency had slipped a subliminal spot into an ad, the bad press the advertiser would receive would overwhelm any potential benefits of the subliminal message.

Does this mean there are no subliminals anywhere in the media? Not quite. In a country as big as the United States or as cosmopolitan as nations in Europe, with so many creative, ambitious, (and slippery) characters, it seems likely that a handful of advertising practitioners subliminally embed sexy messages in ads. (They could do this by airbrushing or using high-powered video editing techniques to insert subliminals in ads, including those that pop up on the Internet.) The major question is: What impact do subliminal messages have on consumers' attitudes or behavior?

Effects

It is important to distinguish between subliminal perception in theory and subliminal perception in the reality of advertising. People can perceive information on a subliminal level and, under certain circumstances, stimuli processed subliminally can affect judgments (Bargh & Pietromonaco, 1982; Bornstein, 1992). But just because something can happen in a rarefied laboratory setting does not mean it does or is likely to happen in the noisy, cluttered world of advertising. Let's review the research.

The first evidence of subliminal advertising effects came in Vicary's report on the effects of "Drink Coca-Cola" and "Eat popcorn" messages. At the time, his study seemed to suggest that subliminals could potently shape human behavior. But when scholars

BOX 13.1 PRODUCT PLACEMENTS

Placement of products into movies, television shows, and video games has become so commonplace it is difficult to imagine an era in which anyone raised eyebrows about the practice. Director Steven Spielberg helped popularize the craze when he inserted Reese Pieces into *E.T.* A later Spielberg movie, *Minority Report*, was jam-packed with brands, including Lexus, Gap, Reebok, and American Express. In the film *Twilight*, Edward famously drives a Volvo. Placements are ubiquitous on reality television shows, with more than 6,000 placements on *The Biggest Loser* and some 4,600 on *American Idol* in the 2008 season alone (Cowley, 2012). Products are placed increasingly into video games and music, like the automobile racing game *Gran Turismo*. Annual spending on product placement stretches into the billions.

What is a **product placement**? It is defined as a paid communication about a product that is designed to influence audience attitudes about the brand through the deliberate and subtle insertion of a product into media entertainment programming. Product placements are similar to advertisements in that they are paid attempts to influence consumers. However, unlike advertising, which identifies the sponsor explicitly, product placements do not indicate that a sponsor has paid for the placement of a product into the media program. Because product placements disguise the attempt of a persuader to influence attitudes, they are regarded by some scholars as less ethical than advertising (Nebenzahl & Jaffe, 1998), and advertising is a medium that has not exactly been free of ethical condemnation. The issue of disguised attempts to influence raises the question of whether product placements are subliminal messages. One could argue that product placements are so incidental to the plot that they are processed on a subliminal level. But recall that subliminal perception occurs when stimuli are detected by the senses but fail to reach conscious awareness, even when attention is directed at them. Product placements are usually transmitted above the threshold of conscious awareness, and people are ordinarily aware they saw a branded candy bar or automobile that was inserted into a movie.

Theories offer insights as to why placements can be effective (Cowley, 2012). Mere exposure and association (discussed later in this chapter) have interesting implications. Repeated exposure to the product over the course of a movie, TV show, or video game can promote positive attitudes. Conditioning and association processes operate, producing a favorable linkage between an attractive character and the brand, as swooning teenage girls who saw *Twilight*'s Edward drive a Volvo might attest.

ELM processes also can operate. For low-involvement products, the placement serves as a peripheral cue. When consumers already harbor an attitude toward the product or can elaborate on the brand, the placement might stimulate thinking about the product.

Narrative perspectives suggest that consumers may elaborate more on placements when they are integrated into the plot or dramatic theme of the entertainment program (see McCarty, 2004). In a study of placements of beverage and candy products in several movies (e.g., *The Client* and *Legally Blonde*), Moonhee Yang and David R. Roskos-Ewoldsen (2007) found that viewers recognized the brand more when it was central to the story or was used by the main character than when it was shown in the background.

Research tells us that product placements capture attention, lead to brand recognition, and can influence attitudes when the brand is novel. Greater involvement with characters or enjoyment of the program in which the brand is embedded can also enhance positive attitudes toward the product (Nelson & Waiguny, 2012). Yet there are limits to product placement effects. Just because viewers recognize or recall a product does not mean they will choose the brand. What's more, it is possible that psychologically memorable product placements can have a boomerang effect. Vividly recalling the placement, viewers may recognize that an advertiser is trying to influence them, resent this influence, and feel reactive toward the product (Nabi & Moyer-Guse, in press). Increasingly, though, consumers are becoming accustomed to product placements and thus may come to view them with the same mixture of interest and skepticism with which they greet ordinary ads.

peered beneath the surface, they discovered that his research had serious flaws. In the first place, there was no control group, an essential requirement of a scientific experiment. Thus, there is no way of knowing whether moviegoers bought more popcorn and Cokes because they happened to be hungry and thirsty that particular day. It is even possible that the movie itself stimulated sales; it was named "Picnic" and showed scenes of people enjoying food and drinks!

More seriously, Vicary never released his data or published his study. Publication and open inspection of data are basic principles in scientific research, and Vicary's reluctance to do so casts doubt on the validity of his results. Shortly after Vicary's findings were revealed, a respected psychological firm tried to replicate his study under controlled conditions. Using more rigorous procedures, the psychologists reported no increase in purchases of either Coke or popcorn. In 1958, a Canadian broadcast network subliminally transmitted the message "Phone now" 352 times during a Sunday night TV show. Telephone calls did not rise during this period, and no one called the station (Pratkanis, 1998).

Although these results cast doubt on the subliminal thesis, they do not disprove it. We are talking about only a couple of studies here. A more rigorous test involves evaluating results from dozens of carefully conducted experiments. Researchers have designed and conducted such studies, embedding messages in ads at levels that elude conscious awareness. They have compared the responses of experimental group participants who receive the subliminal stimuli with control group subjects who view a similar message without subliminals. The findings have stimulated lively debate among scholars. Although a handful of researchers make the case for subliminal advertising effects, they frequently confuse subliminal perception with subliminal persuasion or ignore the preponderance of data that show subliminal messages have few effects on attitudes or behavior (Theus, 1994; Trappey, 1996). According to one scholar, the impact of subliminal advertising on consumers' decision making is roughly the same as "the relationship between alcohol abuse and a tour of duty in Vietnam"—in other words, negligible or nonexistent (Trappey, 1996, p. 517).

This may seem surprising, in view of what you may have read on this topic over the years. However, it makes good psychological sense. Indeed, there are four reasons why one should not expect subliminally transmitted messages to influence consumer attitudes or behavior:

- *People have different thresholds for conscious awareness of stimuli.* To influence a mass audience, a subliminal message would have to be so discreetly beamed that it reached those with normal thresholds of awareness without catching the "attention" of those who are exquisitely sensitive to such stimuli. This would be difficult, perhaps impossible, to achieve using contemporary media.
- *There is no guarantee that consumers "see" or interpret the message in the manner that advertisers intend.* (For example, "Drink Coca-Cola" and "Eat popcorn" moved so quickly across the screen that some moviegoers may have seen "Stink Coke" or "Beat popcorn." This could have had the opposite impact on some viewers.)
- *For a subliminal message to influence attitudes, it must, at the very least, command the viewer's absolute attention.* This can happen in the experimenter's laboratory (Cooper & Cooper, 2002), but is not so likely to occur in the real world. People are

frequently distracted or doing other things when they watch TV or come across magazine advertisements.

■ Let me be clear: it *is* possible that a subliminal message could be perceived on a subconscious level. A sexy picture might "enter" a subterranean portion of the mind. Big deal. *For soon after the picture is processed, it is apt to be overwhelmed by the more powerful images or sounds depicted in the advertisement—the luscious features of the model that can be processed instantly on a conscious level, the obvious beauty of a mountain scene, or jingle-jangle of the advertiser's song.* These attention-grabbing pictures and sounds will swamp the subliminal embed. Just because a message is "in" an ad does not mean it gets "inside" consumers for very long—or at all. If it were that easy, everyone who works for advertising agencies would be very rich.

Self-Fulfilling Prophecies and Beyond

Research makes abundantly clear that subliminally transmitted messages do not influence consumer attitudes or behavior. But could the belief that subliminals are powerful influence attitudes toward a product? Anthony G. Greenwald and colleagues suspected that it could. As true-blue social scientists, they decided to test their intuition. They focused attention on a different kind of persuasive communication: therapeutic self-help tapes that claim subliminally embedded messages can help listeners to solve personal problems.

Greenwald and his associates observed that some self-help tapes promise to enhance self-esteem by subliminally beaming messages like "I have high self-worth and high self-esteem" (Greenwald et al., 1991). Others attempt to improve memory skill by claiming to subliminally transmit messages like "My ability to remember and recall is increasing daily." These words might be embedded underneath sounds, like waves lapping against a shore. Knowing the research as they did, Greenwald and colleagues doubted that such subliminals would have any impact. However, they suspected that consumers' expectations that the subliminals were effective might strongly influence beliefs.

In an elaborate study using careful scientific procedures, Greenwald and his associates (1991) obtained strong support for their hypothesis. Individuals who heard an audiotape that contained the subliminal message "I have high self-worth" did not exhibit any increase in self-esteem. In addition, those who listened to the tape that contained the "My ability to remember is increasing" message did not display improvements in memory. But the belief in subliminals' impact exerted a significant effect. Subjects who thought they had been listening to a tape designed to improve self-esteem (regardless of whether they actually had) believed their self-esteem had improved. Individuals who thought they had been listening to a memory audiotape (regardless of whether they had) were convinced their memory had gotten better!

The researchers argued that what they had discovered was "an illusory placebo effect—placebo, because it was based on expectations; illusory, because it wasn't real" (Pratkanis, 1998, p. 248). Their findings could also be viewed as another demonstration of the power of **self-fulfilling prophecy**. This is the idea that if you expect something to occur, sometimes it will—not because of the objective event itself but, rather, because you altered your thoughts; the alterations in cognitive structure then led to changes in behavior.

Notice that a self-fulfilling prophecy operates on the conscious level, not the secretive, subconscious level at which subliminal ads are supposed to work. And, ironically, it is the conscious level at which subliminal ads may have their greatest impact. Actually, it is not the ads that exert the impact, but rather the *perceptions* of their effects that are influential.

Students sometimes argue that marketers might want to suggest that a particular message has subliminal effects simply to stimulate interest in the product. (One thinks of the grilled cheese sandwich purportedly bearing the image of the Virgin Mary that sold for $28,000 on eBay some years back!) The problem with this strategy is that it could easily backfire. Many consumers might simply reject a product, casting aspersions on a manufacturer who would deliberately insert subliminals into an advertisement.

In view of the exaggerated notions of subliminal message effects, the interesting question for many researchers is not the objective impact of subliminal stimuli, but the subjective issue. Why are so many people convinced that these short, psychologically vacuous messages have so great an impact on attitudes? Laura A. Brannon and Timothy C. Brock put forth several explanations for the persistence in belief in subliminal communications, including the assumption that "if something exists it must be having an effect" (1994, p. 289). People also yearn for simple explanations of complex phenomena like advertising, and the subliminal thesis gives them a foolproof, conspiracy-type theory that seems to explain all of advertising's powerful influences on consumers.

With all this in mind, perhaps next time you read that liquor ads contain subliminally embedded faces or bikini-clad women, you might step back a moment and ask yourself a few questions. First, what evidence is there that these faces or scantily dressed women are actually in the ads, rather than a figment of the writer's sexually active imagination? Second, even if they are "there," what evidence exists that they influence perceptions? Third, assuming that the stimuli influence perceptions (a large "if"), how realistic is it to assume that they influence consumers' attitudes or behavior? By approaching advertising this way, you will quickly recognize that the mad search for subliminals takes you down the wrong trail in the quest to understand advertising effects. By the same token, it is important not to dogmatically take a diametrically opposite approach, in which we assume that consumers are consciously aware of every feature of an advertisement. Just because advertising cannot be explained by subliminal sexual embedded messages does *not* mean that consumers are totally aware of all of the appeals advertisers employ.

Even though subliminal advertising messages (few as there are) do not influence viewers, other subtle commercial appeals *can* affect individuals' feelings and thoughts. Sometimes product placements and clever ads that tell heart-rending stories can tug on the heartstrings. These are not subliminal appeals because viewers can tell you the gist of what they consciously saw. But viewers may not realize how Super Bowl ads that seamlessly associated a man's love of a Clydesdale horse with Budweiser linked the goodness of a farmer with a Dodge Ram truck, or that blended patriotic images of soldiers with a Chrysler Jeep instantly aroused their emotions. People can be conscious of the literal message they saw, but not be entirely aware of how immersed they were in the deeper emotional subtext of the advertisement.

As L. J. Shrum and his colleagues (2013) point out, when consumers saunter through a store, they may be consciously aware that music is being piped into the background. But they may not appreciate that the musical tempo can influence the speed at which they shop for goods. A department store may play slower music to induce consumers to shop for a longer amount of time and shell out more money, while a fast food restaurant may play fast-paced rock and roll to induce people to leave and increase the turnover of customers.

There are a variety of ways that marketing and advertising appeals influence consumers' thoughts and feelings. Some of these work on a conscious level, others on a less conscious level. Sorting out what is very conscious from what is less conscious is a complicated business. From a persuasion perspective, the important point is that advertising appeals can influence the mind in many different ways, cleverly tapping into a variety of mental and emotional processes. In the next sections, I examine theories that help pinpoint these processes, helping us appreciate the many, seemingly magical but actually psychological, ways that advertising influences consumers.

THE PSYCHOLOGY OF LOW INVOLVEMENT

A good way to appreciate the many effects of advertising is to dust off the ELM discussed in Chapter 7 and review its applications to commercial persuasion. Recall that the ELM tells us that people process information differently under high and low involvement and this has important implications for persuasion strategies. Can you think of products that are personally important, mean a lot to you, and fulfill key psychological functions? These are high-involvement purchases. You are highly involved in the consumption of these products, probably thinking about them a lot or reckoning that you have something to lose if you make the wrong choice (Mittal, 1995). For most people, these products include cars, computers, and houses. Now consider the other side of the coin—products that you purchase that are of little personal concern, don't matter much to you, are mundane, and don't stimulate much thought. These are low-involvement purchases. They include soft drinks, countless grocery store products, and convenience goods like paper towels, tissue paper, and toothpaste (see Figure 13.3).

The ELM emphasizes that people process messages peripherally under low involvement and are, therefore, susceptible to simple appeals. Under high involvement, individuals think more centrally and deeply, taking into account the merits of the product and values stimulated by the ad. Advertising for high-involvement products cogently describes tangible benefits associated with the products. Ads also attempt to connect products with deep-seated values. The ELM has many interesting implications for advertising

■ Figure 13.3 Advertisers use a host of peripheral appeals to promote low-involvement products like these.

Photograph by William C. Rieter.

effects, suggesting, as it does, that we look separately at low- and high-involving advertising appeals. The next sections explore this approach.

Mere Exposure

More than 40 years ago, a news story appeared that has nothing—yet everything—to do with advertising:

> A mysterious student has been attending a class at Oregon State University for the past two months enveloped in a big black bag. Only his bare feet show. Each Monday, Wednesday, and Friday at 11:00 A.M. the Black Bag sits on a small table near the back of the classroom. The class is Speech 113-basic persuasion . . . Charles Goetzinger, professor of the class, knows the identity of the person inside. None of the 20 students in the class do. Goetzinger said *the students' attitude changed from hostility toward the Black Bag to curiosity and finally to friendship.*
> (Zajonc, 1968, p. 1)

This story illustrates a fundamental postulate of Robert B. Zajonc's **mere exposure** theory: Through repeated exposure to a neutral stimulus, an individual comes to evaluate the stimulus more favorably. According to the theory, all that is necessary is repetition. The more frequently an individual is exposed to a novel object, the more favorably he or she evaluates it.

Mere exposure has emerged as a robust theory of advertising effects. According to the theory, simple exposure to communications can influence attitudes. Merely seeing a message repeated over and over again leads to liking (Zajonc, 1968). This is a familiar experience. The longer you gaze at a painting in a museum, the more times you hear a hip-hop song on your iPod, and the more frequently you see an advertisement on TV, the more you come to like these stimuli.

Notice that mere exposure makes a prediction opposite to common sense. You have probably heard that "familiarity breeds contempt" or that "absence makes the heart grow fonder." Mere exposure theory suggests that those are nice ideas, but they do not accurately describe how advertising shapes attitudes.

The first studies of mere exposure examined responses to nonsense words, Chinese characters, and photographs—all of which were totally unfamiliar to student participants. Zajonc (pronounced zy-ance) deliberately chose to manipulate exposure to unfamiliar stimuli in order to provide as pure a test as possible of mere exposure theory. In this way he could be sure that whatever treatment differences were obtained were entirely due to the manipulation of mere exposure.

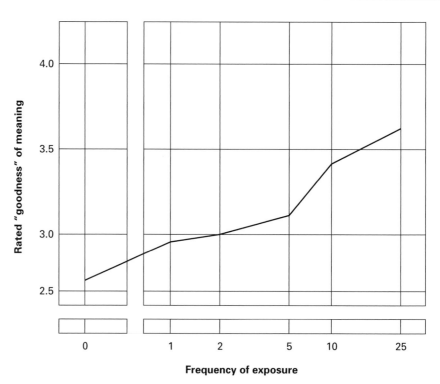

Frequency of exposure

■ Figure 13.4 Mere exposure to nonsense words.

Image from Robert B. Zajonc, R. B. 1968. Attitudinal effects of mere exposure. *Journal of Personality and Social Psychology Monographs Supplement, 9* (2, Pt. 2), 1–27.

In a classic study (Zajonc, 1968), subjects were asked to pronounce a variety of nonsense words (e.g., *afworbu, civrada, jandara, nansoma, iktitaf*). Frequency of exposure was varied and order was counterbalanced so that each word was pronounced 0, 1, 2, 5, 10, or 20 times. The results supported mere exposure: The more frequently a word was pronounced, the more positively it was evaluated. Incredibly, although these words were absolutely incomprehensible to the subjects, with each repetition the words (like the student encased in the black bag) came to elicit a more positive reaction (see Figure 13.4).

Other studies obtained similar findings. With repeated exposure, Chinese characters, men's graduation pictures, and even Pakistani music (a genre unfamiliar to most students outside Kabul) gained in positive affect (Rajecki, 1982). Research over the past decades has provided continued support for the theory, with evidence suggesting that repeated exposure to advertising also enhances favorable attitudes (Grush, McKeough, & Ahlering, 1978).

Why Mere Exposure Works

Mere exposure places more importance on form than content. It is the format—repeated exposure to a neutral stimulus—that matters, not the content of the ad. All that is needed is *mere* exposure.

There are three different explanations for the mere exposure effect (see Fang, Singh, & Ahluwalia, 2007). Some researchers argue that messages are easier to process and encode when they have been seen or heard before (Bornstein, 1992). Second, others proffer a more complex explanation. They suggest that consumers infer that advertisements that come more quickly to mind as a result of mere exposure are ones they like a lot. Still other scholars focus on a third process including the pleasures that come from increased familiarity to an advertisement. According to this view, the first exposure brings an uncomfortable sense of unfamiliarity as different cognitive responses compete for attention. Over time, one settles in on a particular reaction and the ensuring calm is pleasant. The first time television viewers saw the old Taco Bell ad in which the little Chihuahua utters, "Yo quiero Taco Bell" ("I want Taco Bell"), they probably were a little confused by the phrase and put off by the presence of a smirking, talking dog in an ad for a fast-food franchise. But with repetition, they got used to the ad, adjusted to the smug little dog, and developed a sense of what would occur as the quirky ad unfolded. The more they saw the ad, the more comfortable they felt and the more they liked it.

A similar process occurred for the "Can you hear me now?" ads for Verizon cell phones; MasterCard's cute, but incessant, repetition of "For everything else, there's MasterCard"; and McDonald's "I'm lovin' it." In all these cases, the more people saw the ads, the more comfortable they felt, and the more they resonated to the products. People made fun of the old Charmin toilet paper ads ("Please don't squeeze the Charmin"). However, the ads apparently worked, as Charmin, never known to consumers before, captured a significant share of the market after its nonstop advertising campaigns. People made fun of Charmin, but the company's executives had the last repeated laugh, en route to the bank!

When Mere Exposure Is Effective

Is repetition a panacea, a factor that always works? No way! Mere exposure is most effective under certain conditions. First, it works best for neutral products and issues—those to which we have not yet developed a strong attitude. It explains how advertising forms attitudes toward products, not how it *changes* them.

Second, once people have developed an especially negative attitude toward a product, company, or politician, repetition cannot change the attitude. In fact, it may have the opposite effect, producing more negative affect toward the issue as people ruminate about how much they hate the fast-food product, big corporation, or obnoxious politician (Tesser, 1978).

Third, mere exposure works only up to a certain point. After a certain number of exposures, repetition leads to boredom, tedium, and irritation. A phenomenon known as *wear-out* occurs (Bornstein, 1989; Solomon, 1999). Early in the mere exposure curve, repetition is a positive experience, reducing uncertainty, inducing calm, and bringing on a certain amount of pleasure. After a certain point, repetition has the opposite effect, and people become annoyed with the ad. Repetition ceases to lead to positive affect and can induce negative feelings toward the ad or product (see Figure 13.5). This is one reason why companies like McDonald's and Coke frequently switch slogans and change advertising agencies. They want to prevent wear-out and preserve the effect of a novel campaign slogan.

The Magic of Association

There is a marvelous McDonald's ad that was popular some years back. When students watch it, they invariably smile warmly. The ad begins with a football coach lecturing a team of 8-year-old boys. He intones, "A great man once said, 'Winning, gentlemen, isn't everything, it's the only thing.'" Suddenly we hear one of the boys, obviously oblivious to the coach's serious tone, shout, "Look, a grasshopper." All the youngsters jump up to take a look. The coach throws down his hat in mock despair. Another coach,

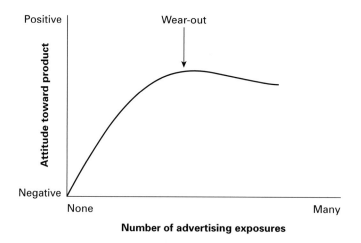

Figure 13.5 Repetition, advertising, and wear-out. After a certain number of repetitions, advertising can lead to wear-out.

kneeling down, says seriously to one of the boys: "I-formation, 34 sweep, on 2. Got it?" When the boy, doing his best to understand but obviously bewildered, shakes his head, the coach says, "Just give the ball to Matt. Tell him to run for his daddy, okay?" The boy nods happily.

As the camera pans the oh-so-cute boys in their blue uniforms, shows us the misty, but picture-perfect, football day, and lets us watch the players do push-ups while fathers feverishly peer through video cameras to record their sons' every movement, we hear the narrator say, "It starts every September with teams like the Turkey Creek Hawks and the Bronx Eagles." Alas, these September days are about more than just winning football games, the narrator goes on to suggest; they're about dads and sons, good times, and—now the pitch—where you go after the game. Soft, sentimental music builds as the scene slowly shifts to what must be a later point in time—the boys smiling and enjoying themselves at McDonald's, no doubt chomping down burgers and fries. And so, the narrator intones, the scene moving back to football, McDonald's would like to salute the players, coaches, and team spirit that are part of these fall September rituals. The visual then profiles a boy, looking up at the "winning isn't everything" coach. "Can we go to McDonald's now, Coach?" he asks. Patiently, kindly, but firmly, the coach notes, "Sit down, Lenny. It's only halftime." The music, playing softly in the background, trails off and fades, as the ad gently comes to a close.

The advertisement illustrates the principle of association. It associates the good feelings produced by football, boys playing pigskin on weekend afternoons, and autumn with the fast-food franchise, McDonald's. McDonald's has not told us the reasons why its hamburgers are tasty (that might be a hard sell, given what we know about fast-food diets!). It has not provided cogent arguments that dining at McDonald's is a healthy, useful activity for budding athletes. In fact, the ad has provided neither argument nor logic. Instead, it has employed the rich language of emotion, telling us a story, associating McDonald's with positive, pleasant images that are peripheral to the purchase decision. If you tried the same technique in a job that required you to provide arguments why clients should purchase your product, trying to associate your product with good times while humming a sentimental tune, you might be fired! Yet McDonald's succeeds because the world of advertising is not purely or primarily rational. It invariably prefers emotion to syllogistic logic. It frequently favors Aristotle's pathos to his deductive logos.

There are countless examples of the use of association in advertising. (See Figure 13.6.)

The most noteworthy example is sex. Displays of nudity, sexual allusions, sexual behavior, and physical attractiveness are . . . everywhere, it seems—in ads on television, in magazines, and on the Internet, the latter employing virtual models (Lambiase, 2003; Reichert, 2003).

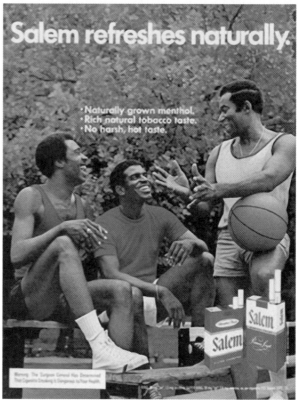

■ **Figure 13.6a–c** Association is used all the time in advertising. By associating products with pleasant, exciting, and beautiful images, advertisers hope the products will take on these desirable attributes. As these examples illustrate, advertising can promote associations for healthy and unhealthy products.

Image courtesy of Budweiser.

Advertisers dream up product names by appeals to association. Think: *Ivory* soap, *Cheer* detergent, *Splash* iced tea, and in the technology area, the internationally famous *Apple*, *BlackBerry*, and *Twitter*. Explaining how product names call on the associational power of metaphor, linguist Christopher Johnson, who helped coin names like these, notes that "the names Apple and BlackBerry metaphorically use the look and feel of fruits to add vividness to technological products. The name Twitter uses the cheerful sound of birds as an instantly recognizable aural image for a new multivocal form of communication" (Johnson, 2011, p. 71).

Yet sometimes a product name can convey more than its creators intended. Many women complained that Apple's iPad tablet elicits uncomfortable associations with feminine hygiene products. "You don't have to be in junior high to make this leap," said a speech writer on her Facebook page. "A lot of women when they hear the word 'pad' are going to think about feminine hygiene." Although "iTampon" emerged as one of the top trending topics on Twitter after the iPad was introduced in 2010, Apple's communications spokespersons diplomatically declined comment on the issue (Stone, 2010, p. 1).

Association is also used in more nefarious ways, as when advertisers pair cigarettes with relaxing images or link drugs like Vioxx (thought to cause heart attacks) with idyllic, happy times. The advertised images contrast sharply with the wretched effects these products exert on the body. (See Box 13.2 for a discussion of cigarette marketing.)

BOX 13.2 CIGARETTE MARKETING

Cigarette marketing, a multibillion-dollar business around the globe, exploits psychological strategies to hook young people into smoking or to convince satisfied customers to stick with their brands. Ads have associated cigarettes with the pristine outdoors, sexuality, and rugged independence (as in the American icon, the Marlboro Man). Appeals geared to young women play on the psychological functions cigarettes serve, like independence and autonomy. The copy in a classic Virginia Slims ad says, "I always take the driver's seat. That way I'm never taken for a ride."

Because cigarettes cannot be advertised on radio or TV in the United States, marketers have relied on a variety of other techniques to promote their products, including billboards, magazine ads, event sponsorship, and linking their logos

Continued

with athletic contests and rock concerts, a practice known as brand-stretching (Campbell, Martin, & Fabos, 2002). Movies like *Basic Instinct, Pulp Fiction, Titanic, Slumdog Millionaire,* and *The Artist* have depicted characters smoking, with apparent enjoyment. Indeed, actors in films smoke almost as frequently today as they did in the 1950s (Walsh-Childers & Brown, 2009). In an effort to reach the burgeoning youth market, multinational cigarette companies have distributed tobacco-branded clothing abroad and, in the United States, have plastered cigarette logos on candy and children's toys.

Another related marketing strategy—point-of-purchase cigarette marketing—appears to be highly effective. One study found that in-store promotions significantly enhanced eighth- and ninth-graders' perceptions of the accessibility and popularity of cigarettes, factors that increase the chances that young people will begin smoking (Henriksen et al., 2002). Yet tobacco executives recognize that, even if point-of-purchase and other marketing strategies generate cigarette sales, smoking has become a cultural taboo and is widely associated with disease and death in the United States. As a consequence, tobacco companies have increasingly begun marketing their product abroad, directing campaigns at psychologically vulnerable children and adolescents in some low-income developing countries. Nearly a fourth of all smokers worldwide started smoking before the age of 10, and as many as 20 percent of adolescents said they owned clothing that showed a cigarette brand logo (McNeil, 2008). "Just at the moment that the cigarette was losing its glamour, sophistication, and sexual allure in the West, the companies sought to recreate these connotations of smoking in developing countries," historian Allan M. Brandt (2007) observes (p. 455).

Particularly problematic are tobacco companies' blatant attempts to hook young people into smoking. "The clearest statement [of this]," reporter Philip J. Hilts discovered, after extensively studying cigarette marketing, "came in a question and answer period at a regional [R. J. Reynolds Company] sales meeting. Someone asked exactly who the young people were that were being targeted, junior high school kids, or even younger?

"The reply came back 'They got lips? We want 'em'" (Hilts, 1996, p. 98).

Association is perhaps the most important reason why advertising succeeds. It explains why things—material objects with no inherent value—acquire powerful meanings in consumers' eyes. Scholars have advanced several theories to explain how association works. They include **classical conditioning, semiotics,** and **accessibility.**

Classical Conditioning

The granddaddy of association concepts, conditioning, dates back to Pavlov. "Does the name Pavlov ring a bell?" Cialdini (2009) asks humorously, reminding us of the Russian psychologist's century-old study that paired an unconditioned stimulus (food) with a conditioned stimulus (bell) to produce a conditioned response (salivation to the bell). Psychologists have applied classical conditioning to social learning, particularly attitude acquisition. In a study conducted in a post-World War II era preoccupied with understanding how Nazi-type prejudice could have developed, Staats and Staats (1958) showed that individuals could acquire negative attitudes toward the word "Dutch" simply by hearing it paired with "higher-order" stimuli, or words that had already acquired unfavorable connotations ("ugly," "failure"). In a similar fashion, consumer psychologists have shown that attitudes toward products can be classically conditioned through association with pleasant images.

In one consumer psychology study, Stuart, Shimp, and Engle (1987) paired a neutral stimulus ("Brand L toothpaste") with higher-order stimuli (nature scenes such as a mountain waterfall or a sunset over an island). For experimental group participants, the toothpaste and beautiful nature scenes were linked over the course of a number of conditioning trials. For control subjects, the toothpaste and nature scenes were presented in random order with respect to each other. The researchers found that experimental group subjects who were exposed to the pairing of toothpaste and beautiful natural scenes displayed significantly more positive attitudes toward Brand L toothpaste than did control group subjects. Similarly, Till and his colleagues found that pairing a fictitious styling gel brand (conditioned stimulus) with a celebrity (higher-order stimulus) produced favorable attitudes toward the brand (Till, Stanley, & Priluck, 2008).

Classical conditioning processes help us understand how people develop favorable attitudes toward products. However, they have drawbacks. Conditioning employs a rather clunky, primitive terminology that does not capture the ways that contemporary advertising operates. Focused as it is on unconditioned stimuli and conditioned responses, it does not appreciate the powerful role that symbols play in advertising or the mental processes by which people come to link images with brands. Consequently, we need to examine other views of association in advertising.

Semiotics

Semiotics is the study of signs and symbols. It helps us understand how signs—visual objects or geometric shapes with no inherent meaning—take on a rich tapestry of social and cultural meaning. A symbol is a sign with substance—a sign that bursts with value and emotional signification. The Cross and Star of David are shapes, but as symbols

Figure 13.7 Well-known signs and symbols in American advertising (see also Goldman & Papson, 1996).

they are much more. The Cross symbolizes Jesus's crucifixion and redemption—an emblem of Christian love. The Star of David, a six-pointed star formed by superimposing two equilateral triangles, is a symbol of Judaism and Jewish culture.

Advertising thrives on signs. It transforms signs into symbols that give a product its meaning or "zip" (Goldman & Papson, 1996). Take a look at the signs in Figure 13.7. Glance first at Coca-Cola, closing your eyes to gain a clearer fix on the image. Do the same for McDonald's, the Nike swoosh, and iPod. What comes to mind? Images, feelings, pictures, people? I'd be willing to bet they did, even if you don't like the products or purchase them. Such is the power of advertising. It attempts to fill commodity signs with meaning, to give value to brands, and to stamp imagery onto products that sometimes differ only trivially from their competitors. Consider that classic entry in the sneaker wars, the Nike swoosh, which was discussed earlier in the chapter. Robert Goldman and Stephen Papson offer a historical perspective:

> Once upon a time, the Nike swoosh symbol possessed no intrinsic value as a sign, but value was added to the sign by drawing on the name and image value of celebrity superstars like Michael Jordan. Michael Jordan possesses value in his own right—the better his performances, the higher his value. The sign of Nike acquired additional value when it joined itself to the image of Jordan.
>
> (1996, p. 10)

This was the Nike "advertising sign machine" of the late 1980s and 1990s, featuring associations between the swoosh and Jordan; Bo Jackson, the professional athlete; and movie director Spike Lee. Since then, Nike has embarked on numerous ad campaigns, including ones that feature commercials resembling MTV videos—brilliant, but blatant, attempts to associate the swoosh with images resonant with a younger market. Nike, like other advertisers, strives constantly to redefine its image in the eyes of new market segments through ever-inventive ways of combining signs with in-vogue celebrities, trends, and images.

Yet, for all of its insights, semiotics does not explain how advertising creeps into the minds of consumers. It is a theory of message content, not message effects. To understand associative advertising impact, we must turn to cognitive psychological concepts. Consider that advertising shapes attitudes toward products by helping to forge an association between the product and a pleasant, memorable image. Once the attitude is formed, it must be retrieved or accessed, particularly at the moment when consumers are making a product decision.

Accessibility

The extent to which people can "call up" an attitude from memory comes to the fore when discussing advertising's effects on attitudes. Research discussed in Chapter 4 suggests that the more exposure consumers have to advertisements that plant the association between a product and image, the more they can quickly get in touch with their attitude when they are trying to decide which soft drink, fast food, or sneakers to purchase. Advertisers recognize this and design messages to encourage consumers to access attitudes from memory (see Shrum et al., 2013).

Thus, McDonald's ads try to induce consumers who are in the mood for fast food to call up the feelings they had when they watched an ad like the one described earlier. Coke tries to access years of internalized associations between its product and positive images. These include mid-20th-century linkages between Coca-Cola and patriotic appeals that call to mind artist Norman Rockwell; the classic 1971 song that associated Coke with global, ethnic diversity ("I'd like to buy the world a Coke and keep it company. It's the real thing"); and current multicultural campaigns that span Egypt, Saudi Arabia, and South Africa.

Other advertisements employ similar strategies. The American commercial icon Campbell's Soup spent much of the 20th century building powerful linkages between its product and down-home days with Mom and Dad (albeit of the White variety). Campbell's ads seemingly left an imprint, as one consumer acknowledged:

> Campbell's tomato soup is the only one that will do. It's like a cozy, comforting thing. It tastes good mainly because you associate it with what it did for you when you were a kid. Maybe it doesn't even taste that good, but somehow it works on a level beyond just your taste buds.
>
> (Langer, 1997, p. 61)

Association appeals can even succeed in convincing consumers to buy products that have no distinctive qualities. Case in point: bottled water. Blind taste tests reveal that most people cannot tell the difference between bottled and tap water. One researcher arrayed 10 bottles of water on a table, including one filled with water from the tap. He asked participants in his informal study to rate samples from each bottle for flavor, aftertaste, feel, and appearance. The majority could not discriminate among the group; indeed, they could not correctly identify the bottle that contained tap water (Standage, 2005). If taste is not the reason why millions buy Aquafina, Evian, Fiji, and other brands, why has bottled water become so popular? A major reason is that bottled water has become fashionable, linked with purity, cleanliness, and good health. "Advertisers used words (*pure*, *natural*) and imagery (waterfalls, mountains) to imply that bottled water tasted better and was healthier than tap," a writer notes (Royte, 2008, p. 34).

Summary

In these diverse ways, marketing builds associations into signs, products, and brands. It transforms things into symbols of hope, desire, and status (Langrehr & Caywood, 1995; McCracken, 1986). An iPod is not a mere MP3 player; instead, it is a life-line, an icon of "techno-chic" (Levy, 2006, p. 67), a connection with worlds more musically majestic than everyday life. Nike shoes are not sneakers but, rather, emblems of excellence, pronouncements of athletic ability. Objects gain this majesty through associational appeals in advertising and the projections of consumers. Although ads do not always exert this impact—the floors of advertising agencies are littered with footage from unsuccessful media campaigns—ads can potently influence affect toward products. In light of advertising's widely recognized ability to shape product attitudes, it is little wonder that people unschooled in advertising effects leapt onto the subliminal seduction bandwagon.

Celebrities as Peripheral Cues

When consumers are in a low-involvement mode—as most are when they encounter ads for soft drink, lip balm, paper towel, and toothpaste products—celebrities can serve as compelling peripheral cues. Celebrities are particularly apt to enhance consumer attitudes when their characteristics "match up with" or are relevant to the product being promoted (Chew, Mehta, & Oldfather, 1994; Lynch & Schuler, 1994; see also Lee & Thorson, 2008). This is known as the advertising match-up hypothesis.

Nike, whose brand conveys athleticism and grace, has selected a legion of sports stars to serve as product representatives. Endorsers, who often simply wear a hat with a salient swoosh, include American basketball stars Michael Jordan and LeBron James, as well as international tennis greats like Spain's Rafael Nadal, Switzerland's Roger Federer, and Maria Sharapova, the stellar Russian competitor.

Celebrity characteristics can net advertisers millions, but they also can be persuasive liabilities. When reports of Tiger Woods' extramarital affairs attracted worldwide publicity, major companies dropped him as a celebrity spokesman. Prior to the scandal, an ad for Accenture, a consulting firm, had featured the golfer looking into the distance, with ominous clouds on the horizon. The advertisement said that it is "tougher than ever to be Tiger." The words took on a totally different meaning after allegations of marital infidelities surfaced.

HIGH INVOLVEMENT

The world of low-involvement advertising is all about promoting products that consumers don't much think about, inducing them to develop positive feelings about these brands. Another category of advertising concerns high-involvement products— those that are important to us personally, touch on our self-concepts, or are big-ticket, expensive items (see Figure 13.8). When consumers are in the market for an ordinarily high-involvement product, like a car, jewelry, computer, or even clothing, they process ads centrally. The ELM emphasizes that, under high-involvement conditions, people consider the merits of the product, connect the product to core values, consider connections with their self-concepts, and otherwise systematically process product commercials (Andrews & Shimp, 1990; Roehm & Haugtvedt, 1999). They carefully process factual information like price and consider the material benefits of the purchase

■ **Figure 13.8 To many consumers, computer, photographic, and electronic products are highly involving. Advertisers use factual, social, and value-based appeals to promote these products.**

Photograph by William C. Rieter.

LOW INVOLVEMENT

HIGH INVOLVEMENT

■ **Figure 13.9 Involvement and brand attitudes. Based on the ELM, and Mitchell, A. A. (1986). Effects of visual and verbal components of advertisements on brand attitudes.** ***Journal of Consumer Research, 13,* 12–24.**

(see Figure 13.9). When they are online and come across banner ads for high-involvement products like cars, consumers may not be influenced by the ads' size or color. Instead, they may be especially likely to click the ads to request more information about the product (Cho, 1999).

The ELM suggests that under moderate to high product involvement, an advertising variable can serve as an argument, intersect with pre-existing attitudes toward the product, catalyze thinking, or bolster confidence in one's own thoughts about the brand. In many instances, strong, cogent arguments on behalf of the product should exert an impact.

But what constitutes a strong, cogent argument on behalf of a product? On this point, as noted in Chapter 7, the ELM's advice is somewhat general. To identify the types of messages that are apt to resonate with people purchasing personally important products, we need to turn to another persuasion theory. Functional theory, discussed in Chapter 5, helps bridge consumer attitudes and persuasion. You may recall that the functional approach says that attitudes serve specific psychological functions or fulfill needs for individuals. Messages are most likely to influence attitudes if they target the function the attitude serves. Let's see how this works in the case of advertising.

Some attitudes serve a *utilitarian* function. People purchase products to gain specific, tangible rewards (Shavitt & Nelson, 2000). Parents who need a minivan to transport their kids, pets, or groceries have utilitarian reasons for purchasing a car. Ads targeted at these parents commonly emphasize the passenger space and roominess of, say, a Chevy Suburban or Honda Odyssey.

People buy products for reasons other than tangible benefits. They buy to fulfill ambitions, dreams, and fantasies. Thus, product attitudes serve symbolic, as well as material, functions. For example, some attitudes serve a social-adjustive function. One obviously upscale mother confessed that she tried to get away with buying her 14-year-old daughter an MP3 player that was $100 cheaper than the most popular brand in her daughter's peer group. "I was in the biggest dog box," she said. Her daughter "went to school, and everyone else had got an iPod for Christmas. It was like, 'How come everyone else got one, and you couldn't buy me an iPod?' So we got one for her birthday two months later" (Williams, 2005, p. 1).

Although the mother's comments might seem silly or petty, they do reflect a common perspective toward products. Advertising designed to reach these mothers would be advised to hype the most expensive, branded products.

Product attitudes also serve a *social identity* function. Consumers purchase cars, jewelry, and other highly involving goods to enhance their identities—to set them apart from others. People buy big-ticket items to gain status, look cool, show off an identity to others, or express love. Ads appeal to these needs, using pictures, images, and the syntax of advertising to suggest that owning products cements a social identity. "May promote feelings of superiority," a tag line for a Nissan car unabashedly stated.

Consumer attitudes also serve a *value-expressive* function. Individuals purchase products to express deep-seated values. Advertisers target environmentally conscious consumers by playing up concern for ecology in their ads. The Body Shop plays up its opposition to scientific testing of animals. Advertisers take code words like *recycling* and *green* and cleverly associate them with their products. An ad for Marcal Small Steps emphasizes that its towels and toilet paper are "100% premium recycled," using "paper from paper, not from trees."

Some consumers purchase green products for value-expressive reasons, but others go green "to be seen" (Griskevicius, Tybur, & Van den Bergh, 2010). Buying green products signifies that you are cool and in this way serves a status function. In support of this notion, researchers found that people were more likely to select pro-environmental products over equally priced, non-green alternatives when individuals were motivated by social status. This helps explain why some consumers gravitate to cars like the Toyota Prius. The fuel-efficient, hybrid car "essentially functions as a mobile, self-promoting billboard for proenvironmentalism" (Griskevicius et al., p. 399).

By knowing the function a product fulfills for an individual consumer or demographic group, marketers can more effectively target the message to the needs of the individual or group. In this way, they can match message to mind, and sell more products.

ETHICAL AND LEGAL ISSUES

Research has established that advertising and marketing shape attitudes toward products. Commercial marketing effects have in turn generated a flurry of ethical and legal questions. Let's explore the ethical conundrums, legal distinctions, and the normative issues surrounding contemporary marketing.

A deontological approach stipulates that the test of ethical communication is whether it treats individuals as an ends, not a means, and operates from honorable motives. Viewed in this way, advertising can fall drastically short of an ethical ideal. Advertisers develop ads that make promises they know products can't deliver. Cigarettes don't offer hedonistic pleasure; cars don't make you rich or famous; and making pancakes for your kids on Saturday won't assuage your guilt about neglecting them all week, despite the plaintive plea of a Bisquik pancake commercial.

Advertisers want consumers to project fantasies onto products in order to hook individuals on the image of the brand. Viewed from a Kantian perspective, advertising is not ethical because advertisers are not truthful. If the decency of the communicators' motives is the criterion for ethical communication, advertising fails. Advertisers deliberately construct fantasies to serve their clients' needs, not to aid the customer in living a healthier, happier life.

In response to these criticisms, defenders of advertising emphasize that consumers recognize that advertising creates untruths. They do not expect ads to tell them "the way things really are in society," Messaris (1997) notes. "Almost by definition," he says, "the portrayals of the good life presented in ads carry with them the implicit understanding that they are idealizations, not documentary reports" (p. 268). In effect, advertising defenders say, "Don't worry; be happy." Advertising is capitalism's playful communication, an attempt to give people an outlet for universal human fantasies.

In the view of defenders, advertising and marketing offer a wealth of positive utilitarian outcomes. They convey information about how to possess nifty things that people desire. Marketers argue that advertising does not create a need for products, but responds to consumers' craving for the latest gadget or thing. On a macro level, advertising keeps the engines of the free market economy rolling. It increases demand and allows companies to sell products, prosper, and employ managers and workers.

And so the debate goes.

If ethical issues are a matter of debate, legal issues are somewhat more amenable to resolution.

The Federal Trade Commission (FTC), which regulates advertising in the United States, has developed regulations, stipulating that deceptive selling practices are unlawful. It is important at the outset to distinguish between falsity and deception. Interestingly enough, an ad can be false, but not deceptive.

A false ad is one that is "misleading in a material respect." An advertisement can contain information that consumers recognize to be false, as they understand that a little falsity is part of the advertising game. Some years back Isuzu automobiles made outrageously, obviously false statements, claiming a truck cost only $19.95. The statements were so deliberately and blatantly exaggerated that no reasonable consumer would consider them to be true (Richards, 1990). Marketers are also allowed to engage in puffery, where they "puff up" or exaggerate the product's virtues. They can use catchwords and superlatives that underscore the superiority of the product, even if the statements are not true. For example, the Army does not let you "be all that you can be." It is not necessarily true that "when you say Budweiser, you've said it all" or that "when you're out of Schlitz you're out of beer." Is it a verifiable fact that "the best part of waking up is Folger's in your cup"? Or that "Bayer works wonders"? You get the drift.

Some scholars (Preston, 1996), upholding the value of truthfulness, lament that advertisers can make even these false, puffed-up claims. However, the FTC has declared that they are legal, regarding them as harmless efforts to promote a product and reasoning that few if any consumers would take them on face value. Thus, the falsity is not material to the consumer's purchase decision.

Most deceptive ads are literally true, but contain deceptive or misleading messages. A classic is a Campbell's Soup ad of the late 1960s. When Campbell's advertisers snapped photographs of the soup, they found the solid vegetable ingredients would not show up clearly in the pictures. The vegetables kept sinking to the bottom of the broth. This did not give the desired image of a delicious soup where the beans and carrots were "so high that they poked right up like periscopes on submarines" (Preston, 1994, p. 34). To manufacture the right image, Campbell's toy department placed loads of marbles in the soup. This prevented the vegetables from sinking to the bottom and made it seem like Campbell's contained more solid ingredients than its competitor's soup. The FTC declared this to be an instance of deceptive advertising, since the pictures misrepresented the product.

What constitutes deception? It's a tough term to define because it is, to a certain degree subjective. In addition, because it requires that the consumer develop false beliefs based on misleading claims, it is, to some degree, a psychological concept that inheres in the receiver's head. How do you measure that objectively? The FTC defines a marketing practice as deceptive if the message contains a representation that "is likely to mislead consumers acting reasonably under the circumstances" and the misrepresentation is material, likely to affect the consumer's decision regarding a product or service.

Scholars have tried to clarify this definition by noting that an advertisement is deceptive if it "leaves intelligent and knowledgeable adults (or a significant percentage of intelligent and knowledgeable adults)" with a belief "different from what would normally be expected if the consumer had reasonable knowledge," and the belief is either "factually untrue or potentially misleading" (e.g., Carson, Wokutch, & Cox, 1985, p. 95). But this raises questions. What percentage of intelligent and knowledgeable adults must hold an inaccurate belief for the ad to be regarded as deceptive? What about adults who are not so intelligent or knowledgeable? Should a different criterion be developed for them? What about our low-involved, low-ability consumers? Are they uniquely vulnerable to misleading peripheral and associational cues? What is "potentially misleading"? And if you adopt a super-strict definition of deception, then you could potentially prosecute advertisers for making claims that have trivial effects on purchase decisions. Is that prudent policy?

These are difficult questions to answer. No law can cover all exceptions. For all their problems, the above definitions allow for some clarity in determining whether an ad is sufficiently deceptive that it warrants punishment and legal action.

High-Tech Marketing and Ethical Quandaries

Advertising is in the throes of change, adapting to the post-Web 2.0 environment and galloping technological innovations. The 30-second advertisement no longer reigns supreme in an era when viewers with TiVos can zap through commercials, and millions of people have become accustomed to getting entertainment for free on Web sites like YouTube. Advertising increasingly must struggle to get its message heard in a noisy, cluttered world (Thaler & Koval, 2003). Advertisers are adapting their psychological appeals, targeting more nonlinear communications on the Internet and cell phones to those who are accustomed to clicking from icon to icon and symbol to symbol (see Figure 13.10).

Tailoring ads to consumer preferences, marketers are an interactive presence on Facebook, where they request users to click if they like an ad, answer survey questions, and accept free samples of products. They are involving consumers in the creation of brands by sponsoring contests on the Internet that invite enthusiasts to submit broadcast-quality ads.

The diffusion of digital technologies has paved the way for new marketing strategies, characterized by increasing intrusion into consumers' personal space. The centerpiece

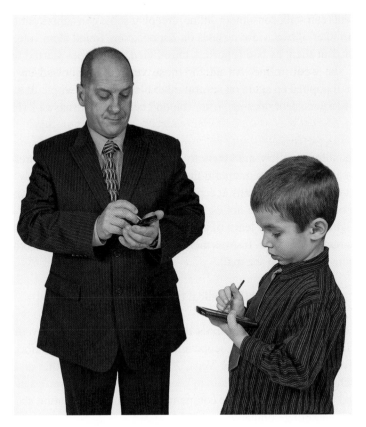

■ **Figure 13.10 With individuals of all ages hooked on their digital devices, marketers have become adept at sending digital persuasive messages, such as advertisements or text messages promoting brands.**

Image courtesy of Shutterstock.

is a cookie, originally a computer science term, but now a word that is bandied about frequently. A cookie encodes and stores information about a user's activity on a Web site. Web site owners and online marketers can retrieve information about the user's preferences, invariably in the absence of the individual's knowledge, permission, or verbal consent. As technology writer Eli Pariser (2011b) notes:

> Search for a word like "depression" on Dictionary.com, and the site installs up to 223 tracking cookies and beacons on your computer so that other Web sites can target you with antidepressants. Share an article about cooking on ABC News, and you may be chased around the Web by ads for Teflon-coated pots.
>
> (p. 6)

Advertisements can stalk consumers online, creeping some consumers out. Julie Matlin, a Montreal mother of two, viewed shoes on Zappos.com, found them cute, but was not ready to buy. But then, as two reporters chronicled, "the shoes started to follow her everywhere she went online. An ad for those very shoes showed up on the blog TechCrunch. It popped up again on several other blogs and on Twitpic. It was if Zappos had unleashed a persistent salesman who wouldn't take no for an answer" (Helft & Vega, 2010, p. A1).

The new technologies allow marketers to gain access to consumers' preferences and buying behavior. Advertisers maintain that these techniques, felicitously called "personalized retargeting," are morally acceptable, noting that they have been used for years in one form or another and are not especially intrusive. Some consumers confess that they are delighted when they learn of a new gadget, wardrobe, or hot product through an adroitly targeted online ad. It saves them time and money they would otherwise have spent shopping online or at the mall.

Others beg to differ, raising philosophical objections.

Retargeting or personalization "illustrates that there is a commercial surveillance system in place online that is sweeping in scope and raises privacy and civil liberties issues," said one privacy advocate (Helft & Vega, 2010, p. B2). One mother and father who recently purchased a software program to keep track of their children's activities online were appalled when they learned the company was selling information about their kids to third-party marketing companies.

It is a classic case of weighing the utilitarian benefit to companies (and consumers) against the psychological costs experienced by individuals when they realize their privacy has been hijacked. It involves considering whether the many opportunities consumers receive from an Internet that minimizes privacy exceed the social drawbacks. Ultimately, one must balance a desire not to intrude on the free market with an appreciation that privacy violations raise deontological issues, telegraphing disrespect for an individual's right to withhold information about the self from strangers with unknown motives. Although Google and Facebook argue that we need to adapt to the inevitability of an all-is-public online world, others worry that the rich and powerful businesses "know a lot more about us than we know about each other—and sometimes, more than we know about ourselves" (Pariser, 2011b, p. 147). What concerns critics is the lack of symmetry between what the powerful know about the powerless and the powerless know about the powerful.

Alas, this too raises a host of philosophical questions. What is meant by privacy? Do people have a right to privacy? Does online marketing facilitated by cookies really constitute a violation of privacy? Most people probably do not know that their online consumer history can be exploited by online businesses. They certainly never gave their verbal consent. Some scholars argue that consumers should be informed that marketers are gathering information about online purchasing preferences, and that they never agreed to this (Tavani, 2000). Others note that, at the very least, we should know who has accumulated information about us and how it is being used. We should also be able to prevent facts gathered about us for one purpose from being exploited for other, less altruistic goals (Pariser, 2011a, b).

Google and Facebook provide numerous utilitarian benefits to consumers. But they frequently see the world differently from ethicists. What is good for Facebook may not be good for us. What helps persuaders may not always be advantageous for individuals. Outcomes that offer lucrative options for consumers may offend their personhood. These are important ethical issues that will become even more daunting in the years to come.

CONCLUSIONS

We all assume we're not affected in the slightest by advertising. We can see through those ploys, we tell ourselves; it's everyone else—the audience, the unwashed masses, who are vulnerable. But this is a fallacy, an illusion (Sagarin et al., 2002). If you are right that other people are influenced by advertisements, then it certainly stands to reason that you, too, should be swayed. On the other hand, if you are correct that you are not influenced and everyone else presumably claims the same lack of influence, then you exaggerate the effects of advertising on others (Perloff, 2009). "In either case," James Tiedge and colleagues note, "most people appear to be willing to subscribe to the logical inconsistency inherent in maintaining that the mass media influence others considerably more than themselves" (Tiedge et al., 1991, p. 152). (Communication researchers call this the **third-person effect**: the notion that persuasive media do not affect "you" or "me"—but, rather, "them"—the third persons. See Andsager & White, 2007 and Box 13.3 for a discussion.)

The reality is that, of course, we are influenced by advertising—sometimes subtly, other times quite directly. Indeed, advertising is such a pervasive part of American culture that it is difficult to conjure up mental images of products that have not been formed through advertising. If you were asked to free-associate about Coca-Cola, Budweiser, Nike, classy perfumes, or cars running the gamut from Mustangs to minivans, your mental images would undoubtedly contain ideas and pictures gleaned from commercials. It is physically difficult, if not impossible, to call to mind an advertising-free image of products. In fact, advertising effects are so deep-seated that exposure to a celebrity who commonly appears in ads and comes across as an expert induces specific brain activity (Klucharev, Smidts, & Fernandez, 2008).

Little wonder that critics have charged that advertising's power comes from subliminally embedded messages that elude conscious awareness. Research finds that subliminal advertisements exert virtually no impact on attitudes. However, the conscious belief that a message contains a subliminal message can influence attitudes. The subliminal notion is more myth than reality, but it persists because people cling to simple ideas about how advertising works.

As suggested by the ELM, advertising works through different pathways under low and high involvement. When viewing ads for low-involvement products, consumers process information peripherally. Repeated exposure, association-based appeals, and celebrity-source endorsements are influential. Association, which encompasses classical conditioning semiotics, and accessibility, is a potent weapon in advertising campaigns.

When considering more personally consequential purchases, consumers process ads centrally, taking into account the benefits that products offer and the psychological functions that products serve. When directing ads at highly involved consumers, advertisers use factual messages and symbolic appeals targeted to particular attitude functions. Advertising frequently invites consumers to imagine that their futures will be brighter if they purchase the product or join the organization the ad is promoting.

BOX 13.3 ADVERTISING AND THE POWER OF PERCEPTION

A new product is advertised. It could be for the latest MP3 player, video game, perfume, beer, or sports car. What happens when people watch commercials like these? Well, many things. They enjoy the ad, remark to themselves the ad is cool (or cheesy), think about the product, decide they don't like it, or alternatively fantasize about partaking in the activities displayed in the ad. But something else happens too. Viewers make a judgment that the ad is going to influence others. This may not be a centrally processed judgment, but people invariably presume that an advertisement will have an impact. And this perception—this belief about the advertisement's impact—has ripple effects that are very interesting and, in some cases, consequential.

This is a somewhat different arena of persuasive effects from what has been discussed up to this point. The focus has been on direct effects of sources, messages, and advertising on attitudes. But this is an indirect influence, and it revolves around perception. We observe this when a consumer assumes that advertisements for a product—like Nintendo Wii sometime ago—will cause others to want to buy the product. Based on this perception, our consumer decides he'd better rush to the mall or quickly make an online purchase before everyone else does the same. The interesting thing is that advertising may not have this effect at all, but it has, through the power of perception, produced a self-fulfilling prophecy.

This notion flows from the third-person effect, as well as what communication researcher Albert C. Gunther calls the presumed influence hypothesis, and Ye Sun (2013) calls simply "the influence of presumed influence." Researchers have examined consequences of simply *presuming* that media influence others. In one study, Gunther and colleagues focused on pre-teens, who tend to be very concerned with perceptions of others, and end up behaving in ways they believe will be popular with peers. These perceptions are especially influential in the case of cigarette smoking.

Gunther and his colleagues (2006) asked sixth and seventh graders to indicate how much exposure they had to smoking advertisements in magazines, the Internet, and stores, as well as to actors smoking on TV and in movies. They also asked students to estimate peer exposure to smoking ads (how often they thought their peers had seen or heard smoking messages); assessed perceptions of smoking prevalence (an estimate of how many students their age smoke cigarettes at least once a week); and measured attitudes toward cigarette smoking.

The ads had intriguing effects. The more exposure students had to smoking messages, the more they thought their peers saw these messages. Perceived peer exposure in turn led students to assume that smoking was prevalent. Importantly, perceiving that their peers smoked cigarettes led students to develop more positive personal attitudes toward smoking. Notice that the ads did not influence smoking attitudes directly. Instead, the ads—indirectly and subtly—led students to infer that their peers were influenced by prosmoking messages and had therefore decided to light up. Presumably, a desire to fit in with a perceived climate of smoking pushed students to evaluate smoking more favorably themselves.

Continued

> There is little doubt that many persuasive messages work in this manner. Teenage girls acknowledge that televised images of thin bodies are unrealistic. However, if they perceive that girls in their peer group buy into these televised images, they may think it is cool to accept these images themselves (Park, 2005; see also Paek, 2009). Thus, advertising may have caused adolescent girls to diet too much or engage in other unhealthy behavior. But the effects were produced indirectly, by influencing their perceptions of what others do or think. These are subtle media effects, but ones that may leave a residual impact on the attitudes and behaviors of vulnerable young consumers.

Ever controversial, advertising has been condemned on deontological grounds by those who point to the obvious falsehoods that ads contain. Other critics lament that advertising inculcates a strange philosophy of life that places great faith in the ability of products to satisfy universal human desires.

Chill out, advertising's defenders respond. People don't believe all of what advertising says and they enjoy watching the clever "magic tricks" ads employ, for example on Super Bowl Sunday. Besides, defenders note, humans' desire to acquire cool gadgets drives advertising. If people did not love things and the status products convey, advertising could not prosper.

Nonetheless, as even defenders acknowledge, advertising and marketing more generally can create mischief if claims advanced in commercial messages are deceptive. The Federal Trade Commission stipulates that a message is deceptive if it contains a representation that is likely to materially mislead consumers acting reasonably under the circumstances. Inevitably, there are gray areas. Advertising can be of questionable moral value, yet legally defensible.

In the final analysis, advertising and commercial marketing remain ethically problematic, but necessary parts of capitalist society. Needed to differentiate and promote products, advertising increases demand, helping business to sell products and employ workers. But questions about falsehood and manipulation persist. Advertising remains, in Schudson's (1986) memorable phrase, an "uneasy persuasion."

Test your knowledge now with interactive exercises

Chapter 14

Health Communication Campaigns

 Listen now to the author's chapter summary

Bill Alcott and Sy Graham were horrified. They were aghast at what people did to their bodies, day after day shoveling unhealthy, even dangerous, food into their mouths. Didn't people know the damage that meat, fried foods, and butter did to the stomach and heart? Convinced that Americans needed to change their diets, Alcott and Graham organized a health food store that supplied fresh fruits and vegetables. A proper diet, in their view, consisted of wheat bread, grains, vegetables, fruits, and nuts. By eating healthy food and avoiding anything that harmed the body, Graham and Alcott emphasized, people could live longer, healthier lives.

Sound familiar? Another example of contemporary activists trying to convince consumers to give up junk food? Well—not exactly. Alcott and Graham were committed health reformers, but they communicated their message some time ago. More than 150 years ago, to be precise! William Alcott and Sylvester Graham, born in the late 1700s, promoted their nutrition reform campaign in the 1830s. They were early advocates of health education, pioneers in a clean-living movement that began in the United States in the 1800s and continues to this day. Alcott's writings can be found in scattered libraries across the country. Graham—or at least his name—is known worldwide through his Graham cracker (Engs, 2000).

Long before it became fashionable to tout one's opposition to smoking or drugs, activists were pounding the pavement, preaching and proselytizing. Campaigns to improve the public health date back to the early 1800s, with Alcott and Graham's vegetarianism, health reformers' condemnation of the "evil, deadly" tobacco, and the Temperance Movement's efforts to promote abstinence from alcohol. Clean-living movements, as Ruth Clifford Engs (2000) calls them, took on special urgency during the 1830s and 1840s, with the outbreak of cholera, an infectious disease that spread through filthy water, a common problem during a time when drainage systems were poor or nonexistent and pigs roamed the streets feeding on uncollected garbage. Although the causes

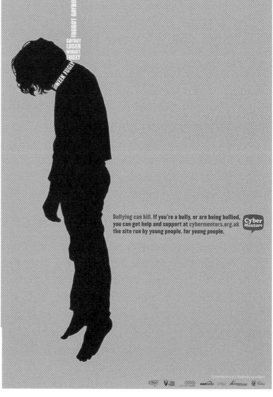

■ **Figure 14.1a–c Contemporary campaigns employ a host of persuasion strategies to change health-related attitudes and behavior. As shown here, a healthy eating campaign employs a slogan and a famous credible source, Michelle Obama. A French breast cancer prevention campaign harnesses social marketing strategies, described later in the chapter, by promoting a race with 4,000 women sporting pink T-shirts. An anti-bullying intervention employs a vivid message appeal. Why are these appeals attention-grabbing? Which do you think are most effective?**

Image courtesy of Getty Images.

of cholera could be traced to the social environment, cholera (like AIDS a century and a half later) was viewed as "God's punishment for vice, sin, and moral flaws" (Rushing, 1995, p. 168).

Health campaigns flourished in the 20th century, with the proliferation of television and realization that activists could change institutions through a combination of persuasion and protest. In the public health arena, campaigns continue apace, with interventions designed to convince people to adopt healthy eating habits, take steps to prevent breast cancer, and quit bullying (see Figure 14.1). Nowadays, campaigns frequently target a specialized audience of young people, relying on Web sites and Facebook. Yet although campaigns adopt a more niche, targeted approach today, they are no less important or dependent on persuasion theories.

Campaigns—colorful, vibrant and controversial—are the focus of this final chapter. The chapter is organized into several sections. The first describes the nature of campaigns. The second portion reviews major theories of campaign effects. The third section summarizes knowledge of campaign effects, focusing on key health campaigns. The final segment touches on ethical issues surrounding campaigns.

THINKING ABOUT CAMPAIGNS

> This is your brain on drugs . . . Parents: The antidrug . . . Welcome to Loserville. Population: You . . . Friends don't let friends drive drunk.

These are some of the most famous emblems of public information campaigns in the United States (see Figure 14.2). However, campaigns involve more than clever slogans. They are systematic, organized efforts to mold health or social attitudes through the use of communication. More formally, **communication campaigns** can be defined broadly as:

> (1) purposive attempts, (2) to inform, persuade, or motivate behavior changes, (3) in a relatively well-defined and large audience, (4) generally for noncommercial benefits to the individuals and/or society at large, (5) typically within a given time period, (6) by means of organized communication activities involving mass media and Internet, and (7) often complemented by interpersonal support.
>
> (Adapted from Rice & Atkin, 2009, p. 436)

People do not devise campaigns with the flick of a wrist. Campaigns require time and effort. Typically, activists or professional organizations hatch a campaign concept. They sculpt the idea, working with marketing and communication specialists; pretest

■ **Figure 14.2** This classic, decades-old anti-drug campaign advertisement is still well known today. Although its effectiveness in reducing drug use has not been conclusively documented, the ad attracted attention, due to its memorable visuals and clever use of parallel phrases.

Image courtesy of zdnet.com.

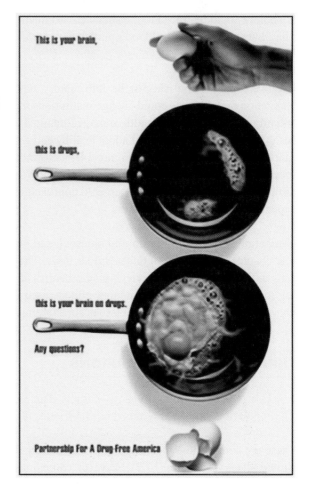

messages; and take their communications to the real world in the hope they will influence behavior.

Like advertising and marketing, health information campaigns apply theories to practical problems. However, classic advertising campaigns differ from their public information counterparts in a variety of ways:

■ Commercial advertising is designed to make a profit for companies. Information campaigns are not purely capitalistic undertakings. They are designed to promote social ideas or improve public health. Typically, pro-social projects have smaller budgets than advertising campaigns. This can limit their effectiveness. What's more, advertising can work at cross-purposes with health campaigns. Campaigns designed to promote healthy eating are thwarted by glitzy advertisements that hype junk food.

■ News plays a greater role in information campaigns than it does in advertising. Advertising involves paid commercial messages. Campaigns utilize ads, but they also attempt to relay messages through the "nonpaid media": news. For example, health education planners have worked with journalists to produce stories that discuss dangers of cigarette smoking and a high-cholesterol diet (Flora, 2001).

■ Interpersonal and organizational communication play a more important role in health campaigns than in commercial advertising. The McGruff "Take a bite out of crime" campaign supplemented media messages with supportive communication from community groups, businesses, and local police forces (O'Keefe et al., 1996; see Figure 14.3). The Stanford cardiovascular risk reduction project involved multiple communication efforts, including hundreds of educational sessions and distribution of thousands of nutrition tip sheets to grocery stores. The D.A.R.E. (Drug Abuse Resistance Education) campaign developed an elaborate school curriculum, with police officers teaching children ways to say no to drugs.

■ Advertising campaigns try to induce people to do something, like buying a six-pack of beer or soft drinks. Information campaigns often try to convince consumers *not* to perform a particular activity (*not* to smoke, litter, or drive after imbibing).

■ Information campaigns invariably face more daunting obstacles than does commercial marketing. It is usually easier to convince someone to buy a commercial product than to "buy into" the idea that she should quit smoking or change her diet.

■ Campaigns frequently target their messages at the 15 percent of the population that is least likely to change its behavior (Harris, 1999). These may be the poorest, least educated members of society, or the most down-and-out intravenous drug users who continue to share HIV-infected needles. By contrast, commercial campaigns focus on the mainstream—on those who are shopping for a product or a dream.

■ Information campaigns involve more highly charged political issues than do commercial efforts. Campaigns frequently encounter strong opposition from powerful industries, such as tobacco companies, beer distributors, oil companies, or gun manufacturers. Antitobacco campaigns, for example, have become embroiled in the politics and economics of tobacco production.

Locating Effects

What impact do campaigns and media have on public health? That's a big question; thus, you need big ideas to help you grapple with it. Communication scholars Kim Walsh-Childers and Jane D. Brown (2009) developed a framework to help explain media influences on personal and public health. They proposed that mass media effects fall into three categories: (a) intention of the message communicator (intended/unintended), (b) level of influence (personal/public), and (c) outcome (positive/negative).

■ Figure 14.3 An advertisement from a classic communication campaign, the McGruff "Take a bite out of crime" campaign. The campaign featured an animated trench-coated dog, called McGruff, who urged viewers to take steps to reduce crime. Through media and community activities, the campaign led to increases in crime prevention behaviors.

Reprinted with permission of the National Crime Prevention Council.

An effect can be intended, as when the National Campaign to Prevent Teen and Unplanned Pregnancy develops messages promoting abstinence; or unintended, as when teenage girls viewing MTV's entertainment program "Teen Mom" rethink their attitudes toward sex without contraception. The bulk of effects discussed in this chapter are intended, since they emanate from campaigns designed to influence attitudes.

A campaign effect can occur at the personal level (a public service ad convinces parents to buy a new child safety seat to protect their infant), or at the public level (a legislator decides, after watching campaign ads, to introduce a bill requiring that all new cars have a special anchoring device to keep the safety seat in place). Finally, effects can be positive, for example, producing primarily healthy outcomes, or negative, leading to mainly unhealthy consequences.

Viewed in this way, campaigns are multifaceted phenomena. They are complex events that can be examined from different points of view. A good way to begin this examination is to look at theories articulated to explain campaign effects.

THEORETICAL PERSPECTIVES

Three major models of campaigns have been developed. The first is a psychological, individual-level perspective. The other two approaches focus on the bigger picture, viewing campaigns from a macro, community-level orientation.

Psychological Approach

The psychological perspective emphasizes that you can't expect a campaign to change behavior instantly, lickety-split. Instead, change occurs gradually, in stages, in line with the ancient Chinese proverb that "a journey of a thousand miles begins with a single step." For example, J. O. Prochaska and colleagues note that people progress through different stages of change, including pre-contemplation, during which they are not aware that they have a psychological problem, contemplation, in which they begin considering how to make a change in behavior, and action, in which they actually modify risky behaviors (Prochaska, DiClemente, & Norcross, 1992; see also Hampton et al., 2009).

The preeminent psychological approach to campaigns combines stages of change with persuasive communication theory. According to McGuire (1989), persuasion can be viewed as a series of input and output steps. In Figure 14.4, the input column labels refer to standard persuasion variables out of which messages can be constructed. The output row headings correspond to the steps that individuals must be persuaded to take if the message is to have its intended impact.

INPUT: Independent (Communication) Variables / OUTPUT: Dependent Variables (Response Steps Mediating Persuasion)	SOURCE (number, unanimity, demographics, attractiveness, credibility)	MESSAGE (type of appeal, type of information, inclusion/omission, organization, repetitiveness)	CHANNEL (modality, directness, context)	RECEIVER (demographics, ability, personality, lifestyle)	DESTINATION (immediacy/delay, prevention/cessation, direct/immunization)
1. Exposure to the communication					
2. Attending to it					
3. Liking, becoming interested in it					
4. Comprehending it (learning what)					
5. Skill acquisition (learning how)					
6. Yielding to it (attitude change)					
7. Memory storage of content and/or agreement					
8. Information search and retrieval					
9. Deciding on basis of retrieval					
10. Behaving in accord with decision					
11. Reinforcement of desired acts					
12. Post-behavioral consolidating					

Figure 14.4 Persuasion and campaign stages.

From McGuire, W. J. (1989). Theoretical foundations of campaigns. In R. E. Rice & C. K. Atkin (Eds.), *Public communication campaigns* (2nd ed., pp. 43–65). Thousand Oaks, CA: Sage. Reprinted by permission of Sage.

As the figure shows, a message must clear many hurdles if it is to successfully influence attitudes and behavior. An antidrug campaign may not clear the first hurdle—exposure—because it never reaches the target audience, or alternatively because receivers, finding the message threatening, tune it out as soon as they view it. Or the message may pass the first few steps, but get knocked out of the box when it threatens deeper values or psychological needs.

The input–output matrix has an optimistic side. It says that campaigns can succeed even if they do not lead to major changes in behavior. Indeed, such changes are not always reasonable to expect, based only on short-term exposure to communications. Campaigns can be regarded as successful if they get people to remember an antidrug ad (Step 4) or if they teach them how to say no to attractive drug-using peers (Step 5). Over time, through subsequent interventions, people can be persuaded to make long-term behavioral changes (Steps 10–12).

Stage-based psychological models are useful. However, they ignore the larger context—the community and society in which campaigns take place. The next two theories address these issues.

Diffusion Theory

Developed by Everett M. Rogers (1995), **diffusion theory** examines the processes by which innovations diffuse, or spread through, society. Campaigns are viewed as large-scale attempts to communicate innovative ideas and practices through mass media and interpersonal communication. The following can be regarded as innovations:

- seat belts
- child safety seats
- designated drivers
- low-cholesterol diets
- sunscreen lotion
- pooper scoopers.

Diffusion theory identifies a number of factors that influence the adoption of innovations. An important variable is the *characteristic of the innovation*. The more compatible an innovation is with people's values and cultural norms, the more likely it is to diffuse rapidly in society. Conversely, the less congruent an innovation is with prevailing values, the less rapidly it is accepted. Environmental recycling and dropping litter in trash cans did not take hold in the 1960s because they diverged from the dominant ideologies: "Bigger is better" and "Commercial growth trumps all." Two decades later, when environmental preservation had emerged as a major cultural value, these practices were more widely adopted.

At the outset of a campaign, one usually finds the greatest resistance to adopting an innovation. Campaigns plant the seeds of cognitive change early on, reaching early adopters, who help spread the word and facilitate change among large numbers of individuals.

Another attribute of an innovation is the degree to which it promises *a clear, salient reward to the individual.* A barrier to condom use is that condoms do not offer an immediate reward. The advantage condoms offer—preventing pregnancy or HIV infection—is not visible immediately after the consummation of sex. As Rogers notes, "The unwanted event that is avoided . . . is difficult to perceive because it is a non-event, the absence of something that otherwise might have happened" (1995, p. 217). Partly because the benefits of condom use are not readily apparent, safer sex practices have not always been a quick, easy sell.

In a similar fashion, Americans have been reluctant to adopt a "green mind-set" (Gertner, 2009), in part because of the absence of rewards for adopting pro-environmental behaviors. Global warming does not viscerally scare many Americans—its effects are more abstract and distant. Diffusion theory suggests that campaigns designed to persuade people to adopt pro-environmental behaviors should either present salient rewards (such as money saved on gas from buying a Prius) or powerfully illustrate symbolic benefits of such actions.

Communication plays a critical role in the spread of innovations. Diffusion theory originally stipulated that mass media are most influential in enhancing knowledge of the innovation, while interpersonal communication is more effective in changing attitudes toward the innovation. Newer approaches suggest that campaigns can influence interpersonal communication, which can then affect health-related beliefs (Hwang, 2012).

Newspapers, television, and the Internet have unquestionably shaped knowledge and beliefs about unhealthy lifestyles. Why do you think so many people know that smoking causes cancer, buckling up can save your life, or unprotected, risky sex can lead to AIDS? The media have conveyed this information. Although the media are frequently criticized, they deserve credit for providing information about unhealthy lifestyles and ways to live a healthier life.

Spurred by activist groups, television producers have increasingly included discussion of such innovations as designated drivers, rape hotlines, and birth control pills in their programs. Other television programs have featured storylines on organ donation, reflecting concern about the 100,000 Americans desperately seeking a transplant, particularly for heart disease and diabetes. Four highly rated television shows, including *Grey's Anatomy* and *House*, devoted episodes to organ donation dilemmas. The programs had an impact on viewers' self-reported organ donation behavior, particularly when the programs encouraged donation explicitly and viewers were emotionally engaged in the narrative (Morgan, Movius, & Cody, 2009; see also Brown & Walsh-Childers, 2002).

A Down Side of Diffusion

It is not all blue skies and rosy fields when it comes to media and campaigns. Consider that poor people or those with little education frequently know less about health issues than people who are wealthier or have more education under their belts (Freimuth, 1990). One objective of campaigns is to narrow the gap between the advantaged and disadvantaged members of society. Unfortunately, just the opposite can occur. Campaigns can widen the disparity so that, by the end of the campaign, the rich and better-educated people are even more knowledgeable of the problem than their poorer, less-educated counterparts (Gaziano, 1983; Viswanath & Finnegan, 1996). This is known as the *knowledge gap*, the tendency for campaigns to increase cognitive differences between haves and have-nots in society (see Figure 14.5).

There are a number of reasons why such knowledge gaps occur. One key reason is that the health information is less likely to reach, or be cognitively accepted by, disadvantaged individuals. Those who have been disadvantaged by society may be so preoccupied with tangible survival needs that they neglect to focus on health issues that are of long-term personal importance. Researchers have identified ways to reduce

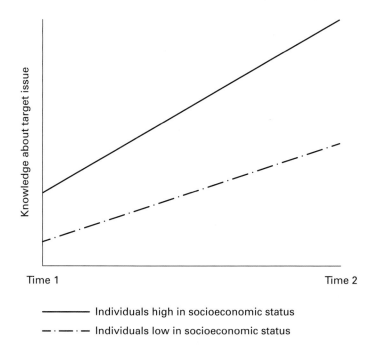

Time 1   Time 2

———— Individuals high in socioeconomic status

— · —— · — Individuals low in socioeconomic status

▨ **Figure 14.5 Schematic diagram of the knowledge gap. Communication occurs between Time 1 and Time 2.**

knowledge gaps—for example by targeting low-income individuals through tailored messages. Nonetheless, the knowledge gap is a down side—or inevitable negative consequence—of communication campaigns.

Social Marketing

Pink.

If you want to understand social marketing, think *pink*. The classic social marketing campaign is breast cancer awareness, originally symbolized by a pink ribbon and now by pink earrings, pink umbrellas, pink tote bags, and even pink clothing donned by performers during a Dallas Cowboys halftime show.

Pink was originally chosen to represent breast cancer because the color symbolizes femininity. But during October, marketed as National Breast Cancer Awareness Month, "'pink' becomes more than a color." It becomes a ubiquitous brand designed to call up concerns about breast cancer, convince women to get mammograms, and raise money for research (Singer, 2011, p. 1; see Figure 14.1). Over the past decades, organizations like the Susan G. Komen for the Cure have successfully harnessed techniques pioneered by commercial marketers, ranging from handing out free products to sponsoring races, all designed to raise consciousness about breast cancer. By employing pink marketing, Komen "has rebranded an entire disease by putting an upbeat spin on fighting it" (Singer, 2011, p. 6). It is vintage social marketing.

Social marketing has a specific definition in the academic literature. It is defined as "a process of designing, implementing, and controlling programs to increase the acceptability of a pro-social idea among population segments of consumers" (Dearing et al., 1996, p. 345). Social marketing is an intriguing concept. It says, in effect: "You know all those great ideas developed to sell products? You can use them to sell people on taking better care of their health. But to do that, you must understand marketing principles." There are five strategic steps in a social marketing campaign: (a) *planning*, (b) *theory*, (c) *communication analysis*, (d) *implementation*, and (e) *evaluation and reorientation* (Maibach, Kreps, & Bonaguro, 1993; see Figure 14.6).

Planning

During this first phase, campaigners make the tough choices. They select campaign goals. They decide whether to focus on creating cognitions or changing existing ones. They deliberate about which beliefs to target and whether to focus on attitudes or behaviors.

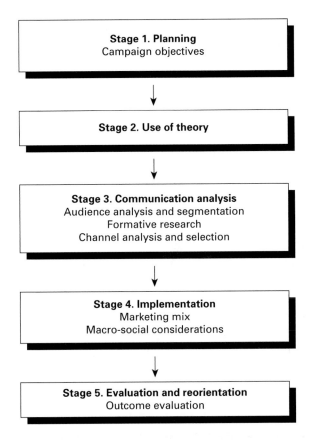

■ Figure 14.6 A strategic health communication campaign model.

Adapted from Maibach, E. W., Kreps, G. L., & Bonaguro, E. W. (1993). Developing strategic communication campaigns for HIV/AIDS prevention. In S. Ratzan (Ed.), *AIDS: Effective health communication
for the 90s* (pp. 15–35).Washington, DC: Taylor & Francis.

Theory

Models, concepts, and theories are the backbone of campaigns (Slater, 2006). You
cannot wage a campaign without some idea of what you want to achieve and how best
to attain your objectives. The central issue is whether your idea is sound, based on concepts, and of sufficient breadth so as to suggest specific hypotheses. Ideas may be cheap,
but good ideas are invaluable. One thing that differentiates effective and ineffective
campaigns is that the former reflect painstaking application of theoretical principles;
the latter are based on "seat of the pants" intuitions.

Communication Analysis

After suitable theory and concepts are selected, they must be aptly applied to the context. This occurs during the down-to-earth communication analysis phase of the campaign. Early on, campaign specialists conduct formative research to explore audience perceptions (Atkin & Freimuth, 2001). They probe targeted audience members' beliefs prior to conducting the campaign, so that they can make sure message arguments will be in sync with audience concerns. In social judgment theory terms, they want to make sure their messages fall within the latitude of acceptance and nudge people toward rethinking risky behaviors.

Implementation

During this phase, the campaign is designed, finalized, and launched. Marketing principles play a critical role here. Of particular importance are the four Ps of marketing: *product*, *price*, *placement*, and *promotion*.

Product? Most of us do not associate products with health campaigns. Yet *products* can be pro-social, as well as commercial. Products marketed in health campaigns include Neighborhood Crime Watch posters, child safety seats, gun trigger locks, and pink ribbon wristbands.

Products come with a *price*. The price can be monetary or psychological. In the AIDS context, planners debate whether to charge a price for condoms (dispensing them free of charge saves people money, but it also can make the product seem "cheap" or "unworthy"). Psychologically, the price of using condoms may be less pleasurable sex or fear of offending a partner. Campaigns devise messages to convince people that these costs are more than offset by the benefits that safe sex provides over the long haul.

Placement involves deciding where to transmit the message. This is critically important, as correct placement can ensure reaching the target audience; incorrect placement can mean that a good message misses its target. The favorite weapon in communication campaigns is the public service advertisement (PSA), a promotional message placed in news, entertainment, or interactive media. Once novel, PSAs are now part of the media landscape—informational sound bites that savvy young people have come to enjoy or ignore. Clever, informative PSAs get noticed and can shatter illusions of invulnerability; dull—or obnoxious—ones are mentally discarded.

The channel—for example, television or Internet—is a key factor in placement decisions. Television allows campaigners to reach lots of people and to arouse emotions through evocative messages. However, it is very expensive. Interactive media offer several advantages. They are usually cheaper than other media, permit upgrading of messages, and allow campaigns to tailor messages to audience subgroups (Kreuter et al., 2000; Lieberman, 2001).

Given its ubiquity and the role that online communities play in young people's everyday communication, it makes sense that campaigns are migrating to the Web and to social networking sites that can build camaraderie. Rice and Atkin (2009) describe a host of such campaigns—a pastiche of interactive games, jazzy Web sites with avatars, and even a memorable viral antismoking intervention that allows users to send smokers' coughs, calibrated by dryness and duration, to individuals to help them kick the habit.

Other health interventions have harnessed popular modalities du jour: YouTube and texting.

RealTalk, a high-tech HIV prevention program, made a funny, teenager-created YouTube video, in which condoms pelt a girl holding an umbrella, while teens shout the refrain from a rap ditty, "Sport Dat Raincoat." Other health interventions capitalize on text messages. Sex-Ed Loop, a Chicago program, provides weekly texts on disease prevention and contraception. ICYC (In Case You're Curious), a text-chat service coordinated by Planned Parenthood of the Rocky Mountains, can text teens back with answers to their questions on sexually transmitted diseases (Hoffman, 2011). The down side of online campaigns is the sheer volume of information people encounter online. Clutter and competing posts can prevent the campaign from capturing receivers' attention (Metzger, 2009).

Promotion, the final marketing P, flows out of the planning process. Promotion involves persuasion—application of theories discussed in this book and implemented in a campaign setting.

Evaluation and Reorientation

Campaign Web sites trumpet campaigns, boasting that they have had whopping, incredible success. They reduce smoking! They curb drug abuse! Before the campaign, things were terrible, and now lives have improved!

It is important to remember that campaigns frequently have a vested interest in heralding success. If the campaign shows improvement, the organizations that spearheaded it can make a forceful case that they should get more money to wage another campaign. This is why it is important to evaluate campaigns as objectively as possible, hopefully using outside agencies that are not connected to the intervention. Campaigns are evaluated through careful empirical studies that use *comparisons* as the basis for judging success.

Evaluators frequently compare those who had exposure to the campaign with a control group of others who did not have exposure. They also make over-time comparisons, looking to see if the problem has declined since the advent of the campaign. Researchers evaluate campaigns on three specific levels: *individual*, *community*, and *state*.

At the individual level, evaluators compare people who viewed or heard many campaign messages with those who were exposed to few, if any. If the intervention worked, individuals with exposure to many campaign communications should change their attitude more in the intended direction than those who were exposed to a handful or none at all.

Researchers also evaluate campaigns at the community level. One town is randomly assigned to be the treatment group. Its citizens receive promotional materials—let's say to persuade people to buckle up when they drive. An equivalent community serves as the control; its residents are not exposed to campaign messages. Researchers then compare the communities, for example, by enlisting police officers to stand on street corners counting the number of drivers wearing safety belts. If a higher proportion of drivers in the treatment community wear safety belts than in the control town, the campaign is declared a success (Roberts & Geller, 1994).

Campaigns can also be assessed at the state level. Let's assume that the number of casualties drops in Indiana shortly after the conclusion of a media campaign promoting seat belt use in the Hoosier state. Let's also assume that casualties in Iowa, a state that shares some demographic features with Indiana, do not decline over a similar time period. These data give us confidence that the Indiana campaign exerted a causal impact on seat belt behavior.

Evaluation is critical because it shows whether campaign objectives have been met. It is not a perfect science. In individual-level surveys, one never knows for sure whether those who saw campaign messages were the same in all other ways as those who did not happen to view the campaign. In community evaluations, researchers can never be 100 percent certain that the treatment and control towns are exactly alike. If the treatment community in the safety belt study had more drivers who were older (and therefore more safety conscious) than the control community, the older age of drivers, rather than the campaign, could have produced the observed effects. In a similar fashion, if the Indiana news media extensively covered an automobile accident that involved the governor's wife, the news coverage—not the campaign—could have caused the concomitant decline in traffic casualties. Researchers take precautions to factor in these extraneous variables, quantifying their contributions in statistical tests.

Online media campaigns pose a different set of procedural problems. It can be difficult to convince individuals, who are randomly assigned to a particular intervention, to attend to a Web-based campaign. Sites that house campaigns can disappear or change without warning, and different subgroups in a particular sample may answer different portions of the questionnaire (Rice & Atkin, 2009).

These difficulties notwithstanding, evaluation research offers a valuable way to assess campaign impact. It gives campaigners useful feedback for future campaigns. It also serves an important political function. Private and public groups spend hundreds of thousands of dollars on campaigns. They are entitled to know if they have gotten their money's worth. When government spends taxpayer money on antismoking or antidrug campaigns, the public has a right to know if socially valuable goals—reducing smoking or drug use—have actually been achieved.

Evaluation in action: Montana Meth Project. Methamphetamine is an addictive synthetic drug that can wreak devastating effects. In Montana the state government has spent close to $50 million each year, trying to deal with costs of meth abuse. In an effort to remedy the problem, a non-profit organization launched an anti-meth campaign some years back, blitzing the airwaves and plastering billboards with hard-hitting, graphic ads. The ads are compelling, capitalizing on fear and vividness appeals (to view them, see http://www.montanameth.org/ads). The Montana Meth Project says the campaign has significantly reduced meth use and meth-related crimes.

But has it? A systematic evaluation, published in a scientific journal, offers a more skeptical conclusion (Erceg-Hurn, 2008). The study concludes that there is no evidence that the campaign reduced use of methamphetamine. Showcasing the important role comparisons play in research, the researcher noted that any reductions in meth usage in Montana could have occurred *not* because of the advertisements, but for another reason. Stricter laws were adopted in 2005, around the time the campaign began. These laws reduced the availability of meth in Montana communities and may have been responsible for some of the positive effects that proponents attributed to the campaign. This is not to say the campaign had no effects. It may have raised awareness about the problem and changed some people's attitudes. However, it does not appear to have exerted the striking effects that its planners claimed. This highlights the importance of conducting hard-nosed empirical evaluations of campaigns (see Figure 14.7).

Real-World Constraints

Campaigns may be based on theory, planned according to marketing principles, and evaluated through high-powered statistics. However, they take place in the real world, with its rough edges, cultural norms, and political constraints. Societal norms and macrosocial factors influence campaigns in a variety of ways. Antismoking campaigns had little chance of changing attitudes so long as most Americans trusted the tobacco

■ **Figure 14.7 There are many campaign message appeals out there that are designed to convince young people not to use methamphetamine. Some campaigns may be effective, others less so. As evaluation research makes clear, we cannot assume campaigns work unless there is evidence documenting their effects.**

Image courtesy of Favors and Voices of Recovery—South Africa.

companies or doubted that smoking caused cancer. As evidence mounted that smoking causes cancer and Americans learned that tobacco companies withheld knowledge that smoking was addictive, antismoking campaigns faced a more receptive audience to their messages. Even so (and not surprisingly), antismoking campaigns attempting to increase public support for regulation of the tobacco industry have faced daunting opposition from the tobacco industry, as the gripping, factually based movie *The Insider* documented.

In a similar vein, the alcohol industry—for example beer manufacturers—fought effort, spearheaded by grassroots groups like Mothers Against Drunk Driving (MADD) to reduce drunk driving. In the 1980s, the industry opposed an innocuous bill that aimed to force states to approve laws that banned the sale of alcohol to individuals under the age of 21 (Lerner, 2011). President Ronald Reagan signed the bill into law, but only after extensive lobbying from MADD.

For much of the 20th century American culture promoted or tolerated drunk driving with a wink and a nod. Anti-drunk driving campaigns, such as those eventually developed by MADD, initially had a hard cultural road to hoe. Little by little, MADD made inroads on cultural beliefs about drinking and driving (see Box 14.1). Its message that drunk driving was a disgrace, young children were routinely killed by drunk drivers, and that laws needed to be changed diffused widely through American culture in the

1980s and 1990s. MADD's campaigns have been stunningly effective over the course of the past decades, but they had to overcome initial cultural and political resistance.

Thus, there are many social and cultural factors that determine campaign success. You cannot understand communication campaigns without appreciating the larger milieu in which they take place. Health campaigns frequently face opposition from entrenched political and business groups. Antismoking and anti-drunk driving campaigns are examples of successful interventions that harnessed principles of persuasion and public relations to change cultural norms. But there is no guarantee that campaigns will succeed.

BOX 14.1 MADD AS HELL AT DRUNK DRIVERS

Candy Lightner was an unlikely leader of a cultural movement. A 33-year-old mother of three children, she was not even registered to vote. She worked in real estate, not social activism. All this changed on May 13, 1980. Her 13-year-old daughter Cari, "who loved to talk on the phone, cook, imitate people, and play basketball and softball," was on her way to a carnival in Fair Oaks, California. Barely a teenager, Cari was walking down a suburban street when a drunk driver suddenly struck and killed her, hurling her body 125 feet (Lerner, 2011, p. 83).

As a grieving Candy moved ahead, making preparations for the funeral, she began to learn details of the hit-and-run accident. The driver, quickly located by police, had been drunk and had four previous drinking-while-intoxicated arrests. Candy asked a patrolman familiar with the case if the driver would go to prison. "Lady," he said bluntly, "you'll be lucky if he sees any time in jail at all, much less prison. That's the way the system works" (Lerner, 2011, p. 83).

Candy was furious. "I was fuming. I felt enraged and helpless," she said. She could not believe that a driver could escape punishment for a crime of this magnitude. Her anger was overpowering. How could she cope? She decided to form an organization to inform the public. "And you are going to call it Mothers Against Drunk Drivers," her friend Leslie presciently announced.

Candy soon became a woman on a mission. Every day she showed up at California Governor Jerry Brown's office and pushed him to launch a task force

Continued

on drunk driving. It took a while, but Brown eventually appointed a commission. Candy became a media darling, appearing on the *Today* show, *60 Minutes*, and the *Phil Donahue Show*. As historian Barron H. Lerner explained, "Lightner was attractive, photogenic, and able to cry in public, fiercely debate opponents, and supply pithy sound bites" (p. 85). "If you want to drink, that's your business. But as soon as you drink and get behind the wheel of a car, it becomes my business," she memorably said.

Employing communication campaign strategies, she worked with another mother whose daughter had been paralyzed by a drunk driver, arousing sympathy. Members of the growing MADD organization spoke at community events, held public vigils, and appealed to reporters for news coverage. Press coverage increased exponentially, helping to build a national movement. The national media campaign, with the Ad Council's brainchild slogan "Friends don't let friends drive drunk," became known to just about everyone with a television set (Lerner, 2011). Working with Hollywood production studios, television networks, and the Harvard School of Public Health, campaigners succeeded in placing dialogue or messages in 160 entertainment programs. Viewers heard a new alliterative phrase: designated driver. It caught on quickly, as it was mentioned in such top-rated 1980s hit programs as *Beverly Hills 90210*, *Growing Pains*, and *Cheers* (Winsten & DeJong, 2001).

Importantly, the media messages played on EPPM and social marketing principles. They aroused fear and provided a simple, readily understandable solution to a problem. They described the price of drunk driving in human terms, and placed promotional spots on TV entertainment programs.

For a long time the campaign experienced nothing but success. President Ronald Reagan signed the Minimum Legal Drinking Age Law. The law employed economic leverage to force states to pass laws that banned the sale of alcohol to individuals under the age of 21. Other laws followed, including a 0.10 percent blood alcohol content limit, license revocation, and required jail time for repeat offenders. No social movement can sustain this level of success. Internal divisions occur, opposition groups organize, and established interests rebound. So it was with MADD. Leaders faced criticism of financial mismanagement. Even MADD's proponents raised eyebrows when in 1993 Lightner, who had developed considerable skills in lobbying, joined a public relations firm that represented the American Beverage Institute, a trade association. The association worked with national restaurant chains that served liquor.

PSAs, which for years had seemed so simple, now stirred controversy. Young people began to complain that popular antidrinking PSAs were corny, cheesy, and preachy (Andsager, Austin, & Pinkleton, 2001; see also Slater et al., 1998). Some PSAs failed to provide a realistic discussion of drinking. Still other campaigns failed to create messages powerful enough to undo the effects of sexy, slick pro-drinking commercial spots.

Faced with these communication and management issues, MADD adapted. It also adopted a stronger presence on the Web and in social media. On balance, the organization has done much good. Thanks to its activists' hard work, the legal blood alcohol content was lowered from .15 percent to .08 percent. The legal drinking age is 21, and the culture of tacit approval of drunk driving has changed dramatically (Lerner, 2011).

Yet in a country where some 16,000 people are killed in drunk driving crashes a year, more persuasion campaign interventions are needed.

CAMPAIGN EFFECTS

Do campaigns work? Do they influence targeted attitudes and behaviors? What do you think? What is your best guess?

There is little question that campaigns face an uphill battle. As McGuire's matrix stipulates, interventions must first attract the target audience and capture its attention. This can be difficult. For a variety of psychological reasons, Caroline Schooler and colleagues note, "Those whom a campaign most seeks to reach with health information are the least motivated to pay attention to it" (1998, p. 414). The last thing addicted smokers, drug users, or gamblers want to do is pay attention to moralistic messages that tell them to stop doing what makes them happy.

Today's teenagers have grown up with health campaigns and have been lectured and hectored by well-meaning, but sometimes-overbearing, adults. When a media campaign tells them that they are engaging in unhealthy behavior, they can become resistant and reactive. The message may evoke a threat to their freedom, leading them to embrace the unhealthy behavior that the communicator condemns (see Burgoon et al., 2002; Dillard & Shen, 2005; Rains, 2013; Shen, 2010). *Psychological reactance theory* suggests that an overly moralistic health message can threaten an individual's freedom and self-determination, sometimes causing the individual to do precisely the opposite of what the communicator recommends (Brehm, 1966). This may be especially likely when the threatened freedom is important (Quick, Shen, & Dillard, 2013). (As parents sang in a song from the musical, *The Fantasticks*: "Why did the kids put beans in their ears? No one can hear with beans in their ears. After a while the reason appears. They did it cause we said no!" Or, as a character in the movie *Hudson Hawk* said, "I hated cigarettes until I saw my first No Smoking sign!")

There is no guarantee a campaign will work. It may fail, and plenty do. There are five major barriers to the success of a health information campaign:

1. Campaigns do not reach or influence those most affected by the problem.
2. Campaign messages may be lost in the clutter of modern Internet and media.
3. Although aims are well intentioned, messages may not be in sync with how the target audience thinks or feels about the problem.
4. Campaigns may arouse **reactance**, turning target audience members off with preachy messages that may smack of middle-aged adult values.
5. Campaign messages are swamped by the prevailing values of mass culture, as when an anti-obesity campaign cannot compete with marketing for fast food and high-calorie junk food.

Okay—but I wouldn't be devoting an entire chapter to this topic if campaigns failed consistently and repeatedly! In fact, a half-century of research indicates that if practitioners know their stuff, apply theory deftly, and utilize principles of social marketing, they can wage effective campaigns (Noar, 2006). Campaigns can and have changed health-related attitudes. Over the past 30 years, there have been sharp declines in adolescent smoking, alcohol and marijuana use, and sexual activity. For example, in 1980, approximately a third of high school seniors had smoked cigarettes in the past month; in 2011 that number had fallen to less than 1 in 5 (Parker-Pope, 2012). While many factors account for these effects, studies suggest that campaigns contributed to declines in adolescent risk taking.

Research has identified a number of concrete steps that campaign planners should take to maximize the likelihood of success. Campaigns are particularly likely to succeed when practitioners:

1. Understand the audience and tailor messages so they connect with the audience needs and preexisting attitudes (Wan, 2008; Cesario, Grant, & Higgins, 2004).
2. Segment the audience into different subgroups, fitting messages ever more exquisitely to the needs of specialized groups.
3. Refine messages so that they are relevant, cogent, and of high production value; this is particularly important when targeting young people, who have grown up with savvy, interactive media.

4. Coordinate efforts across media, and repeat messages over time and in different media and interpersonal channels.
5. Supplement media materials as much as possible with community contacts and participation (McAlister & Fernandez, 2002; Rice & Atkin, 2002).
6. Appreciate that it is frequently easier to promote a new behavior than to convince people to stop a dysfunctional behavior (Snyder, 2001).
7. Design messages so that they cultivate social norms regarding appropriate behavior. (For example, antismoking campaigns capitalized on social norms that it is neither healthy nor cool to smoke.)
8. Adopt a realistic approach. Keep in mind how difficult it is to change deep-seated attitudes and well-learned behaviors. "Set realistic expectations of success . . . , be prepared for a long haul . . . , [and] give more emphasis to relatively attainable impacts, by aiming at more receptive segments of the audience and by creating or promoting more palatable positive products" (Atkin, 2002, p. 37).

With these factors in mind, it is time to turn to specific applications of campaign principles. The next section describes three different types of health campaigns. The first series of campaigns exemplify interventions that have had considerable success. The second group of interventions experienced a mixed record of success, pointing up complexities in health campaigns. The third area of campaigns showcases the inter-section between persuasion and social structural factors.

ANTISMOKING AND CARDIOVASCULAR RISK REDUCTION CAMPAIGNS

Antismoking interventions are among the most famous public information campaigns in America. Many of us recall seeing vivid messages that associate cigarettes with ugly, despicable images or suggest that no one cool smokes anymore. Guided by theory, campaigns have applied cognitive, affective, and behavioral concepts to the development of campaigns (see, for example, Figure 14.8).

Cognitively based campaigns have targeted children's beliefs about smoking and the types of people who smoke. Guided by the Reasoned Action Model, researchers identify perceived drawbacks of smoking. "It's a gross habit, it smells . . . Even just being around people who smoke, you know, my eyes start to water and burn," children told researchers Laura A. Peracchio and David Luna, who used this information to devise antismoking messages (1998, p. 51). Based on findings that short-term negative consequences of smoking (bad smell and harm to eyes) are of central importance to kids, the researchers developed print ads that played on these themes:

■ **Figure 14.8a–c** Antismoking campaigns have employed an endless variety of appeals to change attitudes toward smoking. Over the long haul, the campaigns have helped to reduce smoking levels in the United States.

Image courtesy of Tobacco News.

One of the ads, "Sock," depicts a dirty, grimy sweatsock with the caption, "Gross," next to an ashtray full of cigarette butts with the caption, "Really gross" . . . [A second] ad, "Tailpipe," reads, "Inhale a lethal dose of carbon monoxide and it's called suicide. Inhale a smaller amount and it's called smoking. Believe it or not, cigarette smoke contains the same poisonous gas as automobile exhaust. So if you wouldn't consider sucking on a tailpipe, why would you want to smoke?"

(Peracchio & Luna, 1998, p. 53)

The first ad was simple and concrete; it worked well with 7- and 8-year-olds. The second was more complex and resonated more with 11-year-olds.

A more elaborate intervention, devised by Michael Pfau and his associates, succeeded in stiffening adolescents' resistance to experimenting with cigarettes. Pfau drew on inoculation theory, a cognitive approach discussed in Chapter 7. Persuaders employing inoculations expose audience members to a message they want them to reject, then follow up this initial treatment with a dose of powerful arguments refuting the message. Applying inoculation to antismoking, Pfau and Van Bockern (1994) told seventh-grade students that peer pressure would cause some of them to modify their opposition to smoking and begin to smoke. This was subsequently followed by statements that smoking was cool or won't affect "me," coupled with *refutations* of these arguments. The inoculation treatment intensified negative attitudes toward smoking.

Affectively oriented campaigns focus on feelings associated with smoking. Tobacco advertising has succeeded in linking smoking with relaxation, pleasant affect, and popularity (Romer & Jamieson, 2001). To counter this, campaigns apply association and accessibility concepts, linking smoking with negative images. For example:

In one ad . . . a young male is chewing tobacco and spitting it from time to time into a soft drink paper cup. His female friend, whose attention is absorbed by the movie they are watching, mechanically grabs the cup and reaches it to her mouth without looking inside. A scream is then heard, suggesting that the friend was horrified and disgusted when she tasted the liquid and, by extension, was also horrified and disgusted by her friend's behavior . . . [In another ad], a beautiful girl is smoking a cigarette, but each time she inhales her face is covered with more and more nicotine and tar. This ad creates a huge aesthetic dissonance and shows that, regardless of how attractive you are, smoking makes you repulsive.

(Ohme, 2000, p. 315)

Behavioral interventions draw on social learning theory, a model developed by Albert Bandura. Noting that, unlike rats and pigeons, people do not have to be rewarded to learn new behaviors, Bandura (1977) called attention to the powerful role that observing role models plays in social influence. Theorists have adapted his ideas to public health.

The classic and most elaborate of these interventions were developed at Stanford University in the 1970s (Maccoby & Farquhar, 1975). The campaigns included TV spots, radio PSAs, and a weekly doctor's column that appeared in Spanish-language newspapers. School curricula, workplace classes, and intensive interpersonal instruction supplemented the media messages. During interpersonal sessions, counselors used behavior modification techniques, encouraging smokers to substitute sugar-free lozenges and asking others to keep track of the healthy food they ate each week.

The campaigns had modest effects, smaller than some anticipated, but practically significant (Hornik, 2002). The Stanford communications increased knowledge of healthy eating, diet, and exercise. What's more, communities that received the campaign displayed significant decreases in cholesterol level and blood pressure.

State Antismoking Campaigns

A number of states have launched statewide interventions to curb smoking, calling on monies available from the legal settlement with the tobacco companies. In these cases, states have blitzed the airwaves with antismoking messages. Armed with as much as $90 million, campaigners have enlisted help from creative advertising agencies, developing compelling PSAs. One ad "used actual footage from a congressional hearing, during which the chief executives of each of the major tobacco companies denied, under oath, that nicotine was addictive. The advertisement culminated with the question, 'Do they think we're stupid?'" (Pierce, Emery, & Gilpin, 2002, p. 100).

Campaigns in California, Arizona, Massachusetts, and elsewhere in the United States have significantly influenced smoking attitudes and behavior (Burgoon, Hendriks, & Alvaro, 2001; Pierce et al., 2002; Siegel & Biener, 2002). A multimillion-dollar, decade-long campaign seems to have produced a sharp decline in cigarette consumption in California (see Figure 14.9). An Arizona media campaign that endlessly repeated the hip phrase, "*Tobacco: Tumor-causing, teeth-staining, smelly, puking habit*," pushed young people to evaluate smoking more negatively. In addition, media PSAs, coupled with school-based smoking prevention programs, reduced smoking by 35 percent in portions of the U.S. Northeast and Northwest (Worden & Flynn, 2002).

Summary

At the outset, few believed that tobacco education stood much of a chance, in light of the political and economic power wielded by cigarette companies. However, health

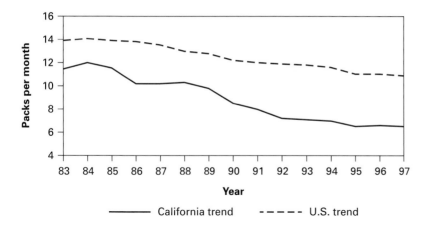

■ **Figure 14.9 Seasonally adjusted trend of per capita cigarette consumption, California versus the United States.**

Note: Smoking dropped in the United States and California from 1983 to 1997, but the rate of decline increased dramatically in California after the state's smoking campaign began in 1989. In the rest of the United States, it did not. Smoking consumption in California was also below that of the rest of the United States.

From Pierce, J. P., Emery, S., & Gilpin, E. (2002). The California tobacco control program: A long-term health communication project. In R. Hornik (Ed.), *Public health communication: Evidence for behavior change* (pp. 97–114). Mahwah, NJ: Lawrence Erlbaum Associates.

communication campaigns have succeeded in changing attitudes toward smoking, promoting bans on secondhand smoke, and creating a public opinion climate that has made it easier for attorneys to sue tobacco companies successfully for damages. Since the advent of antismoking campaigns, the smoking rate among U.S. adults has declined precipitously—from 37 percent in 1974 to just over 20 percent in 2009, with similar drops among teenagers reported more recently (Parker-Pope, 2012; Scott, 2010). By riding the wave of a contemporary public health movement, seizing on antipathy to Big Tobacco, appealing to American values of self-improvement, and helping to pass election referenda to ban smoking in public places, the David of anticigarette marketing has successfully battled the Goliath of American tobacco companies. While many Americans smoke—and they always will, as long as cigarettes are legal—the contemporary antismoking movement will long be remembered for helping create a cleaner, smoke-free environment in the United States.

SOCIAL NORMS MARKETING

It isn't clear whether Leslie Baltz, who was in her fourth year [at the University of Virginia], wanted to drink that much. The 21-year-old honor student, who had a double major in art history and studio art, liked to paint and sketch. Once, at the age of 11, she wrote 31 poems for her mother, one for each day of the month, about love, dreams, and impermanence.

At a party that Saturday, Ms. Baltz drank enough booze-spiked punch that she decided to lie down at a friend's house while her buddies went out. When they returned that night after U. Va.'s 34–20 upset of Virginia Tech, they found her unconscious at the foot of a stairway. Ms. Baltz's blood-alcohol level was 0.27%, more than triple the state's legal limit for drivers, but probably survivable if not for her fall . . . She was declared dead of head injuries. Thus, Ms. Baltz became the fifth Virginia college student to die of alcohol-related causes that autumn, and the 18th at U. Va. since 1990.

(Murray & Gruley, 2000, p. A10)

Unfortunately, Leslie is not the only student to have died as a result of alcohol abuse. Accidents due to drinking claim too many students' lives each year. Drinking, of course, is common on campus. Over 90 percent of students have tried alcohol, close to 25 percent display symptoms of problem drinkers, and others report experiences such as these over the course of a year:

- Had a hangover: 62.8 percent
- Got nauseated or vomited: 53.8 percent
- Drove a car while under the influence: 31.3 percent
- Were taken advantage of sexually: 12.2 percent
- Took advantage of someone else sexually: 5.1 percent.

(Murray & Gruley, 2000)

Still others can be defined as "binge drinkers"—men who consume at least five, and women who drink four or more, drinks in one sitting (see Figure 14.10).

For years, universities used a pastiche of antidrinking appeals, ranging from scare tactics to pictures of cars destroyed by drunk drivers. Convinced that these did not work and searching for something new, they opted to employ a technique based on communication research and social marketing. Called social norms marketing, the strategy draws on the psychology of norms—what we think important others are doing or what we think important others believe we *should* do (Fishbein & Ajzen, 2010; Goldstein & Cialdini, 2007; Park et al., 2009). In the case of drinking, it targets students' perceptions that

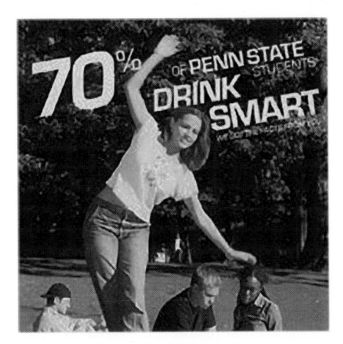

■ **Figure 14.10 Binge drinking has been a major problem on some college campuses. One strategy to alleviate the problem is social norms marketing, as shown in the example above. The strategy has met with mixed success.**

Image courtesy of the Penn State University Collegian.

others drink a lot. The idea is that students overestimate how much alcohol their peers consume. Believing that everyone else drinks a lot and wanting to fit into the dominant college culture, they drink more than they would like. The solution follows logically: *"If students' drinking practices are fostered, or at least maintained, by the erroneous perception that other students feel more positively toward these practices than they do,"* two scholars noted, *"then correcting this misperception should lower their alcohol consumption"* (Schroeder & Prentice, 1998, p. 2153). *Social norms marketing*, appealing to a desire to fit in with the peer culture, devises campaign messages suggesting that students hold incorrect social norms about drinking, believing drinking is more common than it actually is.

A number of universities have adopted this approach in an effort to curb alcohol abuse. The University of Virginia placed posters in the blue and orange school colors in freshman dorms. "Most U. Va. 1st years have 0 to 4 drinks per week," posters declared. A Rutgers University "RU SURE?" campaign devised messages listing the top 10 misperceptions on campus, ranging from the humorous ("It's easy to find a parking place on campus") to the critical ("Everyone who parties gets wasted"). The latter was followed with the answer that two-thirds of Rutgers students stop at three or fewer drinks (Lederman et al., 2001). At Washington State University, Project Culture Change blanketed the campus with posters that said, "Heavy drinking at WSU has decreased every year for the past five years."

What's the verdict? Do social norm campaigns work? The evidence is mixed. Northern Illinois University implemented a social norms campaign in an attempt to reduce the number of students who thought binge drinking was the campus norm. Prior to the campaign, 70 percent of the students believed binge drinking was common practice. By the campaign's conclusion, the percentage had dropped to 51 percent. Self-reported binge drinking decreased by nearly 9 percent during this period (Haines & Spear, 1996). Other studies, using more finely tuned scientific methods, have reported similar findings (Godbold & Pfau, 2000; Perkins & Craig, 2003; Schroeder & Prentice, 1998).

These results have intrigued scholars, but raised questions. Some wonder whether students genuinely changed their views or were just saying they had, in order to comply with the norm of pleasing the faculty investigator. Other scholars doubt that simply providing correct information is sufficient to overcome the more emotional reasons why people choose to drink (Austin & Chen, 1999). Lindsey Polonec and colleagues (2006) raised more serious questions. In a study of Penn State undergraduates' perceptions of social norms, they discovered that over 70 percent of respondents did not believe that most students drank "0 to 4" drinks when they partied. If the social norm is not credible with students, the message will not persuade them. The researchers also found that social norms messages are singularly ineffective in reaching an important target of the campaign: hard-core drinkers. Other carefully conducted studies have also cast doubt on the effectiveness of various university-based social norms campaigns (Cameron & Campo, 2006; Campo & Cameron, 2006; Russell, Clapp, & DeJong, 2005; Yanovitzky, Stewart, & Lederman, 2006).

Thus, we glimpse the complex issues surrounding social norms marketing. It is guided by theory, but its record in practice has been mixed at best. A Washington State University project (see Box 14.2) offers suggestions on how to devise messages that increase the likelihood that a social norm intervention can influence target audience members.

BOX 14.2 PROBING PERCEPTIONS OF AN ANTIDRINKING CAMPAIGN

How do researchers devise messages that are in sync with target audience members? They ask audience members to indicate what they think about campaign messages and seek to revise communications in light of their suggestions. A group of communication researchers employed this approach when they evaluated a social norms intervention some years back (Hansen et al., 2000). The researchers conducted in-depth interviews with a variety of Washington State University (WSU) freshmen, asking them pointed questions about binge drinking and campaign messages. Here is some of what they found:

Moderator: Some of you say that 16 to 17 drinks is binge drinking. Do you think, on average, that's what a lot of people do?

A.C. (a student): Well, for guys and girls, it's, like, different.

Kelly (a student): It depends on the girl.

Moderator: On average, how many drinks do you think the average person has when they go out?

A.C.: If you're drinking to get drunk, then you will have a lot, but if you're drinking to socialize and, like, meet some girls or something like that, then you just want to be buzzed so you're just like sort of loose, and you don't have inhibitions or anything like that.

Moderator: Do you think drinking is a problem on the WSU campus?

A.C.: We drink a lot more than some of the other college campuses I have been on.

Lisa (a student): I think everybody knows about it because Pullman is out in the middle of nowhere. What else is there to do but go out and party?

A.C.: We should form a drinking team (laughter from the group).

Moderator: So at what point do you think that drinking is out of control?

A.C.: I think if you're passing out every time you drink.

Lisa: I think it's either passing out or just blacking out. If you do that every single time you drink, then maybe that's out of control.

Moderator: (Presents an ad with students rock climbing. The copy reads: "Most WSU students drink moderately. Heavy drinking at WSU has decreased every year for the past five years.") Okay, what do you guys think of this one?

Zach: What's with the people climbing?

A.C.: Most people don't drink when they're rock climbing. As that would be very dangerous.

Continued

Moderator: Do you think the ad would be more effective if there were people with alcohol in the pictures? Basically, are you saying that the message in the ad just isn't believable?

Kelly: Well, the message is maybe okay, but the pictures just really don't go.

Zach: That's a believable message though.

Kelly: It's very believable—but just different pictures.

(Excerpts adapted from Hansen et al., 2000)

Note: The interviewers' questions were folksy and tapped into students' beliefs. To their credit, students responded openly and genuinely. Based on the interviews, the researchers concluded that university freshmen were not educated about binge drinking (they defined binge drinking as having 16 drinks or puking, when in fact bingeing involves having 4 to 5 drinks or more on a single occasion). Researchers concluded that messages should emphasize the impact of drinking on students' lives. Ads, they suggested, should contain pictures that relate more to the message. This type of research provides useful insights into students' perceptions, suggesting more effective ways to appeal to a target audience.

INTERVENTIONS TO REDUCE HEALTH-CARE DISPARITIES

"Racial and ethnic minorities tend to receive a lower quality of health care than non-minorities, even when access-related factors, such as patients' insurance status and income, are controlled," concluded the authors of a major book on the topic (Smedley, Stith, & Nelson, 2003, p. 1). The disparities are particularly disturbing in the case of African-Americans. Blacks have the highest mortality rate of any U.S. racial or ethnic group, approximately 1.6 times higher than that of Whites. Blacks have the highest incidence of cancer, diabetes, and infant mortality of any U.S. racial or ethnic group (Kreps, 2006; see also Harrington, 2013).

Recognizing the impact of similarity and personalized appeals that hit home to respondents, campaign specialists have tailored messages to fit individuals' particular needs and values. There has been considerable research in this area over the past decade, typified by an insightful series of studies reported by Marci Kramish Campbell and Lisa M. Quintiliani (2006). Campbell and her colleagues have developed interventions based on the ELM, the source similarity principle, and principles of tailoring messages to fit the needs of target respondents.

Focusing on African-Americans, some living in low-income areas, they designed messages to change attitudes toward diet and exercise, recognizing that modifications in diet and recreational activity may ward off cancer. The researchers adopted a multifaceted approach to campaigns, devising communications that work on different levels. On the psychological level, the researchers crafted personalized newsletters that called on abiding religious values held by respondents, with testimonials from trusted religious sources. Individuals also viewed videotapes that demonstrate how to prepare healthy fruit- and vegetable-based meals. On the organizational level, Campbell and her colleagues worked with Black churches, which command considerable respect in traditional African-American communities. Gaining persuasive support from church pastors, they helped to organize church activities that promote healthy eating. Working on the level of the larger community, the researchers held community events designed to promote awareness of dietary change, such as some that involved the local farmers' markets.

Their interventions exerted significant effects. For example, one tailored intervention produced significant increases in participants' consumption of fruits and vegetables, as well as recreational exercise. It also led to increases in the number of people who sought screening for colorectal cancer, a disease to which Blacks are more susceptible than Whites, for reasons steeped in part in social-structural inequities (Campbell & Quintiliani, 2006).

Positive as these findings are, there remain persistent systemic barriers to the long-term success of campaigns designed to reduce racial (or class) differences in health care. To be sure, a campaign may change attitudes or convince patients that they can exert more control over their health (see, for instance, Smith-McLallen & Fishbein, 2009). However, the intervention may not produce long-term change in behavior because poor minority individuals lack access to health care or transportation to take them to a doctor for a regular check-up. If they do not have a primary care doctor, they may not get regular check-ups that can spot medical problems when a cure is still possible. If they have long harbored a distrust of medical professionals, they may not accept the advice of well-intentioned physicians and nurses. Thus, social-structural factors set limits on the degree to which health campaigns can change attitudes. There is a silver lining, however. Although campaigns cannot relieve structural impediments, they can help individuals rethink their resistance to altering dysfunctional dietary behaviors. This in turn can lead to incremental change in health behaviors that over the long haul may lead to improvements in health. Hopefully, as these improvements become known to other members of a community, via diffusion of health information and the execution of subsequent interventions, more and more people will begin making changes in diet, physical exercise, and use of risky drugs, providing healthy role models for children.

VALUES AND ETHICS

You know the old game "Where's Waldo?" that you played when you were a kid? You would try to spot the cagey character, Waldo, who was hiding somewhere in the picture of a house or outdoors scene. He was always there; you just had to locate his where-abouts. So it is with values and ethical aspects of campaigns, an issue touched on but not directly broached in this chapter. Noted one ethicist, "They are always there, the value judgments: the choices in policy decisions. There are always choices made" (Guttman, 2000, p. 70).

It is nice to think of campaigns as these objective entities, planned by scientifically minded behavioral engineers, implemented by marketing specialists, and evaluated by statisticians. To be sure, campaigns are devised by social science and communication professionals who call on the science and art of persuasive communication in the development of health messages. Yet inevitably, choices must be made. Values and ethics are an inescapable part of persuasion, all the more so in the case of health campaigns which involve larger social and cultural issues. These are six key, value-based issues that face health campaign practitioners:

- *What is the locus of the dilemma?* Planners of a childhood obesity campaign may perceive that the source of the problem is children and their parents. In this case, they would direct messages at kids, moms, and dads, employing media channels they use at home, individually or as a family. Campaign organizers may contend instead that the problem lies with schools that serve lunches kids love—cheese-burgers and fries—but which are filled with transfats. If they locate the dilemma at this level, they would direct messages to school boards and school administrators, as well as to children in the school setting. Alternatively, planners may believe the problem is more social-structural, rooted in American culture's infatuation with fast food and the money restaurants make from serving fatty meals. If so, they might decide to focus their energies on convincing the city board of health to ban the use of transfats in restaurant cooking. Thus, the perceived locus of the problem will influence campaign strategies and choice of social marketing techniques (Dutta, 2006; Dutta-Bergman, 2005).
- *If the goal is to benefit the public good, is the campaign designed to do more good for certain members of the public than for others?* There is no absolute definition of "public good." Instead, the definition inevitably reflects value judgments. Should good be defined in utilitarian terms—a cardiovascular risk reduction campaign designed to reach the greatest number of people? Or should it be viewed in a more deontological fashion, emphasizing values like justice—as when planners of a blood pressure screening campaign, acknowledging that poverty induces stress that can elevate blood pressure, choose to focus primarily on poor people? Should

campaign specialists direct the campaign at a large, heterogeneous population, knowing full well the intervention may increase knowledge gaps? Or should the campaign focus critical attention at low socio-economic individuals to reduce the likelihood of enhanced gaps in knowledge? As Nurit Guttman asks, "Should campaign resources be devoted to target populations believed to be particularly needy or those who are more likely to adopt its recommendations?" (1997, p. 181). Given scarce resources, which strategy makes more sense?

■ *Are the costs of focusing on a particular audience segment worth the benefits?* Segmenting campaign audiences into different demographic groups is usually a worthwhile strategy. Segmentation can make it more likely that the campaign will reached the target audience. However, it can also lead to stigmatization, as when a well-publicized AIDS campaign focuses particular efforts at gay men in a particular city, or an anti-teen pregnancy campaign directs considerable attention on low-income minorities in particular neighborhoods. Campaign planners might reason that the campaign should focus efforts on particular groups from a public health perspective. But if the intervention produces more stigmatization than health gains, were the benefits worth the cost? (See Hornik & Ramirez, 2006 for engaging discussion of these and related issues.)

■ *How are values implicated in the solutions campaigners recommend?* The recommended solution inevitably reflects a particular set of values. An AIDS prevention campaign that urges people to practice safer sex has opted not to communicate the values of abstinence, or waiting to have sex until you are married. Why not? Social norm-based antidrinking campaigns advocate moderate drinking, an option that some parents oppose. Is this the best option?

■ *How do values influence criteria used to proclaim success?* Evaluators must devise benchmarks that can be used to determine if a campaign has succeeded. Values come into play here. For example, an intervention to promote breast cancer screening could be deemed successful if it increased the number of women who had mammograms yearly. However, given that those most likely to get mammograms are women with insurance that covers the procedure, the criterion for success may exclude poor women (Guttman, 2000). Once again, the evaluator may reason that a campaign cannot do everything and note that increases in mammography, even among those with insurance policies, is an achievement. That may be a reasonable call, but it reflects a certain set of value judgments.

■ Finally, although different values shape campaigns, all campaigns are based on a core assumption: *the world will be a better place if social interventions try to change individual behavior.* Campaigns assume that social marketing interventions to change behavior and improve the public health are worthwhile ventures. However, in some cases campaigns launched with good intentions may have unintended effects. Consider the case of campaigns to increase awareness of prostate cancer. These campaigns have caused false alarms, leading people to overestimate their chances of dying from cancer, in turn creating unnecessary anxiety (Singer, 2009). What's more, on a philosophical level, campaigns can be at odds with a strict libertarianism that regards individual liberty as an unshakeable first principle. Libertarians would question why we need campaigns, since people know that smoking causes cancer but choose to smoke, or know all about the risks of HIV but prefer to practice unsafe sex because it's fun. Don't people have a right to make their own choices and live life according to their own rules, even those that strike others as self-destructive?

It is a good question, one that philosophers have been asking in one fashion or another for centuries. Campaigns must necessarily balance individual liberties and the public good. Both are important values. Clearly, when your liberty (to smoke) threatens my good health by exposing me to secondhand smoke, it's a no-brainer for many people. But how far should you go in infringing on smokers for the sake of the larger whole? Is it right to finance public service projects by increasing the tax on cigarettes rather than on other products like candy, salt, or butter, which also cause adverse health outcomes? Should schools become the food police, banning even the most innocuous fatty food from children's diets? Where do we draw the line?

CONCLUSIONS

Communication campaigns are vital activities that use mass media and interpersonal communication to make improvements in public health. They have a long, proud history in this country. Campaigns are broader in scope than most persuasion discussed in this book. They are designed to influence the health and social attitudes of a large audience within a specified amount of time, by means of mediated and interpersonal messages. Unlike commercial campaigns, health campaigns are not designed to make a profit for the sponsoring organizations. They face more daunting obstacles than commercial campaigns, frequently targeting the 15 percent of the population that is least likely to change.

Campaigns are ever changing. The mass media-based antismoking campaigns of the 1980s have given way to new interventions, focused on social problems like obesity and bullying. Television PSA-dominated campaigns still exist, but are increasingly supplemented or even replaced by Web campaigns. Contemporary health interventions have migrated to the Web and social networking sites, bringing forth new challenges on how to effectively reach target audience members in a cluttered environment. Thus, the challenge of developing communications that can alter well-learned attitudes remains. Contemporary theoretical and methodological approaches continue to offer guidelines on how to design effective pro-social interventions.

Three theoretical approaches guide campaigns: a step-by-step psychological approach and two macro perspectives: diffusion, and social marketing. Diffusion calls on theoretical ideas regarding the spread of new ideas throughout society. Social marketing applies the venerable 4 Ps of commercial marketing—product, price, placement, and promotion—to pro-social interventions. Persuasion theories can usefully complement these perspectives, as diffusion and social marketing do not always suggest specific implications for message design.

One cannot assume that campaigns succeed without conducting empirical evaluations. Campaigns are assessed at the individual, community, and state levels. Individuals or groups exposed to the intervention are compared with an equivalent group with little or no exposure to campaign messages. Real-world political factors can influence campaigns, as entrenched, powerful groups can reframe issues, offering competing messages.

Campaigns can face long odds, typified by the difficulty in reaching target audience members who would rather persist in, rather than change, a harmful health habit. Nonetheless, they can succeed when based on theory, and practitioners develop messages congruent with audience needs, employ media messages with high-production value, and supplement media materials with community contacts.

It is tempting to view campaigns as all-powerful weapons in the health communication arsenal. They are not. They can fail if messages are executed poorly. They can fail if individuals fail to internalize the campaign message, and succumb to temptation at a later point in time.

Social and cultural norms play a role in campaign effectiveness. What works in one culture will not succeed in another. Campaign organizers can have brilliant ideas, but if they don't gel with cultural norms or lack the support of prominent opinion leaders, they are unlikely to succeed. And yet research has made it abundantly clear that well-conceptualized, well-executed campaigns can convince people to rethink their resistance to innovation and adopt healthier lifestyles. A generation of antismoking interventions offers strong empirical evidence that communication interventions can alter behavior.

Values and ethics are an inescapable part of health campaigns. A host of ethical issues present themselves, such as determining the locus of the dilemma, deciding if the campaign should be designed to appeal to certain sectors of the public rather than the public-as-a-whole, and favoring one set of morally tinged recommendations rather than another. There is nothing wrong with values intruding on campaigns. We want campaigns to be guided by enlightened moral principles. Still, researchers should try to appreciate how their value judgments, as well as those of community organizers, influence the choice of strategies. It is best to think through these issues, carefully and with as many different perspectives brought to the table as possible, at the outset rather than after the campaign has been launched.

This chapter and the book as a whole have argued that if we understand how people think and feel about communication, we have a pretty good chance of changing their views in socially constructive ways. Stated somewhat differently, the more communicators understand the dynamics of the mind, the better their chances of constructing attitude-altering messages. This is a centerpiece of contemporary persuasion scholarship and seems to have a great deal of empirical support. Yet it is always worth playing devil's advocate with oneself and noting that there are individuals whose attitudes are not amenable to change. There are people who will smoke, no matter how many times they are exposed to an antismoking message, and others who will abuse drugs even after you tell them they can get busted, precisely because they enjoy the thrill of testing the law. Still others will practice unsafe sex, knowing full well that they are HIV-positive.

Persuasive communication, like all forces in life, has limits, a point emphasized at various times in this text. Yet the fact that communication has limits does not mean it is powerless or ineffectual or necessarily plays into the hands of the rich or corrupt. Persuasion can have these effects, of course, but it can also be an instrument of self-insight, healing, and social change.

In the final analysis, it is up to us to harness persuasion for pro-social, humane purposes. We—you, me, the readers of this book—know the theories and the strategies. We also know what constitutes the morally appropriate action. We intuitively know how we want to be treated and how to treat others. As persuaders, we should try to create communications that help people find ways within themselves to make choices that enhance their health and psychological well-being.

 Test your knowledge now with interactive exercises

Glossary

Accessibility: the degree to which an attitude can be automatically activated from memory.

Advertising deception: a representation that contains a message likely to mislead consumers behaving reasonably under the circumstances and likely to influence consumer decision making about a product or service.

Assimilation: perceptual distortion that occurs when an individual assumes that a message is more similar to one's attitude than it actually is.

Attitude: learned global evaluation of an object (person, place, or issue) that influences thought and action.

Authority: power that derives from the communicator's role in a social structure and his or her ability to dispense rewards or punishments.

Balance theory: three-component model of attitude structure that stipulates that people prefer balance or harmony among the components of their attitudes.

Belief: cognition about the world; subjective probability that an object has a particular quality or that an action will lead to a particular outcome.

Central route: processing path characterized by substantial thinking, or consideration of how a message relates to the receiver's values.

Charisma: a certain quality of a communicator that sets him or her apart from ordinary individuals and, in the perceiver's mind, endowed him or her with supernatural, exceptional qualities.

Classical conditioning: Pavlov's theory of association that holds that pairing a conditioned stimulus with an unconditioned stimulus produces a conditioned response.

Coercion: an influence process that occurs when the influence agent delivers a credible threat, raising the prospect of negative physical or emotional consequences; attempts to induce the individual to act contrary to her preferences, and deprives the individual of some measure of freedom or autonomy.

Cognitive dissonance: negative, unpleasant state that occurs whenever an individual holds two thoughts that are psychologically incompatible. Cognitive dissonance theory has intriguing implications for persuasion.

Cognitive response approach to persuasion: emphasizes the role of thoughts, such as counterarguments and proarguments, in the persuasion process.

Communication accommodation theory: an interpersonal communication perspective that examines processes by which individuals adapt their communication behavior toward others—or accommodate them—and the consequences of accommodation on subsequent communication.

Communication campaign: large-scale communicative intervention characterized by purposive attempts to persuade a well-defined audience for noncommercial benefits, typically within a given time period by means of organized communication involving mass media and Internet, and often complemented by interpersonal support.

Compatibility principle: attitude–behavior perspective that says general attitudes predict behaviors across situations, and specific attitudes forecast a specific behavior at a particular time and place.

Compliance-gaining: any communicative interaction in which a communicator tries to convince a message recipient to perform a behavior that he or she would not otherwise perform.

Conclusion drawing: message factor that compares effects of a message that draws a conclusion either explicitly or implicitly.

Contrast: perceptual distortion that occurs when an individual assumes that a message is more different from one's attitude than it actually is.

Credibility: the message receiver's attitude toward the source of a communication; his or her perception of the communicator's qualities.

Cult: a group of individuals who are excessively devoted to a charismatic leader (who is himself or herself an object of worship), effectively isolated from the rest of society, denied access to alternative points of view, and subjected to exploitative social influence techniques.

Danger control: psychological process whereby a fear appeal leads people to focus on the underlying threat and to therefore consider adopting strategies to ward off the danger.

Deontological thought: normative ethical theory that emphasizes universal moral imperatives, such as duty and obligation. Morality is judged in terms of moral obligations, not the consequences of actions.

Diffusion theory: communication theory that describes and explains the process by which innovations spread through society.

Disrupt-then-reframe: a persuader disrupts the message recipient's cognitive view of a persuasion encounter with an entertaining gambit and then reframes the request.

Distraction: process by which environmental distractions can block receivers' cognitive responses to a message, under certain circumstances producing more persuasion.

Door-in-the-face technique: a persuader can gain compliance to a second, smaller request by inducing individuals to turn down an outrageously large initial request.

Elaboration Likelihood Model: a dual-processing model that highlights the processes by which persuasion occurs. It stipulates that there are two distinct ways people process communications: the central and peripheral routes, with the routes differing in the likelihood that people will elaborate on the message.

Evidence: message factor that consists of factual assertions, quantitative information, eyewitness statements, and testimonials advanced by credible sources.

Expectancy–value approach: model of attitude structure that says attitudes are composed of two components (a cognition about the object, an expectation), and an evaluation of this attribute (value).

Extended Parallel Process Model: four-step process model that emphasizes severity, susceptibility, response efficacy, and self-efficacy of a fear-arousing message. The model articulates the processes that a fear appeal must evoke in order to persuade.

Fear appeal: persuasive communication that tries to scare people into changing their attitudes by conjuring up negative consequences that will occur if they do not comply with message recommendations.

Fear control: psychological process whereby a fear appeal leads people to focus on containing their fear rather than developing strategies to ward off danger.

Fear-then-relief: a persuader deliberately places the message recipient in a state of fear, quickly eliminates it, and makes a pitch for the targeted request.

Focus group: a qualitative research strategy that probes the rich meaning people attach to social issues.

Foot-in-the-door technique: a persuader can secure compliance to a second large request by inducing an individual to first go along with a small initial request.

Forewarning: process that occurs when a persuader warns people they will soon be exposed to a persuasive communication. Forewarning can stiffen resistance to persuasion, although the effects can be complex.

Frame: message characteristic that induces persuasion through subtle changes in wording or perspective. To frame is to emphasize a particular definition of the problem or treatment recommendation.

Functional magnetic resonance imaging: neuroscience-based methodology that illuminates brain activity, offering a snapshot of the brain's functioning and structure.

Functional theory: theory of attitudes that argues that people adopt attitudes because they fulfill particular psychological functions.

Gain-framed argument: message that emphasizes benefits of adopting a behavior.

Guttman scale: questionnaire measurement of attitude that progresses from easy-to-accept to difficult-to-accept items.

Heuristic: a simple decision-making strategy.

Heuristic-Systematic Model: a dual-process model of persuasion stipulating that individuals process persuasion through two mechanisms: the systematic and heuristic routes. These dual processes have implications for cognitive processing and persuasion.

Hypocrisy induction: a procedure by which individuals are confronted with examples of their own inconsistency in an effort to harness dissonance to produce attitude change.

Ideological approach to attitudes: model of attitude structure that says attitudes are guided by broad ideological principles.

Illusion of invulnerability: perception that others are more likely to experience negative life outcomes than we are ourselves.

Implicit Association Test: instrument to assess implicit attitude through response time techniques, with the attitude object linked to good and bad labels. The IAT has emerged as a robust measure of prejudice, but has also stimulated considerable controversy.

Implicit attitude: an evaluation that has an unknown origin, is activated automatically, and can influence implicit, uncontrollable responses.

Induced compliance: phenomenon that occurs when an individual freely decides to comply with a dissonance-producing request, sometimes agreeing to perform a counter-attitudinal behavior for a small reward.

Inoculation: persuasion strategy that induces resistance to persuasion by exposing individuals to a small dose of arguments against an idea, followed by criticism of those arguments.

Intense language: evocative speech that includes metaphor, vivid language, emotionally charged words, and obscenities.

Knowledge bias: audience member's perception that a communicator has a biased view of an issue.

Latitudes: the perceived range of psychological acceptability of message positions, derived from social judgment theory, encompassing latitudes of acceptance, rejection, and noncommitment.

Likert scale: questionnaire measurement of attitude that asks respondents to indicate agreement or disagreement with a statement along an equal-interval numerical scale.

Loss-framed argument: message that emphasizes costs of not performing the requested action.

Low-balling: a persuader gains compliance by inducing an individual to comply with an initial request and then "ups the ante" by increasing the costs of compliance.

Manipulation: a persuasion technique that occurs when a communicator disguises his or her true persuasive goals, hoping to mislead the recipient by delivering an overt message that belies its true intent.

Marketing: activities and processes by which a society communicates products and services of value to masses of consumers.

Mere exposure: repeated exposure to a novel, neutral message produces a positive attitude.

Message sidedness: message factor that compares effects of a one-sided message that presents one perspective on the issue with a two-sided message that presents arguments on behalf of both the persuader's position and the opposing side.

Narrative: a coherent story with a clear beginning, middle, and end that offers plot and characters and provides a resolution.

Need for cognition: personality factor that taps individual differences in the tendency to enjoy thinking and to engage in abstract deliberation.

Neuroscience perspective on persuasion: an approach that examines the biological and brain-based underpinnings of attitudes. It can help shed light on neurological processes underlying persuasion and ways in which body and mind exert complementary influences on attitude change.

Norm: an accepted, recommended social behavior in a society. A perceived norm is perceived social pressure to perform a particular action.

Perceived behavioral control: perception of controllability of an action, or the degree to which individuals believe they are capable of performing a particular behavior.

Peripheral route: processing path characterized by superficial thinking and consideration of factors irrelevant or peripheral to the message.

Persuasion: a symbolic process in which communicators try to convince other people to change their attitudes or behaviors regarding an issue through the transmission of a message in an atmosphere of free choice.

Physiological measurements: inference of an attitude from physiological responses such as galvanic skin response, pupil dilation, and facial electromyographic techniques.

Pique technique: a persuader makes the request in an unusual fashion, piquing the target's curiosity.

Powerless/powerful speech: speech that varies in the degree to which it expresses such factors as hesitation, hedges, tag questions, and disclaimers.

Pre-giving: persuader provides the receiver with a reward and then follows this up with the targeted persuasive request.

Product placement: paid communication about a product that is designed to influence audience attitudes about the brand through deliberate and subtle insertion of a product into media entertainment programming.

Propaganda: mass influence that occurs when a group has total control over transmission of information, typically involves mass media, has covert aspects, and elicits negative connotations.

Reactance: psychological tendency to react to a threat to perceived freedom by adopting precisely the opposite of what the communicator recommends.

Reasoned Action Model: a comprehensive theory of attitude and behavior stipulating that behavior can be predicted by inclusion of attitude, norms (descriptive and injunctive), perceived behavioral control, and behavioral intention.

Reporting bias: audience member's perception that the communicator has opted not to report or disclose certain points of view.

Response time measurements: measurement of attitude by assessing latency or length of time that it takes people to indicate agreement with a statement.

Rhetoric: classic concept dating back to ancient Greece that examines the content of argumentation and language in persuasion.

Self-affirmation theory: a psychological perspective that argues individuals are motivated to take a variety of steps to affirm the self.

Self-fulfilling prophecy: event that occurs when an individual's expectation about the outcome—not the objective event itself—influences subsequent behavior.

Self-monitoring: personality trait with persuasion implications that views individuals as varying in the extent to which they are concerned with displaying appropriate behavior in social situations.

Self-perception theory: a psychological theory stipulating that an individual acts as a dispassionate observer of the self, inferring attitudes from behavior.

Semantic differential: questionnaire measurement of attitude that taps meaning assigned to an object using bipolar adjectives.

Semiotics: the study of signs and symbols.

Sequential influence techniques: influence techniques that proceed in stages, in which a prior request creates the communicative foundation for requests that follow.

Sleeper effect: a persuasive message impact increases with the passage of time. A message initially discounted by message receivers, due to its attribution to a low-credibility source, comes to be accepted over the longer haul.

Social judgment theory: attitude theory that emphasizes people's subjective judgments about social issues. People do not evaluate a message purely on its merits, but instead compare the advocated position with their own attitude and determine, on this basis, whether they should accept or reject the message.

Social marketing: a process of creating and implementing programs to enhance the acceptability of a pro-social idea by applying marketing principles to health promotion.

Strong attitude: an attitude of personal importance characterized by such aspects as ego-involvement, extremity, certainty, accessibility, knowledge, and hierarchical organization.

Subliminal perception: perception without awareness of the object being perceived.

Subliminal advertisement: an advertisement that includes a brief, specific message that cannot be perceived at a normal level of conscious awareness.

Symbol: a form of language in which one entity represents a concept or idea, communicating rich psychological and cultural meaning.

Symbolic attitude approach: model of attitude structure that stipulates that large emotional evaluations, prejudices, and symbolic attachments are the core of an attitude.

"That's-not-all" technique: a persuader stipulates that purchase of a product or acceptance of an offer will be accompanied by receipt of an additional product that is also part of the deal.

Third-person effect: distorted perception that persuasive media do not affect "me" or "you, but "them"—everyone else, the third persons.

Transportation: the process whereby fiction imaginatively takes people to different psychological places, sometimes producing a change in attitude or perspective.

Unobtrusive measure: indirect attitude assessment technique in which a researcher observes individuals' behavior without their knowledge.

Utilitarianism: normative ethical theory that judges actions based on whether they produce more positive than negative outcomes, or consequences.

Value: a guiding principle; the idealized conception of desirable outcomes.

Yale Attitude Change Approach: early influential model of persuasion that focused on sources, messages, channels, and receivers of messages and emphasized role of learning in persuasion.

References

Abelson, R. P. (1959). Modes of resolution of belief dilemmas. *Journal of Conflict Resolution*, 343–352.

Abelson, R. P. (1982). Three modes of attitude–behavior consistency. In M. P. Zanna, E. T. Higgins, & C. P. Herman (Eds.), *Consistency in social behavior: The Ontario symposium* (Vol. 2, pp. 131–146). Hillsdale, NJ: Lawrence Erlbaum Associates.

Aberson, C. L., & McVean, A. D. W. (2008). Contact and anxiety as predictors of bias toward the homeless. *Journal of Applied Social Psychology, 38,* 3009–3035.

Abramson, P. R., Aldrich, J. H., & Rohde, D. W. (1994). *Change and continuity in the 1992 elections.* Washington, DC: CQ Press.

Adkins, M., & Brashers, D. E. (1995). The power of language in computer-mediated groups. *Management Communication Quarterly, 8,* 289–322.

Adler, J. (1999, November 29). Living canvas. *Newsweek*, 75–76.

Ajzen, I. (1991). The theory of planned behavior. *Organizational Behavior and Human Decision Processes, 50,* 179–211.

Ajzen, I., & Fishbein, M. (1977). Attitude–behavior relations: A theoretical analysis and review of empirical research. *Psychological Bulletin, 84,* 888–918.

Ajzen, I., & Fishbein, M. (2005). The influence of attitudes on behavior. In D. Albarracín, B. T. Johnson & M. P. Zanna (Eds.), *The handbook of attitudes* (pp. 173–221). Mahwah, NJ: Lawrence Erlbaum Associates.

Ajzen, I., & Fishbein, M. (2008). Scaling and testing multiplicative combinations in the expectancy-value model of attitude. *Journal of Applied Social Psychology, 38,* 2222–2247.

Ajzen, I., Albarracín, D., & Hornik, R. (Eds.) (2007). *Prediction and change of health behavior: Applying the reasoned action approach.* Mahwah, NJ: Lawrence Erlbaum Associates.

Albarracín, D., Johnson, B. T., Fishbein, M., & Muellerleile, P. A. (2001). Theories of reasoned action and planned behavior as models of condom use: A meta-analysis. *Psychological Bulletin, 127,* 142–161.

Albarracín, D., Johnson, B. T., & Zanna, M. P. (2005). Preface. In D. Albarracín, B. T. Johnson, & M. P. Zanna (Eds.), *The handbook of attitudes* (pp. vii–ix). Mahwah, NJ: Lawrence Erlbaum Associates.

Albarracín, D., & Vargas, P. (2010). Attitudes and persuasion: From biology to social responses to persuasive intent. In S. T. Fiske, D. T., Gilbert, & G. Lindzey (Eds.), *Handbook of social psychology* (5th ed., Vol. 1, pp. 394–427). Hoboken, NJ: Wiley.

Alford, J., Funk, C., & Hibbing, J. (2005). Are political orientations genetically transmitted? *American Political Science Review, 99,* 153–167.

Allen, M. (1998). Comparing the persuasive effectiveness of one and two sided messages. In M. Allen & R. W. Preiss (Eds.), *Persuasion: Advances through meta-analysis* (pp. 87–98). Cresskill, NJ: Hampton Press.

Allen, M., Bruflat, R., Fucilla, R., Kramer, M., McKellips, S., Ryan, D. J., & Spiegelhoff, M. (2000). Testing the persuasiveness of evidence: Combining narrative and statistical forms. *Communication Research Reports, 17,* 331–336.

Allen, M., & Preiss, R. (1997a). Persuasion, public address, and progression in the sciences: Where we are at what we do. In G. A. Barnett & F. J. Boster (Eds.), *Progress in communication sciences* (Vol. 13, pp. 107–131). Greenwich, CT: Ablex.

Allen, M., & Stiff, J. B. (1998). An analysis of the sleeper effect. In M. Allen & R. W. Preiss (Eds.), *Persuasion: Advances through meta-analysis* (pp. 175–188). Cresskill, NJ: Hampton Press.

Allport, G. W. (1935). Attitudes. In C. Murchison (Ed.), *A handbook of social psychology* (Vol. 2, pp. 798–844). Worcester, MA: Clark University Press.

Allport, G. W. (1945). The psychology of participation. *Psychological Review, 53,* 117–132.

Ambah, F. S. (2006, July 24). The would-be terrorist's explosive tell-all tale. *The Washington Post,* C1, C4.

Andersen, K. (1971). *Persuasion: Theory and practice.* Boston: Allyn & Bacon.

Anderson, R. B., & McMillion, P. Y. (1995). Effects of similar and diversified modeling on African American women's efficacy expectations and intentions to perform breast self-examination. *Health Communication, 7,* 324–343.

Andrews, J. C., & Shimp, T. A. (1990). Effects of involvement, argument strength, and source characteristics on central and peripheral processing in advertising. *Psychology & Marketing, 7,* 195–214.

Andsager, J. L., Austin, E. W., & Pinkleton, B. E. (2001). Questioning the value of realism: Young adults' processing of messages in alcohol-related public service announcements and advertising. *Journal of Communication, 51(1),* 121–142.

Andsager, J. L., & White, H. A. (2007). *Self versus others: Media, messages, and the third-person effect.* Mahwah, NJ: Lawrence Erlbaum Associates.

Angier, N. (2000a, November 7). Cell phone or pheromone? New props for the mating game. *The New York Times,* D5.

Angier, N. (2000b, November 7). Who is fat? It depends on culture. *The New York Times,* D1–D2.

Angier, N. (2008, December 23). A highly involved propensity for deceit. *The New York Times,* D1, D4.

Arkes, H. R., & Tetlock, P. E. (2004). Attributions of implicit prejudice, or "Would Jesse Jackson 'fail' the Implicit Association Test?" *Psychological Inquiry, 15,* 257–278.

Armitage, C. J., & Conner, M. (2000). Attitudinal ambivalence: A test of three key hypotheses. *Personality and Social Psychology Bulletin, 26,* 1421–1432.

Aron, A., & Aron, E. N. (1989). *The heart of social psychology: A backstage view of a passionate science* (2nd ed.). Lexington, MA: Lexington Books.

Aronson, E. (1968). Dissonance theory: Progress and problems. In R. P. Abelson, E. Aronson, W. J. McGuire, T. M. Newcomb, M. J. Rosenberg & P. H. Tannenbaum (Eds.), *Theories of cognitive consistency: A sourcebook* (pp. 5–27). Chicago: Rand McNally.

Aronson, E., & Mills, J. (1959). The effect of severity of initiation on liking for a group. *Journal of Abnormal and Social Psychology, 59,* 177–181.

Aronson, J., Cohen, G., & Nail, P. R. (1999). Self-affirmation theory: An update and appraisal. In E. Harmon-Jones & J. Mills (Eds.), *Cognitive dissonance: Progress on a pivotal theory in social psychology* (pp. 127–147). Washington, D.C.: American Psychological Association.

Arpan, L., Rhodes, N., & Roskos-Ewoldsen, D. R. (2007). Attitude accessibility: Theory, methods, and future directions. In D. R. Roskos-Ewoldsen & J. L. Monahan (Eds.), *Communication and social cognition: Theories and methods* (pp. 351–376). Mahwah, NJ: Erlbaum Associates.

Atkin, C. (2002). Promising strategies for media health campaigns. In W. D. Crano & M. Burgoon (Eds.), *Mass media and drug prevention: Classic and contemporary theories and research* (pp. 35–64). Mahwah, NJ: Lawrence Erlbaum Associates.

Atkin, C. K., & Freimuth, V. S. (2001). Formative evaluation research in campaign design. In R. E. Rice & C. K. Atkin (Eds.), *Public communication campaigns* (3rd ed., pp. 125–145). Thousand Oaks, CA: Sage.

Atkin, C. K., & Salmon, C. T. (2013). Persuasive strategies in health campaigns. In J. P. Dillard & L. Shen (Eds.), *The Sage handbook of persuasion: Developments in theory and practice* (2nd ed., pp. 278–295). Thousand Oaks, CA: Sage.

Atkinson, M. (2004). Tattooing and civilizing processes: Body modification as self-control. *Canadian Review of Sociology & Anthropology, 41,* 125–146.

Atlas, D., Dodd, J., Lang, A., Bane, V., & Levy, D. S. (2008, April 28). Life in the cult. *People,* 62–67.

Atwood, R. W., & Howell, R. J. (1971). Pupilometric and personality test score differences of female aggressing pedophiliacs and normals. *Psychonomic Science, 22,* 115–116.

Aune, R. K., & Basil, M. D. (1994). A relational obligations approach to the foot-in-the-mouth effect. *Journal of Applied Social Psychology, 24,* 546–556.

Aune, R. K., & Reynolds, R. A. (1994). The empirical development of the normative message processing scale. *Communication Monographs, 61,* 135–160.

Austin, E. W., & Chen, Y. J. (1999, August). *The relationship of parental reinforcement of media messages to college students' alcohol-related behaviors.* Paper presented to the annual convention of the Association for Education in Journalism and Mass Communication, New Orleans.

Axsom, D., Yates, S., & Chaiken, S. (1987). Audience response as a heuristic cue in persuasion. *Journal of Personality and Social Psychology, 53,* 30–40.

Bakker, A. B. (1999). Persuasive communication about AIDS prevention: Need for cognition determines the impact of message format. *AIDS Education and Prevention, 11,* 150–162.

Banaji, M. R., & Heiphetz, L. (2010). Attitudes. In S. T. Fiske, D. T. Gilbert, & G. Lindzey (Eds.), *Handbook of social psychology* (5th ed., Vol. 1, pp. 353–393). New York: Wiley.

Banas, J. A., & Rains, S. A. (2010). A meta-analysis of research on inoculation theory. *Communication Monographs, 77,* 281–311.

Bandura, A. (1971). Analysis of modeling processes. In A. Bandura (Ed.), *Psychological modeling: Conflicting theories* (pp. 1–62). Chicago: Aldine-Atherton.

Bandura, A. (1977). *Social learning theory.* Englewood Cliffs, NJ: Prentice Hall.

Bargh, J. A., & Pietromonaco, P. (1982). Automatic information processing and social perception: The influence of trait information presented outside of conscious awareness on impression formation. *Journal of Personality and Social Psychology, 43,* 437–449.

Baron, A. S., & Banaji, M. R. (2006). The development of implicit attitudes: Evidence of race evaluations from ages 6 and 10 and adulthood. *Psychological Science, 17,* 53–58.

Barstow, D., & Stein, R. (2005, March 13). Is it news or public relations? Under Bush, lines are blurry. *The New York Times,* 1, 18–19.

Bartsch, K., & London, K. (2000). Children's use of mental state information in selecting persuasive arguments. *Developmental Psychology, 36,* 352–365.

Basil, D. Z., Ridgway, N. M., & Basil, M. D. (2006). Guilt appeals: The mediating effect of responsibility. *Psychology & Marketing, 23,* 1035–1054.

Basil, D. Z., Ridgway, N. M., & Basil, M. D. (2008). Guilt and giving: A process model of empathy and efficacy. *Psychology & Marketing, 25,* 1–23.

Bassili, J. N. (1995). Response latency and the accessibility of voting intentions: What contributes to accessibility and how it affects vote choice. *Personality and Social Psychology Bulletin, 21,* 686–695.

Baumrind, D. (1964). Some thoughts on ethics of research: After reading Milgram's "Behavioral study of obedience." *American Psychologist, 19,* 421–423.

Bell, R. A., Cholerton, M., Davison, W., Fraczek, K. E., & Lauter, H. (1996). Making health communication self-funding: Effectiveness of pregiving in an AIDS fundraising/education campaign. *Health Communication, 8,* 331–352.

Belluck, P. (2009, April 26). Yes, looks do matter. *The New York Times* (Sunday Styles), 1, 8.

Bem, D. J. (1970). *Beliefs, attitudes, and human affairs.* Belmont, CA: Brooks/Cole.

Bem, D. J. (1972). Self-perception theory. In L. Berkowitz (Ed.), *Advances in experimental social psychology* (Vol. 6, pp. 1–62). New York: Academic Press.

Bennett, W. J. (1998). *The death of outrage: Bill Clinton and the assault on American ideals.* New York: Free Press.

Benoit, W. L. (1991). Two tests of the mechanism of inoculation theory. *Southern Communication Journal, 56,* 219–229.

Benoit, W. L. (1998). Forewarning and persuasion. In M. Allen & R. W. Preiss (Eds.), *Persuasion: Advances through meta-analysis* (pp. 139–154). Cresskill, NJ: Hampton Press.

Bentler, P. M., & Speckhart, G. (1979). Models of attitude–behavior relations. *Psychological Review, 86,* 452–464.

Berke, R. L., & Elder, J. (2000, November 30). Public splits on party lines over vote and long delay. *The New York Times,* 1, A30.

Berlo, D. K., Lemert, J. B., & Mertz, R. J. (1969). Dimensions for evaluating the acceptability of message sources. *Public Opinion Quarterly, 33,* 563–576.

Berscheid, E. (1966). Opinion change and communicator–communicatee similarity and dissimilarity. *Journal of Personality and Social Psychology, 4,* 670–680.

Bettinghaus, E. P., & Cody, M. J. (1987). *Persuasive communication* (4th ed.). New York: Holt, Rinehart &Winston.

Bilandzic, H., & Busselle, R. (2013). Narrative persuasion. In J. P. Dillard & L. Shen (Ed.), *The Sage handbook of persuasion: Developments in theory and practice* (2nd ed., pp. 200–219). Thousand Oaks, CA: Sage.

Bishop, B. (with R. G. Cushing). (2008). *The big sort: Why the clustering of like-minded America is tearing us apart.* Boston: Houghton-Mifflin.

Bishop, G. F., Tuchfarber, A. J., & Oldendick, R. W. (1986). Opinions on fictitious issues: The pressure to answer survey questions. *Public Opinion Quarterly, 50,* 240–250.

Bishop, G. W. (2005). *The illusion of public opinion: Fact and artifact in American public opinion polls.* Lanham, MD: Rowman & Littlefield.

Blass, T. (1992). The social psychology of Stanley Milgram. In M. P. Zanna (Ed.), *Advances in experimental social psychology* (Vol. 25, pp. 277–329). San Diego: Academic Press.

Blass, T. (1999). The Milgram paradigm after 35 years: Some things we now know about obedience to authority. *Journal of Applied Social Psychology, 29,* 955–978.

Blumenthal, R. (2006, March 30). A preacher's credo: Eliminate the negative, accentuate prosperity. *The New York Times,* B1, B7.

Booth-Butterfield, S., & Reger, B. (2004). The message changes belief and the rest is theory: The "1% or less" milk campaign and reasoned action. *Preventive Medicine, 39,* 581–588.

Borchert, D. M., & Stewart, D. (1986). *Exploring ethics.* New York: Macmillan.

Bornstein, R. F. (1989). Exposure and affect: Overview and meta-analysis of research, 1968–1987. *Psychological Bulletin, 106,* 265–289.

Bornstein, R. F. (1992). Subliminal mere exposure effects. In R. F. Bornstein & T. S. Pittman (Eds.), *Perception without awareness: Cognitive, clinical, and social perspectives* (pp. 191–210). New York: Guilford.

Boster, F. J., & Mongeau, P. (1984). Fear-arousing persuasive messages. In R. N. Bostrom (Ed.), *Communication yearbook 8* (pp. 330–375). Beverly Hills: Sage.

Bowers, J. W. (1964). Some correlates of language intensity. *Quarterly Journal of Speech, 50,* 415–420.

Boxer, S. (2005, September 24). Art of the Internet: A protest song, reloaded. *The New York Times,* A17.

Boyer, M. S. (2006, August 13). Close ties to Far East. *The Plain Dealer,* C1, 10.

Bradley, P. H. (1981). The folk linguistics of women's speech: An empirical examination. *Communication Monographs, 48,* 73–90.

Brandt, A. M. (2007). *The cigarette century: The rise, fall, and deadly persistence of the product that defined America.* New York: Basic Books.

Brannon, L. A., & Brock, T. C. (1994). The subliminal persuasion controversy: Reality, enduring fable, and Polonius's weasel. In S. Shavitt & T. C. Brock (Eds.), *Persuasion: Psychological insights and perspectives* (pp. 279–293). Needham Heights, MA: Allyn & Bacon.

Braverman, J. (2008). Testimonials versus informational persuasive messages: The moderating effect of delivery mode and personal involvement. *Communication Research, 35,* 666–694.

Breckler, S. J. (1984). Empirical validation of affect, behavior, and cognition as distinct components of attitude. *Journal of Personality and Social Psychology, 47,* 1191–1205.

Brehm, J. W. (1966). *A theory of psychological reactance.* New York: Academic Press.

Brinberg, D., & Durand, J. (1983). Eating at fast-food restaurants: An analysis using two behavioral intention models. *Journal of Applied Social Psychology, 13,* 459–472.

Briñol, P., & Petty, R. E. (2005). Individual differences in attitude change. In D. Albarracín, B. T. Johnson, & M. P. Zanna (Eds.), *The handbook of attitudes* (pp. 575–615). Mahwah, NJ: Lawrence Erlbaum Associates.

Broad, W. J., & Shane, S. (2008, August 10). For suspects, anthrax case had big costs. *The New York Times,* 1, 17.

Brock, T. C. (1965). Communicator–recipient similarity and decision change. *Journal of Personality and Social Psychology, 1,* 650–654.

Brock, T. C. (1967). Communication discrepancy and intent to persuade as determinants of counterargument production. *Journal of Experimental Social Psychology, 3,* 296–309.

Brock, T. C., Strange, J. J., & Green, M. C. (2002). Power beyond reckoning: An introduction to narrative impact. In M. C. Green, J. J. Strange, & T. C. Brock (Eds.), *Narrative impact: Social and cognitive foundations* (pp. 1–15). Mahwah, NJ: Lawrence Erlbaum Associates.

Brody, J. E. (2000, April 4). Fresh warnings on the perils of piercing. *The New York Times,* D8.

Brody, J. E. (2011, April 12). Keeping eyes on distracted driving's toll. *The New York Times,* D7.

Brooks, D. (2004, June 29). Age of political segregation. *The New York Times,* A27.

Brooks, D. (2011). *The social animal: The hidden sources of love, character, and achievement.* New York: Random House.

Brown, J. D., & Walsh-Childers, K. (2002). Effects of media on personal and public health. In J. Bryant & D. Zillmann (Eds.), *Media effects: Advances in theory and research* (2nd ed., pp. 453–488). Mahwah, NJ: Lawrence Erlbaum Associates.

Brown, P., & Levinson, S. C. (1987). *Politeness: Some universals in language usage.* Cambridge, UK: Cambridge University Press.

Budesheim, T. L., & DePaola, S. J. (1994). Beauty or the beast? The effects of appearance, personality, and issue information on evaluations of political candidates. *Personality and Social Psychology Bulletin, 20,* 339–348.

Buller, D. B., & Burgoon, J. K. (1996). Interpersonal deception theory. *Communication Theory, 6,* 203–242.

Buller, D. B., & Hall, J. R. (1998). The effects of distraction during persuasion. In M. Allen & R. W. Preiss (Eds.), *Persuasion: Advances through meta-analysis* (pp. 155–173). Cresskill, NJ: Hampton Press.

Buller, D. B., LePoire, B. A., Aune, R. K., & Eloy, S. V. (1992). Social perceptions as mediators of the effect of speech rate similarity on compliance. *Human Communication Research, 19,* 286–311.

Burger, J. M. (1986). Increasing compliance by improving the deal: The that's not all technique. *Journal of Personality and Social Psychology, 51,* 277–283.

Burger, J. M. (1999). The foot-in-the-door compliance procedure: A multiple process analysis and review. *Personality and Social Psychology Review, 3,* 303–325.

Burger, J. M. (2009). Replicating Milgram: Would people still obey today? *American Psychologist, 64,* 1–11.

Burgoon, J. K. (1994). Nonverbal signals. In M. L. Knapp & G. R. Miller (Eds.), *Handbook of interpersonal communication* (2nd ed., pp. 229–285). Thousand Oaks, CA: Sage.

Burgoon, M. (1989). Messages and persuasive effects. In J. J. Bradac (Ed.), *Message effects in communication science* (pp. 129–164). Newbury Park, CA: Sage.

Burgoon, M., Alvaro, E., Grandpre, J., & Voulodakis, M. (2002). Revisiting the theory of psychological reactance: Communicating threats to attitudinal freedom. In J. P. Dillard & M. Pfau (Eds.), *The persuasion handbook: Developments in theory and practice* (pp. 213–232). Thousand Oaks, CA: Sage.

Burgoon, M., Hendriks, A., & Alvaro, E. (2001, May). *Tobacco prevention and cessation: Effectiveness of the Arizona tobacco education and prevention media campaign.* Paper presented to the annual convention of the International Communication Association, Washington, DC.

Burgoon, M., Parrott, R., Burgoon, J., Birk, T., Pfau, M., & Coker, R. (1989). Primary care physicians' selection of verbal compliance-gaining strategies. *Health Communication, 2,* 13–27.

Burke, K. (1950). *A rhetoric of motives.* New York: Prentice Hall.

Burleigh, M. (2000). *The Third Reich: A new history.* New York: Hill and Wang.

Burleson, B. R., Wilson, S. R., Waltman, M. S., Goering, E. M., Ely, T. K., & Whaley, B. B. (1988). Item desirability effects in compliance gaining research: Seven studies documenting artifacts in the strategy selection procedure. *Human Communication Research, 14,* 429–486.

Burrell, N. A., & Koper, R. J. (1998). The efficacy of powerful/powerless language on attitudes and source credibility. In M. Allen & R. W. Preiss (Eds.), *Persuasion: Advances through meta-analysis* (pp. 203–215). Cresskill, NJ: Hampton Press.

Buss, D. M., & Kenrick, D. T. (1998). Evolutionary social psychology. In D. T. Gilbert, S. T. Fiske, & G. Lindzey (Eds.), *The handbook of social psychology* (4th ed., Vol. 2, pp. 982–1026). Boston: McGraw-Hill.

Cacioppo, J. T., Harkins, S. G., & Petty, R. E. (1981). The nature of attitudes and cognitive responses and their relationships to behavior. In R. E. Petty, T. M. Ostrom, & T. C. Brock (Eds.), *Cognitive responses in persuasion* (pp. 31–54). Hillsdale, NJ: Lawrence Erlbaum Associates.

Cacioppo, J. T., Petty, R. E., Feinstein, J. A., & Jarvis, W. B. G. (1996). Dispositional differences in cognitive motivation: The life and times of individuals varying in need for cognition. *Psychological Bulletin, 119,* 197–253.

Cacioppo, J. T., Petty, R. E., & Kao, C. F. (1984). The efficient assessment of need for cognition. *Journal of Personality Assessment, 48,* 306–307.

Cacioppo, J. T., Petty, R. E., & Marshall-Goodell, B. (1984). Electromyographic specificity during simple physical and attitudinal tasks: Location and topographical features of integrated EMG responses. *Biological Psychology, 18,* 85–121.

Cacioppo, J. T., Priester, J. R., & Berntson, G. G. (1993). Rudimentary determinants of attitudes. II: Arm flexion and extension have differential effects on attitudes. *Journal of Personality and Social Psychology, 65,* 5–17.

Caldwell, D. F., & Burger, J. M. (1997). Personality and social influence strategies in the workplace. *Personality and Social Psychology Bulletin, 23,* 1003–1012.

Cameron, K. A., & Campo, S. (2006). Stepping back from social norms campaigns: Comparing normative influences to other predictors of health behaviors. *Health Communication, 20,* 277–288.

Campbell, K. K. (1989). *Man cannot speak for her: A critical study of early feminist rhetoric* (Vol. 1). New York: Greenwood.

Campbell, M. K., & Quintiliani, L. M. (2006). Tailored interventions in public health: Where does tailoring fit in interventions to reduce health disparities? (Communication and racial disparities in health care, R. M. Perloff, Ed.), *American Behavioral Scientist, 49,* 775–793.

Campbell, R., Martin, C. R., & Fabos, B. (2002). *Media & culture: An introduction to mass communication* (3rd ed.). Boston: Bedford/St. Martin's.

Campo, S., & Cameron, K. A. (2006). Differential effects of exposure to social norms campaigns: A cause for concern. *Health Communication, 19,* 209–219.

Carpenter, C., Boster, F. J., & Andrews, K. R. (2013). Functional attitude theory. In J. P. Dillard & L. Shen (Eds.), *The Sage handbook of persuasion: Developments in theory and practice* (2nd ed., pp. 104–119). Thousand Oaks, CA: Sage.

Carpenter, C. J., & Boster, F. J. (2009). A meta-analysis of the effectiveness of the Disrupt-Then-Reframe compliance gaining technique. *Communication Reports, 22,* 55–62.

Carr, D. (2006, January 30). Oprahness trumps truthiness. *The New York Times,* C1, C5.

Carson, T. L., Wokutch, R. E., & Cox, J. E., Jr. (1985). An ethical analysis of deception in advertising. *Journal of Business Ethics, 4,* 93–104.

Cave, D. (2005a, March 27). For recruiters, a hard toll from a hard sell. *The New York Times,* 1, 21.

Cave, D. (2005b, June 3). Growing problem for military recruiters: Parents. *The New York Times,* 1, 23.

Cesario, J., Grant, H., & Higgins, E. T. (2004). Regulatory fit and persuasion: Transfer from "feeling right." *Journal of Personality and Social Psychology, 86,* 388–404.

Chaiken, S. (1979). Communicator's physical attractiveness and persuasion. *Journal of Personality and Social Psychology, 37,* 1387–1397.

Chaiken, S., Liberman, A., & Eagly, A. H. (1989). Heuristic and systematic information processing within and beyond the persuasion context. In J. S. Uleman & J. A. Bargh (Eds.), *Unintended thought: Limits of awareness, intention, and control* (pp. 212–252). New York: Guilford.

Chaiken, S., Wood, W., & Eagly, A. H. (1996). Principles of persuasion. In E. T. Higgins & A. W. Kruglanski (Eds.), *Social psychology: Handbook of basic principles* (pp. 702–742). New York: Guilford Press.

Chapanis, N. P., & Chapanis, A. C. (1964). Cognitive dissonance: Five years later. *Psychological Bulletin, 61,* 1–22.

Chappell, T. (1998). Platonism. In R. Chadwick (Ed.), *Encyclopedia of applied ethics* (Vol. 3, pp. 511–523). San Diego: Academic Press.

Chartrand, T., Pinckert, S., & Burger, J. M. (1999). When manipulation backfires: The effects of time delay and requester on the foot-in-the-door technique. *Journal of Applied Social Psychology, 29,* 211–221.

Chen, S., & Chaiken, S. (1999). The Heuristic–Systematic Model in its broader context. In S. Chaiken & Y. Trope (Eds.), *Dual-process theories in social psychology* (pp. 73–96). New York: Guilford.

Chew, F., Mehta, A., & Oldfather, A. (1994). Applying concept mapping to assess the influence of celebrity message dynamics on communication effectiveness. In K. W. King (Ed.), *Proceedings of the 1994 Conference of the American Academy of Advertising* (pp. 26–39). New York: American Academy of Advertising.

Cho, C. H. (1999). How advertising works on the WWW: Modified Elaboration Likelihood Model. *Journal of Current Issues and Research in Advertising, 21,* 33–50.

Cho, H., & Boster, F. J. (2008). Effects of gain versus loss frame antidrug ads on adolescents. *Journal of Communication, 58,* 428–446.

Cialdini, R. B. (2009). *Influence: Science and practice* (5th ed.). Boston: Pearson Education.

Cialdini, R. B., & Ascani, K. (1976). Test of a concession procedure for inducing verbal, behavioral, and further compliance with a request to give blood. *Journal of Applied Psychology, 61,* 295–300.

Cialdini, R. B., Cacioppo, J. T., Bassett, R., & Miller, J. A. (1978). Low-ball procedure for producing compliance: Commitment then cost. *Journal of Personality and Social Psychology, 36,* 463–476.

Cialdini, R. B., Vincent, J. E., Lewis, S. K., Catalan, J., Wheeler, D., & Darby B. L. (1975). Reciprocal concessions procedure for inducing compliance: The door-in-the-face technique. *Journal of Personality and Social Psychology, 31,* 206–215.

Clary, E. G., Snyder, M., Ridge, R. D., Miene, P. K., & Haugen, J. A. (1994). Matching messages to motives in persuasion: A functional approach to promoting volunteerism. *Journal of Applied Social Psychology, 24,* 1129–1149.

Clines, F. X. (2001, October 21). In uneasy time, seeking comfort in the familiar frights of Halloween. *The New York Times,* B8.

Cody, M. J., & McLaughlin, M. L. (1980). Perceptions of compliance-gaining situations: A dimensional analysis. *Communication Monographs, 47,* 132–148.

Cody, M. J., & McLaughlin, M. L. (1985). The situation as a construct in interpersonal communication research. In M. L. Knapp & G. R. Miller (Eds.), *Handbook of interpersonal communication* (pp. 263–312). Beverly Hills, CA: Sage.

Cody, M. J., McLaughlin, M. L., & Jordan, W. J. (1980). A multidimensional scaling of three sets of compliance-gaining strategies. *Communication Quarterly, 28,* 34–46.

Cody, M. J., & Seiter, J. S. (2001). Compliance principles in retail sales in the United States. In W. Wosinska, R. B. Cialdini, D. W. Barrett, & J. Reykowski (Eds.), *The practice of social influence in multiple cultures* (pp. 325–341). Mahwah, NJ: Lawrence Erlbaum Associates.

Cohen, C., & Regan, T. (2001). *The animal rights debate.* Lanham, MD: Rowman & Littlefield.

Cohen, G. L., Aronson, J., & Steele, C. M. (2000). When beliefs yield to evidence: Reducing biased evaluation by affirming the self. *Personality and Social Psychology Bulletin, 26,* 1151–1164.

Cohen, R. (1999, August 13). Why? New Eichmann notes try to explain. *The New York Times,* A1, A3.

Collins, F. S. (2006). *The language of God: A scientist presents evidence for belief.* New York: Free Press.

Compton, J. (2013). Inoculation theory. In J. P. Dillard & L. Shen (Eds.), *The Sage handbook of persuasion: Developments in theory and practice* (2nd ed., pp. 220–236). Thousand Oaks, CA: Sage.

Condit, C. M. (1990). *Decoding abortion rhetoric: Communicating social change.* Urbana: University of Illinois Press.

Conger, J. A. (1998, May–June). The necessary art of persuasion. *Harvard Business Review, 76,* 84–95.

Connelly, M. (2009, October 29). Framing the debate. *The New York Times,* p. A17.

Conover, P. J., & Feldman, S. (1984). How people organize the political world: A schematic model. *American Journal of Political Science, 28,* 95–126.

Cooper, H., & Peters, J. W. (2012, May 15). For some, same-sex marriage is not politics, it's personal. *The New York Times,* A16.

Cooper, J., & Axsom, D. (1982). Effort justification in psychotherapy. In G. Weary & H. L. Mirels (Eds.), *Integrations of clinical and social psychology* (pp. 214–230). New York: Oxford Press.

Cooper, J., & Cooper, G. (2002). Subliminal motivation: A story revisited. *Journal of Applied Social Psychology, 32,* 2213–2227.

Cooper, J., & Fazio, R. H. (1984). A new look at dissonance theory. In L. Berkowitz (Ed.), *Advances in experimental social psychology* (Vol. 17, pp. 229–266). Orlando, FL: Academic Press.

Cooper, J., & Scher, S. J. (1994). When do our actions affect our attitudes? In S. Shavitt & T. C. Brock (Eds.), *Persuasion: Psychological insights and perspectives* (pp. 95–111). Boston: Allyn and Bacon.

Cooper, M. D., & Nothstine, W. L. (1998). *Power persuasion: Moving an ancient art into the media age* (2nd ed.). Greenwood, IN: Educational Video Group.

Cowley, E. (2012). As a backdrop, part of the plot, or a goal in a game: The ubiquitous product placement. In L. J. Shrum (Ed.), *The psychology of entertainment media: Blurring the lines between entertainment and persuasion* (2nd ed.). New York: Routledge.

Coyne, M. (2000). Paper prepared for course on persuasion and attitude change, Cleveland State University, Cleveland, OH.

Crano, W. D. (2010). Experiments as reforms: Persuasion in the nation's service. In J. P. Forgas, J. Cooper, & W. D. Crano (Eds.), *The psychology of attitudes and attitude change* (pp. 231–248). New York: Psychology Press.

Crano, W. D., Cooper, J., & Forgas, J. P. (2010). Attitudes and attitude change: An introductory review. In J. P. Forgas, J. Cooper, & W. D. Crano (Eds.), *The psychology of attitudes and attitude change* (pp. 3–17). New York: Psychology Press.

Crites, S. L., Jr., Fabrigar, L. R., & Petty, R. E. (1994). Measuring the affective and cognitive properties of attitudes: Conceptual and methodological issues. *Personality and Social Psychological Bulletin, 20,* 619–634.

Cronkhite, G., & Liska, J. (1976). A critique of factor analytic approaches to the study of credibility. *Communication Monographs, 43,* 91–107.

Cross, M. (1996). Reading television texts: The postmodern language of advertising. In M. Cross (Ed.), *Advertising and culture: Theoretical perspectives* (pp. 1–10). Westport, CT: Praeger.

Crossen, C. (1991, November 14). Studies galore support products and positions, but are they reliable? *The Wall Street Journal,* A1, A7.

Crusco, A. H., & Wetzel, C. G. (1984). The Midas touch: The effects of interpersonal touch on restaurant tipping. *Personality and Social Psychology Bulletin, 10,* 512–517.

Cruz, M. G. (1998). Explicit and implicit conclusions in persuasive messages. In M. Allen & R. W. Preiss (Eds.), *Persuasion: Advances through meta-analysis* (pp. 217–230). Cresskill, NJ: Hampton Press.

Cutlip, S. M., Center, A. H., & Broom, G. M. (2006). *Effective public relations* (9th ed.). Upper Saddle River, NJ: Pearson Prentice Hall.

Czopp, A. M., Monteith, M. J., & Mark, A. Y. (2006). Standing up for a change: Reducing bias through interpersonal confrontation. *Journal of Personality and Social Psychology, 90,* 784–803.

Dahl, R. A. (1989). *Democracy and its critics.* New Haven: Yale University Press.

Davidson, E. (1977). *The making of Adolf Hitler.* New York: Macmillan.

Davis, B. P., & Knowles, E. S. (1999). A disrupt-then-reframe technique of social influence. *Journal of Personality and Social Psychology, 76,* 192–199.

Davis, D. (2008, September 13). Do voters want passion, policy or both? *The New York Times* [Letter to the Editor], A28.

Davis, D. (2011, September 8). NE Ohio doctors got $5.8M from drug makers for talks. *The Plain Dealer,* A1, A8.

Dawes, R. M., & Smith, T. L. (1985). Attitude and opinion measurement. In G. L. Lindzey & E. A. Aronson (Eds.), *Handbook of social psychology* (3rd ed., Vol. 1, pp. 509–566). New York: Random House.

Dearing, J. W., Rogers, E. M., Meyer, G., Casey, M. K., Rao, N., Campo, S., & Henderson, G. M. (1996). Social marketing and diffusion-based strategies for communicating with unique populations: HIV prevention in San Francisco. *Journal of Health Communication, 1,* 343–363.

de Botton, A. (2000). *The consolations of philosophy.* New York: Pantheon.

Deci, E. L. (1975). *Intrinsic motivation.* New York: Plenum Press.

DeJong, W. (1979). An examination of self-perception mediation of the foot-in-the-door effect. *Journal of Personality and Social Psychology, 37,* 2221–2239.

Delia, J. G., Kline, S. L., & Burleson, B. R. (1979). The development of persuasive communication strategies in kindergartners through twelfth graders. *Communication Monographs, 46,* 241–256.

Dennett, D. C. (2005, August 28). Show me the science. *The New York Times* [Week in Review], 11.

Denton, R. E., Jr. (Ed.) (1994). *The 1992 presidential campaign: A communication perspective.* Westport, CT: Praeger.

DePaulo, B. M., Kashy, D. A., Kirkendol, S. E., Wyer, M. M., & Epstein, J. A. (1996). Lying in everyday life. *Journal of Personality and Social Psychology, 70,* 979–995.

de Waal, F. (1982). *Chimpanzee politics: Power and sex among apes.* London: Jonathan Cape Ltd.

Dewan, S., & Goodstein, L. (2005, March 16). Hostage's past may have helped win captor's trust. *The New York Times,* A11.

DiClemente, R. J. (Ed.). (1992). *Adolescents and AIDS: A generation in jeopardy.* Thousand Oaks, CA: Sage.

Dijksterhuis, A., Aarts, H., & Smith, P. K. (2005). The power of the subliminal: On subliminal persuasion and other potential applications. In R. R. Hassin, J. S. Uleman, & J. A. Bargh (Eds.), *The new unconscious* (pp. 77–106). New York: Oxford University Press.

Dillard, J. P. (1990a). Self-inference and the foot-in-the-door technique: Quantity of behavior and attitudinal mediation. *Human Communication Research, 16,* 422–447.

Dillard, J. P. (1990b). A goal-driven model of interpersonal influence. In J. P. Dillard (Ed.), *Seeking compliance: The production of interpersonal influence messages* (pp. 41–56). Scottsdale, AZ: Gorsuch-Scarisbrick.

Dillard, J. P. (1993). Persuasion past and present: Attitudes aren't what they used to be. *Communication Monographs, 60,* 90–97.

Dillard, J. P. (1994). Rethinking the study of fear appeals: An emotional perspective. *Communication Theory, 4,* 295–323.

Dillard, J. P. (2010). Persuasion. In C. R. Berger, M. E. Roloff, & D. R. Roskos-Ewoldsen (Eds.), *The handbook of communication science* (2nd ed., pp. 203–218). Thousand Oaks, CA: Sage.

Dillard, J. P., & Anderson, J. W. (2004). The role of fear in persuasion. *Psychology & Marketing, 21,* 909–926.

Dillard, J. P., Hunter, J. E., & Burgoon, M. (1984). Sequential request persuasive strategies: Meta-analysis of foot-in-the-door and door-in-the-face. *Human Communication Research, 10,* 461–488.

Dillard, J. P., Kinney, T. A., & Cruz, M. G. (1996). Influence, appraisals, and emotions in close relationships. *Communication Monographs, 63,* 105–130.

Dillard, J. P., & Knobloch, L. K. (2011). Interpersonal influence. In M. L. Knapp & J. A. Daly (Eds.), *The Sage handbook of interpersonal communication* (4th ed., pp. 389–422). Thousand Oaks, CA: Sage.

Dillard, J. P., Segrin, C., & Harden, J. M. (1989). Primary and secondary goals in the production of interpersonal influence messages. *Communication Monographs, 56,* 19–38.

Dillard, J. P., & Shen, L. (2005). On the nature of reactance and its role in persuasive health communication. *Communication Monographs, 72,* 144–168.

Dillard, J. P., Wilson, S. R., Tusing, K. J., & Kinney, T. A. (1997). Politeness judgments in personal relationships. *Journal of Language and Psychology, 16,* 297–325.

Dolinski, D., & Nawrat, R. (1998). "Fear-then-relief" procedure for producing compliance: Beware when the danger is over. *Journal of Experimental Social Psychology, 34,* 27–50.

Doll, J., & Ajzen, I. (1992). Accessibility and stability of predictors in the theory of planned behavior. *Journal of Personality and Social Psychology, 63,* 754–765.

Doppelt, J. C., & Shearer, E. (1999). *Nonvoters: America's no-shows.* Thousand Oaks, CA: Sage.

Dowd, M. (2006a, June 3). Teaching remedial decency. *The New York Times,* A23.

Dudczak, C. A. (2001, January). *Comments on the Dynamics of Persuasion.* Prepared for Lawrence Erlbaum Associates.

Duff-Adlum, K. (2011, September 11). A mother-in-law will never forget [Letter to the editor]. *The Plain Dealer,* G1.

Dunlop, S. M., Wakefield, M., & Kashima, Y. (2010). Pathways to persuasion: Cognitive and experiential responses to health-promoting mass media messages. *Communication Research, 37,* 133–164.

Dutta, M. J. (2006). Theoretical approaches to entertainment education campaigns: A subaltern critique. *Health Communication, 20,* 221–231.

Dutta-Bergman, M. J. (2004). The impact of completeness and Web use motivation on the credibility of e-health information. *Journal of Communication, 54,* 337–354.

Dutta-Bergman, M. J. (2005). Theory and practice in health communication campaigns: A critical interrogation. *Health Communication, 18,* 103–122.

Dyson, M. E. (2001, January 22). Moral leaders need not be flawless. *The New York Times,* A23.

Dyson, M. E. (2005). *Is Bill Cosby right? Or has the Black middle class lost its mind?* New York: Basic Civitas Books.

Eagly, A. H., & Chaiken, S. (1993). *The psychology of attitudes.* Fort Worth, TX: Harcourt, Brace, Jovanovich.

Eagly, A. H., & Chaiken, S. (1995). Attitude strength, attitude structure, and resistance to change. In R. E. Petty & J. A. Krosnick (Eds.), *Attitude strength: Antecedents and consequences* (pp. 413–432). Hillsdale, NJ: Lawrence Erlbaum Associates.

Eagly, A. H., & Chaiken, S. (1998). Attitude structure and function. In D. T. Gilbert, S. T. Fiske, & G. Lindzey (Eds.), *Handbook of social psychology* (4th ed., Vol. 1, pp. 269–322). Boston: McGraw-Hill.

Eagly, A. H., Mladinic, A., & Otto, S. (1994). Cognitive and affective bases of attitudes toward social groups and social policies. *Journal of Experimental Social Psychology, 30,* 113–137.

Eagly, A. H., Wood, W., & Chaiken, S. (1978). Causal inferences about communicators and their effect on opinion change. *Journal of Personality and Social Psychology, 36,* 424–435.

Easterbrook, G. (2006, May 24). Finally feeling the heat. *The New York Times,* A27.

Edwards, K., & Smith, E. E. (1996). A disconfirmation bias in the evaluation of arguments. *Journal of Personality and Social Psychology, 71,* 5–24.

Eisenstadt, D., Leippe, M. R., Stambush, M. A., Rauch, S. M., & Rivers, J. A. (2005). Dissonance and prejudice: Personal costs, choice, and change in attitudes and racial beliefs following counterattitudinal advocacy that benefits a minority. *Basic and Applied Social Psychology, 27,* 127–141.

Elkin, R. A., & Leippe, M. R. (1986). Physiological arousal, dissonance, and attitude change: Evidence for a dissonance–arousal link and a "don't remind me" effect. *Journal of Personality and Social Psychology, 51,* 55–65.

Elliot, A. J., & Devine, P. G. (1994). On the motivational nature of cognitive dissonance: Dissonance as psychological discomfort. *Journal of Personality and Social Psychology, 67,* 382–394.

Engs, R. C. (2000). *Clean living movements: American cycles of health reform.* Westport, CT: Praeger.

Entman, R. M. (1993). Framing: Toward clarification of a fractured paradigm. *Journal of Communication, 43,* 51–58.

Erceg-Hurn, D. M. (2008). Drugs, money, and graphic ads: A critical review of the Montana Meth Project. *Prevention Science, 9,* 256–263.

Erickson, B., Lind, E. A., Johnson, B. C., & O'Barr, W. M. (1978). Speech style and impression formation in a court setting: The effects of "powerful" and "powerless" speech. *Journal of Experimental Social Psychology, 14,* 266–279.

Falbo, T. (1977). Multidimensional scaling of power strategies. *Journal of Personality and Social Psychology, 35,* 537–547.

Falk, E. B., Berkman, E. T., Mann, T., Harrison, B., & Lieberman, M. D. (2010). Predicting persuasion-induced behavior change from the brain. *Journal of Neuroscience, 30,* 8421–8424.

Fallon, A. (1990). Culture in the mirror: Sociocultural determinants of body image. In T. F. Cash & T. Pruzinsky (Eds.), *Body images: Development, deviance, and change* (pp. 80–109). New York: Guilford.

Fang, X., Singh, S., & Ahluwalia, R. (2007). An examination of different explanations for the mere exposure effect. *Journal of Consumer Research, 34,* 97–103.

Fazio, R. H. (1989). On the power and functionality of attitudes: The role of attitude accessibility. In A. R. Pratkanis, S. J. Breckler, & A. G. Greenwald (Eds.), *Attitude structure and function* (pp. 153–179). Hillsdale, NJ: Lawrence Erlbaum Associates.

Fazio, R. H. (1990). Multiple processes by which attitudes guide behavior: The MODE model as an integrative framework. In M. P. Zanna (Ed.), *Advances in experimental social psychology* (Vol. 23, pp. 75–109). San Diego: Academic Press.

Fazio, R. H. (1995). Attitudes as object-evaluation associations: Determinants, consequences, and correlates of attitude accessibility. In R. E. Petty & J. A. Krosnick (Eds.), *Attitude strength: Antecedents and consequences* (pp. 247–282). Hillsdale, NJ: Lawrence Erlbaum Associates.

Fazio, R. H. (2000). Accessible attitudes as tools for object appraisal: Their costs and benefits. In G. R. Maio & J. M. Olson (Eds.), *Why we evaluate: Functions of attitudes* (pp. 1–36). Mahwah, NJ: Lawrence Erlbaum Associates.

Fazio, R. H., Powell, M. C., & Williams, C. J. (1989). The role of attitude accessibility in the attitude-to-behavior process. *Journal of Consumer Research, 16,* 280–288.

Fazio, R. H., & Roskos-Ewoldsen, D. R. (1994). Acting as we feel: When and how attitudes guide behavior. In S. Shavitt & T. C. Brock (Eds.), *Persuasion: Psychological insights and perspectives* (pp. 71–93). Boston: Allyn and Bacon.

Fazio, R. H., & Williams, C. J. (1986). Attitude accessibility as a moderator of the attitude–perception and attitude–behavior relations: An investigation of the 1984 presidential election. *Journal of Personality and Social Psychology, 51,* 505–514.

Fazio, R. H., & Zanna, M. P. (1978). Attitudinal qualities relating to the strength of the attitude–behavior relationship. *Journal of Experimental Social Psychology, 14,* 398–408.

Fazio, R. H., & Zanna, M. P. (1981). Direct experience and attitude–behavior consistency. In L. Berkowitz (Ed.), *Advances in experimental social psychology* (Vol. 14, pp. 162–202). New York: Academic Press.

Feeley, T. H., Anker, A. E., & Aloe, A .M. (2012). The door-in-the-face persuasive message strategy: A meta-analysis of the first 35 years. *Communication Monographs, 79,* 316–343.

Feinberg, J. (1998). Coercion. In E. Craig (Ed.), *Routledge encyclopedia of philosophy* (pp. 387–390). London: Routledge.

Fern, E. F., Monroe, K. B., & Avila, R. A. (1986). Effectiveness of multiple request strategies: A synthesis of research results. *Journal of Marketing Research, 23,* 144–152.

Festinger, L. (1957). *A theory of cognitive dissonance.* Stanford, CA: Stanford University Press.

Festinger, L., & Carlsmith, J. M. (1959). Cognitive consequences of forced compliance. *Journal of Abnormal and Social Psychology, 58,* 203–210.

Festinger, L., & Maccoby, N. (1964). On resistance to persuasive communications. *Journal of Abnormal and Social Psychology, 68,* 359–366.

Finckenauer, J. O. (1982). *Scared straight and the panacea phenomenon.* Englewood Cliffs, NJ: Prentice Hall.

Fischer, P., Greitemeyer, T., Kastenmuller, A., Vogrincic, C., & Sauer, A. (2011). The effects of risk-glorifying media exposure on risk-positive cognitions, emotions, and behaviors: A meta-analytic review. *Psychological Bulletin, 137,* 367–390.

Fishbein, M., & Ajzen, I. (1974). Attitudes toward objects as predictors of single and multiple behavioral criteria. *Psychological Review, 81,* 59–74.

Fishbein, M., & Ajzen, I. (1975). *Belief, attitude, intention and behavior: An introduction to theory and research.* Reading, MA: Addison–Wesley.

Fishbein, M., & Ajzen, I. (2010). *Predicting and changing behavior: The reasoned action approach.* New York: Psychology Press.

Fitzpatrick, C. (2000, May 18). A new era of male attractiveness? *Plain Dealer,* 5-F.

Fitzpatrick, M. A., & Winke, J. (1979). You always hurt the one you love: Strategies and tactics in interpersonal conflict. *Communication Quarterly, 27,* 1–11.

Flora, J. A. (2001). The Stanford community studies: Campaigns to reduce cardiovascular disease. In R. E. Rice & C. K. Atkin (Eds.), *Public communication campaigns* (3rd ed., pp. 193–213). Thousand Oaks, CA: Sage.

Fogg, B. J. (2003). Motivating, influencing, and persuading users. In J. A. Jacko & A. Sears (Eds.), *The human–computer interaction handbook: Fundamentals, evolving technologies and emerging applications* (pp. 358–370). Mahwah, NJ: Lawrence Erlbaum Associates.

Fountain, H. (2006, October 31). Observatory: The elephant in the mirror. *The New York Times,* D3.

Frankena, W. (1963). *Ethics.* Englewood Cliffs, NJ: Prentice Hall.

Freedman, J. L., & Fraser, S. C. (1966). Compliance without pressure: The foot-in-the-door technique. *Journal of Personality and Social Psychology, 4,* 195–202.

Freimuth, V. (1990). The chronically uninformed: Closing the knowledge gap in health. In E. B. Ray & L. Donohew (Eds.), *Communication and health: Systems and applications* (pp. 171–186). Hillsdale, NJ: Lawrence Erlbaum Associates.

Frey, D. (1986). Recent research on selective exposure to information. In L. Berkowitz (Ed.), *Advances in experimental social psychology* (Vol. 19, pp. 41–80). Orlando, FL: Academic Press.

Frey, K. P., & Eagly, A. H. (1993). Vividness can undermine the persuasiveness of messages. *Journal of Personality and Social Psychology, 65,* 32–44.

Friedman, T. L. (2006, March 1). Who's afraid of a gas tax? *The New York Times,* A25.

Frymier, A. B., & Nadler, M. K. (2011). *Persuasion: Integrating theory, research, and practice* (2nd ed.). Dubuque, IA: Kendall/Hunt.

Gardner, D. (2011). *Future babble: Why expert predictions are next to worthless, and you can do better.* New York: Dutton.

Garland, H. (1990). Throwing good money after bad: The effect of sunk costs on the decision to escalate commitment to an ongoing project. *Journal of Applied Psychology, 75,* 728–731.

Gass, R. H., & Seiter, J. S. (2011). *Persuasion, social influence, and compliance gaining* (4th ed.). Boston: Allyn & Bacon.

Gaziano, C. (1983). The knowledge gap: An analytical review of media effects. *Communication Research, 10,* 447–486.

Genzlinger, N. (2011, May 16). Housewives, sure, but what makes them real? *The New York Times,* C1, C6.

Gerard, H. B., & Mathewson, G. C. (1966). The effect of severity of initiation on liking for a group: A replication. *Journal of Experimental Social Psychology, 2,* 278–287.

Gerrig, R. J. (1993). *Experiencing narrative worlds: On the psychological activities of reading.* New Haven, CT: Yale University Press.

Gerth, J., & Shane, S. (2005, December 1). U.S. is said to pay to plant articles in Iraq papers. *The New York Times,* A1, A18.

Gertner, J. (2009, April 19). Why isn't the brain green? *The New York Times Magazine,* 36–43.

Giles, H., & Street, R. L., Jr. (1994). Communicator characteristics and behavior. In M. L. Knapp & G. R. Miller (Eds.), *Handbook of interpersonal communication* (2nd ed., pp. 103–161). Thousand Oaks, CA: Sage.

Gladwell, M. (2005). *Blink: The power of thinking without thinking.* New York: Little, Brown.

Glick, P., & Fiske, S. T. (1996). The ambivalent sexism inventory: Differentiating hostile and benevolent sexism. *Journal of Personality and Social Psychology, 70,* 491–512.

Glynn, C. J., Herbst, S., O'Keefe, G. J., & Shapiro, R. Y. (1999). *Public opinion.* Boulder, CO: Westview Press.

Godbold, L. C., & Pfau, M. (2000). Conferring resistance to peer pressure among adolescents: Using inoculation theory to discourage alcohol use. *Communication Research, 27,* 411–437.

Goei, R., Lindsey, L. L. M., Boster, F. J., Skalski, P. D., & Bowman, J. M. (2003). The mediating role of liking and obligation on the relationship between favors and compliance. *Communication Research, 30,* 178–197.

Goei, R., Roberto, A., Meyer, G., & Carlyle, K. (2007). The effects of favor and apology on compliance. *Communication Research, 34,* 575–595.

Goethals, G. R., & Nelson, R. E. (1973). Similarity in the influence process: The belief–value distinction. *Journal of Personality and Social Psychology, 25,* 117–122.

Goldberg, J. (2000, June 25). The education of a holy warrior. *The New York Times Magazine,* 32–37, 53, 63–64, 70–71.

Golden, J. L., Berquist, G. F., & Coleman, W. E. (2000). *The rhetoric of Western thought* (7th ed.). Dubuque, IA: Kendall/Hunt.

Goldman, R., & Papson, S. (1996). *Sign wars: The cluttered landscape of advertising.* New York: Guilford Press.

Goldstein, N. J., & Cialdini, R. B. (2007). Using social norms as a lever of social influence. In A. R. Pratkanis (Ed.), *The science of social influence: Advances and future progress* (pp. 167–191). New York: Psychology Press.

Goodman, P. S. (2010). In case of emergency: What not to do. P. R. missteps fueled the fiascos at BP, Toyota and Goldman. *The New York Times* (Sunday Business), 1, 6, 7.

Goodman, P. S., & Morgenson, G. (2008, December 28). Saying yes to anyone, WaMu built empire on shaky loans. *The New York Times,* 1, 21.

Goodstein L. (1997, April 7). No one put a gun to their heads. *The Washington Post National Weekly Edition,* 32.

Granberg, D. (1993). Political perception. In S. Iyengar & W. J. McGuire (Eds.), *Explorations in political psychology* (pp. 70–112). Durham, NC: Duke University Press.

Green, M. C., & Brock, T. C. (2000). The role of transportation in the persuasiveness of public narratives. *Journal of Personality and Social Psychology, 79,* 701–721.

Green, M. C., & Brock, T. C. (2002). In the mind's eye: Transportation-imagery model of narrative persuasion. In M. C. Green, J. J. Strange, & T. C. Brock (Eds.), *Narrative impact: Social and cognitive foundations* (pp. 315–341). Mahwah, NJ: Lawrence Erlbaum Associates.

Green, M. C., & Brock, T. C. (2005). Persuasiveness of narratives. In T. C. Brock & M. C. Green (Eds.), *Persuasion: Psychological insights and perspectives* (pp. 117–142). Thousand Oaks, CA: Sage.

Green, M. C., Kass, S., Carrey, J., Herzig, B., Feeney, R., & Sabini, J. (2008). Transportation across media: Repeated exposure to print and film. *Media Psychology, 11,* 512–539.

Greenberg, B. S., & Miller, G. R. (1966). The effects of low-credible sources on message acceptance. *Speech Monographs, 33,* 127–136.

Greene, J. O., McDaniel, T. L., Buksa, K., & Ravizza, S. M. (1993). Cognitive processes in the production of multiple-goal messages: Evidence from the temporal characteristics of speech. *Western Journal of Communication, 57,* 65–86.

Greenhouse, L. (1999, September 29). Managed care challenge to be heard by high court. *The New York Times,* A22.

Greenwald, A. G. (1968). Cognitive learning, cognitive response to persuasion, and attitude change. In A. G. Greenwald, T. C. Brock, & T. M. Ostrom (Eds.), *Psychological foundations of attitudes* (pp. 147–170). New York: Academic Press.

Greenwald, A. G., McGhee, D. E., & Schwartz, J. L. K. (1998). Measuring individual differences in implicit cognition: The Implicit Association Test. *Journal of Personality and Social Psychology, 74,* 1464–1480.

Greenwald, A. G., Spangenberg, E. R., Pratkanis, A. R., & Eskenazi, J. (1991). Double-blind tests of subliminal self-help audiotapes. *Psychological Science, 2,* 119–122.

Grimes, W. (2005, November 18). Winnowing the field of America to one representative. *The New York Times,* B42.

Griskevicius, V., Tybur, J. M., & Van den Bergh, B. (2010). Going green to be seen: Status, reputation, and conspicuous conservation. *Journal of Personality and Social Psychology, 98,* 392–404.

Gruder, C. L., Cook, T. D., Hennigan, K. M., Flay, B. R., Alessis, C., & Halamaj, J. (1978). Empirical tests of the absolute sleeper effect predicted from the discounting cue hypothesis. *Journal of Personality and Social Psychology, 36,* 1061–1074.

Grush, J. E., McKeough, K. L., & Ahlering, R. F. (1978). Extrapolating laboratory exposure research to actual political elections. *Journal of Personality and Social Psychology, 36,* 257–270.

Gunther, A. C., Bolt, D., Borzekowski, D. L. G., Liebhart, J. L., & Dillard, J. P. (2006). Presumed influence on peer norms: How mass media indirectly affect adolescent smoking. *Journal of Communication, 56,* 52–68.

Gurak, L. J., & Antonijevic, S. (2009). Digital rhetoric and public discourse. In A. A. Lunsford, K. H. Wilson, & R. A. Eberly (Eds.), *The Sage handbook of rhetorical studies* (pp. 497–507). Thousand Oaks, CA: Sage.

Guttman, L. (1944). A basis for scaling qualitative data. *American Sociological Review, 9,* 139–150.

Guttman, N. (1997). Ethical dilemmas in health campaigns. *Health Communication, 9,* 155–190.

Guttman, N. (2000). *Public health communication interventions: Values and ethical dilemmas.* Thousand Oaks, CA: Sage

Haines, M., & Spear, S. F. (1996). Changing the perception of the norm: A strategy to decrease binge drinking among college students. *Journal of American College Health, 45,* 134–140.

Haleta, L. L. (1996). Student perceptions of teachers' use of language: The effects of powerful and powerless language on impression formation and uncertainty. *Communication Education, 45,* 16–28.

Hamermesh, D. S. (2011, August 28). Ugly? You may have a case. *The New York Times* (Sunday Review), 12.

Hamilton, M. A., & Hunter, J. E. (1998). The effect of language intensity on receiver evaluations of message, source, and topic. In M. Allen & R. W. Preiss (Eds.), *Persuasion: Advances through meta-analysis* (pp. 99–138). Cresskill, NJ: Hampton Press.

Hampton, B., Brinberg, D., Peter, P., & Corus, C. (2009). Integrating the unified theory and stages of change to create targeted health messages. *Journal of Applied Social Psychology, 39,* 449–471.

Hannah, D. B., & Sternthal, B. (1984). Detecting and explaining the sleeper effect. *Journal of Consumer Research, 11,* 632–642.

Hansen, M., Kossman, C., Wilbrecht, K., & Andsager, J. (2000). *Culture change on campus.* Unpublished paper, Washington State University, Pullman.

Harmon, A. (2005, November 16). Young, assured and playing pharmacist to friends. *The New York Times,* A1, A17.

Harmon-Jones, E. (2002). A cognitive dissonance theory perspective on persuasion. In J. P. Dillard & M. Pfau (Eds.), *The persuasion handbook: Developments in theory and practice* (pp. 99–116). Thousand Oaks, CA: Sage.

Harmon-Jones, E., & Mills, J. (1999). An introduction to cognitive dissonance theory and an overview of current perspectives on the theory. In E. Harmon-Jones & J. Mills (Eds.), *Cognitive dissonance: Progress on a pivotal theory in social psychology* (pp. 3–21). Washington, DC: American Psychological Association.

Harmon-Jones, E., & Winkielman, P. (2007). A brief overview of social neuroscience. In E. Harmon-Jones & P. Winkielman (Eds.), *Social neuroscience: Integrating biological and psychological explanations of social behavior* (pp. 3–11). New York: Guilford.

Harres, A. (1998). "But basically you're feeling well, are you?" Tag questions in medical consultations. *Health Communication, 10,* 111–123.

Harrington, N. G. (2013). Introduction to the special issue: Communication strategies to reduce health disparities. *Journal of Communication, 63,* 1–7.

Harris, G. (2004, June 27). As doctors write prescriptions, drug companies write checks. *The New York Times,* A1, 19.

Harris, G. R., & Roberts, J. (2007, March 21). A state's files put doctors' ties to drug makers on close view. *The New York Times,* A1, A18.

Harris, R. J. (1999). *A cognitive psychology of mass communication* (3rd ed.). Mahwah, NJ: Lawrence Erlbaum Associates.

Harrison, K., & Cantor, J. (1997). The relationship between media consumption and eating disorders. *Journal of Communication, 47(1)*, 40–67.

Hart, R. P. (1984). *Verbal style and the presidency: A computer-based analysis*. Orlando, FL: Academic Press.

Hart, R. P., Friedrich, G. W., & Brummett, B. (1983). *Public communication* (2nd ed.). New York: Harper & Row.

Hartley, R. E. (2000). *Marketing mistakes* (8th ed.). New York: Wiley.

Hastorf, A., & Cantril, H. (1954). They saw a game: A case study. *Journal of Abnormal and Social Psychology, 49*, 129–134.

Haugtvedt, C. P., Petty, R. E., & Cacioppo, J. T. (1992). Need for cognition and advertising: Understanding the role of personality variables in consumer behavior. *Journal of Consumer Psychology, 1*, 239–260.

Haugtvedt, C. P., & Wegener, D. T. (1994). Message order effects in persuasion: An attitude strength perspective. *Journal of Consumer Research, 21*, 205–218.

Hauser, M. D. (2006). *Moral minds: How nature designed our universal sense of right and wrong*. New York: HarperCollins.

Hazlett, R. L., & Hazlett, S. Y. (1999). Emotional response to television commercials: Facial EMG vs. self-report. *Journal of Advertising Research, 39(2)*, 7–23.

Heider, F. (1958). *The psychology of interpersonal relations*. New York: Wiley.

Helft, M., & Vega, T. (2010, August 30). Seeing that ad on every site? You're right. It's tracking you. *The New York Times*, A1, B2.

Henriksen, L., Flora, J. A., Feighery, E., & Fortmann, S. P. (2002). Effects on youth of exposure to retail tobacco advertising. *Journal of Applied Social Psychology, 32*, 1771–1789.

Henriques, D. B., & Bergman, L. (2000, March 15). Profiting from fine print with Wall Street's help, *The New York Times*, A1, C12–C13.

Herbert, B. (2005a, June 16). Uncle Sam really wants you. *The New York Times*, A29.

Herbert, B. (2005b, August, 22). Truth in recruiting. *The New York Times*, A17.

Hernandez, R. (2006, February 13). At the lectern, critics and admirers agree, Hillary Clinton is no Bill Clinton. *The New York Times*, A19.

Hewitt, B., Fields-Meyer, T., Frankel, B., Jewel, D., Lambert, P., O'Neill, A. M., & Plummer, W. (1997, April14). Who they were. *People*, 40–56.

Hilts, P. J. (1996). *Smokescreen: The truth behind the tobacco industry cover-up*. Reading, MA: Addison-Wesley.

Hinyard, L. J., & Kreuter, M. W. (2007). Using narrative communication as a tool for health behavior change: A conceptual, theoretical, and empirical overview. *Health Education & Behavior, 34*, 777–792.

Hippler, H. J., Schwarz, N., & Sudman, S. (Eds.) (1987). *Social information processing and survey methodology*. New York: Springer-Verlag.

Hoffman, J. (2011, December 31). New medium for sex education is text message. *The New York Times*, A1, A3.

Hogan, J. M. (2013). Persuasion in the rhetorical tradition. In J. P. Dillard & L. Shen (Eds.), *The Sage handbook of persuasion: Developments in theory and practice* (2nd ed., pp 2–19). Thousand Oaks, CA: Sage.

Holbrook, A. L., Berent, M. K., Krosnick, J. A., Visser, P. S., & Boninger, D. S. (2005). Attitude importance and the accumulation of attitude-relevant knowledge in memory. *Journal of Personality and Social Psychology, 88,* 749–769.

Holmes, S. A. (1998, November 20). Klan case transcends racial divide. *The New York Times,* A14.

Holt, J. (2006, December 3). The new, soft paternalism. *The New York Times Magazine,* 15–17.

Holtgraves, T., & Lasky, B. (1999). Linguistic power and persuasion. *Journal of Language and Social Psychology, 18,* 196–205.

Homans, G. C. (1961). *Social behavior: Its elementary forms.* New York: Harcourt, Brace.

Hornik, R. (2002). Public health communication: Making sense of contradictory evidence. In R. Hornik (Ed.), *Public health communication: Evidence for behavior change* (pp. 1–19). Mahwah, NJ: Lawrence Erlbaum Associates.

Hornik, R. C., & Ramirez, A. S. (2006). Race/ethnic disparities and segmentation in communication campaigns. (Communication and racial disparities in health care, R. M. Perloff, Ed.), *American Behavioral Scientist, 49,* 868–894.

Hosman, L. A. (1989). The evaluative consequences of hedges, hesitations, and intensifiers: Powerful and powerless speech styles. *Human Communication Research, 15,* 383–406.

Hosman, L. A. (2002). Language and persuasion. In J. P. Dillard & M. Pfau (Eds.), *The persuasion handbook: Developments in theory and practice* (pp. 371–390). Thousand Oaks, CA: Sage.

Hovland, C. I. (1959). Reconciling conflicting results derived from experimental and survey studies of attitude change. *American Psychologist, 14,* 8–17.

Hovland, C. I., Harvey, O. J., & Sherif, M. (1957). Assimilation and contrast effects in reactions to communication and attitude change. *Journal of Abnormal and Social Psychology, 55,* 244–252.

Hovland, C. I., Janis, I. L., & Kelley, H. H. (1953). *Communication and persuasion: Psychological studies of opinion change.* New Haven, CT: Yale University Press.

Hovland. C. I., Lumsdaine, A. A., & Sheffield, F. D. (1949). *Experiments on mass communication.* Princeton, NJ: Princeton University Press.

Huff, D. (1954). *How to lie with statistics.* New York: Norton.

Hullett, C. R. (2004). Using functional theory to promote sexually transmitted disease (STD) testing: The impact of value-expressive messages and guilt. *Communication Research, 31,* 363–396.

Hullett, C. R. (2006). Using functional theory to promote HIV testing: The impact of value-expressive messages, uncertainty, and fear. *Health Communication, 20,* 57–67.

Hwang, Y. (2012). Social diffusion of campaign effects: Campaign-generated interpersonal communication as a mediator of antitobacco campaign effects. *Communication Research, 39,* 120–141.

Infante, D. A., & Rancer, A. S. (1982). A conceptualization and measure of argumentativeness. *Journal of Personality Assessment, 46,* 72–80.

Infante, D. A., & Rancer, A. S. (1996). Argumentativeness and verbal aggressiveness: A review of recent theory and research. In B. Burleson (Ed.), *Communication yearbook 19* (pp. 319–351). Thousand Oaks, CA: Sage.

Infante, D. A., & Wigley, C. J., III (1986). Verbal aggressiveness: An interpersonal model and measure. *Communication Monographs, 53,* 61–69.

Iyengar, S., & Hahn, K. S. (2009). Red media, blue media: Evidence of ideological selectivity in media use. *Journal of Communication, 59,* 19–39.

Jamieson, K. H. (1988). *Eloquence in an electronic age: The transformation of political speechmaking.* New York: Oxford University Press.

Jarvis, S. E. (2011). The use of focus groups in political communication research. In E. P. Bucy & R. L. Holbert (Eds.), *The sourcebook for political communication research: Methods, measures, and analytical techniques* (pp. 283–299). New York: Routledge.

Jensen, J. D., Bernat, J. K., Wilson, K. M., & Goonewardene, J. (2011). The delay hypothesis: The manifestation of media effects over time. *Human Communication Research, 37,* 509–528.

Jhally, S. (1998). *Advertising and the end of the world* (video). Northampton, MA: Media Education Foundation.

Johnson, B. T., & Boynton, M. H. (2010). Putting attitudes in their place: Behavioral prediction in the face of competing variables. In J. P. Forgas, J. Cooper, & W. D. Crano (Eds.), *The psychology of attitudes and attitude change* (pp. 19–38). New York: Psychology Press.

Johnson, B. T., & Eagly, A. H. (1989). Effects of involvement on persuasion: A meta-analysis. *Psychological Bulletin, 106,* 290–314.

Johnson, C. (2011). *Microstyle: The art of writing little.* New York: W. W. Norton.

Johnston, D. C. (2001, February 14). Dozens of rich Americans join in fight to retain the estate tax. *The New York Times,* A1, A18.

Jordan, J. M., & Roloff, M. E. (1997). Planning skills and negotiator goal accomplishment: The relationship between self-monitoring and plan generation, plan enactment, and plan consequences. *Communication Research, 24,* 31–63.

Julka, D. L., & Marsh, K. L. (2005). An attitude functions approach to increasing organ-donation participation. *Journal of Applied Social Psychology, 35,* 821–849.

Kahle, L. R. (1996). Social values and consumer behavior: Research from the list of values. In C. Seligman, J. M. Olson, & M. P. Zanna (Eds.), *The psychology of values: The Ontario symposium* (Vol. 8, pp. 135–151). Mahwah, NJ: Lawrence Erlbaum Associates.

Kahle, L. R., & Homer, P. M. (1985). Physical attractiveness of the celebrity endorser: A social adaptation perspective. *Journal of Consumer Research, 11,* 954–961.

Kahneman, D. (2011). *Thinking, fast and slow.* New York: Farrar, Straus and Giroux.

Kalichman, S. C., & Coley, B. (1995). Context framing to enhance HIV-antibody testing messages targeted to African American women. *Health Psychology, 14,* 247–254.

Kassan, L. D. (1999). *Second opinions: Sixty psychotherapy patients evaluate their therapists.* Northvale, NJ: Jason Aronson Press.

Katz, D. (1960). The functional approach to the study of attitudes. *Public Opinion Quarterly, 24,* 163–204.

Kaufman, D. Q., Stasson, M. F., & Hart, J. W. (1999). Are the tabloids always wrong or is that just what we think?: Need for cognition and perceptions of articles in print media. *Journal of Applied Social Psychology, 29,* 1984–1997.

Kaufman, L. (2000, September 17). And now, a few more words about breasts. *The New York Times* [Week in Review], 3.

Kazoleas, D. C. (1993). A comparison of the persuasive effectiveness of qualitative versus quantitative evidence: A test of explanatory hypotheses. *Communication Quarterly, 41,* 40–50.

Kellermann, K., & Cole, T. (1994). Classifying compliance gaining messages: Taxonomic disorder and strategic confusion. *Communication Theory, 4,* 3–60.

Kelman, H. C. (1958). Compliance, identification, and internalization: Three processes of attitude change. *Journal of Conflict Resolution, 2,* 51–60.

Kelman, H. C., & Hamilton, V. L. (1989). *Crimes of obedience: Toward a social psychology of authority and responsibility.* New Haven: Yale University Press.

Kennedy, G. (1963). *The art of persuasion in Greece.* Princeton, NJ: Princeton University Press.

Key, W. B. (1974). *Subliminal seduction.* New York: Signet Books.

Kiesler, C. A., Collins, B. E., & Miller, N. (1969). *Attitude change: A critical analysis of theoretical approaches.* New York: Wiley.

Kim, M. S., & Bresnahan, M. (1994). A process model of request tactic evaluation. *Discourse Processes, 18,* 317–344.

Kim, M. S., & Hunter, J. E. (1993). Attitude–behavior relations: A meta-analysis of attitudinal relevance and topic. *Journal of Communication, 43(1),* 101–142.

Kim, M. S., & Sharkey, W. F. (1995). Independent and interdependent construals of self: Explaining cultural patterns of interpersonal communication in multicultural organizational settings. *Communication Quarterly, 43,* 20–38.

Kim, M. S., & Wilson, S. R. (1994). A cross-cultural comparison of implicit theories of requesting. *Communication Monographs, 61,* 210–235.

Kim, S. S., Kaplowitz, S., & Johnston, M. V. (2004). The effects of physician empathy on patient satisfaction and compliance. *Evaluation & the Health Professions, 27,* 237–251.

Kinder, D. R., & Sanders, L. M. (1990). Mimicking political debate with survey questions: The case of White opinion on affirmative action for Blacks. *Social Cognition, 8,* 73–103.

King, C. S. (1969). *My life with Martin Luther King, Jr.* New York: Holt, Rinehart & Winston.

King, S. W., Minami, Y., & Samovar, L. A. (1985). A comparison of Japanese and American perceptions of source credibility. *Communication Research Reports, 2,* 76–79.

Kipnis, D., & Schmidt, S. (1996). The language of persuasion. In E. J. Coats & R. S. Feldman (Eds.), *Classic and contemporary readings in social psychology* (pp. 184–188). Upper Saddle River, NJ: Prentice Hall.

Kleinfield, N. R. (1999, November 15). For three interns, fatigue and healing at top speed. *The New York Times,* A1, A28.

Kleinfield, N. R. (2000, October 19). It's root, root, root, but for which team? *The New York Times,* A1, C27.

Kline, S. L., & Clinton, B. L. (1998). Developments in children's persuasive message practices. *Communication Education, 47,* 120–136.

Klucharev, V., Smidts, A., & Fernandez, G. (2008). Brain mechanisms of persuasion: How "expert power" modulates memory and attitudes. *Social Cognitive and Affective Neuroscience, 3,* 353–366.

Kluckhohn, C. (1951). Values and value-orientations in the theory of action: An exploration in definition and classification. In T. Parsons & E. A. Shils (Eds.), *Toward a general theory of action* (pp. 388–433). Cambridge, MA: Harvard University Press.

Klusendorf, S. (2001). *Why pro-life advocates should use graphic visual aids.* Online: http://realweb.ifastnet.com/articles/graphic./html. (Accessed: May 4, 2013).

Knowles, E. S., Butler, S., & Linn, J. A. (2001). Increasing compliance by reducing resistance. In J. P. Forgas & K. D. Williams (Eds.), *Social influence: Direct and indirect processes* (pp. 41–60). Philadelphia: Taylor & Francis.

Koehler, S. P., & Willis, F. N. (1994). Traffic citations in relation to gender. *Journal of Applied Social Psychology, 24,* 1919–1926.

Kopfman, J. E., Smith, S. W., Ah Yun, J. K., & Hodges, A. (1998). Affective and cognitive reactions to narrative versus statistical evidence organ donation messages. *Journal of Applied Communication Research, 26,* 279–300.

Kotowski, M. R., Levine, T. R., Baker, C. R., and Bolt, J. M. (2009). A multitrait-multimethod validity assessment of the verbal aggressiveness and argumentativeness scales. *Communication Monographs, 76,* 443–462.

Kovach, G. C. (2008, June 6). A sect's families reunite, and start to come home. *The New York Times.* Online: http://www.nytimes.com/2008/06/06/us/06polygamy.html.

Kraus, S. J. (1995). Attitudes and the prediction of behavior: A meta-analysis of the empirical literature. *Personality and Social Psychology Bulletin, 21,* 58–75.

Kreps, G. L. (2006). Communication and racial inequities in health care. (Communication and racial disparities in health care, R. M. Perloff, Ed.), *American Behavioral Scientist, 49,* 760–774.

Kreuter, M., Farrell, D., Olevitch, L., & Brennan, L. (2000). *Tailoring health messages: Customizing communication with computer technology.* Mahwah, NJ: Lawrence Erlbaum Associates.

Kristof, N. D. (2008, September 21). The push to "otherize" Obama. *The New York Times* [Week in Review], 9.

Krosnick, J. A., Judd, C. M., & Wittenbrink, B. (2005). The measurement of attitudes. In D. Albarracín, B. T. Johnson, & M. P. Zanna (Eds.), *The handbook of attitudes* (pp. 21–76). Mahwah, NJ: Lawrence Erlbaum Associates.

Krosnick, J. A., & Petty, R. E. (1995). Attitude strength: An overview. In R. E. Petty & J. A. Krosnick (Eds.), *Attitude strength: Antecedents and consequences* (pp. 1–24). Hillsdale, NJ: Lawrence Erlbaum Associates.

Kruglanski, A. W., & Thompson, E. P. (1999). Persuasion by a single route: A view from the unimodel. *Psychological Inquiry, 10,* 83–109.

Kuczynski, A. (2006). *Beauty junkies: Inside our $15 billion obsession with cosmetic surgery.* New York: Doubleday.

Kumkale, G. T., & Albarracín, D. (2004). The sleeper effect in persuasion: A meta-analytic review. *Psychological Bulletin, 130,* 143–172.

LaBarbera, P. A., & Tucciarone, J. D. (1995). GSR reconsidered: A behavior-based approach to evaluating and improving the sales potency of advertising. *Journal of Advertising Research, 35,* 33–53.

LaFeber, W. (1999). *Michael Jordan and the new global capitalism.* New York: Norton.

Lakoff, G. (1996). *Moral politics: What conservatives know that liberals don't.* Chicago: University of Chicago Press.

Lakoff, G. (2004). *Don't think of an elephant! Know your values and frame the debate.* White River Junction, VT: Chelsea Green Publishing.

Lambiase, J. J. (2003). Sex—Online and in Internet advertising. In T. Reichert & J. Lambiase

(Eds.), *Sex in advertising: Perspectives on the erotic appeal* (pp. 247–269). Mahwah, NJ: Lawrence Erlbaum Associates.

Langer, J. (1997). What consumers wish brand managers knew. *Journal of Advertising Research, 37(6),* 60–65.

Langrehr, F. W., & Caywood, C. L. (1995). A semiotic approach to determining the sins and virtues portrayed in advertising. *Journal of Current Issues and Research in Advertising, 17,* 33–47.

LaPiere, R. T. (1934). Attitudes vs. action. *Social Forces, 13,* 230–237.

Lavin, M. (2001). *Clean new world: Culture, politics, and graphic design.* Cambridge, MA: MIT Press.

Lavine, H., Thomsen, C. J., & Gonzales, M. T. (1997). The development of inter-attitudinal consistency: The shared-consequences model. *Journal of Personality and Social Psychology, 72,* 735–749.

Lavine, H., Thomsen, C. J., Zanna, M. P., & Borgida, E. (1998). On the primacy of affect in the determination of attitudes and behavior: The moderating role of affective–cognitive ambivalence. *Journal of Experimental Social Psychology, 34,* 398–421.

Leave No Sales Pitch Behind (2005, January 4). *The New York Times* [Editorial], A22.

Ledbetter, A. M. (2009). Measuring online communication attitude: Instrument development and validation. *Communication Monographs, 76,* 463–486.

Lederman, L. C., Stewart, L. P., Barr, S. L., Powell, R. L., Laitman, L., & Goodhart, F. W. (2001). RU SURE? Using communication theory to reduce dangerous drinking on a college campus. In R. E. Rice & C. K. Atkin (Eds.), *Public communication campaigns* (3rd ed., pp. 295–299). Thousand Oaks, CA: Sage.

Lee, J. G., & Thorson, E. (2008). The impact of celebrity–product incongruence on the effectiveness of product endorsement. *Journal of Advertising Research, 48,* 433–449.

Leippe, M. R., & Eisenstadt, D. (1994). Generalization of dissonance reduction: Decreasing prejudice through induced compliance. *Journal of Personality and Social Psychology, 67,* 395–413.

Leland, J. (2005, September 18). Under din of abortion debate, an experience shared quietly. *The New York Times,* 1, 29.

Leodoro, G., & Lynn, M. (2007). The effect of server posture on the tips of Whites and Blacks. *Journal of Applied Social Psychology, 37,* 201–209.

Lerner, B. H. (2011). *One for the road: Drunk driving since 1900.* Baltimore: Johns Hopkins Press.

Levine, J. M., & Valle, R. S. (1975). The convert as a credible communicator. *Social Behavior and Personality, 3,* 81–90.

Levine, K. J., Muenchen, R. A., & Brooks, A. M. (2010). Measuring transformational and charismatic leadership: Why isn't charisma measured? *Communication Monographs, 77,* 576–491.

Levy, N. (2005, May 3). Private England pleads guilty to abuses. *The New York Times,* A8.

Levy, S. (2006). *The perfect thing: How the iPod shuffles commerce, culture, and coolness.* New York: Simon & Schuster.

Lewis, I., Watson, B., & White, K.M. (2013). Extending the explanatory utility of the EPPM beyond fear-based persuasion. *Health Communication, 28,* 84-98.

Lieberman, D. A. (2001). Using interactive media in communication campaigns for children and adolescents. In R. E. Rice & C. K. Atkin (Eds.), *Public communication campaigns* (3rd ed., pp. 373–388). Thousand Oaks, CA: Sage.

Lifton, R. J. (2003). Foreword. In M. T. Singer, *Cults in our midst* (Rev. ed., pp. xi–xiii). San Francisco: Jossey-Bass.

Likert, R. (1932). A technique for the measurement of attitudes. *Archives of Psychology, 140,* 1–55.

Lim, J. S., & Ki, E. J. (2007). Resistance to ethically suspicious parody video on YouTube: A test of inoculation theory. *Journalism and Mass Communication Quarterly, 84,* 713–728.

Linz, D. G., & Penrod, S. (1984). Increasing attorney persuasiveness in the courtroom. *Law and Psychology Review, 8,* 1–47.

Lipstadt, D. E. (2011). *The Eichmann trial.* New York: Schocken Books.

Lord, C. G., Lepper, M. R., & Mackie, D. (1984). Attitude prototypes as determinants of attitude–behavior consistency. *Journal of Personality and Social Psychology, 46,* 1254–1266.

Lord, C. G., Ross, L., & Lepper, M. R. (1979). Biased assimilation and attitude polarization: The effects of prior theories on subsequently considered evidence. *Journal of Personality and Social Psychology, 37,* 2098–2109.

Lyon, A., & Mirivel, J. C. (2011). Reconstructing Merck's practical theory of communication: The ethics of pharmaceutical sales representative-physician encounters. *Communication Monographs, 78,* 53–72.

Lynch, J., & Schuler, D. (1994). The matchup effect of spokesperson and product congruency: A schema theory interpretation. *Psychology & Marketing, 11,* 417–445.

Lynn, M., & Mynier, K. (1993). Effect of server posture on restaurant tipping. *Journal of Applied Social Psychology, 23,* 678–685.

Maccoby, N., & Farquhar, J. W. (1975). Communication for health: Unselling heart disease. *Journal of Communication, 25,* 114–126.

Mahler, J. (2005, March 27). The soul of the new exurb. *The New York Times Magazine,* 30–37, 46, 50, 54, 57.

Maibach, E. W., Kreps, G. L., & Bonaguro, E. W. (1993). Developing strategic communication campaigns for HIV/AIDS prevention. In S. Ratzan (Ed.), *AIDS: Effective health communication for the 90s* (pp. 15–35). Washington, DC: Taylor & Francis.

Maio, G. R., & Olson, J. M. (1998). Values as truisms: Evidence and implications. *Journal of Personality and Social Psychology, 74,* 294–311.

Maio, G. R., & Olson, J. M. (Eds.) (2000a). *Why we evaluate: Functions of attitudes.* Mahwah, NJ: Lawrence Erlbaum Associates.

Maio, G. R., & Olson, J. M. (2000b). What is a "value-expressive" attitude? In G. R. Maio & J. M. Olson (Eds.), *Why we evaluate: Functions of attitudes* (pp. 249–269). Mahwah, NJ: Lawrence Erlbaum Associates.

Manstead, A. S. R., Proffitt, C., & Smart, J. L. (1983). Predicting and understanding mothers' infant-feeding intentions and behavior: Testing the theory of reasoned action. *Journal of Personality and Social Psychology, 44,* 657–671.

Marcus, E. N. (2006, November 21). When young doctors strut too much of their stuff. *The New York Times,* D5.

Marklein, M. B. (2000, October 11). Ugly truths about hazing. *USA Today,* 6D.

Martin, M. (2001, March 30). Man sentenced to educate himself. *Plain Dealer,* 1-B, 5-B.

Marwell, G., & Schmitt, D. R. (1967). Dimensions of compliance-gaining behavior: An empirical analysis. *Sociometry, 30,* 350–364.

Max, D. T. (1999, December 26). The Oprah effect. *The New York Times Magazine,* 36–41.

Mazzocco, P. J., & Brock, T. C. (2006). Understanding the role of mental imagery in persuasion: A cognitive resources model analysis. In L. R. Kahle & C.-H. Kim (Eds.), *Creating images and the psychology of marketing communication* (pp. 65–78). Mahwah, NJ: Erlbaum Associates.

McAlister, A. L., & Fernandez, M. (2002). "Behavioral journalism" accelerates diffusion of healthy innovations. In R. Hornik (Ed.), *Public health communication: Evidence for behavior change* (pp. 315–326). Mahwah, NJ: Lawrence Erlbaum Associates.

McBane, D. A. (1995). Empathy and the salesperson: A multidimensional perspective. *Psychology and Marketing, 12,* 349–369.

McCarty, J. A. (2004). Product placement: The nature of the practice and potential avenues of inquiry. In L. J. Shrum (Ed.), *The psychology of entertainment media: Blurring the lines between entertainment and persuasion* (pp. 45–61). Mahwah, NJ: Lawrence Erlbaum Associates.

McCombs, M., & Reynolds, A. (2002). News influence on our pictures of the world. In J. Bryant & D. Zillmann (Eds.), *Media effects: Advances in theory and research* (2nd ed., pp. 1–18). Mahwah, NJ: Lawrence Erlbaum Associates.

McConahay, J. B. (1986). Modern racism, ambivalence, and the Modern Racism Scale. In J. F. Dovidio & S. L. Gaertner (Eds.), *Prejudice, discrimination, and racism* (pp. 91–125). Orlando, FL: Academic Press.

McCracken, G. (1986). Culture and consumption: A theoretical account of the structure and movement of the cultural meaning of consumer goods. *Journal of Consumer Research, 13,* 71–84.

McCroskey, J. C. (1969). A summary of experimental research on the effects of evidence in persuasive communication. *Quarterly Journal of Speech, 55,* 169–176.

McCroskey, J. C. (1972). *An introduction to rhetorical communication.* Englewood Cliffs, NJ: Prentice Hall.

McCroskey, J. C. (1997). *An introduction to rhetorical communication* (7th ed.). Boston: Allyn and Bacon.

McCroskey, J. C., & Teven, J. J. (1999). Goodwill: A reexamination of the construct and its measurement. *Communication Monographs, 66,* 90–103.

McCroskey, J. C., & Young, T. J. (1981). Ethos and credibility: The construct and its measurement after three decades. *Central States Speech Journal, 32,* 24–34.

McGlone, M. S., & Giles, H. (2011). Language and interpersonal communication. In M. L. Knapp & J. A. Daly (Eds.), *The Sage handbook of interpersonal communication* (4th ed., pp. 201–237). Thousand Oaks, CA: Sage.

McGuire, W. J. (1969). The nature of attitudes and attitude change. In G. Lindzey & E. Aronson (Eds.), *Handbook of social psychology* (2nd ed., Vol. 3, pp. 136–314). Reading, MA: Addison-Wesley.

McGuire, W. J. (1970, February). A vaccine for brainwash. *Psychology Today*, pp. 36–39, 63–64.

McGuire, W. J. (1989). Theoretical foundations of campaigns. In R. E. Rice & C. K. Atkin (Eds.), *Public communication campaigns* (2nd ed., pp. 43–65). Thousand Oaks, CA: Sage.

McGuire, W. J., & Papageorgis, D. (1961). The relative efficacy of various types of prior belief-defense in producing immunity against persuasion. *Journal of Abnormal and Social Psychology, 62,* 327–337.

McKelvey, T. (2007). *Monstering: Inside America's policy of secret interrogations and torture in the terror war.* New York: Carroll & Graf.

McLuhan, M. (1967). *The medium is the massage.* New York: Random House.

McNeil, Jr., D. G. (2008, June 3). Global update. *The New York Times,* D6.

Meeus, W. H. J., & Raaijmakers, Q. A. W. (1986). Administrative obedience: Carrying out orders to use psychological-administrative violence. *European Journal of Social Psychology, 16,* 311–324.

Messaris, P. (1997). *Visual persuasion: The role of images in advertising.* Thousand Oaks, CA: Sage.

Messud, C. (2008, September 1). Some like it cool. *Newsweek,* 46–50.

Metzger, M. J. (2009). The study of media effects in the era of Internet communication. In R. L. Nabi & M. B. Oliver (Eds.), *The Sage handbook of media processes and effects* (pp. 561–576). Thousand Oaks, CA: Sage.

Metzger, M. J., Flanagin, A. J., & Medders, R. B. (2010). Social and heuristic approaches to credibility evaluation online. *Journal of Communication, 60,* 413–439.

Meyer, J. R. (2007). Compliance gaining. In D. R. Roskos-Ewoldsen & J. L. Monahan (Eds.), *Communication and social cognition: Theories and methods* (pp. 399–416). Mahwah, NJ: Erlbaum Associates.

Meyerowitz, B. E., & Chaiken, S. (1987). The effect of message framing on breast self-examination attitudes, intentions, and behavior. *Journal of Personality and Social Psychology, 52,* 500–510.

Milburn, M. A. (1991). *Persuasion and politics: The social psychology of public opinion.* Pacific Grove, CA: Brooks/Cole.

Miles, H. L. (1993). Language and the orangutan: The old "person" of the forest. In P. Cavalieri & P. Singer (Eds.), *The great ape project: Equality beyond humanity* (pp. 42–57). New York: St. Martin's Griffin.

Milgram, S. (1963). Behavioral study of obedience. *Journal of Abnormal and Social Psychology, 67,* 371–378.

Milgram, S. (1974). *Obedience to authority: An experimental view.* New York: Harper & Row.

Millar, M. G., & Millar, K. U. (1996). The effects of direct and indirect experience on affective and cognitive responses and the attitude–behavior relation. *Journal of Experimental Social Psychology, 32,* 561–579.

Miller, A. G. (1986). *The obedience experiments: A case study of controversy in social science.* New York: Praeger.

Miller, A. G., Collins, B. E., & Brief, D. E. (1995). Perspectives on obedience to authority: The legacy of the Milgram experiments. *Journal of Social Issues, 51,* 1–19.

Miller, G. R. (1980). On being persuaded: Some basic distinctions. In M. E. Roloff & G. R. Miller (Eds.), *Persuasion: New directions in theory and research* (pp. 11–28). Beverly Hills, CA: Sage.

Miller, G. R., Boster, F., Roloff, M., & Seibold, D. (1977). Compliance-gaining message strategies: A typology and some findings concerning effects of situational differences. *Communication Monographs, 44,* 37–51.

Miller, G. R., & Parks, M. R. (1982). Communication in dissolving relationships. In S. Duck (Ed.), *Personal relationships 4: Dissolving relationships* (pp. 127–154). Orlando, FL: Academic Press.

Miller, K. D. (1992). *Voice of deliverance: The language of Martin Luther King, Jr. and its sources.* New York: Free Press.

Miller, N., Maruyama, G., Beaber, R. J., & Valone, K. (1976). Speed of speech and persuasion. *Journal of Personality and Social Psychology, 34,* 615–624.

Mitchell, A. A. (1986). Effects of visual and verbal components of advertisements on brand attitudes. *Journal of Consumer Research, 13,* 12–24.

Mittal, B. (1995). A comparative analysis of four scales of consumer involvement. *Psychology & Marketing, 12,* 663–682.

Mongeau, P. A. (1998). Another look at fear-arousing persuasive appeals. In M. Allen & R. W. Preiss (Eds.), *Persuasion: Advances through meta-analysis* (pp. 53–68). Cresskill, NJ: Hampton Press.

Mongeau, P. A. (2013). Fear appeals. In J. P. Dillard & L. Shen (Eds.), *The Sage handbook of persuasion: Developments in theory and practice* (2nd ed., pp. 184–199.) Thousand Oaks, CA: Sage.

Moore, M. T. (1993, June 15). Visual overload: Fleeing ad images catch viewers. *USA Today,* B1.

Morgan, S. E., Movius, L., & Cody, M. J. (2009). The power of narratives: The effect of entertainment television organ donation storylines on the attitudes, knowledge, and behaviors of donors and nondonors. *Journal of Communication, 59,* 135–151.

Morin, R. (1997, September 1). The worst of the worst. *The Washington Post National Weekly Edition,* 35.

Morley, D. D., & Walker, K. B. (1987). The role of importance, novelty, and plausibility in producing belief change. *Communication Monographs, 54,* 436–442.

Morris, K. A., & Swann, W. B., Jr. (1996). Denial and the AIDS crisis: On wishing away the threat of AIDS. In S. Oskamp & S. C. Thompson (Eds.), *Understanding and preventing HIV risk behavior: Safer sex and drug use* (pp. 57–79). Thousand Oaks, CA: Sage.

Morrison, D. M., Gillmore, M. R., & Baker, S. A. (1995). Determinants of condom use among high-risk heterosexual adults: A test of the theory of reasoned action. *Journal of Applied Social Psychology, 25,* 651–676.

Morrison, D. M., Gillmore, M. R., Simpson, E. E., Wells, E. A., & Hoppe, M. J. (1996). Children's decisions about substance use: An application and extension of the theory of reasoned action. *Journal of Applied Social Psychology, 26,* 1658–1679.

Mowen, J. C., & Cialdini, R. B. (1980). On implementing the door-in-the-face compliance technique in a business context. *Journal of Marketing Research, 17,* 253–258.

Moyer-Guse, E., Chung, A. H., & Jain, P. (2011). Identification with characters and discussion of taboo topics after exposure to an entertainment narrative about sexual health. *Journal of Communication, 61,* 387–406.

Moyer-Guse, E., & Nabi, R. L. (2010). Explaining the effects of narrative in an entertainment television program: Overcoming resistance to persuasion. *Human Communication Research, 36,* 26–52.

Mulvihill, G., Armas, G. C., & Scolforo, M. (2012, July 3). Penn State staged cover-up. *The (Syracuse) Post-Standard,* A1, A12.

Murphy, S. T., Frank, L. B., Moran, M. B., & Patnoe-Woodley, P. (2011). Involved, transported, or emotional? Exploring the determinants of change in knowledge, attitudes, and behavior in entertainment-education. *Journal of Communication, 61,* 407–431.

Murray, S., & Gruley, B. (2000, November 2). On many campuses, big brewers play a role in new alcohol policies. *The Wall Street Journal,* A1, A10.

Muthusamy, M., Levine, T. R., & Weber, R. (2009). Scaring the already scared: Some problems with HIV/AIDS fear appeals in Namibia. *Journal of Communication, 59,* 317–344.

Mutz, D. C. (2006). *Hearing the other side: Deliberative versus participatory democracy.* Cambridge, UK: Cambridge University Press.

Myers, D. G. (2008). *Exploring psychology* (7th ed.). New York: Worth Publishers.

Nabi, R. L. (2002). Anger, fear, uncertainty, and attitudes: A test of the cognitive-functional model. *Communication Monographs, 69,* 204–216.

Nabi, R. L. (2007). Emotion and persuasion: A social cognitive perspective. In D. R. Roskos-Ewoldsen & J. L. Monahan (Eds.), *Communication and social Cognition: Theories and methods* (pp. 377–398). Mahwah, NJ: Erlbaum Associates.

Nabi, R. L. (2009). Emotion and media effects. In R. L. Nabi & M. B. Oliver (Eds.), *The Sage handbook of media processes and effects* (pp. 205–221). Thousand Oaks, CA: Sage.

Nabi, R. L., & Moyer-Guse, E. (in press). The psychology underlying media-based persuasion. In K. Dill (Ed.), *Oxford handbook of media psychology.* New York: Oxford University Press.

Naftulin, D. H., Ware, J. E., & Donnelly, F. A. (1973). The Doctor Fox lecture: A paradigm of educational seduction. *Journal of Medical Education, 48,* 630–635.

Nagourney, A. (2008, September 2). In political realm, "family problem" emerges as test and distraction. *The New York Times,* A18.

Nagourney, A. (2011, January 20). In an ocean of firearms, Tucson is far away. *The New York Times,* A1, A19.

Nan, X. (2007). The relative persuasive effect of gain- versus loss-framed messages: Exploring the moderating role of the desirability of end-states. *Journalism and Mass Communication Quarterly, 84,* 509–524.

Nan, X. (2012). Relative persuasiveness of gain- versus loss-framed human papillomavirus vaccination messages for the present- and future-minded. *Human Communication Research, 38,* 72–94.

Nebenzahl, I. D., & Jaffe, E. D. (1998). Ethical dimensions of advertising executions. *Journal of Business Ethics, 17,* 805–815.

Nelson, M. R., & Waiguny, M. K. J. (2012). Psychological processing of in-game advertising and advergaming: Branded entertainment or entertaining persuasion? In L. J. Shrum (Ed.), *The psychology of entertainment media: Blurring the lines between entertainment and persuasion* (2nd ed.). New York: Routledge.

Nevid, J. S., & McClelland, N. (2010). Measurement of implicit and explicit attitudes toward Barack Obama. *Psychology & Marketing, 27,* 989–1000.

Niederdeppe, J., Shapiro, M. A., & Porticella, N. (2011). Attributions of responsibility for obesity: Narrative communication reduces reactive counterarguing among liberals. *Human Communication Research, 37,* 295–323.

Nilsen, T. R. (1974). *Ethics of speech communication* (2nd ed.). Indianapolis: Bobbs-Merill.

Nitze, S. P. (2001, April 8). How to be an impostor. *The New York Times Magazine, 38*–40.

Noar, S. M. (2006). A 10-year retrospective of research in health mass media campaigns: Where do we go from here? *Journal of Health Communication, 11,* 21–42.

Nyer, P. U., & Dellande, S. (2010). Public commitment as a motivator for weight loss. *Psychology & Marketing, 27,* 1–12.

O'Brien, T. L. (2005, September 25). Madison Avenue wants you: How to pitch the military when a war drags on? *The New York Times* [Sunday Business], Section 3; 1, 8.

Ohme, R. K. (2000). Social influence in media: Culture and antismoking advertising. In W. Wosinka, R. B. Cialdini, D. W. Barrett, & J. Reykowski (Eds.), *The practice of social influence in multiple cultures* (pp. 309–324). Mahwah, NJ: Lawrence Erlbaum Associates.

O'Keefe, D. J. (1990). *Persuasion: Theory and research.* Newbury Park, CA: Sage.

O'Keefe, D. J. (1997). Standpoint explicitness and persuasive effect: A meta-analytic review of the effects of varying conclusion articulation in persuasive messages. *Argumentation and Advocacy, 34,* 1–12.

O'Keefe, D. J. (1999). How to handle opposing arguments in persuasive messages: A meta-analytic review of the effects of one-sided and two-sided messages. In M. E. Roloff (Ed.), *Communication yearbook 22* (pp. 209–249).

O'Keefe, D. J. (2000). Guilt and social influence. In M. E. Roloff (Ed.), *Communication yearbook 23* (pp. 67–101). Thousand Oaks, CA: Sage.

O'Keefe, D. J. (2002). Guilt as a mechanism of persuasion. In J. P. Dillard & M. Pfau (Eds.), *The persuasion handbook: Developments in theory and practice* (pp. 329–344). Thousand Oaks, CA: Sage.

O'Keefe, D. J. (2003). Message properties, mediating states, and manipulation checks: Claims, evidence, and data analysis in experimental persuasive message effects research. *Communication Theory, 13,* 251–274.

O'Keefe, D.J. (2012). From psychological theory to message design: Lessons from the story of gain-framed and loss-framed persuasive messages. In H. Cho (Ed.), *Health communication message design: Theory and practice* (pp. 3–20). Thousand Oaks, CA: Sage.

O'Keefe, D. J. (2013). The elaboration likelihood model. In J. P. Dillard & L. Shen (Eds.), *The Sage handbook of persuasion: Developments in theory and practice* (2nd ed., pp. 137–149). Thousand Oaks, CA: Sage.

O'Keefe, D. J., & Figgé, M. (1999). Guilt and expected guilt in the door-in-the-face technique. *Communication Monographs, 66,* 312–324.

O'Keefe, D. J., & Hale, S. L. (1998). The door-in-the-face influence strategy: A random-effects meta-analytic review. In M. E. Roloff (Ed.), *Communication yearbook 21* (pp. 1–33). Thousand Oaks, CA: Sage.

O'Keefe, D. J., & Jensen, J. D. (2006). The advantages of compliance or the disadvantages of noncompliance?: A meta-analytic review of the relative persuasive effectiveness of gain-framed and loss-framed messages. In C. S. Beck (Ed.), *Communication yearbook 30* (pp. 1–43). Mahwah, NJ: Erlbaum Associates.

O'Keefe, D. J., & Jensen, J. D. (2009). The relative persuasiveness of gain-framed and loss-framed messages for encouraging disease detection behaviors: A meta-analytic review. *Journal of Communication, 59,* 296–316.

O'Keefe, G. J., Rosenbaum, D. P., Lavrakas, P. J., Reid, K., & Botta, R. A. (1996). *Taking a bite out of crime: The impact of the National Citizens' Crime Prevention Media Campaign.* Thousand Oaks, CA: Sage.

Oldershaw, L., Walters, G. C., & Hall, D. K. (1986). Control strategies and noncompliance in abusive mother-child dyads: An observational study. *Child Development, 57,* 722–732.

Olney, B. (2000, July 9). Hitters vs. pitchers. *The New York Times Magazine,* 38–41.

Olson, M. A., & Fazio, R. H. (2004). Reducing the influence of extrapersonal associations on the Implicit Association Test: Personalizing the IAT. *Journal of Personality and Social Psychology, 86,* 653–667.

Olson, M. A., & Fazio, R. H. (2006). Reducing automatically activated racial prejudice through implicit evaluative conditioning. *Personality and Social Psychology Bulletin, 32,* 421–433.

Orenstein, P. (2000). *Flux: Women on sex, work, kids, love, and life in a half-changed world.* New York: Doubleday.

Orne, M. T., & Holland, C. H. (1968). On the ecological validity of laboratory deceptions. *International Journal of Psychiatry, 6,* 282–293.

Osgood, C. E. (1974). Probing subjective culture/Part I: Cross linguistic tool making. *Journal of Communication, 24 (1),* 21–35.

Osgood, C. E., Suci, G. J., & Tannenbaum, P. H. (1957). *The measurement of meaning.* Urbana: University of Illinois Press.

Osterhouse, R. A., & Brock, T. C. (1970). Distraction increases yielding to propaganda by inhibiting counterarguing. *Journal of Personality and Social Psychology, 15,* 344–358.

Ostrom, T. M., Bond, C. F., Jr., Krosnick, J. A., & Sedikides, C. (1994). Attitude scales: How we measure the unmeasurable. In S. Shavitt & T. C. Brock (Eds.), *Persuasion: Psychological insights and perspectives* (pp. 15–42). Boston: Allyn and Bacon.

O'Sullivan, C. S., Chen, A., Mohapatra, S., Sigelman, L., & Lewis, E. (1988). Voting in ignorance: The politics of smooth-sounding names. *Journal of Applied Social Psychology, 18,* 1094–1106.

Paek, H.-J. (2009). Differential effects of different peers: Further evidence of the peer proximity thesis in perceived peer influence on college students' smoking. *Journal of Communication, 59,* 434–455.

Pariser, E. (2011a, April 26). Welcome to the brave new world of persuasion profiling. *Wired* (Online: http://www.wired.com/magazine/2011/04/st_essay_persuasion_profiling/ (Accessed: December 13, 2011).

Pariser, E. (2011b). *The filter bubble: What the Internet is hiding from you.* New York: Penguin Press.

Park, H. S., Klein, K. A., Smith, S., & Martell, D. (2009). Separating subjective norms, university descriptive and injunctive norms, and U. S. descriptive and injunctive norms for drinking behavior intentions. *Health Communication, 24,* 746–751.

Park, H. S., Levine, T. R., Kingsley Westerman, C. Y., Orfgen, T., & Foregger, S. (2007). The effects of argument quality and involvement type on attitude formation and attitude change: A test of dual-process and social judgment predictions. *Human Communication Research, 33,* 81–102.

Park, H. S., & Smith, S. W. (2007). Distinctiveness and influence of subjective norms, personal descriptive and injunctive norms, and societal descriptive and injunctive norms on behavioral intent: A case of two behaviors critical to organ donation. *Human Communication Research, 33,* 194–218.

Park, S. Y. (2005). The influence of presumed media influence on women's desire to be thin. *Communication Research, 32,* 594–614.

Parker-Pope, T. (2010, June 15). Stupid teenage tricks, for a virtual audience. *The New York Times,* D5.

Parker-Pope, T. (2012, February 5). The kids are more than all right. *The New York Times Magazine,* 14.

Parrott, R., Silk, K., Dorgan, K., Condit, C., & Harris, T. (2005). Risk comprehension and judgments of statistical evidentiary appeals: When a picture is not worth a thousand words. *Human Communication Research, 31,* 423–452.

Paul, P. (2011, December 8). Divisive devices. *The New York Times,* E14.

Peplau, L. A., Hill, C. T., & Rubin, Z. (1993). Sex role attitudes in dating and marriage: A 15-year follow-up of the Boston couples study. *Journal of Social Issues, 49(3),* 31–52.

Peracchio, L. A., & Luna, D. (1998). The development of an advertising campaign to discourage smoking initiation among children and youth. *Journal of Advertising, 27,* 49–56.

Perkins, H. W., & Craig, D. W. (2003). The Hobart and William Smith Colleges experiment: A synergistic social norms approach using print, electronic media, and curriculum infusion to reduce collegiate problem drinking. In H. W. Perkins (Ed.), *The social norms approach to preventing school and college age substance abuse: A handbook for educators, counselors, and clinicians* (pp. 35–64). San Francisco: Jossey-Bass.

Perloff, R. M. (1996). Perceptions and conceptions of political media impact: The third-person effect and beyond. In A. N. Crigler (Ed.), *The psychology of political communication* (pp. 177–197). Ann Arbor: University of Michigan Press.

Perloff, R. M. (1998). *Political communication: Politics, press, and public in America.* Mahwah, NJ: Lawrence Erlbaum Associates.

Perloff, R. M. (2001). *Persuading people to have safer sex: Applications of social science to the AIDS crisis.* Mahwah, NJ: Lawrence Erlbaum Associates.

Perloff, R. M. (2009). Mass media, social perception, and the third-person effect. In J. Bryant & M. B. Oliver (Eds.), *Media effects: Advances in theory and research* (3rd ed., pp. 252–268). New York: Taylor & Francis.

Perloff, R. M., & Brock, T. C. (1980). "And thinking makes it so": Cognitive responses to persuasion. In M. E. Roloff & G. R. Miller (Eds.), *Persuasion: New directions in theory and research* (pp. 67–99). Beverly Hills, CA: Sage.

Petty, R. E., Barden, J., & Wheeler, S. C. (2009). The elaboration likelihood model of persuasion: Developing health promotions for sustained behavioral change. In R. J. DiClemente, R. A. Crosby, & M. C. Kegler (Eds.), *Emerging theories in health promotion practice and research* (pp. 185–214). San Francisco: Wiley.

Petty, R. E., Brinol, P., & Tormala, Z. L. (2002). Thought confidence as a determinant of persuasion: The self-validation hypothesis. *Journal of Personality and Social Psychology, 82,* 722–741.

Petty, R. E., & Cacioppo, J. T. (1977). Forewarning, cognitive responding, and resistance to persuasion. *Journal of Personality and Social Psychology, 35,* 645–655.

Petty, R. E., & Cacioppo, J. T. (1984). The effects of involvement on responses to argument quantity and quality: Central and peripheral routes to persuasion. *Journal of Personality and Social Psychology, 46,* 69–81.

Petty, R. E., & Cacioppo, J. T. (1986). The Elaboration Likelihood Model of persuasion. In L. Berkowitz (Ed.), *Advances in experimental social psychology* (Vol. 19, pp. 123–205). New York: Academic Press.

Petty, R. E., Cacioppo, J. T., & Goldman, R. (1981). Personal involvement as a determinant of argument-based persuasion. *Journal of Personality and Social Psychology, 41,* 847–855.

Petty, R. E., Cacioppo, J. T., Kasmer, J. A., & Haugtvedt, C. P. (1987). A reply to Stiff and Boster. *Communication Monographs, 54,* 257–263.

Petty, R. E., Cacioppo, J. T., Strathman, A. J., & Priester, J. R. (1994). To think or not to think: Exploring two routes to persuasion. In S. Shavitt & T. C. Brock (Eds.), *Persuasion: Psychological insights and perspectives* (pp. 113–147). Boston: Allyn and Bacon.

Petty, R. E., Haugtvedt, C. P., & Smith, S. M. (1995). Elaboration as a determinant of attitude strength: Creating attitudes that are persistent, resistant, and predictive of behavior. In R. E. Petty & J. A. Krosnick (Eds.), *Attitude strength: Antecedents and consequences* (pp. 93–130). Hillsdale, NJ: Lawrence Erlbaum Associates.

Petty, R. E., Ostrom, T. M., & Brock, T. C. (1981a). Historical foundations of the cognitive response approach to attitudes and persuasion. In R. E. Petty, T. M. Ostrom, & T. C. Brock (Eds.), *Cognitive responses in persuasion* (pp. 5–29). Hillsdale, NJ: Lawrence Erlbaum Associates.

Petty, R. E., Ostrom, T. M., & Brock, T. C. (Eds.) (1981b). *Cognitive responses in persuasion.* Hillsdale, NJ: Lawrence Erlbaum Associates.

Petty, R. E., & Wegener, D. T. (1998). Matching versus mismatching attitude functions: Implications for scrutiny of persuasive messages. *Personality and Social Psychology Bulletin, 24,* 227–240.

Petty, R. E., & Wegener, D. T. (1999). The Elaboration Likelihood Model: Current status and controversies. In S. Chaiken & Y. Trope (Eds.), *Dual-process theories in social psychology* (pp. 41–72). New York: Guilford.

Petty, R. E., Wegener, D. T., Fabrigar, L. R., Priester, J. R., & Cacioppo, J. T. (1993). Conceptual and methodological issues in the Elaboration Likelihood Model of persuasion: A reply to the Michigan State critics. *Communication Theory, 3,* 336–363.

Petty, R. E., Wells, G. L., & Brock, T. C. (1976). Distraction can enhance or reduce yielding to propaganda: Thought disruption versus effort justification. *Journal of Personality and Social Psychology, 34,* 874–884.

Petty, R. E., Wheeler, S. C., & Tormala, Z. L. (2003). Persuasion and attitude change. In T. Millon & M. J. Lerner (Eds.), *Handbook of psychology* (Vol. 5, pp. 353–382). Hoboken, NJ: Wiley.

Pew Forum on Religion and Public Life (2008, June). *U. S. religious landscape survey. Religious beliefs and practices: Diverse and politically relevant,* Online. http://religions.pewforum. org/pdf/report2-religious-landscape-study-full.pdf. (Accessed May 4, 2013).

Peyser, M. (2006, February 13). The truthiness teller. Online: http://www.the daily beast.com/newsweek/2006/02/12/the-truthiness-teller.html. (Accessed: May 4, 2013).

Pfau, M. (1997). The inoculation model of resistance to influence. In G. A. Barnett & F. J. Boster (Eds.), *Progress in communication sciences* (Vol. 13, pp. 133–171). Greenwich, CT: Ablex.

Pfau, M., & Burgoon, M. (1988). Inoculation in political campaign communication. *Human Communication Research, 15,* 91–111.

Pfau, M., & Kenski, H. C. (1990). *Attack politics: Strategy and defense.* New York: Praeger.

Pfau, M., Roskos-Ewoldsen, D., Wood, M., Yin, S., Cho, J., Lu, K. H., & Shen, L. (2003). Attitude accessibility as an alternative explanation for how inoculation confers resistance. *Communication Monographs, 70,* 39–51.

Pfau, M., & Van Bockern, S. (1994). The persistence of inoculation in conferring resistance to smoking initiation among adolescents: The second year. *Human Communication Research, 20,* 413–430.

Pharnor, A. (1999, May). Breaking the code. *The Source,* 72.

Phillips, A. (1998, October 2). How much does monogamy tell us? *The New York Times,* A27.

Pierce, J. P., Emery, S., & Gilpin, E. (2002). The California tobacco control program: A long-term health communication project. In R. Hornik (Ed.), *Public health communication: Evidence for behavior change* (pp. 97–114). Mahwah, NJ: Lawrence Erlbaum Associates.

Pigilito says . . . (2006, June 1). *Animal testing is good and proper.* Online: http://pigilito.blogspot.com/2006/06/animal-testing-is-good-and-proper.html. (Accessed: May 4, 2013).

Polonec, L. D., Major, A. M., & Atwood, L. E. (2006). Evaluating the believability and effectiveness of the social norms message "Most students drink 0 to 4 drinks when they party." *Health Communication, 20,* 23–34.

Pratkanis, A. R. (1998). Myths of subliminal persuasion: The cargo-cult science of subliminal persuasion. In K. Frazier (Ed.), *Encounters with the paranormal: Science, knowledge, and belief* (pp. 240–252). Amherst, NY: Prometheus Books.

Pratkanis, A. R. (2007). Social influence analysis: An index of tactics. In A. R. Pratkanis (Ed.), *The science of social influence: Advances and future progress* (pp. 17–82). New York: Psychology Press.

Pratkanis, A. R., & Aronson, E. (1992). *Age of propaganda: The everyday use and abuse of persuasion.* New York: W. H. Freeman.

Preiss, R. W., & Allen, M. (1998). Performing counterattitudinal advocacy: The persuasive impact of incentives. In M. Allen & R. W. Preiss (Eds.), *Persuasion: Advances through meta-analysis* (pp. 231–242). Cresskill, NJ: Hampton Press.

Preston, I. L. (1994). *The tangled web they weave: Truth, falsity, and advertisers.* Madison: University of Wisconsin Press.

Preston, I. L. (1996). *The great American blow-up: Puffery in advertising and selling* (Rev. ed.). Madison: University of Wisconsin Press.

Priester, J., & Petty, R. E. (1995). Source attributions and persuasion: Perceived honesty as a determinant of message scrutiny. *Personality and Social Psychology Bulletin, 21,* 637–654.

Priester, J., Wegener, D., Petty, R., & Fabrigar, L. (1999). Examining the psychological process underlying the sleeper effect: The Elaboration Likelihood Model explanation. *Media Psychology, 1,* 27–48.

Prochaska, J. O., DiClemente, C. C., & Norcross, J. C. (1992). In search of how people change: Applications to addictive behaviors. *American Psychologist, 47,* 1102–1114.

Prochaska, J. O., Redding, C. A., Harlow, L. L., Rossi, J. S., & Velicer, W. F. (1994). The trans-theoretical model of change and HIV prevention: A review. *Health Education Quarterly, 21,* 471–486.

Pryor, J. B., & Reeder, G. D. (1993). Collective and individual representations of HIV/AIDS stigma. In J. B. Pryor & G. D. Reeder (Eds.), *The social psychology of HIV infection* (pp. 263–286). Hillsdale, NJ: Lawrence Erlbaum Associates.

Puente, M. (1999, September 7). Casual clothes hit sour note with some. *USA Today,* 1D–2D.

Putnam, L. L., & Wilson, C. E. (1982). Communicative strategies in organizational conflicts: Reliability and validity of a measurement scale. In M. Burgoon (Ed.), *Communication yearbook 6* (pp. 629–652). Beverly Hills, CA: Sage.

Quick, B. L., Shen, L., & Dillard, J. P. (2013). Reactance theory and persuasion. In J. P. Dillard & L. Shen (Eds.), *The Sage handbook of persuasion: Developments in theory and practice* (2nd ed., pp. 167–183). Thousand Oaks, CA: Sage.

Quinn, J. M., & Wood, W. (2004). Forewarnings of influence appeals: Inducing resistance and acceptance. In E. S. Knowles & J. A. Linn (Eds.), *Resistance and persuasion* (pp. 193–213). Mahwah, NJ: Lawrence Erlbaum Associates.

Rachels, J. (1986). *The elements of moral philosophy.* Philadephia: Temple University Press.

Rains, S. A. (2013).The nature of psychological reactance revisited: A meta-analytic review. *Human Communication Research, 39,* 47–73.

Rajecki, D. W. (1982). *Attitudes: Themes and advances.* Sunderland, MA: Sinauer Associates.

Rancer, A. S. (1998). Argumentativeness. In J. C. McCroskey, J. A. Daly, M. M. Martin, & M. J. Beatty (Eds.), *Communication and personality: Trait perspectives* (pp. 149–170). Cresskill, NJ: Hampton Press.

Rancer, A. S., Whitecap, V. G., Kosberg, R. L., & Avtgis, T. A. (1997). Testing the efficacy of a communication training program to increase argumentativeness and argumentative behavior in adolescents. *Communication Education, 46,* 273–286.

Rankin, B., & Plummer, D. (2005, March 15). "God brought him to my door." *The Plain Dealer,* A1–2.

Ray, G. B., Ray, E. B., & Zahn, C. J. (1991). Speech behavior and social evaluation: An examination of medical messages. *Communication Quarterly, 39,* 119–129.

Redford, R. (2001, May 23). Bush vs. the American landscape. *The New York Times,* A29.

Reichert, T. (2003). What is sex in advertising? Perspectives from consumer behavior and social science research. In T. Reichert & J. Lambiase (Eds.), *Sex in advertising: Perspectives on the erotic appeal* (pp. 11–38). Mahwah, NJ: Lawrence Erlbaum Associates.

Reinard, J. C. (1988). The empirical study of the persuasive effects of evidence: The status after fifty years of research. *Human Communication Research, 15,* 3–59.

Reinard, J. C. (1991). *Foundations of argument: Effective communication for critical thinking.* Dubuque, IA: Wm. C. Brown.

Reinhart, A. M., Marshall, H. M., Feeley, T. H., & Tutzauer, F. (2007). The persuasive effects of message framing in organ donation: The mediating role of psychological reactance. *Communication Monographs, 74,* 229–255.

Remnick, D. (2005, October 3). Letter from Louisiana: High water. *The New Yorker,* pp. 48–57.

Reynolds, R. A., & Reynolds, J. L. (2002). Evidence. In J. E. Dillard & M. Pfau (Eds.), *The persuasion handbook: Developments in theory and practice* (pp. 427–444). Thousand Oaks, CA: Sage.

Rhoads, K. (1997). Everyday influence. In *Working psychology: Introduction to influence.* Online: http.//www.workingpsychology.com/evryinfl.html. (Accessed: 4 May, 2013).

Rhoads, K. V. L., & Cialdini, R. B. (2002). The business of influence: Principles that lead to success in commercial settings. In J. P. Dillard & M. Pfau (Eds.), *The persuasion handbook: Developments in theory and practice* (pp. 513–542). Thousand Oaks, CA: Sage.

Rhodes, N., & Ewoldsen, D. R. (2013). Outcomes of persuasion: Behavioral, cognitive, and social. In J. P. Dillard & L. Shen (Eds.), *The Sage handbook of persuasion: Developments in theory and practice* (2nd ed., pp. 53–69). Thousand Oaks, CA: Sage.

Rice, R. E., & Atkin, C. K. (2002). Communication campaigns: Theory, design, implementation, and evaluation. In J. Bryant & D. Zillmann (Eds.), *Media effects: Advances in theory and research* (2nd ed., pp. 427–451). Mahwah, NJ: Lawrence Erlbaum Associates.

Rice, R. E., & Atkin, C. K. (2009). Public communication campaigns: Theoretical principles and practical applications. In J. Bryant & M. B. Oliver (Eds.), *Media effects: Advances in theory and research* (3rd ed., pp. 436–468). New York: Routledge.

Richards, J. I. (1990). *Deceptive advertising: Behavioral study of a legal concept.* Hillsdale, NJ: Lawrence Erlbaum Associates.

Richardson, L. (2006). *What terrorists want: Understanding the enemy, containing the threat.* New York: Random House.

Riggio, R. E. (1987). *The charisma quotient: What it is, how to get it, how to use it.* New York: Dodd, Mead.

Rimal, R. N., & Real, K. (2003). Perceived risk and efficacy beliefs as motivators of change: Use of the Risk Perception Attitude (RPA) framework to understand health behaviors. *Human Communication Research, 29,* 370–399.

Rind, B., & Bordia, P. (1995). Effect of server's "thank you" and personalization on restaurant tipping. *Journal of Applied Social Psychology, 25,* 745–751.

Rind, B., & Bordia, P. (1996). Effect on restaurant tipping of male and female servers drawing a happy, smiling face on the backs of customers' checks. *Journal of Applied Social Psychology, 26,* 218–225.

Ritter, K., & Henry, D. (1994). *The 1980 Reagan–Carter presidential debate.* In R. V. Friedenberg (Ed.), *Rhetorical studies of national political debates, 1960–1992* (2nd ed., pp. 69–93). Westport, CT: Praeger.

Rittle, R. H. (1981). Changes in helping behavior: Self-versus situational perceptions as mediators of the foot-in-the-door effect. *Personality and Social Psychology Bulletin, 7,* 431–437.

Roberto, A.J. (2013). Editor's note for the extended parallel process model: Two decades later. *Health Communication, 28,* 1-2.

Roberto, A. J., Meyer, G., Johnson, A. J., & Atkin, C. K. (2000). Using the Extended Parallel

Process Model to prevent firearm injury and death: Field experiment results of a video-based intervention. *Journal of Communication, 50(4)*, 157–175.

Roberts, D. S., & Geller, E. S. (1994). A statewide intervention to increase safety belt use: Adding to the impact of a belt use law. *American Journal of Health Promotion, 8,* 172–174.

Robertson, L. S., Kelley, A. B., O'Neill, B., Wixom, C. W., Eiswirth, R. S., & Haddon, W., Jr. (1974). A controlled study of the effect of television messages on safety belt use. *American Journal of Public Health, 64,* 1071–1080.

Robinson, J. P., Shaver, P. R., & Wrightsman, L. S. (Eds.). (1999). *Measures of political attitudes.* San Diego: Academic Press.

Robinson, W. G. (1997). Heaven's Gate: The end? *Journal of Computer Mediated Communication.* Online: http://jcmc.indiana.edu/vol 3/issue 3/robinson/html. (Accessed: 4 May, 2013).

Roehm, H. A., & Haugtvedt, C. P. (1999). Understanding interactivity of cyberspace advertising. In D. W. Schumann & E. Thorson (Eds.), *Advertising and the World Wide Web* (pp. 27–39). Mahwah, NJ: Lawrence Erlbaum Associates.

Rogers, E. M. (1995). *Diffusion of innovations* (4th ed.). New York: Free Press.

Rogers, M., & Seiler, C. A. (1994). The answer is no: A national survey of advertising industry practitioners and their clients about whether they use subliminal advertising. *Journal of Advertising Research, 34,* 2, 36–45.

Rogers, M., & Smith, K. H. (1993, March–April). Public perceptions of subliminal advertising: Why practitioners shouldn't ignore this issue. *Journal of Advertising Research, 33,* 10–18.

Rogers, R. W. (1975). A protection motivation theory of fear appeals and attitude change. *Journal of Psychology, 91,* 93–114.

Rogers, R. W., & Mewborn, C. R. (1976). Fear appeals and attitude change: Effects of a threat's noxiousness, probability of occurrence, and the efficacy of coping responses. *Journal of Personality and Social Psychology, 34,* 54–61.

Rohter, L. (2007, January 14). In the land of bold beauty, a trusted mirror cracks. *The New York Times* [Week in Review], 1, 3.

Rokeach, M. (1973). *The nature of human values.* New York: Free Press.

Romano, L. (1998, October 19). Boss, you want me to do WHAT? *The Washington Post National Weekly Edition,* 29.

Romer, D., & Jamieson, P. (2001). Advertising, smoker imagery, and the diffusion of smoking behavior. In P. Slovic (Ed.), *Smoking: Risk, perception, & policy* (pp. 127–155). Thousand Oaks, CA: Sage.

Rook, K. S. (1987). Effects of case history versus abstract information on health attitudes and behaviors. *Journal of Applied Social Psychology, 17,* 533–553.

Root-Bernstein, R. S. (1993). *Rethinking AIDS: The tragic cost of premature consensus.* New York: Free Press.

Rosenbaum, A. S. (1986). *Coercion and autonomy: Philosophical foundations, issues, and practices.* Westport, CT: Greenwood.

Rosenberg, S. W., & McCafferty, P. (1987). The image and the vote: Manipulating voters' preferences. *Public Opinion Quarterly, 51,* 31–47.

Rosenbloom, S. (2011, January 23). I resolve. World, don't fail me now. *The New York Times* [Sunday Styles], 8.

Roskos-Ewoldsen, D. R. (1997a). Implicit theories of persuasion. *Human Communication Research, 24,* 31–63.

Roskos-Ewoldsen, D. R. (1997b). Attitude accessibility and persuasion: Review and a transactive model. In B. R. Burleson (Ed.), *Communication Yearbook, 20,* 185–225.

Roskos-Ewoldsen, D. R., Arpan-Ralstin, L., & St. Pierre, J. (2002). Attitude accessibility and persuasion: The quick and the strong. In J. P. Dillard & M. Pfau (Eds.), *The persuasion handbook: Developments in theory and practice* (pp. 39–61). Sage: Thousand Oaks, CA: Sage.

Roskos-Ewoldsen, D. R., & Fazio, R. H. (1992). On the orienting value of attitudes: Attitude accessibility as a determinant of an object's attraction of visual attention. *Journal of Personality and Social Psychology, 63,* 198–211.

Roskos-Ewoldsen, D. R., Roskos-Ewoldsen, B., & Carpentier, F. D. (2009). Media priming: An updated synthesis. In J. Bryant & M. B. Oliver (Eds.), *Media effects: Advances in theory and research* (3rd ed., pp. 74–93). New York: Routledge.

Roskos-Ewoldsen, D. R., Yu, H. J., & Rhodes, N. (2004). Fear appeal messages affect accessibility of attitudes toward the threat and adaptive behaviors. *Communication Monographs, 71,* 49–69.

Ross, A. (2011). *Ladies and gentlemen.* New York: Knopf.

Rothman, A. J., Salovey, P., Antone, C., Keough, K., & Martin, C. D. (1993). The influence of message framing on intentions to perform health behaviors. *Journal of Experimental Social Psychology, 29,* 408–433.

Rousseau, F. L., Vallerand, R. J., Ratelle, C. F., Mageau, G. A., & Provencher, P. J. (2002). Passion and gambling: On the validation of the gambling passion scale (GPS). *Journal of Gambling Studies, 18,* 45–66.

Royte, E. (2008). *Bottlemania: How water went on sale and why we bought it.* New York: Bloomsbury.

Rubin, R. B., Palmgreen, P., & Sypher, H. E. (Eds.). (1994). *Communication research measures: A sourcebook.* New York: Guilford.

Rudman, L. A., & Kilianski, S. E. (2000). Implicit and explicit attitudes toward female authority. *Personality and Social Psychology Bulletin, 26,* 1315–1328.

Rushing, W. A. (1995). *The AIDS epidemic: Social dimensions of an infectious disease.* Boulder, CO: Westview.

Russell, C. A., Clapp, J. D., & DeJong, W. (2005). Done 4: Analysis of a failed social norms marketing campaign. *Health Communication, 17,* 57–65.

Sabato, L. J., & Simpson, G. R. (1996). *Dirty little secrets: The persistence of corruption in American politics.* New York: Times Books.

Sagarin, B. J., Cialdini, R. B., Rice, W. E., & Serna, S. B. (2002). Dispelling the illusion of invulnerability: The motivations and mechanisms of resistance to persuasion. *Journal of Personality and Social Psychology, 83,* 526–541.

Salovey, P., & Wegener, D. T. (2002). Communicating about health: Message framing, persuasion, and health behavior. In J. Suls & K. Wallston (Eds.), *Social psychological foundations of health and illness.* Oxford: Blackwell.

Sandel, M. J. (2009). *Justice: What's the right thing to do?* New York: Farrar, Straus and Giroux.

Sandel, M. J. (2012). *What money can't buy: The moral limits of markets.* New York: Farrar, Straus and Giroux.

Sandomir, R. (2011, June 15). Critic of James has a happy ending for his book. *The New York Times,* B14.

Santora, M. (2006, November 25). In diabetes fight, raising cash and keeping trust. *The New York Times,* A1, A13.

Santos, M. D., Leve, C., & Pratkanis, A. R. (1994). Hey buddy, can you spare seventeen cents? Mindful persuasion and the pique technique. *Journal of Applied Social Psychology, 24,* 755–764.

Saul, S. (2005, November 28). Gimme an Rx! Cheerleaders pep up drug sales. *The New York Times,* A1, A16.

Saul, S. (2006, May 20). Unease on industry's role in hypertension debate. *The New York Times,* A1, B9.

Scheibe, K. E. (2000). *The drama of everyday life.* Cambridge, MA: Harvard University Press.

Schein, E. H. (1961). *Coercive persuasion: A socio-psychological analysis of the "brainwashing" of the American civilian prisoners by the Chinese communists.* New York: W. W. Norton.

Scher, S. J., & Cooper, J. (1989). Motivational basis of dissonance: The singular role of behavioral consequences. *Journal of Personality and Social Psychology, 56,* 899–906.

Schmermund, A., Sellers, R., Mueller, B., & Crosby, F. (2001). Attitudes toward affirmative action as a function of racial identity among African American college students. *Political Psychology, 22,* 759–774.

Schmierbach, M., Xu, Q., Bellur-Thandaveshwara, S., Ash, E., Oeldorf-Hirsch, A., & Kegerise, A. (2009). *What do your friends say about you?: Activist group evaluations in a social networking context.* Paper presented to the annual convention of the Association for Education in Journalism and Mass Communication, Boston, August.

Schmitt, E. (2004, August 26). Abuses at prison tied to officers in intelligence. *The New York Times,* A1, A10.

Schooler, C., Chaffee, S. H., Flora, J. A., & Roser, C. (1998). Health campaign channels: Tradeoffs among reach, specificity, and impact. *Human Communication Research, 24,* 410–432.

Schott, B. (2008, December 20). The way we were, 1968. *The New York Times,* A21.

Schroeder, C. M., & Prentice, D. A. (1998). Exposing pluralistic ignorance to reduce alcohol use among college students. *Journal of Applied Social Psychology, 28,* 2150–2180.

Schudson, M. (1986). *Advertising, the uneasy persuasion.* New York: Basic Books.

Schuman, H., & Presser, S. (1981). *Questions and answers in attitude surveys: Experiments on question form, wording, and context.* Orlando, FL: Academic Press.

Schwartz, S. (1996). Value priorities and behavior: Applying a theory of integrated value systems. In C. Seligman, J. M. Olson, & M. P. Zanna (Eds.), *The psychology of values: The Ontario symposium* (Vol. 8, pp. 1–24). Mahwah, NJ: Lawrence Erlbaum Associates.

Schwartz, S. H., & Bilsky, W. (1987). Toward a universal psychological structure of human values. *Journal of Personality and Social Psychology, 53,* 550–562.

Schwarz, N. (1999). Self-reports: How the questions shape the answers. *American Psychologist, 54,* 93–105.

Schwarz, N., & Bless, H. (1992). Scandals and the public's trust in politicians: Assimilation and contrast effects. *Personality and Social Psychology Bulletin, 18,* 574–579.

Scott, E. C. (2004). *Evolution vs. creationism: An introduction.* Berkeley, CA: University of California Press.

Scott, M. (2010, November 18). Americans' attitudes change, but habit remains. *The Plain Dealer,* A1, A10.

Sears, D. O., & Funk, C. L. (1991). The role of self-interest in social and political attitudes. In M. P. Zanna (Ed.), *Advances in experimental social psychology* (Vol. 24, pp. 1–91). San Diego: Academic Press.

Sears, D. O., Henry, P. J., & Kosterman, R. (2000). Egalitarian values and contemporary racial politics. In D. O. Sears, J. Sidanius, & L. Bobo (Eds.), *Racialized politics: The debate about racism in America* (pp. 75–117). Chicago: University of Chicago Press.

Sears, D. O., Lau, R. R., Tyler, T. R., & Allen, H. M., Jr. (1980). The self-interest vs. symbolic politics in policy attitudes and presidential voting. *American Political Science Review, 74,* 670–684.

See, Y. H. M., Petty, R. E., & Evans, L. M. (2009). The impact of perceived message complexity and need for cognition on information processing and attitudes. *Journal of Research in Personality, 43,* 880–889.

Segal, D. (2011, February 12). The dirty little secrets of search. *The New York Times.* Online: http://www.nytimes.com/2011/02/13/business/13search.html.

Segrin, C. (1993). The effects of nonverbal behavior on outcomes of compliance gaining attempts. *Communication Studies, 44,* 169–189.

Seibold, D. R., Cantrill, J. G., & Meyers, R. A. (1994). Communication and interpersonal influence. In M. L. Knapp & G. R. Miller (Eds.), *Handbook of interpersonal communication* (2nd ed., pp. 542–588). Thousand Oaks, CA: Sage.

Sharma, A. (1999). Does the salesperson like customers? A conceptual and empirical examination of the persuasive effect of perceptions of the salesperson's affect toward customers. *Psychology and Marketing, 16,* 141–162.

Shavitt, S., & Nelson, M. R. (2000). The social-identity function in person perception: Communicated meanings of product preferences. In G. R. Maio & J. M. Olson (Eds.), *Why we evaluate: Functions of attitudes* (pp. 37–57). Mahwah, NJ: Lawrence Erlbaum Associates.

Sheeran, P., Abraham, C., & Orbell, S. (1999). Psychosocial correlates of heterosexual condom use: A meta-analysis. *Psychological Bulletin, 125,* 90–132.

Shen, L. (2010). Mitigating psychological reactance: The role of message-induced empathy in persuasion. *Human Communication Research, 36,* 397–422.

Shen, L., & Bigsby, E. (2013). The effects of message features: Content, structure, and style. In J. P. Dillard & L. Shen (Eds.), *The Sage handbook of persuasion: Developments in theory and practice* (2nd ed., pp. 20–35). Thousand Oaks, CA: Sage.

Sherif, C. W., Sherif, M., & Nebergall, R. E. (1965). *Attitude and attitude change: The social judgment-involvement approach.* Philadelphia: W. B. Saunders.

Sherif, M. (1967). Introduction. In C. W. Sherif & M. Sherif (Eds.), *Attitude, ego-involvement, and change* (pp. 1–5). New York: Wiley.

Sherif, M., & Sherif, C. W. (1967). Attitude as the individual's own categories: The social judgment-involvement approach to attitude and attitude change. In C. W. Sherif & M. Sherif (Eds.), *Attitude, ego-involvement, and change* (pp. 105–139). New York: Wiley.

Sherman, D. K., & Cohen, G. L. (2006). The psychology of self-defense: Self-affirmation theory. In M. P. Zanna (Ed.), *Advances in experimental social psychology* (Vol. 38, pp. 183–242). San Diego: Elsevier.

Sherman, D. A. K., Nelson, L. D., & Steele, C. M. (2000). Do messages about health risks threaten the self? Increasing the acceptance of threatening health messages via self-affirmation. *Personality and Social Psychology Bulletin, 26,* 1046–1058.

Shrum, L. J., Liu, M., Nespoli, M., & Lowrey, T. M. (2013). Persuasion in the marketplace: How theories of persuasion apply to marketing and advertising. In J. P. Dillard & L. Shen (Eds.), *The Sage handbook of persuasion: Developments in theory and practice* (2nd ed., pp. 314–330). Thousand Oaks, CA: Sage.

Siebert, F. S., Peterson, T., & Schramm, W. (1956). *Four theories of the press: The authoritarian, libertarian, social responsibility, and Soviet communist concepts of what the press should be and do.* Urbana: University of Illinois Press.

Siegel, M., & Biener, L. (2002). The impact of antismoking media campaigns on progression to established smoking: Results of a longitudinal youth study in Massachusetts. In R. Hornik (Ed.), *Public health communication: Evidence for behavior change* (pp. 115–130). Mahwah, NJ: Lawrence Erlbaum Associates.

Simon, A. F., & Jerit, J. (2007). Toward a theory relating political discourse, media, and public opinion. *Journal of Communication, 57, 2,* 254–271.

Simon, L., Greenberg, J., & Brehm, J. (1995). Trivialization: The forgotten mode of dissonance reduction. *Journal of Personality and Social Psychology, 68,* 247–260.

Singer, N. (2009, July 17). In push for cancer screening, limited benefits. *The New York Times,* A1, A15.

Singer, N. (2011, October 16). Welcome, fans, to the pinking of America. *The New York Times* (Sunday Business), 1, 6.

Skalski, P., Tamborini, R., Glazer, E., & Smith, S. (2009). Effects of humor on presence and recall of persuasive messages. *Communication Quarterly, 57,* 136–163.

Slater, M. D. (2006). Specification and misspecification of theoretical foundations and logic models for health communication campaigns. *Health Communication, 20,* 149–157.

Slater, M. D., Karan, D., Rouner, D., Murphy, K., & Beauvais, F. (1998). Developing and assessing alcohol warning content: Responses to quantitative information and behavioral recommendations in warnings with television beer advertisements. *Journal of Public Policy & Marketing, 17,* 48–60.

Slater, M. D., & Rouner, D. (1996). Value-affirmative and value-protective processing of alcohol education messages that include statistical evidence or anecdotes. *Communication Research, 23,* 210–235.

Slater, M. D., Rouner, D., & Long, M. (2006). Television dramas and support for controversial public policies: Effects and mechanisms. *Journal of Communication, 56,* 235–252.

Smedley, B. D., Stith, A. Y., & Nelson, A. R. (Eds.) (2003). *Unequal treatment: Confronting racial and ethnic disparities in health care.* Washington, DC: National Academies Press.

Smith, B. L., Lasswell, H. D., & Casey. R. D. (1946). *Propaganda, communication, and public opinion.* Princeton, NJ: Princeton University Press.

Smith, M. B., Bruner, J. B., & White, R. S. (1956). *Opinions and personality.* New York: Wiley.

Smith, M. J. (1982). *Persuasion and human action: A review and critique of social influence theories.* Belmont, CA: Wadsworth.

Smith, R. A., Downs, E., & Witte, K. (2007). Drama theory and entertainment education: Exploring the effects of a radio drama on behavioral intentions to limit HIV transmission in Ethiopia. *Communication Monographs, 74,* 133–153.

Smith, R. D. (1993). Psychological type and public relations: Theory, research, and applications. *Journal of Public Relations Research, 5,* 177–199.

Smith, S. M., & Shaffer, D. R. (1995). Speed of speech and persuasion: Evidence for multiple effects. *Personality and Social Psychology Bulletin, 21,* 1051–1060.

Smith, T. W. (1995). Review: The Holocaust denial controversy. *Public Opinion Quarterly, 59,* 269–295.

Smith-McLallen, A., & Fishbein, M. (2009). Predicting intentions to engage in cancer prevention and detection behaviors: Examining differences between Black and White adults. *Psychology, Health & Medicine, 14,* 180–189.

Smythe, T. W. (1999). Moral responsibility. *Journal of Value Inquiry, 33,* 493–506.

Snyder, L. B. (2001). How effective are mediated health campaigns? In R. E. Rice & C. K. Atkin (Eds.), *Public communication campaigns* (3rd ed., pp. 181–190). Thousand Oaks, CA: Sage.

Snyder, M. (1974). Self-monitoring of expressive behavior. *Journal of Personality and Social Psychology, 30,* 526–537.

Snyder, M. (1987). *Public appearances/private realities: The psychology of self-monitoring.* New York: W. H. Freeman.

Snyder, M., Clary, E. G., & Stukas, A. A. (2000). The functional approach to volunteerism. In G. R. Maio & J. M. Olson (Eds.), *Why we evaluate: Functions of attitudes* (pp. 365–393). Mahwah, NJ: Lawrence Erlbaum Associates.

Snyder, M., & Kendzierski, D. (1982). Acting on one's attitudes: Procedures for linking attitude and behavior. *Journal of Experimental Social Psychology, 18,* 165–183.

Snyder, M., & Tanke, E. D. (1976). Behavior and attitude: Some people are more consistent than others. *Journal of Personality, 44,* 510–517.

Sobo, E. J. (1995). *Choosing unsafe sex: AIDS-risk denial among disadvantaged women.* Philadelphia: University of Pennsylvania Press.

Soldat, A. S., Sinclair, R. C., & Mark, M. M. (1997). Color as an environmental processing cue: External affective cues can directly affect processing strategy without affecting mood. *Social Cognition, 15,* 55–71.

Solomon, M. R. (1999). *Consumer behavior: Buying, having, and being* (4th ed.). Boston: Allyn & Bacon.

Sopory, P., & Dillard, J. P. (2002). Figurative language and persuasion. In J. P. Dillard & M. Pfau (Eds.), *The persuasion handbook: Developments in theory and practice* (pp. 407–426). Thousand Oaks, CA: Sage.

Sparks, G. G. (2010). *Rolling in dough: Lessons I learned in a doughnut shop.* Amherst, MA: White River Press.

Sparks, J. R., & Areni, C. S. (2008). Style versus substance: Multiple roles of language power in persuasion. *Journal of Applied Social Psychology, 38,* 37–60.

Spence, J. T., Helmreich, R., & Stapp, J. (1973). A short version of the Attitudes Toward Women Scale (AWS). *Bulletin of the Psychonomic Society, 2,* 219–220.

Sperber, B. M., Fishbein, M., & Ajzen, I. (1980). Predicting and understanding women's occupational orientations: Factors underlying choice intentions. In I. Ajzen & M. Fishbein (Eds.), *Understanding attitudes and predicting social behavior* (pp. 113–129). Englewood Cliffs, NJ: Prentice Hall.

Staats, A. W., & Staats, C. K. (1958). Attitudes established by classical conditioning. *Journal of Abnormal and Social Psychology, 57,* 37–40.

Standage, T. (2005, August 1). Bad to the last drop. *The New York Times,* A17.

Steele, C. M. (1988). The psychology of self-affirmation: Sustaining the integrity of the self. In L. Berkowtiz (Ed.), *Advances in experimental social psychology* (Vol. 21, pp. 261–302). San Diego: Academic Press.

Stengel, R. (2000). *You're too kind: A brief history of flattery.* New York: Simon & Schuster.

Stevens, S. S. (1950). Mathematics, measurement, and psychophysics. In S. S. Stevens (Ed.), *Handbook of experimental psychology* (pp. 1–49). New York: Wiley.

stickK. (2011). The smartest way to set and achieve your goals. Online: http://www.stickk.com/members/commitment.php/cid/52032. (Retrieved April 8, 2011).

Stiff, J. B. (1994). *Persuasive communication.* New York: Guilford.

Stiff, J. B., & Boster, F. J. (1987). Cognitive processing: Additional thoughts and a reply to Petty, Kasmer, Haugtvedt, and Cacioppo. *Communication Monographs, 54,* 250–256.

Stone, B. (2010, January 29). What's in a name? For Apple, iPad said more than intended. *The New York Times,* A1, A3.

Stone, J., Aronson, E., Crain, A. L., Winslow, M. P., & Fried, C. B. (1994). Inducing hypocrisy as a means of encouraging young adults to use condoms. *Personality and Social Psychology Bulletin, 20,* 116–128.

Story, L. (2007, January 15). Anywhere the eye can see, it's now likely to see an ad. *The New York Times,* A1, A14.

Street, R. L., Jr., & Brady, R. M. (1982). Speech rate acceptance ranges as a function of evaluative domain, listener speech rate, and communication context. *Communication Monographs, 49,* 290–308.

Streitfeld, D. (2011, August 20). In a race to out-rave rivals, 5-star web reviews go for $5. *The New York Times,* A1, A3.

Stroud, N. J. (2007). Media effects, selective exposure, and *Fahrenheit 9/11. Political Communication, 24,* 415–432.

Stuart, E. W., Shimp, T. A., & Engle, R. W. (1987). Classical conditioning of consumer attitudes: Four experiments in an advertising context. *Journal of Consumer Research, 14,* 334–349.

Sudman, S., & Bradburn, N. M. (1982). *Asking questions.* San Francisco: Jossey-Bass.

Sun, Y. (2013). When presumed influence turns real: An indirect route of media influence. In J. P. Dillard & L. Shen (Eds.), *The Sage handbook of persuasion: Developments in theory and practice* (2nd ed., pp. 371–387). Thousand Oaks, CA: Sage.

Sutton, S. (1998). Predicting and explaining intentions and behavior: How well are we doing? *Journal of Applied Social Psychology, 28,* 1317–1338.

Swim, J. K., Aikin, K. J., Hall, W. S., & Hunter, B. A. (1995). Sexism and racism: Old-fashioned and modern prejudices. *Journal of Personality and Social Psychology, 68,* 199–214.

Szabo, E. A., & Pfau, M. (2002). Nuances in inoculation: Theory and applications. In J. P. Dillard & M. Pfau (Eds.), *The persuasion handbook: Developments in theory and practice* (pp. 233–258). Thousand Oaks, CA: Sage.

Takaku, S. (2006). Reducing road rage: An application of the dissonance-attribution model of interpersonal forgiveness. *Journal of Applied Social Psychology, 36,* 2362–2378.

Tavani, H. T. (2000). *Privacy and the Internet.* Paper presented to Ethics and Technology conference (Accessed online: http://www.bc.edu/bc_org/avp/law/st_org/iptf/commentary/content/2000041901.html. Retrieved January 3, 2012.)

Tavernise, S. (2011, January 19). Gay parents are thriving in South, census says. *The New York Times,* A1, A15.

Tavris, C., & Aronson, E. (2007). *Mistakes were made (but not by me): Why we justify foolish beliefs, bad decisions, and hurtful acts.* Orlando, FL: Harcourt, Inc.

Taylor, S. E. (1981). The interface of cognitive and social psychology. In J. H. Harvey (Ed.), *Cognition, social behavior, and the environment* (pp. 189–211). Hillsdale, NJ: Lawrence Erlbaum Associates.

Taylor, T., & Booth-Butterfield, S. (1993). Getting a foot in the door with drinking and driving: A field study of healthy influence. *Communication Research Reports, 10,* 95–101.

Tedeschi, J. T., Schlenker, B. R., & Bonoma, T. V. (1971). Cognitive dissonance: Private ratiocination or public spectacle? *American Psychologist, 26,* 685–695.

Tesser, A. (1978). Self-generated attitude change. In L. Berkowitz (Ed.), *Advances in experimental social psychology* (Vol. 11, pp. 181–227). New York: Academic Press.

Tesser, A. (1993). The importance of heritability in psychological research: The case of attitudes. *Psychological Review, 100,* 129–142.

Tetlock, P. E., & Arkes, H. R. (2004). The implicit prejudice exchange: Islands of consensus in a sea of controversy. *Psychological Inquiry, 15,* 311–321.

Tetlock, P. E., Peterson, R. S., & Lerner, J. S. (1996). Revising the value pluralism model: Incorporating social content and context postulates. In C. Seligman, J. M. Olson, & M. P. Zanna (Eds.), *The psychology of values: The Ontario symposium* (Vol. 8, pp. 25–51). Mahwah, NJ: Lawrence Erlbaum Associates.

Tewksbury, D., & Scheufele, D. A. (2009). News framing theory and research. In J. Bryant & M. B. Oliver (Eds.), *Media effects: Advances in theory and research* (3rd ed., pp. 17–33). New York: Routledge.

Thaler, L. K., & Koval, R. (2003). *Bang! Getting your message heard in a noisy world.* New York: Currency/Doubleday.

Thaler, R. H., & Sunstein, C. R. (2008). *Nudge: Improving decisions about health, wealth, and happiness.* New Haven: Yale University Press.

Thernstrom, S., & Thernstrom, A. (1997). *America in black and white: One nation, indivisible.* New York: Simon & Schuster.

Theus, K. T. (1994). Subliminal advertising and the psychology of processing unconscious stimuli: A review of research. *Psychology & Marketing, 11,* 271–290.

Thompson, S. C., Anderson, K., Freedman, D., & Swan, J. (1996). Illusions of safety in a risky world: A study of college students' condom use. *Journal of Applied Social Psychology, 26,* 189–210.

Thompson, M. M., Zanna, M. P., & Griffin, D. W. (1995). Let's not be indifferent about (attitudinal) ambivalence. In R. E. Petty & J. A. Krosnick (Eds.), *Attitude strength: Antecedents and consequences* (pp. 361–386). Hillsdale, NJ: Lawrence Erlbaum Associates.

Thurstone, L. L. (1928). Attitudes can be measured. *American Journal of Sociology, 33,* 529–544.

Tiedge, J. T., Silverblatt, A., Havice, M. J., & Rosenfeld, R. (1991). Discrepancy between perceived first-person and perceived third-person mass media effects. *Journalism Quarterly, 68,* 141–154.

Tierney, J. (2009, August 25). Guilt and atonement on the path to adulthood. *The New York Times,* D1, D3.

Till, B. D., Stanley, S. M., & Priluck, R. (2008). Classical conditioning and celebrity endorsers: An examination of belongingness and resistance to extinction. *Psychology & Marketing, 25,* 179–196.

Todorov, A., Chaiken, S., & Henderson, M. D. (2002). The Heuristic-Systematic Model of social information processing. In J. P. Dillard & M. Pfau (Eds.), *The persuasion handbook: Developments in theory and practice* (pp. 195–211). Thousand Oaks, CA: Sage.

Toulmin, S. (1958). *The uses of argument.* New York: Cambridge University Press.

Tourangeau, R., & Rasinski, K. A. (1988). Cognitive processes underlying context effects in attitude measurement. *Psychological Bulletin, 103,* 299–314.

Trampe, D., Stapel, D. A., Siero, F. W., & Mulder, H. (2010). Beauty as a tool: The effect of model attractiveness, product relevance, and elaboration likelihood on advertising effectiveness. *Psychology & Marketing, 27,* 1101–1121.

Trappey, C. (1996). A meta-analysis of consumer choice and subliminal advertising. *Psychology & Marketing, 13,* 517–530.

Turner, M. M., Tamborini, R., Limon, M. S., & Zuckerman-Hyman, C. (2007). The moderators and mediators of door-in-the-face requests: Is it a negotiation or a helping experience? *Communication Monographs, 74,* 333–356.

Tuttle, S. (2006, December 4). The elusive hunter. *Newsweek,* 50–53.

Twitchell, J. B. (1999). *Lead us into temptation: The triumph of American materialism.* New York: Columbia University Press.

Updike, D. (2010, December 5). Lives: Drinking and driving and paying. *The New York Times Magazine,* 74.

van Knippenberg, B., van Knippenberg, D., Blaauw, E., & Vermunt, R. (1999). Relational considerations in the use of influence tactics. *Journal of Applied Social Psychology, 29,* 806–819.

Verhovek, S. H. (1997, December 14). In poll, Americans reject means but not ends of racial diversity. *The New York Times,* 1, 18.

Vidrine, J. I., Simmons, V. N., & Brandon, T. H. (2007). Construction of smoking relevant risk perceptions among college students. The influence of need for cognition and message content. *Journal of Applied Social Psychology, 37,* 91–114.

Viswanath, K., & Finnegan, J. R., Jr. (1996). The knowledge gap hypothesis: Twenty-five years later. In B. R. Burleson (Ed.), *Communication yearbook 19* (pp. 187–227). Thousand Oaks, CA: Sage.

Waggenspack, B. (2000). Women's role in rhetorical traditions. In J. L. Golden, G. F. Berquist, & W. E. Coleman (Eds.), *The rhetoric of Western thought* (7th ed., pp. 340–370). Dubuque, IA: Kendall/Hunt.

Waldron, V. R., & Applegate, J. L. (1998). Person-centered tactics during verbal disagreements: Effects on student perceptions of persuasiveness and social attraction. *Communication Education, 47,* 53–66.

Wallace, D. S., Paulson, R. M., Lord, C. G., & Bond, C. F., Jr. (2005). Which behaviors do attitudes predict? Meta-analyzing the effects of social pressure and perceived difficulty. *Review of General Psychology, 9,* 214–227.

Wallace, K. R. (1967). An ethical basis of communication. In R. L. Johannesen (Ed.), *Ethics and persuasion: Selected readings* (pp. 41–56). New York: Random House.

Walsh-Childers, K., & Brown, J. D. (2009). Effects of media on personal and public health. In J. Bryant & M. B. Oliver (Eds.), *Media effects: Advances in theory and research* (3rd ed., pp. 469–489). New York: Routledge.

Wan, H.-H. (2008). Resonance as a mediating factor accounting for the message effect in tailored communication—Examining crisis communication in a tourism context. *Journal of Communication, 58,* 472–489.

Wang Erber, M., Hodges, S. D., & Wilson T. D. (1995). Attitude strength, attitude stability, and the effects of analyzing reasons. In R. E. Petty & J. A. Krosnick (Eds.), *Attitude strength: Antecedents and consequences* (pp. 433–454). Hillsdale, NJ: Lawrence Erlbaum Associates.

Ward, J. (2010). *The student's guide to cognitive neuroscience* (2nd ed.). New York: Psychology Press.

Waxman, S. (2004, July 13). Two Americas of "Fahrenheit" and "Passion." *The New York Times,* B1.

Weaver, R. M. (1953). *The ethics of rhetoric.* Chicago: Henry Regnery.

Webb, E. J., Campbell, D. T., Schwartz, R. D., & Sechrest, L. (1966). *Unobtrusive measures: Nonreactive research in the social sciences.* Chicago: Rand McNally.

Weber, M. (1968). *On charisma and institution building.* Chicago: University of Chicago Press.

Wegner, D. M., Schneider, D. J., Carter, S. R., III, & White, T. L. (1987). Paradoxical effects of thought suppression. *Journal of Personality and Social Psychology, 53,* 5–13.

Weigel, R. H., & Newman, L. S. (1976). Increasing attitude–behavior correspondence by broadening the scope of the behavioral measure. *Journal of Personality and Social Psychology, 33,* 793–802.

Weinstein, N. D. (1980). Unrealistic optimism about future life events. *Journal of Personality and Social Psychology, 39,* 806–820.

Weinstein, N. D. (1993). Testing four competing theories of health-protective behavior. *Health Psychology, 12,* 324–333.

West, R., & Turner, L. H. (2010). *Introducing communication theory: Analysis and application* (4th ed.). Boston: McGraw-Hill Higher Education.

Westen, D., Blagov, P. S., Harenski, K., Kilts, C., & Hamann, S. (2006). Neural bases of motivated reasoning: An MRI study of emotional constraints on partisan political judgment in the 2004 U. S. presidential election. *Journal of Cognitive Neuroscience, 18,* 1947–1958.

Whalen, D. J. (1996). *I see what you mean: Persuasive business communication.* Thousand Oaks, CA: Sage.

Wicker, A. W. (1969). Attitudes vs. actions: The relationship of verbal and overt behavioral responses to attitude objects. *Journal of Social Issues, 25,* 41–78.

Wicklund, R. A., & Brehm, J. W. (1976). *Perspectives on cognitive dissonance.* Hillsdale, NJ: Lawrence Erlbaum Associates.

Wigley, C. J., III. (1998). Verbal aggressiveness. In J. C. McCroskey, J. A. Daly, M. M. Martin, & M. J. Beatty (Eds.), *Communication and personality: Trait perspectives* (pp. 191–214). Cresskill, NJ: Hampton Press.

Williams, A. (2005, May 29). "But I neeeeeed it!'" she suggested. *The New York Times* [Sunday Styles], 1, 6.

Williams, A. (2008, August 17). I was there. Just ask Photoshop. *The New York Times* [Sunday Styles], 1, 12.

Williams, K. D., & Dolnik, L. (2001). Revealing the worst first: Stealing thunder as a social influence strategy. In J. P. Forgas & K. D. Williams (Eds.), *Social influence: Direct and indirect processes* (pp. 213–231). Philadelphia: Taylor & Francis.

Williams-Piehota, P., Schneider, T. R., Pizarro, J., Mowad, L., & Salovey, P. (2003). Matching health messages to information-processing styles: Need for cognition and mammography utilization. *Health Communication, 15,* 375–392.

Wilson, M. (2011, May 14). Your palm's telling me you must let go. Of $27,000. *The New York Times,* A15.

Wilson, S. R. (1999). Developing theories of persuasive message production: The next generation. In J. O. Greene (Ed.), *Message production* (pp. 15–44). Mahwah, NJ: Lawrence Erlbaum Associates.

Wilson, S. R. (2002). *Seeking and resisting compliance: Why people say what they do when trying to influence others.* Thousand Oaks, CA: Sage.

Wilson, S. R. (2010). Seeking and resisting compliance. In C. R. Berger, M. E. Roloff, & D. R. Roskos-Ewoldsen (Eds.), *The handbook of communication science* (2nd ed., pp. 219–235). Thousand Oaks, CA: Sage.

Wilson, S. R., Aleman, C. G., & Leatham, G. B. (1998). Identity implications of influence goals: A revised analysis of face-threatening acts and application to seeking compliance with same-sex friends. *Human Communication Research, 25,* 64–96.

Wilson, T. D., LaFleur, S. J., & Anderson, D. E. (1996). The validity and consequences of verbal reports about attitudes. In N. Schwarz & S. Sudman (Eds.), *Answering questions: Methodology for determining cognitive and communicative processes in survey research* (pp. 91–114). San Francisco: Jossey-Bass.

Wilson, T. D., Lindsey, S., & Schooler, T. Y. (2000). A model of dual attitudes. *Psychological Review, 107,* 101–126.

Winfield, B. (1994). *FDR and the news media.* New York: Columbia University Press.

Winsten, J. A., & DeJong, W. (2001). The designated driver campaign. In R. E. Rice & C. K. Atkn (Eds.), *Public communication campaigns* (3rd ed., pp. 290–294). Thousand Oaks, CA: Sage.

Witte, K. (1998). Fear as motivator, fear as inhibitor: Using the Extended Parallel Process Model to explain fear appeal successes and failures. In P. A. Andersen & L. K. Guerrero (Eds.), *Handbook of communication and emotion: Research, theory, applications, and contexts* (pp. 423–450). San Diego: Academic Press.

Witte, K. (2013). Introduction: Pathways. *Health Communication, 28,* 3-4.

Witte, K., & Allen, M. (2000). A meta-analysis of fear appeals: Implications for effective public health campaigns. *Health Education & Behavior, 27,* 591–615.

Witte, K., Meyer, G., & Martell, D. (2001). *Effective health risk messages: A step-by-step guide.* Thousand Oaks, CA: Sage.

Witte, K., & Roberto, A. J. (2009). Fear appeals and public health: Managing fear and creating hope. In L. R. Frey & K. N. Cissna (Eds.), *Routledge handbook of applied communication research* (pp. 584–610). New York: Routledge.

Wolfe, A. (2011). *Political evil: What it is and how to combat it.* New York: Knopf.

Wong, N. C. H., & Cappella, J. N. (2009). Antismoking threat and efficacy appeals: Effects on smoking cessation intentions for smokers with low and high readiness to quit. *Journal of Applied Communication Research, 37,* 1–20.

Wood, W., Kallgren, C. A., & Preisler, R. M. (1985). Access to attitude-relevant information in memory as a determinant of persuasion: The role of message attributes. *Journal of Experimental Social Psychology, 21,* 73–85.

Wood, W., Rhodes, N., & Biek, M. (1995). Working knowledge and attitude strength: An information-processing analysis. In R. E. Petty & J. A. Krosnick (Eds.), *Attitude strength: Antecedents and consequences* (pp. 283–313). Hillsdale, NJ: Lawrence Erlbaum Associates.

Worden, J. K., & Flynn, B. S. (2002). Using mass media to prevent cigarette smoking. In R. Hornik (Ed.), *Public health communication: Evidence for behavior change* (pp. 23–33). Mahwah, NJ: Lawrence Erlbaum Associates.

Yan, C., Dillard, J. P., & Shen, F. (2010). The effects of mood, message framing, and behavioral advocacy on persuasion. *Journal of Communication, 60,* 344–363.

Yang, M., & Roskos-Ewoldsen, D. R. (2007). The effectiveness of brand placements in the movies: Levels of placements, explicit and implicit memory, and brand-choice behavior. *Journal of Communication, 57,* 469–489.

Yanovitzky, I., Stewart, L. P., & Lederman, L. C. (2006). Social distance, perceived drinking by peers, and alcohol use by college students. *Health Communication, 19,* 1–10.

Yousef, F. S. (1982). North Americans in the Middle East: Aspects of the roles of friendliness, religion, and women in cross-cultural relations. In L. A. Samovar & R. E. Porter (Eds.), *Intercultural communication: A reader* (3rd ed., pp. 91–99). Belmont, CA: Wadsworth.

Yzer, M. (2013). Reasoned action theory: Persuasion as belief-based behavior change. In J. P. Dillard & L. Shen (Eds.), *The Sage handbook of persuasion: Developments in theory and practice* (2nd ed., pp 120–136). Thousand Oaks, CA: Sage.

Zajonc, R. B. (1968). Attitudinal effects of mere exposure. *Journal of Personality and Social Psychology Monographs Supplement, 9*(2, Pt. 2), 1–27.

Zakaria, F. (2001, October 15). Why do they hate us? *Newsweek*, 22–30, 32–38, 40.

Zaller, J. R. (1992). *The nature and origins of mass opinion.* New York: Cambridge University Press.

Zanna, M. P., & Fazio, R. H. (1982). The attitude–behavior relation: Moving toward a third generation of research. In M. P. Zanna, E. T. Higgins, & C. P. Herman (Eds.), *Consistency in social behavior: The Ontario symposium* (Vol. 2, pp. 283–301). Hillsdale, NJ: Lawrence Erlbaum Associates.

Zanna, M. P., & Rempel, J. K. (1988). Attitudes: A new look at an old concept. In D. Bar-Tal & A. Kruglanski (Eds.), *The social psychology of knowledge* (pp. 315–334). New York: Cambridge University Press.

Zanot, E. J., Pincus, J. D., & Lamp, E. J. (1983). Public perceptions of subliminal advertising. *Journal of Advertising, 12,* 39–45.

Zarnoth, P., & Sniezek, J. A. (1997). The social influence of confidence in group decision making. *Journal of Experimental Social Psychology, 33,* 345–366.

Zimbardo, P. (2007). *The Lucifer effect: Understanding how good people turn evil.* New York: Random House.

Ziv, L. (1998, February). "I gave him my love, he gave me HIV." *Cosmopolitan,* 240–243.

Subject Index

Author Index